The Idea of Progress

CONCEPTS IN WESTERN THOUGHT SERIES

GENERAL EDITOR: MORTIMER J. ADLER

INSTITUTE FOR PHILOSOPHICAL RESEARCH

The Idea of Progress

by
Charles Van Doren

FREDERICK A. PRAEGER, *Publishers*
New York · Washington · London

FREDERICK A. PRAEGER, Publishers
111 Fourth Avenue, New York, N.Y. 10003, U.S.A.
77-79 Charlotte Street, London W.1, England

Published in the United States of America in 1967
by Frederick A. Praeger, Inc., Publishers

© 1967 by Institute for Philosophical Research

Library of Congress Catalog Card Number: 67–20495

Printed in the United States of America

To

My Mother and Father

Quod spiro et placeo, si placeo, tuum est

Persons Engaged in the Work of
the Institute for Philosophical Research
1961–1967

Acknowledgments

As the title page indicates, and as Dr. Adler states in his Foreword, this work is the product of the Institute for Philosophical Research. The investigations on which it is based have been conducted by members of the staff, and the formulations it advances represent the result of much consultation and collaboration. However, the task of writing the book was assigned to me, and I must bear final responsibility for its form and content, as well as for its faults.

Several members of the Institute's staff gave me special help that I would like to acknowledge here. Paul Cornelius served as a first reader of many important and difficult progress texts, and wrote detailed reports on them. Mortimer Adler and William Gorman read the entire manuscript and made many useful comments. Jeffrey Weiss checked all of the notes and helped prepare the bibliography. Mrs. Celia Wittenber was of great assistance in preparing the manuscript for publication.

My debt to Arthur L. H. Rubin can hardly be described in a few words. He read and commented on two drafts of the manuscript, and made many useful suggestions regarding works that should be investigated. But it was the endless hours that we spent together, discussing the idea of progress and its relation to almost everything else in the world, that were of greatest value to me.

I would also like to record my gratitude to the staffs of the Columbia University Library and of the New York Public Library; to Professor Howard Schless, who made useful suggestions in connection with the medieval conception of regress; and to Professor Richard P. McKeon, who provided me with an initial bibliography of works on progress.

Chicago
March, 1967

CHARLES VAN DOREN

Foreword

The Idea of Progress is one of a series of studies of basic ideas undertaken by the Institute for Philosophical Research. The Institute was established in 1952 with the avowed purpose of taking stock of Western thought on subjects that have been of continuing philosophical interest from the advent of philosophy in ancient Greece to the present day. In pursuing this task, it hopes to clarify the recorded discussion of such basic ideas as freedom, justice, happiness, love, progress, equality, and language. It aims to transform what, in every case, at first appears to be a chaos of differing opinions into an orderly set of clearly defined points of agreement and disagreement that give rise to real issues and make possible the kind of rational debate that constitutes genuine controversy.

What we are given to start with in each case is a diversity of opinions, the pattern of which is seldom clear. To put order into that diversity and to render it intelligible require a creative effort to construct the controversies that are implicit in it. Only by an explicit formulation of the pattern of agreements and disagreements, together with the reasons for the latter, can we delineate the issues and indicate how they have been or might be disputed. Too often reasons have not been given for positions that have been persistently advanced. In consequence, important issues have not been disputed in a way that carries the controversy forward and brings it nearer to a resolution.

The Institute has proceeded on the assumption that the issues in the field of any basic philosophical idea concern matters about which objective truth is ascertainable. The future resolution of these issues depends upon more sustained and more rational efforts to deal with them than the history of Western thought has so far exhibited, and the initiation of such efforts depends in turn upon a clear and precise understanding of the issues. Providing this has been the sole aim of the Institute's work from the beginning.

To accomplish its aim, the Institute has developed certain procedures and a distinctive method of work. Its approach to the study of the recorded discussion of basic philosophical ideas is essentially dialectical. The materials being studied—the major documents in the literature of any philosophical subject—are historical in the sense that each has a date and place in the history of thought about that subject; but the Institute's study of these materials is *non-historical* in aim. It deliberately abstracts from their historical context and pattern. It views them as if they were all contemporary—as if the documents represented the voices of participants confronting one another in actual discussion. The Institute's approach is also *non-philosophical* in the sense that it does not undertake to develop or defend a theory of the idea under consideration. The only truth with which the Institute is directly concerned is truth concerning the body of thought about a particular subject, not truth about the subject thought about. The Institute, therefore, refrains from taking part in the discussion that it attempts to clarify. It makes a sustained effort to be impartial in its treatment of all points of view and to deal with them in an objective and neutral manner. It strives to function as a detached bystander or impartial observer, not as a critic or judge assessing the merits of conflicting claims and awarding a verdict.

It should be clear why an intellectual enterprise thus designed and directed is facilitated by a collaborative effort under institutional auspices; it would be almost impossible for a single person working alone to accomplish effectively. On any basic idea, the volume of literature to be examined and interpreted is tremendous, even if only the most significant and representative documents are selected for study. In the process of interpretation and in the attempt to treat all points of view with impartiality, the desired neutrality is more likely to be achieved by many individuals working together than by the most determined effort of a single individual. Collaboration and consultation tend to offset the idiosyncrasies of individual temperaments and intellectual biases. The advantage of teamwork is not only the pooling of diverse abilities, but also the correction of blind spots and the checking of prejudices.

The first product of the collaborative effort of the Institute's staff was a two-volume study, *The Idea of Freedom*, Volume I of which was published in 1958, and Volume II in 1961. That study exemplified the Institute's dialectical method in the treatment of a basic idea; and its results provided a good measure of what can be achieved by the application of that method. The present study, *The Idea of Progress*, represents an adaptation of the same method to the treatment of another basic idea. Like *The Idea of Freedom*, it is a product of the collaborative effort of the Institute's staff. While the task of writing this book was undertaken by one member of the staff,

Dr. Charles Van Doren, a team formed from other members of the staff helped in the examination and interpretation of the literature under consideration; the formulations proposed by Dr. Van Doren were checked and criticized by his colleagues; and the manuscript was revised in accordance with suggestions made by them. The names of the collaborators specifically engaged in the production of the present volume, together with the names of other members of the Institute's staff and the members of its Board of Directors, will be found on page vi.

The dialectical clarification of the idea of progress closely resembles, in its general outlines, the pattern employed in the clarification of the idea of freedom. In one important respect, however, it is simpler; and in another, it is more complicated.

All the writers who affirm the existence of progress in human affairs define progress in the same way—as irreversible (though not necessarily continuous) change for the better. They may explain it in different ways or conceive it as having different properties, but they all agree that progress consists in (a) irreversible change and (b) change for the better. The same cannot be said for the writers about freedom. In analyzing the literature in which the word "freedom" is used, we found that it stands for five distinct subjects, not one. Each of the five freedoms is affirmed by certain authors and denied by others, but no author denies the existence of human freedom in every sense of that term.

Human progress *is* denied in the one clearly defined sense in which its advocates affirm it. What is more, it is denied in a variety of ways—by those who think that the pattern of historical change is regressive or cyclical, and not progressive at all; and by those who deny either that we are able to discover any over-all pattern of change in history or that we can ever support the judgment that a course of change is truly for the better.

Dr. Van Doren has brought this complex array of conflicting opinions into clear focus for the first time. Anyone who has been puzzled, if not actually bewildered, by discussions of progress that he has read or heard or in which he has himself participated will be grateful for the ordering and clarification that this book provides. It also throws light on the philosophy of history—a field of thought that sorely needs illumination. Few of us can refrain from thinking about and forming some judgment about the whole course of human life on earth. *The Idea of Progress* challenges us to re-examine such thinking as we have done on the matter, and above all, I think, it should induce us to suspend judgment, or at least to be much more circumspect about the opinions that we adopt or reject.

The Institute for Philosophical Research was established on grants from the Ford Foundation and the Old Dominion Foundation. When the Ford Foundation grant expired in 1956, the Old Dominion Foundation continued to support the Institute's work and was subsequently joined by other benefactors. I wish to express the Institute's gratitude to the sources of financial support that made it possible for it to complete its work on the idea of freedom after the expiration of the Ford grant, and beyond that to produce not only the present work on the idea of progress, but also studies of the idea of justice, the idea of love, and the idea of happiness. These four studies are now being published simultaneously. Other studies, one on the idea of equality and one on language and thought, are currently being undertaken and should be ready for publication in the near future.

In the period since 1962, the following foundations have made substantial contributions to the Institute: the Old Dominion Foundation, the Houghton Foundation, the General Service Foundation, the Liberal Arts Foundation, the Olive Bridge Foundation, and the Paul Jones Foundation. These acknowledgements would not be complete without an expression of special gratitude for the friendship and support of three men in particular—Paul Mellon and Ernest Brooks, Jr., of the Old Dominion Foundation, and Arthur Houghton, Jr., of the Houghton Foundation.

MORTIMER J. ADLER

Chicago
May, 1967

Contents

xiii

Book Two The Special Controversy About Progress

The Idea of Progress

General Introduction

O U R subject is the idea of human progress—the progress of the entire human race throughout its whole temporal career on earth. We will adopt the definition of progress that can be extracted from the writings of authors who affirm the existence of progress, *i.e.*, authors who assert that man has made progress in the past and will make progress in the future.[1] Progress, according to them, describes the pattern of change that is manifested in human history: that pattern is, in the long run, irreversible in direction; and its direction is toward an ultimate increase or advance in value—toward that which is better. Progress, in short, is irreversible meliorative change.

More specifically, our subject is the controversy about progress—the various issues or disagreements among writers who have discussed this idea. These issues fall into two groups: (i) the disagreements between those who affirm progress and those who deny it; and (ii) the disagreements about the characteristics or properties of progress among those who

[1] For the sake of brevity, we will use "progress authors" as short for "authors who affirm the existence of progress."

3

affirm it. We will call the former general and the latter special issues; and we will treat the general issues as comprising the general controversy about progress, and the special issues as comprising the special controversy about it.

Our aim is to clarify the controversy about progress as it exists in the literature of the subject—by distinguishing the general from the special issues and by defining, as precisely as possible, each of the issues. The undertaking bespeaks the need. If the distinctions to be made between different types of disagreement and if the various issues to be defined were clearly exhibited in the literature of progress, there would be no need for this effort to clarify it. The fact is that the authors who affirm progress do not confront those who deny it; nor, for the most part, do the progress authors themselves explicitly join issue on questions about the characteristics or properties of progress.

Nevertheless, disagreements do exist in the literature, implicitly if not explicitly. They can be constructed by carefully noting what particular authors assert or deny. If what one author, or one group of authors, asserts can be seen to contradict or otherwise negate what another author, or another group of authors, asserts, then we can formulate the question to which these contrary or contradictory assertions are the opposed answers, and we can construct the issue that is constituted by the opposed answers given to one and the same question. If such constructions were not based on the evidence of what is actually said in the literature, they would be inventions or imaginary concoctions. Hence we will always try to supply sufficient evidence to show that our construction of the issues concerning progress are clarifications or explications of what is to be found in the literature, not inventions of our own.

Here, our concern is simply to give the reader a quick overall view of the general and the special controversies about progress, by giving him an orderly summary of their component issues. The presentation of evidence, point by point, is reserved for the book.

We will first summarize the issues constituting the general controversy, and then the issues constituting the special controversy.

THE GENERAL CONTROVERSY

We have already stated the definition of progress that can be extracted from the writings of those who affirm its existence, past and future. It is now necessary to note the four distinct—or, at least, analytically separable —assertions that are involved in the affirmation of progress. Each of these assertions is capable of being denied in at least one way, and sometimes in more than one. Hence, setting down these four distinct assertions will enable us to construct the issues that result from assertions to the contrary.

Assertion (*a*). *A definite pattern of change exists in the history of mankind.* History is here taken in the broad sense of the entire course of human events—the whole temporal career of mankind on earth. To assert that such a pattern exists is to say that it has been manifested in changes that have taken place; to assert that it will continue to exist is to say that it will be manifested in future changes. While all progress authors do not explicitly make *assertion* (*a*), it is always implied in their affirmation of progress; for progress, as we have seen, is defined by all progress authors as a definite pattern of change; and so, if none existed in history, progress could not be affirmed.

Assertion (*b*). *The pattern of change that is manifested in history is not only discoverable but is also actually known.* While progress authors differ as to how the pattern of history is known, or differ with regard to the evidence for thinking that one exists, such differences do not affect their concurrence in *assertion* (*b*). Once again, it must be pointed out that progress authors seldom make this assertion explicitly; but, here as before, the assertion is plainly presupposed by the affirmation of progress, for, were the pattern of change that exists in history not discoverable or knowable, we could not know that the existent pattern conforms to the conception of progress held by those who affirm its existence.

Before we turn to the *assertions* (*c*) and (*d*), it is important to point out that the first two assertions—(*a*) and (*b*) above—have the logical status of presuppositions of progress. It is possible, in other words, to make *assertions* (*a*) and (*b*) without affirming progress, but it is impossible to affirm progress without making *assertions* (*a*) and (*b*).

Another way of making this same point is also useful. *Assertions* (*c*) and (*d*) consist in declaring that an existent and known pattern of change in history has certain characteristics. *Assertion* (*c*) characterizes the existent and known pattern of change in one way; *assertion* (*d*) characterizes it in another way. But if there were no existent pattern of change in history, or if, though it did exist, it could not be discovered or known by us, we obviously could not characterize it in one way or another. Hence the first two assertions are related to the second two in the following manner: *assertions* (*a*) and (*b*) assert that a pattern of change, capable of being characterized in various ways, exists and is known; *assertions* (*c*) and (*d*) then characterize it in certain ways.

Assertion (*c*). *The existent and known pattern of change in history is, in the long run, irreversible in direction.* The inclusion of the words "in the long run" means that the change need not be *continuously* or *unwaveringly* in one direction. Some progress authors maintain that the change is always in one direction, though they usually concede that the rate of progress varies at different times. Others maintain that there may be and, in fact, are relapses, even long and severe ones. Nevertheless, all agree that, in the long run, the pattern of change moves in one direction, even if to do so it must overcome reversals in direction. To deny this, as we shall presently see, is to assert that the pattern of change in history is repetitive or cyclical—going around and around in a circle of ups and downs instead of ultimately going up (*i.e.*, advancing or ascending), as the progress authors maintain, or ultimately going down (*i.e.*, declining), as the regress authors contend. These two groups of authors agree that the direction of change is irreversible in the long run, and thus together oppose the cyclical view of history; but they part company when the question is no longer whether the pattern of change is irreversible in direction, but what direction it takes.

Assertion (*d*). *The direction of the irreversible pattern of change in history is toward the better; i.e., is an improvement in the state of man or an advance from a less to a more desirable state of affairs.* It is by making this fourth and last assertion that the progress authors set themselves apart from their closest adversaries—authors who agree with them that a pattern of change exists in history and that it can be and is in fact known by us. But they alone among all these authors assert that the pattern consists in changes that are essentially meliorative, *i.e.*, in the long run, always change for the better.

The phrase "change for the better" is the quickest way of saying what progress is, though, as we have seen, it leaves a number of important points unsaid. These other points are presupposed, and this may be the reason why *assertions* (*a*), (*b*), and (*c*) are seldom made explicitly by the progress authors; but they cannot avoid making assertion (*d*), in one form of words or another, because the very core of their understanding of what progress is lies in the notion of change for the better or meliorative change. If it were change for the worse, it would not, in their judgment, be progress; nor, in their view, would it deserve to be called progress if the change were simply a cumulative change in the direction of the more without being either for the better or for the worse.

This last point calls for two explanatory comments. It is, first of all, necessary to remark that meliorative change may be quantitative as well as qualitative. To those who think that truth is better or more desirable than error, the qualitative change from an error to the truth that corrects it is a change for the better. To those who think that having more knowledge is better than having less, the change from less to more is a cumulative quantitative change that is also meliorative or for the better. However, in the sphere of quantitative change it is not always the case that a change from less to more is a change for the better. It may be quite the other way around. With regard to disease, a quantitative decline is meliorative; the fewer the diseases, the better.

Hence, according to the progress authors, a meliorative change may be either qualitative or quantitative, and, if quantitative, it may either be from less of something valued as good to more of it, or from more of something disvalued as bad to less of it. Just as the progress authors would never regard an irreversible change for the worse as progress, so they would oppose extending the use of the word to cover an advance from less to more—a merely quantitative accumulation. To deserve the name of progress, irreversible cumulative change in the positive direction (*i.e.,* from less to more) would also have to be a change for the better—better because whatever has increased in quantity also represents a more desirable state of affairs.

This brings us to our second explanatory comment. A small number of authors, as we shall see, deny progress on the ground that no judgments of value—of better or worse—have any objective validity or certifiable truth. Some of them, nevertheless, wish to retain the word "progress" shorn of its evaluative connotations. It might appear at first as if they could do this simply by dropping the fourth assertion and retaining the first three; but it is not enough to say that (a) the existent and (b) known pattern of change in history is, in the long run, (c) irreversible, because it could be regressive rather than progressive in character—irreversibly in the down rather than the up direction. Hence, these authors, who wish to retain the word "progress" in a sense that they can affirm because it imports no discrimination between better and worse, must point to something that exhibits an upward as opposed to a downward direction. They think that increase in quantity by itself suffices for this purpose. Change from less to more is a positive or upward rather than a negative or downward change, regardless of whether the quantitative increase is in fact for the better or the worse, and regardless of whether such evaluative judgments can be made with any objective validity. Some authors, notably Carl Becker, use the word "progress" in this purely descriptive, nonevaluative sense.

It is also the case that certain progress authors—among them Comte and J. S. Mill—sometimes use the word "progress" for merely cumulative change—change from less to more; but they never use it exclusively in this sense. They always also employ the word in its traditional meaning as signifying irreversible *meliorative* change. A close examination of their writings will show that, when they use the word "progress" for what is merely cumulative not meliorative change, they do so for the purpose of asking whether such progress (*i.e.,* progress in this purely descriptive sense of the word) is truly progress (*i.e.*, progress in the evaluative sense of the word).

In order to avoid the confusion that is latent in these two uses of the same word, and for the purpose of clarifying the literature about this subject, we will always use the word in its evaluative and meliorative sense. Whenever we deal with a text that uses the word in the purely descriptive sense, we will always attach the symbol ICC to that use of the word, in order to indicate that what is being referred to is merely irreversible cumulative change, change from less to more without reference to better or worse. We think this procedure is justified by the fact that all the authors who affirm progress affirm the existence of a pattern of change that is meliorative or for the better, even though they may also use the word "progress" to refer to a merely quantitative increase in order to ask whether such "progress" is genuine progress. In addition, it is justified by the fact that the few authors who maintain that progress exists *only* in this purely descriptive sense (ICC) are at the same time authors who reject the evaluative sense of the term because they reject all value judgments as subjective or emotional.

Before we turn to the denials of progress and the issues in the general controversy that arise from them, it may be useful to present a list of the leading progress authors, which is given below in *Table I*. The authors are listed in chronological order.[2]

The deniers of progress fall into five distinct groups. Instead of naming them in an order that conforms to the order of the assertions that they

TABLE I
PROGRESS AUTHORS

Augustine	J. S. Mill
Joachimites	Marx
Bacon	Bagehot
Pascal	Spencer
Leibniz	Dewey
Turgot	Trotsky
Kant	Maritain
Lessing	Teilhard de Chardin
Robinet	Yves Simon
Condorcet	Hermann J. Muller
Hegel	C. G. Darwin
Comte	E. H. Carr
Buckle	A. C. Clarke

[2] The list is intended to be exemplary rather than exhaustive. More complete listings of progress authors will be found elsewhere in the book. In addition, a diagram of theories of progress appears on p. 31.

deny, I am going to deal with them in an order that represents their position in the controversy—at the heart of it or on the periphery.

At the heart of the controversy are two denials. One is the denial that the pattern of change in history is irreversible in the long run; or the counterassertion that that pattern is cyclical. The other is the denial that the irreversible pattern of change in history is meliorative (from worse to better); or the counterassertion that that pattern is regressive (from better to worse).

The opposition between position (c) and position (c̄), or between progress authors and cyclists, and the opposition between position (d) and position (d̄), or between progress authors and regress authors, constitute the two issues that lie at the heart of the general controversy about progress. In the first of these two issues, we have a disagreement about progress between authors who agree that a pattern of change exists in history and is known by us: the crux of their disagreement lies in the question about the irreversibility of that pattern of change. In the second of these two issues, we have a disagreement about progress between authors who not only agree that a known pattern of historical change exists but also agree that that pattern is, in the long run, irreversible in direction: the crux of their disagreement lies in the question about the direction taken by this pattern of change—from worse to better, or from better to worse. The regress and the progress authors, who disagree on this question, stand together against and are together opposed by the cyclists. The cyclical theory of history denies a regressive pattern as well as a progressive pattern.

Below, in *Table II,* is a chronological enumeration of the leading exponents of the cyclical theory of history; and in *Table III,* a similar

TABLE II
CYCLISTS

Plato	Ibn Khaldun
Aristotle	Vico
Epicurus	Nietzsche
Lucretius	Brooks Adams
Cicero	Spengler

TABLE III
REGRESS AUTHORS

Hesiod	F. G. Juenger
Ovid	Marcuse
Rousseau	Seidenberg
Flammarion	N. O. Brown
Nordau	Ellul

enumeration of the leading authors who assert that the pattern of history is regressive rather than progressive.

Of the remaining three issues in the general controversy—all peripheral —two can be described as antecedent issues in the sense that, instead of denying progress directly, they deny the two presuppositions that underlie the affirmation of progress.

The first of these two denials attacks the presupposition that there exists in human history a definite pattern of change. Authors who take this negative view in the philosophy of history do not necessarily maintain that history is without meaning or significance; their opposition is specifically to those who assert (as progress, regress, and cyclical authors do) the existence in the whole sweep of human history of a single definite pattern of change. The leading exponents of this negative view are named in *Table IV* below.

TABLE IV

AUTHORS WHO DENY THE EXISTENCE OF A PATTERN OF HISTORY

Emerson	A. J. Nock
Burckhardt	M. R. Cohen
Boas	Jaspers

The second of these two denials attacks the presupposition that a definite pattern in history, if one exists, can be known or is known by us. Authors who take this negative view in the philosophy of history do not necessarily deny that an overall pattern of change may exist in history; nor do they deny that a variety of patterns can be discovered in different phases, eras, or epochs of history. Their opposition is specifically to the knowability of a single definite pattern in human history as a whole, including the future as well as the past. This opposition places them in disagreement not only with the progress authors but with the regress authors and the exponents of the cyclical view as well. The difference between the negative position (ā) and the negative position (ƀ) is that the first expresses an existential denial, the second an epistemic denial. The leading authors taking position (ƀ) are listed in *Table V* below.

TABLE V

AUTHORS WHO DENY THE KNOWABILITY OF A PATTERN OF HISTORY

Croce	Collingwood
Mannheim	Popper

Finally, we come to the third of the peripheral issues. Whereas the first two are issues in the philosophy of history antecedent to the controversy about progress as one theory of history, the third is an issue in the sphere of moral philosophy. Looked at one way, it is also antecedent to the controversy about progress, for the validity of value judgments is presupposed by those who evaluate the course of history in their affirmation of progress. That presupposition is denied by those who take a skeptical or relativist view of moral judgments as being nothing more than the expression of personal prejudices or emotional predilections.[3]

However, there is another way of looking at this picture. Those who take one or the other of the two negative positions in the philosophy of history—(ā) or (ɓ)—are denying that there exists, or that there can be known, any pattern in history as a whole that can be characterized as progressive, regressive, or cyclical. Hence, there is some point in examining these two negative positions first, before we deal with the issue in which the progress authors oppose the cyclists and the issue in which the progress authors oppose the regress authors.

Those who take the skeptical or negative position in moral philosophy are attacking any and all characterizations of historical change that are evaluative rather than purely descriptive. They are maintaining that such characterizations cannot be made meaningfully or validly in any transsubjective sense. They are, in effect, dismissing as verbal bickering the controversy about progress, insofar as it involves the issue between the progress authors and the cyclists and the issue between the progress and the regress authors. Hence, there is some point in examining this negative position last, after we have dealt with the two central or core issues. The authors who take this negative position in moral philosophy are too numerous to list here, but we list a few of the leading exponents of this position in *Table VI* below. We have attached an asterisk to the names of those who apply this negative view in moral philosophy to the evaluative judgment that is made in affirming progress.

TABLE VI

AUTHORS WHO DENY THE VALIDITY OF JUDGMENTS OF VALUE
ABOUT THE PATTERN OF HISTORY

Becker*	Stevenson
Ayer	Ross
W. H. Walsh*	Kelsen

What has just been said indicates the manner in which we might have proceeded in the book in constructing the five issues in the general con-

[3] Just as those who deny the presuppositions (a) and (b) oppose the regress authors and the cyclists just as much as they do the progress authors, so those who deny the objective validity of evaluative judgments are also as much opposed to the regress authors as they are to the progress authors.

troversy about progress, and in giving textual evidence to support our construction. We might have presented, first, evidence for the negative view (ā) that a definite pattern of change does not exist in history; and second, evidence for the negative view (b̄), that even if a definite pattern of change does exist it cannot be known by us. We might have then turned to the progress authors who conjunctively assert (a), (b), (c), and (d), examining the evidence for the position they take. By their assertion of (a) and (b), they stand opposed to the two groups of authors previously dealt with. Having presented the progress authors, we might have turned next to the regress authors (d̄) and the cyclists (c̄). This would enable us to present evidence for the core issues in the controversy. Finally, we might have examined the position of those who dismiss all value judgments as subjective. In their view, the foregoing disagreements, especially the one between the progress and the regress authors, are not genuine issues—issues that can be argued or resolved in any meaningful way. No objective validity or meaning attaches to either the affirmation or the denial of progress.

However, that way of presenting the material, though it has analytical advantages, has other disadvantages. The reader of a book about the idea of progress expects to find a discussion of affirmations of progress appearing first; and he probably expects, as well, to find discussion of those more obvious denials of progress constituted by the affirmation of regress or of cycles appearing second. Only then, probably, would he expect to find discussion of the other, less obvious denials of progress constituted by positions (ā) and (b̄), and by the position of those who deny the objective validity of judgments of value.

Hence, in fact, we proceed in the book as follows. We treat, first, affirmations of progress, and present evidence for the various kinds of affirmations that are to be found in the literature. Having done so, we then proceed to discuss, and to present evidence for, the views of the regress authors and the cyclists. Only after this examination of what we have called the core of the general controversy about the subject do we proceed to discuss, and present evidence for, the views—all of them denials of progress—that there is no pattern in history (ā), that, even if there is one, it cannot be known by us (b̄), and that no objective validity attaches to judgments of value regarding the pattern of historical change.

It should be remarked, at the same time, that there is some analytical justification for this order of treatment, too. Positions (ā) and (b̄) are, it is true, *antecedent* denials of progress, but they are nonetheless denials of progress, and if progress had never been affirmed these denials would not have been put forward. Furthermore, treating progress, regress, and cycles first, and treating the issues in the philosophy of history and the issue in the philosophy of value second follows the actual historical order of the discussion of the subject.

The five issues in the general controversy can be briefly summarized by stating the questions to which the progress authors give affirmative answers and their adversaries one or more negative ones.

1. Does there exist in human history as a whole a definite pattern of change?
2. Is that pattern of change discoverable by us?
3. Is it, in the long run, irreversible in direction?
4. Is its direction toward improvement, or an advance in value?
5. Can historical change be objectively evaluated as being for the better or for the worse?

THE SPECIAL CONTROVERSY

Progress authors disagree among themselves on certain questions about the nature or properties of progress and on a number of questions about the respects in which progress has been made. These disagreements constitute the issues in the special controversy. They fall into two groups: a group of three main issues concerning the nature or properties of progress; and a group of five subordinate issues concerning the respects in which progress has been made.

The main issues can best be summarized by stating the three questions to which progress authors give opposed answers.

1. *Is progress necessary or contingent?* Those who hold that progress is necessary are saying, in effect, that the motions of history are governed by a law—the law of progress—just as the motions of the heavenly bodies are governed by the laws of celestial mechanics. Those, on the other hand, who maintain that progress is contingent rather than necessary are saying that its existence is dependent on factors that may or may not operate to produce it.

This issue concerns the future, not the past. With few exceptions, notably that of John Dewey, all progress authors affirm that some progress —perhaps not very much—has taken place in the course of history so far. But when they turn from the past to the future, some assert that progress, in the very nature of the case, must inevitably continue, and some are of the opinion that, while future progress is possible, it is not necessary— it may or may not occur.

The leading authors who hold that progress is necessary, and those, contrary to them, who hold that it is contingent, are listed below in *Table VII*.

TABLE VII

Is Progress Necessary or Contingent?

Progress Is Necessary	Progress Is Contingent
Pascal	Bacon
Leibniz	Bagehot
Kant	Dewey
Lessing	Maritain
Condorcet	Yves Simon
Hegel	Hermann J. Muller
Comte	E. H. Carr
Marx	
Spencer	
Teilhard de Chardin	
C. G. Darwin	

2. *Will progress in the future continue until the end of time?* The issue raised by this question about future progress concerns its extent or duration. On the one hand, there are those who conceive human progress as coextensive with the time of human history: man will make progress from age to age as long as he inhabits the earth. On the other hand, there are those who think that progress will "plateau out"—that it will cease before the end of time, when every improvement in human affairs that can be achieved has been accomplished. With the possible exception of Hegel, who gives apparently contradictory answers to the question, no progress author holds that the apogee of progress has already been reached.

The leading authors who hold that progress will continue indefinitely, and those, contrary to them, who hold that it will "plateau out," are listed below in *Table VIII*.

3. *Does progress consist only in an improvement in man's products and institutions, or does it also consist in an improvement in human nature itself?* All progress authors agree that progress has taken the form of improvement in the products of man's mind and hand and in the institutions or external conditions of human life. But some insist that progress has also been made through improvements in the very nature of man, *i.e.*, that men of later generations are superior in their native capacities to men of an earlier time. Others deny this, maintaining on the contrary that progress has been and can be made in human products or institutions without its being accompanied by any improvement in the nature of man.

TABLE VIII
Will Progress Continue Indefinitely or "Plateau Out"?

Progress Will Continue Indefinitely	*Progress Will "Plateau Out"*
Pascal	Augustine
Leibniz	Joachimites
Kant	Lessing
Condorcet	Hegel
Comte	Marx
Buckle	
J. S. Mill	
Maritain	
E. H. Carr	
C. G. Darwin	

The leading authors who assert that progress has occurred and will occur in man's very nature are listed below, in *Table IX*. All other progress authors maintain that past progress has occurred only in man's products and institutions, although some of these concede that progress in man's nature might possibly occur in the future.

TABLE IX
Authors Who Affirm Progress in Human Nature

Joachimites	Bagehot
Lessing	Spencer
Robinet	Trotsky
Condorcet	Teilhard de Chardin
Comte	Hermann J. Muller
Marx	A. C. Clarke

The five subordinate issues in the special controversy all concern specific ways in which progress manifests itself in human products or institutions. The different respects in which progress is said to be made are in

1. knowledge
2. technology
3. wealth or economic goods
4. social and political institutions
5. morality.[4]

---

[4] In addition, there is discussion in the progress literature of the question whether progress has occurred in the fine arts. This is not a true issue, however, since the disputants do not make or deny the four assertions (a), (b), (c), and (d) about progress in the fine arts that they make about progress in knowledge, in wealth, etc. This question, along with the reasons for saying that it is not a true issue in the special controversy, are examined in an Appendix to this book.

The issues that are concerned with these five respects in which progress occurs refer mainly to the past. Thus, for example, some progress authors assert that progress has been made in morality, and others deny it. Sometimes the issues have a future reference as well. In addition, authors not only disagree about whether progress has been made or will be made in this or that respect, but they also differ about the relation of one type of progress to another.

Attention must be called to two things in connection with these five subordinate issues in the special controversy. First, we must observe that no one disputes the fact of quantitative increase in man's knowledge, in his technological products and ingenuity, and in his supply of economic goods, both consumable and capital. If mere quantitative increase (ICC) were progress, there would, therefore, be no dispute about progress with respect to knowledge, technology, and wealth, at least as far as the past is concerned. But there is a difference of opinion among progress authors about whether increases in knowledge, technology, and wealth represent *changes for the better*—changes in the direction of a more desirable state of affairs. Some progress authors hold that these changes are meliorative; others look upon them as the very opposite. The nub of these disagreements thus lies in opposed evaluations of the same state of facts.

The second point to be observed is that progress authors do not use language uniformly in their discussion of the specific respects in which progress has been or can be made. Some, for example, speak of progress in knowledge; and some refer to this type of progress as intellectual progress. Technological progress is often called progress in the arts, especially by writers before the 19th century; this must be carefully distinguished from progress in art where the reference is to the fine arts, not the industrial or useful arts that have become assimilated to branches of technology. In addition, such phrases as "intellectual progress" or "moral progress" are sometimes used with reference to improvement in the very nature of man —improvements in the power of his mind or the sensitivity of his conscience—as opposed to improvement in his intellectual products or in his moral codes or his moral conduct.

To clarify the discussion of these matters, we must adopt a set of terms and use them unambiguously and uniformly. When we come to the treatment of these five subordinate issues in the special controversy, we set up the necessary terminological conventions for translating the diverse vocabularies of the progress authors into a common neutral language.

OUTLINE OF THE WORK

Our clarification of the discussion of progress is presented in two books. Book One deals with the general controversy about progress, *i.e.*, with the various oppositions between those who affirm and those who deny progress. Book Two deals with the special controversy about progress, *i.e.*, with the differences that divide authors who agree in thinking that progress is manifested in history but who disagree in their conceptions of the progress that has been or will be made.

Book One is divided into three parts, corresponding to the differences we have noted in the general issues about progress. Part I (Chapters 1–11) treats the two core issues in the general controversy about progress—the opposition between those who describe the pattern of history as progressive and those who describe it as regressive, and the opposition to both the progressive and the regressive descriptions on the part of those who view the pattern of history as cyclical. Here we proceed, first, by expounding and documenting the views of those who describe the pattern as progressive; then, by dealing with those who describe it as regressive; and, finally, by presenting the views of those who describe it as cyclical. Part II (Chapters 12–13) treats the two issues in the philosophy of history that are in some sense antecedent to the consideration of progress—the issue concerning the existence of a definite pattern in the whole of human history and the issue concerning the knowability of the pattern, if one exists. In each case, for obvious reasons, we expound and document only the negative position. Part III (Chapter 14) treats the issue about progress that is raised by those who regard judgments of value as lacking in objective validity or meaning. Here we summarize the view of those who take a negative—a skeptical or relativist—position in moral philosophy, and document the application of this view to judgments of progress on the part of writers who concede that irreversible cumulative change has taken place but who deny that there is any objective or meaningful way of saying that such change is for the better or for the worse.

Book Two is divided into two parts, corresponding to the distinction we have made between three main issues and five subordinate ones. Part I (Chapters 15–17) treats the issue concerning the necessity of progress, the issue concerning its duration, and the issue about whether it occurs *only* in human products and institutions or *also* in the very nature of man. Part II (Chapters 18–25) treats the subordinate issues that are concerned with the different respects in which human products or institutions manifest progress: knowledge, technology, wealth, political institutions, morality.

The Appendix treats the difficult question of progress in the (fine) arts.

I

The Core of the General Controversy About Progress: Progress, Regress, and Cyclical Patterns of History

I

The Shape of the
Analysis

THE core of the general controversy about progress is constituted by
two sets of opposing answers to the question: What is the form of
the pattern of history?

On the one hand, there is the opposition between those who answer the
question by saying that the form of the pattern is progressive, and those
who say that it is regressive. On the other hand, there is the opposition between those who say it is progressive and those who say it is repetitive or
cyclical.

In the core of the controversy, all authors agree that there is a single,
overall pattern of human history, and that it is not only knowable but also
actually known by human beings; and none denies that judgments of value
concerning it may be validly made.[1] But they disagree about the description that most accurately fits the pattern. Some hold that the pattern of
history shows consistent, though perhaps not continuous, improvement.
Others hold that it shows consistent, though again not necessarily con-

[1] The cyclists do not place as much emphasis on judgments of value concerning
the pattern of historical change as do the progress and regress authors.

21

tinuous, change for the worse. And still others maintain that the pattern is cyclical—*i.e.*, that either historical events themselves, in their particularity, or the general form of historical events, recur again and again.

Progress

Some authors explicitly assert that progress is the pattern of all of man's history, throughout his entire temporal career on earth. Others emphasize progress in the past; still others turn their attention mainly to the future, in which they see progress as either a necessary or a contingent fact. No writer is considered as affirming progress, however, of whom it may not be said that he affirms it as the overall pattern of history, in both past and future, at least implicitly.[2]

Nor is any author considered as affirming progress who does not, again at least implicitly, assert that progress consists in a change for the better either in man himself, or in the general conditions of human life, or in both. We are not concerned, in other words, with affirmations of progress in limited senses—*e.g.*, the progress of the American people, or of the Negro, or of Communism, or of Democracy, or of any other segment of humanity, or of any human activity or institution considered in isolation from the general conditions of human life.

Some progress authors emphasize such limited senses of progress. It is usually easy to tell, however, whether they are really confining themselves to affirmations of that sort of progress, or are saying that *because of* progress in that limited sense, or in the light of it or on the basis of it, man himself, or the general conditions of human life, may be said to improve in time.

Progress, in short, in the view of this or that author, may consist in this or that particular change for the better. But an affirmation of progress is not counted as such unless its author at least implicitly asserts that *by virtue of this particular change* man himself, or the general conditions of human life, or both, undergo a change that is an improvement in the most general sense—*i.e.*, is better for the human race as a whole.[3]

An *affirmation* of progress comprises the four assertions, some of which

---

[2] Hegel and Dewey may be exceptions to this rule. If it is true that Hegel maintains that progress has ceased, has already "plateaued out," then he does not assert that progress is the pattern of the future. There is some question whether he is actually saying this. Dewey seems to be saying that there has been no progress in the past, but that progress is a possibility in the future. There is some doubt here, as well.

[3] Authors who emphasize particular aspects of human progress are discussed in Book Two, Part II.

may be implied, that were discussed in the General Introduction—*i.e.*, the assertions that there is an overall pattern of history, that the pattern is actually known by men, that the pattern consists in a change that is irreversible in the long run, and that the change is for the better. A *theory* of progress is an affirmation of progress that is accompanied by grounds for the affirmation.

Strictly speaking, theories and not affirmations of progress are considered in what follows. Authors differ regarding the grounds for affirming progress. Theories of progress are classified on the basis of these differences, or, as we say, according to authors' views regarding the *basic source or principle* of progress. A number of different principles of progress are discussed by progress authors, and our analysis reflects this division.

One major difference among progress theories deserves comment here. Some authors hold that the source or principle of progress is in man himself—in what he is, in what he does, in what he learns. They do not see any cosmic progress, or universal principle of progress, and limit their discussion of progress to man alone. Mankind, in short, progresses unaided, in their view, without the help of God or any cosmic principle or law. These authors are said to affirm *anthropogenic progress*.

Other authors hold that the source of progress is in the cosmos. In their view, progress is the design of Providence, or it is the effect or manifestation, in the human sphere, of a cosmic principle that brings about progress—properly so called—in other spheres than the human. These authors are said to affirm *cosmogenic progress*.

Regress

All regress authors agree that there is a known pattern of history, that it consists in a change that is irreversible in the long run, and that the change is for the worse.

No author is considered as affirming regress of whom it may not be said that he affirms it as the overall pattern of history, in both past and future, at least implicitly.[4]

Regress, like progress, may consist in various particular changes in man or in the general conditions of human life. But an affirmation of regress is not counted as such unless its author asserts at least implicitly that by virtue of this particular change there is a change that is for the worse in the most general sense—*i.e.*, is worse for the human race as a whole.

[4] Many regress authors seem to be saying that regress began fairly recently. On the whole, they seem to feel that the relatively distant past was progressive—or at least not marked by change for the worse.

A theory of regress comprises an affirmation of regress plus grounds for the affirmation. Strictly speaking, theories and not affirmations of regress are considered here. As before, theories of regress are classified according to the grounds on which they are said by authors to rest—*i.e.*, according to authors' views as to the basic source or principle of regress.

The distinction between anthropogenic progress and cosmogenic progress finds its analogue here. Theories of regress fall into two main groups. One group of authors sees regress as resulting from the nature or actions of man alone. There is no cosmic regress, in this view, and regress is not the result of God's intervention in history. These writers are said to affirm anthropogenic regress.

The second group of authors finds the source or principle of regress in the cosmos. Regress is either the result of some kind of cosmic or universal regress, or of divine intervention in history. These writers are said to affirm cosmogenic regress.

CYCLES

All authors who affirm a cyclical pattern of history agree that there is a known pattern of history, and that it consists in a change that is reversible in the long run.

No author is considered as affirming a cyclical pattern of history of whom it may not be said that he affirms it as the overall pattern of history, in both past and future, at least implicitly.[5]

Authors who discern cycles in particular aspects of human life—*e.g.*, in economic affairs—but who do not see an overall cyclical pattern of history are not considered as cyclists in what follows.

Cyclists are less likely to discuss the grounds of their affirmation regarding the pattern of history than are progress and regress authors. The term cyclical theory is, therefore, applied to full-fledged descriptions of the cyclical pattern, even if not accompanied by a discussion of grounds, as well as to assertions that the pattern is cyclical when these are accompanied by a discussion of the basic source or principle of cyclicity.

Theories of cosmogenic cycles are distinguished from theories of anthropogenic cycles. In the former, cycles of human history are viewed as resulting from, or as manifestations of, cycles in the universe or cosmos. In the latter, which are sometimes called theories of cultural or historical cycles, cycles of human history are viewed as confined to that sphere alone.

---

5 Brooks Adams is an exception here. He seems to be saying that, while the pattern of the past has been cyclical, the last cycle is "now" (in 1900) coming to an end, and the pattern of the future will either be unchanging or, more likely, regressive.

ISSUES IN THE CORE OF THE
GENERAL CONTROVERSY

There are two general issues in the core of the general controversy about progress. In the first, the progress authors are opposed by the regress authors. In the second, the progress authors are opposed by the cyclists. There is an issue between regress authors and cyclists, but it is not an issue about progress, and is therefore not considered in this work.

The two issues, in one sense, are both explicit in the literature; that is, the three conflicting affirmations regarding the pattern of history—that it is progressive, or regressive, or cyclical—are explicit in the writings of the authors treated. However, the issues as such are constructed, for most progress authors do not explicitly oppose either regress authors or cyclists. The oppositions between progress and regress authors, on the one hand, and between progress authors and cyclists, on the other hand, are manifest in the literature; hence the two issues are explicit it in that sense. But one might wish for more explicit recognition, by the parties to the controversy, of the positions that they implicitly oppose and against which they must be arguing as a result of this opposition.

There being two issues, one would expect that four positions—two affirmatives and two negatives—would have to be considered. However, the affirmative position on each issue is taken by the same group of writers—the progress authors. Hence, Part I may be conceived as being divided into three sections.

In the first section, comprising Chapters 2–6, theories of progress are analyzed, first in general (in Chapter 2), then in particular, and distinguished according to authors' views concerning the basic source or principle of progress.

Chapter 7 is a general treatment of theories both of regress and of cycles. The second section, therefore, comprises a portion of Chapter 7 and Chapters 8–9, in which theories of regress are analyzed. The third section comprises the other portion of Chapter 7, plus Chapters 10–11, in which cyclical theories are examined in detail.

2

Types of Theories
of Progress

T H E major distinction among theories of progress is, as we have seen, the distinction between theories that conceive human progress as the result or manifestation of a cosmic principle or process, and theories that conceive it as limited to the human sphere. Each of these divisions is also divided in two, and each of the four subdivisions is itself divided. As a result, we recognize a total of eleven types of theories of progress, distinguished according to the basic source or principle that is said to bring about progress in history.

ANTHROPOGENIC PROGRESS:
MAN'S COLLECTIVE MEMORY

The first of the four main groups of theories of progress includes theories whose authors see progress as resulting from the fact that man has a collective or social memory. Progress occurs, according to this view, because later generations of men remember, or otherwise retain, the knowledge and skill of earlier generations, and add to this what they know or learn themselves. The means of this retention is, of course, language, usually written language; authors who hold this position often distinguish between man, who is progressive because he has language, and animals, which are not progressive because they do not.

A number of different expressions of this position are found in the literature. Some writers maintain that progress occurs simply through the "transmission of acquired assets"; others hold that man not only inherits knowledge and skill from his forebears, and adds to it for the benefit of generations to come, but also applies or otherwise makes use of his inheritance *in a superior way*. For the authors in the first group, progress occurs without any change in man whatsoever. Progress, for them, is simply a result of the fact that human beings have a collective memory. For the authors in the second group, there are usually changes in man himself as well as in what he knows. For the first group, progress is on the whole a piling up of knowledge and skill. For the second group, it consists in qualitative as well as quantitative changes.

Listed below is a representative sample of authors who hold that the basic source of progress is man's collective memory.

Pascal	Comte
Turgot	J. S. Mill
Condorcet	Henry George
Godwin	Piaget
Madame de Staël	Ortega
Saint-Simon	E. H. Carr

Of the above authors, those in the following list hold that progress occurs through the superior use of assets acquired or inherited from the past.

Turgot	J. S. Mill
Saint-Simon	Piaget
Comte	

ANTHROPOGENIC PROGRESS: MAN'S USE OF REASON

The second main group of theories of anthropogenic progress includes theories whose authors see man's use of reason as the source or principle of progress. For many of these authors, the emphasis is on the future. *If* man uses reason in a certain way, they are saying, *then,* and only then, will he progress.[1] Others conceive man's use of reason in the past as a source of past progress, whether or not they hold that man must continue to be reasonable in order to achieve future progress. It is the first view, however, that is dominant here.

Theories of progress of this type are distinguished according to the particular use or application of reason that is seen as of primary importance. For one group of authors, progress occurs because man uses, or can use, his reason to control external nature. For another group, which includes many modern writers, the control of external nature is not enough. Man, they say, must also control himself, and whatever may have been the case in the past, future progress will occur only if he learns to do this.

A representative list of authors who hold that progress occurs through man's use of reason, in the most general sense, appears below.

Bacon	Dewey
Descartes	Broad
Helvétius	Maritain
Fourier	Simon
Buckle	Mumford
Faraday	C. G. Darwin
Tolstoy	Hermann J. Muller
Morgan	A. C. Clarke

The following indicates which of the above authors feel that the understanding and control of external nature is not enough to bring about progress, and that man must also learn to understand and control himself.

Descartes	Broad
Helvétius	Maritain
Fourier	Simon
Faraday	Mumford
Tolstoy	Hermann J. Muller
Dewey	

COSMOGENIC PROGRESS: DIVINE PRINCIPLES

The third of the four main groups of theories of progress includes theories the authors of which see God or Providence as the source of progress in history. According to these writers, progress occurs through

[1] Hence it is not surprising to find that most of the authors in this group view progress as contingent.

God's design; man enjoys meliorative change because God intends it. Progress is God's plan for the world.

There are several expressions of this position in the literature. One is sufficiently different from the rest so as to require a further division of the group. On the one hand, some authors conceive progress as occurring because of God's general design for man and for the world. On the other hand, a few authors emphasize the agency of God's Church in the occurrence of progress.

A representative sample of authors who see the source of progress as God or Providence follows.

Augustine	Chateaubriand
Joachimites	Guizot
Leibniz	Acton
Edwards	Stace
Kant	James J. Walsh
Lessing	Toynbee[2]
Malthus	

Of the authors shown above, several emphasize the agency of God's Church in the occurrence of progress.

Chateaubriand	James J. Walsh
Acton	Toynbee
Stace	

A large number of authors mention more or less in passing that God is in some sense the ultimate source of human progress. This does not seem to be their main contention regarding the source of progress in history; their theories place emphasis on other grounds for the occurrence of meliorative changes in human life. In a few cases, they seem to be paying a kind of "lip service" to Providence; in others, the intent seems to be a kind of obeisance or humility before God as the ultimate author of all good in the world. A representative sample of such authors appears below. All of these writers are discussed in other connections in this work.

Bacon	Maritain
Descartes	Simon
Pascal	Teilhard de Chardin
Robinet	Rougemont
Hegel	Hocking

[2] Toynbee is also treated as a cyclist in this work.

Cosmogenic Progress: Natural Principles

All of the authors who see progress as the result of a cosmic principle do not hold that God brings it about. On the contrary, many theories of progress conceive melioration in human life as the result or manifestation of a cosmic process that has nothing to do with God or Providence. The principle of progress is natural; progress occurs in the human sphere either because there is a general or universal *progress* of which human progress is a special case, or because there is a cosmic *process*—not in itself meliorative—a result of which is melioration in the human sphere.

Several of the expressions of this position found in the literature are sufficiently different so as to require its division into a number of parts. There is, first, a main division into two groups: theories that conceive the source of progress as conflict or opposition, and theories that conceive its source simply as universal variation.[3] The second of the two groups may stand alone, but the first must be again divided. Four types of conflict or opposition are discussed: these may be termed the dialectic of the spirit, dialectical materialism, economic competition, and biological conflict (the struggle for existence).

The leading authors who hold that the principle of progress is cosmic, but who maintain that the principle is natural rather than divine, appear below.

Mandeville	Spencer
Adam Smith	Sumner
Hegel	Henry Adams
Marx	Bergson
Engels	Bukharin
Charles Darwin	Teilhard de Chardin
Bagehot	Julian Huxley
T. H. Huxley	

Of these, the following see progress as occurring through variation.

Spencer	Bergson
Henry Adams	Teilhard de Chardin

[3] Variation or complexification—the movement from the simple to the complex, or from the homogeneous to the heterogeneous—is a descriptive rather than a causative principle. Authors who conceive it as the principle of progress posit various causes of the phenomenon; they agree, however, that insofar as progress occurs, variation or complexification is its essential form.

THEORIES OF PROGRESS

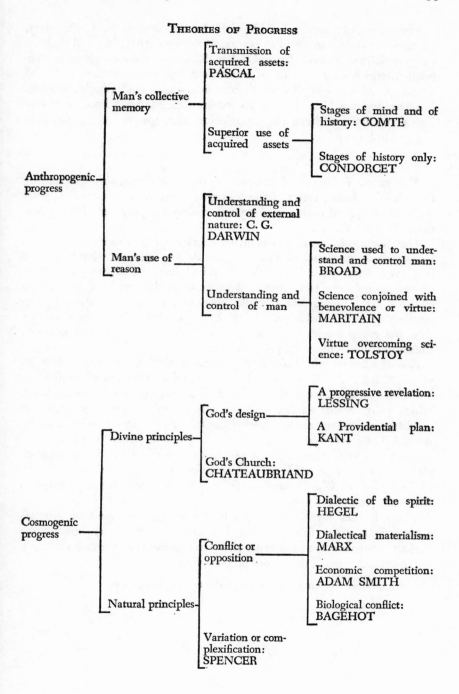

The source of progress for Hegel is the dialectic of the spirit. Marx, Engels, and Bukharin see it as occurring through what they call dialectical materialism. Mandeville and Adam Smith emphasize economic competition, which they conceive as a manifestation, in the human realm, of a principle of wider application than to man alone. And Charles Darwin, Bagehot, and the Huxleys conceive progress as occurring because of biological conflict. For them, the struggle for existence produces meliorative changes in human life.

A diagram of theories of progress, as they are distinguished according to authors' differing views of the source or principle of progress, appears on p. 31. A typical author is associated, mainly for purposes of identification, with each theory.

The diagram indicates three further breakdowns of theories of progress besides those discussed in this chapter. Among authors who hold that progress is anthropogenic and that its principle is the superior use of acquired assets, some view historical progress as the result of progressive changes in the human mind, while others affirm stages of historical progress but do not describe underlying stages or phases in man's thinking. The first group combines notions of historical and psychological progress; the second affirms historical progress alone.

Among authors who hold that progress is anthropogenic and that its principle is man's use of reason to understand and control himself, some assert that science itself should be used to understand human nature; others maintain that science is useful only if conjoined with benevolence or virtue; and some feel that science, at least as it operates now, must be discarded altogether, and some other use of reason put in its place.

Among authors who hold that progress is cosmogenic and that its principle is God's design, some see it as manifested in a progressive revelation of God to man, while others speak of a general and universal progress that is the plan of Providence.

These further breakdowns are reflected in the treatment of progress authors in the next four chapters. However, the differences among the various groups are not sufficiently sharp to require us to increase the number of distinct types of theories of progress.[4]

  [4] That number remains eleven, as was indicated on p. 26, above.

3

Anthropogenic Progress:
Man's Collective Memory

T H E theory that sees progress as occurring because mankind has a social or collective memory, such that the knowledge of past ages is handed down to later generations, which in turn add to it, is probably the most familiar, and is, in one sense, the most basic of all theories of progress.[1]

[1] The progress theories analyzed in Chapters 3 and 4 are divided into several categories. The groupings do not always correspond, however, to sharp differences between theories. All of the authors considered see progress as occurring because of the nature of man's mind, because of the way he uses—indeed, for many writers, must use—his "mental apparatus." But the authors emphasize, in their discussions of progress, one or another aspect of the human mind. Some see progress occurring because man has a social or collective memory, others because he has a mind susceptible to development, still others because of his application of some sort of "right method" to the control of nature and of human nature. The groupings correspond to these various points of view, and reflect conceptions sufficiently different to require separate treatment.

However, it is not to be supposed, because a progress author is placed in one group of anthropogenic theories, that he has that view of the nature and use of the human mind exclusively. Rather, he is placed there because he emphasizes that view of the mind particularly, or because he is particularly illuminating on that aspect of the question. Indeed, the likenesses among authors, with regard to their

33

The theory was proposed in the seventeenth century, by Pascal and others, in a simple form. In the eighteenth and nineteenth centuries, the notion was added that man progresses not only because he "stands on the shoulders of all past ages" but that later generations make a superior use of their intellectual and artistic inheritance. Comte is perhaps the leading author here.

Modern times have seen a revival of this traditional position, in both its simple and its more sophisticated form, in the work of such writers as Ortega and E. H. Carr.

The authors below hold that progress occurs because mankind has a social or collective memory.

Hobbes	Enfantin
Pascal	Comte
Perrault	J. S. Mill
Fontenelle	Henry George
Turgot	Piaget
Robertson	Freud
Condorcet	Inge
Volney	Ortega
Madame de Staël	Casson
Godwin	E. H. Carr
Saint-Simon	Whyte

PROGRESS THROUGH THE TRANSMISSION OF ACQUIRED ASSETS

The following authors maintain that progress is simply the result of the fact that men of later generations inherit intellectual "assets" from earlier generations.

Hobbes	Madame de Staël
Pascal	Godwin
Perrault	Henry George
Fontenelle	Inge
Robertson	Ortega
Volney	E. H. Carr

views concerning the principle of progress, on this side of the main division of progress theories—that is, between cosmogenic theories and anthropogenic theories—are more striking than the differences. Again and again the same themes, often expressed in the same language, are found to recur.

According to Pascal, progress consists in and is measured by the accumulating knowledge that is the result of the fact that one generation remembers, can use, and can build on the knowledge of earlier generations.

Pascal draws an analogy between the human race as a whole and a single individual. The same thing happens in the succession of men, he says, as in the life of a single man. Hence the entire series of human beings may be considered as one persistent individual, who not only persists but also learns continually.[2] This comparison is one of the fundamental notions underlying the idea of progress.

Pascal makes several other points that often recur in the literature. He distinguishes between two kinds of knowledge, the one of subjects where we defer to authority, the other of subjects "accessible to sense or reasoning." The first includes matters in which we seek to know only what authors have written, as in history, geography, jurisprudence, languages, "and above all in theology," where "we must necessarily have recourse to books." Geometry, arithmetic, music, physics, medicine, architecture, and all the sciences susceptible to experiment and reason must, on the other hand, "be added to if they are to become perfect."[3] The secrets of nature are hidden, and are only discovered from generation to generation; "although always the same in herself, [nature] is not always equally known." On the contrary, experiments into nature's secrets "multiply continually"; the experiments of the ancients, and the truths they discovered, can therefore serve as "steps to our own." We enjoy the advantage of a position that is "higher" than theirs because they have helped to place us at the height which we have attained. "Placed by them part way up the ladder, we are carried higher by our slightest effort, and with less labor and less glory find ourselves above them."[4]

Pascal goes on in a paragraph remarkable for its mention of a number of recurrent themes to carry the argument a step or two farther than it was usually carried by proponents of the Moderns in the controversy against those who exalted the Ancients and said they could never be equaled.

---

[2] The validity of this comparison seems to be accepted by almost all anthropogenic progress authors. Comte, for one, declares that the "scientific" idea of progress has its birth in this "immortal aphorism" of Pascal (*Positive Philosophy*, p. 441).

[3] *Preface to the Treatise on the Vacuum*, in *Great Books of the Western World*, Vol. 33, pp. 355–6. An English translation of "these few immortal pages," as Comte called them, will also be found in Teggart (ed.), *The Idea of Progress*, pp. 164–9.

[4] *Ibid.*, p. 357; see Teggart, p. 166. Remarks of this sort are not uncommon among those who defend the Moderns in the great controversy between Ancients and Moderns that raged throughout the seventeenth century. See, for example, Swift's *Battle of the Books*. An overall view of the controversy is given in R. F. Jones, *Ancients and Moderns*, where many additional affirmations and denials of progress may be found.

It is a strange thing how we reverence their [the ancients'] opinions. To contradict them counts as a crime and to add to them is an outrage, as if they had left no more truths to know. Is not this to treat man's reason with indignity and to put it on a level with animal instinct, since we thereby take away the main difference, which consists in this that the effects of reason increase continually whereas instinct always remains in the same state? Beehives were as well laid out a thousand years ago as today. . . . It is the same with everything animals make by that hidden motion. Nature teaches them in response to the pressure of necessity; but this frail knowledge dies with its need: as they receive it without study, they do not have the happiness of preserving it; and every time they are given it, they find it new, because nature, whose object is merely to maintain animals in an order of limited perfection, infuses in them this necessary knowledge, always the same, lest they perish, and does not allow them to add to it lest they go beyond the boundaries prescribed to them.[5]

"It is different with man," Pascal declares, "made only for infinity.[6] He is ignorant in his life's first age, but he never ceases to learn as he goes forward, for he has the advantage not only of his own experience but also of his predecessors', because he always has in his memory the knowledge he has once acquired, and that of the ancients is always at hand in the books they have left."[7]

And since he keeps his knowledge, he can also easily increase it, so that men today are in a certain sense in the same condition in which those ancient philosophers would be if they could have prolonged their old age until now, adding to the knowledge they had what their studies might have won for them by the grace of so many centuries.[8]

"Hence it is that by a special prerogative not only does each man advance from day to day in the sciences," says Pascal, "but all men together make a continual progress as the universe grows old, *because the same thing happens in the succession of men as in the different ages of an individual man.* So that the whole series of men during the course of so many centuries should be considered as *one self-same man, always in existence and continually learning.*"[9]

Pascal concludes that it is unjust to respect antiquity "in the person of its philosophers," for the old age of "this universal man should be sought not in the times near his birth but in those which are most distant from it."

[5] *Ibid.;* see Teggart, p. 167.
[6] One might seek far to find a phrase more expressive of the attitude of the earlier progress authors regarding the future career of man on earth.
[7] *Ibid.*
[8] *Ibid.*
[9] *Ibid.* Emphasis added.

Those whom we call ancients were in truth new in every respect, and actually formed the childhood of man; and since we have added to their knowledge the experience of the succeeding centuries, it is in ourselves that that antiquity can be found which we revere in others.[10]

Pascal, in drawing this analogy between the whole succession of men and the life of one single man who persists forever and learns continually, seems to admit that this "universal man" grows old, for ours is the old age of the race. However, this of course raises the question whether progress can be expected to continue indefinitely. In order to remove this difficulty, it must be claimed that the single man who stands for the whole race, in some sense *never* grows old. The point is made by Fontenelle, who, like Pascal, takes the Moderns' side in the famous controversy.

The comparison . . . between the men of all ages and a single man is applicable to our whole problem of the ancients and moderns. A good cultivated mind contains, so to speak, all the minds of preceding centuries; it is but a single identical mind which has been developing and improving itself all this time.[11]

In his infancy, "this man, who has lived since the beginning of the world up to the present," was occupied by the pressing needs of existence; in his youth, he pursued poetry and eloquence and "even began to reason a little, though with less soundness and fire"; he is now in his prime and would be farther advanced had not the passion for war diverted him from the sciences.[12] We are not, however, to extend the analogy further.

It is annoying not to be able to prosecute to the end a comparison which is in such a fair way; but I am obliged to confess that *the man in question will have no old age*, he will always be equally capable of those things for which his youth was suited, and he will be ever more and more capable of those things which are suited to his prime; that is to say, to abandon the allegory, men will never degenerate, and there will be no end to the growth and development of human wisdom.[13]

Fontenelle makes another point that is often made by later progress authors. "Once clearly understood," he says, "the whole question of preeminence between the ancients and moderns reduces itself to knowing whether the trees of yesterday were greater than those of today."[14] This mysterious remark is explained by the observation that if the ancients had

[10] *Ibid.*, pp. 357–8; see Teggart, p. 168.
[11] *On the Ancients and Moderns*, in Teggart, p. 184.
[12] *Ibid.* Vico and other cyclists have a similar view of the character of early man.
[13] *Ibid.* Emphasis added.
[14] *Ibid.*, p. 176.

had superior intellects, this would be because nature was "at that time younger and more vigorous," in which case the trees would have been more vigorous, too. But such was not the case, says Fontenelle. There is no natural difference between the men and the trees of ancient and modern times.

> Nature possesses a kind of paste which is always the same, which she cease-lessly moulds and remoulds in a thousand ways, and of which she forms men, animals, and plants; and certainly she did not form Plato, Demosthenes, or Homer of a finer or better kneaded clay than our philosophers, our orators, and our poets of today.[15]

Fontenelle emphasizes this point, with which he begins his essay, for reasons that are probably obvious enough. For, if men are not claimed to be the same at all times and places, then the simple theory of cumulative progress that he puts forward, and that is here being discussed, could be invalidated by the assertion that mankind has undergone a sudden, or even a gradual, degeneration in its nature. Most later proponents of this sort of progress accept Fontenelle's contention.

Widespread support for the Pascal-Fontenelle position is to be found in the literature. What is the law of human progress—the law under which civilization advances? asks Henry George. It is not difficult to discover such a law, he declares. The incentives to progress are the desires inherent in human nature, and its instrument is mind; the law or principle whereby progress occurs he describes as follows:

> Though he may not by taking thought add a cubit to his stature, man may by taking thought extend his knowledge of the universe and his power over it, in what, so far as we can see, is an infinite degree. The narrow span of human life allows the individual to go but a short distance, but though each generation may do but little, yet generations, succeeding to the gain of their predecessors, may gradually elevate the status of man-kind, as coral polyps, building one generation upon the work of the other, gradually elevate themselves from the bottom of the sea.[16]

Even more modern support is provided by E. H. Carr, who draws a distinction between "biological inheritance, which is the source of evolu-tion, [and] social acquisition, which is the source of progress."

> The essence of man as a rational being is that he develops his potential capacities by accumulating the experiences of past generations. Modern man is said to have no larger a brain, and no greater innate capacity of

15 *Ibid.*
16 *Progress and Poverty,* p. 507. This colorful image is found in several later writers.

thought, than his ancestor 5,000 years ago. But the effectiveness of his thinking has been multiplied many times by learning and incorporating in his experience the experience of the intervening generations.[17]

"The transmission of acquired characteristics, which is rejected by biologists, is the very foundation of social progress," Carr goes on to say. "*History is progress through the transmission of acquired skills* from one generation to another."[18]

Ortega concurs, at the same time emphasizing a point that had been made by Pascal. That our life possesses a "simply progressive character," he declares, "this we can affirm *a priori* with full evidence and with a surety."[19] One reason is man's mutability, "our ontological privilege. Progress is only possible to one who is not linked to what he was yesterday, who is not caught forever in that being which is already, but can migrate from it to another."[20]

Ortega goes on to distinguish between the progress that is natural to man and the stasis, based on instinct, that is natural to animals. Ortega's example of an animal bound by instinct in the same old round is the tiger; it will be recalled that Pascal's was the bee. The difference between a bee and a tiger may denote some kind of difference between Pascal and Ortega as to their conception of animality or instinct, but their notions of the principle of progress appear to be the same.[21]

The fabulist Charles Perrault, in still another contribution to the controversy between Ancients and Moderns, adds to the basic argument a figure of speech that is often used by its proponents. *A Comparison of the Ancients and Moderns* is in dialogue form, and several participants—the Président, the Chevalier, the Abbé—have different things to say; all agree, however, that progress occurs. The Chevalier is the one who draws the familiar analogy between the race and the individual; the Abbé remarks that

> the latest arrivals have, as it were, inherited the estate of their predecessors, and have added to it a great many new acquisitions which they have acquired through their own study and effort.[22]

However, the Abbé must meet an objection raised by the Président. If progress in knowledge is merely a question of the passage of time, then

[17] *What Is History?*, pp. 150–1.
[18] *Ibid.*, p. 151. Emphasis added.
[19] *History as a System*, p. 218.
[20] *Ibid.*, p. 219.
[21] The bee seems to be a common example among progress authors. Ortega may be alone in choosing the tiger.
[22] *A Comparison of the Ancients and Moderns*, in Teggart, p. 189.

"the men of the ninth and tenth centuries would have been more capable than all those of antiquity";[23] but this, patently, is not true. The Abbé replies:

> It is not strange that the arts and sciences disappear for a time and that ignorance and barbarism rule in their place. The sciences and arts may be likened in this connection to those rivers which are suddenly swallowed up, but which, after having flooded underground for a space, come finally upon an outlet in some neighboring province, whence they are seen to reissue with the same abundance with which they vanished from sight.[24]

Human progress, by this argument, is continuous; however, it is not continuous in one place or among one people. Such factors as climate, situation, national character, and so forth, have critical effects on its occurrence—or rather, on the rate at which it occurs, for the Abbé does not appear to be saying that progress in general can be stopped, but only that it can be slowed.

This point is concurred in by several of the authors discussed above. Carr, for instance, declares that "whatever progress we can observe in history is certainly not continuous either in time or place. . . . What seems for one group a period of decline may seem to another the birth of a new advance. Progress does not and cannot mean equal and simultaneous progress for all."[25]

A host of progress authors agree that one source at least of progress is man's social nature, his capacity to remember and build on what his forefathers have learned and experienced, his faculty of transmitting "acquired assets" through the medium of language. The position is clearly enough expressed, perhaps, by the authors mentioned.

However, a variant of the position requires discussion here. A relatively small number of progress authors appear to base their affirmation of progress on the same grounds as those considered here, but they make little or no mention of this. Instead, they seem to be saying that man progresses simply because he is progressive.

Progress occurs in every respect, says Madame de Staël; the reason, however, is merely that man is perfectible.

> As I survey the revolution of the globe, and the succession of ages, one great idea is ever uppermost in my mind, from which I never allow my attention

23 *Ibid.*
24 *Ibid.* This figure of speech recurs, as will be seen.
25 *Op. cit.*, p. 154.

to be diverted; I mean that of the perfectibility of the human race. I cannot bring myself to think, that this grand work of moral nature has ever been abandoned: in the ages of light, as well as in those of darkness, the gradual advancement of the human intellect has never been interrupted.[26]

Madame de Staël's theory, in one sense, is complex. She distinguishes literally dozens of stages, or "aeras," in history, all of which "discover . . . the natural progress of the human mind."[27] But she does not indicate how progress operates, or by what institutions it was brought about and is to be continued. Man progresses, it appears, merely because it is in the nature of man to progress.

The same lack of grounds is found in Godwin. His notion, too, of the source of progress is simplicity itself. "Man," he declares, "is perfectible."

> By perfectible, it is not meant that he is capable of being brought to perfection. But the word becomes sufficiently adapted to express the faculty of being continually made better and receiving perpetual improvement; and in this sense it is here to be understood. The term perfectible, thus explained, not only does not imply the capacity of being brought to perfection, but stands in express opposition to it. If we could arrive at perfection, there would be an end to our improvement. There is however one thing of great importance that it does imply: every perfection of excellence that human beings are competent to conceive, human beings, unless in cases that are palpably and unequivocally excluded by the structure of their frames, are competent to obtain.[28]

This seems to reduce, once again, to the proposition that man progresses because he is progressive.

Progress, for Godwin, is continuous, a belief he shares with Madame de Staël; moreover, its future occurrence is assured. "We will . . . simply remind the reader," he writes, "of the great changes which man has undergone as an intellectual being, entitling us to infer the probability of improvements not less essential, to be realized in the future."[29] This inference, though it seemed to Malthus highly tenuous,[30] is for Godwin as solid as bedrock. The only conceivable change in man that Godwin does *not* envisage is that he should change for the worse, that is, cease to be perfectible.

[26] *The Influence of Literature Upon Society,* Vol. I, pp. 72–3.
[27] *Ibid.,* p. 83.
[28] *An Enquiry Concerning Political Justice,* Vol. I, p. 93.
[29] *Ibid.,* p. 110.
[30] Malthus attacks the "facile optimism" of Godwin in *Population.* For an account of this dispute, see Chapter 16.

Progress Through the Superior Use of Acquired Assets

The authors who hold that progress occurs, not only because man inherits knowledge from the past and builds thereon but also because he uses his inherited knowledge in a superior way, are listed below.

Turgot	J. S. Mill
Condorcet	Piaget
Saint-Simon	Freud
Comte	Whyte
Enfantin	

In addition, several authors are discussed in the following pages—notably Childe and Mumford—who appear to conceive past progress in the same light as do the above writers, but who conceive future progress as largely contingent on man's use of his reason. They properly belong in another group of progress authors, and are so considered in the next chapter.

The progress theories discussed in the preceding section put emphasis on the fact that knowledge is transmitted from one generation to the next, and also on the essential sameness of human beings at all times and places. The authors of the theories now to be considered concur in holding that man as a social animal inherits knowledge from the past, and increases it before handing it on to the future, but they also see some kind of evolution or development, itself meliorative, occurring in the human mind. The authors of these theories usually maintain that this mental development follows a prescribed course through a number of clearly defined stages or steps.

Comte proposes such a scheme at the beginning of his *Positive Philosophy*.

> In order to understand the true value and character of the Positive Philosophy, we must take a brief general view of the progressive course of the human mind, regarded as a whole; for no conception can be understood otherwise than through its history.
>
> From the study of the development of human intelligence, in all directions, and through all times, the discovery arises of a great fundamental law, to which it is necessarily subject, and which has a solid foundation of proof, both in the facts of our organization and in our historical experience. The law is this:—that each of our leading conceptions—each branch of our knowledge—passes successively through three different theoretical conditions: the Theological, or fictitious; the Metaphysical, or

abstract; and the Scientific, or positive. In other words, the human mind, by its nature, employs in its progress three methods of philosophizing, the character of which is essentially different, and even radically opposed: viz., the theological method, the metaphysical, and the positive. Hence arise three philosophies, or general systems of conceptions on the aggregate of phenomena. The first is the necessary point of departure of the human understanding; and the third is its fixed and definite state. The second is merely a state of transition.

. . . The importance of the working of this general law will be established hereafter. At present, it must suffice to point out some of the grounds of it.

There is no science which, having attained the positive stage, does not bear marks of having passed through the others. Some time since it was (whatever it might be) composed, as we can now perceive, of metaphysical abstractions; and, further back in the course of time, it took its form from theological conceptions. We shall have only too much occasion to see, as we proceed, that our most advanced sciences still bear very evident marks of the two earlier periods through which they have passed.[31]

Comte does not fail to make the comparison that has been found in Pascal and other writers. "The progress of the individual mind is not only an illustration," he declares, "but an indirect evidence of that of the general mind. The point of departure of the individual and of the race being the same, the phases of the mind of a man correspond to the epochs of the mind of the race."[32] He goes on to observe that each of us is aware, if he looks back on his own intellectual history, that "he was a theologian in his childhood, a metaphysician in his youth, and a natural philosopher in his manhood."[33] He writes, furthermore, that

> it is the slow, continuous accumulation of . . . successive changes which gradually constitutes the social movement, whose steps are ordinarily marked by generations, as the most appreciable elementary variations are wrought by the constant renewal of adults. At a time when the average rapidity of this progression seems to all eyes to be remarkably accelerated, the reality of the movement cannot be disputed, even by those who most abhor it.[34]

The source or principle of progress for Comte is therefore twofold, rather than, as for Pascal, singular. Progress for Comte rests on two great facts about man. The first is that, as is true for Pascal, mankind accumulates experience and knowledge through the passage of time, in the

[31] *The Positive Philosophy*, pp. 25–6. Comte claims that there are even more compelling "historical evidences" for the law.
[32] *Ibid.*, pp. 26–7.
[33] *Ibid.*, p. 27.
[34] *Ibid.*, p. 464.

same fashion as an individual learns as he grows older.[35] The second is that the human mind is so constituted that it develops in a certain way— through the three intellectual states—and that these in turn affect the conditions of human life.[36]

Progress for Comte is not only incontrovertible, it is also continuous. In this belief he differs with most progress authors. The reason is because progress results from the conflict between two states of mind, the passage from one to the other of which is inevitable; the intermediate or metaphysical stage is merely transitional.

> The general, like the individual mind, is governed by imagination first, and then, after a sufficient exercise of the faculties at large, more and more by reason. The same grounds on which the process takes place in the individual determine that of the whole species.[37]

If history is the record of the conflict between these two opposing states of mind, and if imagination must always give way to reason, then any apparent regress is merely a manifestation of the conflict itself. At certain moments in history, at certain places on earth, when and where the positive state of mind is struggling to assert itself, it may encounter resistance, it may even *seem* to be losing ground. But these apparent losses are really gains.[38]

Progress, in short, can never be halted; it can only be retarded. However, the fact that its rate can be slowed means that it can be quickened as well.

> In a dynamical view, the progress of the race must be considered susceptible of modification only with regard to its speed, and without any reversal in the order of development, or any interval of any importance being over-leaped.[39]

[35] It is a corollary of this fact that the past determines the present, to some extent at least, and that history is consequently intelligible. As Comte likes to quote Leibniz in saying, "The past subsists in the present, and the present is big with the future."

[36] It is true that Comte holds that progress is, from "the highest scientific point of view," an aspect of the progress (evolution) of nature as a whole. Underlying the two facts, therefore, may be another, an even more basic fact, namely, that nature shows a total progress from inorganic to organic, from organic to animal, from animal to human—finally, to the "intellectual and moral" sphere. Comte, in short, has affinities to several of the cosmogenic progress authors discussed in Chapter 6. However, his main emphasis is on the anthropogenic character of progress. Human progress —social progression—is natural to man, and proceeds because of, and according to, the two facts about man that have been described.

[37] *Op. cit.,* p. 531.

[38] This is Comte's version of the underground river of progress.

[39] *Ibid.,* p. 470.

Comte mentions several factors that affect the rate of progress. Among them are boredom (*ennui*),[40] the "actual duration of human life,"[41] the "natural increase of population," and the tendency, also natural, of increasing population to condense in cities.[42]

The factor that most effectively slows the rate of progress is, for Comte, the intransigence of men, which means, at bottom, their refusal to heed reason. Turgot, Condorcet, and others hold that the very fact of human error and intransigence is a spring of progress; not so for Comte. Progress, in his view, continues to occur *in spite of* the efforts of powerful men to obstruct it. But they do succeed in slowing it down.

In *A System of Logic*, which is divided, like *The Positive Philosophy*, into six books, J. S. Mill considers in his Book Six many of the questions that are dealt with in the last part of Comte's work. Among these are the questions, whether there is a science of human nature, whether there are laws of the mind and its development, what are the methods of social science, and what is the law of history. In general, Mill comes to the same conclusions as does Comte.

He is agreeing with Comte when he says that the primary problem of social science "is to find the laws according to which any state of society produces the state which succeeds it and takes its place."[43] History, in short, is a phenomenon that can be, and should be, studied in the same way as other natural phenomena. With respect to the direction history takes, or the pattern it shows, Mill says that this must be (on the analogy of the solar system) either cyclical or "a trajectory—a course not returning into itself. One or the other of these must be the type to which human affairs conform."[44]

Vico, in the *Scienza Nuova*, "adopted the former of these opinions," says Mill. But

> though there were not wanting circumstances tending to give some plausibility to this view, it would not bear a close scrutiny; and those who have succeeded Vico in this kind of speculation have universally adopted the idea of a trajectory or progress, in lieu of an orbit or cycle.[45]

[40] *Ibid.*, pp. 517–8. For Kant and Malthus, boredom is rather a kind of obstacle to progress, for mankind has a tendency to accept it and to rest in its spurious "content."

[41] *Ibid.*, pp. 518–9. The average duration of human life, Comte declares, is exactly right to promote progress. If men lived longer lives, they would incline too much toward conservatism. If shorter, they would change too often and too radically.

[42] *Ibid.*, pp. 519–21. Increasing population tends to condense in cities, cities lead to civilization, and civilization promotes progress.

[43] *A System of Logic*, p. 595.

[44] *Ibid.*, p. 596.

[45] *Ibid.*

The basic reason why progress is the pattern of history, rather than the cycle, is, as for Comte, the first or Pascalian fact about man. "It is sufficient," says Mill,

> that there is a progressive change, both in the character of the human race and in their outward circumstances so far as moulded by themselves; that in each successive age the principal phenomena of society are different from what they were in the age preceding, and still more different from any previous age; the periods which most distinctly mark these successive changes being intervals of one generation, during which a new set of human beings have been educated, have grown up from childhood, and taken possession of society.[46]

Any law of the succession of social states can only, Mill declares, be an empirical law, not an absolute law. And it must furthermore be based on an understanding of human nature and psychology, for

> the order of human progression in all respects will mainly depend on the order of progression in the intellectual convictions of mankind, that is, on the law of the successive transformations of human opinions.[47]

These conditions being laid down, Mill declares that "the important generalization, which Comte regards as the fundamental law of the progress of human knowledge,"[48] is the very conception sought. Of this, Comte's law of the three intellectual states, Mill writes:

> This generalization appears to me to have that high degree of scientific evidence which is derived from the concurrence of the indications of history with the probabilities derived from the constitution of the human mind. Nor could it easily be conceived, from the mere enunciation of such a proposition, what a flood of light it lets in upon the whole course of history, when its consequences are traced, by connecting with each of the three states of human intellect which it distinguishes, and with each successive modification of these three states, the correlative condition of other social phenomena.[49]

Mill, finally, concludes from all this what Comte also concludes, namely, that "a Philosophy of History is . . . at once the verification and the initial form of the Philosophy of the Progress of Society."[50]

[46] *Ibid.*
[47] *Ibid.*, p. 605.
[48] *Ibid.*, p. 606.
[49] *Ibid.*
[50] *Ibid.*, p. 607. The impression should not be had that Mill agrees with Comte about everything, even concerning progress. Indeed, he holds that many of Comte's predictions regarding the future development of mankind are inaccurate, not to say absurd. He criticizes Comte for supposing that he had completely formed the science

Mill emphasizes the necessity of "connecting all our generalizations from history with the laws of human nature," and contends that Comte alone, "among the new historical school," has seen this requirement, and observed it.[51] The reference is probably to writers like Condorcet and Godwin, who, while they speak of the "development" of the human mind and of institutions, propose no precise law of human nature to account for it. Godwin has been discussed above; we shall consider Condorcet below. For the moment, mention should be made of one or two authors who appear to satisfy Mill's criteria.

In a number of works, the psychologist Piaget studied the mentality of the child, in order, he says, to arrive at conclusions about the development of the human mind. His emphasis is on the individual mind; but he accepts the Pascalian analogy between the individual and humanity as a whole.

> If we examine the intellectual development of the individual or of the whole of humanity, we shall find that the human spirit goes through a certain number of stages, each different from the others, but such that during each, the mind believes itself to be apprehending an external reality that is independent of the thinking subject. The content of this reality varies according to the stages: for the young child it is alive and permeated with finality, intentions, etc., whereas for the scientist, reality is characterized by its physical determinism.[52]

Piaget's scheme is complex: he distinguishes three "processes," five "adherences," and seventeen "types of causal relation in child thought."[53] However, the complex superstructure does not hide the fact that the underlying notions are Comtian. For Piaget, the five adherences are of primary importance, just as, for Comte, the fact that humanity drags behind it the lengthening chain of the past is most striking. The adherences are: dynamic participation, animism, artificialism, finalism, and the notion of force;[54] all represent states of mind out of which humanity must break as it passes on to scientific conceptions, as well as phases through

---

of society, and "that it was already sufficiently solid for attempting to build upon its foundation the entire fabric of the Political Art" (*Auguste Comte and Positivism*, p. 113). The later speculations of Comte, in his *Positive Polity*, about the future of humanity, among them the proposal of a "religion of humanity," in which man himself is the Godhead, come in for especially stringent rebuke on the part of Mill. However, these differences are not really germane to the question at hand. Mill's conception of the grounds for progress and the manner of its occurrence is the same as Comte's.

[51] *Op. cit.*, p. 597.
[52] *The Child's Conception of Physical Causality*, p. 237.
[53] *Ibid.*, pp. 244, 258, 267.
[54] *Ibid.*, pp. 244–5.

which the child passes on its way to maturity. In a statement that would be equally applicable to humanity as a whole, Piaget writes of the child mind:

> Both the area of application and the strength of resistance of these adherences decrease progessively throughout the mental development of the child. And not only do these adherences lose ground little by little in correlation with each other, but their progressive disappearance seems to be proportional to the increasing clarity with which the child becomes conscious of his subjectivity.[55]

Freud proposes a similar theory in one of his earlier works. In *Totem and Taboo* he writes:

> If we take the now established omnipotence of thought among primitive races as a proof of their narcism, we may venture to compare the various evolutionary stages of man's conception of the universe with the stages of the libidinous evolution of the individual. We find that the animistic phase corresponds in time as well as in content with narcism, the religious phase corresponds to that stage of object finding which is characterized by dependence on the parents, while the scientific stage has its full counterpart in the individual's taste of maturity where, having renounced the pleasure principle and having adapted himself to reality, he seeks his object in the outer world.[56]

The animistic, religious, and scientific phases of evolutionary development may not coincide exactly with Comte's theological, metaphysical, and positive states of mind. But the likeness is close enough for our purposes. [57]

For Comte and those whom he inspires, the "development" of the human mind is along a threefold course, running in general from a state in which "thought" or "imagination" is dominant, to one (a final state) in which "reason" or "positive or scientific conception" is dominant. A

[55] *Ibid.*, pp. 245–6.
[56] In *Basic Writings of Sigmund Freud*, pp. 876–7.
[57] We will discover that neo-Freudians like Marcuse and N. O. Brown derive their theories of regress from later works of Freud—notably *Civilization and Its Discontents*. Must we conclude from this fact, however, that there is a contradiction in Freud's thinking on the subject of progress? It is true that Freud's later writings are more "pessimistic" than his earlier ones, but he does not deny in them that progress occurs in history; rather, he points out that progress does not insure a certain type of happiness. Progress may decrease the amount of this happiness, while at the same time increasing man's desire for it. But progress is not the same as the increase of this type of happiness, which is characterized by freedom from guilt. "The price of progress in civilization is paid in forfeiting happiness through the heightening of the sense of guilt," says Freud (*Civilization and Its Discontents*, p. 90). Statements of this kind are probably the source of the view that Freud denies progress. However, the price that man pays for progress an individual also pays for his own development. It is the price that has to be paid for growing up.

number of other writers have a similar notion, whether or not they take
the basic pattern from Comte. Indeed, one of them may have supplied
Comte with the pattern.

This is Turgot, who, in the second of his two lectures to the Sorbonne
on the subject of human progress, asserts that progress occurs in almost
every sphere of human life except the artistic, and who suggests a threefold developmental scheme.

The lecture begins with distinctions and comparisons that are by now
familiar. "The phenomena of nature" are to be distinguished from "the
succession of men," says Turgot, and for the same reasons that Pascal had
given. "The human race, considered from its origin, appears to the eyes
of the philosopher to be an immense whole, having like every individual
its own childhood and its own stages of growth."[58]

> The total mass of human kind, through alternations of calm and agitation,
> of evil days and good, ever advances, though with dragging pace, towards a
> higher degree of perfection.[59]

Progress is continuous, although there appear to be periods of regress.
During the Dark Ages, progress did, indeed, cease in some respects, and
its overall rate was slowed. But even then it was "working unawares."
"What a surge of inventions unknown to the ancients and due to these
barbaric centuries!" Turgot cries.[60] Particularly notable are three inventions often cited by progress authors: printing, gunpowder, and the compass. In the process of defending the Middle Ages against the charge of
regression, Turgot makes use of Perrault's figure of speech:

> Facts were being amassed in the obscurity of the times of ignorance, and the
> sciences whose progress was not the less real for being hidden were destined
> one day to reappear increased by these new riches, just as those streams
> which, after being concealed from our sight in a subterranean channel,
> come to the surface further on, swollen with all the waters filtered into
> them through the earth.[61]

[58] *Tableau philosophique des progrès successifs de l'esprit humain*, p. 8. Turgot did
not complete the ambitious historical work that he proposed at an early age, and of
which the two Sorbonne lectures might have been parts. The work was to be in
opposition to Bishop Bossuet's *Discourse on Universal History* (1688), which, while
recognizing the concept of universal history (the history of mankind as a whole), did
not view it as progressive. "Turgot's objective," says G. H. Hildebrand, "was to provide an alternative picture of the 'general' history of the human race in terms of the
idea of progress, and with central emphasis upon the advancement of 'the human
mind'" (in Teggart, p. 15).

[59] *Op. cit.*, p. 5. Comte also speaks of the dragging pace of progress.

[60] *Ibid.*, p. 17.

[61] *Ibid.* It is noteworthy, in fact, that Perrault's metaphor does not imply what he
means it to. His stream emerges from underground "with the same abundance" with
which it vanished. While that may mean that *regress* does not occur, it does not
add up to an affirmation of progress. Turgot has the thing right.

Turgot's scheme of the development of the mind is sketched in the first of the two Sorbonne lectures. J. B. Bury shows the similarity between this pattern and Comte's:

> "Before man understood the causal connection of physical phenomena, nothing was so natural as to suppose they were produced by intelligent beings, invisible and resembling ourselves; for what else would they have resembled?" That is Comte's theological stage. "When philosophers recognised the absurdity of the fables about the gods, they thought to explain the causes of phenomena by abstract expressions such as essences and faculties." That is the metaphysical stage. "It was only at a later period, that by observing the reciprocal mechanical action of bodies hypotheses were formed which could be developed by mathematics and verified by experience." That is the positive stage.[62]

Bury adds that "the observation assuredly does not possess [for Turgot] the far-reaching importance which Comte attached to it; but whatever value it has, Turgot deserves the credit of having been the first to state it."[63]

Bury also remarks that Turgot held that "the development of human societies has not been guided by human reason. . . . They have been conducted by passion and ambition and have never known to what goal they were moving."[64] In this respect Turgot differs with Comte. According to the latter, progress can be accelerated by the judicious application of reason to human affairs. For Turgot, it may be wiser to leave progress to proceed by itself. He emphasizes the disparity of human desires.

> Interest, ambition, and vainglory at every instant change the face of the world and inundate the world with blood. In the midst of their ravages, manners grow refined, the mind of man becomes enlightened, nations leave their isolation to draw near to one another; commerce and politics unite at last all the parts of the globe; and the total mass of human kind . . . ever advances.[65]

It may even be that Turgot is suggesting that some kind of conflict accelerates, if it does not by itself produce, progress in society. At least there is little doubt that he has affinities with writers like Mandeville and Adam Smith, who do say this, and with certain other cosmogenic progress authors such as Malthus, Kant, and Hegel.

We have seen how Mill criticizes the "new historical school" for affirming progress without finding a basis for it in the "laws" of human nature.

---

[62] Bury, *The Idea of Progress*, p. 157. Bury is quoting Turgot here.
[63] *Ibid.*
[64] *Ibid.*, p. 155.
[65] *Op. cit.*, p. 5.

A criticism not entirely dissimilar is found in the so-called Doctrine of Saint-Simon.

> The imperfectly conceived idea of perfectibility remained sterile in the hands of Vico, Lessing, Turgot, Kant, Herder, and Condorcet because none of these philosophers knew how to describe the character of progress. None of them indicated in what it consisted, how it operated, or by what institutions it was brought about and was to be continued; none of them, when confronted by the great number of historical events, could classify them into progressive and retrogressive events or coordinate them into homogeneous series, the terms of which would be linked together according to a law of growth and decline.[66]

Several of the writers mentioned here are discussed in other parts of this study; Vico, in our opinion, is not a progress author at all. Nevertheless, the criticism seems accurate in regard to Condorcet, if to no other of the writers listed; and it may be applied to still other progress authors, of whom the Saint-Simonians could not have heard.

Condorcet's theory of progress has in common with both Pascal's and Comte's that the progress of the human mind

> is subject to the same general laws that can be observed in the development of the faculties of the individual, and it is indeed no more than the sum of that development realized in a large number of individuals together in society. What happens at any particular moment is the result of what

[66] *The Doctrine of Saint-Simon,* p. 32, Note. The quotation continues: "All of them finally overlooked the fact that the only elements that have appeared repeatedly in the past and would interest the future were the Fine Arts, the Sciences, and Industry, and that the study of this triple manifestation of human activity was to constitute social science, because it served to verify the moral, intellectual, and physical development of the human race, its ceaseless progress towards the unity of affection, doctrine, and activity." This, of course, is a doctrinal statement; it conveys the progress theory of the Saint-Simonians themselves. Saint-Simon, whom Comte, as a young man, served as secretary, has three terms of reference: "feeling," "intellect," and "material activity"; these are "the three modes of human activity." There is progress in each, but the progress of mankind consists in a more and more ordered relation among them. Of the three, the last is the most important; it is ultimately to be ordered according to feeling, which is defined as "affectionate relations" among men. From hatred man turns to social love, and military fierceness is converted to peaceful production. At the same time, the intellect, "which had been kept down by brutality, occupies a successively higher place" (*ibid.*, pp. 26–9).

An early Saint-Simonian, Eugène Rodrigues, makes this comparison between Saint-Simon, Comte, and Enfantin: "The classification into three is shared by Saint-Simon, Auguste Comte and Enfantin. But Saint-Simon puts feeling and science on the same plane and subordinates both to industry and action. Auguste Comte subordinates feeling to science. Enfantin . . . subordinates science (as well as action) to feeling" (*ibid.*, pp. 28–9, Note). Rodrigues goes on to observe that "actually, when the Saint-Simonian doctrine was transformed into a religious dogma, its adherents began to see a trinity manifesting the divine life, namely, Love, Wisdom, and Power."

has happened at all previous moments, and itself has an influence on what
will happen in the future.[67]

However, Condorcet does not take the further step that is taken by
Comte. That is, Condorcet has no explicit theory of the development of
the human mind; no notion of intellectual or mental states through which
every kind of speculation, and consequently every kind of social institution, must pass; and no idea, beyond vague references, of the "laws of
human nature" on which Comte's theory essentially depends.

Condorcet has moved beyond Pascal, however, for he does have an
idea of social development, though it is not closely related to mental development. The outline of his work reflects this notion; it is divided into
ten chapters, each treating a "stage" of human progress. Although Condorcet uses the term "stage" to describe the various epochs through which
man has passed, he does not have the same conception of a stage of development as do, for example, Comte and Saint-Simon, or even Turgot.
Condorcet's stages are merely historical epochs or periods. They are eras
in which certain events occurred, and certain social institutions were dominant. They are not based on fundamental changes in the mind of man.

Nevertheless, like all of the authors being treated in this section, Condorcet views the history of man as having followed, and as continuing
to follow, a certain comprehensible course. The direction of human development is not reversible, nor could it have followed any other course
than the one it did follow. In this respect he, like the others, is beyond
Pascal, who offers only a formal principle of progress, and does not show
how this actually operates in history.

V. Gordon Childe also superimposes a scheme of social development
on the basic Pascalian theory of progress. He accepts the validity of the
analogy between the race and the individual; he notes the difference between history and cultural progress, on the one hand, and natural history
and organic evolution, on the other—this corresponds to Pascal's distinction between "instinct" and "intelligence"; and he appears, like Condorcet, to hold that progress is continuous, that it can be retarded but
not stopped altogether. But the development, for Childe, is social only,
not psychological.

The stages in man's progress (Childe calls them "revolutions") are
marked by sharp increases in population. Revolutions

[67] *Sketch for a Historical Picture of the Progress of the Human Mind*, p. 4.
Condorcet's famous *Sketch (Esquisse)* was in large part written under the threat of
death; it was composed at a time when the Marquis was hiding from the Jacobins.
On completion of the manuscript, in March 1794, Condorcet was arrested and confined. He was found dead in his cell the next day; it is supposed that he took
poison to escape the guillotine. Few commentators have failed to note the irony in
the fact that Condorcet's book is among the most enthusiastic of all progress works.

manifest themselves in the same way as the "Industrial Revolution"—in an upward kink in the population curve. They must be judged by the same standard. The chief aim of this book is to examine prehistory and ancient history from this angle. It is hoped that a consideration of revolutions, so remote that it is impossible to get angry or enthusiastic about them, may help to vindicate the idea of progress against sentimentalists and mystics.[68]

Childe discusses five revolutions: first, the "neolithic revolution," when man began to control his food supply; second, the conversion of small, isolated communities into populous cities; third, the "urban revolution," which involved the discovery of the division of labor, the building of surplus wealth, and the emergence of a leisure class, which in turn brought about further and accelerated progress; fourth, the "revolution in human knowledge," or the beginning of the "scientific tradition"; and fifth, the "industrial revolution." He also lays out nineteen "social mutations," which seem to correspond on the whole to technological innovations.[69]

Progress consists in two advances—the increase of population and the accumulation of knowledge. The spring of progress is the latter, although knowledge does not accumulate steadily; the various revolutions change the character and direction of increasing knowledge. Condorcet concurs. And Childe's revolutions are very similar to Condorcet's stages of history.[70]

C. G. Darwin agrees with Childe in several respects. He views progress as occurring—or as having occurred in the past—because of man's capacity to transmit social experience; he measures progress by population jumps; and he speaks of revolutions in history. But for Darwin, the emphasis is on increase in "intellectual stature," rather than, as for Childe, advances to "higher" social states. Hence Darwin's revolutions are somewhat different from Childe's.[71]

Mumford speaks not of stages or revolutions, but of the "transformations of man." There are five of these; the last brings about a radical crisis in history, a crucial point at which man may either degenerate or continue to advance.

---

[68] *Man Makes Himself*, p. 19. The title implies that progress is anthropogenic.
[69] Childe's discussion of the various revolutions occupies the bulk of his book.
[70] Up to the point, at least, where Childe stops; he does not carry his story beyond the age of the classical Greeks. Condorcet's later stages bring him to the "present" (1794), and his tenth stage is "the future progress of the human mind."
   The difference between Childe and Condorcet, on the one hand, and Godwin and Madame de Staël, on the other hand, is that the former pair see human development occurring in a specific and intelligible series of social states, where the latter pair do not. This difference should not mask the difference between all four writers and Comte, who has a conception of the relation between these social states and psychological modes in the development of the human mind.
[71] Darwin's theory of progress is treated in the next chapter. The decision to discuss him there is somewhat arbitrary.

The transformations of man are marked by changes in both intellectual attitudes and social institutions, though the former appear to be the result of the latter. The first transformation was that by which the animal became human, by which man escaped the world of 'instinctual cyclism" and took over his own social or cultural evolution. "Of all the labor-saving devices that man has invented," says Mumford, "this earliest invention, that of detachment from the organic, seems beyond any doubt the most important."[72] The second transformation resulted in what Mumford calls "Archaic Man."[73] The third brought into existence "Civilized Man."

> The prime mark of civilization . . . is the bringing together of larger bodies of men, by means of technical agents, symbolic abstractions, and centralized political authority, into a greater community of purpose than had ever existed before.[74]

However, the ambivalent character of progress is indicated by the fact that there were invented, at the same time,

> slavery, compulsory labor, social regimentation, economic exploitation, and organized warfare: this is the darker side of the "progress of civilization."[75]

From the fourth transformation emerged "Axial Man," who "concentrates upon inner growth."[76] But the sum of the four transformations was still only "Old World Culture," which was limited and susceptible of becoming once more cyclic and unchanging. The fifth transformation, that by which Old World Man become "New World Man," was brought about by the scientific and technological "revolutions" of the last several centuries.

We are at present in the midst of this fifth transformation, says Mumford, and, barring a nuclear catastrophe, we can now turn in one of two directions. It is possible, perhaps even probable, that the next (and consequently the last) stage will be that of "posthistoric man," as it is conceived by Seidenberg.[77] However, Mumford differs with Seidenberg in holding that the posthistoric stage is not inevitable. The antlike existence of posthistoric man can be avoided; a "miracle" can bring about another trans-

---

[72] *The Transformations of Man*, p. 13.

[73] Most of Mumford's book is devoted to discussion of the various revolutions. This second one corresponds to Childe's "neolithic," and Darwin's "agricultural," revolution.

[74] *Ibid.*, p. 44. This corresponds to Childe's and Darwin's "urban" revolution.

[75] *Ibid.*, p. 50. Childe also refers to these melancholy side effects of the urban revolution.

[76] *Ibid.*, p. 64.

[77] Seidenberg is a regress author. His theory of regress is discussed in Chapter 8.

formation, from "New World Culture" to "World Culture." The integrating purpose of World Culture

> is to provide a means of bringing into relations of reciprocity and willing amity the entire family of man, so that they may share, as never before, not only what they have gained through their historic experience, but what they have still to create through their deliberate intermingling and cultural interchange.[78]

World Culture will be marked by a "wholeness" of the personality, and there will be reciprocal relations between the wholeness of the individual and that of the culture.

> In the fulness of time, a unified self will bring a world culture into existence, and that world culture will in turn sustain and bring to a higher pitch of development this new self.[79]

Mumford accepts the idea that man advances because of his capacity to transmit tradition, and, like all of the authors discussed in this section, he sees man as developing along a certain course. He adds, however, the assertion that

> the other source of man's veritable humanness was his capacity to dream; for this is the forward-moving counterpart to memory. In origin derived perhaps from man's anxiety, the dream took on a positive function—it became the great instrument of anticipation, invention, projection, creative transformation.[80]

This is perhaps another way of saying what Godwin says—namely, that man is capable of achieving everything that he is capable of conceiving, with the exception of the physically impossible; or it may mean simply that the capacity to "dream" of progress makes progress, if not likely, at least a possibility. At any rate, Mumford can conclude that

> unified man is no terminal point. For who can set bounds to man's emergence or to his power of surpassing his provisional achievements? So far we have found no limits to the imagination, nor yet to the sources on which

---

[78] *Ibid.*, p. 141.

[79] *Ibid.*, p. 170.

[80] *Ibid.*, p. 16. Mumford here, and in other places in this book, seems to be hopeful about man's chances for progress. In other works, his pessimism is more evident. For example, in a review of Jung's *Memories, Dreams, Reflections,* Mumford makes reference to the matters treated in *The Transformations of Man,* but implies that there is little likelihood of making progress in that direction. He also quotes Jung speaking disparagingly of "the cult of progress" (*The New Yorker,* May 23, 1964).

it may draw. Every goal man reaches provides a new starting point, and the sum of all man's days is just a beginning.[81]

As Pascal puts it, man is "made only for infinity."

All of the authors discussed in this section concur in accepting the Pascalian analogy between the race as a whole and an individual man, with its attendant notion that progress occurs through the transmission of knowledge and other intellectual assets from one generation to the next. They also concur in taking a further step; that is, they agree in holding that man's progress or development is manifested in a series of three or more stages, steps, phases, revolutions, or transformations. However, a difference is discovered among them on the question, raised by Mill and the Saint-Simonians, whether the stages of history are based on the laws of human nature. In the case of Comte and Mill, and also of Saint-Simon and Enfantin, the stages are so based. In the case of Condorcet, Childe, Darwin, and Mumford, the stages do not seem to be so based. The latter writers appear to offer no more than a descriptive scheme of progressive stages in history. It is significant that some members of this group—notably Mumford and Childe—also emphasize the ambivalent or contingent character of future progress. Past progress, they seem to be saying, has taken the form of changes from one stage of human life to another. Future progress will be dependent, however, on man's use of reason, and on his desire to bring progress about.

[81] *Ibid.*, p. 184. Hence the "miracle" is perhaps to be expected, after all. But see Note 80, above. Compare also the last sentences of Freud's *Civilization and Its Discontents,* where the scientist appears to put his ultimate faith in the actions of a "principle" more or less mysterious.

In large part, future progress depends, for Mumford, on man's use of his reason.

4

Anthropogenic Progress:
Man's Use of Reason

W E turn next to a large number of progress authors who, while in large part not disagreeing with the views of those considered in the previous chapter, are more explicit in describing the particular mental activities and functions of the mind that bring about human progress. In general, these writers do not deny that knowledge accumulates in time; and some of them have an idea of a developmental scheme in history. For them, too, progress remains anthropogenic; its principle is human, and its source is to be found not in the wide universe but in the littler world of man, in the microcosm rather than the macrocosm. However, they differ in that they place the main emphasis on man's use of reason to confront human problems and to deal with human affairs, rather than on this or that conception of the nature of man himself, as the source of progress.

In a sense, the difference between these authors and those discussed in Chapter 3 is that the latter see progress as resulting mainly from the characteristics of the human species—from what man is; while the former see it as a product of certain of man's activities and attainments—from what he does, by his own efforts.[1] It is not surprising, therefore, to find many of these authors holding that progress is not "necessary," that it is not a "law of history." Consideration of this point is, however, reserved for another chapter.

The progress authors who maintain that progress mainly results from man's use of reason are listed below.[2]

Bacon	Ginsberg
Descartes	Simon
Voltaire	Einstein
Rousseau	Carrel
Helvétius	Rougemont
Lavoisier	Childe
Tocqueville	Mumford
Woodberry	C. G. Darwin
Buckle	H. Brown
Fourier	Dunning
Faraday	Dobzhansky
Tolstoy	Skinner
Bryce	Calder
Morgan	Frankel
Dewey	Hermann J. Muller
Todd	Boulding
Marvin	Heilbroner
Broad	Herbert J. Muller
Hobhouse	Dedijer
Maritain	A. C. Clarke
Stace	McNeil

Progress Through Man's Control of Nature

The above authors have various conceptions of the relation between man's use of reason and the occurrence of progress, but one major distinction among their theories is of primary importance. For a relatively

[1] The difference between the authors considered in this chapter and Comte, for instance, is this: Comte holds that the application of positive methods (scientific thinking) to all kinds of human problems accelerates progress. But for him, progress occurs *in any event*. Such application is not the basic source of progress. These authors either say that progress does not occur at all if intelligence is not used by men, or they emphasize the importance of such use to the point where the progress that may occur despite man's misuse of his mind is hardly considered.

[2] The list could be greatly extended by the addition of numerous contemporary authors.

small group of authors—several of them early writers, although they are joined by some contemporary figures—man's use of his reason to understand and control external nature is enough to bring about progress. In their view, progress consists in that increasing control, and any melioration in the general conditions of human life is a result of it. For the majority of the authors listed above, however, such control is not enough, in itself, to bring about progress. Progress, in their view, may be a result of such control, but it is also the result of the use of reason in other spheres. We shall return to the views of the latter authors in a moment.

The authors below hold that progress occurs through man's control of nature, and that this in itself constitutes progress.

Bacon	Childe
Woodberry	C. G. Darwin
Buckle	Dedijer
Morgan	Clarke

One way to argue that progress occurs through man's control of nature is to say that the advancement of science is the equivalent of progress. This is the view of Bacon; it is expressed in many of his writings; it is in the *Novum Organon,* however, that he is most explicit. In a series of chapters he discusses the errors and misconceptions that have inhibited the advance of the sciences. All are shown to be avoidable. Among the most important is this: that "it is impossible to advance properly in the course when the goal is not properly fixed." But the goal *is* fixed, says Bacon. "The real and legitimate goal of the sciences, is the endowment of human life with new inventions and riches."[3] The result of the advancement of science, in short, is human progress, and not the increase of knowledge alone.

The question, then, is not how to bring about progress but how to advance science, for the other will follow from this. By far the greatest obstacle to this advance, Bacon writes,

> is to be found in men's despair and the idea of impossibility; for men of a prudent and exact turn of thought are altogether diffident in matters of this nature, considering the obscurity of nature, the shortness of life, the deception of the senses, and weakness of the judgment. They think, therefore, that in the revolutions of ages and of the world there are certain floods and ebbs of the sciences, and that they grow and flourish at one time, and wither and fall off at another, that when they have attained a certain degree and condition they can proceed no further.[4]

[3] *Advancement of Learning and Novum Organon,* p. 339.
[4] *Ibid.,* pp. 347–8.

This objection, however, is easily overcome. Men have only to apply the same effort and intelligence to "the contemplation of things as they are, free from superstition or imposture, error or confusion," as they apply to their other enterprises, and the sciences will be regenerated, and the human race will progress. Even the objection that scientific discoveries might be used for unworthy purposes is overruled,

> for the same can be said of every worldly good; talent, courage, strength, beauty, riches, light itself, and the rest. Only let mankind regain their rights over nature, assigned to them by the gift of God, and obtain that power, whose exercise will be governed by right reason and true religion.[5]

Buckle also holds that the source of progress is the application of reason, as scientific thinking, to the control of external nature. It is true that Buckle places emphasis on climatic and environmental conditions in the occurrence of progress,[6] but these affect only its rate, which differs at different places and times. A combination of environmental factors has enabled Europe to attain to levels of intellectual and practical achievement not equaled elsewhere, but progress properly consists, in Buckle's view, in our increasing capacity to master physical nature and bend it to to our will.

Buckle's treatment is complicated by his insistence that progress be understood as resulting from the interaction of various fundamental and universal laws, but he is willing to describe the gist of the matter thus:

> The progress is one, not of internal power, but of external advantage. The child born in a civilized land is not likely, as such, to be superior to one born among barbarians; and the difference which ensues between the acts of the two children will be caused, so far as we know, solely by the pressure of external circumstances; by which I mean the surrounding opinions, knowledge, associations; in a word, the entire mental atmosphere in which the two children are respectively nurtured.[7]

Since the difference of "external advantage" is almost entirely the result of the application of rational intelligence to the control of nature, progress must be based on such application.

C. G. Darwin was mentioned, along with Childe and Mumford, in Chapter 3; he is one who has a more complex scheme of mental development than do Bacon and Buckle, and most of the other writers in the above list. However, Darwin's "revolutions" are based on technological developments. Each reflects the attainment of a new, and unlosable, bit of knowledge about nature. The first results from the discovery of fire, the second from the discovery of agriculture, the third from the discovery of

[5] *Ibid.,* p. 366.
[6] He draws largely, it appears, on Montesquieu.
[7] *History of Civilization in England,* Vol. I, p. 176.

civilization (the "urban revolution"), and the fourth is the "scientific revolution," which is

> based on the discovery that it is possible consciously to make discoveries about the fundamental nature of the world; so that by their means man can intentionally and deliberately alter his way of life.[8]

Hence future progress, at least, will be of the sort being discussed in this section.

Darwin, like Freud, does not hold that progress will insure, or even that it means, an increase in future happiness. Indeed, the opposite seems likely, for we are now living in a "Golden Age" marked by the exploitation of "capital resources"—*i.e.*, fossil fuels. We are like a man who lives off principal rather than income; life seems good as long as the principal lasts, but eventually he will have to go back to living on income alone. The course of human development over the next million years can be foreseen, Darwin believes; it will not be particularly pleasant. It will, indeed, be similar to the history of China.

> The regions of the world will fall into provinces of everchanging extent, which most of the time will be competing against one another. Occasionally —more rarely, than has been the case in China—they will be united by some strong arm into an uneasy world government, which will endure for a period until it falls by the inevitable decay that destroys all dynasties. There will be periods when some of the provinces relapse into barbarism, but all the time civilization will survive in some of them.[9]

"It will survive," Darwin declares, "because it will be based on a single universal culture, derived from the understanding of science; for it is only through this understanding that the multitudes can continue to live."

> On this basic culture there will be overlaid other cultures, often possessing a greater emotional appeal, which will vary according to climate and race from one province to another. Most of the time and over most of the earth there will be severe pressure from excess populations, and there will be periodic famines. There will be a consequent callousness about the value of the individual's life, and often there will be cruelty to a degree of which we do not willingly think.[10]

This, however, is but one side of the story. Religion and morals, and political and other institutions, may undergo a cyclical pattern of rise and fall. But true progress will go on and on. "On the other side," Darwin

[8] *The Next Million Years,* p. 36.
[9] *Ibid.,* p. 149.
[10] *Ibid.*

tells us, "there will be vast stores of learning, far beyond anything we can now imagine, and the intellectual stature of man will rise to ever higher levels. And sometimes new discoveries will for a time relieve the human race from its fears, and there will be golden ages, when man may for a time be free to create wonderful flowerings in science, philosophy and the arts."[11]

Many progress authors hold the position here expressed by Bacon, by Buckle, and somewhat differently by Darwin. It is always important to observe, however, whether they are saying, as these authors do, that the source of progress is in the increasing control of external or physical nature alone (or primarily), and not in the increase of scientific control of human nature as well. With this in mind, it is of particular interest to mention the Greek poets Aeschylus, Sophocles, and Euripedes, who, in the opinion of at least one commentator, hold ideas about progress that are strikingly modern.[12]

PROGRESS THROUGH MAN'S CONTROL OF MAN

In a fragment titled "The Sphinx," Bacon writes:

> Now of the Sphinx's riddles there are in all two kinds: one concerning the nature of things, another concerning the nature of man; and in like manner

---

[11] *Ibid.*

[12] In *The Liberal Temper in Greek Politics,* E. A. Havelock outlines what he calls "the historically regressive Hesiodic scheme," and then shows how the conception of man's history in *Prometheus Bound, Antigone,* and Euripedes' *Suppliants* differs from it.

Prometheus is "a fire-giver only by accident," says Havelock; "his significant function is to serve as the channel by which men are endowed with technology" (p. 54; Havelock supports this interpretation by numerous quotations from *Prometheus Bound*). Prometheus, however, is not human, and we must ask, therefore, whether for Aeschylus, progress is anthropogenic or cosmogenic. For Sophocles, there seems to be no question of divine intervention in human progress. According to Havelock, the choral ode at *Antigone* 332–375 recounts the technical advances of which man himself, unaided, can be proud. "The figure of Prometheus has disappeared," Havelock comments. "Man is now truly self-taught" (p. 68).

A similar historical analysis is to be found (according to Havelock) at *Suppliants* 196–217, which ends thus:

> What luxury for us if God had given
> This life's resources when we had none of it!
> Yet man's intelligence would seek a power
> Higher than God's. We get verve in our hearts,
> And think our skill surpasses the divine.

And Havelock finds the same theme in Diodorus Siculus, who appears to draw some of his inspiration from Egyptian as well as Greek models (pp. 71–86).

In general, Havelock traces an important strain of affirmations of progress in ancient Greek literature. Its source, he thinks, was the scientific school of Leucippus, Democritus, and others, the main works of whom are now lost. It was submerged, he says, after its "emasculation" in Aristotle's *Ethics,* and its "rejection" in his *Politics.*

there are two kinds of kingdom offered as the reward of solving them: one over nature, and the other over man.[13]

Bacon seems to imply that progress of the latter sort is not likely; in any event, it need not occur for human progress to occur. Progress, properly so called, consists in the increase of man's knowledge of external nature. Man, knowing no more than he does of human nature, may be trusted to use that other knowledge wisely.

This opinion is not shared by the majority of the authors in the list above. Most of them maintain that man's increasing knowledge of the physical world (which increase they do not deny) is not human progress in itself. That properly consists, for them, in increasing knowledge of man, and in the meliorative effects of this growing understanding on human affairs and institutions, to say nothing of its effects on human nature itself.

Agreeing on that, they do not, however, agree on the role that science plays in the process. As will be seen, some hold that the same type of scientific thinking may be applied to man as to external nature, and that progress will be the result. Others maintain that science is not enough, that man must control his own science above all, that science must be in the service of humanity and not the other way about. These may be said to distrust science but to recognize its usefulness when coupled with a benevolent intent. Others carry their distrust so far as to say that science is intrinsically antiprogressive, that it necessarily leads to the domination of man by man, and perhaps even to the ultimate destruction of the entire human race. For them, some other use of reason is called for besides the scientific.

Descartes is a leading spokesman of the position that progress, while occurring in the natural sciences, is more appropriately to be seen as resulting from the application of scientific thinking to human life.

"The end of study," he declares, "should be to direct the mind towards the enunciation of sound and correct judgments *on all matters that come before it.*" And he goes on to remark that "the sciences taken altogether are identical with human wisdom."

> If, therefore, anyone wishes to search out the truth of things in serious earnest, he ought not to select one special science; for all the sciences are conjoined with each other and interdependent: he ought rather to think how to increase the natural light of reason, not for the purpose of resolving this or that difficulty of scholastic type, but in order that *his understanding may light his will to its proper choice in all the contingencies of life.*[14]

[13] *Gateway to the Great Books,* Vol. 8, p. 3.
[14] *Rules for the Direction of the Mind,* I, in Vol. I, *The Philosophical Works of Descartes,* pp. 1–2. Emphasis added.

Right thinking, for Descartes, consists in the investigation of "what we can clearly and perspicuously behold and with certainty deduce; for knowledge is not won in any other way."[15] Scientific or right thinking must be applied to every sphere of human life, and progress will result therefrom.[16]

C. D. Broad concurs, although he sounds a warning of which Descartes makes no mention. "The greatest immediate threat to the further progress of the human mind," Broad writes, "is the *unequal development*" of the three main branches of knowledge, namely, physics and chemistry, biology and genetics, and psychology and sociology. "It therefore seems not unlikely," Broad declares,

> that there is a great and growing disharmony between human organisms and their environment; and that, unless this can be corrected, the physical and mental qualities of the human race may degenerate. Now it cannot be corrected except by a *deliberate* modification of human organisms, which shall proceed as fast as the deliberate modification of their environment now proceeds.[17]

This is possible, he goes on to say, only if we have a scientific knowledge of biology, physiology, and genetics comparable in extent and accuracy to our knowledge of physics and chemistry. In the final analysis, the possibility of progress

> depends on our getting an adequate knowledge and control of life and mind before the combination of ignorance on these subjects with knowledge of physics and chemistry wrecks the whole social system.[18]

Broad is not saying, as many writers do—they are considered below— that science is not enough. No other use of reason, no benevolence or generosity or love of man for man is called for or necessary. Broad wants more science rather than less, but he wants it applied to areas in which it has so far, in his opinion, shed little light.

15 *Ibid.*, Vol. III, p. 5.
16 It may be objected that Descartes's theory conceives progress as cosmogenic. Charles Frankel writes: "In his omnipotence God could have established other laws for nature. He could have made clear and distinct ideas false, unclear and indistinct ones true. He did not do so because he was benevolent. Consequently, the proof of Descartes's essential discovery—that his method is a revolutionary contribution guaranteeing the future progress of mankind in wisdom—rests ultimately on the recognition of God's grace and is not supportable by an acquaintance with man's intellect alone. The revelation of the method owes nothing to past philosophy; and the progress which follows the revelation is a work and a reminder of Providence" (*The Faith of Reason*, p. 26). But this may be to figure a little too fine. On these grounds, almost no Christian writer could be said to have a theory of anthropogenic progress.
17 *The Mind and Its Place in Nature*, pp. 664–5.
18 *Ibid.*, p. 666.

Skinner's theory of progress is the same as Broad's, although he is considerably more hopeful about the possibility of progress. Men have so far designed their cultures largely by guesswork, he declares, but the time is near when this can be changed. "Our decision in favor of sanitation and medicine seems to make for survival," he says, but we cannot be certain of this as yet; we do not know enough about the effects such decisions, however beneficial they may seem to be, will have on the future. But we already know enough to make some decisions intelligently; the "disinterested scientist" now has, or soon will have, the capacity "to make human behavior vastly more effective through cultural invention."[19]

Skinner, like Broad, envisions a wide application of science to human life and behavior. More specifically, a number of biologists and geneticists hold that the application of scientific methods to the investigation and control of human reproduction will bring about beneficial results and promote human progress. Hermann J. Muller is a leading exponent of this opinion. He sees progress occurring in all areas of human life, and concludes:

And so, I believe, not only our cultural, but also our biological evolution will go on and on, to new, undreamed of heights, each of these two means reenforcing each other, and again with a positive feedback, but with an enormously more effective one than heretofore.[20]

In a similar strain, Carrel writes that "science, which has transformed the material world, gives man the power of transforming himself."[21] The transformation will be the result of a choice made "among the multitude of civilized human beings."

We must single out the children who are endowed with high potentialities, and develop them as completely as possible. And in this manner give to the nation a nonhereditary aristocracy.[22]

For the first time in the history of humanity, Carrel declares, "a crumbling civilization is capable of discerning the causes of its decay." This capability is given by science; and science, having discerned the causes of decay, can be used to escape "the fate common to all great civilizations of

[19] "The Design of Cultures," in *Daedalus*, Summer, 1961, pp. 545–6. Compare the same author's *Walden II*, the thesis of which—that a technically planned society is preferable to an unplanned, "organic" one—has met with sharp opposition.

[20] "Should We Weaken or Strengthen Our Genetic Heritage?", in *Daedalus*, Summer, 1961, p. 450.

[21] *Man, the Unknown*, p. 179.

[22] *Ibid.*, p. 192. Socrates suggests a similar procedure in *The Republic*.

the past. Our destiny is in our hands. On the new road, we must now go forward."[23]

Remarks of this sort are not uncommon among writers who hold that man's use of reason is the spring of progress. The position is maintained by Voltaire, who considers science a better guarantor of progress than religion. Helvétius puts his faith in "scientific education," but his general view is similar.[24] Faraday suggests that scientific habits of thought can be effectively applied, in the service of progress, to many moral and social problems. "I am persuaded," he writes,

> that all persons may find in natural things an admirable school for self-instruction, and a field for the necessary mental exercise; that they may easily apply their habits of thought, thus formed, to a social use; and that they ought to do this, as a duty to themselves and their generation.[25]

Dewey holds that advances in science offer the opportunity for human progress but are not, strictly speaking, to be construed as progress itself. Modern man is deceived about the amount of progress he has made, Dewey declares, "and especially deceived about the automatic certainty of progress." Nevertheless, he is "right in thinking that for the first time in history mankind is in command of the possibility of progress."

> I might almost as well stop there. For it seems to me that about all which I can say about the future of progress at the present time is that it depends upon man to say whether he wants it or not. If we want it, we can have it—if we are willing to pay the price in effort, especially in effort and intelligence.[26]

More is needed than science alone, which, Dewey is saying, can only carry us a small part of the way. Beyond science lies something that Dewey terms "devotion" and "acceptance of responsibility."

[23] *Ibid.*, p. 207.

[24] See Helvétius' *De L'Esprit; or, Essays on the Mind and Its Several Faculties;* Helvétius' views are considered elsewhere in this study. Havelock sees Plato and Aristotle as holding a similar opinion of the value of education. "Their genius," he writes, "had made a social discovery of immense importance. . . . This was nothing less than the perception that a system of university education had now become socially indispensable for the progress of western culture." (*op. cit.*, p. 20)

[25] "Observations on Mental Education," in *Gateway to the Great Books*, Vol. 7, p. 216. Lavoisier also argues for this procedure for the improvement of the mind in his *Elements of Chemistry*.

[26] "Progress," in *International Journal of Ethics*, April 1916, p. 314.

Bryce, admitting some progress in social morality during the last century or so, raises the same objection as Dewey when he asks:

> Does our increased knowledge and command of nature, do all these benefits and comforts which the mastery of nature has secured, so greatly facilitate intellectual and moral progress that there will be an increase in intelligence, in virtue, and in all that is covered by the word "Happiness"?[27]

The point here is that Bryce, while he allows some progress in these, the important respects, finds no close connection between them and scientific advance. And he sees a growing need for science to be controlled in the future by "altruism" and "benevolence."

The advent of the atomic age has given new force to the position that progress depends on the *controlled* use of science to further human purposes. Thus the resolution of the quarrels between nations that endanger the modern world is a condition of progress in the view of many contemporary authors. The *Einstein-Russell Manifesto* warns that mankind faces a fearful choice.

> There lies before us, if we choose, continual progress in happiness, knowledge and wisdom. Shall we, instead, choose death because we cannot forget our quarrels? We appeal as human beings to human beings: remember your humanity and forget the rest. If you can do so, the way lies open to a new paradise; if you cannot there lies before you the risk of universal death.[28]

The atom offers untold riches; science may harness it to make "a new paradise." But if science is not controlled by "humanity," the same atom may produce the destruction of the entire race. Possibly no position about progress is more widely held in our time.[29]

Maritain's theory of progress is both subtle and complex. He accepts, although with certain reservations, the Pascalian analogy between the individual and the race; for Maritain, indeed, knowledge is intrinsically progressive, as will be seen. He has some notion of the development of the

27 "What Is Progress?", in *Atlantic Monthly*, August 1907, p. 150.

28 Qu. in Gerard Piel, *Science in the Cause of Man*, p. 148. Piel in this work makes the same point, as the title indicates. According to the dust jacket, he "affirms his belief in the sciences as entities inseparable from our broadest humanistic concerns." This is indeed the heart of the position being discussed here. If there are "two cultures," then one might contribute to progress, and the other hinder or nullify it. But if science can be seen as going hand in hand with benevolence or altruism or humanism, then progress is, or can be, the result of both kinds of thinking.

29 E.g., by Herrick in *The Evolution of Human Nature*, H. Brown in *The Challenge of Man's Future*, Ginsberg in *Reason and Unreason in Society*, J. Huxley in *Evolution: A Modern Synthesis*, Herbert J. Muller in *Freedom in the Western World*, and Calder in *After the Seventh Day*.

human mind, although he is critical of some of the developmental schemes that were described in Chapter 3. Enthusiasts of progress "flit away from one kind of movement to another," he says, and

> abandon metaphors drawn from the movement of growth to revel in those furnished by movement in space. Hence all the *stages* and *steps*, all the *ons* and *forwards*, all the *ascents, movements,* and *élans* which contribute, if not to the enrichment, at any rate to the embellishment, of modern thought.[30]

He also shares, to some extent at least, the notion that God is a partner with man in progress.[31] Nevertheless, in spite of the eclectic character of his theory, his more carefully reasoned position appears to be the one that is being considered here, namely, that progress will occur through the application of science, controlled by benevolence, to human affairs.

"If it is a question of minor victories over inert matter," says Maritain's protagonist in the dialogue *Theonas,*

> we are easily more cunning than matter: also in the order of material making, progress will be the rule—not only progress but indefinite progress, at least within the limits of one continuous period. . . . Progress of this order has held the stage for roughly a century with a shower of marvels.[32]

But this fact is not enough to support the contention that human progress in a broader sense occurs. It would be a waste of time, Theonas goes on to say,

[30] *Theonas,* pp. 117–8.

[31] With respect to the question whether progress, for Maritain, is anthropogenic or cosmogenic, it is to be admitted that, from the religious point of view, it is a matter in which Providence is deeply involved. "At one and the same time," says Maritain (expressing a common idea in his writings), "this world is on the march—it is the growing of the wheat—towards the Kingdom of God; it is also on the march—it is the growth of the tares, inextricably mixed with the wheat—towards the kingdom of reprobation" (*True Humanism,* p. 101). However, the Kingdom of God will not come "in and as a part of history. Prepared by the growth of history, and by the progressive mixing and refining of the human being that it involves, it will come *at the end* of history, at that hour of the resurrection of the dead to which all history tends" (*ibid.,* p. 52). Thus progress is not, strictly, in the religious order. Providence is the source of progress as final cause; it is that for which progress occurs. But the spring of progress is better seen as subsisting in the secular life. Indeed, progress can fruitfully and meaningfully be viewed as a natural process. "Let us say," Maritain writes, "that civilization or culture is that flowering which gives space for a rightly human life; is concerned not only with the necessary material development which permits the leading of a proper life here below, but also and primarily with man's moral development, the development of those spiritual and practical (artistic and ethical) activities which rightly merit the name of human progress. Civilization is thus seen to be a natural thing in the same sense as are the workings of reason and virtue, whose fruit and accomplishment it is. It answers to an essential impulse of human nature, but is in itself a work of our spirit and our freedom acting in co-operation with nature" (*ibid.,* p. 88).

[32] *Theonas,* pp. 152–3.

to remind you that of itself [material progress] contributes nothing either to the moral perfection of men nor even to their earthly happiness—since concupiscence is limitless and human needs grow faster than the means of satisfying them. . . . What is more important, this purely material progress—good of course in its own order, but definitely of a low order—puts civilization in presence of a measureless peril. . . . If it definitely took the preponderance and the directing role, it would mean for the West decadence beyond remedy.[33]

In a somewhat different sense, knowledge—"the speculative order"—is progressive. "It is not to change, to the law of the other as other," says Theonas, "that [knowledge] is primarily submitted: but to progress, to the law of augmentation and movement towards perfection."

Thus we may understand why, despite accidental failings, the mathematical sciences—which of all sciences are best proportioned to the human mind—present an admirable example of progressive development. . . . We see the same history of progress—even, may be, more strikingly—since the time of Galileo in the physico-mathematical sciences—that is to say in the art of translating sensible phenomena into quantitative symbols: and this is precisely because those studies are in truth the poorest of all in intelligibility, the least exacting in intellectuality, hence the easiest.[34]

However, metaphysics, too, is progressive, since "in it, better than in any other [science], is realized the absolutely essential condition of . . . progress, namely, fixity of principles and stability of tradition."[35]

In spite of the splendor of their achievements, material and speculative progress are not enough, in Maritain's opinion, to insure real or true progress. The truth is, he says in another work,

that it is not the business of science to regulate our life; that is the office of wisdom. . . . Really to make the machine, technical developments, and industry serve man implies making them the servants of an ethic of personality, of love and liberty.[36]

This indeed is Maritain's main point. Future progress—whatever may be said of progress in the past—will depend on the erection of an "essentially human" civilization, one that is based on Christian principles, and one that is "communal," "pluralist," and "personalist."[37] In such a civiliza-

[33] *Ibid.*, p. 153.
[34] *Ibid.*, p. 158. The last statement is noteworthy. Behind it there lies, of course, a whole theory of knowledge.
[35] *Ibid.*, p. 159.
[36] *True Humanism*, p. 188.
[37] Maritain's conception of this society is discussed elsewhere in this study. He does not expect its attainment without the intervening "historic liquidation" of bourgeois society.

tion, progress will occur along the two lines that its essentially ambiguous nature requires.

> Progress has two poles, one economic, on the side of the most urgent necessities of the ethico-biological order; the other religious, on the side of the most urgent necessities of the life of the soul.[38]

Thus the Christian ought to strive for, and may to some extent attain, a "proportionate realization . . . of the claims of the Gospel and of practical Christian wisdom in the socio-temporal order."[39] But this will require a different kind of thinking than the scientific, a kind that Maritain considers to be rare. Thus Maritain is not hopeful about any real progress in the near future.[40]

Civilization, says Maritain, and therefore progress, are allied with "reason and virtue." The last term, though not often used by the writers being considered here, might well stand for the state or activity of mind that they conceive as a necessary accompaniment to science in the production of human progress.

Simon concurs in this view; he actually uses the word virtue to describe what is, for him, the source of real progress. Scientific and technical advances do not entail inevitable evil consequences, he declares; nor are their consequences necessarily beneficial. A great deal of ink is wasted on the assertion that technology may be used for good or for ill. Nothing could be more obvious, says Simon.

> It is virtue alone that can be put to no bad use. It is to virtue, not to science or technique, that it falls to make men good, absolutely speaking.[41]

Simon's statement may serve as a touchstone for positions about man's use of reason in relation to progress. Regress authors like Juenger and Seidenberg, who see science and technology bringing about regress, not progress, hold, in opposition to Simon, that reason, as it may be called, not virtue, determines the course of history—and that reason works for man's ill.[42] Progress authors like Bacon and C. G. Darwin, who also see reason determining the course of history, view it as working for man's good, although they speak of it as primarily operative in the sphere of external nature. Progress authors like Descartes and Broad see reason as applicable to human nature as well as to external nature; for them, reason might

[38] *Ibid.*, p. 89.
[39] *Ibid.*, p. 120.
[40] Maritain returns to many of the subject matters of *Theonas* in *Philosophy of History*, which work is discussed elsewhere in this study.
[41] *Community of the Free*, p. 124.
[42] The theories of regress of Juenger and Seidenberg are treated in Chapter 8.

be said to perform the same function as virtue does for writers like Maritain and Simon. In the opinion of the latter, reason, in the sense of science and technique, is not enough. Reason must be combined with virtue to bring about real human progress.

It is evident, from an inspection of the terms used in the last paragraph, that still another position is possible, namely, that reason (*i.e.*, science and technology) works for man's ill, but that virtue may overcome it and bring about progress in spite of reason. This appears to be the position of Tolstoy, Fourier, and one or two others.

Union or community, says Tolstoy, is the destiny of mankind.

> However differently in form people belonging to our Christian world may define the destiny of man . . . all men in our times admit that the highest well-being attainable by men is to be reached by their union with one another.[43]

If union is man's destiny, then movement toward it is his progress. Science, however, not only does not contribute to this progress; it hinders it. For

> one side of science, including theology and philosophy adapted to the existing order, as also history and political economy of the same sort, is chiefly occupied in proving that the existing order is the very thing which ought to endure; that it has come into existence and continues to exist by the operation of immutable laws not amenable to human will, and that all efforts to change it are therefore harmful and wrong. The other part, experimental science—including mathematics, astronomy, chemistry, physics, botany, and all the natural sciences—is exclusively occupied with things that have no direct relation to the purpose of human life: with what is curious, and with things of which practical application advantageous to people of the upper classes can be made. . . .
> So that one side of science, instead of studying how people should live in order to fulfil their mission in life, demonstrates the righteousness and immutability of the bad and false arrangements of life which exist around us; while the other part, experimental science, occupies itself with questions of simple curiosity, or with technical applications.[44]

The first kind of science is harmful, Tolstoy charges, not only because it confuses people's perceptions and forces them to make false decisions "but also by its mere existence." His main attack, however, is directed at "the second division"—experimental science—the kind of science of

[43] *What Is Art?*, p. 264.
[44] *Ibid.*, pp. 278–9.

which (as he points out) the modern world is so proud, and which it sometimes considers the only real science. This is harmful in that "it diverts attention from the really important subjects to insignificant subjects." It is

> also directly harmful in that under the evil system of society which the first division of science justifies and supports, a great part of the technical gains of science are turned not to the advantage, but to the injury, of mankind.[45]

In this situation, Tolstoy says, we must look to art to remedy matters, for art alone can accomplish a cure and bring about a society in which man experiences freedom and joy. What this means we shall try to ascertain in another place; for the moment we observe that, in Tolstoy's opinion, science and reason (at least in their current aspect) hinder progress, while the large, generous, and communal thinking that is the essence of great art can help to bring it about.

If art accomplishes the changes that Tolstoy desires, then science, too, will be transformed; then, and then only, will "real art, aided by science, guided by religion," bring about "that peaceful co-operation of man which is now maintained by external means. . . . Art should cause violence to be set aside."[46]

Where Tolstoy allows that science may be transformed in the new order, Charles Fourier declares that it must be exiled from it. This is his *écart absolu*, as he calls it.

> I assumed that the most certain means of arriving at useful discoveries was to remove oneself in every sense from the methods followed by the dubious sciences which never contributed an invention that was of the remotest utility to society and which, despite the immense progress of industry, had not even succeeded in preventing poverty; I therefore undertook to stand in constant opposition to these sciences.[47]

Instead of art, Fourier proposes instinct as the remedy for the manifold ills of civilization, which has to be destroyed, for it cannot be amended. Civilization, science, philosophy—all must go down in this prophet's vision of a better world. All offer but an ethic of self-denial, when men really crave pleasure. Even Liberty, Equality, and Fraternity are the watchwords of repression. In their place, the hope of man and of progress is to be found in the "orderly satisfaction of the passions."

[45] *Ibid.*, p. 279.
[46] *Ibid.*, pp. 286–7.
[47] *Théorie des quatres mouvements*, qu. in Frank E. Manuel, *The Prophets of Paris*, p. 209.

Human passions are constant, says Fourier, and history is merely the story of varying methods—more or less successful—of inhibiting them.[48]

> Civilization is therefore a society that is contrary to nature, a reign of violence and cunning, and political science and morality, which have taken three thousand years to create this monstrosity, are sciences that are contrary to nature and worthy of profound contempt.[49]

Fourier offers in place of civilization the "phalanstery," a closed society (of which there would be many examples), each containing 1,620 persons (since there are 810 different passions, and each should be represented by a male and a female), in which passionate attraction will transform labor into joy and life into constant but ever new love. Man is by nature cooperative, loving, and philanthropic, says Fourier, and only requires to live in a society that is based on this fact to be happy. Every mature person will have at least one partner in love, probably several—Fourier considers mankind to be naturally polygamous—and the sanitary needs of the community will be served by children, because of their "natural penchant . . . for filth." With all of these matters taken care of, mankind may look forward to indefinite progress.

> When the globe shall have been organized and brought to the total of three billion inhabitants, there will normally be on earth thirty-seven million poets the equal of Homer, thirty-seven million mathematicians the equal of Newton, thirty-seven million authors of comedies the equal of Molière, and the same number in all other conceivable talents (these are estimates).[50]

What is more, Fourier predicts, the sea will turn to lemonade.

In this chapter we have examined the theories of progress of a large number of authors who agree in holding that progress occurs through man's use of reason. We may have seemed to stray from this position in the latter part of the chapter; several of the authors mentioned appear to hold that progress occurs in spite of man's use of reason, not because of it; one or two even seem to be saying that reason is the great obstacle to progress, and must be overcome.

This apparent inconsistency is removed if it is recognized that we use the term "reason" to mean one thing, whereas progress authors use it to mean several things. When we speak of the occurrence of progress through

[48] Compare on this point the psychoanalytical theory of history of N. O. Brown. See Chapter 8.
[49] Manuel, *op. cit.*, p. 215.
[50] *Ibid.*, p. 237.

man's use of reason, we mean that progress is the result of the application of thought to the problems that confront the human species, the solution of which constitutes human progress. Such application can take the form of scientific investigation of external nature, or of human nature; it can take the form of benevolence, wisdom, or communal thinking; it can take the form of art; it can even take the form of the creation of a society based on instinct.

The progress authors treated here disagree, then, about the meaning of reason; they also disagree as to whether man's reason is good for him. But they concur in holding that progress occurs if, or whenever, man thinks about himself and the world in a way that they approve.

5

Cosmogenic Progress:
Divine Principles

T HE authors who see God or Providence as the source of progress in history are listed below.

Augustine	Coleridge
Joachimites	Guizot
Dante	Acton
Leibniz	Trench
Edwards	Stace
Kant	Sorokin[1]
Lessing	Toynbee
Herder	Dawson
Malthus	James J. Walsh
Chateaubriand	Jehovah's Witnesses

[1] Sorokin, like Toynbee, is treated both as a progress author and as a cyclist in this work.

Progress Through God's Design

The position that progress occurs through God's design finds various expressions in the literature. Some authors hold that God gives to man a progressive revelation of Himself, and that human progress therefore consists in man's knowing God more and more fully with the passage of time. Others say that progress is an overall pattern imposed by God on history, which is manifested in meliorative changes of many kinds. Still others describe a kind of conflict in human life which they hold to be ordained by God, and which results in human progress. And there are other versions of this position as well.

The authors who hold that progress occurs through God's design are listed below.

Augustine	Schelling
Joachimites	Malthus
Dante	Coleridge
Leibniz	Guizot
Edwards	Trench
Kant	Sorokin
Lessing	Dawson
Herder	Jehovah's Witnesses

The position that God determines and brings about human progress is usually stated by the above authors in one or the other, or both, of two propositions:

1. It is the design of God that the world (and mankind within it) shall be perfected in time.
2. It is the design of God that there shall be progress in the knowledge of God; that is, God reveals Himself progressively to man.

The notion that God progressively reveals Himself to man is the main theme of Lessing's *Education of the Human Race*. The analogy between education and revelation is emphasized by Lessing throughout this work.

> Just as in education, since not everything can be brought to pass at once, the order of the development of the powers of man is not a matter of indifference; so God, in His revelation, felt constrained to maintain a certain system, a certain moderation.[2]

[2] *Lessing's Education of the Human Race*, p. 34.

The system is this. During the early history of the human race, mankind was plagued by many different kinds of errors. Little by little, however, God cleared man's mind. At first He revealed Himself only to individuals. Then He revealed Himself to an entire race—the Jews.

> When He no longer could or would reveal Himself to the *individual man,* He selected for His particular education an *individual people,* and that, the most rude and most barbarous, in order to begin with it from the beginning.[3]

The reason for thus instructing the Jews was, "later on, to be able to use, with greater certainty, as instruments of all other peoples, several of them. He developed in them the future teachers of the human race. They were Jews; they must have been Jews; they must have been men from a people educated in that way."[4]

But God kept certain truths back from the Jews, just as a teacher keeps back certain matters from the children in his charge. What God taught the Jews was contained in the Old Testament; but this was, in effect, only the first "primer" of the race, and could not, and should not, be dwelt over too long or too curiously. "A better teacher must come," Lessing says, "and snatch from the child's hand the spent primer. Christ came."[5] And the New Testament became the "new primer" of the human race.

Lessing concludes his book by saying that the ultimate aim of divine education is that man will be able, one day, to will the good, not because he knows that he will be rewarded but simply because it is the good. In that third and last period of education (the periods of the Old and New Testaments being the first two), men will pursue virtue for its own sake. Hence there emerges a threefold plan of development, ordained and directed by God, that is based on a progressive revelation and the stages of which are measured by moral criteria.[6]

Lessing recognizes that his plan is not new. It may be, he says,

> that even certain visionaries of the thirteenth and fourteenth centuries had caught the gleam of this new, eternal gospel and erred only in announcing its dawn as so near. Perhaps their threefold age of the world was no mere empty vagary, and certainly they had no evil aim when they taught that the New Covenant must become just as antiquated as the Old. There

[3] *Ibid.,* p. 35.
[4] *Ibid.,* p. 37.
[5] *Ibid.,* p. 47.
[6] Todd (*Theories of Social Progress,* p. 465) remarks that Coleridge "likewise treated all history as an education of the mind of the race," and refers us to *Friend,* Vol. III, Essay 10. And Archbishop Trench asserts that "the very idea of God's kingdom is that of a progress, of a gradually fuller communication . . . of Himself to men" (*Notes on the Miracles of Our Lord*).

remained even with them always the same economy of the same God, always—to let them use my phrase—the same plan for the universal education of the human race. But they were too hasty in that they thought they could make their contemporaries, who had hardly outgrown childhood, without enlightenment, without preparation, at one stroke, men, worthy of their third age![7]

The reference here is to the Joachimite literature that flourished in Europe from the twelfth to the sixteenth century.[8] The doctrinal essence of Joachism is at the same time an idea of universal history and a theory of progress. The history of humanity is divided into three periods. These are defined as the Age of the Law, or of the Father; the Age of the Gospel, or of the Son; and the Age of the *viri spirituales,* or of the Spirit, which will bring the ages to an end.

This trinitarian view of history is, for the Joachimites, both a formal pattern and an historical fact. Thus, the Jews were slaves under the law of the Father. The Christians of the second epoch were partly, although not completely, spiritual and free; this is seen when early Christianity is compared with the moral legality of the first dispensation. In the third epoch, which is beginning "just now" (*i.e.,* toward the end of the twelfth century), St. Paul's prophecy will come true, that we know and prophesy now only in part, "but when that which is perfect is come, that which is in part shall be done away." And "already we can apprehend the unveiling of the final liberation of the spirit in its plenitude."[9]

> The first epoch was inaugurated by Adam in fear and under the sign of the law; since Abraham it had borne fruit to become fulfilled in Jesus Christ. The second was inaugurated by Uzziah in faith and humility under the sign of the gospel; since Zechariah, the father of John the Baptist, it had borne fruit to become fulfilled in future times. The third was inaugurated by St. Benedict in love and joy under the sign of the Spirit; it will come to pass with the reappearance of Elijah at the end of the world.[10]

The three stages overlap; the second epoch begins in the first, the third in the second. Various levels of spirituality are coexistent. The church of monks already exists within the church of clerics.

[7] Lessing, *op. cit.,* pp. 55–6.

[8] The Joachimite literature is traced to the twelfth-century monk Joachim of Floris, who wrote a number of treatises that influenced his many followers; there is question whether any of his own writings survive. Joachim founded his own monastic order, the *ordo Florensis,* which initiated and sustained a spiritual, antipapal movement in the Church. It did not prevail, and some of Joachim's views were declared anathema.

[9] We follow Lowith's commentary on Joachim, in *Meaning in History,* pp. 145–59.

[10] *Ibid.,* p. 148.

The first dispensation is historically an order of the married, dependent on the Father; the second an order of clerics, dependent on the Son; the third an order of monks, dependent on the Spirit of Truth.[11]

The first age is ruled by labor and work, and possesses *scientia*. The second is ruled by learning and discipline, and possesses *sapientia ex parte*. The third is ruled by contemplation and praise, and possesses *plenitude intellectus*.[12]

The Joachimite theory is not an allegory; it is a true theory of historical progress. Progress occurs in the real past, present, and future.[13] The theory nevertheless differs sharply in its notion of the *eschaton* from that of more orthodox Christian thinkers. The *eschaton*, for the Joachimites, is twofold: there is to be, and will be soon, an historical phase; this will be followed by the transcendent *eschaton*, the New Jerusalem, which will be ushered in by the second coming of Christ. For many Christian writers, the "Kingdom of God" is without or beyond history. The Joachimites predict an earlier stage of the Kingdom that will be within and a part of history. The existing church will yield to the coming church of the Spirit, but the latter will be a terrestrial reality.

This ultimate transition . . . implies the liquidation of preaching and sacraments, the mediating power of which becomes obsolete when the

[11] *Ibid.*

[12] *Ibid.* Another description of the Joachimite theory of progress is found in Cohn's study, *The Pursuit of the Millennium.* "In his exegese of the Scriptures, Joachim elaborated an interpretation of history as an ascent through three successive ages," says Cohn, "each of them presided over by one of the Persons of the Trinity. The first age was the Age of the Father or of the Law; the second age was the Age of the Son or of the Gospel; the third age would be the Age of the Spirit and that would be the culmination of human history. This third age would be to its predecessors as broad daylight compared with starlight and the dawn, as high summer compared with winter and spring. The laws of the first and second ages were contained in the Old and New Testaments respectively, but in the third age the 'everlasting gospel' was to replace the precepts of the New Testament. If the first age had been one of fear and servitude and the second one of faith and filial submission, the third age would be one of love, joy and freedom, when the knowledge of God would be revealed directly in the hearts of all men. The Age of the Spirit was to be the sabbath or resting-time of mankind. In it there would be no wealth or even property, for everyone would live in voluntary poverty; there would be no work, for human beings would possess only spiritual bodies and would need no food; there would be no institutional authority of any kind. The Empire would be no more and the Church of Rome would give place to a free community of perfected beings who would have no need of clergy or sacraments or Bible. In fact the world would be one vast monastery, in which all men would be contemplative monks rapt in mystical ecstasy and united in singing the praises of God. And this new version of the Kingdom of the Saints would endure until the Last Judgment" (p. 100).

[13] In the supposedly "nonhistorical Middle Ages" there is thus to be found an idea of real human progress that is deserving of comparison on its own terms with the theories of modern writers.

spiritual order is realized which possesses knowledge of God by direct vision and contemplation.[14] The real significance of the sacraments is not, as with Augustine, the significance of a transcendent reality but the indication of a potentiality which becomes realized within the framework of history.[15]

For the Joachimites, specifically human progress is a result of God's care for men and control of history. The third stage is, moreover, decidedly secular; or it is easily converted into a secular paradise. The church will cease to be a clerical hierarchy and will become instead a monastic community of saints, "destined to cure, by an ultimate effort, a disintegrating world."[16] The similarity to Lessing's last stage of history or revelation, in which men pursue virtue for its own sake, is obvious; but the Joachimite scheme is similar to others as well.[17]

Augustine's progress theory, despite its likeness to that of the Joachimites, is less clearly an affirmation of historical progress.

A main intent of *The City of God* is to refute the classical pagan theories of historical cycles; for if any such theory were valid, Christ would have to undergo His passion repeatedly. Furthermore, Augustine frequently declares in this work that the world was made; it has a beginning, a middle, and an end. And the world's history may be divided into six epochs. Augustine compares these to infancy, childhood, youth, early manhood, later manhood, and old age, and he suggests that the childhood of the human race is that period during which man did not yet have the law; manhood, the period under the law; and old age, the period in which grace is present. Nevertheless, Augustine's primary objection to the pagan theory of cycles is moral or religious, rather than purely

[14] Many cyclical and regress theories place "direct vision" of God at the beginning rather than the end of history.

[15] Lowith, *op. cit.*, p. 151.

[16] *Ibid.*, p. 146.

[17] This is recognized by Lowith and Cohn. Lowith writes: "The revolution which had been proclaimed within the framework of an eschatological faith and with reference to a perfect monastic life was taken over, five centuries later, by a philosophical priesthood, which interpreted the process of secularization in terms of a 'spiritual' realization of the Kingdom of God on earth. As an attempt at realization, the spiritual pattern of Lessing, Fichte, Schelling, and Hegel could be transposed into the positivistic and materialistic schemes of Comte and Marx. The third dispensation of the Joachites reappeared as a third International and a third Reich, inaugurated by a *dux* or *Führer* who was acclaimed as a savior and greeted by millions with *Heil!*" (p. 159). Compare also Lowith's "Appendix I: Modern Transfigurations of Joachism" (pp. 208–13). Cohn traces the Joachimite ideas through the Middle Ages and to Comte, to the Marxist writers on history, and to the Third Reich, which "would have had but little emotional significance if the phantasy of a third and most glorious dispensation had not, over the centuries, entered into the common stock of European social mythology" (p. 101). We have not seen it noted, in addition to the above, that Rabelais' conception of the ideal monastic community, as described in his picture of the Abbey of Thélème, shows the influence of Joachimite notions.

historical. For him, history is the pilgrimage of mankind, just as every man's life is a pilgrimage, toward a consummation that is above and beyond terrestrial life as it is known to us. Indeed, it sometimes seems that Augustine is saying that the *saeculum*, the history of the City of Man, shows only a nonprogressive—and almost cyclical—succession of generations of men.

In one sense there is undoubted progress for Augustine. The Incarnation represents an absolute increase in man's potential for salvation. The old Adam is present in the new, just as the Old Testament prefigures the New; but the new in each case is a step forward, and reflects the fact that there is something in the world that was not there before. The Incarnation is an historical fact, and therefore constitutes progress in history.[18]

At the same time, Augustine's refutation of the theory of cycles makes other theories of progress possible. It is only required to show that the City of Man itself is susceptible to or actually sustains irreversible meliorative change. This, as we have seen, is what the Joachimites do.

It is what the Jehovah's Witnesses also do, although there is some question in their case, as there is in that of Augustine, whether the future progress that they proclaim will actually occur in history. "See the happy people on the cover of this booklet," one of the pamphlets distributed by this sect of modern millennialists begins.

> Would you not like to be one of them? Why, yes, you say. For here is the peace and harmony desired by all mankind. People of all races—the black, the white, the yellow—are mingling as one family. What joy! What unity! Obviously these people are not worrying about nuclear fallouts, or the threat of hydrogen bombs. Jet warplanes do not shatter the peaceful skies above this lovely park. There are no soldiers, no tanks, no guns. Not even a police baton is needed to keep order. War and crimes simply do not exist. And no housing shortages, for everyone has a beautiful home to call his own.[19]

The booklet goes on to describe in detail the delights of a paradise that is, nevertheless, terrestrial. The children do not play with ordinary, certainly not with plastic, toys; instead they cavort with the animals; the lion and the lamb have become friends, not only of each other but of man. The odor of the flowers is something never before experienced, the tingling warmth of the sun something never felt, and everyone is healthy and no one ever dies of old age. In fact, "all earth is being transformed into a paradise park. It will be paradise restored earth-wide."[20]

[18] See, in *The City of God*, especially V, 9; X, 14; XI, 26; XII, 10–20; XV, 7; XXII, 24. For a discussion of Augustine's theory of progress, see Lowith, pp. 160–73.
[19] "Look! I Am Making All Things New!" (distributed by the Watch Tower Bible and Tract Society of Pennsylvania), p. 3.
[20] *Ibid.,* pp. 3–4.

Now this is not the earth as we know it; however, it is not heaven either. In a sense this paradisaical condition is not a part of history; on this count the millennialists disagree with the Joachimites, for whom the third dispensation is explicitly an historical phase. But in another sense the paradise of the pamphlet is no different from the "world of tomorrow" that is conceived and described by other progress authors. This is reflected in the particular anxieties and problems that the millennium will put an end to; these are all current problems, and their resolution is promised by politicians as well as by preachers. It is also reflected in the secular tone of the invitation that is extended by the pamphlet to all men—an invitation couched in phrases reminiscent of modern advertising. "Unbelievable, did you say?" the pamphlet asks.

> First, though, consider the facts in proof. It is possible for you and your family to survive the passing of the present troubled world, and to enter the new world represented on our cover.[21]

Leibniz speaks of a "progressive revelation" of God, but he is also concerned to show that the progress of the world at large is the design of God. Lessing sees progress occurring in history because of God's desire that it should occur. Leibniz's is a wider view. He writes:

> To realize in its completeness the universal beauty and perfection of the works of God, we must recognize a certain perpetual and very free progress of the whole universe, such that it is always going forward to greater improvement [*cultus*]. So even now a great part of our earth has received cultivation [*cultura*][22] and will receive it more and more. And although it is true that sometimes certain parts of it grow wild again, or again suffer destruction or degeneration, yet this is to be understood in [this] way . . . that this very destruction and degeneration leads to some greater end, so that somehow we profit by the loss itself.[23]

21 *Ibid.*, p. 4.
22 *I.e.*, civilization.
23 R. Latta (ed.), *The Monadology and Other Philosophical Writings*, p. 350. "There are," says Lovejoy in *The Great Chain of Being*, "two Leibnitian systems of philosophy, quite irreconcilable with one another—though their author was seemingly unaware of the fact. The first is a vision of a world which is through and through rational. . . . It was, therefore, in its essential structure, an immutable world. . . . In the other vision, the time-process, conceived as a continuous augmentation of realized values, is the *most* significant aspect of reality—and change is the most indispensable mark of excellence." According to the second "vision," the world is *"not now, and, indeed, never will be, 'the best of possible worlds';* it is only a world which is in process of growing better. It is true, however, that, for Leibniz, a world thus forever falling short of perfection was better than the optimist's 'best,' because a finite good incapable of being transcended lacks the first essential of value" (pp. 261–2). The first system or vision is more commonly associated with Leibniz; it

These remarks do not contradict Leibniz's notion of a pre-established harmony, or of a world that is, at any one time, as good as it can be. For the best is only the best at a given moment; the future will see more and better. It is true that "all is regulated in things, once and for all, with as much order and mutual connexion as possible, since supreme wisdom and goodness can act only with perfect harmony." But this is not all that must be said. It is also true that "the present is big with the future, the future might be read in the past, the distant is expressed in the near."[24] The world is not the static manifestation but the dynamic unfolding of the divine plan.

In return for God's gift of progress, we must love God.

> Besides the present pleasure it affords, nothing can be of more advantage for the future than this love of God, for it fulfils our expectations also and leads us in the way of supreme happiness.[25]

This is man's obligation, man's side of the bargain; it is by loving God that man assists in the work of Providence. But this happiness is not really "supreme," for it, too, is dynamic, progressive.

> Supreme felicity . . . can never be complete, because God, being infinite, cannot be entirely known. Thus our happiness will never consist (and it is right that it should not consist) in complete enjoyment, which would leave nothing more to be desired and would make our mind [*esprit*] stupid; but it must consist in a perpetual progress to new pleasures and new perfections.[26]

For Herder, too, the world reveals God's greatness, which is in and above all things, and is always changing, growing, and developing. Creation is inexhaustible at the same time that a balance or harmony pervades all of its operations.

Herder regards man as a special creation, the highest link in "the great chain of beings"; but man is not thereby complete or perfect. On the contrary, he is to expect untold powers, perfections, and glories in the future.

---

is the second that is being discussed here. For an extended treatment of the conversion of the idea of the great chain of being as immutable—the so-called optimistic philosophy—to that of a world sustaining continuous improvement—the so-called melioristic philosophy—see Lovejoy, pp. 242–87.

Acton entertains a notion concerning progress that is similar to Leibniz's. "The wisdom of divine rule," he says, "appears not in the perfection but in the improvement of the world" (*Essays on Freedom and Power*, p. 36).

[24] Latta, *op. cit.*, p. 419. Comte quotes the latter remark repeatedly.
[25] *Ibid.*, p. 423.
[26] *Ibid.*, p. 424.

There is no doubt . . . that what has not yet appeared upon earth will at some future period appear: for no prescription is a bar to the rights of man, and the powers, that God has implanted in him, are ineradicable.[27]

Progress is not, for Herder, the result of God's direct intervention in human affairs; rather, nature is created by God in such a way that man may progress. Man is not deprived of his freedom; he is not, as it were, forced to progress; yet he will necessarily do so, for such is God's decree.

> When God had created the earth, and all its irrational inhabitants, he formed man, and said to him: "Be my image; a god upon earth; rule and dispose. Whatever of noble and excellent thy nature will permit thee to produce, bring forth: I will assist thee by no miracle; for I have placed thy own fate in thy own hand: but all my sacred, eternal laws of nature will be thy aids."[28]

Guizot, like Herder, emphasizes man's freedom—not his freedom *not* to progress, but his freedom *to* progress. One reason man cannot *not* progress is because he does not fully comprehend the divine plan. "Man advances," Guizot declares, "in the execution of a plan which he has not conceived, and of which he is not even aware. He is the free and intelligent artificer of a work which is not his own."[29] Guizot goes on to propose a "model" of human progress that is proposed by other writers as well.

> Conceive a great machine, the design of which is centered in a single mind, though its various parts are intrusted to various workmen, separated from, and strangers to each other. None of them understands the work as a whole, nor the general result which he concurs in producing; but everyone executes, with intelligence and freedom, by rational and voluntary acts, the particular task assigned to him.[30]

"It is thus," Guizot concludes, "that by the hand of man, the designs of Providence are wrought out by the government of the world."

Kant's theory of progress has much in common with those described above. He writes, in terms that are reminiscent of Leibniz's, that

> I will . . . venture to assume that as the human race is continually advancing in civilization and culture as its natural purpose, so it is continually making progress for the better in the moral end of its existence, and that this progress although it may be sometimes interrupted, will never be entirely broken off or stopped.[31]

[27] *Outlines of a Philosophy of the History of Man*, Book IV, pp. 441–2.
[28] *Ibid.*, p. 442.
[29] *General History of Civilization in Europe*, p. 291.
[30] *Ibid.*
[31] "On the Saying: That a Thing May Be Right in Theory, but May Not Hold in Practice," in W. Hastie (ed.), *Principles of Politics*, p. 69. See also Teggart (ed.), *The Idea of Progress*, p. 305.

Evidence from history that men have not grown better or, indeed, that they have grown worse is not relevant, Kant declares; even his doubts that men might attain a better and happier condition would be irrelevant, if he had them. The *hope* of improvement, since it is felt by every person, is enough to insure the ultimate attainment of improvement. Any other conclusion would, Kant says, offend not only God but "even the commonest well-disposed man"; a world not so ordained would be a "farce."[32]

Kant does not view progress here as anthropogenic, although he allows man a role in bringing about progress, as in Guizot's great machine that is incomprehensible to an individual workman. Kant writes that

> it is from human Nature in general, or rather—since supreme wisdom is requisite for the accomplishment of this end—it is from *Providence* alone that we can expect a result which proceeds by relation to the whole and reacts through the whole upon the parts.[33]

In another work, Kant offers a more extended argument for progress, and at the same time indicates by what means God brings about the progress of mankind. In the essay *Idea for a Universal History with Cosmopolitan Intent,* Kant declares that any such history would allow

> that what appears to be complicated and accidental in individuals, may yet be understood as a steady, progressive, though slow, evolution of the original endowments of the entire species.[34]

His argument runs as follows. It is to be assumed, he says, that all of any creature's natural faculties must "unfold completely and according to their end." Reason is one of man's natural faculties; hence the "use of reason shall be fully developed in the species," though not, perhaps, ever in any individual member of it.[35] Furthermore,

> nature has intended that man develop everything which transcends the mechanical ordering of his animal existence entirely by himself and that he does not partake of any other happiness or perfection except that which he has secured himself by his own reason and free of instinct.[36]

This is not to say, of course, that Providence is not the ultimate source of human progress. Kant is here making the point insisted on by both Herder and Guizot; progress is brought about by God *through* nature, and

[32] *Ibid.*, p. 70; see Teggart, p. 306.

[33] *Ibid.*; see Teggart p. 307.

[34] C. J. Friedrich (ed.), *The Philosophy of Kant,* p. 116. The title of this essay is variously translated. Another version (that of Hastie) is: *Idea of a Universal History from a Cosmopolitical Point of View.*

[35] *Ibid.*, p. 118.

[36] *Ibid.*, p. 119.

not by God directly. Human nature is created by God in such a way as to produce progress in human history.

But how does nature bring about progress? Having assumed that "an animal species is to have reason, and is to arrive at a complete development of its faculties as a class of reasonable beings," Kant answers the question in this fashion:

> The means which nature employs to accomplish the development of all faculties is the antagonism of men in society, since this antagonism becomes, in the end, the cause of a lawful order of this society.[37]

The last statement is the heart of Kant's position. Man, he says, has a "propensity to be lazy";[38] however, he is "impelled by vainglory, ambition and avarice," and seeks standing among his fellows, "whom he cannot *leave*."

> Thus the first steps from barbarism to culture are achieved; for culture actually consists in the social value of man.[39]

Humanity's talents are gradually unfolded in due course. But without the "essentially unlovely qualities of associability," Kant declares, man would not progress; all talents would have remained "hidden germs." Hence, thanks are due to nature—which is to say, to Providence—for man's

> quarrelsomeness, his enviously competitive vanity, and for his insatiable desire to possess or to rule, for without them all the excellent natural faculties of mankind would remain forever undeveloped. Man wants concord but nature knows better what is good for his kind; nature wants discord.[40]

Men desire to live comfortably and pleasurably, but nature raises them out of lethargy and "inactive contentment" into work and strife. The natural impulses,

> from which so many evils spring, but which at the same time drive man to a new exertion of his powers and thus to a development of his natural faculties, suggest the arrangement of a wise creator and not the hand of an evil spirit who might have ruined this excellent enterprise or spoiled it out of envy.[41]

Progress, in short, is ultimately the work of God, not the devil.

Malthus' theory of progress has much in common with Kant's, although,

---

[37] *Ibid.*, p. 120.
[38] *Ibid.* Herder and Malthus agree that man is naturally lazy.
[39] *Ibid.*
[40] *Ibid.*, p. 121.
[41] *Ibid.*

in keeping with the pessimistic tone of his essay on population, his world is both darker and more violent. "The world and this life," he writes,

> are the mighty process of God, not for the trial, but for the creation and formation of mind, a process necessary to awaken inert, chaotic matter into spirit, to sublimate the dust of earth into soul, to elicit an ethereal spark from the clod of clay.[42]

In this view of the subject, Malthus goes on, the various impressions and excitements which man receives through life may be considered as "the forming hand of the Creator," acting by general laws, and

> awakening his sluggish existence, by the animating touches of the Divinity, into a capacity of superior enjoyment. The original sin of man is the torpor and corruption of the chaotic matter in which he may be said to be born.[43]

Malthus and Kant, for whom the principle of conflict or opposition is clearly operative in the production of progress, have much in common with several of the authors discussed in Chapter 6, for whom the source of progress is the cosmic principle of conflict or opposition. However, Malthus and Kant—and Herder and Schelling, as well—do not conceive this principle as nondivine, as do writers like Marx, Engels, Mandeville, Bagehot, and Julian Huxley. For the latter, conflict is far from being ordained by God for the betterment of men.

PROGRESS THROUGH GOD'S CHURCH

The authors listed below are those who hold that progress occurs primarily through God's Church, although none of them denies that progress ultimately is the design of Providence.

Chateaubriand	Toynbee
Acton	James J. Walsh
Stace	

"There are not a few people, in our time particularly," writes Father Walsh,

> who are quite ready to declare that because of fixing man's gaze on another world Christianity has really hampered human progress, and that great

---

[42] *Population,* p. 123.
[43] *Ibid.,* p. 124.

advances have only come when the influence of the Church has not been much felt.[44]

Father Walsh asks, in effect, whether Christianity *as an institution* has hindered progress in the secular realm. His answer, of course, is that it has not. And he enumerates many of the technological advances and political improvements that we owe to the Middle Ages, when the Church, as he says, reigned supreme. These include such things as printing, the compass, and gunpowder, as well as the first steps taken by Western man toward democracy. His conclusion is that the Church not only did not hinder these developments, but in most cases actively fostered them.

Chateaubriand also recognizes an opposition between Christianity and progress in the popular mind. In his time, he observes, men are deluded into thinking that the Christian religion has been a serious obstacle in the way of human amelioration;

> that, having been invented in a barbarous age, its dogmas were absurd and its ceremonies ridiculous; that it tended to enslave the world, opposed the arts and sciences, and was in general hostile to the liberty of men and the advancement of civilization.[45]

But all of this is far from the truth, Chateaubriand declares. He finds evidence of the progressive effect of Christianity in almost every sphere of human life. It goes without saying, he asserts, that morals have improved as a result of the spread of Christian doctrine. But Christianity has not been hostile to art and science, either. There is improvement, directly owing to the Church, in poetry, in painting, in music, and in architecture. Government is more humane, and laws are more just. Charity is more widely practiced, and even warfare has undergone changes that are desirable; indeed, war is on the way to extinction as a means of settling disputes between nations and peoples. Not least important, in his view, is the fact that modes of prayer have become more civilized, and funerary monuments more beautiful. His aim is,

> in a word, to show . . . not that the Christian religion is excellent because it comes from God, but that it comes from God because it is excellent.[46]

Other writers might be cited as holding this position. However, most of them either agree with Walsh in holding that the Church does not hinder progress and indeed has fostered it more often than not, or with Chateaubriand that the Church has directly brought about meliorative changes in human life.

[44] *Modern Progress and History*, p. 257.
[45] *The Genius of Christianity*, p. 7.
[46] *Ibid.*

6

Cosmogenic Progress:
Natural Principles

T HE authors discussed in Chapter 5 hold that progress is the gift of God, the work of Providence, or the result of divine intervention in history. The authors about to be discussed agree that some force or principle *that is greater than man* brings about progress (or helps to bring it about), but they deny, either implicitly or explicitly, that this principle is divine.

Instead, they maintain that human progress is a manifestation—*merely one example*—of a phenomenon that is to be observed in the universe at large, and not merely in the world of man. These authors hold, with more or less emphasis on the human aspect of the process, that the universe as a whole undergoes a change that, in the human sphere, may be called the progress of mankind.

In that sphere, indeed, and from a limited point of view, human progress as such may appear to be anthropogenic. But in a larger view, it is the result of a process of change that affects all things, or all living things —at any rate, a larger group of things than the totality of human beings and human institutions and concerns.[1]

[1] Certain widely held views concerning the development of mankind are, by the foregoing, and also by the limitations of our analysis, ruled out of consideration

89

To be treated in this chapter, then, authors must agree on the following three points:

1. Human progress occurs.
2. The universe as a whole (or a part of it that is greater than man but includes man) develops or evolves.
3. The principle of human progress is the same as the principle of cosmic evolution.

The authors who conceive progress as the result or manifestation of some natural cosmic principle are listed below.

Mandeville	Bellamy
Adam Smith	Henry Adams
Robinet	Bergson
Hegel[2]	Lenin
Marx	Bukharin
Engels	Trotsky
Charles Darwin	Teilhard de Chardin
Bagehot	J. Huxley
T. H. Huxley	Nouÿs
Fiske	Herrick
Spencer	Simpson
Sumner	Clough

PROGRESS THROUGH CONFLICT OR OPPOSITION

Conflict or opposition is conceived, by the authors who hold that it is the principle of progress, in various ways.[3] However, all of the authors

here. In particular, if an author says that a universal process which he calls progressive produces man, and even if he holds that man is in some sense the goal of the process, but if he either denies that man himself progresses or does not affirm his progress, then he cannot be considered here. He is not talking about human progress *per se*. He has a theory of cosmic progress, not of human progress. He uses the term, but does not apply it to man.

Alternatively, an author who says that some cosmic process (which he may call evolution) produces man, and that man thereafter, by reason of his place in nature, continues to evolve, but does not term the process progressive, and particularly does not call man's evolution progressive, is also ruled out. He is not talking about human progress, either. He discusses the phenomenon that the first-mentioned author does not discuss, but he does not call it progress.

Finally, authors who posit an evolutionary or other process that they do not term progressive, the goal of which may or may not be man, and who in addition do not speak of changes in man once he is produced by the process, are clearly ruled out of the discussion. They do not speak of human progress *or* of cosmic progress.

[2] From one point of view, Hegel does not belong in this list. See below, Note 12.
[3] See Chapter 2.

who appear below agree that the natural conflict that obtains in the world at large results in progress in history.

Mandeville	Bellamy
Adam Smith	Lenin
Hegel	Bukharin
Marx	Trotsky
Engels	J. Huxley
Charles Darwin	Nouÿs
Bagehot	Herrick
T. H. Huxley	Simpson
Sumner	Clough

DIALECTIC OF THE SPIRIT

Hegel's basic notion concerning the career of anything in time (as opposed to its static aspect) is revealed in his apparently paradoxical use of such a word as *aufheben*.[4] This verb, one of Hegel's characteristic key words, is employed by him to convey three distinct meanings: to annul or cancel, to preserve or conserve, and to elevate or exalt. It is true of anything that persists in time that it is canceled or annulled, conserved or preserved, and elevated or exalted; in short, a rhythmic pattern is to be observed in all phenomena. Everything vanishes into its opposite, in some sense; but nothing ever passes away entirely; on the contrary, it is raised to a higher state or stage. Everything comes to fruition, then to grief, then to a higher truth. This process is called by Hegel dialectical, and is described by him, with respect to the career of what he calls Spirit, thus:

> Spirit—consuming the envelope of its existence—does not merely pass into another envelope, nor rise rejuvenescent from the ashes of its previous form; it comes forth exalted, glorified, a purer spirit. It certainly makes war upon itself—consumes its own existence; but in this very destruction it works up that existence into a new form, and each successive phase becomes in its turn a material, working on which it exalts itself to a new grade.[5]

This process occurs in history as a whole, in what Hegel calls universal history. For history in general is, he says, the development of Spirit in time. The history of the world presents us with a rational process, which is to be understood in terms of the dialectic of the world spirit—its rational necessary course. As such, the world spirit manifests itself in a progressive sequence of states of consciousness.

[4] This point is made by Loewenberg. See Hegel, *Selections*, pp. xii–xiii.
[5] *The Philosophy of History*, p. 73.

Universal history . . . is the exhibition of Spirit in the process of working out the knowledge of that which it is potentially.[6]

That which spirit is potentially, is freedom; hence the states or stages of world history are measured by degrees of freedom. These stages are three: first, as among the Orientals, one man, the despot, is free; second, as among the Greeks and Romans, some men (those not enslaved) are free; third and finally, as among the German nations, all men are free.

The German nations, under the influence of Christianity, were the first to attain the consciousness, that man, as man, is free: that it is the *freedom* of Spirit which constitutes its essence.[7]

In short, "the History of the world is none other than the progress of the consciousness of Freedom."[8]

In terms of Hegelian dialectics, the progress of the world is described thus:

Universal History exhibits the *gradation* in the development of that principle whose substantial *purport* is the consciousness of Freedom. . . . The first step in the process presents that immersion of Spirit in Nature. . . . The second shows it as advancing to the consciousness of its own freedom. But this initial separation from Nature is imperfect and partial, since it is derived immediately from the merely natural state, is consequently related to it, and is still encumbered with it as an essentially connected element. The third step is the elevation of the soul from this still limited and special form of freedom to its pure universal form; that state in which the spiritual essence attains the consciousness and feeling of itself.[9]

The means by which freedom progressively manifests itself in the world are the actions and, perhaps even more important, the passions of men. "This may be called the *cunning of reason,*" says Hegel, that it sets the passions to work for it, and uses (and sacrifices) individuals, who are merely "phenomenal," to its ends.[10] This being so, progress is neither simple nor continuous, since it is the result of conflict between antagonistic or antithetical forces. When the antithesis is not active—in periods of "historical stagnation"—progress ceases. The history of the world, Hegel declares,

[6] *Ibid.,* pp. 17–8.
[7] *Ibid.,* p. 18.
[8] *Ibid.,* p. 19.
[9] *Ibid.,* p. 56. This scheme has affinities to other schemes of threefold development, particularly that of the Joachimites. But Hegel is akin to Comte, as well, and even to cyclists like Vico.
[10] *Ibid.,* p. 33. Here Hegel's theory seems close to Kant's. There is little difference between Hegel's "cunning reason" and Kant's "wise nature," both of which know what is best for man. See Note 12, below.

is not the theatre of happiness. Periods of happiness are blank pages in it, for they are periods of harmony, periods when the antithesis is in abeyance.[11]

Although many other authors hold that universal conflict is the source of human progress, none conceives this conflict in quite the same way. Hence, Hegel's theory of progress is *sui generis,* despite the fact that it is similar to other theories in the respects noted, and in other respects as well.[12]

DIALECTICAL MATERIALISM

Marx and Engels are in many places careful to point out the difference between Hegel's dialectics and their own. "My dialectical method," writes Marx,

> is not only different from the Hegelian, but its direct opposite. To Hegel, the life process of the human brain, *i.e.,* the process of thinking, which, under the name of "the Idea," he even transforms into an independent subject, is the demiurge of the real world, and the real world is only the external, phenomenal form of "the Idea." With me, on the contrary, the ideal is nothing else than the material world reflected by the human mind, and translated in forms of thought.[13]

"With him," Marx continues, dialectic "is standing on its head. It must be turned right side up again, if you would discover the rational kernel within the mystical shell."[14]

[11] *Ibid.,* pp. 26–7. Once more compare Kant's theory of progress; for Kant agrees that man must be thwarted in his desire for "inactive contentment" and driven to progress.

[12] This analysis indicates that Hegel belongs with the other writers treated in this chapter. However, it would have been possible to treat him elsewhere in this work. "This *good,* this *reason,*" he says, "is God. God governs the world; the actual working of His government, the carrying out of His plan, is the history of the world" (*ibid.,* p. 36). Such a statement calls for grouping Hegel with the writers who hold that God or Providence is the principle of progress.

Hegel is a complex and difficult writer, and his theory of progress has several elements. It was necessary to make a rather arbitrary decision as to the group in which to place him. It might be fair to say that for Hegel, history religiously conceived is the work of Providence, while history conceived in itself is the progressive unfolding of a world spirit which is not, strictly speaking, the same thing as God or Providence (cf. *ibid.,* p. 56).

[13] *Capital* (Preface to the Second Edition), p. 25.

[14] *Ibid.* Engels criticizes Hegel in the same terms. Hegel was, he says, an "idealist." "To him the thoughts within his brain were not the more or less abstract pictures of actual things and processes, but, conversely, things and their evolution were only the realized pictures of the 'Idea,' existing somewhere from eternity before the world was. This way of thinking turned everything upside down, and completely reversed the actual connection of things in the world" (*Socialism: Utopian and Scientific,* p. 122).

Hegel conceives progress as a dialectical movement in the realm of Spirit, contrasting this with the realm of Matter or Nature, which is unchanging.[15] Marx and Engels conceive progress as a result of the conflict—the dialectical opposition—of material forces. Hence they name their philosophy dialectical materialism.[16] Engels calls earlier thought "metaphysical." Metaphysical thinking, while it may assert the occurrence of progress in the human sphere, fails to see the connection between progress and the general laws of nature. It is progress intuitively, rather than scientifically, conceived. With the French of the eighteenth century, Engels writes,

> and even with Hegel, the conception obtained of Nature as a whole, moving in narrow circles, and forever immutable, with its eternal celestial bodies, as Newton, and unalterable organic species, as Linnaeus, taught.[17]

Man may indeed be said to progress while at the same time it is held that nature moves in the same old, recurrent pattern, but the assertion of progress is groundless, Engels declares, as long as human history is viewed as separate from natural history. Man is a part of nature, and his institutions, especially his economic institutions, develop according to the same laws that determine the development of all (living) things. For Marx and Engels, human progress is the manifestation in man's history of the line of development along which the world, or at least all living nature, has gradually advanced, and will continue to advance.[18]

Historical evolution is not quite the same, Marx and Engels make clear, as biological evolution. The latter results from conflict among individual living things. The former is brought about by conflict among social classes. This, the "fundamental proposition" of their idea of history, is explicated by Engels in his preface to *The Communist Manifesto*. The fundamental proposition is, he says,

> that in every historical epoch the prevailing mode of economic production and exchange, and the social organization necessarily following from it, form the basis upon which is built up, and from which alone can be ex-

[15] See *op. cit.,* p. 54.
[16] Marx, *op. cit.*
[17] *Op. cit.,* p. 123.
[18] If human progress is the same, or nearly the same, as biological evolution, it must be shown that dialectical materialism applies to the animal world. This Engels attempts to do in the unfinished book, *Dialectics of Nature,* in which he records remarkable insights into the connections between the sciences and the facts that underlie them and give them their meaning and validity, all from a dialectical point of view. Dialectical materialism is thus seen to be "not merely a philosophy of history, but a philosophy which illuminates all events whatever, from the falling of a stone to a poet's imaginings."

plained, the political and intellectual history of that epoch; that, consequently, the whole history of mankind (since the dissolution of tribal
society, holding land in common ownership) has been a history of class
struggles, contests between exploiting and exploited, ruling and oppressed
classes.[19]

This insight is, Engels says, due to Marx; in Engels' opinion it "is destined
to do for history what Darwin's theory has done for biology."[20]

Economic Competition

Economic competition among individuals rather than social classes—
although these may be involved—is seen as the source of progress by
several eighteenth-century authors. Their progenitor may be Mandeville,
the thesis of whose *Fable of the Bees* is neatly summed up in its subtitle:
"Private Vices, Publick Benefits." The point is that civilization advances
because of the vices, not the reasoned cooperation, of men. "I flatter myself to have demonstrated," says Mandeville,

> that neither the friendly qualities and kind affections that are natural to
> man nor the real virtues that he is capable of acquiring by reason and self-
> denial are the foundations of society; but that what we call evil in this
> world, moral as well as natural, is the grand principle that makes us so-
> ciable creatures, the solid basis, the life and support of all trades and em-
> ployments without exception; that there we must look for the true origin
> of all arts and sciences, and that the moment evil ceases, the society must
> be spoiled, if not totally dissolved.[21]

Mandeville's fable tells how, at first, the hive was naturally full of
vice, yet the whole mass was "a Paradise." Millions of bees worked to supply each other's "lust and vanity." The most vicious bees, however, cried
out the loudest against vice: "All the rogues cry'd brazenly, / Good Gods,
had we but honesty!" An indignant Jove, offended more by hypocrisy
than by wrongdoing, made the hive honest. The results were catastrophic.
Luxury diminished; trade and industry declined. A flourishing society
founded on natural selfishness became degenerate and vulnerable to
enemies. The hive was attacked by outsiders, and the few remaining bees

[19] *The Communist Manifesto* (Preface), in *Capital*, p. 318.
[20] *Ibid.*, p. 319. Marxist writers usually concur in the views here associated with
Marx and Engels. The progress theory of Bukharin, Lenin, and Trotsky is indistinguishable from that of the founders of the philosophy; and it is unchanged in essential respects in the *Program of the Communist Party of the Soviet Union* (*Draft*),
1961.
[21] *The Fable of the Bees*, p. 188.

retreated to a hollow tree, there to lead temperate and frugal lives "Blest with content and honesty."[22]

It is clear that the "blessings" of this primitive condition represent regress, not progress. Progress occurs through the conflict that obtains in the natural world, and that is inhibited in an artificially "honest" community. As Mandeville says,

> hunger, thirst, and nakedness are the first tyrants that force us to stir; afterwards our pride, sloth, sensuality, and fickleness are the great patrons that promote all arts and sciences, trades, handicrafts and callings; while the great taskmasters, necessity, avarice, envy, and ambition, each in the class that belongs to him, keep the members of the society to their labour, and make them all submit, most of them cheerfully, to the drudgery of their station, kings and princes not excepted.[23]

Adam Smith has a somewhat more elevated view of human nature than does Mandeville, but his conception of the principle of progress is very similar. "Every individual," he declares,

> is continually exerting himself to find out the most advantageous employment for whatever capital he can command. It is his own advantage, indeed, and not that of the society, which he has in view. But the study of his own advantage naturally, or rather necessarily, leads him to prefer that employment which is most advantageous to the society.[24]

What is more, "by pursuing his own interest he frequently promotes that of the society more effectually than when he really intends to promote it." He is in this, Smith adds, "as in many other cases, led by an invisible hand to promote an end which was not part of his intentions."[25]

The notion of an "invisible hand" that directs, controls, and secures the progress of nations is, of course, akin to the notion that Providence does these things, but Smith's director is not the Hand of God. It is in the nature of the case that man advances through economic competition and individual selfishness; no Divinity need be involved in the process. Indeed, the system of free trade and its meliorative effects is based, for Smith, on a primary natural characteristic of man, namely, that he has the "propensity to truck, barter, and exchange one thing for another."[26] It follows in his view that no restraints should be placed on this pro-

22 *Ibid.*, p. 34. Cf. the cyclical theories of Ibn Khaldun and Vico, to which Mandeville's scheme shows a striking resemblance. However, his is a progress theory.

23 *Ibid.*, p. 186. It is well to remember that (in the view of Mandeville) while men are really vicious, civilization really progresses—*i.e.*, changes for the better—too.

24 *The Wealth of Nations*, Vol. I, p. 398.

25 *Ibid.*, p. 400.

26 *Ibid.*, p. 12.

pensity; economic legislation should always promote the freedom, rather than the limitation in any way, of trade.

Dugald Stewart describes Smith's position thus:

> The great and leading object of his speculations is, to illustrate the provisions made by nature in the principles of the human mind, and in the circumstances of man's external situation, for a gradual and progressive augmentation in the means of national wealth; and to demonstrate that the most effectual plan for advancing a people to greatness, is to maintain that order of things which nature has pointed out; by allowing every man, as long as he observes the rules of justice, to pursue his own interest in his own way, and to bring both his industry and his capital into the freest competition with those of his fellow-citizens. Every system of policy which endeavours, either by extraordinary encouragements, to draw towards a particular species of industry a greater share of the capital of the society than what would naturally go to it, or, by extraordinary restraints, to force from a particular species of industry some share of the capital which would otherwise be employed in it, is, in reality, subversive of the great purpose which it means to promote.[27]

These ideas are found in the writings of other "liberal" economists.

BIOLOGICAL CONFLICT
(THE STRUGGLE FOR EXISTENCE)

Bagehot also emphasizes the importance for progress of free competition, but he speaks rather of the conflict of ideas than of economic ambitions. His theory is couched in terms drawn from biology, specifically from Darwin's *The Origin of Species*. "Civilization begins," says Bagehot, "because the beginning of civilization is a military advantage."[28] The heart of the theory is in that sentence.

The situation, however, is somewhat more complex, for Bagehot is concerned with the problem of why certain nations and peoples do not progress, where others do. We must concede, he declares, that civilization *begins* because it confers immense advantages in primitive life. But this is only a first step. Mankind is at the beginning wild and free. By a great effort control is achieved by means of the "yoke" or "cake" of custom, as Bagehot terms it. However, this first step is not sufficient for continuing progress, for the yoke of custom may inhibit further advance.

[27] *Adam Smith, Works, with an Account of His Life and Writings*, Vol. V, pp. 492–3; see Teggart (ed.), *The Idea of Progress*, pp. 284–5.
[28] *Physics and Politics*, p. 39.

The great difficulty which history records is not that of the first step, but
that of the second step. What is most evident is not the difficulty of getting
a fixed law, but of getting out of a fixed law; not of cementing . . . a
cake of custom, but of breaking the cake of custom; not of making the
first preservative habit, but of breaking through it, and reaching something better.[29]

The importance of free conflict or competition is seen at this point.
Only those nations can progress, Bagehot declares, that preserve and use
"the fundamental peculiarity" of all organisms, including man. This is,
that

there is a tendency in descendants to be like their progenitors, and yet
a tendency also in descendants to *differ* from their progenitors.[30]

An "arrested civilization"—*i.e.*, one in which the cake of custom is unbroken—tends to "kill out varieties at birth almost—that is, in early childhood, and before they can develop."[31] Such a civilization, in order to progress, must "break out" by gaining the habit of free discussion. This is
the source of the variety, tempered by likeness, that confers advantages on
certain nations over others. There is a basic conservative tendency in
mankind, and this tendency, "in a thousand cases—in the great majority
of cases"—has arrested progress. It is "government by discussion" that
breaks "the bond of ages" and sets free man's originality. Then, and then
only, "the tendency in every man to ameliorate his own condition" begins
to be important, because only then can man alter his condition; then
only does

the tendency in each mechanical art towards perfection begin to have force,
because the artist is at last allowed to seek perfection, after having been
forced for ages to move in the straight furrow of the old fixed way.[32]

Charles Darwin accepts, although with some hesitation, Bagehot's
application of his (Darwin's) biological theory to social history. "It is . . .
highly probable," he declares, "that with mankind the intellectual faculties have been maintained and gradually perfected through natural
selection."[33] And he writes:

Obedience, as Mr. Bagehot has well shewn, is of the highest value, for
any form of government is better than none. . . . A tribe rich in [the

29 *Ibid.*
30 *Ibid.*, p. 40.
31 *Ibid.*
32 *Ibid.*, p. 159. Hence progress, in a sense, is not "natural," and therefore not
"necessary."
33 *The Descent of Man*, p. 497.

qualities of sympathy, fidelity and courage] would spread and be victorious over other tribes. . . . Thus the social and moral qualities would tend slowly to advance and be diffused throughout the world.[34]

However, such remarks are very general, Darwin warns, and have little or no scientific validity. Such validity as they have refers rather to the first advance of savages toward civilization than to subsequent advances. For example, supposing that sympathy confers an advantage in the primitive condition of mankind, it must be recognized that it tends to perpetuate, and perhaps even to increase, the number of inferior members of the species. The indigent and stupid in modern societies are allowed, out of charity, to breed, and this may be to the ultimate detriment of the race as a whole.[35] In reality, Darwin is saying it is difficult to decide whether, even if the principle of natural selection was once operative in human progress, it continues to be so. There is evidence for and against the assertion. Darwin concludes, however, that

> to believe that man was aboriginally civilized and then suffered utter degradation in so many regions, is to take a pitiably low view of human nature. It is apparently a truer and more cheerful view that progress has been more general than retrogression; that man has risen, though by slow and interrupted steps, from a lowly condition to the highest standard as yet attained by him in knowledge, morals and religion.[36]

If this is indeed the case, the principle of natural selection has undoubtedly had an important part in man's advance.

Other authors are less hesitant than Darwin in asserting the importance of the principle. Sumner, for example, combines the theory of Adam Smith and other "liberal" economists—that progress occurs through the pursuit of each man's economic self-interest—with the theory of Bagehot and other "social Darwinists"—that progress occurs through natural conflict, as manifested in the world of man. Sumner points to several "great facts" that determine man's life, and that the sociologist, he declares, must take into account. These are, first, that man is born under the necessity of struggling with nature to sustain his existence; second, that weapons and tools are required to subjugate nature; third, that capital is needed for the effective application of such tools and weapons to the struggle; fourth, that the pressure of population must everywhere become intense, if it is not already so; and fifth, that liberty is necessary in order that

[34] *Ibid.*, p. 498.
[35] This same point is made by Crow, a regress author, and by C. G. Darwin, a progress author.
[36] *Ibid.*, p. 511.

competition among men may bear fruit. Viewed in the light of these facts, it is not surprising, says Sumner, that

> the progress which men have made in developing the possibilities of human existence has never been made by jumps and strides. It has never resulted from the schemes of philosophers and reformers.[37]

Indeed, progress may be converted into regress—"corruption and decay through luxury and vice"—by the "folly" of mankind. But progress does occur, nevertheless, especially in the expansion of man's power over nature, and its rate can be accelerated if men are left free to compete with one another in the economic as well as in other spheres of human life.[38]

Shephard Clough's position is similar. He maintains that

> degrees of civilization are measured by the extent of control over physical and human environment and by the quality and quantity of intellectual and aesthetic accomplishments,[39]

and he holds that advances in civilization do not occur, or at least tend not to occur, in societies that are "rigidly structured." "Indeed," he says, "the range of opportunities for alternative decisions is a useful concept in analyzing civilizing forces." And he goes on to say:

> Everything which contributes to the extension of that range, whether it be economic surplus, the use of leisure, the development of cities, or the absence of stultifying rigidities, is of the utmost significance in furthering the process of civilization.[40]

Clough is spelling out here the different sorts of freedom that allow the principle of natural selection to operate in behalf of progress. "Government by decision," a condition of things in which new ideas can be put forward and considered by the whole community, is a leading type of this freedom.

The idea that conflict or opposition is a productive principle was by no means new when it was proposed as the source of progress by Kant, Malthus, Hegel, Marx, Engels, Bagehot, and others from one to two cen-

---

[37] "The Challenge of Facts," in *The People Shall Judge,* Vol. II, p. 91.
[38] See also "The Absurd Effort to Make the World Over," in *War and Other Essays,* pp. 195–9, 208–10.
[39] *The Rise and Fall of Civilization,* p. 258.
[40] *Ibid.,* p. 11. Clough here uses "process" instead of "progress." Many modern writers have an aversion to the latter term.

turies ago.[41] According to Augustine, the beauty and perfection of the course of this world is achieved by the opposition of contraries.[42] Empedocles held that strife is the principle of movement and change; the idea may be found in Plato and Aristotle, as well.

Empedocles is not a progress author, nor are Plato and Aristotle. Indeed, an assertion that opposition is a productive or generative principle is not necessarily an affirmation of progress. Milton, for instance, in saying that "we bring not innocence into the world, we bring impurity much rather; that which purifies us is trial, and trial is by what is contrary,"[43] is not saying that progress occurs in history. Similarly, Christian's "progress" through this world and toward eternal bliss is the result of obstacles faced and battles won against many and powerful adversaries, but Bunyan does not see the human race as facing obstacles or winning battles, nor does he affirm human progress.

Nevertheless, the idea that conflict or opposition is connected with progress, even if it is not its basic source or principle, is to be found in the work of a very large number of writers of the last two or three centuries. A representative sample appears below; the list includes authors who emphasize some other principle of progress, and who are therefore discussed elsewhere in this study, but who nevertheless refer to the idea being considered here.

Hobbes	Spencer
Turgot	Tolstoy
Rousseau	Freud
Kant	Maritain
Herder	Ortega
Malthus	Ginsberg
Saint-Simon	C. G. Darwin
Comte	Rougemont
Buckle	Rostow

PROGRESS THROUGH VARIATION

Movement or change from the simple to the complex is conceived as the principle of progress by a relatively small number of authors, several of whom, however, are of major importance.[44]

---

[41] Kant and Malthus were treated in the previous chapter; they nevertheless see conflict or opposition as important in progress.

[42] This is one of the underlying ideas of *The City of God*.

[43] *Aeropagitica and Other Prose Writings*, p. 22.

[44] The list could be lengthened by including the many disciples of Herbert Spencer.

Robinet   Henry Adams
Spencer   Bergson
Fiske   Teilhard de Chardin

Spencer's theory of progress can be stated in a sentence: Progress, which may be defined as motion from homogeneity to heterogeneity, results from the universal fact that an active force produces more than one effect or change.

The theory is outlined in "Progress: Its Law and Cause." Spencer writes:

> The investigations of Wolff, Goethe, and von Baer have established the truth that the series of changes gone through during the development of a seed into a tree, or an ovum into an animal, constitute an advance from homogeneity of structure to heterogeneity of structure. . . . Now . . . this law of organic progress is the law of all progress. Whether it be in the development of the earth, in the development of life upon its surface, in the development of society, of government, of manufactures, of commerce, of language, literature, science, art, this same evolution of the simple into the complex, through successive differentiations, holds throughout.[45]

Many examples of the working of this "law" are given by Spencer. These include the formation of the solar system (on "the nebular hypothesis"), the "development" of the earth itself, biological evolution in general, and "the progress of the latest and most heterogeneous creature—man."[46] The law is exemplified in man's physical nature, says Spencer, and even more so in "humanity as socially embodied."

> The change from the homogeneous to the heterogeneous is displayed in the progress of civilization as a whole, as well as in the progress of every nation; and is still going on with increasing rapidity.[47]

This is true in government, in the division of labor, in language, in art, and in science, all of which are growing more complex and heterogeneous. Indeed,

> the law thus clearly exemplified in the evolution of the social organism, is exemplified with equal clearness in the evolution of all products of human thought and action; whether concrete or abstract, real or ideal.[48]

If the law is universally exemplified, Spencer asks, must there not be some universal cause that underlies it?

[45] "Progress: Its Law and Cause," in Teggart (ed.), *The Idea of Progress*, p. 436.
[46] *Ibid.*, pp. 436–7.
[47] *Ibid.*, p. 438.
[48] *Ibid.*, p. 441.

Must not this uniformity of procedure be a consequence of some fundamental necessity? May we not rationally seek for some all-pervading principle which determines this all-pervading process of things? Does not the universality of the law imply a universal cause?[49]

That such a cause could be "comprehended, noumenally considered," is not, Spencer says, to be supposed. To do so would be to solve the "ultimate mystery." But it still may be possible to reduce the law of progress from the condition of "an empirical generalization, to the condition of a rational generalization."

We may be able to affiliate all these varied evolutions of the homogeneous into the heterogeneous, upon certain facts of immediate experience, which, in virtue of endless repetition, we regard as necessary.[50]

The problem, then, is to discover some fact, of a high degree of abstractness, that is common to "such infinitely varied phenomena." In order to do so, it is necessary to consider progress as it were in the abstract, and not "this or that form of progress." From this point of view,

the only obvious respect in which all kinds of progress are alike, is, that they are modes of change; and hence, in some characteristic of changes in general, the desired solution will probably be found.[51]

For we may expect *a priori*, Spencer contends, that in some universal law of change lies the explanation of this universal transformation of the homogeneous into the heterogeneous.

Thus much premised, Spencer goes on,

we pass at once to the statement of the law, which is this—Every active force produces more than one change—every cause produces more than one effect.[52]

The rest of the essay is devoted to examples of *this* law. "Illustrations to the same effect might be indefinitely accumulated," Spencer concludes, "but they are needless."

Endless facts go to show that every kind of progress is from the homogeneous to the heterogeneous; and that it is so because each change is followed by many changes. And it is significant that where the facts are most accessible and abundant, there these truths are most manifest.[53]

In his *First Principles*, Spencer argues that there is a fundamental law of matter, called by him the law of the persistence of force, which re-

[49] *Ibid.*
[50] *Ibid.*, pp. 441–2.
[51] *Ibid.*, p. 442.
[52] *Ibid.*
[53] *Ibid.*, p. 447.

quires that nothing homogeneous can remain so if acted upon, for whatever acts upon it must affect its different parts in different ways. Hence an increasing variety is the result of any action, and this law of the multiplication of effects is the clue to all development, cosmic as well as biological. The question remains of how the entire process is begun. Spencer solves this difficulty by positing an unknown and unknowable absolute force that continuously operates on the material world. The ultimate cause of progress of all kinds is, therefore, this hypothetical primary force; but the principle of progress is variation, or the universally observed movement from homogeneity to heterogeneity.[54]

The notion of force is also basic to Henry Adams' theory of progress.[55] For him, it appears, everything is a force. "Man is a force; so is the sun; so is a mathematical point, though without dimensions or known existence." A force is "anything that does or helps to do work." And, according to Adams, "progress is the development and economy of Forces."[56]

Just as man uses, and acts on, lesser forces, so he is "captured" and moved by forces greater than himself.

> A dynamic theory, assigning attractive force to opposing bodies in proportion to the law of mass, takes for granted that the forces of nature capture man. A sum of force attracts; the feeble atom or molecule called man is attracted; he suffers education or growth; he is the sum of forces that attract him; his body and his thought are alike their product; the movement of the forces controls the progress of his mind, since he can know nothing but the motions which impinge on his senses, whose sum makes education.[57]

Man is "pulled" through history by the various forces that attract him. Indeed, he is subject to a multiplicity of forces and "lines of force" that are "higher" than those that affect other living things, all of which he cannot know, nor can he know their number, which may be infinite. And

[54] It may be asked whether variation can continue indefinitely; and Spencer is not unaware of the problem raised by the question. Indeed, there is in his *First Principles* the suggestion that some sort of absolute integration will ultimately follow the absolute differentiation and variation toward which the world is now moving, and that a sequence of integrations and differentiations is thus the overall pattern of events in the cosmos. Within the limits, however, of mankind's career on earth, the pattern appears to be only progressive. See Part II, xxiv, "Summary and Conclusion," in *First Principles*, pp. 551–72.

Spencer's cosmic theory—if it deserves the name—is to be compared to Gamow's theory of the expanding universe. It is now held by some cosmogonists that the universe undergoes a cycle of expansion and contraction once every eighty billion years or so. The "big bang" that initiated the present expansive phase of the cycle began some ten billion years ago, so mankind will probably not see the end of this phase, to say nothing of seeing the contraction that will follow.

[55] Adams' theory of progress is not presented in any one work; a synthesis of several of his works has here been made.

[56] *The Education of Henry Adams*, p. 474.

[57] *Ibid.*

his movement, development, or education—these terms appear to be interchangeable—is human progress.

> Science has proved that forces, sensible and occult, physical and metaphysical, simple and complex, surround, traverse, vibrate, rotate, repel, attract, without stop; that man's senses are conscious of a few, and only to a partial degree; but that, from the beginning of organic existence his consciousness has been induced, expanded, trained in the lines of sensitiveness; and that the rise of his faculties from a lower power to a higher, or from a narrower to a wider field, may be due to the function of assimilating and storing outside force or forces.[58]

The above constitutes an affirmation of progress, but it is not yet a theory of progress. In Adams' paper on the phase theory of Willard Gibbs, he applies his notion of force to history, and attempts to construct a language in which to talk about progress scientifically.

Gibbs's Rule of Phase has to do with the passing of substances from the solid to the liquid to the gaseous state. Phase itself is a state of equilibrium; as Adams says, "the common idea of phase is that of the solution itself, as when salt is dissolved in water. It is the whole equilibrium or state of apparent rest."[59] The scientist, however, is interested in relations between phases: "the various conditions of temperature, pressure and volume have become more important than the atoms and molecules themselves."[60] What is more, the rule lends itself to mathematical treatment, whereby it goes beyond material substances, since they can be reduced mathematically to immaterial energy—magneto-electricity and ether. Expanding on this idea, Adams writes:

> Thenceforward nothing prevented the mathematical physicist from assuming the existence of as many phases, and calculating the values of as many mutations as he liked, up to the last thinkable stage of hyperthought and hyperspace which he knew as pure mathematics, and in which all motion, all relation, and all form, were merged.[61]

Not only, then, is thought a phase of matter but it has gone through phases analogous to those through which matter passes. Hence the Rule of Phase is applicable to history.

> In this long and—for our purposes—infinite stretch of time, the substance called thought has—like the substance called water or gas—passed through a variety of phases, or changes, or states of equilibrium, with which we are more or less familiar.[62]

---

[58] *Ibid.*, p. 487.
[59] "The Rule of Phase Applied to History," in *The Degradation of the Democratic Dogma*, p. 262.
[60] *Ibid.*, p. 263.
[61] *Ibid.*, p. 271.
[62] *Ibid.*, p. 276.

It remains only to apply the rule to specific historical epochs, and this Adams attempts to do. He suggests that Comte's theory of phases was a first and not unrespectable approximation; however, it lacked a precise mathematical formulation, and a means of measuring exactly when thought passed from one phase to the next. In fact, Adams himself admits to failure in the attempt to state such a formula and discover such a measure. Nevertheless, he proposes that the period between 1600–1900 might be termed the Mechanical Phase, and that the coal output of the world, which "doubled every ten years between 1840 and 1900, in the form of utilized power, for every ton of coal yielded three or four times as much power in 1900 as in 1840,"[63] might serve as a rough measure.

A Religious Phase, Adams declares, lasting about 90,000 years, ended in 1600; the next, or Electric Phase, would start in 1900 and

> would have a half life equal to $\sqrt{300}$, or about seventeen and a half years, when—that is, in 1917—it would pass into another or Ethereal Phase, which, for half a century, science has been promising, and which would last only $\sqrt{17.5}$, or about four years, and bring Thought to the limit of its possibilities in the year 1921. It may well be! Nothing whatever is beyond the range of possibility; but even if the life of the previous phase, 1600–1900, were extended another hundred years, the difference to the last term of the series would be negligible. In that case, the Ethereal Phase would last till about 2025.[64]

Progress, then, is the development or economy of forces. History is the record of phases of thought that manifest themselves in transformations of these forces; it is subject to a law of acceleration. The process as a whole is described by Adams as "movement from unity to multiplicity."[65] Such a movement is the principle of progress.

Teilhard de Chardin also holds that the direction of evolution is from

[63] *Education,* p. 490.
[64] "Rule of Phase," p. 302. On the basis of such estimates, Adams makes a number of prophecies. "At the rate of progress since 1800, every American who lived into the year 2000 would know how to control unlimited power." He would think in "complexities unimaginable to an earlier mind." He would deal with problems "altogether beyond the range of an earlier society." "To him the nineteenth century would stand on the same plane with the fourth—equally childlike—and he would only wonder how both of them, knowing so little, and so weak in force, should have done so much" (*Education,* pp. 496–7). Adams adds, with typical nostalgia, that his hypothetical American might even "go back, in 1964, to sit with Gibbon on the steps of Ara Coeli."
[65] "The movement from unity to multiplicity, between 1200 and 1900, was unbroken in sequence, and rapid in acceleration. Prolonged one generation longer, it would require a new social mind. As though thought were common salt in indefinite solution it must enter a new phase subject to new laws. Thus far, since five or ten thousand years, the mind had successfully reacted, and nothing yet proved that it would fail to react—but it would need to jump" (*Education,* p. 498).

the simple to the complex. In a statement that, he says, sums up his thinking on the subject, he writes:

> If the universe, regarded sidereally, is in process of spatial expansion (from the infinitesimal to the immense), in the same way and still more clearly it presents itself to us, physico-chemically, as in process of organic *involution* upon itself (from the extremely simple to the extremely complex)—and moreover this particular involution "of complexity" is experimentally bound up with a correlative increase in interiorization, that is to say in the psyche or consciousness.[66]

Although Teilhard declares that consciousness is not a particular subsistent entity, but an "effect," the " 'specific effect' of complexity,"[67] the specific effect is of greater interest to him than the general phenomenon. Evolution or progress—in the limited human sphere they are the same thing—is ultimately the movement from the simple to the complex; and this movement is manifested in a cosmic rise or advance of consciousness that can be observed at every level of being.

The notion of universal consciousness[68] is essential to Teilhard's theory of progress. Consciousness as we usually think of it is, he says, only the local manifestation and expression of a cosmic trend. In fact, consciousness "transcends by far the ridiculously narrow limits within which our eyes can directly perceive it." The most rudimentary corpuscles, even the "megamolecules," have some sort of psyche, which is, however, imperceptible because of its extreme diffuseness. In such "primitive" entities involution has not yet occurred sufficiently to produce a perceptible radiation of consciousness.[69]

The notion of involution is also essential to the theory. Just as in the development of the embryo the outer layers turn inward and enclose what becomes the most important parts of the organism, so,

> regarded along its axis of complexity, the universe is, both on the whole and at each of its points, in a continual tension of organic doubling-back upon itself, and thus of interiorization.[70]

"The involuting universe," Teilhard continues, "considered in its pre-reflective zones, proceeds step by step by dint of billion-fold trial and error."[71] The process results in what is called the biosphere—the world of

[66] *The Phenomenon of Man*, p. 300.
[67] *Ibid.*
[68] The notion is sometimes called panpsychism. See Lovejoy, *The Great Chain of Being*, p. 276.
[69] *Op. cit.*, p. 301.
[70] *Ibid.*
[71] *Ibid.*

living things. Man is in turn a production or result of the biosphere. But he is more than merely a member of it. Just as the biosphere represents a step forward in evolution, so does man's "power of reflection" have the "value of a 'threshold' or a change of state."

> From the theshold of reflection onwards, we are at what is nothing less than a new form of biological existence, characterized, among other peculiarities, by the following properties:
>
> *a.* The decisive emergence in individual life of factors of internal arrangement (*invention*) above the factors of external arrangement (utilization of the play of chance).
>
> *b.* The equally decisive appearance between elements of true forces of attraction and repulsion (sympathy and antipathy), replacing the pseudo-attractions and pseudo-repulsions of pre-life or even of the lower forms of life. . . .
>
> *c.* Lastly, the awakening in the consciousness of each particular element . . . of a demand for "unlimited survival." That is to say the passage, for life, from a state of relative irreversibility (the physical impossibility of the cosmic involution to stop, once it has begun) to a state of absolute irreversibility (the radical dynamic incompatibility of a certain prospect of total death with the continuation of an evolution that has become reflective).[72]

Involved here is the notion of a further "sphere" beyond the biosphere, called the noosphere. This "second fanning out" (the first being the so-called tree of life) is not, Teilhard declares, antievolutionary, nor is it in any sense beyond evolution. Universal evolution does not cease because man now controls his own evolution—because, in a word, he thinks. Just the contrary is the case.

> How can we fail to see that after rolling us on individually—all of us, you and me—upon our own axes, it is still the same cyclone (only now on the social scale) which is still blowing over our heads, driving us together into a contact which tends to perfect each one of us by linking him organically to each and all of his neighbours?[73]

The noosphere, in short, is not merely the aggregation of thinking men; while as yet rudimentary, it can be expected to develop into a type of shared consciousness of which we may now have but a faint conception. Such a notion explains history, and allows us to predict the future. For "if above the elementary hominisation that culminates in each individual,

[72] *Ibid.*, pp. 302–3.
[73] *Ibid.*, p. 304.

there is really developing above us another hominisation, a collective one of the whole species," then it is natural that we should observe—as in fact we do—the "same three psycho-biological properties" advancing on the earth that had produced the original step to individual reflection.

a. Firstly the power of invention, so rapidly intensified at the present time by the rationalised recoil of all the forces of research that it is already possible to speak of a forward leap of evolution.

b. Next, capacity for attraction (or repulsion), still operating in a chaotic way throughout the world but rising so rapidly around us that (whatever be said to the contrary) economics will soon count for very little in comparison with the ideological and the emotional factors in the arrangement of the world.

c. Lastly and above all, the demand for irreversibility. This emerges from the still somewhat hesitating zone of individual aspirations, so as to find categorical expression in consciousness and through the voice of the species. . . . The effort to push the earth forward is much too heavy, and the task threatens to go on much too long, for us to continue to accept it, unless we are to work in what is incorruptible.[74]

The above, along with other assembled pointers, constitutes, Teilhard declares, a serious scientific proof that man is not drifting biologically, nor simply declining toward a catastrophe or senility, but on the contrary that

the human group is in fact turning, by arrangement and planetary convergence of all elemental terrestrial reflection, towards a second critical pole of reflection of a collective and higher order; towards a point beyond which (precisely because it is critical) we can see nothing directly, but a point through which we can nevertheless prognosticate the contact between thought, born of involution upon itself of the stuff of the universe, and that transcendent focus we call Omega, the principle which at one and the same time makes this involution irreversible and moves and collects it.[75]

Teilhard's panpsychism is not new. The French *philosophe* J. B. Robinet, following Leibniz, also sees an infinitely graduated continuity

[74] *Ibid.,* p. 305. Cf. Ellul on technology: "Technique is the totality of methods rationally arrived at and having absolute efficiency (for a given stage of development) in every field of human activity" (*The Technological Society,* p. xxv). Ellul believes that the "solution" of the "problem of technology" offered by Teilhard belongs to "the realm of fancy and [has] no bearing on reality" (*ibid.,* p. xxxi). The correctness of this judgment is irrelevant to our analysis, but it is important to recognize, as Ellul does, that Teilhard is indeed offering a solution to the problem.
[75] *Ibid.,* p. 306.

of being such that consciousness is shared by all things. For every purely qualitative difference between two things is necessarily a discontinuity. *All* things must therefore be supposed to have some degree of any quality that is possessed by *any*thing.

> What continuity can there be between the organic and the inorganic, between the animate and the inanimate, between the rational and the non-rational? It is evident that there is no mean between the positive and the negative, and consequently, that there are no intermediate beings which link the two together. If there were such beings, it would be necessary that their constitution should simultaneously participate in two mutually exclusive contraries. . . . If we wish to allow Nature to pass insensibly from one of her productions to another, without compelling her to make leaps, we must not admit the existence of any inorganic beings, or any inanimate, or any non-rational.[76]

"For myself," Robinet adds, "I would rather give even intelligence to the last atom of matter . . . than refuse organization to the fossils and make of them isolated beings, having no connection with others. It is to no purpose to tell me this is a bizarre opinion, and that it is not possible that a stone thinks."[77] For if the law of continuity be admitted, we must, he declares, likewise admit all that follows from it.

Nature, says Robinet, works by means of a vast number of fumbling experimentations in order to reach her goal—mankind. She must err before she can find the right way; and in order to find it, she must take every possible path. Progress is by trial-and-error; variation is its principle.

> All the varieties intermediate between the prototype and man I regard as so many essays of Nature, aiming at the most perfect, yet unable to attain it except through this innumerable sequence of sketches. I think that we may call the collection of the preliminary studies the apprenticeship of Nature in learning to make a man.[78]

For Robinet, "brute matter" and "spontaneous activity" are polar opposites, and the direction of progress or evolution is from the former to the

---

[76] *De la Nature*, IV, 4–5. We are indebted to Lovejoy's analysis of Robinet. See *The Great Chain of Being*, pp. 269–83. This quotation is translated by Lovejoy, p. 276.

[77] *Ibid.*, 11–12. See Lovejoy, p. 277.

[78] *Ibid.*, V. See Lovejoy, p. 280. Robinet holds that all living things are merely natural variations of a prototypical entity he describes as "an elongated tube or hollow cylinder, naturally active." Elsewhere he calls this an *organe,* which is the equivalent of a protoplasmic cell. All living things are built up of units of the same shape and homogeneous in their properties (*De la Nature,* IV).

latter.[79] In the lower grades of being, brute matter is dominant; the tendency to spontaneous activity is almost wholly inhibited. Little by little, as Nature makes more experiments, spontaneity gains strength, and, finally, in man, establishes a dominance so complete that matter becomes less an obstacle than an instrument whereby activity achieves its ends.[80]

> In man . . . it is evident that matter is only the organ through which the active principle brings its faculties into play. The former is an envelope which modifies the action of the latter, one without which it would perhaps act more freely, but also without which, perhaps, it could not act at all, and without which it assuredly could not render its activities sensible. Does it not . . . seem that the active power grows and perfects itself in being, in proportion as it raises itself above matter?[81]

Man has not yet attained perfection, Robinet declares. Society itself is the work of nature, and it is advancing as are all her works; "arts and sciences, laws, the diversity of forms of government, war and commerce— everything, in short, is only a development."

> The seeds of all were latent in Nature; they have unfolded, each in its own time. Perhaps she still retains in her womb other germs, of slower growth, of which future races will reap the fruits. Then genius will expand and take on a still greater form. The tree of science will acquire new branches. As the catalogue of arts is extended, their scope will become more ample.[82]

And in another place, he asserts that "*la progression n'est pas finie.*"

> There may be forms more subtle, potencies more active, than those which compose man. The force may, indeed, be able to rid itself insensibly of all materiality, and so to begin a new world—but we must not let ourselves go astray in the boundless regions of the possible.[83]

A comparison among Teilhard's Omega Point, Adams' phase beyond the Ethereal, and this new world of Robinet's, which has rid itself insensibly of all materiality, is not without interest. It may be coincidence that these three writers share a vision of the future of humanity in which

---

[79] Bergson sees the course of evolution as moving from "instinct" to "intelligence," of which the latter is marked by "freedom." Bergson might have been discussed at length in this place. His theory of progress is not essentially different from that of the authors treated in this section. See *Creative Evolution*, pp. 149 ff.

[80] Teilhard concurs with Robinet on this point; but Ellul fears that matter, through technology, will dominate man, and not the other way about. Ellul's theory of regress is treated in Chapter 8.

[81] *Vue philosophique de la gradation naturelle des formes de l'être*, pp. 8–10. See Lovejoy, p. 282.

[82] *De la Nature*, I, 25. See Lovejoy, p. 273.

[83] *Vue philosophique*, p. 12. See Lovejoy, p. 282.

man will attain a kind of superior consciousness, unalloyed by matter, and to be described, perhaps, in pure mathematics alone. However, the idea that the principle of progress is variation would seem to lead naturally enough to such speculations.[84]

[84] Robinet shares with Teilhard and Adams a kind of wonder as to what the new world will be like. What will this shared consciousness, to be attained by mankind at the Omega Point, really mean? Will men "see" into each other's minds? Will individuals become, as it were, the organs of some kind of superorganism, just as the arms and eyes are now organs of a single mind? Will humanity be truly one, capable of drawing on the senses and intellects of all its members, and able to exert all their energies at the behest of some unified, organized, and superior will? Such speculations remain unvoiced in these authors, but they are commonplaces of science fiction. A. C. Clarke, for example, imagines a further step in the "evolution of mind" that puts an end to *Homo sapiens*, and by which is forged a new race of beings "who will not possess minds as you know them. They will be a single entity, as you yourselves are the sums of your myriad cells" (*Childhood's End*, in *Across the Sea of Stars*, p. 405).

Clarke's speculations raise a serious question about the theory being considered here. Robinet and Teilhard, if not Adams, emphasize the principle of continuity in their discussions of progress. But it would seem that the Omega Point marks a discontinuity of some sort in the cosmic evolution of which human progress is a part.

7

Denials of Progress:
Types of Theories
of Regress and of Cycles

IF we let an upward-moving line represent a progressive pattern of history—thus:

(1)

then there are two lines that represent patterns that are inconsistent with a progressive pattern and that therefore represent denials of progress. They are:

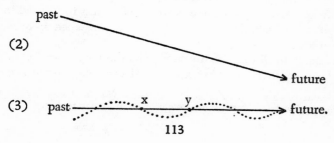

(2)

(3)

Line (2) represents regress—an irreversible change for the worse in the conditions of human life. This need not be continuous; some regress authors hold that there are temporary advances and improvements from time to time. But the general or overall pattern or tendency of history that is represented by this line is downward. In the long run, man loses more than he gains.

Line (3) represents the position that there is no significant change in the conditions of human life. It reflects the denial of a prime tenet of both progress and regress theories, namely, that history shows irreversible change, either for the better or for the worse. According to this position, there are cycles of history—as was said long ago, there is nothing new under the sun.

The dotted line signifies changes in man's nature or condition. Such changes are observable and no cyclist denies their occurrence. But, according to the cyclist view, they are not significant in the context of a search for a pattern of irreversible change in history. At x, regress seems to be occurring, but apparent progress later on will cancel it out. At y, the pattern of history seems to be progressive; but this "progress" will be canceled by later "regress."

Types of Theories of Regress

As we have observed, regress authors are divided into two main groups. For one group, the changes for the worse that occur in history reflect a universal or cosmic pattern, usually itself regressive.[1] For the other group, historical regress occurs independently of any cosmic pattern. The one group of theories is called cosmogenic, the other anthropogenic.

Theories of Anthropogenic Regress

For the most part, theories of anthropogenic regress do not state explicitly that historical regress is independent of the cosmos. However, most such theories posit some specific cause, inherent in human nature or in the human condition, for the occurrence of regress in history. In a few cases, regress is merely described. A cause of regress apart from man and the human world is never given.

It is difficult to distinguish theories of anthropogenic regress substantively. However, they can be distinguished according to their use of a

---

[1] The cosmic process itself need not be regressive (*i.e.*, a change for the worse). Cosmic changes involving no pejoration might result in human regress.

few sets of characteristic terms. Several authors speak of an original "state of nature" from which man fell. Others see history as the conflict between "intelligence" and "instinct," and hold that the inevitable victory of the former over the latter is the sign of regress. Still others hold that technological progress is really regress for mankind; the advance of technology is at the same time the degeneration or corruption of humanity. All of these authors have much in common, and their ideas about what regress is, and about why it occurs, overlap in many respects.[2]

Rousseau is, traditionally, the leading proponent of this position, but F. G. Juenger, Herbert Marcuse, Roderick Seidenberg, N. O. Brown, and Jacques Ellul are also worthy of note. The position that anthropogenic regress occurs is discussed in Chapter 8.

THEORIES OF COSMOGENIC REGRESS

Two types of theories of cosmogenic regress are found in the literature; the distinction between them parallels the distinction between progress as a divine gift and progress as the result of a natural cosmic principle. First, there are theories that assert that a succession of gods or mythical figures controls history—a succession the essential character of which is regressive. Such theories usually involve the notion of an original golden age, from which man apparently fell by no fault of his own.[3] Second, there are theories that assert that the universe as a whole is wearing out or running down. History is affected by this cosmic process; mankind cannot escape the fate of the world at large. Such theories often involve the notion that the second law of thermodynamics has a valid application to

---

[2] Many of the authors who have theories of regress state that the earliest stage of human life, which they hold to be preferable to later ones, was "childlike" or "innocent." It is possible that these writers feel that childhood is a preferable state, in the individual, to maturity, and that they extend this judgment (which all men may feel from time to time) to the entire human race. Or they may feel (an attitude also widely shared) that the price of maturity, in the race as well as in the individual, is too high. The fact that many authors cite the acquisition of the arts and sciences (the advance of technology) as a sign or even a cause of regress may lend weight to the latter view. The attainment of power over nature and human nature by means of technology may correspond to the understanding achieved by individuals as they mature, the price of which, traditionally, is suffering and woe.

[3] There are few exceptions to this rule; in most Greek and Roman versions of the myth of the ages of man, humanity is not responsible for its first downward step, for its fall from the first or golden age. Some classical theories seem to say that later downward steps are taken by man himself.

If the story told in *Genesis* may be classed with these, then it is worth noting that, in the Christian tradition, man is responsible even for his first departure from innocence.

history. As before, man is not at fault. He cannot be blamed for the nature of things.[4]

Hesiod and Ovid are especially notable among the authors who hold that a regressive sequence of divinities brings about regress in history. Henry Adams assembles a large number of quotations from authors who see the second law of thermodynamics as affecting historical regress,[5] and James Jeans and Norbert Wiener hold similar views. Theories of cosmogenic regress are treated in Chapter 9.[6]

[4] Nevertheless, the proponents of such theories often charge man with hastening his regress.

[5] In *A Letter to American Teachers of History,* where Adams attempts to meet the denials of his affirmation of progress constituted by such views.

[6] None of the theories of cosmogenic regress that are discussed is a specifically Christian theory. Modern Christian writers, at least since the seventeenth century, seem to hold that regress occurs for reasons having little to do with Providence. And we have not found a true theory of regress in the writings of any older Christian thinker.

This is the more surprising, perhaps, in the light of the almost universally held modern scholarly opinion that Medieval thinkers saw man's history as on the whole degenerative. This opinion is hinted at in Bury's *The Idea of Progress* (pp. 78–97), and is documented, as well as it can be documented, by Cross in his article "Microcosm and Macrocosm in Old English" (in *Festschrift for A. G. Brodeur,* ed. Stanley Greenfield). See also Maurice de Wulf's *Philosophy and Civilization,* Chapter 12, Haskins' *12th-Century Renaissance,* and Jacques le Goff's *Les Intellectuels au Moyen Age.* The last work compares Bernard and Abelard, and suggests that Bernard is a regress author and Abelard a progress author, though both are far from having what we would call a theory regarding the pattern of history. R. F. Jones, in *Ancients and Moderns,* also discusses many of the "pessimistic" views of the relative excellence of modern as opposed to ancient authors, views that were opposed by such indubitably progress authors as Pascal, Perrault, and Fontenelle. And there are other such works, as well.

Despite this wealth of scholarly comment, we have not, as we have said, been able to find any argued theory of regress before modern times—and we have doubts about even these, which are indicated in this chapter and in its notes. Why should this be so?

Perhaps the answer is that Medieval thought, while undoubtedly "pessimistic" about the career of man on earth, had no real conception, capable of being compared with modern conceptions, of universal history—of the history of mankind throughout its entire temporal career. If this is correct, then we should not be at all surprised to find no true theory of regress in the Middle Ages. Such a theory is hinted at in *The Divine Comedy.* There were many other Medieval writers who made reference to the classical myth of the Ages of Man, as originally expressed by Hesiod and Ovid, and saw it as in some way relevant to their view of history. But the Medieval emphasis was primarily—indeed, almost exclusively—on the career of the individual soul, and not on that of mankind or humanity considered as a whole. Thus, by extension, regress, degeneration, or deterioration was man's lot, but no strong and unequivocal affirmation of regress was necessary or even conceivable. Mankind was not considered, in short, as having a career; only men had histories, and possibly institutions and states; the idea of universal history had yet to be discovered or invented.

In the light of this, it is the more remarkable to find the Joachimites and other millennialists of the Middle Ages developing a true theory of progress. The millen-

Types of Theories of Cycles

Cyclists, like regress authors, are divided into two main groups. For the first, the cyclical changes that occur in history reflect a cosmic pattern, itself cyclical or repetitive. For the second, cyclical historical changes occur independently of any cosmic pattern. The one group of theories is called cosmogenic, the other anthropogenic.

Theories of Anthropogenic Cycles

All authors who have theories of cosmogenic cycles either state explicitly or strongly imply that the cyclical pattern to be observed in history is dependent on, or closely related to, repetitive occurrences in the cosmos. Authors of theories of anthropogenic cycles concur in asserting that history shows a cyclical pattern, but they either make no mention of cosmic cycles, or deny that these have any effect on man's career on earth.

The major theories of anthropogenic cycles are remarkably similar; there are few grounds on which to classify them into types, and little need for such a classification. It is true that the terminology of most of these writers is complex, and it differs from author to author. But the characterizations of the different phases of history that are found in their writings are much the same.

One distinction among theories of anthropogenic cycles deserves mention, although it is not sharp enough to support a classification into types. Some writers, notably Spengler, say that cultures or civilizations change in a pattern that is like that of (other) living things. Cultures are born, grow, reach maturity (a climax), wane or decay, and die or are destroyed, much as plants or animals undergo these changes. Other writers, notably Toynbee, deny that this organic analogy has validity. A culture is not alive, they say, in the way that an animal or plant is alive. Nevertheless, one cannot escape the impression that the analogy between the career of

---

nialist position was by no means the dominant one; "pessimism" was the order of the day. But it is noteworthy that the only group of thinkers who conceived, however faintly, that mankind as a whole might be considered as having a history, were either progress authors or, perhaps, more accurately, proto-progress authors. This leads, of course, to the speculation, discussed in this chapter and in its notes, that the notion of universal history is more intimately related to the notion of a progressive pattern of history than has been realized. If, in short, one conceives mankind as having a history, can that history be considered as being anything other than progressive?

living things and that of cultures or civilizations is of importance for all of
these writers.[7]

Among the leading authors taking this position are Ibn Khaldun, Vico,
Brooks Adams, Spengler, and Toynbee. The position is discussed in Chapter 10.

THEORIES OF COSMOGENIC CYCLES

Theories of cosmogenic cycles are most commonly found among archaic
and primitive peoples, and among Oriental writers.[8] Eastern works are not
considered in this study; however, such theories are also proposed by some
Western authors, both simple and sophisticated, both ancient and modern.

Two possible assertions about history seem to underlie all theories of

[7] All authors of theories of anthropogenic cycles either state explicitly or strongly
imply that the evolution of cultures or civilizations is subject to some sort of "law."
The question is whether this is the same "law" that determines and guides the
growth and decay of living things.

[8] The idea that the universe or cosmos changes according to a cyclical pattern is
primarily associated, it seems, with the ancient world, and, in more recent times, with
the East. This point is made by many writers. Eliade, for example, in *Cosmos and
History*, distinguishes between two kinds of time—profane time, which is characterized by a state of "becoming," and sacred or mythical time, which is characterized
by "being," and in which "the individual is truly himself" (p. 35). Profane time "is
without meaning"; the man of archaic culture "tolerates 'history' with difficulty and
attempts periodically to abolish it" (p. 36). This is effected, says Eliade, by "arche-
typal thinking." That is, every action has an archetype; it is a repetition of an
original action that is sacred; only the original action has meaning. This kind of
thinking is necessary, says Eliade, because the life of primitive man is highly undesirable; he lives in extreme discomfort, with little or no hope for improvement.
The only available relief is in the supposition that what is apparently "real life" is
not real at all; even his discomfort is an appearance. And this kind of thinking leads
to the view that there is nothing really new; time is "regenerated," and the world
renews itself at stated intervals. No "historical event" has real significance, nor does
any "historical epoch" (pp. 34–92).

De Rougemont writes in a similar vein. "The West is individualist," he declares,
"and the East traditional" (*Man's Western Quest*, p. 13). He adds that "the adjective 'traditional' is used . . . with its strict initiatory and religious meaning, and
must not be confused with 'conservative'" (p. 13, Note). Hence, for the Eastern
thinker, "all magic goes beyond the person, or, rather, dissolves the person in meta-
morphosis. Animal, man, demon, symbol, the god or saint—everything communicates
in magic, everything is transmuted without obstacle, measure, limit, or distance—
in an inexpressible identity within which our conceptions of liberty, action, person,
and history no longer have either point or purpose" (p. 15). One result of this state
of mind is the notion that the pattern of change is cyclical; everything is endlessly
repeated, and no person or thing will "escape the necessity of rebirth into a thousand
or a hundred thousand successive lives" (p. 20).

Grace E. Cairns differentiates, in *Philosophies of History*, among various archaic
and Oriental cyclical views. The reader is referred to her thorough treatment of these
topics, which cannot be considered here. Miss Cairns' notion as to the source of
archaic and mythical cyclism is similar to that of Eliade and De Rougemont; she
agrees, in short, that primitive peoples tend to desire to deny or repudiate "history."

cosmogenic cycles. The first is that there are regular cosmic cycles that directly influence historical events. The second is that exactly the same historical events occur again and again. The various combinations of affirmations and denials of these two assertions result in three positions that constitute a classification of theories of cosmogenic cycles into three types:

1. Regular cosmic cycles cause regular and exact recurrences of historical events. This position is taken by the Pythagoreans and Stoics, among others.

2. Irregular (noncyclical) cosmic recurrences produce the recurrence of exactly the same historical events at irregular intervals. This position is taken by the Epicureans and, in the nineteenth century, by Nietzsche and others.

3. Regular cosmic cycles bring about roughly similar but not identical historical events. This position, the most widely held of the three, is taken by Plato and Aristotle; they are joined by Polybius, Florus, and other classical writers, as well as by some modern cyclists.

These three types of theories of cosmogenic cycles are treated in Chapter 11.

THEORIES OF REGRESS AND OF CYCLES COMPARED

Theories of regress and of cycles are of course clearly distinguished by our analysis. Any theory of regress involves the assertion that history shows irreversible change; no theory of cycles does. Yet there are, nevertheless, marked similarities between the two kinds of antiprogress theory.

Of particular note is the fact that all of the theories of cycles we have examined concur in holding that the human race is "now" (*i.e.*, at the time of appearance of the theory) in the downward or regressive phase of a cycle of history. We know of no cyclist who asserts, at the time when he proposes his theory, that the human race is moving upward or forward. This striking fact raises the question whether theories of cycles are in some sense theories of regress in disguise.[9]

The question becomes of even greater interest when it is seen that almost all theories of regress include a note of warning. In spite of the force of the affirmation of regress, which may be very great, almost all regress authors hold out some hope for man. Instead of saying flatly that the pattern of history is regressive and that things will inevitably go from bad to worse, they seem to be saying that things will go from bad to worse if men do not change their ways.

[9] The observation applies more to theories of anthropogenic cycles, perhaps, than to theories of cosmogenic cycles. However, even for such authors as the Pythagoreans and Stoics, the present age is always as bad, or nearly as bad, as it can be.

However, if an author implies, even faintly, that there is a possibility that the human race might change its ways and thereby escape either the regressive or the cyclical pattern that he discerns in history, is his theory truly one of regress or of cycles?

Of importance here is the relation of theories of *contingent* progress to theories of regress, and of theories both of contingent progress and regress to theories of cycles. A theory of contingent progress, by definition, concedes that the future pattern of history *may not be* progressive, whatever has been the pattern of the past. If the future is not progressive, it may be regressive, or even cyclical. In addition, several cyclists suggest that the cyclical pattern is now coming to an end, or will shortly come to an end. In that case, the pattern of history may change from cyclical to either regressive or progressive.

The solutions offered in this study to the problems raised by the foregoing are admittedly somewhat artificial. With regard to the relation of theories of contingent progress to theories of regress, we are obliged to assume that all regress authors are necessitarians—in other words, that a theory of contingent progress is not a theory of regress by virtue of its contingent character. This means, of course, that we do not consider that there is such a thing as a theory of contingent regress; an author who holds that both regress and progess are future possibilities would be treated by us as a contingent progress author.

With regard to the relation of theories of cycles to both theories of progress and of regress, we must concede the existence in the literature of what have been called spiral theories. Such a term might be applied to the theories of writers like Brooks Adams, Toynbee, Sorokin, and Hegel. We treat Adams, Toynbee, and Sorokin primarily as cyclists, at the same time observing that there is a progress note in Sorokin and Toynbee, a regress note in Adams. Hegel is treated as a progress author, on somewhat surer grounds than the other three.[10]

[10] Sorokin and Toynbee, although as cyclists they are necessitarians, seem to allow a greater measure of freedom to mankind to "escape" from the pattern of history than do the other cyclists who have been studied. The injection of freedom into a cyclical theory tends to convert it into some other kind of theory. Both Sorokin and Toynbee seem to be saying that while history is largely determined, and as such is cyclical, man is at the same time free in certain respects to advance. They are primarily cyclists, but they admit the possibility of progress in some areas. Hence they become to a certain extent contingent progress authors.

Brooks Adams and Hegel do not suggest that mankind can "escape" from the cyclical pattern of history; they convert their theories in other ways. Adams holds that an essential element in cultural cyclicity is lacking "now" (in 1900); this element is the existence, somewhere on earth, of a "barbarian" group that can "infuse" energy into the exhausted civilization. Hence the present age constitutes the downward curve of the *last possible cycle* of history, and the theory is converted into a regress theory. Hegel also says that the cycles come to an end, but in his

These concessions made, and those problems recognized, it should be said in all fairness that most of the authors we have studied leave little doubt as to the positions they hold about the pattern of history. To take an extreme case: there is usually little difficulty in distinguishing between a contingent progress author, even one who emphasizes the contingency of future progress very strongly, and a regress author, even one who seems to hold out considerable hope that mankind might change its ways and escape the regressive pattern of history. At this point, the emotional attitude of the author toward the future—is he of optimistic or pessimistic temperament?—probably becomes relevant. We have found it impossible, however, to take matters of this sort into consideration.[11]

---

case this occurs at the highest point rather than the lowest. Both men deny that the cyclical pattern is unending, but for different reasons. The injection of a terminal date or epoch into a cyclical theory tends, therefore, as does the injection of freedom, to convert it into another kind of theory.

[11] Further analysis of regress positions might reveal groupings of authors on the question whether regress is necessary or may possibly be averted, on the question whether regress occurs in human nature or only in institutions, and on the question which institutions are particularly prone to regress—do morals regress faster or farther than political institutions? Does art regress farther or faster than science? It was not possible, however, to do this without encroaching on the analysis of progress positions. Regress is, schematically, the reverse of progress; but this does not mean that it is always possible to convert a negative statement about regress into a positive one about progress. That is, denials of regress are not necessarily affirmations of progress.

The questions raised about the genuineness of theories of regress and of cycles become particularly relevant here. As was seen, cyclical theories place the author's own time at the (lower) end of a cycle. One explanation is that cyclical theories (at least in the West) are really theories of regress in disguise—that is, subtle, complicated, and to some extent masked assertions that things are growing worse and worse. It was also pointed out that all theories of regress hold out some hope that mankind, by wrenching history out of its disastrous course, might change the pattern and avoid the ultimate catastrophe.

If all cyclical theories are disguised theories of regress, and if all theories of regress, in turn, are either disguised theories of contingent progress or, more simply, jeremiads against the practice of human life as it is now lived (that is, prophecies of doom *if* the author's warning is not heeded), then a final question must be asked. Are there, in the West at least, any genuine denials of progress? Does any Western author flatly and finally deny that progress occurs *or may occur in the future?*

It would seem that the occurrence of progress is truly and genuinely denied by the authors (considered in Part II) who hold that the pattern of history is unknowable, or that there is no such pattern at all. There is no progress if there is no meaning in history, for progress is inherently meaningful.

But do the authors considered in Part I really deny progress? It is here that doubt enters. It is difficult to answer the question with certainty.

However, if the answer is no—if, that is, affirmations of cyclical and regressive patterns of history do not constitute true and genuine denials of progress—then this conclusion appears inescapable: In the West, at least, the assertion that history shows a pattern is equivalent, or nearly equivalent, to the assertion that progress is the pattern of history. Western authors, if they see a pattern at all, see a progressive pattern. If there is a meaning of history, it is that human progress occurs.

8

Anthropogenic Regress

Among the writers who have theories of anthropogenic regress are those listed below. Many others could be mentioned; this position is hinted at, if it is not carefully argued, by a host of modern authors.

Rousseau	Seidenberg
Nordau	Crow
Coblentz	N. O. Brown
Juenger	C. P. Richter
Marcuse	Ellul

THE DESCENT FROM THE STATE OF NATURE

The notion that history shows a descent from an original and desirable "state of nature" is perhaps most commonly associated with Rousseau. Rousseau's ideas on the subject, which are presented in his *Dissertation on the Origin and Foundation of the Inequality of Mankind*, have often been misinterpreted.[1] Nevertheless, Rousseau's theory, as it appears in this work, is a true theory of regress.

The theory may be outlined thus: Man in the state of nature was healthy and free because he was content with his limited existence.[2] But man also had the ability to perfect himself—the faculty of perfectibility; by this there came about an "expansion of human faculties." Hence there was a second stage of human development (after that of the state of nature); it was the happiest epoch of man's history.[3] Soon, however, degradation set in, as man, becoming dependent on new inventions and the wants they engendered, grew weaker. Eventually he was the slave of the civilization he had created and was thus no longer free. In the end occurs a kind of despotism, which is a "new state of nature." But this is the

---

[1] Rousseau's place in the progress literature is peculiarly ambivalent. In spite of the fame of his theory of regress, as expressed in the *Origin of Inequality,* Rousseau in other works—notably *The Social Contract*—is a progress author.

Several commentators have pointed to this ambivalence in Rousseau. In "The Supposed Primitivism of Rousseau's *Origin of Inequality,*" Lovejoy shows that the French philosopher's ideas do not add up to the simple regress affirmation that many have seen. Lovejoy carefully examines the different stages discerned by Rousseau in history, observes that none of these is said to be really happy, and suggests that the essay combines a traditional affirmation of regress with an "innovating" affirmation of "evolution," if not progress ("The Supposed Primitivism of Rousseau's *Discourse on Inequality,*" in *Essays in the History of Ideas,* pp. 14–37).

Charles Frankel also questions the traditional view of Rousseau. "Rousseau has sometimes been regarded as a primitivist opponent of any belief in progress," Frankel declares. "It is doubtful, however, that Rousseau was so widely removed from the aspirations of his contemporaries" (*The Faith of Reason,* p. 76). He sums up the situation thus: "When men forgot the original drives, capacities, and limitations of human nature, he [Rousseau] referred to man's primitive beginnings, as in the *Discourse on the Origin of Inequality.* When men forgot, as, for example, in the individualistic doctrine of 'natural rights,' the direction in which men must move to be complete, he used [another] notion of nature, as in *The Social Contract.* For Rousseau, the natural man was completed in the citizen" (p. 80).

For our purposes, Rousseau's essay is a prime example of a theory of regress—that is, of an argued regress affirmation. We may admit the relevance of Lovejoy's and Frankel's wider view of Rousseau, and at the same time examine the *Discourse* for the ideas *it* contains about the pattern of human history.

[2] For a discussion of what Rousseau means by the "state of nature," see the Lovejoy essay referred to in Note 1.

[3] "Though men had less endurance, and though natural sympathy (*pitié*) had suffered some diminution, this period of the development of the human faculties," says Rousseau, "holding a just mean between the indolence of the primitive state and the petulant activity of our self-esteem, must have been the happiest and the most lasting epoch. The more one reflects upon it, the more one perceives that it was the state least subject to revolutions, the best state for man; and that he can have departed from it only by some unhappy chance, which in the interest of the general good (*utilité*) ought never to have occurred" (qu. in Lovejoy, *op. cit.,* p. 30). Lovejoy's main point is that Rousseau maintains that the state of nature was not the most desirable condition, but that this second, later state was more desirable. Nevertheless, whichever state was most desirable, man fell from it, and has continued to regress ever since. Hence Rousseau is counted as a regress author.

result of corruption, not innocence, and man now *knows* that he is enslaved.

> The times of which I . . . speak are very remote: how much are you changed from what you once were! It is, so to speak, the life of your species which I . . . write, after the qualities which you have received, which your education and habits may have depraved, but cannot have entirely destroyed. . . . Discontented with your present state, for reasons which threaten your unfortunate descendants with still greater discontent, you will perhaps wish it were in your power to go back; and this feeling should be a panegyric on your first ancestors, a criticism of your contemporaries, and a terror to the unfortunates who will come after you.[4]

It is the faculty of self-improvement, Rousseau declares, that is the source of all human misfortunes. It is this that draws man out of his original state; it is this that makes him "at length a tyrant over himself and over nature."[5] Perfectibility makes civilized man unhealthier than the primitive, for "we bring on ourselves more diseases than medicine can furnish remedies."[6] The same faculty has "improved the human understanding while depraving the species, and made man wicked while making him sociable."[7] And it is ultimately the source of the political, social, and intellectual inequality that is the prime curse of the world.

Rousseau's arguments for his theory are interesting, since almost the same story is used by later writers—Condorcet, for example—to exemplify man's progress.[8] As the race grew—as the pressure of population became more and more intense[9]—men's cares increased. New problems were presented, and these were solved with an ingenuity that grew at an equal pace. This had its effect:

> This repeated relevance of various things to himself, and one to another, would naturally give rise in the human mind to the perceptions of certain relations between them. . . . The new intelligence which resulted from this development increased his superiority over other animals, by making him sensible of it.[10]

[4] *A Discourse on the Origin of Inequality*, in *The Social Contract and Discourses*, p. 176.

[5] *Ibid.*, p. 185.

[6] *Ibid.*, p. 181.

[7] *Ibid.*, pp. 205–6.

[8] Lovejoy notes that "the term 'perfectibility' to which—though it was apparently invented by Turgot in 1750—Rousseau probably did more than anyone else to give currency, became the catchword of Condorcet and other subsequent believers in the reality, necessity, and desirability of human progress through a fixed sequence of stages, in both past and future" (*op. cit.*, p. 25).

[9] Comte, for one, maintains that the pressure of increasing population is an important source of progress.

[10] *Discourse*, p. 208.

Man became proud, but also may have insensibly acquired some gross ideas of mutual undertakings, and of the advantages of fulfilling them. Language was invented, and thereby these first advances enabled men to make others with equal rapidity. Families were established, and man soon discovered leisure, which he employed to furnish himself with many conveniences unknown to his fathers; at length, however, all became necessities. Love, "a tender and pleasant feeling," insinuated itself into the lives of men; but "the least opposition turned it into an impetuous fury: with love arose jealousy; discord triumphed, and human blood was sacrificed to the gentlest of all passions."[11] Wildness was laid aside; men had been wild rather than wicked in the state of nature. Men assembled, at first to sing and to dance, and then to discover inequalities among themselves. For "whoever sang or danced best, the strongest, the most dextrous, or the most eloquent, came to be of most consideration; and this was the first step towards inequality, and at the same time towards vice."[12] Thus envy came into existence; and hence arose the first obligations of civility even among savages. The result was that "revenge became terrible, and men bloody and cruel."[13]

In a society in which love, jealousy, envy, and revenge had come to exist, discontent must grow apace. And with this discontent was born the idea of property. This, it seems, is near to the root of all social evil, for the idea of property led to the defense of property, and this to the use of iron, that is, to war. At the same time corn was discovered, which led to the cultivation of the earth; but this brought about the unequal distribution of land. Hence one may declare, as Rousseau does in one of his most memorable epigrams, that "the poets tell us it was gold and silver, but, for the philosophers, it was iron and corn, which first civilized man, and ruined humanity."[14]

In this state of affairs, equality might have been sustained had the talents of individuals been equal, and had, for example, the use of iron and consumption of commodities always exactly balanced each other; but, as there was nothing to preserve this balance, it was soon disturbed; the strongest did most work; the most skilful turned his labour to best account; the most ingenious devised methods of diminishing his labour: the husbandman wanted more iron, or the smith more corn, and, while both laboured equally, the one gained a great deal by his work, while the other could hardly support himself. Thus natural inequality unfolds itself insensibly with that of combination, and the difference between men, developed by

11 *Ibid.*, p. 212.
12 *Ibid.*, pp. 212–3.
13 *Ibid.*, p. 213.
14 *Ibid.*, p. 215. One of the poets referred to is probably Ovid.

their different circumstances, becomes more sensible and permanent in its effects, and begins to have an influence in the same proportion, over the lot of individuals.[15]

"Matters once at this pitch," Rousseau declares, "it is easy to imagine the rest."[16] Indeed, society had arrived at a point not far distant from the one Rousseau's readers knew, except that it still lacked law and government. These relative goods—good in the same sense as medical remedies, which would not be needed were it not for the diseases that civilization brings in its train—were developed slowly but inevitably.[17] However, the final term of the "progress" of the human race is a kind of despotism, if not of a tyrant then of luxuries, if not of an illegitimate government then of vicious desires. Rousseau ends his essay with a series of exhortations. The most unwavering opposition to "progress," as ordinarily conceived—that is, as the "advance of the human mind"—is expressed, and the absurdity of the goals toward which this "advance" tends is revealed. For example:

> It follows from this survey that, as there is hardly any inequality in the state of nature, all the inequality which now prevails owes its strength and growth to the development of our faculties and the advance of the human mind, and becomes at last permanent and legitimate by the establishment of property and laws. Secondly, it follows that moral inequality, authorized by positive right alone, clashes with natural right, whenever it is not proportionate to physical inequality; a distinction which sufficiently determines what we ought to think of that species of inequalities which prevail in all civilized countries; since it is plainly contrary to the law of nature, that children should command old men, fools wise men, and that the privileged few should gorge themselves with superfluities, while the starving multitude are in want of the bare necessities of life.[18]

Man's liberty is conceived by regress authors in various ways. Some psychologists hold that it consists in the free play of Eros, or the love instinct, which in turn manifests itself in the free play of the Pleasure Principle. Opposed to the Pleasure Principle is the Reality Principle; hence

[15] *Ibid.*, p. 217.

[16] *Ibid.*

[17] "I regard it . . . as certain," Rousseau says, "that government did not begin with arbitrary power, but that this is the depravation, the extreme term, of government, and brings it back, finally, to just the law of the strongest, which it was originally designed to remedy" (*ibid.*, p. 228). On this point Rousseau differs with many of his contemporaries, who held that government was the legitimization of the right of the strongest. Rousseau's views are argued more extensively in *The Social Contract.*

[18] *Discourse*, p. 238.

if it can be shown that the "progress" of civilization reflects the increasing subjugation of Eros by the Reality Principle, then the pattern of history is regressive. This Marcuse attempts to show.

Freud's proposition that civilization is based on the permanent subjugation of the human instincts has been taken for granted, Marcuse declares,[19] and goes on:

> His question whether the suffering thereby inflicted upon individuals has been worth the benefits of culture has not been taken too seriously—the less so since Freud himself considered the process to be inevitable and irreversible. Free gratification of man's instinctual needs is incompatible with civilized society: renunciation and delay in satisfaction are the prerequisites of progress. . . . The sacrifice has paid off well. . . . The continual increase of productivity makes constantly more realistic the promise of an even better life for all.
>
> However, intensified progress seems to be bound up with intensified unfreedom.[20]

Marcuse outlines the process in terms that make it clear that it applies both to the individual and the race. The animal man becomes a human being only through a fundamental transformation of its (his) nature, he says. This change affects not only the instinctual aims but also the instinctual values—that is, the principles that govern the attainment of the aims. The transformation of governing value systems is revealed thus:

from	*to*
immediate satisfaction	delayed satisfaction
pleasure	restraint of pleasure
joy (play)	toil (work)
receptiveness	productiveness
absence of repression	security

"The difference between these two dimensions is a genetic-historical as well as a structural one," he explains. "The replacement of the pleasure principle by the reality principle is the great traumatic event in the development of man—in the development of the genus (phylogenesis) as well as of the individual (ontogenesis)."[21]

In *Totem and Taboo*, as we have seen, Freud combines a psychoanalytic with a Comtian view of history. The animistic or religious phase corresponds to infantile narcism; the metaphysical phase to the stage

---

[19] Freud is taken in this study as a progress author; however, he agrees with Marcuse that progress does not necessarily mean increasing happiness.

[20] *Eros and Civilization*, pp. 3–4.

[21] *Ibid.*, pp. 12–14.

of object-finding in which parental dependence is paramount; and the positive or scientific phase to maturity, in which the individual, having renounced the Pleasure Principle and accepted the Reality Principle, seeks his objects in the outer world. In terms of the objects sought, the sequence is: self, parents, outer (real) world. This process, for Freud, is not regress; for N. O. Brown, however, who bases his work on that of Freud, the pattern of history is regressive.

According to Brown, man's history is a *Krankheitsgeschichte*—the history of a disease,[22] a neurosis that is based on the repression of love (Eros). "Repressed Eros is the energy of history and labor must be seen as sublimated Eros."[23]

> Psychoanalysis can provide a theory of "progress," but only by viewing history as a neurosis. By defining man as the neurotic animal, psychoanalysis not merely assumes man's Faustian character but also explains why man is so.[24]

However, man remains, at bottom, a pleasure-seeking animal. The repressive morality that produces apparent progress does not, and cannot, obliterate his nature.

> Parental discipline, religious denunciation of bodily pleasure, and philosophic exaltation of the life of reason have all left man overtly docile, but secretly in his unconscious unconvinced, and therefore neurotic. Man remains unconvinced because in infancy he tasted the fruit of the tree of life, and knows that it is good, and never forgets.[25]

"History-making"—which, for Brown, is progress—is always the quest for group-immortality. But this quest, he declares, is a dream from which man cannot awake—a psychosis.[26] The primary symbol of the psychosis is money and the insane scramble for wealth. Money confers a kind of immortality. It cannot be carried to the other world, but it can be left behind to perpetuate one's name in this. However, money is a representation of unconscious anal fantasies; hence the piling up of wealth is a progressive anality that accumulates to humanity's woe.[27]

---

[22] The "progress" of a disease is sometimes spoken of in a sense in which the term denotes degeneration, at least of the host.

[23] *Life Against Death: The Psychoanalytic Meaning of History*, p. 17.

[24] *Ibid.*, p. 19.

[25] *Ibid.*, p. 31.

[26] The notion that a psychosis is a dream from which one cannot wake is put forward by Freud in *An Outline of Psychoanalysis*, p. 61.

[27] Not only are money and the search for wealth anal, but science is also a "morbid" search for security where none can be found. Knowledge as such is not morbid, says Brown; rather, "the unconscious schemata governing the pursuit of knowledge in modern civilization—specifically the aim of possession or mastery

Brown is able to map the history of mankind in terms of accumulating guilt as well as of accumulating anality. Psychoanalytic theory suggests that the race underwent a universal trauma, corresponding to the Oedipus Complex in the life of an individual.[28] This primal guilt is traceable up to and through the invention of society. There it is mitigated by being shared.

Man entered social organization in order to share guilt. Social organization (including the division of labor) is a structure of shared guilt. Social organization brings the repressed unconscious guilt to consciousness (in a distorted form of course). . . . Social organization is a symbolic mutual confession of guilt.[29]

This notion of the origin of society is far from being the same as Rousseau's. For the latter, men first assembled to express their "primitive" joy in song and dance. But subsequent events are similar in the view of the two writers.

Indeed, Brown, like Rousseau, discovers regress in almost every area of possible progress. He sees it occurring (in the form of some kind of distorted anal sadism) in the intellectual, technological, economic, moral, and artistic activities of man.[30] The accumulation of knowledge, skill, wealth, and power represents a movement away from the Eden of childhood; mankind goes deeper and deeper into the guilt-ridden dream that is history, from which it can hardly hope to awake.[31]

---

over objects (Freud), and the principle of economizing in the means (Ferenczi). . . . In contrast, what would a nonmorbid science look like? It would presumably be erotic rather than sadistic in aim. Its aim would not be mastery over but union with nature. And its means would not be economizing but exotic exuberance. And finally, it would be based on the whole body and not just a part; that is to say, it would be based on the polymorphous perverse body" (*ibid.*, p. 236).

The polymorphous perverse body is the one that we knew in childhood, according to psychoanalysts; such a science would thus be an example of a return to the state of nature. One wonders what Rousseau would make of the anal interpretation of history. In any event, Juenger agrees with Brown's judgment of modern science. See below, p. 139.

[28] Freud writes: "In the history of the species something happened similar to the events in the life of the individual. That is to say, mankind as a whole passed through conflicts of a sexual-aggressive nature, which left permanent traces, but which were for the most part warded off and forgotten; later, after a long period of latency, they came to life again and created phenomena similar in structure and tendency to neurotic symptoms" (*Moses and Monotheism*, qu. in Brown, p. 12).

[29] *Ibid.*, p. 269.

[30] Brown's critique, in the light of his theory of anal repression, of the writings of Swift is particularly impressive.

[31] In common with many regress authors, Brown suggests a possible cure for the problem. As might be expected, it is through psychoanalysis. Psychoanalysis "offers a theoretical framework for exploring the possibility of a way out of the nightmare of endless 'progress' and endless Faustian discontent, a way out of the human neurosis, a way out of history. . . . If historical consciousness is finally transformed

Rousseau differs in important respects with Marcuse and Brown. His theory of the origin of the state is not the same as theirs, and it is probable that he views man's deepest nature as *méchant* rather than *bon*.[32] Freud, too, although he is a progress author, holds that man is at heart not a loving creature toward his kind.[33] The accumulation of wealth is not as important, for Rousseau, as the advance of technology; Brown seems to reverse this order. Nevertheless, the three authors have much in common. All agree that the cause of regress is in human nature, although they disagree as to the specific cause. And they see this cause working itself out in history in epochs and stages that have a remarkable similarity, considering the disparity of terminology.[34]

Coblentz sees regress in the physical rather than the psychical side of man's nature, but his argument also runs on grounds made familiar by Rousseau. According to Coblentz,

> the example of the great extinct Brontosaurus is fraught with warning for the human race; the very forces exterminating the dinosaur may be operating directly upon the body of man, and . . . they may have visible analogies in human society.[35]

Brontosaurus was the largest and the last of the dinosaurs. Its brain was tiny despite its vast bulk, and it became extinct because of a radical maladjustment to a changing environment. Coblentz sees a marked similarity between this story and the situation of modern man.

> The human race . . . is to be regarded as senile rather than youthful, wizened and decrepit rather than rosy-cheeked and adolescent; and among the signs of its old age is the fact that the brain power of the average man has shown a constant tendency to decrease during historic times and is distinctly on the decline today. Accompanying this unfavorable change in

into psychoanalytical consciousness, the grip of the dead hand of the past on life in the present would be loosened, and man would be ready to live instead of making history, to enjoy instead of paying back old scores and debts, and to enter into that state of Being which was the goal of his Becoming" (*op. cit.*, p. 19). Freud has a similar notion; for him, the discovery of psychoanalysis is a sign of progress. However, in Brown's opinion, the possibility described here is extremely remote.

[32] On this point cf. Lovejoy, *op. cit.*

[33] Cf. *Civilization and Its Discontents*, pp. 84–8.

[34] It is not being suggested that Rousseau is a precursor of psychoanalysis; however, his *Confessions* has been said to contain the germs of almost all modern ideas.

[35] *The Decline of Man*, p. 236.

the individual . . . are numerous equally unfavorable developments in society; and the most conspicuous of these are its excessive specializations. . . .[36]

Overspecialization is to be observed in many areas, Coblentz declares. Even the recent increase in the average size of human beings is, on the Brontosaurian analogy, disquieting. "Excessive size, of course, does not necessarily imply impending extinction . . . yet man's relatively great bulk is at least an indication that he is racially at a stage of decrepitude rather than of youth."[37]

Max Nordau is another who sees the human species degenerating. He feels that our complex civilization has placed too much of a strain on man's limited nervous organization. Degeneration is everywhere: in the increase in crime that is "a fact proved by official statistics of all countries"; in "the great increase of lunacy in all civilized lands"; in the "preachings of a Schopenhauer, a Hartmann, a Mainländer, a Bakunin, a Max Steiner, a Nietzsche"; in "the teachings of degenerate half-fools"; in the general "loosening of morality"; in the "disappearance of logic from thought and action, a morbid inability and vacillation of public opinion, a relaxation of character." Degeneration attacks not only "the pinnacle of the social building, but also its broad base; not a privileged class, but the whole stratum."[38] Finally, the contemporary spirit, says Nordau, is

a mixture of febrile restlessness and defeatist discouragement, of fear for the future and sulking resignation. The prevalent sense is one of impending destruction and extinction. . . . The sunlight and starlight are gradually fading, and the human race with all its institutions is dying out amidst a dying world.[39]

His view is shared by C. P. Richter, who also foresees the biological degeneration of the human race as the result of various cultural influences. Our ancestors lived the healthy, wholesome life of wild animals, he declares. They struggled and fought; natural selection winnowed the worst of them; the best survived, and the poorest and weakest succumbed. Hence the development of man's finest qualities; but in advanced societies natural selection no longer holds sway. Birth and death rates are both low, the necessities of human life are everywhere assured, environmental hazards are controlled, diseases are conquered—with the result that the unfit survive and reproduce their kind. The same process that has transformed the vigorous wild rat (*rattus norvegicus*) into the domesticated

[36] *Ibid.* The opposite assertion—that human brain power is increasing—is made by many progress authors.

[37] *Ibid.*, p. 39.

[38] "Degeneration," *The Hibbert Journal*, Vol. X (October 1911–July 1912), pp. 745–65.

[39] Qu. in A. J. Nock, *Memoirs of a Superfluous Man*, p. 108. Nordau's language is similar to that of Flammarion and other writers quoted by Adams. See Chapter 9.

laboratory rat, unable to live outside its cage, is also working in human evolution.[40]

REGRESS AS THE CONQUEST OF "INSTINCT" BY "INTELLIGENCE"

"The whole evolution of the animal kingdom," says Bergson, "apart from retrogressions toward vegetable life, has taken place on two divergent paths, one of which led to instinct and the other to intelligence." These two great evolutionary principles are "opposite and complementary." The difference between them is not a "difference of intensity, nor, more generally, of degree, but of kind"; nevertheless, they were originally "interpenetrating." Indeed, neither "is ever found in a pure state."

> In reality, they accompany each other only because they are complementary, and they are complementary only because they are different, what is instinctive in instinct being opposite to what is intelligent in intelligence.[41]

The difference between the two faculties is to be observed in regard to the use of tools. Intelligence, considered in what seems to be its original feature, is the faculty of manufacturing artificial objects, especially tools to make tools, and of indefinitely varying the manufacture. Instinct, on the other hand, is the faculty of using the tools that intelligence has manufactured. But the distinction is not so simple as it appears. For instinct perfected is a faculty of using and even of constructing organized instruments; while intelligence perfected is the faculty of making and using unorganized instruments. Instruments constructed and used by instinct are perfect ones; they perform exactly the tasks for which they were made.

> The instrument constructed intelligently, on the contrary, is an imperfect instrument. It costs an effort. It is generally troublesome to handle. But, as it is made of unorganized matter, it can take any form whatsoever, serve any purpose, and free the living being from every new difficulty that arises and bestow on it an unlimited number of powers. Whilst it is inferior to the natural instrument for the satisfaction of immediate wants, its advantage over it is the greater, the less urgent the need.[42]

[40] "Rats, Man, and the Welfare State," *American Psychologist,* 14:18–28. Theodosius Dobzhansky (*Mankind Evolving,* p. 326) discusses Richter's argument and points out that the laboratory rat, though doubtless more timid than its wild ancestor, is admirably suited to its environment. This objection might also be made to Rousseau's theory.
[41] *Creative Evolution,* pp. 149–50.
[42] *Ibid.,* p. 155.

Furthermore, the instrument that is constructed intelligently reacts on its maker. For each need that it satisfies, it creates a new need, with the result that the animal making and using it is "made more and more free."[43] Instead of being trapped in an instinctive "round of action," the intelligent animal lives in an ever expanding and opening world.[44]

The advantage of intelligence over instinct is not evident at first. The two faculties "represent two divergent solutions, equally fitting, of one and the same problem."[45] In time, however, intelligence solves the problem with greater success.

The evolutionary function of intelligence, according to Bergson, is the creation of "mechanisms" for the furtherance of life; once created, however, these serve, in most cases, but to stultify the very life they made possible. Thus

> everywhere except in man, consciousness has let itself be caught in the net whose meshes it tried to pass through: it has remained the captive of the mechanisms it has set up. Automatism, which it tries to draw in the direction of freedom, winds about it and drags it down. It has not the power to escape, because the energy it has provided for acts is almost all employed in maintaining the infinitely subtle and essentially unstable equilibrium into which it has brought matter. But man not only maintains his machine, he succeeds in using it as he pleases.[46]

Hence, although there is not, properly speaking, any project or plan to evolution; although it is incorrect to speak of the rest of nature as existing for the sake of man; and although it "would be wrong to regard humanity, such as we have it before our eyes, as prefigured in the evolutionary movement,"[47] there is nevertheless a sense in which man is the "term" and "end" of evolution. There are other "ends" to evolution, with an equal right to the name: "evolution has been accomplished on several divergent lines, and while the human species is at the end of one of them, other lines have been followed with other species at their end."[48] But it is nonetheless true that "everywhere but in man, consciousness has had to come to a stand; in man alone it has kept on its way."[49] And the further prospects of man are seemingly without limit, for he is "able to beat down

---

[43] Rousseau infers just the opposite; he holds that increasing needs and desires enslave rather than free mankind.

[44] *Ibid.*, pp. 153–6.

[45] *Ibid.*, p. 158.

[46] *Ibid.*, p. 288.

[47] *Ibid.*, p. 289.

[48] *Ibid.*, pp. 289–90.

[49] *Ibid.*, p. 290.

every resistance and clear the most formidable obstacles, perhaps even death."[50]

Bergson is a progress author. His theory is outlined here because several writers make use of his terms and even of his arguments to show that the pattern of history is regressive.[51]

Such a writer is Seidenberg, who sees the trend of history as movement from the "organic" to the "organized." Instinct, he declares, is associated with the organism, intelligence with the organization. "Under the headings of Organism and Organization we may list," he says, "related groups of qualities and attributes that bear in each case a similar correlation to each other."

ORGANISM	ORGANIZATION
Instinct	Intelligence
Innate	Acquired
Implicit	Explicit
Preconscious	Conscious
Faith and Belief	Knowledge
Religion	Science
Customs	Laws
Culture	Civilization
Ends	Means
Growth	Progress
Introversion	Extroversion[52]

"The movement from instinct to intelligence," Seidenberg writes, "is seen to exhibit a kind of determinism—historic or morphological but inherent, in any case—in the evolution of man's development."

Three conditions were noted in respect to this trend: first, that at some point, tentatively assumed to lie within the historic era, the weight of influence of instinct and intelligence upon the affairs of man would reach an unstable equilibrium; second, that such a point would constitute a vital moment or era of transition dividing man's development into two phases—an earlier phase under the domination of the instincts, and a later phase under that of intelligence; and, finally, that organization was a modulus of the increasing dominance of intelligence.[53]

50 *Ibid.*, p. 295.
51 They may misuse, distort, or even misunderstand his terms.
52 *Posthistoric Man: An Inquiry*, p. 47.
53 *Ibid.*, p. 55.

A diagram helps to explain the theory.[54]

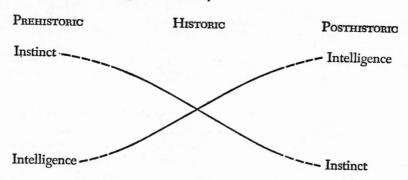

The diagram shows, according to Seidenberg, that history is marked off as a "transitional interregnum." His theory contemplates a final posthistoric phase, more or less symmetrical with the prehistoric phase. The historical period is one of

> ever increasing change, tending toward a climax, after which man may again attain, in perhaps an equally long interval of time, a relatively fixed state of stability and permanence.[55]

The modern age represents the vital moment or era of transition between the dominance of instinct and of intelligence; in other words, the climax has already been, or is about to be, reached; and man is already entering upon his final, posthistoric phase.

A theory of this sort is not necessarily incompatible with a progress theory. The observation that instinct and intelligence are opposite but complementary aims of evolution does not keep Bergson, for example, from affirming at least contingent progress. And perhaps some authors who believe that progress will "plateau out" would be willing to accept a scheme of historical development similar to Seidenberg's. But for Seidenberg himself, the process is anything but progressive. He foresees instead an ultimate, and inevitable, regress.

> The organization of society will unquestionably proceed until its final crystallization shall have been achieved ecumenically, because of the relationship of this trend with the inherent dominance of the principle of intelligence. But the process, once dominant, implies in turn a steady decrease and retardation of social change—the gradual slowing down of the momentum of history until, indeed, we shall be confronted by the inverse of our historical ascent in ever more delayed sequences of stability and

[54] *Ibid.*
[55] *Ibid.*, p. 56.

permanence in the conditions of life. And thus, in a period devoid of change, we may truly say that man will enter upon a posthistoric age in which, perhaps, he will remain encased in an endless routine and sequence of events, not unlike that of the ants, the bees, and the termites. Their essentially unchanging survival during some sixty million years testifies to the perfection of their adjustment, internally and externally, to the conditions of life: man may likewise find himself entombed in a perpetual round of perfectly adjusted responses.[56]

The primary symbol and example of organization is the machine, in which is found the pattern of the goal toward which mankind is moving. The machine, defined in its most abstract terms, "constitutes in itself a unique and perfect paradigm of organization: it consists of a series of interrelated means contrived to achieve an explicit end. The deepest significance of the machine, in its effect upon the social fabric of man, lies precisely in its own rigid organizational structure."[57] Indeed, Seidenberg declares that posthistoric society will be one great machine, running of itself, under the "momentum" of which

> the individual will . . . find himself churned into an ever smaller particle, into a minute and at length irreducible atom of the social system. As the significance of the individual is thus steadily diminished, his status and identity must necessarily approach that of a statistical average, while at the same time the mass will become correspondingly enlarged and dominating in its new and terrifying totality.[58]

It is on the last count that Seidenberg most markedly departs from Bergson. The latter admits that "everywhere except in man, consciousness has let itself be caught in the net whose meshes it tried to pass through. . . . But man not only maintains his machine, he succeeds in using it as he pleases."[59] Seidenberg might argue that Bergson was as yet unable (in 1911) to see the fearful tendency toward organization that is evident to Seidenberg (in 1950). However, using Bergson's terminology, Seidenberg appears to have almost completely inverted its meaning. For Bergson, the faculty associated with organization is instinct; for Seidenberg it is intelligence. For Bergson, the faculty associated with freedom and change is intelligence; for Seidenberg it is instinct.[60] It appears that Bergson ought to judge Seidenberg's thesis to be that the trend of human development, if it is toward organization, is thereby in the direction of the

[56] *Ibid.*, p. 179.
[57] *Ibid.*, p. 27.
[58] *Ibid.*, p. 13.
[59] Bergson, *op. cit.*, p. 288.
[60] However paradoxical this may seem.

instinctual: witness Seidenberg's assertion that human social life might ultimately be like that of the ants, bees, and termites. For Bergson the insects are the very opposite of intelligent; they represent a course of evolution that is entirely distinct from man's. Yet this same course is called by Seidenberg a trend toward intelligence.

Whether or not Seidenberg is justified in deriving his theory from Bergson (as he indicates that he does), his view is shared by several other modern writers. Some of them are cited by Seidenberg himself. For instance, in Eugene Zamiatin's satirical novel *We,* "the characters are no longer identified by names but merely by impersonal numbers, and . . . we read derisively of a time . . . when human beings still lived in a state of freedom, that is, in an unorganized primitive state."[61] In Orwell's *1984* the primary object of the social organization "is summed up in these dire and significant words: 'But the purpose of all of them was to arrest progress and freeze history at a chosen moment!' "[62] Aldous Huxley's *Brave New World,* along with other modern "distopias," makes much the same point. And in *The Transformations of Man,* Mumford follows Seidenberg's analysis, declaring, however, that the posthistoric phase is only one of the alternatives that face mankind.[63] Seidenberg, of course, as a regress author, holds that posthistoricism is inevitable.

Regress in the Guise of Technological Progress

The modern progress literature is deeply concerned[64] with the problem of technology, the advance of which—in itself, denied by no one—is seen in various lights. For many writers, it is a sign, if not the primary source, of human progress. For others, it forces man to recognize the danger inherent in his progress.[65] For still others, it accompanies but is not the source of regress. A fourth group views advancing technology as intrinsically evil, and the cause of human regress.

For Friedrich Georg Juenger, technology is essentially demonic. "All things mechanical harness elemental forces," he declares; and these forces by their very nature are perilous.

> The surplus of elemental power that man has obtained by his destructive exploitation of nature . . . turns against him and threatens to destroy

61 Seidenberg, *op. cit.,* p. 12.
62 Qu. in *ibid.,* pp. 12–13.
63 *The Transformations of Man,* pp. 117–32. Mumford, as a (contingent) progress author, was treated in Chapter 4.
64 "Obsessed" might be the more accurate word.
65 De Rougemont, for example, emphasizes the "ambivalence" of progress.

him. In terms of an older language, it is the vengeance of the elemental
spirits which the modern magician has conjured up. With a hostility no
longer disguised, the accumulated elemental forces harnessed in our mechanics are rebelling against their masters. *This is the regression that proceeds in exactly the same proportion as technology progresses.*[66]

Why do myths have so many evil deeds and disasters to report in connection with the art of metalworking, asks Juenger? The answer is that
"the gods manifestly do not love man the maker; they oppose him violently
at times, while at other times they suffer him as a half-burlesque figure
by their side, like Hephaistos. . . . All technology is of titanic mold, and
man the maker is always of the race of the Titans." Man is thus hated
by the gods, who wish to destroy him.[67]

An important point in Juenger's theory is that the regress that is based
on technological advance is necessary, for this sort of advance is inevitable. If the essence of technology were production, then it might not have
to increase constantly; but technology is not essentially productive. Rather,
its essence is consumption; it feeds on all that it touches—nature, man, even
itself—and its hunger grows at an increasing rate. Technology is intrinsically rapacious. It is the art, or science, of rapaciously "organizing," or
exploiting, the earth and all that it contains. Man is the preferred object
of this rapine, and Juenger sees technology shifting, in our time, from
the control and organization of nature to the control and organization of
men. Hence technological advance, or progress in "rationalization,"[68]
denotes, and insures, regress in every area of human life.

Even human nature is changing. "Lifeless time" invades "life time,"
the symbol of lifeless time being the clock; technology has brought about
a situation "where man no longer has time, where he is destitute of time,
where he is hungry for time."[69] Technology also drives out imagination.
The technician engages in "functional thinking," which is "an unimagina-
tive way of thought, thought denuded of all images, a pauperized mentality. . . . Its very language betrays its loss of vitality."[70] Indeed, technology brings about a kind of living death.

A machine is dead though it never lived. It is dead because its motions
are subject to functionalism throughout. And there can be deadness of
the same kind in a living man, a deadness that never had life and therefore

[66] *The Failure of Technology*, pp. 177–8. The word "failure" in the title is a
translation of the German *Perfektion*, which more accurately expresses the tone of
the work.
[67] *Ibid.*, pp. 184–5.
[68] "Rationalization" is similar to Seidenberg's "intelligence."
[69] *Ibid.*, p. 44.
[70] *Ibid.*, pp. 77–8.

cannot die, but can only disintegrate, vanish, or erode. Such a human being has dead spots, dead parts, dead sections, in him. He shows a lifelessness that is manifested even in the midst of activity. His youth is without vigor, his age synthetic; maturity is lacking. . . . The masklike quality in the face of such a man reveals that here life is merely being imitated.[71]

Death itself is changed. Juenger remembers the battlefields of the First World War; they are symbolic, he declares, of the destructive bent of technology. Machinery tears apart, crushes, obliterates machinery in modern warfare. But this inhuman carnage and destruction spills over into the human sphere.

This can best be seen where machinery tears itself apart, where it is ripped open, where, in destruction, it loses its mechanical form, just as man who is tied to it is torn apart with utter disregard of his organic form and structure, which is to say, mechanically. He is not even cut up like an animal that is taken to the butcher, nor neatly carved and disjointed like a chicken: he is blown to pieces, crushed, torn to shreds.[72]

Worst of all, the reaction of mankind to the advance of technology is a kind of mass insanity. All men are anxious, says Juenger; they are fearful of any strange sound, they tremble with nameless fears. "To the extent in which the masses become subjected to rational organization, they become supercharged with blind elemental powers and bereft of all spiritual powers to oppose them. The masses are running berserk."[73]

Juenger's theory is perhaps unique in that he sees regress in every area of life, without exception. Knowledge, for example—factual knowledge—being empirical, is

thereby as infinite as are the endless rows of causes and effects whereby it is described. . . . But this knowledge is a *mare tenebrosum* . . . a knowledge that has become boundless has become also formless. If to the human mind all things are equally worth knowing, then knowledge loses all value.[74]

Science—indeed all rational thought—is inextricably intertwined with technology. Doubtless, technology cannot exist, certainly cannot advance, without thought; the point is, for Juenger, that thought cannot exist any longer without furthering technology, and increasing its despotism over mankind.

[71] *Ibid.*, pp. 108–9. Charlie Chaplin gave this masklike face dramatic reality in the movie *Modern Times*.
[72] *Ibid.*, p. 122. One wonders whether the alternative deaths are any more desirable. Should a man wish to be cut up as neatly as a chicken?
[73] *Ibid.*, p. 144.
[74] *Ibid.*, p. 90. Cf. N. O. Brown; see Note 27, above.

Juenger also maintains that technological advance means the decrease, rather than the increase, of wealth. His opinion follows from his fundamental proposition, that technology is essentially consumptive, not productive.

> By definition, technology is really nothing but a rationalism of the work process. But when have riches ever been created by rationalization? Is rationalization a sign of riches at all? Does it stem from abundance? Is its aim abundance? Or is it not rather a method which is used whenever a lack is felt, where want is suffered?[75]

If technology produced wealth, we should have been wealthy long ago. If it were so, the signs of wealth would be apparent everywhere, in greater freedom, greater abundance, greater happiness. But there are no such signs. Indeed, just the opposite is the case. The truth is that

> every rationalization is the consequence of scarcity. The expansion and constant perfection of the technical apparatus are not merely the result of the technician's urge for power; they are just as much the result of want. That is why the human situation characteristic of our machine world is poverty. And this poverty cannot be overcome by any technological efforts; it is inherent in technology itself; it has marched in step with the industrial age and it will do so to the end.[76]

The clear and infallible sign of poverty is the "progressive rationalization of organization." For in an economy that is based, as a technological one necessarily is, on the exhaustion of resources, "the organization alone survives intact and unimpaired—its power grows as poverty spreads."[77] As poverty spreads, as resources are exhausted, the technical apparatus becomes more efficient, and the pressure on men grows, for it becomes more and more necessary to squeeze from them the last drop. Technology

> does not work according to economic laws. It is economic life that becomes ever more subservient to technology. We are approaching a point—here and there we have already reached it—where technological rationalization in production is more important than the profit produced. In other words, technological improvement must go on even if it spells financial loss.[78]

Finally, technology reaches a point where it expends a maximum of rationalized effort on the production of a minimum return—a situation in

[75] *Ibid.*, p. 12.
[76] *Ibid.*, pp. 13–14.
[77] *Ibid.*, p. 17.
[78] *Ibid.*, p. 29.

which a giant organization produces almost nothing at all, but merely exists for its own sake.

Regress is as marked in the moral and spiritual as in the economic and political realms. Juenger sees anxiety, nervousness, mental devastation and desolation, continuous nervous work destroying leisure—everywhere, and increasingly. There are feelings of depression, of boredom, of futility, lack of purpose, nervousness and mechanical restlessness. The masses are bereft of spiritual powers.[79] Even sports betray the rationalized destruction of healthy, natural activity.

> The physique of the modern athlete betrays the onesided training to which it is subjected. His body is trained, but it is anything but beautiful. . . . Modern sports are incompatible with any kind of artistic life and activity; they are essentially unartistic and unspiritual by nature.[80]

What is more, they are totally lacking in gaiety and delight.

The modern technological slave gives up his freedom in the hope, Juenger declares, of achieving security. But he is once more tricked and cheated. The same argument applies here as applies to wealth. "Not actual security, but want of security produces those powerful organizations we see growing up around us, not only labor parties and unions but also private insurance companies and governmental social-security bureaus."[81] In short, advancing technology is the cause of all the evils of modern life. It forces us to work more rather than less, it perverts science and religion and crushes freedom, it creates bureaucracy with all its viciousness, it destroys money, it befouls education (which is replaced by "training"), it distorts even nutrition ("scientific" nutrition is a "fraud"), it impoverishes the arts (men are "self-deceived" by such arts as photography), it produces synthetic emotions and a pathetic longing for vitality of any kind, and, finally, but not least, it brings about ever and ever greater wars.

> Total war presupposes total technical organization. By its very concept, total war rejects all limitations of means and purposes. Its corollary appears to be nothing less than total annihilation—from the writings of modern war theorists this goal emerges forever more clearly. This war is total not only in its preparation, its strategic and tactical means and ends; it is total above

---

[79] Juenger echoes the charge of Nordau—that the nerves of mankind will not stand up to the pressures of the modern world.

[80] *Ibid.*, p. 153.

[81] *Ibid.*, p. 140. Juenger adds: "The whole weakness of the human being who lives within the technical organization, his whole peculiar uprootedness, his crying need for guidance and aid, his isolation—they find expression in this striving for security that shrinks from no act of subjection, that surrenders itself into dependence with a definite eagerness" (*ibid.*, pp. 140–1).

all in its mentality of ruthless extermination which no longer recognizes any barriers. This destructive mentality is the counterpart of technological progress.[82]

Most of the authors who are associated with the general theme of Juenger's work agree that many of the phenomena of regress he describes are to be observed, but they do not agree that all are to be ascribed to the advance of technology. For Juenger, all the ills of modern life are brought about by the increase in rationalized, organized, technical exploitation of nature and of man. The others do not say this, for they do not appear to agree with Juenger that technology is *essentially* rapacious and exploitative. Usually, they see it as merely a means to an end that is good in itself—or that used to be a good, or that might some time be a good; the trouble is, in their view, that the means have obscured the end. Their position is that a method that was good in its place and that might still be good if it were controlled has become autonomous. Humanity, mesmerized by the success of technology, can do nothing to stop it. This is not Juenger's position. Technology, for him, must be destructive and evil, that being its very nature. It is not a tool that men can use for good or for ill. It can only be used for ill. And it cannot *not* be used.

Juenger's is therefore the strong position on the advance of technology; the weaker position might be represented by Ellul. He maintains that technology has become autonomous, and he finds manifestations and ramifications of this autonomy—which is also autocracy—everywhere. Technology invades science, is prior to it in time, and controls it in fact; it dominates all intellectual activity of any kind; and, under the guise of the desirability of "organization," undertakes the conquest of all social, political, moral, and artistic arrangements. The rule of technology is sometimes subtle, but it is always thorough. *La technique* is omnipresent.

However, although the results of these invasions and conquests are bad, they are so for somewhat different reasons than for Juenger. In Ellul's opinion, technology is not evil in itself; rather, as a methodology, it is neither good nor evil; but since it has become autonomous and runs by itself, and since it is not itself intelligent and certainly is not concerned with man's good, it necessarily leads to consequences that cannot be foreseen. These are likely—highly likely, given the innate ignorance, stupidity, and viciousness of men—to be evil. For Ellul, the probability that technology will end up, and mankind with it, in an *ersatz* golden age in which men will be unhappy without even knowing it, verges on certainty. But

[82] *Ibid.*, p. 165. Juenger wrote before the Second World War.

it is nevertheless not certain, as it is for Juenger, who is uncompromising in his prophecies of doom.[83]

Ellul agrees with Juenger on many particular points,[84] although the matter of the increase of wealth is an exception. (Ellul maintains that technology produces real wealth; he questions, however, whether this wealth is well used, or can be well used, in a technological society.) They disagree on one major point. Juenger holds that there is regress in human nature as well as in institutions; man himself is changing for the worse, as well as the conditions of human life. Ellul denies this. The changes for the worse that he describes occur without man, and not within him.

Indeed, Ellul makes much of the application of technical advances to eugenics; he suggests that there is a movement among biological technologists to create a "better" world by means of the controlled manipulation of germ plasma. Ellul does not seem to deny that better men might be produced; but he does deny that they would live in a better world. Perhaps some sort of progress in human nature might occur, but it would not cancel out the general regress that is the dominant note in technological society.[85]

By no means do all biologists agree that technology can produce better men, to say nothing of a better world. James F. Crow sums up the arguments against the position; he sees regress in human nature as a result of technological tampering with heredity. The cause is biological rather than moral or social. Because of advances in medical and public-health

[83] Ellul's ideas are presented in *The Technological Society*, which several critics have held to be the best book on the subject. It is hard to escape the feeling, however, that Ellul himself has something of the technician about him. Gone is the rhetoric of a Rousseau, a Flammarion, a Juenger. Ellul's prose is measured, moderate, cool. He describes coming disasters with calm.

[84] Mumford, in a number of books, also agrees on several points, notably the deleterious effect of technology on artistic and social life, especially the life of cities. See, for instance, *The City in History* and *Art and Technics*. Nicolas Berdyaev, in *The Fate of Man in the Modern World*, declares that "in all of the present historical process a greater role than that of war is played by another force, a force of far longer duration, a force of almost cosmic significance: technics and the mechanization of life" (p. 14). Technics results in "dehumanization," "centralization," "falsity," "anxiety"—all of these terms in common use. Ortega coined a famous phrase—*The Revolt of the Masses*—and discusses the bad effects of technology on man and culture, in this and other books.

The list of general indictments of technology might be extended almost at will. Reference could be made to the work of Coblentz and Crow (on the biological side), to that of Dubos (on the general scientific side), to that of Guardini, Niebuhr, and Barth (on the philosophical and religious side), to that of Jung and Neumann (on the psychological side). However, perhaps nothing essentially new would be added to the argument.

[85] Such genetic "progress" in human nature is a *bête noire* of the distopians like Huxley. Hermann J. Muller, on the contrary, has high hopes for just the eventuality that frightens the distopians.

techniques, the low death rate has reduced the opportunity for selection by death. At the same time, the index of selection because of differential fertility has risen in many technologically advanced countries.

> The important conclusion is this: the amount of differential reproduction that now exists, a differential of which we are hardly conscious and which we do not ordinarily regard as a social burden, would, if applied to a highly heritable trait, be such as to make possible a rapid change in that trait. The loss of opportunity for selection because of a lower death rate is approximately compensated for by a greater opportunity, one that is inherent in the pattern of birth rates.[86]

However, if, as seems true, for the past several thousand years the major selective factor in human survival has been resistance to disease, and if, as is also true, today these diseases have virtually disappeared from much of the world, then man may be left with certain kinds of resistant genes involving highly specific mechanisms that are of no use in other contexts and may be harmful.

> An example is the sickle-cell anemia gene (common in Africa), because in some manner it confers a measure of resistance to one type of malaria. Despite the fact that a double dose of the gene causes a severe anemia that would nearly always be fatal in a rigorous environment, the gene is retained because in a single dose it leads to increased malaria resistance. Today many populations, well on the way to freedom from malaria, thanks to modern sanitation and insecticides, still carry a gene which still exacts its price in anemia deaths with no longer any compensating benefit from malaria resistance. There is the possibility that several genes whose present function is obscure are relics of former disease resistance mechanisms in which they were some way involved, or were selected for other less obvious reasons that are no longer relevant.[87]

The importance of this becomes even more clear in the case where there is radical change in the environment. In the history of most evolving species a change in the environment is almost always bad, says Crow. In the case of man, changes are brought about by himself and are not necessarily bad. However, in the majority of cases a changed environment ameliorates rather than obliterates the harmful effect of a mutant gene. A gene that is harmful in one environment is harmful in another, although it may be less so. But if the effect of an environmental change is to lessen rather than to remove completely the harm caused by a gene, the effect is

[86] "Mechanisms and Trends in Human Evolution," in *Daedalus*, Summer, 1961, pp. 420–1.

[87] *Ibid.*, p. 423. Recent reports cast doubt on the capacity of insecticides to rid large areas of mosquitoes, and hence of malaria.

one of postponement rather than of prevention of the harmful effect. Such a postponement may increase the harm by spreading it over a long period of time, even though in the short view it appears to decrease it.

As human beings, we are primarily interested, not in the effect of a gene on fitness *per se*, but in its associated effects on health, happiness, intelligence, and other aspects of human well-being. From the standpoint of long-range human welfare, the most beneficial kind of environmental advance is one that reduces the amount of suffering and unhappiness caused by a mutant gene by a greater degree than the increase in fitness. On the other hand, an environmental change that, for example, increases the fertility of persons with a severe or painful disease without a corresponding decrease in the amount of suffering caused by the disease will in the long run cause an increase in human misery.[88]

At the present time, genetic regress is actually going on, says Crow. The issue is not *whether* man is influencing his evolution, but in what direction. "To the extent that [genetically selective deaths] no longer occur or are reduced in number, the genetic makeup of the population is deteriorating."[89] The solution, interestingly enough, is, for Crow, more technology rather than less. In this he agrees with the progressive eugenecists. But, unlike them, he seems to regard the attainment of a sufficient technology in this regard as almost impossible. Hence regress is to be expected in the future.[90]

Modern "total" war is often cited by regress authors as an example of the deterioration and degeneration that follows on technological advance.[91] This view, which is widely held in the twentieth century, is starkly presented in *Community of Fear*, a pamphlet by Harrison Brown and James Real. Their picture of the future is dark indeed. They are cognizant of the newest weapons, and of the horrors that men can create with them. They also indicate the lines of development in weaponry that may be expected in the future. The horrors do not abate.

[88] *Ibid.*, p. 424.
[89] *Ibid.*, p. 428.
[90] Crow does not explicitly assert what his argument seems to imply—that is, necessary and unavoidable genetic regress. He holds out some hope that we can use birth selection in an effective and socially acceptable way to compensate for decreased death selection. The point is that he attacks the eugenecists—even the most technical among them—on their own ground. Eugenics may lead, he is saying, to genetic deterioration as well as to social and moral regress. The eugenecists are attacked by many writers who do not approve of the utopias they hope to achieve. But it is usually regarded as certain that the utopias *can be achieved*—it is merely a question of whether they are desirable. Crow seems to be throwing doubt on the attainment itself of any sort of genetic improvement.
[91] Cf. Juenger on this point. See above, p. 141.

The new developments will cause people to burrow more deeply into the ground. Factories will be built in caves, as will apartment houses and stores. Eventually most human life will be underground, confronted by arsenals capable of destroying all life over the land areas of the earth. Deep under the ground people will be relatively safe—at least until such time as we learn how to make explosives capable of pulverizing the earth to great depths.[92]

Once people are convinced that they can survive the present state of the "art of killing," Brown and Real declare, a significant new habit pattern will have been introduced and accepted. But it will be "grotesquely different from any we have known for thousands of years." The new habit pattern will consist in "adjusting ourselves to the idea of living in holes. From that time onward it will be simple to adjust ourselves to living in *deeper* holes."

Tens of thousands of years ago our Mousterian and Aurignacian ancestors lived in caves. The vast knowledge which we have accumulated during the intervening millennia will have brought us full circle. The epic of man's journey into the light will have ended.[93]

Harrison Brown is treated elsewhere in this study as a contingent progress author; in other writings he maintains that mankind is at a crossroads of its history, and that there is still time for it to change its ways.[94] But the position that human regress is occurring in the guise of technological progress—a position often hinted at, if not always explicitly affirmed, at the present day—is well expressed by the sentences quoted here.

[92] *Community of Fear*, pp. 38–9.
[93] *Ibid.*, p. 39. Brown's and Real's theory might be termed a "one-great-cycle" theory as to the pattern of history. However, it appears that in the long run, regress is the final result—that is, the future will be worse than the past ever was.
[94] Cf. *The Challenge of Man's Future*.

9

Cosmogenic Regress

Among the many writers who have theories of cosmogenic regress —*i.e.*, regress in human affairs that is caused by regress in the cosmos or among the gods—are those listed below. The list would be greatly lengthened, of course, if Eastern authors were included.

Hesiod	Von Hartmann
Aratus	Jeans
Ovid	Russell
Flammarion	Wiener

THE MYTH OF THE AGES OF MAN

Many cyclical theories posit an initial golden age in which men live the happy life of children, close to nature and to the gods of nature, with all their simple and reasonable wants satisfied directly out of the immediate environment, and in which they feel no unreasonable and "vicious" desires whatever. Indeed, this notion is a commonplace in Eastern cyclical theories.[1] However, since the theories are cyclical, the golden age is attained in them over and over again.

It has been suggested that Western versions of such theories make use of this initial golden age but combine it with a theory of regress in history.[2] Whatever the truth of this suggestion, for many Western writers the cycle occurs only once in man's history. There is no return to the golden age once it is lost. Things go from good to bad, and from bad to worse, irreversibly.

A familiar version of the tale of the ages of man is given by Ovid, in the *Metamorphoses*.

> Golden was that first age, which, with no one to compel, without a law, of its own will, kept faith and did the right. There was no fear of punishment, no threatening words were to be read on brazen tablets; no suppliant throng gazed fearfully upon its judge's face; but without judges lived secure. Not yet had the pine-tree, felled on its native mountains, descended thence into the watery plain to visit other lands; men knew no shores except their own. Not yet were cities begirt with steep moats; there were no trumpets of straight, no horns of curving brass, no swords or helmets. There was no need at all of armed men, for nations, secure from war's alarms, passed the years in gentle ease. The earth herself, without compulsion, untouched by hoe or plowshare, of herself gave all things needful. And men, content with food which came with no one's seeking, gathered the arbute fruit, strawberries from the mountain-sides, cornel-cherries, berries hanging thick upon the prickly bramble, and acorns fallen from the spreading tree of Jove. Then spring was everlasting, and gentle zephyrs with warm breath played with the flowers that sprang unplanted. Anon the earth, untilled, brought forth her stores of grain, and the fields, though unfallowed, grew white with the heavy, bearded wheat. Streams of milk and streams of sweet nectar flowed, and yellow honey was distilled from the verdant oak.[3]

> After Saturn had been banished to the dark world of death, and the world was under the sway of Jove,[4] the silver race came in, lower in the scale than gold, but of greater worth than yellow brass. Jove now shortened the bounds of the old-time spring, and through winter, summer, variable autumn, and brief spring extended the year in four seasons. Then first the parched air glared white with burning heat, and icicles hung down congealed by freezing winds. In that age men first sought the shelter of

[1] In some Western cyclical theories (for example, Plato's), the first age is miserable. Men are naked and helpless, the prey of disease, want, and wild beasts. Only with the help of such figures as Prometheus are they able to survive in a hostile environment.

[2] See Grace E. Cairns, *Philosophies of History*, pp. 202–3.

[3] The men of the golden age have no technology whatever.

[4] Ovid does not suggest that the men of the golden age brought this catastrophe on themselves. The cause is a quarrel among divinities.

houses. Their homes had heretofore been caves, dense thickets, and branches bound together with bark. Then first the seeds of grain were planted in long furrows, and bullocks groaned beneath the heavy yoke.

Next after this and third in order came the brazen race, of sterner disposition, and more ready to fly to arms, savage, but not yet impious. The age of hard iron came last. Straightway all evil burst forth into this age of baser vein: modesty and truth and faith fled the earth, and in their place came tricks and plots and snares, violence and cursed love of gain. Men now spread sails to the winds, though the sailor as yet scarce knew them; and keels of pine which long had stood upon high mountain-sides, now leaped insolently over unknown waves. And the ground, which had hitherto been a common possession like the sunlight and the air, the careful surveyor now marked out with long-drawn boundary-line. Not only did men demand of the bounteous fields the crops and sustenance they owed, but they delved as well into the very bowels of the earth; and the wealth which the creator had hidden away and buried deep amidst the very Stygian shades, was brought to light, wealth that pricks men on to crime.[5] And now baneful iron had appeared, and gold more baneful still; war came, which fights with both, and brandished in its bloody hands the clashing arms. Men lived on plunder. Guest was not safe from host, nor father-in-law from son-in-law; even among brothers 'twas rare to find affection. The husband longed for the death of his wife, she of her husband; murderous stepmothers brewed deadly poisons, and sons inquired into their fathers' years before the time. Piety lay vanquished, and the maiden Astraea, last of the immortals, abandoned the blood-soaked earth.[6]

The fourth and last stage in the series is, of course, our own. Ovid gives no hint of a return to the happy beginnings of the race.

Hesiod's scheme includes five ages, rather than the customary four.[7] The first is that of gold:

First of all the deathless gods who dwell on Olympus made a golden race of mortal men who lived in the time of Cronos when he was reigning in heaven. And they lived like gods without sorrow of heart, remote and free from toil and grief: miserable age rested not on them; but with legs and arms never failing they made merry with feasting beyond the reach of all evils. When they died, it was as though they were overcome with sleep, and they had all good things; for the fruitful earth unforced bare them fruit

[5] Mumford and Juenger, among modern writers, also imply that man's efforts to mine the interior of the earth are symbolic of his fall from happiness.

[6] *Metamorphoses*, Vol. I, pp. 9, 11, 13.

[7] It has been suggested that Hesiod's pattern fuses a pre-Hesiodic myth of four ages and a legend about the age of heroes "which Hesiod, or some precursor, interpolated between the third and the last of the other ages" (Lovejoy and Boas, *Primitivism and Related Ideas in Antiquity*, p. 25).

abundantly and without stint. They dwelt in ease and peace upon their lands with many good things, rich in flocks and loved by the blessed gods.[8]

The second or silver race of men "lived only a little time and that in sorrow because of their foolishness, for they could not keep from sinning and from wronging one another, nor would they serve the immortals, nor sacrifice on the holy altars."[9] They were destroyed by Zeus, in anger. The third race was the bronze. They were "terrible and strong," and delighted in deeds of war and violence. They were destroyed by their own hands.[10]

The fourth race was that of heroes, men like Achilles and the others at Troy, Oedipus and his children, Theseus and his companions, Jason and his crew. They too were destroyed, perhaps by their own fierceness. Zeus, in pity for them, sent them to a heaven after their death, where they dwell "untouched by sorrow in the islands of the blessed."[11]

The fifth race or age is that of iron. Hesiod beweeps this age, which is his own.

> And again far-seeing Zeus made yet another generation, the fifth, of men who are upon the bounteous earth.
> Thereafter, would that I were not among the men of the fifth generation, but either had died before or been born afterwards.[12] For now truly is a race of iron, and men never rest from labour and sorrow by day, and from perishing by night; and the gods shall lay sore trouble upon them. But, notwithstanding, even these shall have some good mingled with their evils. And Zeus will destroy this race of mortal men also when they come to have grey hair on the temples at their birth.[13] The father will not agree with his children, nor the children with their father; nor guest with his host, nor comrade with comrade; nor will brother be dear to brother as aforetime. Men will dishonour their parents as they grow quickly old, and will carp at them, chiding them with bitter words, hard-hearted they, not knowing the fear of the gods. They will not repay their aged parents the cost of their nurture, for might shall be their right: and one man will sack

---

[8] *Works and Days*, p. 11. Miss Cairns declares: "The Golden Age is similar to that in all myths of the ancient world, Mesopotamian, Egyptian, Indian, Zoroastrian, Hebrew. As in the Garden-of-Eden days of Adam and Eve as well as the primeval dawn of history described in all other ancient cultures, The Golden Age knew no moral or physical evil and did not have to labor" (*op. cit.*, p. 197).

[9] *Ibid.*, p. 13. Hence the silver race, unlike the golden, brought on its own destruction. On this point Hesiod differs with Ovid.

[10] Once more Hesiod differs.

[11] *Ibid.*, p. 15. Hesiod does not say whether the heroes brought on their own destruction. He gives the impression, however, that they were by temperament not adapted to continued existence.

[12] Hesiod may be hinting here that there is to be a return to the first or golden age. This interpretation, however, seems to contradict the general tone of the work.

[13] That is, when they are so degenerate that even the newborn have gray hair.

another's city. There will be no favour for the man who keeps his oath or for the just or for the good; but rather men will praise the evil-doer and his violent dealing. Strength will be right and reverence will cease to be; and the wicked will hurt the worthy man, speaking false words against him, and will swear an oath upon them. Envy, foul-mouthed, delighting in evil, with scowling face, will go along with wretched men one and all. And then Aidôs and Nemesis, with their sweet forms wrapped in white robes, will go from the wide-pathed earth and forsake mankind to join the company of the deathless gods: and bitter sorrows will be left for mortal men, and there will be no help against evil.[14]

There is no explicit suggestion in Hesiod that the cycle will renew itself. Hesiod does not say what will happen when this fifth and last race is destroyed.

Aratus offers a version of the tale that has three rather than four or five stages. Justice, as represented by a Maiden (Astraea or Virgo), is the central figure in the myth.[15] There was first a golden race. As long as the earth nurtured them, the Maiden dwelt on earth. "But with the Silver Race only a little and no longer with utter readiness did she mingle, for that she yearned for the ways of the men of old. Yet in that Silver Age was she still upon the earth; but from the echoing hills at eventide she came alone, nor spake to any man in gentle words."[16] Finally, a brazen race replaced that of silver, and then "verily did Justice loathe that race of men and fly heavenward and took up that abode, where even now in the night time the Maiden is seen of men, established near to far-seen Boötes."[17]

The story of the four (three, five) regressive ages of man is symbolized in *Daniel*[18] and in Dante's *Inferno*, as well as other places. Dante says:

Within the mountain [Ida] stands a great old man, who keeps his back turned to Damietta and gazes on Rome as on his mirror; his head is fashioned of fine gold, his breast and arms are pure silver, then to the fork he is of brass, and from there down all of choice iron except that the right foot is baked clay, and he rests more on this than on the other.[19]

14 *Ibid.*, pp. 15, 17.
15 Astraea or Virgo, the maiden who flees the earth to reside among the stars when man becomes too evil and corrupt, is mentioned by Virgil and Dante, and is a favorite symbol in the Renaissance. John Donne, for instance, constructs complex conceits around her story.
16 *Aratus [Phaenomena]*, pp. 389, 391.
17 *Ibid.*, p. 391. One is not sure whether the Maiden (Justice) flees because men are no longer just, or they are no longer just because she flees. In either case, a cosmic upheaval is associated with the change of phase.
18 *Daniel* ii, 31 ff.
19 *Inferno* xiv, 103–111. The translator (J. D. Sinclair) notes that "the four metals represent the successive degenerating ages of history."

Many other versions of the myth of the ages of man are to be found in the literature. There are usually four stages, sometimes three (as with Aratus), occasionally five (as with Hesiod). It seems that it is never said in these tales that there will be a return to the first, often called the golden age. And no reason other than the will of the gods is given for the descent from that first age, although, once man has stepped down from his first eminence, he may bring about his further fall.

It is the lack of a specifically human cause of degeneration that distinguishes these theories, based on myth, from the theories of anthropogenic regress that are put forward by a number of authors who also have a conception of an original golden age, or state of nature or innocence. As has been seen, however, the descriptions of the first and subsequent ages to be found in writers such as Ovid and Hesiod are similar to those found in Rousseau and other modern authors.[20]

It is the lack of a specifically human cause of degeneration—and a consequent dependence on some principle of cosmic regress—that makes it desirable to treat the myths discussed above with the theories of the authors to be considered in the next section. The latter also view history as essentially regressive, not because of any fault in man but because of the nature of things.

The Second Law of Thermodynamics in Relation to History

Henry Adams discusses the second law of thermodynamics, and treats the problem it poses for historians, and particularly for progress authors, in *A Letter to American Teachers of History*. "The mechanical theory of the universe governed physical science for three hundred years," he writes. "Under this Law the quantity of matter in the universe remained invariable; the sum of movement remained constant; energy was indestructible; 'nothing was added; nothing was lost'; nothing was created, nothing was destroyed."[21]

Toward the middle of the nineteenth century, Adams says, a new school of physicists appeared in Europe. This new school "announced a second law of dynamics. The first law said that Energy was never lost; the second said that it was never saved; that, while the sum of energy in the universe might remain constant . . . the higher powers of energy tended always to fall lower, and that this process had no known limit."[22]

[20] Rousseau views a specifically human cause—man's "perfectibility"—as operating in the state of nature to bring about degeneration.
[21] *The Degradation of the Democratic Dogma*, p. 136.
[22] *Ibid.*, pp. 136–7.

The application of this law to the history of the universe meant, Adams declares, that the universe had been "tossed . . . into the ash-heap." The law held that "the Entropy of the Universe tends toward a maximum"; this meant "to the vulgar and ignorant historian . . . that the ash-heap was constantly increasing in size."[23]

> Kelvin and Tait . . . affirmed . . . that all nature's energies were slowly converting themselves into heat and vanishing in space, until, at the last, nothing would be left except a dead ocean of energy at its lowest possible level—say of heat at 1° Centrigrade, or −252° C. below freezing point of water—and incapable of doing any work whatever, since work could only be done by a fall of tension, as water does work in falling to sea-level.[24]

Social or "Vital" energy might, of course, be of another sort than mechanical energy, and thus not liable to decay. Adams reviews the theories that proposed this. But the evidence against the position is, in his view, overwhelming. And he quotes a number of perorations that fairly threaten mankind, as he says, with its doom. "Faye, in his 'Origin of the World,' " says this, for example:

> We must . . . renounce those brilliant fancies by which we try to deceive ourselves in order to endow man with unlimited posterity, and to regard the universe as the immense theatre on which is to be developed a spontaneous progress without end. On the contrary, life must disappear, and the grandest material works of the human race will have to be effaced by degrees under the action of a few physical forces which will survive man for a time. Nothing will remain: *"etiam periere ruinae!"*[25]

All work is done, Adams explains, by conversion of one energy, or intensity, into another, and a lower. If this conversion is prevented, "all processes which involve such conversion must cease, and among these are vital processes."

> It will be the height of imprudence to trust to the prospect, not infrequently referred to, at the present time, of drawing on the energy locked up in the atomic structure of matter. . . . After a large part of the whole existent energy has gone to raise the dead level of things, no difference of temperature, adequate to work between, will be possible, and the inevitable death of all things will approach with headlong rapidity.[26]

Adams discusses the application of this theory of energy to social and historical change. He quotes Eduard von Hartmann:

[23] *Ibid.*, p. 138.
[24] *Ibid.*, p. 141.
[25] Qu. in *ibid.*, pp. 145–6.
[26] *Ibid.*, p. 147. Adams is here quoting "the sketch of Kelvin's Life and Work by Professor Andrew Gray."

If the social consciousness of to-day rebels so strongly against the thought that vital processes will come to an end in the world, the chief reason is because society has indeed absorbed the first principle of thermodynamics —the conservation of energy—but not the second, the progressive degradation of energy by dissipation and leveling of intensities; and, in consequence, has erroneously interpreted the first law as though it contained an eternal guaranty of the endlessness of vital processes.[27]

The implication is, however, that mankind will become ever more conscious of its inevitable fate, now ensured by science, and will ultimately accept it.[28]

There is usually little or no similarity between the regress resulting from the second law of thermodynamics and that based on the conflicts of the gods. But such an authority as Saporta seems to supply a link. "We recognize," he says, ". . . that the world was once young; then adolescent; that it has even passed the age of maturity; man has come late, when a beginning of physical decadence had struck the globe, his domain."[29] Adams goes on to comment:

The steady decline continued until the convulsion of the glacial epoch, when, in the midst of a wrecked solar system, man suddenly appeared. "Since this great event occurred," according to Lapparent (III, 1655), "the organic world has enriched itself with no new species, but several forms have disappeared, among them those that surrounded the first men; and the great herbivorous mammals, already on their decline, have seen their principal representatives, little by little, quit the scene of the world."[30]

That would not be out of place in Hesiod, in Ovid, in Lucretius.[31] And this paragraph of Camille Flammarion, also quoted by Adams, might well have been written by a proponent of the myth of the ages of man:

Life and human activity will insensibly be shut up within the tropical zones. Saint Petersburg, Berlin, London, Paris, Vienna, Constantinople, Rome, will successively sink to sleep under their eternal cerements. . . . No longer will man live—no longer will he breathe—except in the equatorial zone, down to the day when the last tribe, already expiring in cold

27 *Ibid.*, pp. 147–8.
28 Adams quotes from many other scientific and philosophical figures of his time, all of whom are in agreement on the basic problem. The reader is referred to Adams' work for the wealth of evidence assembled for this view.
29 Quoted by Adams, *op. cit.*, p. 157.
30 *Ibid.*, pp. 163–4.
31 For instance, Lucretius declares that "the age is enfeebled and the earth, exhausted by bearing, scarce produces little living creatures, she who produced all races and gave birth to the huge bodies of wild beasts . . . Moreover she first spontaneously of herself produced for mortals goodly corn-crops and joyous vineyards; of herself gave sweet fruits and glad pastures; which now-a-days scarce attain any size when furthered by our labour" (*On the Nature of Things*, II, in *The Stoic and Epicurean Philosophers*, p. 113).

and hunger, shall camp on the shores of the last sea in the rays of a pale sun which will henceforth illumine an earth that is only a wandering tomb, turning around a useless light and a barren heat. Surprised by the cold, the last human family has been touched by the finger of death, and soon their bones will be buried under the shroud of eternal ice. The historian of nature would then be able to write—Here lies the entire humanity of a world which has lived! Here lie all the dreams of ambition, all the conquests of military glory, all the resounding affairs of finance, all the systems of an imperfect science, and also all the oaths of mortals' love! Here lie all the beauties of earth!—But no mortuary stone will mark the spot where the poor planet shall have rendered its last sigh![32]

Norbert Wiener also regards the second law of thermodynamics as relevant to theories of the history of mankind. He remarks:

Sooner or later we shall die, and it is highly probable[33] that the whole universe around us will die the heat death, in which the world shall be reduced to one vast temperature equilibrium in which nothing really new ever happens. There will be nothing left but a drab uniformity out of which we can expect only minor and insignificant local fluctuations.[34]

We are immersed, he says, in a life in which the world as a whole obeys the second law of thermodynamics: confusion increases and order decreases. But this is not, he assures us, a cause for immediate and total despair. The law "may be a valid statement about the whole of a closed system," but it is "definitely not valid concerning a non-isolated part of it." Thus the fact that "there are local and temporary islands of decreasing entropy in a world in which the entropy as a whole tends to increase"

[32] Qu. in Adams, pp. 178–9. Rhetoric of this sort is a commonplace of science fiction. In H. G. Wells's story, *The Time Machine,* there is a memorable description of the world in its last days, when the sun has become a red disk on the horizon, and the last heir of man hops fitfully on the shores of the blood-red ocean. "A horror of this great darkness came on me. The cold, that smote my marrow, and the pain I felt in breathing overcame me. I shivered, and a deadly nausea seized me. Then like a red-hot bow in the sky appeared the edge of the sun. I got off the machine to recover myself. As I stood sick and confused I saw again the moving thing upon the shoal—there was no mistake now that it was a moving thing—against the red water of the sea. It was a round thing, the size of a football perhaps, or, it may be, bigger, and tentacles trailed from it; it seemed black against the weltering blood-red water, and it was hopping fitfully about. Then I felt I was fainting. But a terrible dread of lying helpless in that remote and awful twilight sustained me while I clambered upon the saddle" (*Three Prophetic Novels of H. G. Wells,* p. 330). Wells is here clearly accepting the validity of the application of the second law of thermodynamics to history.

[33] Wiener emphasizes what Adams does not concede, that the law is a probabilistic and not a certain one. It is very likely that entropy will increase with time; it is not, however, certain that it will.

[34] *The Human Use of Human Beings,* pp. 30–1.

can be the source of a measured hope, for "the existence of these islands enables some of us to assert the existence of progress."[35]

The question, he goes on, whether the law of entropy should be interpreted "pessimistically or not" depends on the relative importance assigned to the universe at large. If our notion of progress involves the universe, then the second law of thermodynamics makes progress an impossibility. But if we regard particularly the "islands of locally decreasing entropy," the situation is quite different. There progress is possible. It is quite conceivable, says Wiener, that life "belongs to a limited stretch of time." Nevertheless,

> to those of us who are aware of the extremely limited range of physical conditions under which the chemical reactions necessary to life as we know it can take place, it is a foregone conclusion that the lucky accident which permits the continuation of life in any form on this earth, even without restricting life to something like human life, is bound to come to . . . an end.[36]

We may succeed in so framing our values, says Wiener, that this temporary accident of living existence, and this much more temporary accident of human existence, may be taken as all-important, notwithstanding their fugitive character. In other words, Wiener seems to suggest, it might be proper to ask whether progress is the pattern of history, and even to reply in the affirmative, even when we are at the same time forced to concede that mankind will not endure forever.[37]

However, Wiener himself does not hold out much hope, even from this limited point of view. "The best we can hope for the role of progress in a universe running downhill," he declares, "is that the vision of our attempts to progress in the face of overwhelming necessity may have the purging terror of Greek tragedy."[38] All that can be said is that it may be a long time yet before our civilization and our human race perish, though perish they will even as all of us are born to die. However, should this fact, Wiener asks, be entirely disheartening?

> The prospect of a final death is far from a complete frustration of life and this is equally true for a civilization and for the human race as it is for any of its component individuals. May we have the courage to face the eventual doom of our civilization as we have the courage to face the certainty of our personal doom. The simple faith in progress is not a conviction

[35] *Ibid.*, pp. 36–7.
[36] *Ibid.*, p. 40.
[37] In the present work we treat theories that view mankind throughout its entire career on earth; however, they need not conceive the race as enduring forever. Hence Wiener is here accepting a limitation accepted by most progress authors.
[38] *Ibid.*, p. 41.

belonging to strength, but one belonging to acquiescence and hence to weakness.[39]

Other writers share Wiener's attitude toward the situation as he describes it. Bertrand Russell, for example, in "A Free Man's Worship," has this to say:

That Man is the product of causes which had no prevision of the end they were achieving; that his origin, his growth, his hopes and fears, his loves and beliefs, are but the outcome of accidental collocations of atoms; that no fire, no heroism, no intensity of thought and feeling, can preserve an individual life beyond the grave; that all the labours of the ages, all the devotion, all the inspiration, all the noonday brightness of human genius, are destined to extinction in the vast death of the solar system, and that the whole temple of Man's achievement must inevitably be buried beneath the debris of a universe in ruins—all these things, if not quite beyond dispute, are yet so nearly certain, that no philosophy which rejects them can hope to stand.[40]

Russell, like Wiener, sees a kind of tragic beauty in all this.

Sir James Jeans, who does not dispute the main point, sees a ray of hope. He writes:

Taking a very gloomy view of the future of the human race, let us suppose that it can only expect to survive for two thousand million years longer, a period about equal to the past age of the earth. Then regarded as a being destined to live three-score years and ten, Humanity, although it has been born in a house only seventy years old, is itself only three days old. . . . Utterly inexperienced beings, we are standing at the first flush of the dawn of civilization. . . . In time the glory of the morning must fade into the light of common day, and this, in some far distant age, will give place to evening twilight, presaging the final eternal night. But we children of the dawn need give but little thought to the far-off sunset.[41]

---

[39] *Ibid.*, p. 47.

[40] *Mysticism and Logic*, p. 45.

[41] *Eos: or the Wider Aspects of Astronomy*, qu. by Toynbee, *A Study of History*, one volume edition, pp. 247–8. Jeans's remarks are interesting because, while he does not deny the application of the concept of entropy to history, he has a somewhat hopeful view of man's prospects. Indeed, Toynbee cites this text as testimony from a leading scientist that man still has much to look forward to.

It should be noted that more recent estimates of the age of the earth differ sharply from Jeans's. The twentieth century has seen the estimates doubled about every decade. Gamow assumes that our universe has existed for an eternity of time; that until about five billion years ago it was collapsing uniformly from a state of infinite rarefaction; that five billion years ago it arrived at a state of maximum compression in which the density of all matter may have been as great as that of the particles packed in the nucleus of an atom (*i.e.*, 100 million million times the density of water); and that the universe is now on the rebound, dispersing irreversibly toward a state of infinite rarefaction (cf. *The Modern Astronomy*, pp. 23 ff.). Gamow's view

In other words, while it is true that regress is the ultimate pattern of history, the human race has plenty of time before it in which to progress, ephemeral though this progress must necessarily be. And what vast changes may overtake man in the millions and billions of years that are before him? May he not even discover some way, as yet unforeseen, of overcoming the second law of thermodynamics? This possibility is suggested by a few of the authors who affirm the relevance of the law to theories of progress.[42]

The majority of the authors, however, who explicitly take into account the relation of entropy to the question of human progress either agree with the writers quoted by Adams, that the second law of therodynamics dooms the race utterly, or with Wiener and the others like him, that the law sets an ultimate limit to man's hopes, before which some progress nevertheless may be made.[43]

---

is, incidentally, formally the same as the one here being discussed. It posits a cosmic process which must ultimately bring to an end all human progress, whatever man might do to try to avert this result.

Even more recent estimates of the age of the universe place it at between ten and twenty billion years, and posit a cyclical or repetitive alternation of compressions and rarefactions. They give no hint, however, of whether man will exist again, and perform the same actions, in the next cycle, some eighty billion years hence.

[42] Among them is C. D. Broad, who is treated in this study as a progress author. Henry Adams is another who sees a way to avoid the workings of the law. His theory of progress is considered in Chapter 6.

[43] There is no sign, in the two or three generations that have passed since the second law of thermodynamics was first proposed, that anyone has disproved it, or even tried to disprove it. Hence this law, and its consequences for the future of man, must in some sense underlie all modern affirmations of progress. Since the strict assertion that cosmic regress determines human regress is a flat denial of progress, at least over the long run, it may be asked how it is possible for any modern writer to assert that progress will, or even may, occur.

The question seems to have been answered recently in the same way that it was before the law was proposed. That is, the possibility that the universe would eventually "run down" or "wear out" had always been recognized by at least a few progress authors. In the face of this possibility, they followed one of two courses. Either they said nothing about it, in which case it is to be assumed that they did not suppose the possibility to be a relevant consideration; or they explicitly affirmed that it was irrelevant—that is, they said that the progress they were talking about was to be thought of as occurring within the limits, whatever they were, of the world's span of existence. These two courses seem, on the whole, to be the ones followed in the modern epoch, too. Therefore, in one sense, the discovery of the second law of thermodynamics has no effect on the discussion of the idea of progress.

In another sense, of course, it needs to be said that the affirmation of progress is no longer possible, because the final degradation of the universe, *which is denied by no one*, rules it out as a valid hypothesis. But such a position runs counter to the explicit assertions of many authors, both old and new. This paradox cannot be resolved here. Our methods require us to take all assertions on their own terms. If one author says that progress will occur, and another proposes a theory of the world that makes the first assertion untenable, we can do no more than record the difference in views.

IO

Anthropogenic Cycles

THE following authors are the leading proponents of theories of anthropogenic cycles. Others also hold this position, but since all such cyclists tell much the same story, it is not necessary to list them.

Ibn Khaldun	Spengler
Vico	Toynbee
Lasaulx	Sorokin
Brooks Adams	

The *Muqaddimah* of Ibn Khaldun was completed in 1377, some 350 years before the publication of Vico's *New Science* and nearly 500 years before Comte's *Positive Philosophy*. Yet Ibn Khaldun calls history a science, and what is more a social science. The field of inquiry of this "independent science"[1] is, he says, "information about human social organization, which itself is identical with world civilization."[2] This science

[1] *Muqaddimah*, Vol. I, p. 77.
[2] *Ibid.*, p. 71.

has its own peculiar object—that is, human civilization and social organization. It also has its own peculiar problems—that is, explaining the conditions
that attach themselves to the essence of civilization, one after the other.
. . . The discussion of this topic is something new, extraordinary, and
highly useful. . . . In fact, I have not come across a discussion along
these lines by anyone.[3]

The key phrase in the above is "the conditions that attach themselves
to the essence of civilization, one after the other"—a phrase that might
almost be found in Comte. These conditions, according to Ibn Khaldun,
follow one another in cyclical fashion.[4]

That human affairs are cyclical becomes evident, according to Ibn
Khaldun, when we compare the life of an individual man (120 years)
to that of a dynastic cycle, which has the same life-span.[5] A dynastic
cycle endures for three generations of forty years each, which correspond
to spring, summer, and autumn. In the fourth generation (winter) the
dynasty comes to an end. One explanation for this is that all things that
are born and grow also decline and die.

The world of the elements and all it contains comes into being and decays.
This applies to both its essences and its conditions. Minerals, plants, all
the animals, including man, and the other created things come into being
and decay, as one can see with one's own eyes. The same applies to the
conditions that affect created things, and especially the conditions that
affect man. Sciences grow up and then are wiped out. The same applies
to crafts, and to similar things.[6]

Civilizations (Bedouin dynasties) are marked, in the first generation,
by "desert qualities" of courage, toughness, and savagery; "group feeling
continues to be preserved." The second generation sees the accumulation
of wealth and a consequent waning of the desert qualities. The ruler
now "claims all the glory for himself while the others are too lazy to
strive for [glory]." They become subservient, and group feeling is lessened. Some strength of character remains because of the memory that
is retained of the first generation.

In the third generation, "luxury" reaches its peak and the desert qualities
are forgotten. The culture becomes "sedentary." The ruler governs by
force and his people become "more cowardly than women upon their

[3] *Ibid.*, p. 77. These claims are the more striking, since Arabic writers usually
underplayed any originality in their work.
[4] Ibn Khaldun traces only the rise and fall of (Bedouin) dynasties, but we may
generalize, as he intended us to do, to cultures or civilizations (in the sense in which
Spengler and Toynbee employ these terms).
[5] Ibn Khaldun concedes that the lives of most Muslims last "between sixty and
seventy years"; 120 years is the "ideal" life-span. See *ibid.*, pp. 343–4.
[6] *Ibid.*, p. 278.

backs." All group feeling is gone, and without it there is no impetus to risk life for the dynasty. Mercenaries are hired but are not able to defend the royal house. The fourth generation sees the final destruction of the dynasty. A provincial family takes over the royal power, or a foreign force invades and conquers. The new dynasty will undergo the same pattern of change.[7]

Elsewhere, Ibn Khaldun adds another stage. The last stage is now the fifth and is preceded by a period of "resting on one's oars," during which the ruler is "content with what his predecessors have built."[8] The addition does not change the pattern much, but it is significant because it permits the theory to avoid too much dependence on the seasonal analogy. The pattern of cultural change is independent of the pattern of seasonal change, though it is similar to it.

To avert any misconception on this point, Ibn Khaldun gives a reason why any dynasty (or civilization) must decline. "Sedentary culture is the goal of civilization," he says. But sedentary culture also means "the end of its life span and brings about its corruption."[9] The two propositions taken together show that the rise and fall of dynasties is determined by what they are. The cause of decline is in human nature, not in the stars. Hence, Ibn Khaldun is a true anthropogenic cyclist. In his view, the cosmos has little or nothing to do with the pattern of history.[10]

Spengler's cyclical theory has several elements in common with Ibn Khaldun's. For both men, cultures (Spengler) or civilizations (Ibn Khaldun) are similar to organisms and are subject to a pattern of growth and decay.[11] For both, though they speak occasionally of the childhood, youth, and maturity of cultures, the favored analogue is the seasons. And for both, permanent progress appears to be impossible. Neither sees any kind of pattern of advance superimposed on the cyclical pattern of growth and decline, as Sorokin and Toynbee seem to do.[12]

According to Spengler, each culture has a life-span of about a thousand years. Within this life-span, each stage—childhood-spring, youth-summer, maturity-autumn, and old age–winter—must occur, and in that order. For

[7] For a summary description of the four stages, see *ibid.*, pp. 342–6. They are discussed extensively throughout the work.

[8] *Ibid.*, p. 354.

[9] *Ibid.*, Vol. II, p. 291.

[10] The two propositions taken together satisfy Aristotle's demand in the *Politics* for a cause of decay that is specific to the situation in question (see Chapter 11, Note 43). Ibn Khaldun knew Aristotle well and often cites him as an authority.

[11] Spengler may actually conceive of cultures as living things.

[12] In other words, Spengler's and Ibn Khaldun's cyclical theories are not convertible into spiral theories.

a culture is an organic macrocosm, "a superlative human organism," with its own distinctive personality or style. Each culture, too, has an instinctive goal: the concrete expression of its style or soul in all possible forms. This distinctive goal is termed the Destiny-idea.[13]

The childhood or spring of a culture is marked by an awakening of religious consciousness, by "god-feeling," "world-fear," and "world-longing." Poetry and myth are characteristic of this age, as they are of the childish mind.[14] Such characteristics find expression in all culture forms: in art, in philosophy, in politico-economic organization, and so forth.

In the summer of a culture, a critical spirit awakes, bringing reformations in religion (*e.g.*, Luther and Calvin in Western culture), in philosophy (*e.g.*, the Ionians and Eleatics in Classical culture), in art (*e.g.*, the Islamic-Moorish style in Arabian culture), and in other areas. In the politico-economic sphere, city life begins.

The autumn of a culture sees its full maturity. There is an age of enlightenment; the "zenith of strict intellectual creativeness" is attained. Religion is rationalized. Cities become dominant.

Winter is marked by the triumph of the megalopolis. In the great cities the people degenerate into "masses" that are not, however, held together by any human bond. In the midst of crowds, individuals feel themselves alone.[15] Religion declines and skepticism invades philosophy. Everywhere there is disillusion and "world-weariness." The outlook is materialistic; the age is imbued with the "cult of science, utility, and prosperity." The dominant political form is imperialism, called by Spengler Caesarism. The culture has now reached the end of its life cycle.[16]

Cultures are formally the same but differ in details; they are differentiated by the meaning they "intuitively" attach to the concept of time.[17] But the "prime symbol" of a culture is its space-form, its "kind of extension."[18] Art is in general the expression of a culture's style. A cycle of art

[13] *The Decline of the West*, Vol. I, p. 346. Spengler mainly emphasizes three cultures—the Classical, the Arabian, and the Western. The styles of the three cultures are termed, respectively, Apollinian, Magian, and Faustian.

[14] This point is also made by many progress authors, for example, Comte, Hegel, and Piaget.

[15] Cf. Vico on this point; see below, p. 170, and Note 46.

[16] This description of Spengler's scheme is largely drawn from his "Tables Illustrating the Comparative Morphology of History," at the end of the first volume of *The Decline of the West*.

[17] The conception of time is related to the possibility of tragedy; "consequently 'tragedy' of the grand order has only developed in the Culture which has most passionately affirmed, and in that which has most passionately denied Time" (Vol. I, p. 130). The former is the Classical; the latter, the Western.

[18] Classical culture, which affirms Time, also affirms Space; the Apollinian culture-soul experiences depth as finite, sensuous, concrete. Sculpture is its characteristic plastic art form. The Faustian soul "stretches out into infinite time and infinite space"; indeed, infinite space is its prime symbol; this is expressible satisfactorily only in music. Hence the "real heir" of Michelangelo is Palestrina (see *ibid.*, p. 277).

tells the story of a culture, and the examination of the art of a culture gives an insight into its soul or Destiny-idea. Thus Spengler is able to distinguish cultures even by such a detail as the favored colors of their painters.[19]

The Decline of the West provides similarly detailed analyses of drama, architecture, and music. In the politico-economic order, Spengler finds all cultures divided into peasantry and society. The peasantry is relatively historyless; the society is class-structured and carries the burden of the culture's history.[20] Characteristic of the first stage of a culture is patriarchism or feudalism; the dominant classes are the nobles and the priests. Later arise towns and cities, and a third class, the *bourgeoisie*, comes into being. It originates in protest against the nobles but degenerates into revolution and "Napoleonism." A fourth class is born in winter, or the "stage of Civilization" of a culture; this is the Fourth Estate, the "masses." At first there is political democracy, but this passes to Caesarism, which terminates all.[21] We in the West find ourselves "now" (in 1918) at a late moment of our cycle—

> the moment when money is celebrating its last victories, and the Caesarism that is to succeed approaches with quiet, firm step—[and] our direction, willed and obligatory at once, is set for us within narrow limits. . . . We have not the freedom to reach to this or that, but the freedom to do the necessary or to do nothing. . . . *Ducunt Fata volentem, nolentem trahunt.*[22]

" 'Mankind' . . . has no aim, no idea, no plan, any more than the family of butterflies or orchids," Spengler declares. " 'Mankind' is a zoological expression, or an empty word."[23] Such extreme cultural rela-

---

[19] The typical Classical colors are yellow, red, black, and white. Blue and blue-green are avoided because they give an impression of distance; "they are cold, they disembody, and they evoke impressions of expanse and distance and boundlessness." Yellow and red are colors "of the crowd, of children, of women, and of savages," but blue and green—"Faustian, monotheistic colors—are those of loneliness, of care, of a present that is related to a past and a future, of destiny." Brown is "the unrealest color that there is. It is the one major color that does not exist in the rainbow." But it is the favored color of artists from Giorgione through the great Dutch painters. It "possesses a mightier power over things than the greens of Leonardo's, Shongauer's, and Gruenewald's backgrounds, [and] carries the battle of Space against Matter to a decisive close. It creates an atmosphere of purest spatiality, which enveloped and rendered, no longer body,—the human body as a shape—but the soul unconfined. And thus was attained the inwardness that in the deepest works of Rembrandt and of Beethoven is able to unlock the last secrets of themselves—the inwardness which Apollinian man has sought with his strictly somatic art to keep at bay" (see *ibid.*, pp. 245–50).
[20] *Ibid.*, Vol. II, p. 331.
[21] For an analysis of these classes, see *ibid.*, pp. 327–58.
[22] *Ibid.*, p. 507.
[23] *Ibid.*, Vol. I, p. 21.

tivism is of the essence of Spengler's theory. He sees no buildup or carry-over from one culture to the next. Indeed, this is just the point.

> Every Culture has *its own* Civilization. . . . The Civilization is the inevitable *destiny* of the Culture, and in this principle we obtain the viewpoint from which the deepest and gravest problems of historical morphology become capable of solution. Civilizations are the most external and artificial states of which a species of developed humanity is capable. . . . They are an end, irrevocable, yet by inward necessity reached again and again.[24]

Hence each culture is complete in itself, and enjoys—or suffers—its own necessities. And it is distinct from every other. Only the form of cultures persists; that form does not, and cannot, change. But all of the concrete elements—persons, things, ideas—disappear.[25]

In a sense, Brooks Adams' view is even darker than Spengler's. Spengler at least affirms that there will be a future, even if it will involve the total "going under" of the West. Adams has no such hope. According to him, the current regressive phase is the end of the last cycle of man's history.

Adams' theory is based, he says, "upon the accepted scientific principle that the law of force and energy is of universal application in nature, and that animal life is one of the outlets through which solar energy is dissipated."[26] In short, the second law of thermodynamics applies to history.[27]

> Starting from this fundamental proposition, the first deduction is, that, as human societies are forms of animal life, these societies must differ among themselves in energy, in proportion as nature has endowed them, more or less abundantly, with energetic material.
>
> Thought is one of the manifestations of human energy, and among the earlier and simpler phases of thought, two stand conspicuous—Fear and Greed. Fear, which by stimulating the imagination, creates a belief in an

---

24 *Ibid.*, p. 31.

25 The Pythagoreans, with their conception of exactly repeating cycles of history; Plato and Empedocles and Aristotle, with their idea of a cosmic motion, no matter how distant, somehow determining events; even Machiavelli, with his cold and passionless figure of Fortuna—for all of these there is some kind of world order, some Logos, some being that endures beneath "the wilderness of changes." Only the Epicureans, with their conception of an elemental universe ruled by chance, seem to approach the degree of relativeness, the lack of any permanence, of Spengler. The Epicureans, however, posit the lasting value (it is a paradox of their system) of certain moral habits. Spengler does not concede even this.

26 *The Law of Civilization and Decay*, pp. 5–6.

27 The application of this law to history usually results in a regress theory; see Chapter 10. Most of the authors who make the application see the final results of entropy as occurring far in the future. Adams appears to be alone in holding that they have already (in 1900) occurred, or are about to occur.

invisible world, and ultimately develops a priesthood; and Greed, which dissipates energy in war and trade.[28]

Fear is dominant at first, but as consolidation advances, fear yields to greed, and the economic organism tends to supersede the emotional and martial. As a result, a surplus may be stored in the shape of wealth. Economic organization is radically different from emotional and martial, and the effect of economic competition has been, perhaps invariably, to dissipate the energy massed by war.

The tendency of human organizations is toward unification, says Adams.

Probably the velocity of the social movement of any community is proportionate to its energy and mass, and its centralization is proportionate to its velocity; therefore, as human movement is accelerated, societies centralize.[29]

A result of this is that wealth tends to accumulate and becomes the controlling social force. Capital becomes autocratic, and "in this last stage of consolidation, the economic, and, perhaps, the scientific intellect is propagated, while the imagination fades, and the emotional, the martial, and the artistic types of manhood decay."[30] Lost energy no longer reproduces itself, and two "extreme economic types" are developed: the usurer and the peasant.

At length a point must be reached when pressure can go no further, and then, perhaps, one of two results may follow: A stationary period may supervene, which may last until ended by war, by exhaustion, or by both combined, as seems to have been the case with the Eastern Empire; or, as in the Western, disintegration may set in, the civilized population may perish, and a reversion may take place to the primitive form of organism.[31]

The cause of decline and degeneration is clearly stated. A "highly centralized society disintegrates . . . because the energy of the race has been exhausted." The survivors lack the power to resuscitate themselves and to concentrate anew, and must remain "inert until supplied with fresh energetic material by the infusion of barbarian blood."[32]

This is Adams' argument; the main part of his book consists of analyses of various historical epochs, which show that the theory applies. Examples

[28] *Ibid.*, p. 6.
[29] *Ibid.*
[30] *Ibid.* Cf. Ibn Khaldun on this point, which comes close to being a commonplace for anthropogenic cyclists. However, some *progress* authors share the opinion that mankind moves from a condition in which art dominates life to one in which science and wealth are sovereign.
[31] *Ibid.*, pp. 6–7.
[32] *Ibid.*, p. 7. The supply of barbarian blood is, however, not infinite, which gives Adams' theory its unique place in the literature; for when there are no more barbarians, the cycle cannot begin again.

are taken from the history of political and economic institutions, from
the history of art (including the coinage—a degenerate coinage is a sign
of a degenerate society), from the history of warfare, of morals, and of
philosophy.

Analyses of such matters are customary for cyclists. But Adams concludes as no other anthropogenic cyclist does. Something is now lacking
that has always before been present, he declares. He writes:

> No poetry can bloom in the arid modern soil, the drama has died, and the
> patrons of art are no longer even conscious of shame at profaning the most
> sacred of ideals. The ecstatic dream, which some twelfth-century monk cut
> into the stones of the sanctuary hallowed by the presence of his God, is
> reproduced to bedizen a warehouse; or the plan of an abbey, which Saint
> Hugh may have consecrated, is adapted to a railway station.[33]

This sort of criticism of "the modern temper" is common enough among
the authors being treated in this chapter. But Adams goes on:

> Decade by decade, for some four hundred years, these phenomena have
> grown more sharply marked in Europe, and, as consolidation apparently
> nears its climax, art seems to presage approaching disintegration. The archi-
> tecture, the sculpture, and the coinage of London at the close of the nine-
> teenth century, when compared with those of the Paris of Saint Louis,
> recall the Rome of Caracalla as contrasted with the Athens of Pericles,
> *save that we lack the stream of barbarian blood which made the Middle
> Age.*[34]

Ibn Khaldun, Spengler, and Adams agree that the first phase in a
cycle is marked by "imagination," "awe," "superstitious fear," or some
such characteristic; they agree, too, that this aids in the creation of a
priesthood or priestly class.[35] But they do not carry this a step further
and suggest that a certain type of religious feeling—which may differ from
one culture or civilization to another—is the key to the cycle, and gives
it its particular style or tone.[36]

Ernest von Lasaulx[37] applies the classical theory of historical cycles, as

[33] *Ibid.*, p. 308.

[34] *Ibid.* Emphasis added.

[35] In the case of Ibn Khaldun, the characteristic feeling at the beginning of
dynasties expresses itself in art and a hunger for glory rather than in religion or
superstition. Nevertheless, he appears to be describing much the same feeling.

[36] Spengler holds that each culture has a style, but this is given mainly by its
art, not its religious beliefs.

[37] Lasaulx (1805–61) was a German archaeologist and philosopher. He was the
author of several books on the history of the fine arts and on other subjects, none of
which seems to be available in English. We depend in the following on an account of his theory by James Nichols, the editor of Burckhardt's *Force and Freedom* (*q.v.*, pp. 59–60). Burckhardt often ridiculed Lasaulx's ideas, which he considered absurd.

found in Plato, Aristotle, Polybius, and others, to the demonstration of the West's decline. Every people is allotted, according to his theory, a determinate quota or portion of vital energy,[38] which they live out much as plants do, passing through stages of childhood, youth, maturity, old age, and death. The cycle is about two thousand years in duration, and always follows the Platonic or Aristotelian sequence of types of government, from monarchy and aristocracy, and through democracy to final military despotism. The development of the arts and sciences also follows a regular pattern in every case.

However, the cyclical change of cultures is described by Lasaulx in terms of their orderly "emancipation" from the religious cult that in every case gives them birth. Each people—each cycle—has a "religious core." And this is the key to the cycle, for, after it creates, inevitably, a secular culture, the religious core is always attacked by rationalism and skepticism. Its native vigor is lost, and the civilization which it created becomes a mighty framework without the belief and sense of duty that alone could maintain it. At this point—sooner or later—barbarian invaders find conquest easy, and the cycle begins anew.

Despite its obvious similarities to the theories already discussed, Lasaulx's scheme is different in several respects. For Ibn Khaldun and Adams, the cause of degeneration is wealth or success; these, which are in some sense the necessary goals of any culture, also bring about the culture's downfall. Lasaulx does not share this view. Spengler seems to agree with Lasaulx, but he really does not. According to Spengler, the conflict between a "religious core" and the secular culture which it helps to bring into being is only one of the *signs* of decline, and is not the cause of it. For Lasaulx, the pattern is simple enough. A culture is born at the same time that a new religious insight is gained by a people. They are unified by the insight, and given strength by it. But their very success in promulgating the insight—its infusion, for example, into institutions —is the cause of ultimate decay.

A question remains that Lasaulx does not appear to answer. Is it possible to compare the religious cores of various cultures? Can one be said to be better than another? Do the later ones build on the ones that went before? If so, then progress of a sort, outside and beyond the cultural cycles that set the pattern for secular life, might be conceivable.

Vico agrees with Lasaulx, and differs with Spengler, in proposing a theory of historical cycles on which might be superimposed a linear pattern of progress in religion. Vico does not clearly assert that such religious

[38] This seems to be a classical notion—cf. Polybius on the point. It is not the notion of Brooks Adams.

progress occurs, but the possibility is obviously there in his theory, as it is not in Spengler's, and as it is only faintly in Lasaulx's. In some later developments of anthropogenic cyclism—*e.g.*, in the theories of Sorokin and Toynbee—this possibility becomes an actuality.

Vico does not fail to make use of the seasonal analogy when speaking of the various stages of culture, but he prefers, and emphasizes, the analogy to the life of an individual man. Thus he speaks of the childhood, adolescence, and maturity of cultures, and calls these, respectively, the Age of Gods, of Heroes, and of Men.[39]

As with the other anthropogenic cyclists, the first stage is marked by fable and myth, and by a condition of religious fear and awe. A primitive morality is born, and the first form of social organization—the family—is developed. The birth of language is associated with myth; poetry is more ancient than prose. Reason is weak, imagination strong. Rule is by one—the father-despot—who has the power of life and death over the members of his "family."

In the Age of Heroes, government is by the few. An aristocracy is established by force—the might of men such as Achilles. Language is symbolic and metaphorical, as in Homer. The characteristic social organization at this epoch is feudal, but cities begin to appear. This age also sees the birth of trade, commerce, and war. In the first age, law was oracular; now it is "what the Roman juriconsults called civil equity and we call reason of state."

> And if, as a consequence of this equity, the laws turned out in a given case to be not harsh but actually cruel they naturally bore it because they thought their law was naturally such. Furthermore they were led to observe their laws by their own highest interest, with which, we find, the heroes identified that of their fatherlands, of which they were the only citizens.[40]

In the heroic age, the natural law of force reigned supreme, and people looked upon each other as perpetual enemies, and pillage and piracy were continual because, as war was eternal between them, there was no need of declaration. In this regard, Vico compares the first Age of Heroes (that of Achilles) to the second (that of feudalism in Europe).

> There was a return of heroic raids. As the heroes had counted it an honor to be called robbers, so now it was a title of nobility to be a corsair.[41]

The Age of Men began in Greece with the Seven Sages; in Rome, with the fall of Carthage. It is an age of humanism that corresponds to Ibn

[39] *The New Science*, p. 5, and *passim*.
[40] *Ibid.*, p. 7.
[41] *Ibid.*, p. 353.

Khaldun's sedentary culture and to Spengler's Civilization. All men consider themselves equal in human nature, and, therefore, are established "first the popular commonwealths and then the monarchies, both of which are forms of human government."[42] Written language is developed, and law is based on equity and truth. Judgments are "ordinary" and are based on the "merits of the case," as opposed to the divine judgments and judgments based on force of the earlier stages. Reason thrives, and self-conscious philosophies are developed. Theories are proposed of external nature and of human and social nature.

The Age of Men is divided into two phases: the era of the free popular commonwealth (*e.g.*, the republics of Greece, Rome, and Florence), and the era of monarchy (*e.g.*, the empires of Alexander and Augustus, and the kingdoms of France, Britain, and Spain). In the earlier phase, men devote their energy to the attainment of private ends, public affairs are forgotten, the republic decays, and soon a central monarchy is the only solution. It is inevitable, says Vico—"an eternal natural royal law"—that "nations come to rest under monarchies." This is, he declares, "the form of government best adapted to human nature when reason is fully developed."[43]

In the Age of Men, first, many rule, then all, and finally one.[44] But the last now governs on a higher level than in the first age; he is no longer merely a father-despot; his domain is absolute and includes the whole of society, and pervades the spiritual as well as the secular realm. However, monarchy is not the final solution. It is a palliative for the civil disorder that follows the breakdown of the commonwealth, but monarchic states are neither lasting nor secure. They become decadent, and the nation is either conquered by another or becomes subject to the "extreme remedy."

> But if the peoples are rotting in this last civil illness and cannot agree upon a monarch from within, and are not conquered and preserved by better nations from without, then providence[45] for their extreme ill has its extreme

[42] *Ibid.*, p. 3. Vico follows the traditional sequence, after Plato, Aristotle, and Polybius.

[43] *Ibid.*, p. 334.

[44] We may be reminded of Hegel's sequence in which one, then a few, then all are free—a sequence that ends, as does Vico's, in monarchy. However, Hegel's pattern is progressive; the final monarchy is the highest state for man, and it endures, there being no cyclical return to a lower and less desirable condition.

[45] It is difficult to discover what "providence" is in Vico's story. Sometimes the term seems to stand simply for the "law" of cyclical evolution; at other times, for a directing Power and Will. Nevertheless, Vico's theory appears to be primarily, if not exclusively, anthropogenic. Men themselves bring about the changes that occur in history.

remedy at hand. For such peoples, like so many beasts, have fallen into the custom of each man thinking only of his own private interests and have reached the extreme of delicacy, or better of pride, in which like wild animals they bristle and lash out at the slightest displeasure. Thus in the midst of their greatest festivities, though physically thronging together, they live like wild beasts in a deep solitude of spirit and will, scarcely any two being able to agree since each follows his own pleasure or caprice.[46] By reason of all this, providence declares that, through obstinate factions and desperate civil wars, they shall turn their cities into forests and the forests into dens and lairs of men.[47] In this way, through long centuries of barbarism, rust will consume the misbegotten subtleties of malicious wits, that have turned them into beasts made more inhuman by the barbarism of reflection[48] than the first men had been made by the barbarism of sense. . . . Peoples who have reached this point of premeditated malice, when they receive this last remedy of providence and are thereby stunned and brutalized, are sensible no longer of comforts, delicacies, pleasures and pomp, but only of the sheer necessities of life. And the few survivors in the midst of the abundance of the things necessary for life naturally [49] become well behaved and, returning to the primitive simplicity of the first world of peoples, are again religious, truthful, and faithful.[50]

After all of this, the cycle begins anew, there is a new Age of Gods, and civilization develops once more. But this too must inevitably decay.

It has been noted that Vico's idea of "providence" is complex, perhaps even contradictory. Providence works, according to him, in mysterious ways.

This world without doubt has issued from a mind often diverse, at times quite contrary, and always superior to the particular ends that men have proposed to themselves; which narrow ends, made means to serve wider ends, it has always employed to preserve the human race on earth.[51]

Thus men mean to gratify lust and to abandon their offspring, but instead they establish the chastity of marriage, and from this the family

[46] This description is remarkably similar to Spengler's, written some 250 years later; see Note 15. Vico seems to be speaking here of a phenomenon often discussed by modern authors, and called by them "alienation" or some such term.

[47] In a modern formulation, "grass will grow in the streets of a hundred cities." The similarity between this description and Mandeville's vision of the conditions of life if all men were virtuous is striking; but Mandeville, of course, is a progress author.

[48] This seems to be an attack, not dissimilar to Lasaulx's and Spengler's, on the "rationalism" and "skepticism" that are said to invade religion and philosophy toward the end of a cultural cycle.

[49] The operations of "nature" in Vico's scheme are also obscure. Is nature the equivalent of providence at this juncture?

[50] *Ibid.,* p. 381.

[51] *Ibid.,* p. 382.

is born. Fathers intend to exercise paternal power without restraint over their *clientes,* but, instead, subject them to the civil powers from which cities arise. The nobles mean to abuse their lordly freedom over the plebeians, but are instead obliged to submit to the laws that establish popular liberty. Free peoples intend to shake off the yoke of these laws, but, instead, become subject to monarchs. Monarchs mean to strengthen their position by debasing their subjects with the vices of dissoluteness, but end up, instead, by exposing them to enduring slavery at the hands of other nations. The nations, desperate and confused, mean to "dissolve themselves, and their remnants flee for safety to the wilderness, whence, like the phoenix they rise again."[52]

The cycles are determined; man is a pawn; he knows not what he does, nor what the future brings. Such is the view of any anthropogenic cyclist. But Vico is here offering more. The cycles are a means, it seems, to the preservation of the race. Growth and decay are equally preservative, that much is clear. But if there is such care for man, why is not progress of a sort to be expected, and not this weary circling? Indeed, since Vico's pattern is merely formal, and the same events do not recur, the possibility of progress exists; and Vico does not actually deny that it might occur. It appears that he does not oppose—though he has many opportunities to do so—the widely held opinion of his time that his own Age of Men was built on the ruins of the corresponding era in the classical world, and contained significant elements of it. In particular, he does not deny the claim of an author such as Augustine, that at least one great religious awakening, that which inaugurated the Christian era, had lasting and beneficial effects.[53] He does not, however, offer an explicit theory of progress in religion. It remains for authors like Sorokin and Toynbee to make explicit what is implicit in Vico's thought.

Sorokin's theory has many elements in common with those already treated.[54] Each cycle has three "movements": the ideational, the idealistic, and the sensate. The first is religious and "superrational"; it develops into an idealistic phase which is a combination of the ideational and the sensate, or empirical; this in turn develops into a purely empirical phase. The last epoch in a cycle is characterized by the dominance of empirical, sensuous, and secular elements in all areas of life.

[52] *Ibid.,* pp. 382–3.
[53] Vico here reveals the difficulty in which any believing Christian who supports a true cyclical theory must find himself.
[54] Sorokin's theory is argued extensively in his four-volume *Social and Cultural Dynamics* and sketched in *The Crisis of Our Age,* on which we draw in the following.

The major principle of medieval culture made it predominantly other-worldly and religious, oriented toward the supersensuous and permeated by this value. The major principle of the idealistic culture was partly super-sensory and partly 'thisworldly' and secular. Finally, the major principle of our modern sensate culture is predominantly 'thisworldly', secular, and utilitarian. All these types—ideational, idealistic, and sensate—are exempli-fied in the history of Egyptian and Babylonian, Graeco-Roman, Hindu, Chinese, and other great cultures.[55]

The essential element in Sorokin's theory is his notion of a rhythmic pattern of history, a "creative 'eternal cycle' [that] will persist, as long as human history endures."[56] But while asserting that this formal pattern will always be followed, he holds that one similarly patterned culture can build on another, even though all is done in a new way and, perhaps, for what appear to be new reasons. He suggests that the "new style" for the cultural cycle that he sees as dawning in our own time must have as its basis "creative altruism." He maintains that the transfiguration of man—at least of some men—is essential if civilization is to endure. He seems to differ with Vico, and certainly differs with Ibn Khaldun and Spengler, in hinting that such a change is possible.

According to Toynbee, there are four phases or stages in a cycle: first, challenge and response; second, the growth of civilizations; third, the breakdown of civilizations; and fourth, the disintegration of civilizations. In the first stage, man is challenged out of the Yin condition of sloth into the Yang condition of creative activity.[57] Some civilizations arise out of the primitive, some out of the ruins of earlier civilizations; in either case, a creative minority, or "internal proletariat," develops a new religious idea round which others rally, and a new civilization is born.[58] In the second stage, further challenges from the physical and social en-vironment are met creatively. For instance, the new civilization may move

[55] *The Crisis of Our Age*, p. 21. Sorokin's theory resembles Hegel's theory of progress, but is even more like Comte's. For Hegel, however, the third stage is a synthesis of the two earlier ones, and is furthermore enduring; for Comte, there is a continuous advance as civilization develops through the theological, metaphysical, and positive stages. Thus, where Sorokin merely concedes the possibility of progress, Hegel and Comte see it as inherent in the pattern. Sorokin therefore remains a cyclist, at least in part.

[56] *Ibid.*, p. 132.

[57] The agent of this first change of condition seems to be God, who thereby brings about further creation. This is not enough, however, to call Toynbee a cosmogenic cyclist.

[58] The similarities between Toynbee and Lasaulx are many and striking, and may not have been previously noted. Lasaulx is not mentioned by Toynbee in *A Study of History*.

to "new ground" as the result of persecution, overcome "blows" (*e.g.*, the blows dealt Athens by Persia), or withstand continuing pressure of some sort (*e.g.*, the pressure of the Danes on the French and English in the eighth and ninth centuries A.D.).

The criterion of growth, which is characteristic of the second stage, is not expansion (though this may occur), but "progress toward self-determination; and progress toward self-determination is a prosaic formula for describing the miracle by which Life enters into its Kingdom."[59] In the third stage, the breakdown of civilizations is caused by the "loss of self-determination." This results in schism of the body social; the creative minority becomes dominant, and the proletariat secedes. This occurs in many ways.

In the fourth stage disintegration is brought on by "a time of troubles"; this is followed by a universal state;[60] and this by an interregnum or by petrifaction. In the latter event a civilization may endure for a long time (*e.g.*, the Egyptian) or may become a "fossil" (*e.g.*, the Hebraic). In the time of troubles, the body social is split into three groups: the dominant minority (evolved from the creative minority), the internal proletariat, and the external proletariat. The first builds the universal state, the second a universal church,[61] and the third consists of exiles—"barbarian war bands," or guerillas. Eventually, a new civilization arises out of the chaos brought about by this radical division.

Like the other authors who have been treated in this chapter, Toynbee shows how his pattern applies to the history of art, philosophy, science, political and economic arrangements, and so forth—indeed, to every aspect of life. In the sphere of religion, however, he departs even further than Sorokin from his forebears. For he maintains that the "One True God" of the Hebrews, Christians, and Muslims has won the "supreme role" in the "mystery play which has for its plot the revelation of God to man."[62]

Such a statement could have been made by many progress authors. It could not have been made by Spengler or Ibn Khaldun, not to mention Nietzsche, and nothing of the sort is to be found in Vico's writings. The point is that the statement (there are many like it in *A Study of History*) is a clear assertion that some progress—if only in the religious or spiritual realm—has occurred in the past. Toynbee is equally clear that progress —again of this limited sort, perhaps—*may* occur in the future.

Our own civilization is now in the fourth stage, that of disintegration.

---

[59] *A Study of History*, one-volume edition, p. 208.
[60] This seems to be the equivalent of Spengler's Caesarism and of Vico's monarchy.
[61] This may correspond to the secularistic invasion of religion described by Lasaulx and other cyclists.
[62] *Ibid.*, p. 502. *Cf.* Lessing; see Chapter 5.

It is well into its time of troubles and is perhaps on the verge of that last phase in which a universal state and church are opposed by barbarian war bands. Yet it is not *necessarily* doomed. It may also be on the verge of "a wholly new chapter in the history of Mankind."[63] For

> inasmuch as it cannot be supposed that God's nature is less constant than Man's, we may and must pray that a reprieve . . . will not be refused if we ask for it . . . in a humble spirit and with a contrite heart.[64]

In Chapter 7, we considered the two related questions: whether theories of cycles are actually theories of regress in disguise, and whether theories of regress, in turn, are actually theories of contingent progress in disguise. These questions are raised by the fact that almost all theories of regress seem to hold out some faint hope that man can escape the regressive pattern of history *if* certain things are done (or not done), and by the fact that almost all theories of cycles are framed at a time, according to their authors, when man is on the downward swing of a cycle, or indeed at the bottom of one.

These questions become particularly apt when we approach the study of theories of anthropogenic cycles; for the authors of these theories, without exception, see mankind in the regressive phase of a cycle. We may wonder why every anthropogenic cyclist sees his own time as decadent. Why does every one of them, no matter how many stages his theory comprises or how complex it is, assert that his own era or epoch is the last?

---

[63] *Ibid.*, p. 149.

[64] *Ibid.*, p. 554. With this statement, if not before, we see that Toynbee is not a true anthropogenic cyclist. For a pattern of history from which mankind can escape by means of prayer is not a pattern at all, as it is conceived by the authors on whom Toynbee draws. Perhaps a theory of cycles is compatible with the idea of a God or Providence having the power to break or end the cyclical pattern. But Toynbee seems to be saying that man himself can evade or escape the determinate pattern of the past.

Our judgment is that Toynbee is at heart a (contingent) progress author, but all critics do not concur. Geyl, for instance, declares that, according to Toynbee's system, our civilization is irrevocably doomed, and there is no way out for it. "His system," Geyl writes, "lays it down that the civilization which has been overtaken by a breakdown is doomed. Now Toynbee has repeatedly suggested that our Western civilization did suffer a breakdown as long ago as the sixteenth century, and that consequently, try as we may, we cannot avoid disaster. Except in one way, except in case we allow ourselves to be reconverted to the faith of our fathers. And here Toynbee exclaims: 'You see, I am not so gloomy after all.' Perhaps not. But if one happens to hold a different opinion both of the efficacy and of the likelihood of application of this particular remedy, one cannot help thinking that Toynbee is but offering us cold comfort" ("Can We Know the Pattern of the Past?—A Debate," in Gardiner (ed.), *Theories of History*, p. 315).

The latter question appears to have two possible answers. The first is that anthropogenic cycles are not evident to historians except toward their close. When humanity is advancing forward and upward in a cycle, as it must do as often as it moves backward and down, historians cannot see, or have no interest in seeing, that the course of history is determined by laws that will also determine a subsequent descent and degeneration.

If this answer is correct, it seems to raise other difficulties.

The second answer is that theories of anthropogenic cycles are no more than complicated and perhaps subtle ways of charging that one's own time is decadent and corrupt. If this is the correct answer, then anthropogenic cyclical theories are essentially theories of regress, for they merely assert that the present is worse than the past.

The second answer is supported by a marked characteristic of anthropogenic cyclists. These authors tend to place emphasis on past cycles rather than future ones; by and large, they are not of a hopeful disposition. But this would seem to be unexpected. Anthropogenic cyclists agree that at some times, mankind is happy and successful, at other times, unsuccessful and miserable. They also agree that the present is a time of relative misery and unsuccess. Now this ought to mean, in their view, that the future holds much promise for mankind, for things cannot be worse, on the cyclical hypothesis, than they are at the end of a cycle. This ought to mean, in turn, that cyclists are hopeful. For, if the present is a time of misery, their science ought to tell them that the future cannot help but be better. In short they ought to be, *in a limited view*, enthusiastic progress authors!

However, anthropogenic cyclists are usually gloomy and despondent. This paradox may derive from one of two possible circumstances. Either they are gloomy and despondent because they have particular regard for their own epoch and sympathize with its sufferings, even though they know that these will soon be alleviated, or they do not mean what they seem to mean when they say that history is subject to "laws" of growth and decline and subsequent growth. The former circumstance is not in accord with the usual pose of these authors, who often take a very long view of man's career on earth. The latter circumstance leads, of course, to the suspicion that these theories are actually theories of regress in disguise.

The paradoxes and problems raised by these questions cannot be resolved here. However, it seems that the suggestion that was made in Chapter 7 should be seriously considered.[65] This is the suggestion, made it is true with hesitation, that all Western authors (at least since the

[65] See above, pp. 119–121, and Note 11.

seventeenth century) who discuss the entire career of man on earth hold, more or less explicitly, that the pattern of history is at least contingently progressive.

Is there in fact any modern author who flatly and incontrovertibly asserts that the future of man *cannot* be progressive? Is there any modern author who flatly and incontrovertibly asserts that man is *necessarily* doomed to a regressive or a cyclical pattern of history?

II

Cosmogenic Cycles

T H E authors who have theories of cosmogenic cycles are listed below. The list could be expanded by the inclusion of other nineteenth-century followers of Nietzsche.

Pythagoreans	Cicero
Stoics	Lucretius
Plato	Seneca
Aristotle	Florus
Epicurus	Machiavelli
Polybius	Nietzsche

CYCLICAL REPETITION BASED ON REGULAR COSMIC CYCLES

The Pythagoreans, whose views survive only in commentaries, are supposed to have asserted the occurrence of regularly recurrent and repetitive cycles, both in the cosmos and in history. For the Pythagoreans, number was the essence of things. They were impressed with the regularity of celestial motions, and were able to express these in numerical terms. It was not a long step to finding a mathematical relation between celestial phenomena and the seasons and other periodic terrestrial happenings.

Porphyry outlines the theory thus:

> The following became universally known: first, that he [Pythagoras] maintains that the soul is immortal; next, that it changes into other kinds of living things; also that events recur in certain cycles, and that nothing is ever absolutely new; and finally, that all living things should be regarded as akin.[1]

Porphyry does not say here that exactly the same things will recur. This point is, however, made by Eudemus. "If one were to believe the Pythagoreans," he says, "with the result that the same individual things will recur, then I shall be talking to you again sitting as you are now, with this pointer in my hand, and everything else will be just as it is now, and it is reasonable to suppose that the time then is the same as now."[2]

The Ionian thinkers—notably Thales, Anaximander, and Anaximenes —were said by later Stoic commentators and critics to have asserted that exactly repetitious cosmic and celestial cycles occur. This judgment has been called in question.[3] In the case of Heraclitus, there is even more doubt that this difficult thinker held the extreme cyclical position being discussed here. Nevertheless, the Stoics adopted Heraclitus as their intellectual and spiritual forebear. In order to understand their cyclical theory it is desirable to treat Heraclitus' ideas. In common with the other Ionians, Heraclitus was a material monist; the material substratum of the universe was, in his view, fire. Fire gave rise to the other elements; it was also called Logos; in effect, it was ordered change, and it operated in such fashion that there were regular cycles of elemental evolution. All things were made out of fire and returned to it in an *ecpyrosis*, or universal conflagration.[4]

The Stoics took from Heraclitus the notion of fire as Logos, and the notion of the *ecpyrosis*. From the Pythagoreans they are supposed to have taken the idea of the exact repetition of historical events, although some

[1] For this quotation from the *Vita Pythagorae* and for an extended review of Pythagorean ideas on this and associated topics, see Kirk and Raven, *The Pre-Socratic Philosophers*, pp. 223 ff.

[2] *Ibid.*, p. 223.

[3] For a discussion of these Stoic assertions, see *ibid.*, pp. 74 ff.

[4] For a review of Heraclitus' philosophical ideas, see *ibid.*, pp. 182–215, esp. 214–15.

ancient commentators dispute this.[5] Whatever is the truth in this complex intellectual genealogy, the Stoic position is clear. The fifth-century writer Nemesius offers this version of it:

> The Stoics say that the planets will be restored to the same zodiacal sign, both in longitude and latitude, as they had in the beginning when the cosmos was first put together; that in stated periods of time a conflagration [*ecpyrosis*] and destruction of things will be accomplished, and once more there will be a restitution of the cosmos as it was in the very beginning. And when the stars move in the same way as before, each thing which occurred in the previous period will without variation be brought to pass again. For again there will exist Socrates and Plato and every man, with the same friends and fellow citizens, and he will suffer the same fate and will meet with the same experiences and undertake the same deeds. And every city and village and field will be restored. And there will be a complete restoration of the whole, not once only but many times, or rather interminably, and the same things will be restored without end.[6]

The Stoics could wax lyrical about the *ecpyrosis* and the subsequent reconstitution of the world. "A single day will see the burial of all mankind," Seneca declares. "All that the long forbearance of fortune has produced, all that has been reared to eminence, all that is famous and all that is beautiful, great thrones, great nations—all will descend into the same abyss, will be overthrown in one hour." Soon, however,

> the ancient order of things will be recalled. Every living creature will be created afresh. The earth will receive a new man ignorant of sin, born under happier stars. But they, too, will retain their innocence only while they are new. Vice creeps quickly in; virtue is difficult to find; she requires ruler and guide. But vice can be acquired even without a tutor.[7]

Seneca seems to allow for progress of a sort in the arts and even, perhaps, in morality. Philosophy in particular plays a large part in the "progress" of mankind. "Who can doubt," he asks, ". . . that life is the gift of the immortal gods, but that living well is the gift of philosophy?"[8] But such advances as occur are not, and cannot be, permanent. They

---

[5] Eudemus holds that the source of this idea was Pythagoras; the second-century writer Tatianus says that it was Zeno. "Zeno has shown," he says, "that after the *ecpyrosis* these men will be resurrected as they were. And I say that this must imply that Anytus and Meletus will again bring their accusation, and Busiris slay the strangers, and Hercules perform his labors" (qu. in Lovejoy and Boas, *Primitivism and Related Ideas in Antiquity*, p. 84).

[6] Qu. in Lovejoy and Boas, *ibid.*

[7] *Physical Science in the Time of Nero* [*Quaestiones Naturales*], pp. 152, 156.

[8] *Epistulae Morales*, Vol. II, p. 395.

will be utterly annulled by the *ecpyrosis,* and will have to be achieved all over again in the next age of the world.

The Stoics and Pythagoreans held that the recurrent ages are dependent on the regular motions of the heavenly bodies. For instance, Cicero, speaking of the five stars "which are falsely called wandering," writes:

> On their dissimilar movements mathematicians have based what they call the Great Year, which is completed when the sun and moon and the five wandering stars, having accomplished their several courses, have come round again to the same relative positions. How long the revolution takes is a much disputed point, but that it is fixed and definite is a matter of necessity.[9]

There was much disagreement among the ancients as to the exact length of the Great Year. Some held it to be 36,000 solar years, some suggested other figures;[10] sometimes its duration was measured in months or seasons. The important thing is that for these authors (as opposed to the Atomists and Epicureans) the Great Year had a definite length. And when the time is up, as Cicero says,

> the thing which one used to be told Panetius was inclined to doubt, will come to pass, I mean the final conflagration of the whole universe; for when moisture has been exhausted the earth could not be nourished, and there would be no returning stream of air, as its creation would be impossible when the water had all been used up; nothing, therefore, they say, is left except fire as the agency, vivifying and divine, by which the universe should be renewed again, and the same external order called into being.[11]

[9] *De Natura Deorum,* p. 101. Cicero derives comfort from the close relation between celestial and terrestrial events. "The man who is not impressed by this connection between things," he says, "conspiring, as it were, for the safety of the universe, has never, I am quite sure, taken any of these facts into consideration" (p. 135).

[10] See Kirk and Raven, pp. 74–162.

[11] *Op. cit.,* pp. 134–5. The Stoic position as such is probably not held in modern times. But when Auguste Blanqui, for instance, says: "That which I write at this moment in a dungeon in the Fort of the Bull, I have written already, and I shall write it for eternity on the same table, with the same pen, in the same clothes and in the same circumstances. The universe repeats itself to eternity" (*L'Eternité par les astres,* qu. in Dawson, *Progress and Religion,* p. 223), he is taking the position, whether or not he is entirely aware of the cosmogonical tradition lying behind his words. However, Blanqui may be expressing Nietzschean ideas here.

Goethe expressed similar views in conversation with Eckermann. "Men will become more clever and more acute," he declared; "but not better, happier, and stronger in action—or at least only at epochs. I foresee the time when God will have no more joy in them, but will break up everything for a renewed creation. I am certain that everything is planned to this end, and that the time and hour in the distant future for the occurrence of the renovating epoch are already fixed. But a long time will elapse first, and we may still for thousands and thousands of years amuse ourselves on this dear old surface" [Oct. 28, 1828]. The passage, says Bury, is "a plan rejection of perfectibility" (*The Idea of Progress,* p. 259). There is some doubt whether Goethe is saying that he (and Eckermann) will return to talk again.

CYCLICAL REPETITION BASED ON
IRREGULAR COSMIC OCCURRENCES

The authors discussed in the previous section agree on two points: first, that exactly the same historical situations and events, as well as the persons involved in them, recur; and second, that they do so as the result of regular cycles in the cosmos. The Stoic position is perhaps the simplest version. There, an *ecpyrosis* occurs at stated intervals—at the end of each Great Year—whereupon the world is reconstituted precisely as before.

Another group of writers holds with the above that exactly the same events recur, but sees this as the result not of regular cosmic cycles but of chance combinations of natural elements. Hence, though it is certain that a given person or situation will "return eternally" (to use Nietzsche's phrase), it is impossible to predict exactly when the return will occur.

The Epicurean version of this cyclical theory is outlined in Epicurus' *Letter to Herodotus.* "The universe is bodies and space"; the "first-beginnings are indivisible corporeal existences," *i.e.*, atoms, which, in combination with space or void, make up the universe; "moreover, the universe is boundless."

> Furthermore, the infinite is boundless both in the number of the bodies and in the extent of the void. . . . Besides this the indivisible and solid bodies, out of which too the compounds are created and into which they are dissolved, have an incomprehensible number of varieties of shapes. . . . And so in each shape the atoms are quite infinite in number, but their differences of shape are not quite infinite, but only incomprehensible in number.[12]

The size, weight, and shape of the atoms differ; they are continuously in motion; moreover, they "swerve." Hence they impinge on one another and form compounds; and, from time to time, out of the amalgamation of vast numbers of atoms and compounds, a world comes into being. There are many worlds; indeed, there is an infinite number of them.

> For those atoms, which are of such nature that a world could be created out of them or made by them, have not been used up either on one world or on a limited number of worlds, nor again on all the worlds which are alike, or on those which are different from these. So that there nowhere exists an obstacle to the infinite number of worlds.[13]

There is an infinite number of worlds, but each is not unique, for there is not an infinite—only an incomprehensible—number of different

[12] *Letter to Herodotus,* in *The Stoic and Epicurean Philosophers,* p. 4.
[13] *Ibid.,* p. 5.

shapes of the atoms. Hence, among the infinite worlds now in existence, there are some that are exactly like our own. But worlds, like men and all other things, having come into being, will also pass away. In the words of the Epicurean poet Lucretius,

> the walls too of the great world around shall be stormed and fall to decay and crumbling ruin. . . . All things are gradually wasting away and passing to the grave, quite forspent by age and length of days.[14]

There are no bounds to the universe, either in time or space. Hence, in infinite time, our world will recur, exactly as it is now, an infinite number of times.

There is not, however, any definite sequence of worlds. *When* our world will exist again cannot be known; it is a matter for chance to decide; there is not, in short, any sort of cosmic *logos*. And there is room for a kind of progress within the life-span of a given world; Lucretius, in the Fifth Book of *On the Nature of Things*, describes much past progress, and even predicts that, in certain respects, there will be some future progress.[15] But of course the Epicurean theory is, on the whole, a complete denial of progress. The pattern of history is not a line moving ever upward; it is a great half circle, and ends, for this and any other world, at the lowest point, at the point of dissolution; for the universe at large, it shows repeating though irregular cycles and cycles of cycles. Worlds grow and die. But every advance must finally be annulled.

Some of the Epicureans do not place the same emphasis as do the Stoics on the recurrence in exactly the same form of individual persons and situations. One is not certain that the Stoic assertion is not a disguised affirmation of immortality; however, Lucretius, for one, declares that death is the definite and everlasting end for an individual. His words are well known:

> What evil lust of life is this which constrains us with such force to be so mightily troubled in doubts and dangers? A sure term of life is fixed for mortals, and death cannot be shunned, but meet it we must. . . . Quite doubtful it is what fortune the future will carry with it or what change

14 *On the Nature of Things,* II, in *ibid.,* pp. 113–4.

15 This part of Lucretius' poem is an admirable expression of ancient anthropological ideas, including the notion that men have "progressed" from a primitive condition to the one we "now" (*i.e.,* in 40 B.C.) enjoy. In a larger context it is not an affirmation of progress. Nevertheless, Lucretius closes the book with a description of what, in another context, might be called irreversible cumulative change: "Thus time by degrees brings several things forth before men's eyes and reason raises it up into the borders of light; for things must be brought to light one after the other and in due order in the different arts, until these have reached their highest point of development" (p. 80). For a discussion of these anthropological ideas as expressed by the pre-Socratic physicists, see Havelock, *The Liberal Temper in Greek Politics.*

will bring us or what end is at hand. Nor by prolonging life do we take
one title from the time past in death nor can we fret anything away,
whereby we may haply be a less long time in the condition of the dead.
Therefore you may complete as many generations as you please during
your life; none the less however will that everlasting death await you; and
for no less long time will he be no more in being, who beginning with
to-day has ended his life, than the man who has died many months and
years ago.[16]

In other words, although Lucretius agrees with the Stoics that exactly
the same world as our own will recur again and again (and may even be
in existence now in some other part of the universe), he does not hold
the same notion of the recreation or reincarnation of individual persons
with, presumably, the same thoughts, desires, and perhaps even memories.[17]

Nietzsche takes the more traditional Epicurean view. His argument,
though it is based, he says, on the discoveries of nineteenth-century
physics, is similar to that of the first-century *Letter to Herodotus*. The
principle of the conservation of energy indicates, Nietzsche declares, that
the amount of matter or energy in the universe is constant, and that,
consequently, there is a vast but not infinite number of what he calls
"power quanta." From these are made up all things, including worlds,
but since the elements are finite in number, their configurations, no matter
how complex, must be repeated if enough time is available. There is, in
fact, an infinite amount of time available, for there is no beginning nor is
there any end of the universe.[18] It follows that

This life, as thou livest it now, as thou hast lived it, thou needst must live
again, and an infinite number of times; and there will be in it nothing new;
but every grief and every joy, every thought and every sigh, all the infinitely great and the infinitely little in thy life must return for thee, and
all this in the same sequence and the same order. And also this spider and
the moonlight through the trees, and also this moment and myself. The

[16] *On the Nature of Things*, III, in *ibid.*, p. 136.
[17] The Epicureans' primary concern was with ethics, which may explain why
they did not always carry out their physical theories to their ultimate conclusion.
[18] For Nietzsche's scientific speculations see his *Complete Works*, Levy (ed.), Vol.
XVI. With respect to the possibility of an end to the universe, Nietzsche argues: If
energy could attain a state of equilibrium it would be possible for a last combination
to occur. But this is impossible, for if it were possible then it would already (in infinite time) have happened. In that event the present world would not exist, for a
state of equilibrium would, by definition, persist. But the present world, which
patently, is not in a state of equilibrium, *does* exist.
Nietzsche's attitude toward the idea of progress is summed up in *Antichrist*,
Sect. 4, where he writes: Progress is "merely a modern idea, that is, a false idea."

eternal hour-glass of existence will ever be turned again, and thou with it, dust of dust.[19]

With respect to the question whether the individual returns with exactly the same thoughts, feelings, memories, and so forth—whether, in short, there is a kind of interrupted immortality—Nietzsche is quite explicit. He has Zarathustra say:

Now do I die and disappear. . . . In a moment I am nothing. Souls are as mortal as bodies.[20]

But the plexus of causes returneth in which I am intertwined,—and it will again create me! I myself pertain to the causes of the eternal return.

I come again with this sun, with this earth, with this eagle, with this serpent—*not* to a new life, or a better life, or a similar life:

—I come again eternally to this identical and selfsame life, in its greatest and its smallest, to teach again the eternal return of all things,—

—To speak again the word of the great noontide of earth and man, to announce again to man the Superman.[21]

Nietzsche supports his argument with analogies from physics. "Space like matter is a subjective form, time is not," he writes. "The notion of space first arose from the assumption that space should be empty. But there is no such thing as empty space. Everything is energy."[22] Finite energy quanta, in infinite time, produce, as we have seen, the eternal return. All possible combinations of quanta must recur an infinite number of times. It is not, however, possible, since the combinations are owing wholly to chance, to estimate the amount of time between any two recurrences. The time might be short; usually, however, it would be very long.

The difference between the Stoic and Epicurean-Nietzschean theories is as important as the similarity. They share the notion of the recurrence

19 *The Joyful Wisdom*, No. 341, qu. in Dawson, *Progress and Religion*, p. 223.

20 One of the main points of Lucretius' third book is that the soul is as mortal as the body. The fact that he concurs with Nietzsche on this point, and that Nietzsche is able, nevertheless, to assert that we will return in another world in exactly the same physical and intellectual form, raises the question whether this is not Lucretius' position as well. Indeed it may be so; the Latin poet may be affirming the finality of death in this world, but not affirming it for the entire career of the universe at large. In that case, the final death of an individual would occur many times over in exactly the same way.

21 *Thus Spake Zarathustra*, LVII, "The Convalescent," p. 226. It seems (from experience) that the returned soul does not recall having been in existence before.

22 *Complete Works*, Vol. XVI, p. 240; qu. in Cairns, *Philosophies of History*, p. 227.

of exactly the same persons and situations; but they depart from one another on the question of what brings about this recurrence. The Stoics hold that the alternate creations and destructions of the world—which is, for them, unique—depend on celestial phenomena; the period of the Great Year is usually the ruling consideration. The Epicureans maintain that there are infinite coexisting worlds;[23] and they conceive the endless cycles of worlds as happening entirely according to chance, and not according to any comprehensible pattern or design. Hence in one sense they have no idea of a "pattern of history"; the moment when you or I will be reborn cannot be determined. In another sense they do, of course, have such an idea; for *that* we will be reborn they can confidently predict.

CYCLES OF HISTORY BASED ON REGULAR COSMIC CYCLES

We turn now to the most widely held of Western cosmogenic cyclical theories—the theory that some sort of historical cyclism (but *not* the exact repetition of situations and persons) is based on more or less well-discerned cyclical changes in the cosmos.

Plato's theory of cosmogenic cycles is based on the conception of the world as turning upon itself. The Great or Perfect Year is the interval of time which must elapse before the planets return to the same relative positions. Timaeus describes this:

> There is no difficulty in seeing that the perfect number of time fulfils the perfect year when all the eight revolutions, having their relative degree of swiftness, are accomplished together and attain their completion at the same time, measured by the rotation of the same and equally moving.[24]

[23] The conceit that there are many coexisting worlds that may differ only slightly from our own is a favorite one of contemporary science fiction, which often has agents traveling from one world to another. Sometimes the other worlds are better than our own, sometimes worse. Usually the differences point up undesirable aspects of our own.

The poets have also played with the idea that other worlds exist to which we might escape. E. E. Cummings, for instance, expresses the notion, not uncommon in our day, that the world is "diseased" with progress, and offers a way out:

> pity this busy monster, manunkind,
> not. Progress is a comfortable disease:
> . . . .
> We doctors know
> a hopeless cause if—listen: there's a hell
> of a good universe next door; let's go

[24] *Timaeus*, in *The Dialogues of Plato*, Vol. II, p. 21.

At the end of each Great Year[25] the world is destroyed, but not utterly, for a remnant of mankind is left from which a new world comes into existence. The agent of destruction is sometimes fire (the Heraclitean tradition), sometimes water (the Thalean tradition). If the world is burned, "those who live upon the mountains and in dry and lofty places are more liable to destruction than those who dwell by rivers or on the seashore."[26] If the world is drowned, "the survivors . . . are herdsmen and shepherds who dwell on the mountains, but those . . . living in cities are carried by the rivers into the sea."[27]

In the *Timaeus*, Critias relates Solon's tale of a great disaster that befell the Athenians some 9,000 years before: all save a remnant were destoyed in a great flood. Solon was told, says Critias, that

> there have been, and will be again, many destructions of mankind arising out of many causes; the greatest have been brought about by the agencies of fire and water, and other lesser ones by innumerable other causes. . . . A great conflagration of things upon the earth . . . recurs after long intervals.[28]

In the *Statesman*, the Eleatic Stranger discourses on the nature of the world's cycles. There is a pattern of three phases or stages. In the first, God is at the helm of the universe; it is an age of bliss. After a time, the universe is let go to run by itself, whereupon it reverses its motion: "this is due to its perfect balance, to its vast size, and to the fact that it turns on the smallest pivot." This reversal

> may be supposed to result in the greatest changes to the human beings who are the inhabitants of the world at the time. . . . There necessarily occurs a great destruction of [animals], which extends also to the life of man; few survivors of the race are left, and those who remain become the subjects of several novel and remarkable phenomena.[29]

Among these phenomena are: the old, instead of dying, become young again; the young become children; and babies dissolve away. Once more

[25] Plato does not here, nor, it seems, in any of the dialogues, tell us exactly how many years make up the Great Year. Scholars differ on the question: some propose 36,000 solar years, others 10,800 solar years (the so-called Heraclitean number); perhaps the majority hold that for Plato, the Great Year had the Perfect Number (10,000) of solar years. For a review of the various theories, see Cairns, *op. cit.*, pp. 207–11.

[26] *Timaeus*, p. 8.

[27] *Ibid.* Cf. *Laws*, III.

[28] *Timaeus, ibid.*

[29] *Statesman*, in *The Dialogues of Plato*, Vol. II, pp. 300–301. The description of the various ages is extremely hard to follow and has baffled many commentators. Grube, for instance, suggests that "there is humour here, but it is rather crabbed," and declares that "there is no need to seek any deep meaning in the details of the story" (*Plato's Thought*, pp. 278–9).

the world is subjected to the shock of reversal. Now a third age begins, one in which God does not, as at first, superintend all human actions. Instead, the World-Creature is made imperishable and immortal, and living beings, including man, imitate it by generating their own species out of themselves.

The third and last phase is our own and shows progress within limits. Men are first miserable, and are then assisted by Prometheus, who gives fire; by Hephaestus and Athene, who give the arts; and by other divinities, from whom is derived all that has helped to frame human life. But the progress symbolized by these gifts is not permanent, for the world will, at the end of the present age, reverse itself again, and all the arts will be lost.

Socrates, in the *Republic*, describes what seems to be the same process as it affects the career of men in states.

> A city which is thus constituted can hardly be shaken; but, seeing that everything which has a beginning, has also an end, will not last forever, but will in time be dissolved. And this is the dissolution:—In plants that grow in the earth, as well as in animals that live on the earth's surface, fertility and sterility of soul and body occur when the circumference of the circles of each are completed, which in short-lived existences pass over a short space, and in long-lived ones over a long space. But to the knowledge of human fecundity and sterility all the wisdom and education of your rulers will not attain; the laws which regulate them will not be discovered by an intelligence which is alloyed with sense.[30]

"And so," Socrates continues, "iron will be mingled with silver, and brass with gold, and hence there will arise dissimilarity and inequality and irregularity, which always and in all places are causes of hatred and war." The ideal aristocratic state will degenerate to a timocracy, this to an oligarchy, this to a democracy, and this to a tyranny. If—or perhaps when —the tyrant is or becomes a philosopher, then the cycle starts again.[31]

Plato's true position on any given matter is always hard to ascertain, but his theory of history may be summed up in some such fashion as this: There are cosmic cycles that repeat at definite intervals; these determine, or at least are closely related to, human cultural cycles, since all living things are part of one great world organism. History shows a cyclic pattern of rise, climax, degeneration, and death or destruction, with a saving remnant beginning the cycle anew. Events and persons do not, however, repeat themselves in identical form, and some cycles reach higher than others. The cause of decline is variously said to be contempt for wisdom,

[30] *Republic*, VIII, in *The Dialogues of Plato*, Vol. I, pp. 803–4.
[31] See *ibid.*, pp. 803–28. Socrates does not point to any inherent cause of degeneration, a failure for which he is criticized by Aristotle. See Note 43, below.

greed, and desire for personal power, on the one hand, and to be in the nature of the case, on the other hand.[32]

Aristotle asks in *On Generation and Corruption:*

> Why do some things manifestly come-to-be in this cyclical fashion (as, *e.g.,* showers and air . . .), while men and animals do not "return upon them-selves" so that the same individual comes-to-be a second time (for though your coming-to-be presupposes your father's, his coming-to-be does not pre-suppose yours)? Why, on the contrary, does this coming-to-be seem to con-stitute a rectilinear sequence?[33]

The answer is that all things do not "return upon themselves" in the same way. "In some sequences what recurs is *numerically* the same, in other sequences it is the same *only in species.*" Those things whose substance is imperishable will be "numerically, as well as specifically, the same in their recurrence." And those things whose substance—"that which is un-dergoing the process"—itself comes-to-be will recur specifically but not numerically.[34]

For Aristotle, the world as a whole is imperishable,[35] but it is not changeless. On the contrary, it moves; its fundamental motion is circular; it turns upon itself, or around itself. Hence the world's sequential motions are "numerically" the same, *i.e.,* exactly repetitive. The circular motion of the world also gives rise to cyclical recurrences in things whose subject is not imperishable.[36] Hence these things—animals, men, ideas, institu-tions, and the like—do not recur exactly but only formally ("specifically"). History repeats itself in general but not in detail.

In the *Meteorology,* Aristotle speaks of a "great year," in the "great win-

---

[32] Passages from other dialogues throw some light on Plato's views. In the *Protagoras,* this philosopher discourses on the myth of Prometheus and Epimetheus. In the unfinished *Critias* is related a story about the ancient Athenians and the Atlantides that is at the same time an analogue of the war between Sparta and Athens and a description of the golden age. And in the *Laws,* the Athenian Stranger expands on the description of the cultural and political cycles discussed in the *Republic.* But Plato's expressions of his theory never fail to be infused with myth.

For a treatment of the relation between Plato's cyclical theory and that of the pre-Socratic anthropologists, who are held by Havelock to have affirmed progress, see the latter's *Liberal Temper in Greek Politics.*

[33] *On Generation and Corruption,* II, 11, in *The Works of Aristotle,* Vol. II, 338b.

[34] *Ibid.*

[35] Aristotle opposes Empedocles and Heraclitus on this point, showing that what they consider to be successive creations and destructions of distinct worlds are really only different orders or dispositions of a single, continuing world. Cf. *On the Heavens,* I, 10.

[36] Cf. *On Generation and Corruption,* II, 10–11.

ter" of which there is excessive rain.[37] However, this does not seem to be the same conception as that held by Plato and the Stoics. A modern meteorologist might well subscribe to this notion of a "great" meterological year.[38] In *On Generation and Corruption*, Aristotle declares that there is "an Order controlling all things, and every time (*i.e.*, every life) is measured by a period."[39] But this does not mean that the life of a man and of a state and the duration of civilizations and epochs are measured by a determinate number, as these are for Empedocles and the Pythagoreans. Aristotle is careful to limit his assertion to "living things," by which he means things whose substance is perishable. Such things have what may be termed an average life-span, but the life-span of individuals varies. The world endures, but no man does, nor does any institution.

Human affairs in particular are subject to a cyclical pattern of coming-to-be and passing-away (or birth, death, and rebirth). For instance, in discussing the proposition that the heavenly bodies are gods, Aristotle declares that "we must regard this as an inspired utterance, and reflect that, while probably each art and science has often been developed as far as possible and has again perished, these opinions have been preserved."[40]

Speaking of the organization of states into classes, he says: "It is true indeed that these and many other things have been invented several times over in the course of ages, or rather times without number."[41] And in discussing the eternality of the "primary body," and the primordial knowledge men have had of it, he writes: "The same ideas, one must believe, recur in men's minds not once or twice but again and again."[42]

Although Aristotle holds, in short, that the cosmos changes according to a definite pattern, suffering regular, cyclic change, and that this has an effect on the changes in man's history, he does not hold that the cyclic changes are exact recurrences, or even that they are necessarily periodic. There is no Great Year of the world having a beginning, middle, and end. There is instead a constant coming-to-be and passing-away of things, both living and nonliving, as manifestations of different, and in themselves cyclical, dispositions of the universe as a whole.[43]

---

[37] *Meteorology*, I, 14, in *Works*, Vol. III, 352a.
[38] See below, Note 51.
[39] *On Generation and Corruption*, II, 10, 336b.
[40] *Metaphysics*, XII, 8, in *Works*, Vol. VIII, 1074a.
[41] *Politics*, VII, 10, in *Works*, Vol. X, 1329b.
[42] *On the Heavens*, I, 3, in *Works*, Vol. II, 270a.
[43] The differences between Plato's and Aristotle's cyclical theories might be described thus: Where Plato makes much of the exact periodicity of the Great Year, Aristotle seems to underplay it, and perhaps merely assumes it without comment; and where Plato insists on the direct relation between the Great Year and the cycles of history, Aristotle seems to suggest that the relation, though present, is not direct, and can in any event not be easily determined. Plato takes what may be termed a

Of the many authors who hold the position being discussed, which persists to the present day, some seem to follow the Platonic, some the Aristotelian, model; that is, some emphasize the directness of the relation between cosmic and historical cycles, while others de-emphasize this, or at least do not mention it explicitly.

Of the former, Polybius is a leading example. He records his debt to Plato:

> Perhaps this theory of the natural transformations into each other of the different forms of government is more elaborately set forth by Plato and certain other philosophers; but as the arguments are subtle and are stated at great length, they are beyond the reach of all but a few. I therefore will attempt to give a short summary of the theory, as far as I consider it to apply to the actual history of facts and to appeal to the common intelligence of mankind.[44]

Polybius summarizes the evolution and devolution described by Plato in *Republic* VIII and at other places, and declares:

> Such is the cycle of political revolution, the course appointed by nature in which constitutions change, disappear, and finally return to the point from which they started. Anyone who clearly perceives this may indeed in speaking of the future of any state be wrong in his estimate of the time the process will take, but if his judgment is not tainted by animosity or jealousy, he will very seldom be mistaken as to the stage of growth or decline it has reached, and as to the form into which it will change.[45]

poetical view of the cyclical pattern of history; his discussions of the matter are always infused with mythical conceptions and replete with fabulous examples. Aristotle is more skeptical and seems willing to assert only that things recur formally (*i.e.*, specifically, not numerically) from time to time. He is firm in his denial that details recur. Plato does not say that they do, but he does not strongly deny it. For an example of a point on which they are directly opposed, the question of the cause of the evolution of political states or conditions may be mentioned. Plato suggests that governments evolve in some sort of imitation of the circling of the spheres. Aristotle admits the evolution, but he seems to cast doubt on its being directly imitative of a cosmic process. The evolution is ultimately to be traced to the cosmos, which is changeable. But the relation between the changes in the cosmos and those of men in states is not very close. Aristotle says: "In the *Republic* of Plato, Socrates treats of revolutions, but not well, for he mentions no cause of change which peculiarly affects the first, or perfect state. He only says that the cause is that nothing is abiding, but all things change in a certain cycle" (*Politics*, V, 12, in *Works*, Vol. VIII, 1316b). Aristotle goes on to point out that the various stages of political evolution have lasted for different amounts of time in different states, and declares that it is not enough simply to say that "seeing that everything which has a beginning has also an end, even a constitution like ours will not last forever."

44 *The Histories*, VI, 5, in Teggart (ed.), *The Idea of Progress*, p. 78.
45 *Ibid.*, 9, pp. 78–9.

Polybius gives evidence of his own objectivity and lack of animosity or jealousy by noting that "especially in the case of the Roman state will this method enable us to arrive at a knowledge of its formation, growth, and greatest perfection, and likewise of the change for the worse which is sure to follow some day. For . . . this state, more than any other, has been formed and has grown naturally, and will undergo a natural decline and change to its contrary."[46] Polybius also applies his method to the history of Carthage, observing that

> at the time when they entered on the Hannibalic War, the Carthaginian constitution had degenerated, and that of Rome was better. For as every body or state or action has its natural periods first of growth, then of prime, and finally of decay, and as everything in them is at its best when they are in their prime, it was for this reason that the difference between the two states manifested itself at this time.[47]

It is quite clear that the "natural" cycles are ultimately ruled by the cyclicity of the heavens.

Florus also points to the career of Rome as exemplary of cycles of history. His terms differ somewhat from those of the authors considered above; he compares the history of a state to the life of a man, remarking that states, like men, are first young, then mature, and then old. Rome's "infancy," he says, was under the kings; its next period, "during which it subdued Italy . . . was a time of action for men and arms, and we may therefore call it its youth."

> The next period was one of two hundred years, to the time of Caesar Augustus, in which it subdued the whole world; this may accordingly be called the manhood, the robust maturity, of the empire. From the reign of Caesar Augustus to our own age is a period of little less than two hundred years, in which, from the inactivity of the Caesars, it has grown old and lost its strength, except that it now raises its arms under the emperor Trajan, and, contrary to the expectation of all, the old age of the empire, as if youth were restored to it, renews its vigour.[48]

The last point is of interest. As we have seen, it is a commonplace among progress authors to compare the life of the race to that of a man, with the important proviso that the race, unlike an individual man, never grows old. Florus hints at such an idea, but he does not follow it up. For him, there is the same inevitable decline in states that there is in the life of an individual, and it is inevitable, for the same reason; namely,

[46] *Ibid.*, p. 79.
[47] *Ibid.*, 51, p. 79.
[48] *Epitome Rerum Romanorum*, in Teggart, *op. cit.*, p. 109.

the relation between the cycling cosmos and the career of the sublunar world.

If Polybius and Florus lean to the Platonic version of the theory, Machiavelli leans to the Aristotelian. In the course of a disquisition on the history of his own city, Florence, he declares that

> nations, as a rule, when making a change in their system of government pass from order to disorder, because nature permits no stability in human affairs. When nations reach their final perfection and can mount no higher they commence to descend; and equally when they have descended and reached a depth where they can fall no longer, necessity compels them to rise again. Thus states will always be falling from prosperity to adversity, and from adversity they will ascend again to prosperity. Because valour brings peace, peace idleness, idleness disorder, and disorder ruin; once more from ruin arises good order, from order valour, and from valour success and glory.[49]

Here, one Aristotelian touch is the last sentence, in which a specific reason is given for the decline from a condition of perfection. States do not degenerate *merely* because the cosmos changes. In another place, Machiavelli offers another reason for the decline, or rather for the constant motion that is sometimes decline, sometimes not. "Since the desires of men are insatiable," he says,

> Nature prompting them to desire all things and Fortune permitting them to enjoy but few, there results a constant discontent in their minds, and a loathing of what they possess, prompting them to find fault with the present, praise the past, and long for the future, even though they be not moved thereto by any reasonable cause.[50]

It appears, however, that the ultimate cause of the rise and fall of states is not human disquiet but Fortune, who attains for Machiavelli, as she does for many of his contemporaries, at least semi-divine status. Hence it is the cosmos that is behind historical cycles; the cause does not lie exclusively in human nature.

R. H. Wheeler is a modern author who seems to reflect the Aristotelian version of this position. Wheeler has plotted the course of world history against a "drought clock," worked out in detail over the last 1,500 years, which indicates that "the climate of the earth shifts from warmer to colder periods and back again, frequently in rhythms."

> History shows that nations are built on shifts from cold periods to warm, when the human energy level temporarily reaches a maximum. Nations

[49] *Florentine History,* V, 183.
[50] *Discourses,* II, in Teggart, *op. cit.,* p. 128.

crumble on the shift from warm to cold. International wars are mostly warm, civil wars cold.

The phases of warm and cold are associated with a phasic change in the amount of rainfall. Both warm and cold phases begin wet and end dry. Cold droughts and centers of civil-war epochs generally coincide.

A major cold drought and civil war period occurs about every 510 years; generally less severe ones every 170 years. There are also shorter rhythms.

It seemed to Wheeler, in 1943, that the world was near the beginning of a cold period, since it had been "generally warm for about 45 years." There was some comfort to be found in this, for "totalitarianism is typical of late half-warm periods; democracy is revived during cold times."[51]

Wheeler, like the other writers treated in this chapter, sees the pattern of history as cyclical, and holds that the pattern is determined, or at least strongly affected, by natural or cosmic cycles that are beyond the reach of human control. In so saying, whatever the differences among them, they concur in opposing the position of the anthropogenic cyclists who are treated in Chapter 10.

[51] "The Effect of Climate on Human Behavior in History." Reference to this work is made in *Cycles,* published in Pittsburgh, Pa., by the Foundation for the Study of Cycles. This organization is probably the foremost contemporary proponent of cosmogenic cyclical theories of history. Studies undertaken by it have found cycles of varying "wave length" in everything from prices of grain to prices of stocks, and from strength of sunspots to frequency of battles.

II

Issues in the
Philosophy of History

12

Does a Definite Pattern of Change
Exist in Human History
as a Whole?

THE affirmative answer to the question whether there is a definite pattern of change in human history as a whole is given—implicitly for the most part—by the progress authors. It is also given, again implicitly, by the regress authors and by the cyclists. Hence, in the discussion of this issue that follows, the affirmative answer is not dealt with extensively, and the emphasis is mainly on the negative answer.

There appear to be two ways of saying that there is no single, overall pattern of change in man and in the conditions of human life. The first is to say that there is no change in these things whatsoever; the human being remains the same, and the general conditions of human life do not differ significantly from one epoch to the next. The second is to say that the changes in question are so radical as to bar meaningful comparison of human life at different epochs.

The foregoing are extreme statements; authors do not state their positions in quite these terms. However, the various denials—which are also, *ipso facto*, denials of progress—fall in one or the other category.

Representative authors making the first denial are the following:

Emerson	Cram
Burckhardt	Nock
Shaw	

Representative authors making the second denial are listed below.[1]

Schopenhauer	Berdyaev
Boas	Adams
Cohen	Strong
Jaspers	

THE POSITION THAT THERE IS NO SIGNIFICANT CHANGE IN HUMAN LIFE FROM ONE EPOCH TO ANOTHER

Progress, says Jacob Burckhardt, is an "optical illusion"; it is merely a manifestation of the "ridiculous vanity" of the modern bourgeois mind. The belief in progress forms "part of the fussy baggage of public opinion" that, in general, is the "deadly [enemy] of true historical insight."[2]

Burckhardt denies not only affirmations of progress. He also criticizes the notion that history exhibits a cyclical pattern; he directs his barbs especially against Lasaulx, who in many respects is the nineteenth-century counterpart of Toynbee.[3]

It is the idea of progress, however, that comes in for Burckhardt's most scornful remarks.

> Arguments based on the corruption, debauchery and even more the violence of times past, or on the cruelty and perfidy of barbarians, are misleading. For we judge everything by that standard of morality without which *we* could no longer exist, and condemn the past by pointing out that our atmosphere did not exist in it, forgetting that even now, the moment security is suspended—in war, for instance—every conceivable horror shows its head. . . . Our assumption that we live in the age of moral progress is supremely ridiculous. . . . Morality as a power stands no higher, nor is there more of it, than in so-called barbarous times. We may be sure that even among the lake-dwellers men gave their lives for one another.[4]

So much might be said by an author who denied moral progress but allowed progress in other respects—and who thus conceded that there is

[1] This list could doubtless be longer. Some of the authors discussed in Chapter 13, who deny that the pattern of history is knowable, might, from one point of view, belong in it. For further candidates for the list, see Chapter 13, Note 2.

[2] *Force and Freedom*, pp. 149, 351.

[3] For a discussion of Lasaulx's cyclical theory, see above, pp. 166-7.

[4] *Op. cit.*, pp. 148-9.

some kind of overall pattern of history. But Burckhardt makes his denial quite general. "Even progress in intellectual development is open to doubt," he declares, "since, as civilization advanced, the division of labor may have steadily narrowed the consciousness of the individual. In the sciences, a host of discoveries of isolated facts already threatens to obscure any general outlook. In no sphere of life does individual ability develop uniformly with the expansion of the whole; culture might easily stumble over its own feet."[5]

Two main notions underlie Burckhardt's denial that there is any single, overall pattern of history. One is that in every developed civilization, various aspects of culture continually affect and modify one another so that all that we can see at any given moment is the temporarily dominant factor. History presents a constant shifting of values; progress in one respect is made at the expense of regress in another, with the result that both progress and regress are merely apparent. In short, gains are canceled by losses, and the sum remains zero. The other notion is that human nature remains essentially the same at all times.

The first point is concurred in by Emerson. "Society never advances," he says.

> It recedes as fast on one side as it gains on the other. It undergoes continual changes; it is barbarous, it is civilized, it is Christianized, it is rich, it is scientific; but this change is not amelioration. For everything that is given something is taken. Society acquires new arts and loses old instincts. . . . The civilized man has built a coach, but has lost the use of his feet. He is supported on crutches, but lacks so much support of muscle. He has a fine Geneva watch, but he fails of the skill to tell the hour by the sun. . . . His notebooks impair his memory; his libraries overload his wit; the insurance office increases the number of accidents; and it may be a question whether machinery does not encumber; whether we have not lost by refinement some energy, by a Christianity, entrenched in establishments and forms, some vigor of wild virtue. For every Stoic was a Stoic; but in Christendom where is the Christian?[6]

Emerson also agrees on the second point. He declares that "there is no more deviation in the moral standard than in the standard of height or bulk. No greater men are now than ever were. A singular equality may be observed between the great men of the first and of the last ages; nor can all the science, art, religion, and philosophy of the nineteenth century avail to educate greater men than Plutarch's heroes, three or four and

---

[5] *Ibid.,* p. 150.

[6] "Self-Reliance," in *The Complete Essays and Other Writings of Ralph Waldo Emerson,* pp. 166–7.

twenty centuries ago. Not in time is the race progressive."[7] These remarks echo Burckhardt's claim that "neither the spirit nor the brain of man has visibly developed in historical times, and his faculties were in any case complete long before then."[8]

G. B. Shaw is entirely in agreement. For him, too, progress is a ridiculous presumption; and his attack on it is at the same time an attack on the position that there is any overall pattern of history. "The more ignorant men are," he says,

> the more convinced are they that their little parish and their little chapter is an apex to which civilization and philosophy have painfully struggled up the pyramid of time from a desert of savagery. . . . The whole process is summed up as Progress with a capital P. And any elderly gentleman of Progressive temperament will testify that the improvement since he was a boy is enormous.[9]

However, such testimony, according to Shaw, is without weight. Murder with a Mauser rifle, he observes, is no less grievous than murder with a poisoned arrow. The supposed "increased command over nature" is a great illusion. The condition of the American Negro is hardly an index of human progress. Most so-called progress is mere Tweedle-dum and Tweedle-dee, mere "transfigurations of institutions." Occasionally there is to be observed the appearance of progress. But

> we might as well make up our minds that Man will return to his idols and his cupidities, in spite of all "movements" and all revolutions, until his nature is changed. . . . Whilst Man remains what he is, there can be no progress beyond the point already attained and fallen headlong from at every attempt at civilization; and since that point is but a pinnacle to which a few people cling in giddy terror above an abyss of squalor, mere progress should no longer charm us. . . . We must therefore frankly give up the notion that man as he exists is capable of net progress.[10]

The idea that human nature remains so absolutely constant that progress is impossible is taken up by R. A. Cram, although with a good deal more bitterness than is brought to it by Shaw. Progress is an absurd delusion, says Cram, which the First World War showed to be such. This terrible conflict brought men back to the realities of human nature, which they had forgotten.

[7] *Ibid.*, p. 167.
[8] *Op. cit.*, p. 149.
[9] These sentiments are expressed in Shaw's notes to *Caesar and Cleopatra*, in *Three Plays for Puritans*, pp. 199–203.
[10] "The Revolutionist's Handbook." Qu. in A. J. Todd, *Theories of Social Progress*, pp. 136–7.

It is a salutary proceeding that has issue in manifold revelations, while its implications are singularly valuable in the light they throw on the dissolving dream of progressive evolution.[11]

History, says Cram, shows no picture of progress, indeed no pattern of change of any sort. The more carefully we look, the more clearly we see that the great mass of men at all times are no more than members of "the obscene mob." They are, on the whole, brutish, immoral, "Neolithic." If there is any pattern of human life, it is this:

> Millennium after millennium [an] endless flood of basic raw material sweeps on. It is the everlasting Neolithic man, the same that it was five or ten thousand years B.C. It is the matrix of the human being, the stuff of which he is made.[12]

Cram's notion of human nature is more complex than that of Burckhardt, Emerson, and Shaw, who merely observe that at all times there are a few great men and many men who are not great or good. Cram seems to say that there are in fact two different kinds of human beings; indeed, most men are not, strictly speaking, human at all. History always " 'fountains' in fine personalities, eminent and of historic record, or obscure yet of equal nobility, and these are the 'human beings' on whose personality, character and achievements we establish our standard."[13] These few—they are Emerson's and Shaw's great men, and possibly Schopenhauer's "men of genius," too—are admirable. But there are not enough of them to bring about progress, indeed to produce any significant change in the general conditions of human life. The great mass of "Neolithic or more probably Paleolithic submen" weighs down the race. "The cause of comprehensive failure and bar to recovery is the persistence of the everlasting Neolithic Man and his assumption of human control."[14]

A. J. Nock accepts Cram's notion of a twofold human nature, or of a division of the race into two species. "Mr. Cram's thesis is," he writes,

> that we do not behave like human beings because the great majority of us, the masses of mankind, are not human beings. . . . They are merely the subhuman raw material out of which the occasional human being is produced by an evolutionary process as yet unexplained, but no doubt catastrophic in character, certainly not progressive.[15]

[11] "Why We Do Not Behave Like Human Beings," in *Convictions and Controversies*, p. 142.

[12] *Ibid.*, p. 151.

[13] *Ibid.*

[14] *Ibid.*, p. 154. Cram's conception of a twofold human nature reappears—but as a theory of progress—in Nouÿ's *Human Destiny*. For a discussion of this work see below, pp. 300–301.

[15] *Memoirs of a Superfluous Man*, p. 137.

In addition, there are, according to Nock, three "natural laws" that tend to nullify any important change in the conditions of human life, and certainly any progressive change. Revolutions do occur, he says; they are usually initiated by "human beings," and they are intended to improve matters. But as soon as a revolution succeeds, the three laws subvert it. The first is "Epstean's law," that "man tends always to satisfy his needs and desires with the least possible exertion." Hence,

> at the moment when the revolution becomes a going concern, Epstean's law brings in a waiting troop of political adventurers whose interest is not social but institutional. . . . Their aim is to make the revolution serve this institutional interest, and in virtue of their numbers and peculiar aptitudes they rather easily do so.[16]

The second law is developed from Gresham's famous dictum, that bad money drives out good. Nock applies this universally, holding that bad literature drives out good literature, bad morals drive out good morals, bad institutions drive out good institutions, and so forth. Social interest in general is rapidly driven out, and those who represent it are lucky to escape with their lives.

The third law is the "law of diminishing returns."

> As the institution grows in size and strength, as its confiscations of social power increase in frequency and magnitude, as its coercions upon society multiply, the welfare of society (which the original intention of the revolution was to promote) becomes increasingly depleted and attenuated.[17]

The net result is that "these three laws dog the progress of every organization of mankind's effort." The absurdity of progress in such circumstances is manifest.

At first glance, Nock's remarks may seem to add up to an affirmation of regress. However, on closer examination, this is seen to be incorrect. If ameliorating revolutions—or, rather, revolutions with an ameliorative intent—did not occur, or ceased to occur, things would indeed go from bad to worse, and regress would be the pattern of history. But the existence of a few scattered "human beings" insures that revolutions do occur from time to time. Their effect is never lasting, however, and thus the general conditions of human life are much the same at all epochs.

Several of the authors discussed in this section make mention of the fact that progress is an illusion fostered by our preference for the conditions of life in our own time, and our inability to conceive how a different sort of life could also be desirable or admirable. This point is made by

16 *Ibid.*, p. 133.
17 *Ibid.*, pp. 165–6.

some of the authors discussed in the next section; it is strongly emphasized by several of the writers, discussed in Chapter 13, who deny the knowability of the pattern of history. There is, indeed, some overlapping of views on the negative side of the two issues in the philosophy of history that are being considered here and in the next chapter. Nevertheless, the main purport of the statements discussed above is that there is no single, overall pattern of history, because the general conditions of human life, as well as man himself, are at all times much the same. And the fact that there are no significant changes in these respects means, of course, that progress does not occur.

THE POSITION THAT RADICAL CHANGES OCCUR IN HUMAN LIFE FROM ONE EPOCH TO ANOTHER

Franz Boas, in arguing against any theory of the superiority of one race as against another, argues also against any affirmation of progress, and, by extension, against the idea that there is a single, overall pattern of change in history. "Ever since the time when the study of human cultures was recognized as a problem," he observes, "attempts have been made to interpret it as a unit phenomenon."[18] These attempts, however, he goes on to show, must always fail.

He cites a number of theories about the evolutionary development of culture and discards them all. Society is *not* like an organism, he declares, which is developing (as the social Darwinians maintain) a kind of collective consciousness. Primitive men are *not* children, as others hold, nor are they to be thought of as "mental defectives." The theory of parallel development does not stand up, for "the facts, so far as known at the present time, are entirely contrary to this view."[19] There is no real evidence to support the theory of economic determinism, or the theory of geographic determinism, or the theory of similar development based on the similarity of psychic structure. Even the theory that the history of culture may be "reconstructed by means of the application of the principle that the simple precedes the complex" is open to serious question, since cultures that are "simple" according to one index of comparison are often "complex" according to another.[20] It is still more difficult, Boas declares,

> to define progress in social organization. The extreme individualist considers anarchy as his ideal, while others believe in voluntary regimentation.

[18] *The Mind of Primitive Man*, p. 162.
[19] *Ibid.*, p. 165.
[20] *Ibid.*, pp. 180–1.

Control of the individual by society or subjection to leadership, individual freedom or the attainment of power by the group as a whole may be considered the ideal. Progress can be defined only in regard to the special ideal that we have in mind.[21]

"There is no absolute progress," Boas is forced to conclude. Nor, it is clear, is there any "absolute" regress, or any "absolute" pattern of cycles in history.

The reason lies, Boas tells us, in the "lack of comparability of the data" with which the anthropologist deals.

Attention is directed essentially to the similarity of ethnic phenomena, while the individual variations are disregarded. As soon as we turn our attention to these we notice that the sameness of ethnic phenomena is more superficial than essential, more apparent than real. The unexpected similarities have attracted our attention to such an extent that we have disregarded differences.[22]

The value that we attribute to our own civilization is owing to the fact that we participate in it, Boas goes on to say, and that it controls all our activities and habits of thought from the time of our birth. One conclusion to be drawn from this is that

the general theory of valuation of human activities, as developed by anthropological research, teaches us a higher tolerance than the one we now profess.[23]

Another is that we must approach the problem of patterns of history in the same way that we approach the problem of racial differences. In the latter realm, "freedom of judgment can be attained only when we learn to estimate an individual according to his own ability and character. . . . Then we shall treasure and cultivate the variety of forms that human thought and activity have taken, and abhor, as leading to complete stagnation, all attempts to impress one pattern of thought upon whole nations or even upon the whole world."[24]

Boas' point is that civilizations and cultures are *sui generis;* the relations between them that any overall pattern of history would have to find are therefore merely apparent. (This is not to deny, of course, that there *are* real analogies between cultures, the result, for example, of "cultural contact.") George P. Adams is saying the same thing when he declares that "the only legitimate use of the term civilization . . . is to denote a class of civilizations."

21 *Ibid.*, p. 187.
22 *Ibid.*, p. 171.
23 *Ibid.*, p. 203.
24 *Ibid.*, p. 242.

What exists and is actual is always some particular pattern of human life and society, a persistent set of institutions, habits, and interests. Each concrete civilization is a historical episode. It is a theme exemplified within certain boundaries of historical time and geography. The boundaries may be imprecise and vague rather than sharp and clear. The transition from one culture epoch to another may be slow or rapid, gradual or revolutionary. . . . But it remains true that there are diverse and distinguishable civilizations in the plural, for the historian to describe as best he may.[25]

Indeed, this is the historian's real task; the task is emphatically not to compare civilizations, nor to propose theories of how they must always develop from one another, and especially not to evaluate one as against the other. Evaluations could only be made in the light of our own ideals. It is

quite meaningless to entertain any notion that it is incumbent upon any one concrete historical civilization, such as our own, to further the ends of civilization as such, to devote its energies to the realization of any ideal denoted by the term civilization in the singular. That term is the name of a class, and a class name is not to be confused with any type of prescriptive ideal or principle.[26]

Adams concedes that a given civilization undergoes cumulative change and development, involving growth and decay; in short, there is, and there can be discovered, the pattern of *a* civilization. He also asserts that the notion of civilization, like the notions of science, morality, law, religion, art, and technology, are not "exclusively descriptive class names" except when looked at from without—"when viewed, phenomenally, as observed facts." He frowns on the idea that one should refuse, on the basis of his own or similar arguments, to try to improve the world. "A nominalistic theory of universals," he observes, "goes hand in hand with a naturalistic theory of value," and the latter—"the view that the source of all prescriptive ideals is to be looked for in what somebody happens to like"—is not adequate, he suggests, to the practice of a civilized man, whatever the adjective may mean. However, affirmations of progress imply the existence of an overall pattern of history when history is looked at from without, when it is viewed, phenomenally, as a set of observed facts. From this point of view, according to Adams, "civilization" is an exclusively class name, and has no intrinsic meaning apart from the concrete examples of it that have actually existed.[27]

Edward W. Strong agrees on this point. "The persistence of the human

[25] "The Idea of Civilization," in W. R. Dennes (ed.), *Civilization*, pp. 48–9.
[26] *Ibid.*, p. 49.
[27] *Ibid.*, pp. 49–67.

race on earth is the biological condition and continuity for all other human continuities," he observes.

> Such persistence, however, does not constitute any identifying nucleus of social relations with respect to which cultural transmissions take place. Philosophers of history have, indeed, been aware that it was illegitimate to assert mankind as a continuant linking a temporal sequence of events. Either the idea of universal progress was thereby illegitimate, or it was saved by recourse to a metaphysical fiction.[28]

The argument is conclusive against a progressive pattern of history. However, it is equally conclusive against any other pattern. Either the notion of any single, overall pattern is illegitimate, or it must be saved by a "metaphysical fiction," such, for example, as the hypothesis that the Mayan society developed by a kind of sympathetic parallelism of events.

> On the unilinear interpretation of history, we must either deny that this society was a civilization at the expense of a descriptive classification, or else strain credulity by an Atlantic leap to save continuity in Spirit where it cannot be shown in evidence.[29]

The fact that there is no overall pattern of history does not mean, both Strong and Adams insist, that we cannot look forward to future improvements in our civilization. Strong even suggests that a "relativist" position with regard to progress—*i.e.*, the position that there is no single, overall pattern of history—might be more likely to result in local progress than the belief in progress itself. It is not paradoxical, he declares,

> to assert that a conviction of valuational relativity holds more promise for efforts to realize [a world] civilization than a conviction of absolute justification when claimed by any class or nation of men.[30]

But this does not contradict the main point that is made by both writers. There is no single progressive pattern of the human race, taken as a whole and throughout its entire career on earth, even though improvement in the near future may be more than a mere pious hope.

The authors discussed above emphasize the incommensurability of cultures or civilizations, and thereby deny progress. Another group of writers emphasizes the incommensurability of the lives of individual men, and thereby make the denial even stronger.

28 "Civilizations in Historical Perspective," in *ibid.*, p. 99.
29 *Ibid.*, p. 98–9.
30 *Ibid.*, p. 120.

Schopenhauer is a famous pessimist; he is surely no affirmer of progress! Yet a pessimist might affirm at least a regressive pattern of history. However, Schopenhauer does not do so. His argument runs like this.

Human life, he proclaims, is simply a mistake. No other conclusion is rationally possible. Nevertheless, in the face of all the evidence to the contrary, men continue to hope for improvement. Hence they live in a world of illusions. Men could only be joined, intellectually, by knowledge of reality. But reality is just what men refuse to face. The fact that each of our private worlds is illusory means that our lives are essentially incommensurable with those of others. Each man's "solution" of the problem of life is unique, and utterly different from that of any other man. The only thing these solutions have in common is their note of desperation.[31]

The foregoing constitutes a denial not only of progress—one of man's leading "illusions"—but of any pattern of history. In denying the reality of time, Schopenhauer makes the point in another way. The past might as well never have been, he declares, and the future is a delusion toward which we strive, but which produces only frustration. That which is, is in the present, and all the rest is nothing.[32]

This contention, which is of course a denial that there is any pattern of history, is shared by several modern writers who do not necessarily share Schopenhauer's other views. Nicolas Berdyaev, for example, maintains that the "doctrine of progress"—and, it goes without saying, the doctrines of regress and of cycles as well—is "inadmissible,"

> because by its very nature it excludes a solution to the tragic torments, conflicts, and contradictions of life valid for all mankind, for all the generations who have lived and suffered.[33]

This doctrine, he observes, forces us to regard past generations as merely the means and instruments to some ultimate goal. This is unacceptable. In reality, the only thing that can be said to advance or retreat is our recognition of our tragic destiny. An advance of this sort is occurring now.

> The dual and profoundly tragic character of the historical process becomes increasingly manifest. There is no such thing in history as progress from good to perfect on a single plane of development, in virtue of which some future generation may exhalt itself at the expense of all those that have

[31] See "On the Vanity and Suffering of Life," in *The Will to Live: Selected Writings of Arthur Schopenhauer*, pp. 199–214. The passages there quoted are taken from the fourth book of *The World As Will and Idea*.

[32] See "The Vanity of Existence," in *ibid.*, pp. 229–33. The passages there quoted are taken from *Parerga*.

[33] *The Meaning of History*, p. 189.

gone before. There is no such thing in history as progress in human happiness. There is only progress in the tragic sense of the inner principles of being, of the good-evil, divine-demonic antithesis, of the principles of good and evil in collaboration.[34]

Progress means putting "the future on a pedestal," says Berdyaev. The "faith and trust" that the idea of progress calls forth in us should instead "inspire us to do away once and for all with the disintegration of time into present, past and future, and set up the time era of eternity."[35] Berdyaev's argument is couched in very different terms from Schopenhauer's, but his conclusion is the same. Progress, regress, and cycles can only be meaningful if time is meaningful. If the present alone is significant for human beings, then there is no pattern of history.

Karl Jaspers shifts the emphasis slightly, but his position is the same. The past is not without meaning, he declares, and one may legitimately hope for the future. But one should not *live* in or for either the past or the future. The "eternal Present" is the proper object of our concern.

> What is the present that is eternal? It is the clairvoyant love of humans sharing their destinies in rational union; it is the consciousness of doing right; it is the strength of advancing on the path of reason; it is the resistance that checks my self-will, my drifting, my untruthfulness, my anger, my arrogance, like the flaming sword of an angel parrying whatever would revolt in my existence; it is what happens in the deepest recesses of my being, by myself and not by myself alone; it is what guides my outward actions.[36]

This is far from the pessimism of a Schopenhauer. Jaspers recognizes the possibility of individual improvement—a kind of private or individual progress. But no single, overall pattern of history can exist when all that matters is how an individual man faces the world and his own particular destiny.

Morris R. Cohen also emphasizes the tragic nature of life and of history, and maintains that a man ought to study history, if at all, to gain insight into his own private "agony," and not to find patterns of overall change. Like some of the other writers discussed in this chapter, he does not deny the possibility of local improvement in human affairs; indeed, he asserts that we should hope that this will occur. Nevertheless, he denies that progress is the enduring pattern; we should not expect things

[34] *Ibid.*, p. 192.
[35] *Ibid.*, p. 195. For other expressions of this viewpoint, see Berdyaev's *The Fate of Man in the Modern World*.
[36] *The Future of Mankind*, p. 341. Other expressions of the existentialist position regarding progress are found in Camus' *The Myth of Sisyphus*—although there tinged, as they are not in Jaspers, with a profound pessimism, not to say despair.

always to grow better. In so saying, he provides additional support for the negative position on the issue whether there is a pattern of history.[37]

[37] See *The Meaning of Human History*, pp. 260–96. Cohen seems to be saying that there is no meaning *of* history but only meaning *in* it—and this meaning is to be found in its tragic aspect. He credits Felix Adler with having been the founder and main proponent of what he calls "the tragic view of history."

13

Is the Pattern of Historical Change, If One Exists, Discoverable or Knowable by Us?

LIKE the assertion that there is a pattern of history, the assertion that this pattern is actually known by us is at least implicit in all affirmations of progress, regress, and cycles. Hence the affirmative answer to this question is not treated extensively in this chapter.[1]

Where there are two ways of saying that there is no pattern of history, there appears to be only one way of saying that the pattern, even if it exists, cannot be known by us. There are many different expressions of the position in the literature, but they all reduce to the assertion that the task of discovering a single, overall pattern of historical change is beyond the capacity of the human mind. The pattern would involve, it is said, too many elements; furthermore, much of the evidence that would be needed to affirm such a pattern is lost forever. Man will never be able to learn all that is necessary in order to assert with assurance that the pattern of history is this and not that.

The denial of man's capacity to comprehend such a vast thing as the

[1] Occasionally, affirmative authors on these issues make their assertions that there is a pattern of history, and that it is knowable, explicit. Toynbee, for example, in a debate with Geyl, attempts to answer the latter's denial of the knowability of the pattern of history. See Note 18, below.

overall pattern of human history does not preclude historical knowledge of a sort. Human beings are not absolutely barred from understanding the past; the relations of particular events are discoverable, and local patterns of change may be discerned. What is denied by this position is that man can ever know the overall pattern. This is beyond him, and it will always be so.

Representative authors taking this position, which is of course a denial of progress, are listed below.[2]

Croce	Fisher
Mannheim	Geyl
Collingwood	W. H. Walsh
Popper	

Of the authors listed, R. G. Collingwood and Karl Popper are perhaps clearest in taking the position that the pattern of history cannot be known by us. Collingwood turns his attention mainly to the knowability of a progressive pattern of history, but his argument applies, by extension, to the knowability of any pattern. Popper makes his denial somewhat more general, as will be seen.

The ideal of historical progress, says Collingwood,

> if it refers to anything, refers to the coming into existence not merely of new actions or thoughts or situations belonging to the same specific type, but of new specific types. It therefore presupposes such specific novelties, and consists in the conception of these as improvements.[3]

This means, among other things, that "progress is not the replacement of the bad by the good, but of the good by the better."

> In order to conceive a change as a progress, then, the person who has made it must think of what he has abolished as good, and good in certain definite

---

[2] This list, like those at the beginning of Chapter 12, could doubtless be expanded. For example, it might appropriately include Berlin, Blake, Donagan, Dray, Frankel, Gallie, Gellner, Hempel, Mandelbaum, Nagel, Pareto, Scriven, Watkins, and White, all of whom are represented in Gardiner's *Theories of History* as expressing differing views concerning historical knowledge and explanation. Some of the authors included in the above additional list are clearer than others on the point that the pattern of history, even if there is such a thing, is not knowable by men. And some, such as Hempel, suggest that the pattern of history is as knowable as some other matters, the knowability of which is not usually brought into question. For further treatment of the issue, which is primarily one in the philosophy of history and is only distantly connected to the controversy about progress, the reader should refer to Gardiner's collection. His short introductions to the selections quoted are particularly revealing.

[3] *The Idea of History,* p. 324.

ways. This he can only do on condition of his knowing what the old way of life was like.[4]

One result of this is that the "revolutionary" can only regard his revolution as a progress if he is, and insofar as he is, an historian. Another is that he must be able to enter "sympathetically" into the life of another epoch. This is extraordinarily difficult, Collingwood declares.

Such are the conditions of an affirmation of local progress, of a particular manifestation of progress in the context of a specific cultural milieu. What is the situation of an historian who is placed outside of the cultural milieu, as any historian must be who affirms an overall pattern of the entire history of the race? In effect, says Collingwood, he "must judge the relative value of two different ways of life, taken as two wholes."

> Now, in order to do this, he must be able to enter with equal sympathy into the essential features and values of each way of life: he must re-experience them both in his own mind, as objects of historical knowledge. What makes him a qualified judge, therefore, is just the fact that he does not look at his object from a detached point of view, but re-lives it in himself.[5]

The question is, whether the historian is capable of such knowledge. Collingwood declares that he is not. For the historian can never, he says, take any period as a whole. There must be large tracts of its life for which he either has no data, or no data that he is in a position to interpret. For example, we cannot understand Greek music, although we know that the Greeks greatly enjoyed it; we have much data about Roman religion, but our own religious experience bars us from reconstructing in our own minds what it meant to them; and we are absolutely disqualified from speaking of progress in happiness or comfort or satisfaction, since

> different ways of life are differentiated by nothing more clearly than by differences between the things that people habitually enjoy, the conditions which they find comfortable, and the achievements they regard as satisfactory. The problem of being comfortable in a medieval cottage is so different from the problem of being comfortable in a modern slum that there is no comparing them; the happiness of a peasant is not contained in the happiness of a millionaire.[6]

Collingwood concedes that progress is possible in certain realms. Science, for example, seems to be able to improve; so does philosophy, although the evidence here is more dubious; conceivably there is progress in institutional morality; and the change from the Judaic to the Christian God

---

[4] *Ibid.*, p. 326.
[5] *Ibid.*, p. 327.
[6] *Ibid.*, p. 330. See also pp. 328–9.

"was a progress, and a momentous one, in the history of the religious consciousness."[7] Progress within limits may occur; whether it has actually occurred, and where and when and in what ways, are questions for historical thought to answer. But there is no overall progress of the human race, taken as a whole. Knowledge that such occurs would involve judging the "value of a certain way of life taken in its entirety," and this is, Collingwood declares, an impossible task.[8]

The attempt to know what we have no way of knowing is an infallible way to generate illusions, Collingwood goes on to observe, and

> this attempt to judge whether one period of history or phase of human life, taken as a whole, shows progress as compared with its predecessor, generates illusions of an easily recognizable type. Their characteristic feature is the labelling of certain historical periods as good periods, or ages of historical greatness, and of others as bad periods, ages of historical failure or poverty.[9]

The good periods are those whose spirit is comprehensible to the historian; the bad are those whose spirit he cannot sympathize with, either because of scanty evidence or because his own way of life is in some essential respect antipathetic. Good and bad periods tend to alternate; the bad periods are divided into the primitive and the decadent, depending on whether they come before or after the good ones. But "this distinction between periods of primitiveness, periods of greatness, and periods of decadence, is not and never can be historically true. It tells us much about the historians who study the facts, but nothing about the facts they study."[10] The reason is, of course, as before, that the affirmation of any overall pattern of history is invalid because it would require a kind of historical knowledge that is beyond the capacity of the human mind.[11]

The finding of a single, overall pattern of human history is given a name by Popper: he calls it "historicism," and the methods by which affirmations of progress, regress, and the like are arrived at are termed by him "historicist."

Collingwood argues that we cannot know the pattern of history because

[7] *Ibid.*, p. 333.
[8] *Ibid.*, p. 327.
[9] *Ibid.*
[10] *Ibid.*
[11] The notion that historical knowledge involves—indeed, demands—some kind of intuitive sympathy with the objects with which it is concerned may be traced to Dilthey. But Dilthey, unlike Collingwood, seems to be saying that such sympathetic understanding of "other persons and their life-expressions" is possible. See Gardiner, *op. cit.*, pp. 211–25.

we cannot know the past in its entirety. Popper approaches the problem from another point of view. He observes that any affirmation of progress must involve a prediction concerning the future course of man's history. He outlines his "refutation of historicism," which is argued extensively in *The Poverty of Historicism* and *The Open Society and Its Enemies,* thus:

1. The course of human history is strongly influenced by the growth of human knowledge.
2. We cannot predict, by rational or scientific methods, the future growth of our scientific knowledge.
3. We cannot, therefore, predict the future course of human history.
4. This means that we must reject the possibility of a *theoretical history;* that is to say, of a historical social science that would correspond to *theoretical physics.* There can be no scientific theory of historical development serving as a basis for historical prediction.
5. The fundamental aim of historicist methods . . . is therefore misconceived; and historicism collapses.[12]

Popper observes that the decisive step in the argument is the second statement. He believes that the statement is convincing in itself, for, as he says, if there is such a thing as growing human knowledge, then we cannot anticipate today what we shall know only tomorrow. His proof of the statement consists in showing that

> *no scientific predictor*—whether a human scientist or a calculating machine —*can possibly predict, by scientific methods, its own future results.* Attempts to do so can attain their result only after the event, when it is too late for a prediction; they can attain their result only after the prediction has turned into a retrodiction.[13]

Popper concedes that scientific prediction of events is possible in limited areas; for example, economic theories can be tested "by way of predicting that certain developments will take place under certain conditions."[14] But no scientific prediction of the future course of history, taken in its entirety, is within the capacity of the human mind, since the future must be affected by the knowledge that men of the future, and only they, will have. And if the future is not knowable in its entirety, then the overall

12 *The Poverty of Historicism,* pp. vi-vii.
13 *Ibid.,* pp. vii–viii.
14 *Ibid.,* p. vii. It may be observed, in general, regarding Popper's views that most progress authors maintain that progress in knowledge, at least, is incontestable, and that it is in some sense the basis of all other progress. But Popper turns this argument against them when he says that the advance of knowledge is the insurmountable obstacle to any affirmation of progress.

pattern is not knowable either. Popper's argument is thus conclusive against any affirmation of a pattern of history, taken as a whole.

Collingwood's argument against man's capacity to have sufficient knowledge of the past, and Popper's against man's ability to predict the future, are concurred in by the other authors who take the negative position on the issue about the knowability of the pattern of history, although with differing emphases. Karl Mannheim tends in the direction of Popper; he questions whether a truly scientific social science is possible, and observes that "the very principles, in the light of which knowledge is to be criticized, are themselves found to be socially and historically conditioned. Hence their application appears to be limited to given historical periods and the particular types of knowledge then prevalent."[15] This makes Popper's point, although in a slightly different way. W. H. Walsh, on the other hand, appears to be making Collingwood's point when he remarks that "it is . . . one thing to look for meaning in history, another to seek for the meaning of history."[16] All historians seek meaning *in* history, he avers, and their search is not vain. The trouble lies in their attempting to discover *the* meaning in history, which is the same as the meaning *of* history. History has no single meaning, which is but another way of saying that man cannot know the overall pattern of events.

H. A. L. Fisher, too, emphasizes the complexity of past occurrences and of their relations to one another, and declares, in a statement often quoted by those who take the negative position on this issue:

> Men wiser and more learned than I have discerned in History a plot, a rhythm, a predetermined pattern. These harmonies are concealed from me. I can see only one great emergency following upon another as wave follows upon wave; only one great fact with respect to which, since it is unique, there can be no generalizations; only one safe rule for the historian: that he should recognize in the development of human destinies the play of the contingent and the unforeseen.[17]

[15] *Ideology and Utopia*, p. 259. Qu. in W. R. Dennes (ed.), *Civilization*, p. 126.
[16] " 'Meaning' in History," in Gardiner, *op. cit.*, p. 302. "That history is meaningful, *i.e.* intelligible in the light of such explanatory procedures as we can bring to bear on it, is," says Walsh, "so far from being a matter of dispute that every historian assumes it. But of course," he goes on, "those who claim that history has *a* meaning must do much more than repeat this comparatively uninteresting proposition" (*ibid.*, p. 299). Walsh's essay is particularly concerned with Toynbee's *A Study of History*, which has brought forth, in the decade or so since it was published, a large number of reviews and other writings more or less making Walsh's point, and in effect taking the negative position on the issue about the knowability of the pattern of history.
[17] The passage is from the preface to Fisher's *History of Europe*. It is quoted by Walsh and Frankel, among others, in Gardiner, *op. cit.*, pp. 300, 419.

And Pieter Geyl expresses a similar humility before the task of discovering the unique meaning of history—the single, overall pattern of the past
and the future. "I have not been convinced," he says, "of the essential
difference between the phases of civilization."

> There are evil tendencies and there are good tendencies simultaneously
> present at every stage of human history, and the human intellect is not
> sufficiently comprehensive to weigh them off against each other, and to tell,
> before the event, which is to have the upper hand.[18]

Collingwood maintains that the affirmation of a single, overall pattern of history is an infallible generator of illusions. Popper sees a grave
danger in historicism, which he terms the "enemy" of the open society,
that is, of human freedom. Croce seems to combine these views when he
declares that the "philosophy of history" is the realm of myth. The void
of logical thought in this area is filled, he says,

> with *praxis*, or what is called sentiment, which then appears as poetry, by
> theoretical refraction. There is an evident poetical character running through
> all "philosophies of history."[19]

---

[18] "Can We Know the Pattern of the Past?—A Debate," in Gardiner, *op. cit.*, p.
311. The two main points made by Geyl in this B.B.C. debate (on Jan. 4 and Mar.
7, 1948) are, first, that Toynbee's notion of cycles of history is "gloomy" because it
tends to predict an unavoidably calamitous future for our civilization; and, second,
that the particular cases chosen by Toynbee to support his contention that the
histories of past civilizations have been at least similar are not convincing. "The
twenty cases are selected cases," says Geyl, "—selected out of two hundred, or two
hundred thousand!" Furthermore, "even the twenty cases selected could most of
them be presented in a slightly, or radically, different way, with the result that they
would no longer support the argument" (*ibid.*, p. 309). In short, Geyl objects that
Toynbee's cases are both arbitrarily chosen and arbitrarily interpreted. Toynbee
replies to the first point by observing that " 'gloomy' and 'cheerful' are one thing,
'true' and 'false' quite another," and by claiming that his predictions are actually
not gloomy at all, because he does not predict the inevitable destruction of our
civilization. As to the second point, Toynbee charges that what he calls "the
nonsense view of history" does not hold water. Even though this view has been
fashionable among Western historians for the last few generations, as Toynbee
concedes, it has never, he says, been the *practice* of historians to consider the past as
essentially without overall meaning. He defends his own practice by remarking that
he puts *his* "general ideas"—his "trump cards"—"face upwards on the table." All
historians have general ideas, he claims; those who deny the knowability of the
overall pattern of the past merely refuse to reveal theirs, or at least fail to recognize
their unconscious prejudices and predilections (*ibid.*, pp. 311–12, 313, 316, 318).
Geyl counters, in his turn, that "one of the great things to realize about history
is its infinite complexity," and adds that when he says "infinite" he means that "not
only the number of the phenomena and incidents but often their shadowy and
changing nature is such that the attempt to reduce them to a fixed relationship and
to a scheme of absolute validity can never lead to anything but disappointment"
(*ibid.*, p. 318).
[19] "Historical Determinism and the 'Philosophy of History,' " in Gardiner, *op. cit.*,
pp. 236–7. The passage quoted is from Chapter IV of Croce's *History—Its Theory
and Practice.* See also his *History as the Story of Liberty*, pp. 140–6, 310–20.

Those of antiquity viewed history as the battleground of the gods of peoples.

> The most modern of modern forms is that inspired by various national and ethnic feelings (the Italian, the Germanic, the Slav, etc.), which represents the course of history as leading to the kingdom of liberty, through the Middle Ages of slavery, servitude, and wages, toward the restoration of communism, which shall no longer be unconscious but conscious, no longer Edenic but human.[20]

In poetry, facts are no longer facts but words, not reality but images, "and so there would be no occasion to censure them, if it remained pure poetry." But it does not, because the words and images are conceived as facts and ideas—"that is to say, as myths: progress, liberty, economy, technique, science are myths, in so far as they are looked upon as agents external to the facts. They are myths no less than God and the Devil, Mars and Venus, Jove and Baal, or any other cruder forms of divinity."[21] As myths, they may be studied by the historian; but he should not himself fall into the practice of mythmaking.

The notion that affirmations of progress, of regress, and of historical cycles are myths or poetical fancies is probably shared by most of the authors who deny the knowability of the pattern of history. The poet has been said to have another kind of knowledge from that of the scientist or historian; some have even claimed that his knowledge is higher, and in some sense more true. This claim is not recognized by the authors studied. The charge that progress is a myth is, for them, the most telling argument against it. For what is mythical is precisely what is not known; and it is the burden of their contention that, whatever man's attitude toward the pattern of history ought to be, he does not and cannot know what it is.

[20] Gardiner, *op. cit.*, p. 237.
[21] *Ibid.*

III

The Issue About Progress
in Moral Philosophy

14

Can Judgments of Value Regarding
Historical Change Be Validly Made?

I N the General Introduction to this book, we showed that four assertions are basic to any affirmation of progress. These are the assertions (a) that there is a definite pattern of history; (b) that the pattern is known by men; (c) that it consists in an irreversible change; and (d) that the change is for the better. We showed further that the denial of any of these assertions constitutes a denial of progress itself. The four denials—namely, (ā) that there is no pattern of history; (b̄) that even if there is a pattern, it cannot be known by men; (c̄) that the pattern is reversible (*i.e.*, cyclical); and (d̄) that the change instead of being for the better is for the worse (*i.e.*, regressive)—have been treated in Chapters 7–13.

There is a fifth denial of progress, as was also pointed out in the General Introduction, which has not yet been considered. This denial comes about from the fact that the fourth assertion—that progress consists in a change that is for the better—can be denied in two different ways, not just in one. Progress can be denied by saying that the pattern of history consists in a change for the worse instead of a change for the better: this regress position was analyzed in Chapters 8 and 9. Progress can also be denied by saying that judgments of value regarding historical changes, even if these reveal an overall pattern, are not objectively valid or meaningful. In effect, this is not only to deny progress itself but to characterize the discussion of it in the literature as mere verbal bickering, as the expression of personal prejudices and preferences having no final, transsubjective importance or value. This position is treated in the present chapter, which closes the analysis of the general controversy about progress.

In considering this position, it is important to keep in mind the distinction between it and the issues in the philosophy of history that were considered in Chapters 12 and 13. There, the emphasis was on the preconditions, so to speak, of an affirmation of progress; the authors whose views were analyzed denied these preconditions—namely, that there is a pattern of history, and that it can be known by men and in fact is known by them —preconditions that are usually only implicitly affirmed by progress authors. The issues were therefore seen as in a sense prior to the core of the general controversy, for the issues in that core—issues developed from the conflict between various descriptions of the known pattern of history, as progressive, regressive, or cyclical—obviously depend on the prior affirmation that there is such a pattern, and that it is known. Here, the emphasis is differently placed.

The authors about to be considered do not usually deny, at least not explicitly, that there is a pattern of history, or that it can be and is known; nor do they all deny—and this is of first importance—that the pattern consists in a change that is irreversible. What they deny is that the change, even if it is irreversible in the long run, can be said to be for the better in the sense of positive and lasting amelioration or improvement for the human race as a whole. The emphasis is on the making of moral judgments, not on the finding of historical patterns, which, in fact, the authors may concede to be not only possible but valid and appropriate for historians to do. The issue, therefore, may be properly said to be in moral philosophy rather than in the philosophy of history. As such, it is in a sense posterior to the core of the general controversy about our subject.

GENERAL DENIALS OF THE OBJECTIVE VALIDITY AND MEANING OF JUDGMENTS OF VALUE

It is hard to find authors who discuss progress saying explicitly that judgments of value regarding the pattern of history are inadmissible because not objectively valid or meaningful. (The one author who does say this clearly and explicitly—Carl Becker—is discussed in the next section.) The position may, however, be implicit in the views of writers who deny progress on the grounds that if there is such a pattern, it cannot be known by men. A case in point is the position, discussed in Chapters 12 and 13, that all historical value judgments are necessarily relative to the historian's own social and intellectual situation.[1] And the opponents of "historicism," for example, Karl Popper, also seem to make this denial implicitly. Their main attack is on the assertion that a definite pattern of history can be seen and described; they thus deny not only progress but regress and cycles as well. In effect, however, their denial of progress is twofold, for they deny progress explicitly by holding that there is no pattern of history, and by saying that, even if there is one, it cannot be known; and implicitly by suggesting that even if there were such a pattern and even if it could be known, judgments of value regarding it—judgments that the present is better than the past, and that the future will be even better—are questionable at the best.

As J. H. Steward and D. B. Shimkin put it in an article that takes strong exception to Hermann J. Muller's great hopes for genetic improvement,

> the assumption that individuals can be bred for a superior culture not only lacks scientific validation of the relation between genetics and culture but presupposes indefensible conclusions concerning the superiority of any culture. *There are no ethical grounds for maintaining that modern culture is inherently superior to primitive culture or that either science or philosophy can blueprint a better culture for the future.*[2]

In the absence of explicit denials in the progress literature, a group of writers that includes A. J. Ayer, Alf Ross, C. L. Stevenson, and Hans Kelsen can provide the terms for a general denial of the objective validity and meaning of such judgments of value as are involved in any affirmation of progress. These writers, who are adherents of what Ayer calls the "emotive theory of values," hold that statements like "mankind is moving in a desirable direction" express no more than personal preferences; to say that man has progressed is to say merely that the speaker prefers the present to the past, and implies no objective improvement in the general conditions of human life. According to Ross, words like "progress" and "progressive" are emotive, subjective, nonscientific and noncognitive; ultimately, they are void of meaning, at least of the kind of meaning that progress authors evidently suppose them to bear. To say that the human race progresses is meaningful as expressing the opinion of the

---

[1] Among the authors who may be found to hold this position are Boas and Collingwood. Karl Mannheim might also be mentioned in this connection. See the selection from his *Ideology and Utopia* that appears in Gardiner (ed.), *Theories of History*, pp. 242–9. For additional names that are relevant to this discussion see above, Chapter 13, Note 2.

[2] "Sociocultural Evolution," in *Daedalus*, Summer, 1961, p. 494, Note. Emphasis added.

speaker, but it does not express anything that is really meaningful about the human race itself as it is subjected to historical change in time.

The fundamental diversity or opposition for which Ross argues can be exhibited by listing in parallel columns certain terms that he would contrast as belonging to entirely different realms.

concept	emotion
fact	value
true-false	good-bad
is	ought
rational	irrational
theoretical	practical
scientific	nonscientific
objective	subjective
descriptive	normative
representative meaning	expressive meaning
argument	persuasion[3]

The words "progress" and "progressive" would fall in the second, or right-hand, column; the words "evolution" and "evolutionary," or "development" and "developmental," would fall in the first, or left-hand, column.

It is objectively meaningful to say that the human race undergoes some sort of evolution or development. It is only subjectively and emotively meaningful to say that mankind progresses, in the sense of advancing from a condition of things that is relatively worse to one that is relatively better. It is not necessarily *true* that the human race evolves socially; but the statement that it does so can be declared true or false on the basis of appropriate evidence and argument. There is no appropriate evidence, capable of scientific and rational assessment, for or against the proposition that the human race progresses or has progressed.

The combination of this explicit denial of the objective validity or meaning of value judgments, in the work of men like Stevenson and Ayer, with the implicit denial of such judgments in the work of authors like Mannheim, G. P. Adams, A. I. Melden, W. R. Dennes,[4] and Croce,

[3] *On Law and Justice*, pp. 274, 299–305. For a discussion of Ross's theory in another connection, see Otto Bird, *The Idea of Justice*, Chapter III, where Kelsen and Ayer are also considered. And for a general treatment of the emotive theory of values, see Mary Warnock, *Ethics Since 1900*, Chapter 4. Mrs. Warnock there provides lengthy analyses of the views of Ayer and Stevenson, and also discusses Ogden and Richards, Dewey, Ralph Barton Perry, and Wittgenstein. She suggests that the last named is the progenitor of the position.

[4] Essays by Adams, Melden, and Dennes appear in W. R. Dennes (ed.), *Civilization*. In "Judgments in the Social Sciences," Melden includes a lengthy discussion of Mannheim's relativistic theory of values, as originally propounded in *Ideology and Utopia*.

who question the validity of affirmations of progress, leads to the kind of denial of progress we are considering in this chapter. The leading adherent of this position is the historian Carl Becker.

Becker's Theory of "Non-Meliorative Progress": Irreversible Cumulative Change in History

Becker's philosophy of history was thoroughly and fundamentally pragmatic, says Leo Gershoy; and, Gershoy goes on to say, Becker

> linked this pragmatism to his much-disputed idea of history, his famous relativist position that absolute norms did not exist, that the observer for all his presumed detachment was part of the observed. Reason, truth, and value judgments were purely relative, having neither objective validity nor meaning apart from the social situation in which they were framed and from which they arose. Long before he elaborated this heresy in a challenging presidential address before the American Historical Association in 1931, Becker had solemnly apostrophized the muse with the words: "O History, how many truths have been committed in thy name!"[5]

Becker's theory of "non-meliorative progress" is propounded in his book *Progress and Power*. He quotes G. K. Chesterton as saying that "nobody has any right to use the word 'progress' unless he has a definite creed. . . . For progress by its very name indicates a direction; and the moment we are doubtful about the direction, we become to the same degree doubtful about the progress."[6] But, after all, Becker asks, is this really true? Must we cease to talk about progress if we have ceased, as he concedes that he has, to be doctrinal? Are there not "absolute criteria" for progress—for example, happiness, longevity, material well-being, intelligence, morality? What can be said for these criteria as standards for measuring the progress of mankind toward a good end?

"I think," says Becker, "that very little can be said for them." Happiness is incommensurable, and longevity, though measurable, is of no value unless one's life is satisfying. Material well-being is only the means to

---

[5] *Progress and Power*, Introductory Essay, p. xviii. Gershoy gives the impression that Becker originated this idea. But Burckhardt, and perhaps others, as we showed in Chapter 12, hold similar views.

[6] *Ibid.*, pp. 11–12. "On this account of it, we can all easily recognize Mr. Chesterton's right to talk about progress," Becker declares, "since he has the courage to be doctrinal: he may not be infallible, but at least he manages, every bright morning, to convey the impression of having recently and pleasantly communed with some infallibility."

something better, and, concerning intelligence, we must ask, intelligence for what?

> Intelligence is a specialized quality, specific for the task: and how can we tell whether the intelligence of Einstein is better or worse than that of Aristotle?

"Finally, as for morality, what, if anything, is it but custom, which is admittedly nothing if not infinitely variable?"[7]

All these criteria are empty words until we give them a content, Becker declares, and the only content we can give them is the temporary and conflicting values of our own times. These values are valid for us and our own times, and it is therefore right, and indeed necessary, that we should endeavor to make them prevail. But that is a very different thing from making an objective judgment regarding the entire history of the human race, to the effect that it shows a consistent change for the better. To make such a judgment on the basis of these personal values would be to recreate the world in our own image.

> Recreating the world in my own image is, however, what I wish particularly to avoid doing—at least in so far as it can be avoided. Mankind, taking it by and large, has as yet paid so little attention to my values and aversions that it seems presumptuous to erect them into absolute standards for judging it; and it is therefore futile . . . to inquire whether the human race is moving toward either a good or a bad end until some less fallible intelligence than mine turns up to tell me what that end is.[8]

"I thus conclude," Becker goes on to say, "that my ethical and moral judgments are, as Justice Holmes said of Truth, no more than 'the system of my limitations.' "[9] These limitations cannot be transcended in the realm of practical activities, but they can be ignored in "the conceptual realm of thought."

> I will, therefore, for the purpose of this discussion [of human progress], dismiss all ethical and moral judgments, forget about the final or relatively good end toward which man may be moving, and endeavor to estimate human progress in terms of what man has in fact done, and of the means that have enabled him to do it, without prejudice to the values which, at any moment of time, may have seemed to him valid grounds for his activities. By taking a sufficiently long-time view of these activities, it may be possible to note in what essential respects man has become different from what he was, from his cousins the apes—those friendly enemies with whom, in "the dark backward and abysm of time," he associated on scarcely more

[7] *Ibid.*, p. 14.
[8] *Ibid.*, p. 16.
[9] *Ibid.*, p. 18.

than equal terms. *The extent and character of this difference, whether the difference itself is to be judged good or ill, will be taken as the measure of human progress.*[10]

According to Becker, there is such a difference, as is clear enough from the fact that men put apes into zoos, and not the other way around.[11] The difference is manifested in an "expansion of human power," by which, Becker says, "I mean no more than the capacity of men to do something, whether in the mental or the physical realm, that they could not do before."

All that has happened to man in 506,000 years may be symbolized by this fact—at the end of the Time-Scale he can, with ease and expedition, put his ancestors in cages: he has somehow learned the trick of having conveniently at hand and at his disposal powers not provided by his biological inheritance. *From the beginning of the Time-Scale man has increasingly implemented himself with power.*[12]

Indeed, had he not done so, man would have had no history, nor even the consciousness of not having any; he would still be what he was at the beginning, *Pithecanthropus erectus.* "Without power no progress."[13]

Man has progressed—but only in this sense. Indeed, it may be that improvement of the human condition is not to be expected until progress in *this* sense stops, until science ceases to provide men with "dangerous new powers."

It is conceivable, even probable, that the possibility of discovering and applying new sources and implements of power will in the course of time gradually diminish, or even be altogether exhausted.[14]

In that event, Becker declares, the conditions of life will change less and less rapidly, will in time become sufficiently stable perhaps to be comprehended, sufficiently stable therefore for a relatively complete adjustment of ideas and habits to the relatively unchanging body of matter-of-fact knowledge of man and the world in which he lives. In that far-off condition of things,

in such a stabilized and scientifically adjusted society, the idea of progress would no doubt become irrelevant as progress itself became imperceptible or nonexistent.[15]

[10] *Ibid.,* pp. 18–19. Emphasis added.
[11] A science-fiction novel by L. Sprague de Camp takes as its premise that a few men have been transported into a future in which apes place men in zoos.
[12] *Op. cit.,* p. 24. Emphasis added.
[13] *Ibid.*
[14] *Ibid.,* p. 112.
[15] *Ibid.*

Becker speaks of progress almost as if it were the technological progress of which so many other authors write; indeed, he calls his subject technological progress in several places. Nevertheless, his subject is not progress, or even technological progress, as it is understood in the present work. It is not change for the better that he is discussing; nor is it change for the worse—what we have called regress in the guise of technological progress.[16] It is a phenomenon in all other respects the same as that which is discussed by others; but it differs in this one essential respect—that Becker refuses to judge it to be for good or for ill. He consistently uses the word "progress" to apply to this phenomenon.

> In the long-time perspective, from *Pithecanthropus* to Einstein, the progress of mankind, irrespective of the rise and fall of particular civilizations, has been accomplished by the slow, often interrupted, but fairly persistent extension of matter-of-fact knowledge and matter-of-fact apprehension to an ever widening realm of experience.[17]

And he foresees a time when this kind of matter-of-fact knowledge and apprehension will be extended to include the whole world of human relations, an extension, it appears, of which he approves. But even that will not be progress in the sense of a change for the better; for Becker holds that no such judgment can be made with objective meaning and validity.

The analytical difficulty caused by Becker's discussion of a phenomenon that he actually calls "progress" but that is not progress as we understand it may be resolved by our use of a new term. Disregarding Becker's use of the word "progress," let us say that he writes not of progress but of what we may call nonmeliorative *irreversible cumulative change*—a steady change in one direction, that of ever expanding power, which is, in his view, the most marked characteristic of man's career on earth considered over the last half million years at least. We observe that Becker holds that this phenomenon, which we may refer to by the mnemonic "ICC," is to some extent or in some sense necessary—that is, it appears to satisfy an exigency of man's very nature—but that it may nevertheless come to an end in the far distant future.

Such a resolution of the analytical difficulty is all the more desirable since ICC seems to be discussed, sometimes very obliquely and never very consistently, by a number of leading progress authors. How the phenomenon is conceived by some representative writers, and what is its relationship to progress itself, are questions that are considered in the next section.

[16] See Chapter 8.
[17] *Op. cit.*, p. 110.

Progress and ICC

If we refer back to the four assertions that underlie any affirmation of progress—the four assertions that are discussed in the General Introduction, and that are listed at the beginning of this chapter—we see that progress may be defined by the phrase *irreversible meliorative change.* That is, progress is a change that is not essentially reversible (though it may be temporarily reversed), and furthermore constitutes an improvement in the general conditions of human life, or in some aspect thereof. The phrase *irreversible cumulative change,* then, clearly distinguishes this phenomenon—the one discussed by Becker—from progress itself. ICC, like progress, is a patterned change in the general conditions of human life; and it is a change that is not essentially reversible, though it too may be temporarily reversed (for a longer or shorter period, man's power might decrease rather than increase, but in the long run it increases). But the change represented by ICC is not meliorative, like progress; it cannot be said to be for the better. Instead, it is a cumulative change in the general conditions of human life.

If, now, we remove from the conception of ICC the notion that it represents a more or less constant increase in human power, and view it only as representing the more or less constant (irreversible) cumulative increase of something (which might or might not be power), we begin to comprehend a conception that seems to underlie, or at least to be connected with, the idea of progress as it is discussed in the works of some major writers. In general, we find that these writers have four different views of the relation of ICC to progress:

1. ICC is the same as progress. That is, the historical pattern of irreversible cumulative change in the general conditions of human life is inherently meliorative.

2. ICC is the cause or condition of progress. That is, the historical pattern of irreversible cumulative change in the general conditions of human life underlies or precedes progress. Progress cannot occur without ICC; but ICC is not necessarily, or not always or in every respect, progress.

3. ICC either is, or is the condition of, regress. That is, the historical pattern of irreversible cumulative change in the general conditions of human life either is inherently for the worse—is pejorative—or leads to or brings about a worsening of those conditions.

4. ICC, while it definitely occurs, cannot be said to be either meliorative or pejorative, or even to be the condition of melioration or pejoration.

That is, the historical pattern of irreversible cumulative change in the general conditions of human life cannot be judged to be either an improvement or a worsening of those conditions.

This last view is held by Becker, as we have seen, and perhaps by some other writers. The first three views require some further comment.

ICC as Inherently Meliorative

The view that the pattern of history shows irreversible cumulative change, and, furthermore, that this change is inherently meliorative or for the better, is primarily associated with the Marxist authors. According to them, history shows a more or less constant increase in man's power and also an advance in the degree or character of human social organization. They hold, in addition, that despite the appearances, and despite temporary real regressions reflected in the sufferings of this or that generation, the general course of history is for the better, since history is moving necessarily and inevitably toward the condition of things that they call true communism. In other words, history is justified by its end or goal; since this is good, and since history tends toward it, this tendency is in itself a change for the better.

Some other writers, for example, Augustine, millennialists like the Joachimites and Lessing, Leibniz, Hegel, and a few modern writers like Henry Adams, may hold what are essentially similar views. All of these authors either explicitly recognize or seem inclined to consider the fact, as it seems to them, that history often or even typically shows changes in the general conditions of human life that are undesirable, at least to some people. But this does not hinder them from affirming overall progress with confidence. History, though it sometimes involves undesirable changes, is basically meliorative, because it is moving toward an end or goal that is basically desirable.

This end or goal, for many of these writers, is a kind of millennium—a condition of things than which no better or more desirable can exist, or can be conceived. But this is not always true for them. Leibniz, for example, does not affirm a fixed end or goal of history. He nevertheless concurs with these writers in many ways.

ICC as the Condition of Melioration

The view that ICC is the cause or condition of true or real progress is held by a relatively large number of authors, although the position is not always explicitly expressed in their works. Dewey, for example, maintains that past technological and economic advances are not progress in themselves, though, as he says, we often think they were or act as if they were; instead, they are the condition of progress, which we can have, he declares, if we want it—but only at the cost of great effort. Hence, for him, ICC is the condition of progress, but progress does not always follow from it.

A similar position seems to be taken by Ortega, who distinguishes between "simple progress" and "progress toward the better."

> Now concerning man it must be said, not only that his being is variable, but also that his being grows and, in this sense, that it progresses. The error of the old doctrine of progress lay in affirming *a priori* that man progresses towards the better. That is something that can only be determined *a posteriori* by concrete historical reason. . . . But that our life does possess a simply progressive character, this we can affirm *a priori* with full evidence and with a surety. . . . The same knowledge that discovers to us man's variation makes patent his progressive consistency.[18]

"To progress," Ortega adds, "is to accumulate being, to store up reality." This is a cumulative change; it is obviously irreversible; but it is not always—not "necessarily" or "inevitably"—meliorative. The accumulation of being, the storing up of reality—by means, we may conclude, though Ortega does not make this clear, of the transmission of acquired knowledge and experience through tradition—is ICC. (This notion is different from Becker's increase of power; it is a more fundamental or rudimentary notion.) But it is not progress in the sense of an irreversible meliorative change. Whether or not that occurs, whether or not that is the pattern of history, can only be determined after the fact—*a posteriori*. In fact, Ortega does not seem to feel that progress is the pattern of history at the present time, although he concedes that progress has occurred in the past and may occur in the future.

Others also see a phenomenon of historical change that may be called ICC as underlying progress, or as in some way acting as a cause or condition of it, but they differ with Dewey and Ortega in holding that progress always—necessarily or inevitably—follows from it. A case in point is Comte, who sometimes, though not always, speaks of what he calls "social evolution" or "development" as being in itself a necessary historical phenomenon, and also as necessarily or inevitably resulting in progress—a change for the better in the general conditions of human life. Social evolution or

[18] *History as a System*, pp. 217–218.

development, though it is variously conceived by Comte,[19] is akin to our ICC. In speaking of the relation between this underlying process and progress itself, Comte declares that "the only ground of discussion is whether development and improvement . . . are one; whether the development is necessarily *accompanied by* a corresponding amelioration, or progress, properly so called." And he adds that "to me it appears that the amelioration is as unquestionable as the development *from which it proceeds.*"[20]

Mill seems to concur with Comte on this point, as do a number of others. However, they are not so clear and unambiguous in their discussion of it as he is.[21]

ICC as Inherently Regressive, or as the Condition of Regress

The view that the pattern of history shows irreversible cumulative change, either in power or in some other respect, and that this change is either inherently regressive or always—"necessarily" or "inevitably"— leads to regress, is primarily represented by the "anti-technologists" like Juenger, Seidenberg, and Ellul, who were discussed in Chapter 8. Juenger takes the position more uncompromisingly than the others, but they all seem to concur in holding that advancing technology—a variant of ICC

[19] Sometimes, social evolution or development seems for Comte to mean no more than the increase of knowledge and experience brought about by the transmission of social acquisitions from one generation to all subsequent generations. At other times, the notion is more complex and involves the law of the three states of the human mind—theological, metaphysical, and positive. When the latter notion is in Comte's mind he seems to feel that the process is inherently meliorative, and is not merely the condition of melioration.

[20] *Positive Philosophy*, p. 467. Emphasis added.

[21] For example, in *A System of Logic*, Mill writes: "The words Progress and Progressive are not here understood as synonymous with improvement and tendency to improvement. It is conceivable that the laws of human nature might determine, and even necessitate, a certain series of changes in man and society, which might not in every case, or which might not on the whole, be improvements. It is my belief indeed," he adds, "that the general tendency is, and will continue to be, saving occasional and temporary exceptions, one of improvement—a tendency towards a better and happier state" (p. 596).

These remarks, and a very few others of the same kind, were the cause of much difficulty until it was understood that Mill, and the few others who speak thus, do in fact—at least in those of their works that have been examined—take the words "progress" and "progressive" as synonymous with improvement and a tendency to improvement, in spite of their assertions to the contrary. See for example the following three or four pages in Mill's *A System of Logic*, where he seems to take the words in exactly the sense in which he says he is not taking them.

in general—either is, or results in, a change for the worse in the general conditions of human life.

They differ in their view of the irreversibility of the underlying process. N. O. Brown seems to hint that ICC—which for him is perhaps more economic than technological—might be stopped, or at least changed in direction, by means of a universal psychoanalysis. This of course would convert regress into progress. Ellul seems to suggest that technology can be controlled if we fully understand its nature and the problems that it inevitably raises, which again is to affirm, albeit very hesitantly, contingent progress in the future. Their position is hard to comprehend for the reasons that we have more than once discussed: namely, that regress authors never affirm regress as incontrovertibly as at least some progress authors affirm progress. However, the gist of their arguments seems to be fairly summed up in the propositions that ICC is the pattern of history, and that it tends to lead, if it does not inevitably lead, to regress—to a change for the worse in the general conditions of human life.

In any event, their position is clearly distinguished from that of Becker and those who, like him, maintain that no judgment of melioration *or* of pejoration may properly be made regarding ICC or its results. These writers seem to have no difficulty in judging that ICC either is in itself or results in a change for the worse.

Let us return now to the issue in moral philosophy that is the real subject of this chapter. We see on reflection that all of the authors discussed in the previous section are directly opposed on this issue both to those who explicitly deny that objective and meaningful (moral) judgments regarding historical changes can validly be made, and to those, at the same time, who only implicitly deny this. That is, they are opposed to writers like Mannheim, Collingwood, Boas, and Popper, insofar as they judge that history shows *either* progress *or* regress (*i.e.*, shows a change that is *either* objectively and meaningfully for the better *or* objectively and meaningfully for the worse); and they are opposed to Becker and others like him insofar as they hold that a process that he calls "progress" is actually either for the better or for the worse, which he denies.

On one side of the issue, then, stands a group of authors who may or may not use the word "progress" to refer to changes that occur in history, but who in fact deny progress by taking the negative position on the issue in question. And on the other side stands a group of authors who may—and often do—have the same doubts about the real occurrence of improvement or melioration as their opponents, and who may discuss the underlying process of change—ICC—in much the same terms as they, but who nevertheless affirm at least contingent progress by taking the affirmative side of the issue, and of course by making the other assertions mentioned at the beginning of this chapter as well.

Becker is the most troublesome figure here. The other opponents of the progress authors—that is, mainly, the writers we discussed in Chapters 12 and 13—deny progress by denying one or more of the four assertions *besides* the assertion that progress always means a change for the better. Becker is the only writer we have found, although there are probably others who have like ideas, who goes so far along, as it were, with the progress authors—to the extent of even using their key word—and then, at the last moment, parts company from them. It is to be hoped, nevertheless, that this chapter has helped to make his position clear.

I

Issues About the Nature or Properties of Progress

15

Is Progress Necessary
or Contingent?

THE issue, whether progress is necessary and must occur, or whether it is contingent on factors that may or may not operate to bring it about, is probably the most explicit in the literature of the subject. In this chapter, we will treat first the position that progress must occur, and second, the position that it need not. The position that progress *will not* occur is of course a denial of progress, and hence cannot be treated here.

The assertion that there is a *de jure* necessity for progress—that progress is the law of history—is usually sufficient to place an author on the affirmative side of the issue, but this is not always so. Whether or not he maintains that there is a *de jure* necessity for progress, an author must state that progress will occur *in fact* to be so placed. An author is therefore not counted as a necessary progress author unless he asserts—or may be inferred to hold—that progress will actually occur in the future.[1]

---

[1] There is a sense, of course, in which all progress in the past was necessary. What happened happened, and if it was an improvement so much the better, but there is no changing it now. It is in this sense that Childe, for example, can define progress as "what actually happened—the content of history" (*Man Makes Himself*, p. 11).

This does not mean, however, that necessary progress need be continuous. The position that progress must occur does not always imply that "every day, in every way, we are getting better and better." While a few authors, notably Comte, maintain that progress is both necessary and continuous, and that it is only the *rate* of progress that is subject to contingencies, others allow for gaps, missteps, and wrong turnings in the advance of mankind, and assert only that progress must occur in the long run.

Similarly, many authors see the difficulty of holding that the situation of every single human being must improve. Here it is important to recall that our topic is the progress of the human race considered as a whole, not any part of it, nor indeed all of it during but a part of the time it exists on earth. Thus the progress of mankind is admitted by some necessary progress authors—though not all—to be a change that is not particularly desirable or beneficial for at least some individuals, even for entire nations or races. It is only the general, average, or overall situation that must improve.

To be counted as a necessary progress author, then, one must assert or be inferred to hold that mankind in general, or the general conditions of human life, will necessarily, in the long future and taking into account possible regressive periods, change for the better and undergo improvement. A contingent progress author, on the contrary, is one who asserts or may be inferred to hold that progress *may* occur in the future, but that it also may not.[2]

Necessary progress authors give three reasons for saying that progress is necessary. The differences among the reasons reflect differences among theories of progress.

1. Progress is necessary because it is willed and thus assured by Providence.
2. Progress is necessary because it is assured by a natural cosmic principle that is not exclusively in human nature.
3. Progress is necessary because it is inherent in human nature.

Authors who hold that progress is necessary are listed on the next page.

2 Perhaps the most general term employed by progress authors to denote the capacity of mankind for progress is perfectibility. The issue, then, is whether mankind must be perfected in time, or whether it may not be. Perfected is not equivalent to perfect, as several writers point out. And they disagree on what it means to be perfected.

Augustine	Guizot
Joachimites	Saint-Simon
Pascal	Comte
Leibniz	Buckle
Fontenelle	J. S. Mill
Turgot	Marx
Kant	Engels
Robinet	Spencer
Lessing	Henry Adams
Herder	Lenin
Condorcet	Trotsky
Godwin	Bukharin
Malthus	Teilhard de Chardin
Chateaubriand	C. G. Darwin
Madame de Staël	E. H. Carr
Hegel	

Although contingent progress authors discuss many factors on which progress is in their view dependent, all of these actually reduce to one—human freedom. Man is free, according to these authors, to progress or not.

The following authors are those who hold that progress is contingent on man's desire or willingness to bring it about.[3]

Bacon	Broad
Descartes	Maritain
Voltaire	Simon
Helvétius	Ginsberg
Fourier	Carrel
Bagehot	Einstein
Henry George	Hermann J. Muller
Charles Darwin	Toynbee
T. H. Huxley	Mumford
Tolstoy	Rougemont
Bryce	H. Brown
Dewey	Calder

THE POSITION THAT PROGRESS IS NECESSARY

"There is no doubt, generally speaking, that what has not yet appeared upon earth will at some future period appear," says Herder; "for no

[3] This list could be expanded by the inclusion of many contemporary writers.

prescription is a bar to the rights of man, and the powers, that God has implanted in him, are ineradicable."[4] Hence every sort of improvement must ultimately become fact. The reason is that

> the general composition of powers and forms is neither retrograde, nor stationary, but progressive. This position appears self-evident: for how can we conceive any living power in nature to stand still, or retrograde, unless it be circumscribed, or repelled, by some inimical superiour power? It acts as an organ of the Almighty, *as an active idea of his permanent plan of creation;* and thus it must actively increase its powers.[5]

Here God is the ultimate assurance of progress; but it is God working through nature. Kant entertains a similar notion. All the capacities implanted in a creature by nature, he declares, are destined to unfold themselves, completely and conformably to their end, in the course of time. But what are the means, he asks, by which "this continuous progress to the better may be maintained and even hastened?"

> When carefully considered, we soon see that as this process must go on to an incalculable distance of time, it cannot depend so much on what we may do of ourselves . . . as on what human *Nature* as such will do *in* and with us, to compel us to move in a track into which we would not readily have betaken ourselves.[6]

However, it is not human nature alone that insures progress; nor is it nature alone, either. In another work, Kant writes:

> For, it is from human Nature in general, or rather—since supreme wisdom is requisite for the accomplishment of this end—it is from *Providence* alone that we can expect a result which proceeds by relation to the whole and reacts through the whole upon the parts.[7]

Leibniz' position, although not so explicit, is similar. "We must recognize," he declares, "a certain perpetual and very free progress of the whole universe, such that it is always going forward to greater improvement."[8] This is manifested, among other ways, in a progressive revelation of God's being to man. And since

[4] *Outlines of a Philosophy of the History of Man,* Book XV, p. 438. See also Teggart (ed.), *The Idea of Progress,* p. 319.
[5] *Ibid.,* Book V, p. 114; see Teggart, pp. 310–311.
[6] *Idea of a Universal History,* in W. Hastie (ed.), *Principles of Politics,* p. 4. See also Teggart, p. 293. As such, the statement does not imply that it is Providence that assures the unfolding. In this work, Kant makes no mention of Providence, speaking only of nature as the source of necessary melioration.
[7] "On the Saying: That a Thing May Be Right in Theory, But May Not Hold in Practice," in Hastie, p. 71; see Teggart, p. 307.
[8] *On the Ultimate Origination of Things,* in R. Latta (ed.), *The Monadology and Other Philosophical Writings,* p. 350; see also Teggart, p. 203.

God, being infinite, cannot be entirely known . . . our happiness will never consist . . . in complete enjoyment, which would leave nothing more to be desired and would make our mind stupid; but it *must consist* in a perpetual progress to new pleasures and new perfections.[9]

Necessary progress also consists for Augustine, Lessing, and the Joachimites in a progressive revelation of God to man. God wills, in Lessing's phrase, "the education of the human race"; if He did not will it, it would not occur. Thus, with respect to man, melioration *must* occur, and progress is necessary; man could not avert or avoid it even if he wanted to; but this does not mean, of course, that God is bound by the same necessity. Nor, in another sense, is mankind bound, at least to the extent that it loses its freedom; for if this were so, the change would not be for the better.

This point is made by several writers. The "defective beginning"—his near animality—of man's history is, says Herder, "a proof of his endless progress."

For man must himself acquire by exercise this degree of light and security, so as under the guidance of his father to become a nobler, freer creature, by his own exertions; and this he will become. Thus the simular of man will become man in reality: thus the bud of humanity, benumbed by cold, and parched by heat, will expand in its true form, in its proper and full beauty.[10]

Man's freedom, here affirmed, is not a contingency on which progress depends. Progress is necessary; melioration will occur in fact. Herder's point is that man will choose it freely, will work for it freely, and will therefore deserve it. Progress will occur no matter what happens; what will *not* happen, Herder is careful to remind us, is that man will choose not to improve. And the source of this disposition in man is Providence.

Kant concurs. Nature has willed, he declares,

that man shall produce wholly out of himself all that goes beyond the mechanical structure and arrangement of his animal existence, and that he shall participate in no other happiness or perfection but what he has procured for himself, apart from instinct, by his own reason.[11]

Hence, as before, man will deserve the progress that is nevertheless secured to him by God.[12] A formulation of this view that probably would not be rejected by either Kant or Herder is provided by Guizot.

[9] *Principles of Nature and of Grace*, in Latta, p. 424; see Teggart, p. 208. Emphasis added. There is a similarity here to Carr, who also rejects the notion of a fixed goal of progress. See Note 39, below.
[10] *Op. cit.*, Book V, p. 125; see Teggart, p. 312.
[11] *Idea of a Universal History*, in Hastie, pp. 5–6; see Teggart, p. 294.
[12] Similar remarks were made concerning salvation in an earlier Christian tradition.

Conceive a great machine, the design of which is centered in a single mind, though its various parts are entrusted to various workmen, separated from and strangers to each other. None of them understands the work as a whole, nor the general result which he concurs in producing; but everyone executes, *with intelligence and freedom*, the particular task assigned to him. It is thus, that, by the hand of man, the designs of Providence are wrought out in the government of the world.[13]

And Malthus' view of the matter, based as it is on the conception of the world and this life as the mighty process of God for the creation and formation of mind, is essentially the same. Man is free, yet he *must* undergo change for the better. He cannot avoid progress.[14]

It may be remarked that all of the authors who are cited in Chapter 5 as holding that the source of progress is God or Providence, also hold that progress is necessary.

Since all things proceed in accordance with law, it is clear, says Bukharin, that there is no such thing as accident in history.

Each historical event, however accidental it may appear, is absolutely and completely conditioned by certain causes; historical accidentalism also simply means the intersection of certain causal series of which only one series is known. . . . Strictly speaking, there is no such thing as an accidental phenomenon in the historical evolution of society. . . . *All* events from the most petty and insignificant to the most epoch-making events of our time, are *equally not accidental*, are equally conditioned by causes, *i.e.*, are equally the result of causal necessity.[15]

These remarks apply above all to the "historical evolution of society," which is progressive, *i.e.*, consists in change for the better. For "does not humanity propose for itself a great goal; namely communism?" Bukharin

[13] *History of Civilization in Europe*, p. 291.

[14] Malthus' first essay on population, which is, unlike later versions, primarily an essay on history, devotes its main attention to the refutation of the "easy optimism" of Godwin and Condorcet about future progress. However, Malthus does not, as we have seen, deny progress in his attacks on their beliefs; nor does he differ markedly with them on the question whether progress is necessary. Instead, he takes issue with Condorcet mainly on the question whether there is progress in "human nature" as well as in the exterior conditions of human life; and he takes issue with Godwin mainly on the question whether progress will be unlimited in certain respects. These disputes are treated elsewhere in this study. Despite his reputation for pessimism, it is worth noting that Malthus holds that some progress must occur. But it is rather a distant progress, far removed from the present day; in the practical, everyday world, progress is not at all automatic, and it is this notion that is most memorable in the essay.

[15] *Historical Materialism*, pp. 44–6.

asks. "Does not the entire evolution of history move toward this goal?" And even if communism be not attained, progress is still inevitable. Bukharin writes:

> Let us consider human society. No matter how we imagine the future of this society to be (whether this future will be socialism, or any other form of society), is it not apparent that the human type is growing, that man is becoming more "cultivated," that he is perfecting himself, and that we, the lords of creation, are advancing on the road of civilization and progress?[16]

That progress is necessary has taken on the character of a Marxist dogma. In the *1961 Draft Program* we find these declarations, for example:

> The epoch-making turn of mankind from capitalism to socialism, initiated by the October Revolution, is a natural result of the development of society. Marxism-Leninism discovered the objective laws of social development and revealed the contradictions inherent in capitalism, the inevitability of their bringing about a revolutionary explosion and of the transition of society to communism.[17]

And Engels is hardly less explicit in his formulation of the "fundamental proposition" of Marx's thought, in which the key words are "necessarily" and "evolution."[18] According to Engels, social evolution is as necessary as evolution itself, and the latter is necessary in the same way as all natural processes.

> To expect any other division of the products from the capitalistic mode of production is the same as expecting the electrodes of a battery not to decompose acidulated water, not to liberate oxygen at the positive, hydrogen at the negative pole, so long as they are connected with the battery.[19]

The fact that progress is inevitable does not mean for the Marxist authors any more than for Guizot, Herder, and Kant that mankind should not act to accelerate its pace. "The highroad to Socialism has been paved"

[16] *Ibid.*, p. 24. Bukharin continues, in language very much like that of Herder and Kant, to remark on the analogies between society and nature. "Precisely as the structure of the animal is becoming better adapted to its purpose," he says, "so also is society becoming more perfected in its structure, *i.e.*, more adapted to plan. Here the goal (perfection) is revealed in the course of evolution. It is not designed in advance by divinity, but blows forth like the rose from its blossom, simultaneously with the development of this blossom into the rose, by virtue of certain causes" (*ibid.*). The difference between Bukharin, and Kant and Herder, of course, is that for the former God or Providence has no part in the process.

[17] *Program of the Communist Party of Soviet Union (Draft)*, 1961, p. 107.

[18] See "Preface" to the *Communist Manifesto*, in Marx, *Capital, The Communist Manifesto, and Other Writings*, p. 318.

[19] *Socialism: Utopian and Scientific*, p. 135.

by the Russian Socialist state, declares the *1961 Draft Program;* "many persons are already marching along it, and it will be taken sooner or later by all peoples."[20] Nevertheless, this document urges "the peoples" on to more and more intensive efforts to bring about socialism with all its attendant benefits. These efforts affect only the rate of progress, however, which is necessary because of the nature of the dialectical process. The classless society will come sooner if men work for it; but it will come sooner or later whatever they do.

Engels, indeed, sees mankind gaining freedom as progress proceeds. Man is less free in "the present epoch"—in pre-Socialist society—than he will be later. After the socialist revolution "the objective, external forces which have hitherto dominated history will pass under the control of men themselves," he declares.

> It is only from this point that men, with full consciousness, will fashion their own history; it is only at this point that the social causes set in motion by men will have, predominantly, and in constantly increasing measure, the effects willed by men. It is humanity's leap from the realm of necessity to the realm of freedom.[21]

Similar statements are to be found in *Capital* and in Lenin's *The State and Revolution.*[22] Is the point that in *these* times progress is *unconsciously* willed by mankind? And that afterward it will be consciously willed? Whatever the answer, progress is necessary and must occur.[23]

Hegel[24] shares with the Marxists the belief that progress is necessary. Progress develops "according to the necessity of its nature," he declares, which is that of a "rational process." This we know both *a priori* and *a posteriori.* For in philosophy this is no hypothesis; it is there proved by speculative cognition. At the same time, "it is . . . an inference from the history of the world, that its development has been a rational process; that the history in question has constituted the rational necessary course of the World-Spirit."[25]

In a discussion of the "grades" or "stages" of progress, Hegel has this to say:

[20] *Loc. cit.,* p. 118.
[21] *Anti-Duhring,* qu. in R. L. Heilbroner, *The Future as History,* p. 43.
[22] See, for example, *The State and Revolution,* pp. 160–6.
[23] Will progress cease when the realm of freedom is attained? The answer is yes, in a sense. For a discussion of this point see Chapter 16.
[24] As before, Hegel is considered in this study in company with the Marxists and the other writers who hold that progress results from a natural principle, not divine. For a discussion of the hesitation that we feel in so placing him, see Chapter 16, Note 6.
[25] *The Philosophy of History,* p. 10.

To realize these grades is the boundless impulse of the World-Spirit—the goal of its irresistible urging; for this division into organic members, and the full development of each, is its Idea.[26]

So far, Kant, Herder, Guizot, and the Marxists might agree. But Hegel goes farther and shows—as the others may, indeed, believe—that progress is not only necessary but continuous. He is concerned by the fact that "there are many considerable periods in history in which [progress] seems to have been intermitted; in which, we might rather say, the whole enormous gain of previous culture appears to have been entirely lost."[27] The answer is that regress is only apparent at these periods, for

> in actual existence Progress appears an an advancing from the imperfect to the more perfect; but the former must not be understood abstractly as *only* the imperfect, but as something which involves the very opposite of itself— the so-called perfect—as a *germ* or impulse. . . . Thus the Imperfect, as involving its opposite, is a contradiction, which certainly exists, but which is continually annulled and solved.[28]

This "dialectic of transition" is the explanation of the fact that progress sometimes seems—but only to those who conceive it as mere growth, or mere formal development—not to occur. Progress involves a "stern reluctant working against itself," and thereby does not occur simply; nevertheless, it does not cease to occur.

The natural principle that not only brings about progress but assures it is, for Hegel and the Marxists, conflict or opposition. We have seen that another group of cosmogenic progress authors holds that progress is the result of the natural principle that, in the course of time, the simple becomes complex, the homogeneous heterogeneous. This principle also insures that progress will inevitably occur.

Progress, Spencer declares,

> is not an accident, but a necessity. Instead of civilization being artificial, it is a part of nature; all of a piece with the development of the embryo or the unfolding of a flower. The modifications mankind have undergone, and are still undergoing, result from a law underlying the whole organic creation.[29]

This law, we recall, is that every cause produces a multiplicity of effects. In comprehending it, we see, according to Spencer,

[26] *Ibid.*, p. 53.
[27] *Ibid.*, p. 56.
[28] *Ibid.*, p. 57. At the same time that progress is necessary, man remains free— indeed becomes more free as progress occurs; for "the History of the world is none other than the progress of the consciousness of Freedom" (*ibid.*, p. 19).
[29] *Social Statics*, p. 80.

that as in each event of to-day, so from the beginning, the decomposition of every expended force into several forces has been perpetually producing a higher complication; that the increase of heterogeneity so brought about is still going on and must continue to go on; and that thus progress is not an accident, not a thing within human control, but a beneficent necessity.[30]

Progress is equally inevitable for Henry Adams.

In the earlier stages of progress, the forces to be assimilated were simple and easy to absorb, but, as the mind of man enlarged its range, it enlarged the field of complexity, *and must continue to do so.*[31]

And Teilhard de Chardin, agreeing with these two writers that progress is characterized by a movement toward complexity, agrees too that the process must continue to occur. "Life, by its very structure," he declares, "having once been lifted to its stage of thought, cannot go on at all without requiring to ascend ever higher."

Man is irreplaceable. Therefore, however improbable it might seem, *he must reach his goal,* not necessarily, doubtless, but infallibly.[32]

Pascal and Fontenelle hold that progress is necessary because it is in the nature of the case. The argument for the necessity of progress is the same as the argument for progress itself: the human race is like an individual man, who must advance in knowledge and understanding as he ages. "Not only does each individual man progress from day to day," Pascal declares, "but mankind as a whole constantly progresses . . . in proportion as the universe grows older."[33] And Fontenelle observes that "a good cultivated mind contains, so to speak, all the minds of preceding centuries; it is but a single identical mind which has been developing and improving itself all this time." Moreover,

the man in question will have no old age, he will always be equally capable of those things for which his youth was suited, and he will be ever more and more capable of those things which are suited to his prime; that is to say, to abandon the allegory, men will never degenerate, and there will be no end to the growth and development of human wisdom.[34]

Many writers affirm the necessity of progress on the same grounds. Condorcet, for instance, declares that

[30] *Progress: Its Law and Cause,* in Teggart, p. 447.
[31] *The Education of Henry Adams,* p. 487. Emphasis added.
[32] *The Phenomenon of Man,* p. 232.
[33] *Preface to the Treatise on the Vacuum,* in GBWW, Vol. 33, p. 357. See also Teggart, p. 167.
[34] *On the Ancients and Moderns,* in Teggart, p. 184.

progress is subject to the same general laws that can be observed in the development of the faculties of the individual, and it is indeed no more than the sum of that development realized in a large number of individuals joined together in society.

From this it follows, Condorcet says, that man's progress

has no other limit than the duration of the globe upon which nature has cast us. This progress will doubtless vary in speed, but it will never be reversed.[35]

In like manner, according to Comte, "the progress of the race must be considered susceptible of modification only with regard to its speed, and without any reversal in the order of development, or any interval of importance being overleaped."[36] Mill rests his belief in the necessity of progress on the fact

that there is a progressive change, both in the character of the human race and in their outward circumstances so far as moulded by themselves; that in each successive age the principal phenomena of society are different from what they were in the age preceding, and still more different from any previous age.[37]

Indeed, this kind of progressive differentiation, in Mill's view, is the basis of social science. It is the fact on which that science rests.

And Carr, declaring that

the essence of man as a rational being is that he develops his potential capacities by accumulating the experience of past generations,[38]

takes what is essentially the same position. Progress is inevitable because it is in man's very nature to transmit his "acquired social assets." Some social "forgetting" doubtless occurs, but in the long run mankind "remembers" more than it "forgets," and gains more than it loses.[39]

[35] *Sketch of an Historical Picture of the Progress of the Human Mind*, p. 4.
[36] *Positive Philosophy*, p. 470.
[37] *A System of Logic*, p. 596.
[38] *What Is History?*, p. 150.
[39] *Ibid.* We have noted that Carr concurs with Leibniz (and others) in rejecting the notion of a fixed goal of (necessary) progress. He writes: "The notion of a finite and clearly definable goal of progress in history, so often postulated by nineteenth-century thinkers, has proved inapplicable and barren. . . . Progress is an abstract term; and the concrete ends pursued by mankind arise from time to time out of the course of history, not from some source outside it." This appears to oppose Leibniz' idea, and that of others. However, Carr goes on to say that "I shall be content with the possibility of unlimited progress—or progress subject to no limits that we can or need envisage—towards goals which can be defined only as we advance towards them, and the validity of which can be verified only in a process of attaining them"

The rational and scientific bent of the modern mind is cited by a number of writers as the sign that progress in the future is inevitable, even if it was not always so. Godwin, for example, declares that

> everything may be trusted to the tranquil and wholesome progress of knowledge, and . . . the office of the enlightened friend of political justice, for the most part, consists in this only, a vigilant and perpetual endeavour to assist the progress.[40]

Madame de Staël concurs on the importance of such "assistance"; her words are somewhat wistful.

> It is easy to see how much our progress . . . would be accelerated, if all these prejudices which now stand in the way of truth were removed, and if nothing remained to philosophy, but to proceed directly from demonstration to demonstration.[41]

Nevertheless, she declares (in a statement that probably would satisfy all of the authors here being discussed) that it is "in the nature of the human understanding always to improve."[42] For the method that proceeds "directly from demonstration to demonstration" is, she explains, the one "adopted by the sciences, which every day advance to some new discovery, and *never lose what they have gained.*"[43] C. G. Darwin's view is similar. The scientific revolution that occurred in the seventeenth century has changed the world in innumerable ways, he says,

> but perhaps the most important of all is that it has provided a universality in methods of thought that was wanting before. So there is an even stronger reason to believe that the new culture cannot die, than ever held for any of the old civilizations; it has only got to survive in one part of the earth for it to be recoverable everywhere. . . . It can be regarded as certain that the new culture will be inextinguishable.[44]

According to Darwin, progress has been going on for a long time—for thousands of years at least. He suggests here that it *became necessary*

(*ibid.,* pp. 157–8). This "relativization" of the goals of history does not change the situation much. It remains true that mankind can attain whatever it desires; progress is therefore always in a desirable direction (though the direction may change). The defect is not in progress but in our vision; it is presumptuous to say in what perfectibility consists, but mankind will nevertheless become perfected. One is reminded of Godwin's claim that mankind can attain whatever it can conceive as desirable. Carr's position seems, therefore, to be a modern version of the nineteenth-century one that he opposes.

40 *Enquiry Concerning Political Justice,* Vol. I, p. 362.
41 *Influence of Literature upon Society,* Vol. I, p. 96.
42 *Ibid.,* p. 219.
43 *Ibid.,* p. 96. Emphasis added.
44 *The Next Million Years,* p. 146.

only a short time ago. Nevertheless, he is saying that progress is now necessary, and hence will necessarily occur in the future as long as there are men alive who have any cognizance whatever of scientific methods of thought. If, however, the human race ceased to have such individuals among it, it would no longer be the human race as we know it. Thus progress is necessary as long as man remains man, which is all that any necessitarian of progress is required to hold.[45]

THE POSITION THAT PROGRESS IS CONTINGENT

Simon holds that the idea of necessary progress admits of several forms and of several degrees. To be distinguished from one another are, he says, a mere exigency, an exigency accompanied by a *de jure* necessity, and an exigency accompanied by a *de jure* necessity and a *de facto* necessity. First,

> by saying that progress is a necessary thing, one can merely mean that it is the object of an aspiration, of a demand, of an imperious exigency of human nature. Progress is necessary just as virtue is necessary—that is, as a *sine qua non* of man's fidelity to his vocation. . . . If humanity progresses, it obeys the law of its nature; if it does not progress, its natural law is transgressed.[46]

This is not necessary progress as the authors on the affirmative side of the present issue understand it. Obviously, according to this view, progress, no matter how exigent, need not occur; it ought to occur, perhaps, and men desire that it shall, but it may not. Having in mind the concession in the last sentence of the quotation, an author who said no more than this would be counted as holding that progress is contingent.

By necessary progress one can also mean, Simon goes on to say, that progress

> has not only, like virtue, the necessity of an exigency, but also the necessity of an essentially indefectible determination, like every process of proper

[45] D. J. de Solla Price examines, in *Little Science, Big Science,* the growth of science in the period discussed by Darwin, and suggests that it is chimerical to expect that its development (he never uses the word progress) will continue at the same "exponential" rate or in the same way. The fact that De Solla Price is clearly not talking about the progress of the human race rules him out of consideration here. However, a number of writers seem to agree with Darwin's contention that the scientific revolution constitutes the attainment of an "unlosable" civilization, among them W. G. Sumner and Herbert Butterfield.

[46] *Community of the Free,* pp. 94–5. Here Simon's remarks seem to be directed at the authors' discussion in the last section who see progress as necessary because inherent in human nature. Simon is suggesting that they have no more to stand on than an exigency, and that there is no real ground for their assertion.

causation in the physical world. . . . The law of progress does not conjecture as to fact; it announces only a *de jure* necessity. The coincidence of
the fact and the law depends upon circumstances which no essential determination guarantees.[47]

This is not necessary progress, either, as we understand it, for there is
no assertion here that progress *will* occur, only that, in some sense, it
must. Indeed, these remarks seem most applicable to the assertion that
progress is not only necessary but continuous. But we have shown that
progress may be held to be necessary without being held to be continuous.
In any event, Simon disputes even this weak meaning of the idea of necessary progress.

His main opposition, however, is directed to the belief that progress
is subject to a *de facto* necessity—the position, in fact, of the authors on
the affirmative side of the issue. He writes:

> Finally, by saying that progress is a necessary thing, one can mean that it is
> necessary as a factual development. One then affirms that no contingency
> and no liberty can arrest it. This position has no foundation in a rational
> analysis of human nature, which reveals only possibilities of progress and
> exigencies for progress. It does violence to experience. It supposes a quasi-
> theological concept of the government of history, for which neither histori-
> cal knowledge nor philosophy affords the least shred of justification. . . .
> Belief in a factually determined progress, destined to become a reality *no
> matter what happens,* can be nothing but a substitute for belief in para-
> dise.[48]

Simon thus places himself squarely on the negative side of the issue, in
opposition to the authors considered in the first section of this chapter.

According to Maritain, the idea of necessary progress contains a contradiction. For, on the one hand, "all progress . . . demands," he declares,

---

47 *Ibid.*, pp. 95–6.

48 *Ibid.*, p. 96. In spite of Simon's assertion that there is no justification for the
position in question, it is, or at least was, widely held, as has been shown. Actually,
his assertion shows only that he does not hold the position himself. His own view
seems to be that there is an exigency for progress in human nature, and perhaps a
law of progress with regard to the increase rather than the decrease of knowledge in
time, but that there is no *de facto* necessity that progress occur.

His opposition to necessary progress authors seems to be based on his belief that
the affirmation of an exigency, no matter how compelling, cannot guarantee progress
in fact, and that the affirmation of a *de jure* necessity is not much stronger grounds
for the assertion that progress must in fact occur. This of course follows from his
notion that progress by its nature cannot be said to be subject to a *de facto* necessity,
since it depends on human freedom. An author who disputed this point—Comte, for
example—would probably place more value and importance on the affirmation of a
compelling exigency and a *de jure* necessity. For him, this affirmation would be
enough to make progress necessary in fact.

"that the future should conserve, in one way or another, the gains acquired by the past."[49] This follows from the likeness of progress to growth, which demands the incorporation of new matter with the old. At the same time, if "the law of Progress is . . . a metaphysically necessary law of human history . . . then its domain must be universal and nothing, absolutely nothing, can escape it."[50] On the other hand, however, that being so,

> there is absolutely nothing of the past which is not less good than the present, and this, in its turn, is less good than the future. . . . From which it follows that if anything of the past subsists in the present and claims to subsist in the future, it is an evil, a thing intolerable. . . . The law of Progress, then, demands for its full realization the destruction of all that comes from the past.[51]

This contradicts the earlier statement. Similarly, if it be assumed that progress is absolutely necessary and that it also has an absolutely universal domain, then

> the things that we call foundations and principles—whether in the order of knowledge or in the order of the moral life—must absolutely change like everything else. . . . But the foundations being changed, all that rested on them must break down. . . . But then it follows that since the law of Progress demands the ceaseless changing of the foundations and principles admitted in the past, it also demands that the movement of humanity toward the Better must take place by means of a process of breaking down and radical destruction, everlastingly repeated. . . . We shall then have to say that progress, as progress, demands some kind of conservation of the gains acquired by the past; but we shall have to say that Necessary Progress, in as much as it expresses a law which you claim to be metaphysically necessary and universal in its operation, demands the regular destruction and disappearance of these same gains. Thus real progress is devoured by Progress, the idea-myth.[52]

This argument is found in an early work of Maritain; in later works he expresses his opposition to the Marxists, holding, against them, that progress is contingent on human freedom. Progress is indeed "an essential impulse of human nature," he declares, in so saying seeming to agree with Simon, "but it is in itself a work of our spirit and our freedom acting in co-operation with nature."[53] Thus history and progress are not —as they are, Maritain is saying, for the Marxists—

[49] *Theonas*, p. 124.
[50] *Ibid.*
[51] *Ibid.*, pp. 124–5.
[52] *Ibid.*, pp. 127–8.
[53] *True Humanism*, p. 88.

fixed in advance by evolution; rather [they depend] on an enormous mass of accumulated necessities and fatalities, but one in which the interventions of that freedom can take effect; [they are] only fixed in advance in the degree . . . to which man renounces his own freedom.[54]

But the renunciation of freedom would in itself be regressive; hence progress is contingent on man's free choice to bring it about or not.

Few progress authors[55] are as explicit as Simon and Maritain in their denials of the necessity of progress. That progress is contingent, may, however, be inferred in the case of many writers. For instance, the assertion, made familiar by a large number of contemporary books, that mankind stands at a crossroads of history, is usually an indication that their authors hold progress to be contingent. Einstein and Russell speak of the crisis facing the race in a manifesto signed by a number of leading scientists. They speak, they say,

> as human beings, members of the species man, whose continued existence is in doubt. The world is full of conflicts. . . . Almost everybody who is politically conscious has strong feelings about one or more of these conflicts that divide mankind, but we want you, if you can, to set aside such feelings and consider yourselves only as members of a biological species which has had a remarkable history, and whose disappearance none of us can desire.
> We shall try to say no single word which would appeal to one group rather than to another. All, equally, are in peril, and, if the peril is understood, there is hope that that may collectively avert it.

These scientists, it is clear, are posing a question for the whole of mankind; the race is in peril, and, it goes without saying, progress may come to an end. After detailing the stark facts of physics "underlying the prospect of the Third World War"—they have found, they say, "that the men who know the most are the most gloomy"—they describe the alternatives thus:

> There lies before us, if we choose, continued progress in happiness, knowledge and wisdom. Shall we, instead, choose death because we cannot forget our quarrels? We appeal as human beings to human beings: remember your humanity and forget the rest. If you can do so, the way lies open to a new paradise; if you cannot there lies before you the risk of universal death.[56]

54 *Ibid.,* p. 124.
55 That is, authors who *affirm* progress rather than merely discussing it.
56 Qu. in Gerard Piel, *Science in the Cause of Man,* pp. 147–8. It should be observed that the familiar assertion that man stands at a crossroads cannot be considered in this study unless its author spells out what the alternatives are that face the human race, and in particular unless he indicates that one of them is change for the better. The *Einstein-Russell Manifesto,* of course, satisfies this condition. For no one

The signers of the *Einstein-Russell Manifesto* imply that man may continue to advance if he controls science and uses it in the right way. C. D. Broad makes some careful distinctions with regard to this general view. He shows ingeniously that "perpetual progress" is not only "logically possible," but also "causally possible"; that is, it is not only conceivable but it may actually occur.[57] However, he questions whether the "special configurations of matter in the actual Universe" may retard or even end progress. These special configurations are, it turns out, men themselves, and particularly the amount and kind of knowledge men have of different subjects. So far, men know more about inorganic matter than about living things; so far, they are better physicists and chemists than biologists and psychologists. The result is that while perpetual mental progress is certainly not logically impossible, it is also "certainly not causally inevitable, in the sense of being bound to happen whatever we may do." In the final analysis, the possibility of progress.

> depends on our getting an adequate knowledge and control of life and mind before the combination of ignorance on these subjects with knowledge of physics and chemistry wrecks the whole system. Which of the runners in this very interesting race will win, it is impossible to foretell. But physics and death have a long start over psychology and life.[58]

Einstein and Broad write at the end of a long revolutionary period in science, and plead with men to turn their efforts in another direction from the one they see leading to disaster. Bacon and Descartes, writing at the beginning of this period, do not warn of disaster, but equally urge men to act in a certain way to bring about progress. "Our only hope," says Bacon,

> is in the regeneration of the sciences, by regularly raising them on the foundation of experience and building them anew, which I think none can venture to affirm to have been already done or even thought of.[59]

---

would deny that "progress in happiness, knowledge and wisdom," and the attainment of a "new paradise," is truly a progressive change.

[57] *The Mind and Its Place in Nature*, pp. 656–62. In the process, Broad manages to get around the objection that the second law of thermodynamics constitutes the final obstacle to progress. He concedes that this law requires that the universe as a whole necessarily tends to "run down," but he points out that the law does not apply to a particular part of the universe—to a limited portion of it—and that the world of man might be such a limited portion and thus capable of enjoying ever increasing organization and centralization. In the very long run, of course, the general law would affect even the world of man, but this might occur so far in the future that man would have long since ceased to be man; or, indeed, he might have found an answer to the second law of thermodynamics! (*ibid.*, pp. 661–2).

[58] *Ibid.*, p. 666.

[59] *Novum Organon*, I, 97, in *The Advancement of Learning and Novum Organon*, p. 350.

One who maintains that "our only hope" for progress is an action never yet performed is of course saying that progress is contingent on that action, and that it will not occur if the action is not performed. Descartes has a similar view of the matter. "There is need of a method," he declares, "for finding out the truth."[60] The method is his own and has never been tried; without it truth cannot be found.

> In the subjects we propose to investigate, our inquiries should be directed, not to what others have thought, nor to what we ourselves conjecture, but to what we can clearly and perspicuously behold and with certainty deduce; for *knowledge is not won in any other way*.[61]

Progress, for Helvétius, is contingent not so much on the regeneration of the sciences or on the use of a certain method of investigation as it is on education, for, as he asserts,

> the inequality observable among men . . . depends on the government under which they lie; on the greater or less happiness of the age in which they are born; on their education; on their desire of improvement, and on the importance of the ideas that are the subject of their contemplations.[62]

Of these factors, education is by far the most important. Improvements could be effected by enlightened legislation, but this is finally dependent, Helvétius declares, on the education that the legislators have received. For all men have naturally equal capacities; if exterior conditions (mainly their education) are of the right sort, anyone can become a "Turenne, Rony, Colbert, Descartes."[63]

For Charles Darwin, Bagehot, and T. H. Huxley, progress (as opposed to evolution) is contingent not on education simply, but on what may be termed a certain disposition of the will. Bagehot devotes his main attention to the question of why some peoples progress and others do not; he finds the source of continuing progress in "free discussion," or, in other words, the willingness to listen to the other side of any argument.[64] Darwin is not so categorical, although he agrees that free discussion is desirable. The problem of the first advance of savages toward civilization is at present much too difficult to be solved, he declares; progress, as one result, is

---

[60] *Rules for the Direction of the Mind*, IV, in *Philosophical Works*, Vol. I, p. 9.

[61] *Ibid.*, III, p. 5. Descartes' method applies to the search for every kind of truth, of course, and not just to the study of the external world of nature.

[62] *De l'Esprit; or, Essays on the Mind and Its Several Faculties*, p. 363.

[63] *Ibid.*, p. 339. Helvétius' view is shared by Locke, Voltaire, La Mettrie, Condillac, and even Rousseau, among writers of the Enlightenment. See Frankel, *The Cause of Reason*.

[64] *Physics and Politics*, pp. 114–48. Bagehot's position might be summed up in the famous phrase of Justice Holmes, "free trade in ideas."

not at all necessary in his view; he seems to feel that it is contingent mainly on early education, and on sympathy and fellow feeling.[65] T. H. Huxley conceives the required disposition to be the willingness to give up some of the natural aggressiveness that is, at the same time, the source of evolutionary advance. He warns that what

> lies before the human race is a constant struggle to maintain and improve, in opposition to the State of Nature, the State of Art of an organized polity; in which, and by which, man may develop a worthy civilization.[66]

In a similar vein, Dewey lays down no specific conditions for future progress, but asserts, nonetheless, that it is a possibility. "All which I can say about the future of progress at the present time," he says, "is that it depends upon man to say whether he wants it or not. If we want it, we can have it—if we are willing to pay the price in effort, especially in effort and intelligence."[67] And Bryce, as well, when he asks whether technological advances mean greater happiness for mankind, seems to suggest that progress is a possibility but by no means a necessity. Like Darwin, Bagehot, Huxley, and Dewey, he is saying that progress depends on man's acting or feeling in such a way as to bring it about.[68] But the implication is unavoidable in the case of all of these authors, that if man does not act or feel in this way, progress will not occur.

A large number of writers, finally, hold that the contingency on which progress mainly depends is not merely man's desire to have it, or even his willingness to work for it, but the actual creation of a state or condition of human life that will promote it. Thus, for Charles Fourier, progress depends on the formation of the special communities, the existence of which will, he believes, insure an eternal golden age; but without these, progress is no more than a vain hope. Lewis Mumford describes the two roads that lie before mankind, one leading toward "One-World Man," the other toward "Post-Historic Man"; the choice is ours to make, and on it the possibility of progress depends. Maritain, Simon, and De Rougemont all emphasize the importance for progress of the formation of a society based on the "person," and modeled, at least according to Maritain, on the Gospels. And there are to be found numerous other expressions of the same or similar views.

All, however, reduce, as we have observed, to the proposition that

[65] *The Descent of Man,* pp. 496–511.
[66] *Evolution and Ethics,* p. 45.
[67] "Progress," in *International Journal of Ethics,* 1916, p. 314.
[68] "What is Progress?", in *Atlantic Monthly,* August, 1907, pp. 148 ff.

future progress is not necessary, that it depends instead on man's free decision to move forward rather than backward. Progress, in short, is contingent on human freedom. Neither it nor regress is the inevitable pattern of future history; man can choose his own path, either upward to what are perhaps unimaginable glories, or downward to what are, considering man's new scientific capacities, equally unimaginable horrors. Change for the better is far from being in the nature of the case. There is nothing in heaven or earth that insures it; indeed, the belief that progress is inevitable may even retard if not end it. Progress will not necessarily happen. It *may* happen—if.[69]

Contingent progress authors differ as much in their actual expectations in regard to progress as they do in their notions of what men ought freely to do to bring it about. Some are hopeful, some are not; some feel that progress is very likely, others that it is very unlikely, though of course still a possibility. Since these disparate views seem to depend more on a given writer's intellectual disposition than on any conceptual difference between him and another writer, they are not discussed here. It should be borne in mind, however, that an author may affirm the high probability of progress or the high probability of regress and still be, for the purposes of this analysis, a progress author.

On the Necessity of ICC

In Chapter 14 we discussed the historical phenomenon that we termed irreversible cumulative change (ICC), and showed that, while a small

[69] We have held throughout this chapter that contingent progress authors conceive only one real contingency for progress, that is, human freedom. It must be conceded that some necessary progress authors mention what is in one sense a contingency on which progress might be said to depend. Progress, for them, is contingent on the continuance of the universe, or at least the solar system, more or less in its present state, including the natural laws that govern its operations. Thus Condorcet writes: "Progress will doubtless vary in speed, but it will never be reversed as long as the earth occupies its present place in the system of the universe, and as long as the general laws of this system produce neither a general cataclysm nor such changes as will deprive the human race of its present faculties and its present resources" (*Sketch*, p. 5). Comte mentions this proviso also, as do several others. But such an eventuality as the one described by Condorcet does not seem to be taken very seriously. Barring total catastrophe, progress will occur. Modern authors, however, realizing man's new capacity (by means of the hydrogen bomb) to bring just such a catastrophe on himself and the world, tend to emphasize the contingency of progress. But such an event would not be natural; it would be produced by man himself. Thus progress is ultimately contingent on human freedom.

It should be observed that some modern thinkers have raised the question of whether the "general laws" of nature are changing along with everything else. If so, this would make Condorcet's remark more important. See Toulmin and Goodfield, *The Discovery of Time*, pp. 269–72, for a discussion of such contemporary speculations.

number of writers hold that this is not progress (*i.e.*, is not for the better), a relatively larger number maintain that the phenomenon either underlies true progress or, indeed, is itself intrinsically meliorative. We also showed that, for most of the authors who discuss this process, it is associated with or based on the Pascalian analogy between the race and an individual man. It is perhaps not surprising, therefore, to find that ICC is held to be necessary. For if mankind is like an individual who grows and develops to maturity in time, then in the case of mankind, as in that of an individual, the sum of experience (given the faculty of memory that conserves it) *must* increase and can never become less. Living things—and by the analogy the human race is conceived as a living thing—cannot grow backward, cannot undevelop, with the passage of time. Only in myth do animals and men become younger as time grows older. It is more than merely an empirical law—the sum of all observations so far—that tells us this. Inherent in organic growth and mental development is the necessity of these being, so to speak, one-way. It is exactly as necessary that ICC occur as that time always advance and never regress or go backward.[70]

The Pascalian analogy deals with the accumulation of knowledge and experience only—given, as it is always required to state, the faculty of memory to conserve them. Comte and Mill, among others, realize that a theory of progress may involve more than that. In the case of the individual, the bare analogy seems to demand (if it does not necessarily require) a *conscious* conservative faculty; but this means, when the analogy is extended to the race as a whole, that mankind must have some sort of conscious memory of its entire past. The difficulty is lessened by the introduction by Comte and Mill of the notion of social development or evolution. Just as, in the phrase Comte likes to quote from Leibniz, "the present is big with the future," so the present is affected by, and contains determinations of, the past. This may be seen in the fact, which Comte emphasizes, that at any given time there are in the world individuals of different ages. The old, he says, tend to conserve the past and hence to some extent limit the capacity of future change, while the young discard the past and actively promote changes that will be most evident in the future. The process goes on all the time and accounts, without having to bring in the notion of a *conscious* racial memory, for the fact that the world is always changing but also staying the same.[71]

[70] The twentieth century has seen several studies of time that have raised the question whether its "direction" is as easily determined as used to be supposed. Eddington's *The Nature of the Physical World* and Blum's *Time's Arrow and Evolution* are representative works in this literature. The notion of absolute time as found in Newton is of course no longer accepted by physicists. The last sentence in the paragraph should be read in this light.

[71] It is often observed by progress authors that books and libraries constitute such a racial memory.

ICC, then, whether it be conceived simply as the accumulation of knowledge in time or, more complexly, as social evolution, is always held to be necessary by the writers who discuss it. But ICC is not, in the view of the majority of those writers, in itself progress. Is there a relation between ICC and necessary progress? Do authors who discuss ICC tend to affirm that progress is necessary? Can ICC be affirmed and progress be held to be contingent?

In the case of those authors who hold that progress is based on ICC, progress is usually held to be necessary. Mill and Comte are examples here, as well as Condorcet and Carr, to name two otherwise very different figures. As Comte declares, social development inevitably brings improvement after it; the necessity of the one is assured by the necessity of the other.

The Marxists and a few other writers seem to be saying that development—ICC—is intrinsically meliorative; progress is not based on ICC, but ICC is itself progress. For them, too, progress is necessary.

Even if ICC is affirmed as necessary, however, progress can be held to be contingent. It might be said, for example, that an individual who simply grows, who merely suffers things to happen to him, to impinge upon him, as time passes, does not develop in any meaningful way—does not progress. The individual who only *passes through life* might be said not to progress unless he gains wisdom, where wisdom is conceived as something higher and better than mere accumulated experience. It might be asked what the individual does with his growing knowledge, and whether he acts better as the result of his increased experience. It might be claimed that while the knowledge, or at least the experience, of an individual does necessarily increase in time (given a nondefective memory), wisdom is not necessarily attained thereby, but is, instead, contingent on the will of the individual, on his choosing to use his growing knowledge well.[72] And all of these remarks apply, by the Pascalian analogy, to the human race. It might be asked whether mankind has gained something like wisdom as a result of its long experience, and whether it acts better or is actually better off as a result of its passage through history.

Indeed, this question may underlie the position of many of the contingent progress authors discussed in this chapter. Maritain is perhaps the best example. Growth—ICC—is necessary; but growth is not progress. Progress consists in the introduction of something new, something that

---

[72] An aphorism in a novel of Leo Rosten's may be enlightening in this connection. "Most men never mature," says a character in *Captain Newman, M.D.*; "they only grow taller."

was not present before. And the introduction of a new good for man is contingent, according to Maritain, on man's free choice.

Wisdom, or its equivalent for the race as a whole, might be such a new thing. A new and more beneficent determination of the will might be another. Still another is suggested by Aristotle when he speaks in the *Politics* of the development of civil society out of primitive conditions of life.

> When several villages are united in a single complete community, large enough to be nearly or quite self-sufficing, the state comes into existence, originating in the bare needs of life, and continuing in existence for the sake of a good life.[73]

This is change for the better, but it is not ICC. It is quite a different thing to exist for the sake of life, and to exist for the sake of a good life; and although the former is not destroyed in the latter, the latter does not necessarily follow from the former. The good life implies life, but life does not imply the good life.[74]

Contingent progress is usually of the sort suggested by the examples of racial wisdom and existence for the sake of the good life. These are, from the point of view of one who affirms ICC, undetermined, unpredictable, "emergent" eventualities. Wisdom can be said not to follow necessarily from the accumulation of knowledge; it is an "emergent" attainment. The search for the good life need not follow from the creation of a self-sufficient community; it is an "emergent" characteristic of men in large groups. Similarly, the advent of Christianity is not usually thought of as following necessarily from man's prior history; it is a free and undetermined gift of God. And a mutation that is also an improvement[75] is usually viewed as a fortunate chance, not as something that one had a right to expect would result from the accumulation of challenges presented to an organism by its environment.

However, each of these meliorative changes—each of these examples of progress—may be said to be necessary in a different sense. They do not follow directly from ICC; ICC may be their necessary, but it is not

---

[73] *Politics*, 1, 2, in *Works*, Vol. X, 1252b.

[74] The change from simply existing to existing for the sake of a good life constitutes progress—or would do so (for Aristotle) if he held that it was an irreversible process affecting and benefiting the whole human race. In fact, he does not hold this, since he believes that the passage from primitive conditions of life to those in which the state exists and men can seek the good life must be won over and over, by different groups of men, and has been so won and will be won again without end. That Aristotle is, however, with respect to this investigation, a cyclist and not a progress author does not deprive the example of its value.

[75] It appears that such mutations are rare, if they occur at all.

their sufficient, condition. But it may be said that each of them follows necessarily from a determination *on the part of some higher power*. It is at this juncture that Providence is called upon by a large number of progress authors. For if progress cannot be seen as *intrinsically* necessary —and it appears that it is difficult to see it thus if it is not based on ICC— then recourse must be had to a supervening power. Providence, as we have seen, is exactly what is required.

16

Will Progress Continue
Indefinitely or "Plateau Out"?

THE question whether progress will continue indefinitely or terminate
—"plateau out"—is discussed by a number of progress authors. Moreover, it is a question on which some of them take specific issue with opponents whom they name and try to refute.[1]

Before treating the diverse answers to the question that are found in
the literature, it is desirable to recall the limits we have imposed on the
terms in which the question is framed.

Our topic is human progress. As such, we are concerned with the
world's history within certain definite temporal limits. These are, in the
past, that moment (whenever it was, and *if* it was) when man first appeared on earth, and in the future, that moment (whenever it is to be,
and *if* it is to be) when man will cease to exist or inhabit the earth.[2]

[1] Unfortunately, most of these attempts to meet the issue squarely are found
only on one side of it. Authors take specific issue with the view that progress
"plateaus out," but the opposite is not true.

[2] It is of course conceivable that mankind may continue to exist on another planet
after leaving the earth. This possibility is seldom if ever discussed by progress authors
and is not considered in this study.

We are not concerned with the career of the earth, the solar system, or the universe, except insofar as they determine (as for some writers they do) the duration of human progress.

An author's assertion, therefore, that the earth, the solar system, or the universe will some day cease to exist or be hospitable to man need not, in itself, constitute a denial that progress will continue indefinitely. Indefinite or indeterminate progress is taken in this work to mean progress that continues *as long as man endures on earth*. Terminating progress, contrarily, is taken to mean progress that stops *before* mankind stops, that ceases *before* humanity ceases to live on earth (if that is ever to happen). It follows from this that the position that progress "plateaus out" requires the assertion that mankind will continue to live on earth in a "perfect" state or condition of life *after* progress stops.

The state or condition of "perfection"—the "plateau"—need not be one in which change does not occur. What no longer occurs in this state or condition of life is progress; that is, there is no longer any change for the better in what an author considers to be the significant respects, from the point of view of his conception of progress. Advance may indeed continue to occur in some respects. For example, men may advance or improve as individuals. But in other respects, in those that are held by the author to be significant or denominative for progress, advance no longer occurs. Progress has therefore ceased when this state or condition of life is attained.[3]

The majority of our authors hold that progress will continue to occur indefinitely, if it occurs at all.[4] These writers are divided into two groups, according to whether they maintain that progress will continue indefinitely but within limits, or indefinitely without limit. The former group holds that progress will not cease but that the *amount* of progress to be expected is limited; the latter says that progress will not only continue to occur indefinitely but that its amount cannot be limited. A minority— notably the Marxists—assert that progress will cease when certain historical conditions have been satisfied, conditions that they describe.

[3] No author who affirms the occurrence of irreversible cumulative change (ICC)— with the possible exception of Becker—fails to maintain that this phenomenon is of indefinite duration. Indeed, the notion of a "plateau" above or beyond which man cannot advance seems to be ruled out by the nature of the process we have called ICC.

[4] It is of some moment in considering this issue whether an author holds that progress is necessary or contingent. It would seem that an author who holds that progress will "plateau out" ought to be a necessitarian; in any event, we know of no contingent progress author who says that progress will "plateau out." However, necessary progress authors divide on this issue. Some say that progress will continue, others that it will stop when a condition of "perfection" is attained. Thus the position that progress will "plateau out" is associated with the position that it is necessary, but the position that it will continue indefinitely is associated both with the position that it is necessary and that it is contingent.

The position that progress "plateaus out" suggests important implications for the remainder of this study. These implications are discussed at the end of the chapter.

It should be observed here that the question at issue is not whether progress will *actually* continue indefinitely—that assertion can only be made by an author who holds that progress is necessary—but whether there is anything in the nature of progress itself that implies that it will either continue indefinitely or "plateau out." Thus it is possible for an author who holds that progress is contingent to assert that *if* progress occurs in the future *then* it will go on and on without stopping. There is no reason to suppose, in other words, that progress will ever cease unless man does something to stop it, such as destroying the earth in a nuclear war.

Progress authors who hold that progress will "plateau out" are listed below.

Augustine	Engels
Joachimites	Lenin
Lessing	Bukharin
Hegel	Trotsky
Marx	Jeans

The following authors maintain that progress will continue as long as man endures on earth.[5]

Pascal	J. S. Mill
Leibniz	Henry George
Fontenelle	Spencer
Adam Smith	Dewey
Kant	Broad
Herder	Maritain
Condorcet	Simon
Godwin	Ortega
Malthus	Teilhard de Chardin
Madame de Staël	Mumford
Guizot	C. G. Darwin
Comte	E. H. Carr
Buckle	A. C. Clarke

[5] Both lists could probably be expanded. Authors who are discussed elsewhere in this work but who do not appear on either list are absent because they have little or nothing to say on the question at issue; there is, therefore, no good reason to assign them to one list or the other. It is likely, however, that most of the progress authors missing from both lists belong in the first list. A few, for example, Acton and Henry Adams, may belong in the second list.

The Position that Progress Will "Plateau Out"

The Marxists, and millennialists like Lessing and the Joachimites, give the same answer to the question we are considering about the duration of progress. Marxist authors hold that a time will come when mankind will live under "real" or "true" communism, the state will "wither away," possibilities for further economic, political, and social improvement will no longer exist, and progress will cease. In this condition of life, it will still be possible for advances, even improvements, of certain kinds to occur —in art, for example, or in knowledge, or in morality. The Marxist millennium is not absolutely static and unchanging. But the class struggle will have come to an end, and progress will have become unnecessary, and therefore impossible.

The Joachimites, Lessing, and others hold similarly—though for different reasons—that some sort of "perfect" state or condition (a millennium) will be attained *in time,* and before the last age of the world "wherein we shall all be changed." This eschatology is not traditional. According to the traditional view, the world will regress before its final judgment; the last judgment will be followed by an earthly paradise, but that will *not* be in time. The traditional view is not a progress position, for it involves the notion that man changes for the worse in time, however much better things may be after time has had a stop. The millennialist position *is* a progress one, since it involves the assertion that man improves *before* the last judgment. That the millennialists also envisage an earthly paradise *after* the millennium (and after the last judgment) does not change the situation.

Besides the Marxists and the Christian millennialists, a few other authors—notably Hegel—hold that progress will cease and "plateau out" before the end of history.[6]

The basic source of progress, for Marx and Engels, is a kind of conflict or opposition that they call class struggle when it is manifested in

[6] Hegel takes a position that in some sense forms a bridge between that of the Marxists and that of the millennialists. Hegel is not a Marxist, as the Marxists are the first to point out; nevertheless, his "paradise" is decidedly more secular than that of the millennialists. It may be indeed that the view of such writers as Hegel and Lessing, to say nothing of the Marxists, is a "radical secularization" of the millennialist position regarding the future of man. Such at least is the suggestion of several commentators. See the article, "Progress," in *Encyclopedia of the Social Sciences,* and, particularly, *The Belief in Progress,* by John Baillie. Baillie's work is mainly based on this notion.

the realm of human history (as distinguished from natural history). Class struggle is the cause of progress; it ensures progress as long as it continues; if it were to stop then progress would stop, too. Hence when Marx speaks of that

> class whose vocation in history is the overthrow of the capitalist mode of production and the final abolition of all classes—the proletariat,[7]

he is by the same token speaking of the end of progress. When Engels declares that

> the history of these class struggles forms a series of evolutions in which, nowadays, a stage has been reached where the exploited and oppressed class —the proletariat—cannot attain its emancipation from the sway of the exploiting and ruling class—the bourgeoisie—without at the same time, *and once and for all*, emancipating society at large from all exploitation, oppression, class distinctions and class struggles,[8]

he is in effect saying the same thing. And when Marx and Engels write together, in *The Communist Manifesto*, that

> in place of the old bourgeois society, with its classes and class antagonisms, we shall have an association in which the free development of each is the condition for the free development of all,[9]

they are saying it once more.

Lenin, commenting on the statement of Engels, that "the State will not be 'abolished'; it will wither away," makes the general point in a political context. He writes:

> In using the term, "withering away," Engels refers quite clearly and definitely to the period *after* "the taking over of the means of production by the State on behalf of the whole of Society," that is, after the Socialist Revolution.[10]

The State at this period will be "complete Democracy," but even this will "wither away." The existence of the State is a manifestation of the class struggle and of class antagonism, and when these cease the State can no longer exist. Political progress will have come to an end. But not only "political progress" in a narrow sense; for these authors, social evolution in the political and economic spheres *is* progress, is the basic constituent of melioration. "The free development of all" that is envisaged by Engels is not progress in their terms, although of course it is desirable. It

[7] *Capital*, "Author's Preface to the Second Edition," p. 20.
[8] *Manifesto of the Communist Party*, "Preface," in *Capital, The Communist Manifesto and Other Writings*, p. 318.
[9] *Ibid.*, p. 343.
[10] *The State and Revolution*, p. 162.

is a matter for individuals, it is not *history;* strictly speaking, only history progresses; and the very freedom of individuals to "develop" after the Socialist Revolution is the sign that human progress has ceased to occur. As Engels himself writes:

> With the seizing of the means of production by society, production of commodities is done away with, and, simultaneously, the mastery of the product over the producer. Anarchy in social production is replaced by systematic, definite organization. The struggle for individual existence disappears. Then for the first time, man, in a certain sense, is finally marked off from the rest of the animal kingdom, and emerges from mere animal conditions of existence into really human ones. . . . Man's own social organization, heretofore confronting him as a necessity imposed by Nature and history, now becomes the result of his own free action. The extraneous objective forces that have hitherto governed history, pass under the control of man himself. Only from that time will man himself, more and more consciously, make his own history—only from that time will the social causes set in motion by him have, in the main and in a constantly growing measure, the results intended by him.[11]

Trotsky sees "the man of the future" in a different light in *Literature and Revolution,* but he makes the same point as Marx, Engels, and Lenin. "Life in the future will not be monotonous," he tells us. Man will "master his own feelings," "raise his instincts to the heights of consciousness," and "create . . . if you please, a superman."

> Man will become immeasurably stronger, wiser and subtler; his body will become more harmonized, his movements more rhythmic, his voice more musical. The forms of life will become dynamically dramatic. The average human type will rise to the heights of an Aristotle, a Goethe, or a Marx. And above this ridge new peaks will rise.[12]

These remarkable improvements, in spite of their likeness to the prophecies of such writers as Godwin, Condorcet, and even Fourier, are not progress in the sense in which the term is to be understood in the present epoch. Now, progress is the "iron law of history"; it is the absolutely determined advance of the whole society *toward* the condition in which the free development of each is the condition for the free development of all.

---

[11] *Socialism: Utopian and Scientific,* p. 144. The whole complex question of the kind of freedom conceived by these authors is extensively treated in Mortimer J. Adler's *The Idea of Freedom,* esp. Vol. II, pp. 184–222 and 626–33. According to Adler, this freedom—which he terms collective—is only achieved upon the attainment of a certain kind of social order. Progress in or toward freedom is considered, from another point of view, elsewhere in the present study. See Chapter 23.

[12] *Literature and Revolution,* pp. 254–6.

Bukharin also discusses the matter in similar terms. He cites Heraclitus to the effect that "conflict is the mother of all happenings," and Hegel to the effect that "contradiction is the power that moves things." But with the coming of the Revolution, contradiction and conflict will cease, and the

> entire aggregate of humanity, a mass which will have ceased to be a mass . . . will become a single, harmoniously constructed human society.[13]

The cessation of conflict between classes will not create a stagnant society, but one, on the contrary, in which individuals will have the opportunity to develop all of their talents. In such a society progress in the old sense will no longer occur.

Hegel, who in many respects is an influential precursor of the Marxists, holds the same position as they do on this issue. The German World corresponds, he declares, to the "old age" of the world, but as to that, a difference between nature and spirit is relevant:

> The Old Age of *nature* is weakness; but that of *Spirit* is its perfect maturity and *strength,* in which it returns to unity with itself, but in its fully developed character as *Spirit.*[14]

Now, the state no longer occupies a position of inferiority to the church; the latter asserts no prerogative, and the spiritual is no longer an element foreign to the state.

> Freedom has found the means of realizing its ideal—its true existence. This is the ultimate result which the process of history is intended to accomplish.[15]

The implication, of course, is that progress must come to an end, indeed has already stopped, for the German World, which embodies the last stage in the development of spirit, is already in existence.

However, although the history of the world is the development of the idea of freedom, and although the present last stage is marked by a universal consciousness of freedom, and although the German World embodies the true ideal of freedom, all men are not yet free *as individuals.* There is still evil in the world, force is still applied to bend the wills of human beings, and the consciousness of freedom is in many places no more than desire for it.

[13] *Historical Materialism,* p. 311; see also pp. 40–41. And cf. "Marx's Thinking and Its Historical Importance," in *Marxism and Modern Thought,* pp. 1–29.
[14] *The Philosophy of History,* pp. 108–9.
[15] *Ibid.,* pp. 109–10.

"Society and the State are the very conditions in which Freedom is realized," says Hegel.[16] At the same time,

> Freedom is nothing but the recognition and adoption of such universal substantial objects as Right and Law, and the production of a reality that is accordant with them—the State.[17]

In order that these two statements may not be contradictory, "freedom" must be taken in two senses. First, there is the overall "philosophical" conception; from this point of view, progress, as the development of the idea of freedom, comes to an end when there is universal consciousness of freedom. Second, there is the conception of freedom from the point of view of the individual; in this sense the existence of the state is not in itself the development of (perfect) freedom, but its *condition*. In the state, and only in the state, is it possible for men to be free; but even the most advanced society, which insists that all men are free theoretically, and incorporates this insistence in laws and institutions, does not as yet assure that they are all free in fact. In the second sense there remains much room for improvement. Hegel conceives progress in the first sense and not in the second. In this respect his position is similar to that of the Marxist authors.[18]

In discussing the tripartite division of the history of the German World and of the world as a whole, Hegel also shows that he has affinities to the millennialists.

> We may distinguish these periods as Kingdoms of the Father, the Son, and the Spirit. The Kingdom of the Father is the consolidated, undistinguished mass, presenting a self-repeating cycle, mere change—like that sovereignty of Chronos engulfing his offspring. The Kingdom of the Son is the manifestation of God merely in a *relation* to secular existence—shining upon it as upon an alien object. The Kingdom of the Spirit is the harmonizing of the antithesis.[19]

To make this clear, Hegel compares Charlemagne's time with the Persian Empire (each was a "period of substantial unity," in which one man alone was truly free); the "time preceding Charles V" with the "Greek world and its merely *ideal* unity" (when only some were free); and the third and present epoch with the "Roman world" (when "peoples will

[16] *Ibid.*, p. 41.
[17] *Ibid.*, p. 59.
[18] According to *The Idea of Freedom,* Hegel is not a proponent of the kind of freedom—termed collective freedom—that is there associated with the Marxist authors. With regard to their answers to the question about the duration of progress, however, Hegel and the Marxists concur.
[19] *Ibid.*, p. 345.

the Right in and for itself"). In the German world this last stage is on a higher plane, for there is now universal consciousness of freedom.[20]

The statement that in this last stage "peoples will the Right in and for itself" recalls the belief of the Joachimites, who held, in the twelfth century, that such a stage was imminent. This final stage is also similar to Lessing's third and last Gospel, that is to come shortly, one supposes, and which will be an age in which men pursue virtue for its own sake.

Lowith shows how Lessing's version of Joachimite millennialism affected the thinking of Hegel, Fichte, and Schelling.[21] He also suggests that the doctrine survived into the twentieth century, to appear in some of the historical predictions of Mussolini and Hitler. Thus even they may have supported the position being discussed here—the position that progress, conceived as a succession of different historical stages, will end when the last stage is attained.

Progress, conceived as the development or amelioration of human beings themselves—in short, of human nature—can hardly be said to cease just at the moment when the conditions for it are most propitious; but these authors do not speak of progress in that sense. The seeeming paradox presented by this situation is discussed at the end of this chapter.[22]

---

[20] *Ibid.*, pp. 345–6.

[21] Cf. *Meaning in History*, pp. 208–11. Fichte and Schelling probably also hold the position being discussed.

[22] It is rare for authors who affirm ICC to hold that this phenomenon will not continue indefinitely. Perhaps it is obvious why this is so. Most conceptions of this kind of advance derive from the analogy between the race and the individual, both of which continue to accumulate knowledge as long as they exist.

Becker appears to be an exception to this rule, as he is also an exception to the rule that ICC is always held to be necessary—and for the same reason. For Becker, ICC (he calls it progress but denies that it is improvement) is equivalent to "the expansion of human power"; the question, therefore, is whether this expansion will ever stop. "It is conceivable, even probable," Becker writes, "that the possibility of discovering new sources and implements of power will in the course of time gradually diminish, or even be altogether exhausted. In that event the outward conditions of life will change less and less rapidly, will in time become sufficiently stable perhaps to be comprehended, sufficiently stable therefore for a relatively complete adjustment of ideas and habits to the relatively unchanging body of matter-of-fact knowledge of man and his outer world in which he lives. In such a stabilized and scientifically adjusted society the idea of progress would no doubt become irrelevant as progress itself becomes imperceptible or nonexistent" (*Progress and Power*, pp. 111–2). This same point is touched on by Jeans. "It seems," he writes, "that if the solar system is left to the natural course of evolution, the earth is likely to remain a possible abode of life for thousands of millions of years to come. If so, we may perhaps be glad that our lives have fallen in the beginning, rather than at the end, of this great stretch of time. We may well imagine that if man survives to the end of it, he will have infinitely more knowledge than now, but one thing he will no longer have—the thrill of pleasure of the pioneer who opens up new realms of knowledge" (*The Universe Around Us*, p. 287).

Both of these statements depend on an extremely rare notion of knowledge,

The Position that Progress Will Continue as Long as Man Endures on Earth

The position that progress is interminable, unlike the position that progress will "plateau out," is held by progress authors in two markedly different ways; two subpositions may therefore be distinguished. The difference between them is indicated by several writers. C. D. Broad lays the groundwork for the distinction by first differentiating, as he says, between perpetual and uniform progress. "To say that *s* perpetually progresses is to assert the following two propositions," he declares.

> (a) If *x* be any state of *s* there is a state of *s* which succeeds *x* and is better than *x* itself and all *x*'s predecessors. And (b) if *x* be any state of *s* there is no state of *s* which succeeds *x* and is worse than *x* itself and all *x*'s predecessors.

"This of course leaves it quite open," he continues, "that some of the successors of any state of *s* are worse than this state or than some of its predecessors. The definition is meant to allow of fluctuations of value, provided that their maxima increase and their minima do not as time goes on." Having shown that progress need not be continuous to be perpetual, Broad goes on to make the distinction referred to; for perpetual progress, thus defined, is perfectly compatible with the view that the value of no state of *s* will surpass a certain finite magnitude.

> For, although the successive maxima always increase, they may increase at a diminishing rate as time goes on. It is also consistent with the definition that the successive minima should continually decrease, and that they should approach the same limit as the successive maxima. In that case *s*, though perpetually progressing, would perpetually approach (though it would never exactly reach) a permanent condition of finite value.[23]

Condorcet makes the same distinction. Discussing the future extension of the average life-span of human beings, he takes "the opportunity of explaining the two meanings that can be attached to the word *indefinite*."

> In truth, this average span of life which we suppose will increase indefinitely as time passes, may grow in conformity either with a law such that it continually approaches a limitless length but without ever reaching it, or

---

particularly of knowledge of nature—the notion that knowledge is essentially limited, and that the time may come when all that there is to know is known. Most progress authors do not concur in this notion of knowledge.

[23] *The Mind and Its Place in Nature*, p. 656.

with a law that through the centuries it reaches a length greater than any determinate quantity that we may assign to it as its limit. In the latter case such an increase is truly indefinite in the strictest sense of the word, since there is no term on this side of which it must of necessity stop. In the former case it is equally indefinite in relation to us, if we cannot fix the limit it always approaches without ever reaching, and particularly if, knowing only that it will never stop, we are ignorant in which of the two senses the term "indefinite" can be applied to it.[24]

In other words, it may be said—and it is said by some writers—that progress will continue indefinitely, as long as man endures on earth, but that its rate tends to slow down as time goes on, and that in given respects progress approaches a (finite) limit. Since progress in these respects never reaches the limit *but always approaches it*, progress is interminable; but since it never goes beyond the limit, indeed never quite reaches it, the rate of progress must decrease as time goes on.[25]

That is one version of the position that progress continues as long as man endures on earth. The other version is that progress is interminable and unlimited.

THE POSITION THAT PROGRESS IS INTERMINABLE BUT LIMITED

Comte, who, like the authors discussed in the first section—the authors who hold that progress will "plateau out"—has a theory of stages through which the development of mankind must pass, might be expected to hold, like them, that progress will come to an end when the last stage is reached. In a sense, this expectation is justified. Comte declares at the end of the *Positive Philosophy*:

> The positive philosophy will lead us on to a social condition the most conformable to human nature, in which our characteristic qualities will find their most perfect respective confirmation, their completest mutual harmony, and the freest expansion for each and all.[26]

[24] *Sketch of an Historical Picture of the Progress of the Human Mind*, p. 200.

[25] The position that progress is interminable but limited is the refuge of several "pessimistic" progress authors, among them Comte and Malthus. C. G. Darwin seems to share their tone, but he holds that progress in knowledge, at least, is limitless.

The similarity between this position and that of the Marxists is obvious: both conceive a "plateau" or level beyond which progress cannot go. The difference is also obvious: the Marxists contend that the "plateau" will be reached, these writers that it never will be.

[26] *Positive Philosophy*, p. 838. The last phrase is similar to the phrase of Marx and Engels: "The free development of each is the condition for the free development of all."

In short, if the positive is the last stage through which mankind must develop, then, when it is most fully realized in society, mankind can develop no further, and progress will cease.

However, is Comte saying that society will actually realize the positive stage? Is he saying that the "perfect" society will ever be attained? Or does he maintain that there are natural limits to progress such that it will advance more and more slowly, and never cease?

The latter is, in fact, his position. "To me it appears," he says,

> that the amelioration is as unquestionable as the development from which it proceeds, provided we regard it as subject, like the development itself, to limits, general and specific, which science will be found to proscribe.[27]

Progress, he declares, must be generally conceived as occurring at a slower and slower rate as time goes on. There are, for example, "general limits of political action."

> No enlightened man can be blind to the necessary existence of such limits, which can be ignored only on the old theological supposition of the legislator being merely the organ of a direct and continuous Providence, which admits of no limits.[28]

The future is limited by the present; every decision has its consequences, every choice results in a lessening of available choices. "The dead hand of the past" narrows the future. The rate of progress decreases as there is less and less for it to accomplish.

The physical improvement of man also is limited, as is his intellectual potentiality; "the chimerical notion of unlimited perfectibility is . . . at once excluded."[29] Limits must be set even in the sphere of positive knowledge of nature.

> Because it is proposed to consolidate the whole of our acquired knowledge into one body of homogeneous doctrine, it must not be supposed that we are going to study this vast variety as proceeding from a single principle, and as subjected to a single law. . . . *Our intellectual resources are too narrow, and the universe is too complex, to leave any hope that it will ever be within our power to carry scientific perfection to its last degree of simplicity.* . . . While pursuing the philosophical aim of all science, the lessening of the number of general laws requisite for the explanation of natural phenomena, we shall regard as presumptuous every attempt, in all future time, to reduce them rigorously to one.[30]

[27] *Ibid.*, p. 467.
[28] *Ibid.*, p. 469.
[29] *Ibid.*, p. 467.
[30] *Ibid.*, pp. 37–8. Emphasis added.

The final stage of the progress of mankind is desirable but not attainable. That final condition, in which knowledge is one and is reflected in the positive society, must be sought and will inevitably be to some extent attained, but it cannot be completely attained. Man is too little and weak, the universe too big and complex, for that.[31]

A similar view, though by no means so sophisticated a one, is held by Malthus. Almost the main purpose of his first essay on population is to refute the "easy optimism" of Condorcet and Godwin, and he declares that "in the sense in which Mr. Godwin understands the word perfectible, the perfectibility of man cannot be asserted." In Godwin's sense of the term, Malthus asserts, perfectibility is essentially unlimited.

> There is, however, one sense, which the truth will bear, in which [this view] is, perhaps, just [Malthus says]. It may be said with truth that man is always susceptible of improvement, or that there never has been, or will be, a period of his history, in which he can be said to have reached his possible acme of perfection.[32]

Hence, progress is essentially indefinite or interminable; it will never cease. Yet it does not follow from this, he goes on to say, that

> our efforts to improve man will always succeed, or even, that he will ever make, in the greatest number of ages, any extraordinary strides toward perfection. The only inference that can be drawn, is that the precise limit of his improvement cannot possibly be known. And I cannot help again reminding the reader of a distinction which, it appears to me, ought particularly to be attended to in the present question: I mean, the essential difference there is, between an unlimited improvement and an improvement the limit of which cannot be ascertained. The former is an improvement not applicable to man under the present laws of his nature. The latter, undoubtedly, is applicable.[33]

Progress, therefore, although no end of it is to be expected, is sharply limited by the nature of man. Malthus declares that he does not in fact hope for

> any great and decided amelioration of the condition of the lower classes of mankind, the most numerous, and, consequently, in a general view of the subject, the most important part of the human race.[34]

[31] This is probably an accurate reading of Comte's *Positive Philosophy*. In later works, notably the *Positive Polity*, Comte expresses greater certainty that the last political phase, at least, will be reached. Adler, in *The Idea of Freedom*, considers him in this light. Thus, from the point of view of Adler, Comte is in the company of Marx. Here he is opposed to him.

[32] *Population*, p. 95.

[33] *Ibid.*

[34] *Ibid.*, p. 97. Malthus draws the same distinction drawn by Broad and Condorcet. See pp. 95–6.

It is in this connection that Malthus' "dismal theorem" comes into play. The theorem, simply, is that the power of population is indefinitely greater than the power in the earth to produce sustenance for man. The only checks on population are misery and vice. "Consequently, if the premises are just, the argument is conclusive against the perfectibility of the mass of mankind."[35] Since that mass must significantly lower or impede the average progress of man, considered as an entire species, progress is sharply limited, whatever heights individuals may hope to reach.

Maritain also holds that progress is limited though indefinite. That it is indefinite is the more important point, which he argues in many places against the Marxists. For instance, he declares in *True Humanism* that the

> fundamental process which it [Marxism] recognizes, the dialectical process, must needs be a movement which is endless; yet, on the other hand, revolutionary dynamism has its object and aim in a communistic society which will mark the end of "the quarrel between man and nature and between man and man" and the *final* triumph of man over his destiny. In other words . . . its aim is the Kingdom of God *in* history, as a part of history.[36]

This is unacceptable to Maritain. "It is absurd to think," he says, that the Kingdom of God "will come *in and as a part* of history."[37] It is true indeed that

> the world . . . is on the march towards the Kingdom of God, and that is why it is treachery towards that Kingdom not to seek with all our power . . . a realization, or more truly, the refraction in this world of the exigencies of the Gospel. *Nevertheless this realization, even a relative one, will always, in one way or another, be deficient.*[38]

"The conditions of life of the members of the temporal city," he declares, "must not be confounded with an earthly beatitude, nor with any restful felicity or ease."[39]

The major point of attack of Maritain's argument is the Marxist contention that progress will "plateau out," that a "perfect" state or condition of man and society will be attained in time. As such, Maritain stands in direct opposition to the Marxists (and millennialists) on this issue. But he is also saying that the future progress of mankind must be conceived as sharply limited by the nature of man himself. The basic reason for this is that any condition of society, when compared to the Kingdom of God, will be seen as relatively deficient. *Any* "earthly paradise" would be no

35 *Ibid.*, p. 6.
36 *True Humanism*, p. 47. The argument applies as well to the millennialists as to the Marxists.
37 *Ibid.*, p. 52.
38 *Ibid.*, p. 101. Emphasis added.
39 *Ibid.*, p. 130.

more than a refraction of Gospel demands—and, one feels, a radical distortion at that.[40]

Kant's position is not dissimilar to Maritain's. The burden of proof that progress is *not* perpetual rests, Kant says, on his opponents. Perpetual "progress for the better" is to be expected because if it did not happen the world would be a "farce," and its history "altogether opposed to the morality of a wise Creator and Governor."[41] Underlying these assumptions is the principle that

> all the capacities implanted in a creature by nature, are destined to unfold themselves, completely and conformably to their end, in the course of time.[42]

For, Kant goes on to say, "if we turn away from that fundamental principle, we have then before us a nature moving without purpose, and no longer conformable to law; and the cheerless gloom of chance takes the place of the guiding light of reason."

As a result of these tendencies, "perpetual peace" can be expected in time, Kant declares. But this does not mean that progress will cease when peace is attained. Although Kant may supply some terms and concepts to authors like Hegel and Marx, he himself does not foresee a "plateau." The rational society that may confidently be predicted for the future is not the end of progress; it is instead the condition of further progress, progress that will go on and on.

Nevertheless, progress remains limited by the nature of man. Even if all men were to become "perfect"—an event that will occur, if it occurs at all, in a future so distant as to be almost inconceivable—progress toward this condition would not have been unlimited. Human nature is fixed and does not change, even though individual men may develop their capacities in the direction of full humanity.

The Position that Progress Is Interminable and Unlimited

The main intent of his *Sketch* of man's progress, Condorcet writes in his introduction to the work, will be to show that

[40] Maritain's position is similar to Malthus'. Both hold that progress will not "plateau out," and that man will never attain "perfection"; both hold that there is a limit beyond which progress cannot go; both hold that this limit cannot be precisely known; and both hold that the limit is not far beyond what has already been attained. Yves Simon probably concurs in all these points.

[41] "On the Saying: That a Thing May Be Right in Theory But Does Not Hold in Practice," in W. Hastie (ed.), *Principles of Politics*, p. 69; see also F. J. Teggart (ed.), *The Idea of Progress*, p. 305.

[42] *Idea of a Universal History*, in Hastie, p. 4; see also Teggart, p. 293.

nature has set no term to the perfection of human faculties; that the perfectibility of man is truly indefinite; and that the progress of this perfectibility, from now onwards independent of any power that might wish to halt it, has no other limit than the duration of the globe upon which nature has cast us.[43]

The general grounds for this assertion, Condorcet declares, are that there are "natural tendencies" in the direction, first, of the equality of nations; second, of the equality of individuals; and third, of more and better education. All of these tendencies work in such a way as to promote each other. In the intellectual sphere, for example, considering man as susceptible of no natural improvement (as not progressive in his nature), it is obvious, Condorcet says, that as more and more is known, it becomes ever easier to learn even more, and "methods that lead genius to the discovery of truth increase at once the force and the speed of its operation."

> Therefore, since these developments are themselves the necessary consequences of progress in detailed knowledge, and since the need for new methods in fact only arises in circumstances that give rise to new methods, it is evident that, within the body of the sciences of observation, calculation and experiment, the actual number of truths may always increase, and that every part of this body may develop, and yet man's faculties be of the same strength, activity and extent.[44]

This type of argument applies, Condorcet indicates, to every kind of progress that occurs.

However, for Condorcet it is almost a certainty that man's physical, intellectual, and moral faculties will *not* remain the same, but will themselves progress. Therefore, since indefinite progress is to be expected even if man remains the same, it is so much the more certain if man himself improves. The conclusion is that progress must continue as long as man inhabits the earth, and that progress is unlimited.

This is Condorcet's general position. On one or two specific points he is somewhat more hesitant. "Would it be absurd then to suppose," he asks,

> that this perfection of the human species might be capable of indefinite progress; that the day will come when death will be due only to extraordinary events or to the decay of the vital forces, and that ultimately the average span between birth and decay will have no assignable value? Certainly man will not become immortal, but will not the interval between the first breath that he draws and the time when in the natural course of events, without disease or accident, he expires, increase indefinitely?[45]

[43] *Op. cit.*, p. 4.
[44] *Ibid.*, p. 185.
[45] *Ibid.*, p. 200.

This seems to indicate that even in this respect progress is *both* indefinite and unlimited. But Condorcet here distinguishes between the two senses of "indefinite," as has been seen, and declares:

> So . . . we are bound to believe that the average length of human life will for ever increase *unless this is prevented by physical revolutions;* we do not know what the limit is which it can never exceed. We cannot even tell whether the general laws of nature have determined such a limit or not.[46]

Condorcet thus concedes that the position of Malthus may be correct in part: in this respect, at least, progress may be indefinite but limited. However, he is really opposed to the position of Malthus even here. For, if there is actually no limit on the average life-span determined by "the general laws of nature," then he is clearly opposed; but even if such a limit exists (Condorcet does not and cannot know what it is, he says), he still differs strongly. Malthus, although he too does not know what the limit is, believes that it exists, and believes furthermore that it is not very much greater than the present figure. Condorcet supposes that even if there is a natural limit, it is vastly greater than the present figure. The impression is given that he would not be surprised to find men of the future living for thousands of years.[47]

Godwin is as certain as Condorcet that man can expect perpetual progress, as Godwin calls it. He means by this that progress will never cease and is not limited. We recall his proposition that the perfectibility of man implies that

> every perfection of excellence that human beings are competent to conceive, human beings, unless in cases that are palpably and unequivocally excluded by the structure of their frames, are competent to obtain.[48]

He conceives a future society in which men will be almost perfectly healthy, in which they will live almost forever and enjoy almost infinite physical strength and capacities, and furthermore one in which

> there will be no war, no crimes, no administration of justice, as it is called, and no government. Besides this, there will be neither disease, anguish, melancholy, nor resentment. Every man will seek, with ineffable ardour, the good of all.[49]

[46] *Ibid.,* p. 201. Emphasis added.
[47] Malthus writes: "A few observations will be sufficient to show how completely [Condorcet's] theory is contradicted when it is applied to the real, and not to an imaginary, state of things" (*Population,* p. 51).
[48] *An Enquiry Concerning Political Justice,* Vol. I, p. 93.
[49] *Ibid.,* p. 528.

Since such a society is not, according to Godwin, excluded by the structure of the human frame, it must, by his hypothesis, be attainable. It is obvious enough that in these circumstances perpetual progress is no chimera.

Malthus mocks all of Godwin's predictions, and in effect asserts that the nature of man is an immovable obstacle to the attainment of any such society. Malthus appears to be made most indignant by Godwin's belief, which, as we have seen, Condorcet shares, that the average life-span of humans will increase without limit. This would lead, Malthus declares, to a monstrous absurdity.

> They [*i.e.*, Godwin and Condorcet] suppose that all the great, virtuous, and exalted minds, that have ever existed or that may exist for some thousands, perhaps millions of years, will be sunk in annihilation, and that only a few beings, not greater in number than can exist at once upon the earth, will be ultimately crowned with immortality.[50] Had such a tenet been advanced as a tenet of revelation I am very sure that all the enemies of religion, and probably Mr. Godwin, and Mr. Condorcet among the rest, would have exhausted the whole force of their ridicule upon it, as the most puerile, the most absurd, the poorest, the most pitiful, the most iniquitously unjust, and, consequently, the most unworthy of the Deity that the superstitious folly of man could invent.[51]

A number of other writers hold that progress—such progress as may be expected, at least[52]—will not cease as long as man inhabits the earth, and will surpass any limits that may be set on it. Carr, for example, declares that "we need not and should not conceive progress as having a finite beginning or end." Civilization was "surely not an invention, but an infinitely slow process of development, in which spectacular leaps probably occurred from time to time," and it may be expected to continue to advance in the future.[53] He concurs with Maritain's censure of Hegel and the Marxists, and for the same reasons. It is absurd that Hegel should have seen "the end of progress in the Prussian monarchy," he declares, and Marx' prediction that "the proletarian revolution would realize the ultimate aim of a classless society" is a characteristic error of the theologico-historian.

> The presumption of an end of history has an eschatological ring more appropriate to the theologian than to the historian, and reverts to the fallacy of a goal outside history. No doubt a finite end has attractions for the human mind. . . . But if the historian is to save his hypothesis of progress, I think

[50] Condorcet actually denies that men will ever become immortal. See p. 276 above.
[51] *Population*, p. 84.
[52] This is an important proviso. We do not insist that an author hold that progress of every type will continue indefinitely.
[53] *What Is History?*, p. 151.

he must be prepared to treat it as a process into which the demands and conditions of successive periods will put their own specific content. . . . For the historian the end of progress is not already evolved. It is something still infinitely remote; and pointers toward it come in sight only as we advance.[54]

However, despite his concurrence with Maritain on the main point being discussed here, Carr does not, as is evident from the last two sentences in the above passage, agree that progress is limited, at least in the same sense as it is for Maritain. The limits are set, Maritain holds, by the demands of the Gospel; mankind can never advance very far toward them, though it will continue to advance. For Carr, since the goals of progress are seen to be different as we advance toward them, any "final" or limiting goal must be only an appearance. Progress is logically illimitable, if it is not factually limitless. It is indefinite and tends to exceed any assignable limit.[55]

Leibniz and Guizot also hold that progress is "perpetual"—*i.e.*, indefinite and unlimited. This follows, says Leibniz, from "the infinite divisibility of the continuous."

There always . . . remain parts which have yet to be awakened, to grow in size and worth, and in a word, to advance to a more perfect state. And hence no end of progress is ever reached.[56]

Our happiness must consist in a perpetual progress to new pleasures and new perfections; the notion of a "plateau" is an error. Complete enjoyment, which makes the mind stupid, is not happiness; there is no happiness where nothing more is to be desired.

Guizot expects "infinite" progress, but for different reasons.

We shall not, I think, proceed far in this study [he writes], without being convinced that civilization is still in its infancy. How distant is the human mind from the perfection to which it may attain—from the perfection for which it was created! How incapable are we of grasping the whole future destiny of man! Let any one even descend into his own mind—let him picture there the highest point of perfection to which man, to which society may attain, that he can conceive, that he can hope—let him then contrast

---

[54] *Ibid.*, pp. 151–3.

[55] This relativistic view is held by other progress authors, among them Calder, Carrel, J. Huxley, Hermann J. Muller, and Skinner.

It should be observed again that most of these writers do not maintain that progress will *necessarily* continue to occur. Many of them hold that progress is contingent on man's willingness and effort to bring it about. But if man does will to bring about progress, and does succeed in so doing, then progress by its very nature is indefinite in duration and unlimited in extent and amount.

[56] *On the Ultimate Origination of Things*, in R. Latta (ed.), *The Monadology and Other Philosophical Writings*, p. 351.

this picture with the present state of the world, and he will feel assured that society and civilization are still in their childhood: that however great the distance they have advanced, that which they have before them is incomparable, is infinitely greater.[57]

Guizot does not state explicitly that mankind will never actually reach the "perfection" toward which it moves, nor is it explicitly stated that progress is limitless. Nevertheless, the tone of the passage gives both impressions. Guizot has much in common with Carr, whose notion of shifting goals of progress is hinted at here, and with Godwin, whose notion of the inevitable attainment of the conceivable is also implied.[58]

Progress in the sense of man's increasing knowledge and his power over nature is unlimited, in the view of many authors. Buckle, for example, writes:

> The powers of nature, notwithstanding their apparent magnitude, are limited and stationary; at all events, we have not the slightest proof that they have ever increased, or that they ever will be able to increase. But the powers of man, so far as experience and analogy can guide us, are unlimited; nor are we possessed of any evidence which authorizes us to assign even an imaginary boundary at which the human intellect will, of necessity, be brought to stand.[59]

Pascal, Fontenelle, and C. G. Darwin also hold that progress in this sense will go on and on, for there is no reason to think that it will ever cease, and no conceivable limit beyond which it cannot go. The future will see "vast stores of learning, far beyond anything we can now imagine," says Darwin, "and the intellectual stature of man will rise to ever higher levels."[60] "Not only does each individual man progress from day to day in the sciences," Pascal declares, "but mankind as a whole constantly progresses in them in proportion as the universe grows older."[61] And Fontenelle asserts that "the man in question"—that is, the man who stands for the whole human race—

> will have no old age, he will always be equally capable of those things for which his youth is suited, and he will be ever more and more capable of

---

57 *History of Civilization in Europe*, pp. 23–4.

58 It is interesting to compare Guizot's position with Maritain's. Guizot considers that the almost infinite dissimilarity between the conceivable and the actual is a sign that progress will continue to occur indefinitely. Maritain considers that the same dissimilarity is a sign that progress is essentially limited.

59 *History of Civilization in England*, p. 51.

60 *The Next Million Years*, p. 149.

61 *Preface to the Treatise on the Vacuum*, in GBWW, Vol. 33, p. 357; see also Teggart, *op. cit.*, p. 167.

those things which are suited to his prime; that is to say . . . man will never degenerate, and there will be no end to the growth of human wisdom.[62]

IMPLICATIONS OF THE POSITION THAT PROGRESS WILL "PLATEAU OUT"

The majority of progress authors concur in holding that there is no reason to believe progress will ever cease (unless man arbitrarily stops it); most also agree that there is no reason to assign limits to the amount or degree of progress, at least in some respects, that is to be expected.

A few authors concur in holding that progress will continue indefinitely, but maintain that it is limited in significant respects. They do not, however, differ markedly from the writers described in the previous paragraph. They give the same answer to the main question about the duration of progress.

Opposed to all of the foregoing authors are the writers who hold that progress, by its very nature, will come to an end before the end of man's history on earth, and that mankind can look forward to living in some sort of "perfect" society in the near or far—but nonetheless real, and historical—future.

The attack of such writers as Maritain and Carr on the Marxist position—namely, that the affirmation of a stopping place in history has an "eschatological ring" that is unbecoming to historians, and especially to "materialist" historians—is, interestingly enough, leveled by Engels, and in much the same terms, against the view of Hegel that progress had already ceased in his time.

The Hegelian system, in itself, was a miscarriage [says Engels]—it was also the last of its kind. It was suffering, in fact, from an internal and incurable contradiction. Upon the one hand, its essential proposition was the conception that human history is a process of evolution, which, by its very nature, cannot find its intellectual final term in the discovery of any so-called absolute truth. But, on the other hand, it laid claim to being the very essence of this absolute truth. A system of natural and historical knowledge, embracing everything, and final for all time, is a contradiction to the fundamental law of dialectical reasoning. This law, indeed, by no means excludes, but, on the contrary, includes the idea that the systematic knowledge of the external universe can make gigantic strides from age to age.[63]

[62] *On the Ancients and Moderns,* in Teggart, p. 182.
[63] *Socialism: Utopian and Scientific,* pp. 122–3.

This criticism of Hegel may not be valid. If it is valid, however, it is hard to see why it may not be applied to the Marxist view of history, too, and to that of the Joachimites, of Lessing, and of other millennialists, as well.

True, the emphasis in Engels' remarks is on our *knowledge* of the world and of the historical process. If we say that we *now know* what that process is, and at the same time say that we *now know* that it is evolutionary, developmental, or progressive, we are involved in a contradiction —for how can we be sure that some future conception of the process will not be more correct than the one we have now? However, his remarks seem to apply as well to history in the other sense of the term—history as what actually happened. That is, if we say that the present (or some future) stage of development is the best that man can attain, and at the same time say that it is the result of an historical evolution, development, or progress, then how can we be sure that some stage even farther in the future will not be better than the one we now call the best?

Marxist authors are probably recognizing this puzzling paradox when they declare insistently that the condition of society after the Revolution, although not progressive, will not be dull, stagnant, or unchanging, or even unmarked by improvement. From one point of view, their insistence on this point seems to confound rather than clarify the paradox. If progress is improvement, then how can there be improvement but no progress? From another point of view, however, a way out is seen. There are two types or kinds of improvement, perhaps; one is progress, the other is not. This way out is suggested by several commentators. For example:

> There may be some answer to this question in a second aspect of the theory of progress which goes with the dialectic of history. The progress which the successive stages of history represent resides in the quality of human institutions rather than in the nature of man. If more economic justice or greater political liberty is achieved, it is not because the later generations of men are born with a nature more disposed to goodness or virtue, but because better institutions have evolved from the conflict of historical forces. . . . Hence though institutional progress may arrive at its historical goal with the establishment of the ideal economy, it may be possible for further progress to be made throughout the rest of time by the improvement of men themselves, when at last their natures can develop under ideal circumstances.[64]

The implications, for our investigation, of a distinction between two types or kinds of progress—progress in human nature and progress in institutions—are far-reaching. Until now, we have not had to consider dif-

[64] "Progress," in *The Great Ideas: A Syntopicon,* in GBWW, Vol. 3, pp. 439–40.

ferences in authors' conceptions of the content of progress, of the respects or realms, as it may be said, in which progress occurs. We appear now to be faced with the necessity of adjusting our conception of our topic to fit at least two different notions of it that are found in the literature.[65]

To distinguish two or more kinds or types of progress goes far toward resolving the paradox revealed in our treatment of the question whether progress will continue indefinitely or "plateau out."[66] If there are two types of improvement, the one in institutions and the other in individuals, and if the first is called progress and the second not, then the puzzling assertions of the Marxists and some of the millennialists become clear. This is probably the traditional resolution of the paradox, and seems to be the one accepted by the Marxists themselves.[67]

A simpler way out of the dilemma might be found, however, in an examination of the analogy between the human race and an individual that is central to so many affirmations of progress. A glance at the first list of authors at the beginning of this chapter—the authors who maintain that progress will "plateau out"—reveals that most of them conceive progress as occurring in steps or phases. This characteristic helps to resolve the difficulty. In the case of an individual, if it is said, for example, that his progress consists in the advance from infancy to adolescence to maturity, then progress stops when maturity is reached. However, this does not mean that from another point of view—that, for example, of his intellectual development conceived as a cumulative process—he cannot continue to develop or progress even after reaching maturity. He may indeed develop faster and farther after attaining the state of "perfection" in which all of his powers are at his command and conditions are most propitious for intellectual and moral growth. And the same considerations would seem to apply to mankind when it is conceived as analogous to an individual man.

[65] The remainder of this study reflects the distinction.

[66] Not only does the distinction between types of progress—the one in institutions, the other in human nature—help to resolve the paradox here described, but the distinction is made by progress authors themselves. See, for example, the remarks of Comte, quoted in the next chapter (pp. 288–9).

[67] Cf. Trotsky, p. 266, above.

17

Is There Progress in
Human Nature?

W H A T do progress authors mean by progress in human nature? Or, in other words, what is meant by the "perfectibility" of man?

Progress, in general, means an irreversible change for the better. When this notion is applied to the present case, progress in human nature is seen to be an irreversible improvement in man's very nature, in man himself, as distinguished from his environment or the conditions of his life.

Involved here is the perennial distinction between nature and nurture. Human beings, at birth, have certain inherited capacities. No one denies that the realization of these capacities is influenced by the environment in which human beings live. A human being, whatever his innate capacities, is less likely to develop or realize them if the environment is subject to privations of various kinds, and he is more likely to realize them if the environment is not subject to privations. In spite of the obvious interaction between nature and nurture, however, a distinction between them should be retained. Man's nature is his inherited or innate capacities. Nurture—the environment—has an affect on the development of nature, and is, in turn, affected by it.

For example, the average human being is born with the capacity for what Comte calls "mental combinations"—in short, with the capacity to do some kind of thinking. There is no question that in many cases the realization of this innate capacity can be improved by education. Doubtless some men can learn to think without education; education cannot bring some other men to think very well, if at all. On the whole, however, education helps to realize the capacity to think. Without any education, most men never learn to think very well.

Similarly, the average man is born with a body capable of living for about 70 or 80 years. The figure is an average one, and is, furthermore, in dispute, but within limits it is accurate enough. (It is agreed by everyone that the average man is born with the capacity to live more than, say, 50 years, but less than, say, 120 years.) There is no question that this capacity—the capacity to live for 70 or 80 years—is more adequately realized in an environment not subject to privations. As far back as we go in history we find individuals who lived to be 70 or 80 or even 90 years old, but they were very few in number and constituted a minute proportion of the population. Today, a higher proportion of human beings, when they live in an environment not subject to privations, probably live to be 70 or 80 years old. And the life expectancy of the human race taken as a whole may increase even more in the future.

The kinds of changes represented by these examples do not, however, constitute progress in human nature. They are not changes in the innate capacities of human beings. The fact that the average man thinks better, acts better, or lives longer does not need to mean that mankind has changed for the better in its nature. For that to occur, the innate capacities of man must themselves improve.

For example, if later men are born with a greater capacity for mental combinations than were earlier men, then progress in human nature has occurred. This would mean that later men, given the same education, would, on the average, be able to think better than their ancestors. With a better education, they might be able to think *much* better; even with a worse education, they might be able to think as well. They would, on the whole, be born with better minds.

Similarly, if later men are born with bodies capable of living for 200 years, instead of 70 or 80 years, then progress in human nature has occurred. This would not mean, of course, that all men would live to be 200 years old. Some might die of childhood disease, others might be killed off by accidents of one sort or another. In addition, the environment might be subject to so many privations that few men, if any, would live out their full ten score. But most men, given an evironment not essentially different from that which obtains today, would, on this hypothesis, live much longer than men live today. They would, on the whole, be born with better bodies.

Progress authors, then, who give the affirmative answer to the question being considered in this chapter must say that men born at a later time are actually better men than those born at an earlier time. They must say that later men have better minds or better bodies. Furthermore, since progress is an irreversible change, they must say that later men are permanently improved in their nature over earlier men. There will never be an even later time when the improvements in innate capacities will be lost. In modern terms, the improvements are not superficial but are in the genetic makeup of the species.

Progress authors who give the negative answer to the question must deny that assertion. They must say that improvements in behavior, in average life expectancy, in reading ability, and so forth are merely superficial and the result of improved conditions of life. They indeed maintain that conditions improve, for if they did not, they would not be progress authors.[1] But they must maintain that they are the *only* improvements that occur. Human nature remains the same.

The foregoing, which may seem to dwell too much on the obvious, is justified, perhaps, by the fact that many progress authors appear to misunderstand the distinctions involved. On few other subjects in the literature of progress is the discussion so hazy.

All progress authors affirm progress in institutions, *i.e.*, say that there is improvement in the conditions of human life, but all do not affirm progress in man's very nature. Hence, for some authors, both kinds of progress occur. In their view, what is the relation between the two kinds of progress? Is one kind the cause or condition of the other? Do they occur independently? Or are they involved in a process of reciprocal causality?

The position that progress in institutions brings about progress in human nature has a number of adherents. This view need not be based, as it is in the case of Comte, on a Lamarckian notion of evolution; some writers maintain, instead, that culture tends to select for certain qualities, with the result that they become more common as time goes on. If the qualities are desirable, then progress in human nature occurs.

The position that the two kinds of progress are in a relation of reciprocal causality also has adherents, although authors taking this position are not always clear in saying what the relationship is. A number of writers seem to imply, however, that both kinds of progress occur, and that each affects the occurrence of the other.

The position that progress in human nature occurs independently

[1] As in Chapters 15 and 16, only progress authors are treated here.

of progress in the conditions of human life is taken by few if any progress authors.[2]

In this chapter, we treat first the authors who affirm progress in human nature, second the authors who deny this kind of progress.

The Position that Progress Occurs in Human Nature

Authors who affirm progress in human nature may be divided into four groups. The first includes writers like Condorcet and Comte, who see this kind of progress occurring as the result of changes for the better in the conditions of human life. Some of these writers see a reciprocal relation of causality between the two kinds of progress. The irreversibility of the improvements in man's nature is assured, for many of these authors, by the necessity of progress in institutions. Since the conditions of life must improve, and since improvement of the conditions brings about improvement in man's nature, then the latter improvement is irreversible.

The second group includes writers like Hermann J. Muller, who see the possibility of applying modern biological knowledge to the creation of a race of superior human beings. Here, irreversibility is assured by the fact that the improvements are in the genetic makeup of the species. These writers do not, however, usually hold that the application of the required biological techniques is inevitable. This position is a variant of the one discussed in the previous paragraph; here the change in the environment that results in improvement in man's nature is of a very special kind.

The third group includes the Marxist authors, who, strictly, deny that there is any such thing as "human nature," but who predict that better men will be the result of better conditions of life in the future. The irreversibility of the improvements is assured by the inevitability of future progress in institutions. This position, too, is a variant of the first one.

The fourth group includes authors like Teilhard de Chardin and Nouÿs, who seem to suggest that progress in human nature occurs independently of improvements in the conditions of human life. The irreversibility of progress in man's nature seems, in this case, to be assured by some sort of mechanism, genetic or otherwise, regarding which these authors tend to be somewhat vague.

The progress authors who hold that there is progress in man's nature are listed below.

[2] In other words, progress authors seem to find it hard to conceive of progress in human nature occurring without any parallel or consequent progress in institutions.

Joachimites   Lenin
Lessing   Trotsky
Condorcet   Bukharin
Godwin   Nouÿs
Madame de Staël   Carrel
Fourier   Hermann J. Muller
Saint-Simon   Teilhard de Chardin
Comte   Julian Huxley
Marx   A. C. Clarke
Engels   Dobzhansky
Bagehot   Hoyle
Spencer

Progress in Human Nature as the Result of Improvements in the Conditions of Human Life

Comte carefully distinguishes between progress in human nature and progress in the external conditions of life, declares that both kinds of progress occur, and furthermore indicates how they are related. "Taking the human race as a whole," he writes,

> and not any one people, it appears that human development brings after it, in two ways, an ever-growing amelioration, first, in the radical condition of Man, which no one disputes; and next, in his corresponding faculties, which is a view much less attended to.[3]

"There is no need to dwell," says Comte, "upon the improvements in the conditions of human existence."[4] These are admitted by all.

> As for the other aspect of the question, the gradual and slow improvement of human nature, within narrow limits, it seems to me impossible to reject altogether the principle proposed (with great exaggeration, however) by Lamarck, of the necessary influence of a homogeneous and continuous exercise in producing, in every animal organism, and especially in Man, an organic improvement, susceptible of being established in the race, after a sufficient persistence.[5]

If we take "the best-marked case—that of intellectual development," Comte goes on to say,

> it seems to me unquestionable that there is a superior aptitude for mental combinations, independent of all culture, among highly-civilized people; or, what comes to the same thing, an inferior aptitude among nations that are

[3] *Positive Philosophy*, p. 467.
[4] *Ibid.*
[5] *Ibid.*, p. 468.

less advanced—the average intellect of the members of those societies being taken for observation.[6]

The same remarks apply, Comte declares, to morals; it seems to him indisputable that the gradual development of humanity favors a growing preponderance of the noblest tendencies of man's nature.

> The lower instincts continue to manifest themselves in modified action, but their less sustained and more repressed exercise must tend to debilitate them by degrees; and their increasing regulation certainly brings them into involuntary concurrence in the maintenance of a good social economy.[7]

Condorcet concurs in many of these points. He writes:

> Organic perfectibility or deterioration amongst the various strains in the vegetable and animal kingdoms can be regarded as one of the general laws of nature. This law applies to the human race.[8]

Since deterioration is out of the question because of the inevitable progress in the conditions of life that is assured by the advance of knowledge, organic improvement or perfectibility must occur.

> No-one can doubt that, as preventative medicine improves and food and housing become healthier, as a way of life is established that develops our physical powers by exercise without ruining them by excess, as the two most virulent causes of deterioration, misery and excessive wealth, are eliminated, the average length of human life will be increased and a better health and a stronger physical constitution will be insured. . . . Finally may we not extend such hopes to the intellectual and moral faculties? . . . Is it not probable that education, in perfecting these qualities, will at the same time influence, modify and perfect the organization itself?[9]

Godwin also maintains that the establishment of a social organization based on reason, and not on "greed, fear or envy"—the bases, according to Condorcet, of present-day society—will result in organic improvements of many kinds. According to Godwin, the mind (which is intrinsically progressive) has power over the body, and when it is allowed to exert that power unobstructed, will change the body in many desirable ways. For example, a proper and healthy frame of mind—to be generally expected in the future—will put an end to bodily fatigue.

> How often do we find a piece of good news dissipating a distemper? How common is the remark that those accidents which are to the indolent a source of disease are forgotten in the busy and active? I walk twenty miles in an indolent and half determined temper and am extremely fatigued. I walk

6 *Ibid.*
7 *Ibid.*
8 *Sketch of an Historical Picture of the Progress of the Human Mind*, p. 199.
9 *Ibid.*, pp. 199–201.

twenty miles full of ardour, and with a motive that engrosses my soul, and I come in as fresh and alert as when I began my journey.[10]

Bagehot takes the same position, although he emphasizes, as Godwin does not, the fact that a natural principle underlies the improvement in man's nature that he observes in the past, and that he predicts in the future. This principle is that of natural selection; it operates to increase the incidence of desirable qualities in the human species. There is a probability, Bagehot declares,

> greater or less according to circumstances, but always considerable, that the descendants of cultivated parents will have, by born nervous organization, a greater aptitude for cultivation than the descendants of such as are not cultivated; and . . . this tendency augments, in some enhanced ratio, for many generations.[11]

The proof that such progress occurs is seen when the "power" of primitive and of civilized men is compared. This power is "not external only," Bagehot says; "it is also internal. The English not only possess better machines for moving nature, but are themselves better machines."[12] Further evidence is found when we compare ourselves to the ancients.

> Savages in the first year of the Christian era were pretty much what they were in the 1800th; and if they stood the contact of ancient civilized men, and cannot stand ours, it follows that our race is presumably tougher than the ancient; for we have to bear, and do bear, the seeds of greater diseases than those the ancients carried with them. We may use, perhaps, the unvarying savage as a meter to gauge the vigor of the constitutions to whose contact he is exposed.[13]

Bagehot's notion of progress in human nature resulting from a process of natural selection is retained by some contemporary evolutionists, although with more hesitation. Dobzhansky, for example, declares that

> the ability to study geometry, let alone higher mathematics, had no selective value in the ancestors of our species, and it is not certain that such abilities are biologically advantageous even at present.[14]

However, he goes on to say,

> the ability of abstract thinking, or of perceiving causal relationships between events, did confer tremendous adaptive advantages on the human species.

---

[10] *Inquiry Concerning Political Justice,* qu. by Malthus, *Population,* p. 77. For Malthus' animadversions on Godwin's views as here expressed, see below, pp. 307–9.

[11] *Physics and Politics,* p. 7.

[12] *Ibid.,* p. 151.

[13] *Ibid.,* p. 36.

[14] *The Biological Basis of Human Freedom,* p. 132.

. . . If natural selection has not developed genes for philosophy, it has favored genetic endowments which enable their carriers to become, among other things, philosophers.[15]

Dobzhansky makes few if any predictions about future melioration as the result of natural selection. Fred Hoyle, however, does see improvement occurring in the future. He looks forward to "a series of organizational break-downs, or catastrophes, occasioned by over-population."[16] These will not be totally disastrous for the race, because "during the beginning of the re-expansion phases there will be selection for greater sociability and for higher intelligence."

The degree of selection in any one cycle need not be dramatically large because the effects of the repeated cycles are cumulative. Indeed I expect the number of cycles—the number that occurs before they are damped away —to be determined by how much selection occurs per cycle. If this is large the number of cycles will be small, and vice versa, the net effect being the same.[17]

"The ultimate outcome," Hoyle believes, "will be a highly sociable, highly intelligent creature."[18] This will doubtless constitute progress in man's very nature.

Progress in Human Nature as the Result of the Modern Science of Genetics

Other writers, taking into account modern advances in biological techniques, and imagining their application to the task of making a race of superior human beings, are hopeful regarding the future improvement of man.

[15] *Ibid.*, p. 133. In another work, Dobzhansky concurs in Lancelot White's statement that "an 'appreciable' change in the 'biological factor' of human mental ability during the last fifty thousand years [cannot] be rigorously proven." Dobzhansky observes that "there is no way to make the experiments necessary to secure such a proof. We cannot plant identical twins to be reared by Peking man or by the Neanderthalians and leave cotwins to grow up in a modern society. . . . The 'proof' has to be based on inference" (*Mankind Evolving*, p. 321). Nevertheless, he feels that proofs based on inference have some weight. He points out that Darwin himself claimed no more than that "evolution can be inferred from what he did observe." Dobzhansky appears to say that although rigorous proof cannot be found, the inference is fair enough that there has been progress in human mental nature over the past 100,000 years or so.

[16] *Encounter with the Future*, p. 36.

[17] *Ibid.*, pp. 36–7. Despite his use of the term "cycles," Hoyle's is not a theory of cycles of history.

[18] *Ibid.*, p. 37. Hoyle's statement is somewhat complicated by his remark that the improved man will be "a new species." If that is so in fact, this is not progress in human nature *per se*.

Hermann J. Muller accepts the notion that some "biological better-ment" occurred in the past, because culture afforded an increasing relative advantage in the struggle for existence to those individuals who had cer-tain faculties regarded by him as desirable. However, our "genetic 'laissez faire'" cannot be expected, Muller declares, to bring about much, if any, further progress along this line. New techniques, on the other hand, offer the possibility of great advances. It is now within the capacity of scien-tists, or it will soon be so, to change the genetic makeup of human beings in any direction desired. That being taken for granted, Muller says, the problem becomes one of determining the most desirable direction.

> Among the qualities of man most generally valued [Muller writes] are a genuine warmth and fellow feeling and a cooperative disposition, a depth and breadth of intellectual capacity, moral courage and integrity, an appre-ciation of music and art, and an aptness of expression and communication.[19]

Marked improvement in all of these respects is practically assured by the new techniques—as well as by cultural selection, Muller concedes. And progress need not be confined to the spirit and mind of man. It will also be feasible

> to strive for real progress in what is called the physical side: to better the genetic foundations of health, vigor, and longevity; to reduce the need for sleep; to bring the induction of sedation and stimulation under more effective voluntary control; and to develop increasing physical tolerances and aptitudes in general.[20]

[19] "Should We Weaken or Strengthen Our Genetic Heritage?", in *Daedalus*, Summer, 1961, p. 445.

[20] *Ibid.*, p. 447. Muller concludes his article by declaring that he believes that "not only our cultural but also our biological evolution will go on and on, to new, undreamed of heights, each of these two means reenforcing the other, and again with a positive feedback, but with an enormously more effective one than hitherto" (p. 450).

Muller's views are subjected to severe criticism—and are also defended—in a sym-posium reported in *ibid.*, pp. 451–76. One point that is made by several critics is also expressed by Dobzhansky in *Mankind Evolving* (p. 330). "Muller's implied assumption," Dobzhansky declares, "that there is, or can be, *the* ideal human genetype which it would be desirable to bestow upon everybody is not only un-appealing but almost certainly wrong—it is human diversity that acted as a leaven of creative effort in the past and will so act in the future." However, at least in his *Daedalus* article, Muller does not seem to insist upon one ideal genetype. He declares that the intellectual and moral progress that he foresees need not involve a progres-sive conformity to rigid standards of thought and behavior, and observes that, on the contrary, "in a wiser, kindlier age than ours, men may more safely and calmly con-sider how this spice of life, variety, can be turned to even better account" (*op. cit.*, p. 447).

Muller's views are presented at greater length in *Out of the Night: A Biologist's View of the Future.*

Muller does not assert that progress of this kind will necessarily occur. He is a contingent progress author, as we have seen. Nevertheless, he gives the impression that he thinks it likely that biological techniques will be used to improve the human breed.[21] Carrel makes no predictions regarding what will actually happen, but he declares that if the race is not improved, catastrophe will ensue. Thus, for example, artificial health does not suffice for human happiness—the sort of health, that is, that is based on medical examinations and care. We need to produce a race of humans who enjoy natural health and other desirable qualities. Carrel declares that many improvements can be brought about by the application of educational techniques to the bodies and minds of existing human beings. This is not progress in human nature, but rather progress in the conditions of life that results in better human beings—with no assurance, however, that humans of the next generation will be any more likely to possess the desirable qualities.

Scientific eugenics is another question. Here true progress in human nature becomes a possibility.

> Eugenics may exercise a great influence upon the destiny of the civilized races. Of course, the reproduction of human beings cannot be regulated as in animals. The propagation of the insane and the feebleminded, nevertheless, must be prevented.[22]

Even though we are incapable, according to Carrel, of inducing a progressive evolution of germ-plasm—a point on which Muller does not concur—much might be effected by careful control of human breeding, by "facilitating the union of the best elements of the race through education and certain economic advantages."[23]

Julian Huxley emphasizes the contingent character of future progress in human nature. Progress is a "major fact of past evolution," he declares. "It may continue in the future, but it is not inevitable; man, by now become the trustee of evolution, must work and plan if he is to achieve further progress for himself and so for life."[24] Nevertheless, on the biological side,

> there are many obvious ways in which the brain's level of performance could be genetically raised—in acuteness of perception, memory, synthetic

[21] Others, such as the modern "distopians," while they agree that the techniques referred to by Muller will probably be used in the future, question whether the results will be improvements. Huxley's *Brave New World* is a case in point. However, the "distopians" are seldom progress authors and are therefore not treated here.

[22] *Man, the Unknown*, p. 194.

[23] *Ibid.*, p. 195.

[24] *Evolution: The Modern Synthesis*, p. 578.

grasp and intuition, analytic capacity, mental energy, creative power, balance, and judgment. If for all these attributes of mind the average of our population could be raised to the level now attained by the best endowed ten-thousandth or even thousandth, that alone would be of far-reaching evolutionary significance. Nor is there any reason to suppose that such quantitative increase could not be pushed beyond its present upper limit.[25]

Huxley also sees the possibility that the men of the future will be born with a much improved capacity for telepathy and other extra-sensory activities of mind.

A. C. Clarke touches upon all of the matters discussed by the authors we have considered here. He seems to say that many of the improvements they foresee can be brought about by education of special kinds. In other words, he does not see the necessity, in every case, for improvements in man's very nature in order to bring about the existence of better human beings—human beings with better memories, better senses, better bodies in general, and more ability to think. He suggests, for example, that it will be quite possible to "gain conscious or artificial control of memory," with the result that nothing need be forgotten, and that "new memories" may be created.

> It is hard to think of any invention that would be more valuable than . . . a "mechanical educator" [that] . . . could impress on the brain, in a matter of a few minutes, knowledge and skills which might otherwise take a life-time to acquire. A very good analogy is the manufacture of a phonograph record; the music may take an hour to perform, but the disc is stamped out in a fraction of a second, and the plastic "remembers" the performance perfectly.[26]

Clarke concedes that impressing information directly onto the brain, so that we can know things without ever learning them, seems impossible today. But the need for such a tool is, he declares, imperative; "for this reason, though I have no idea how it would really operate . . . I feel fairly convinced that the mechanical educator will be invented."[27] He adds that if it is not, "the end of human culture is already in sight," a warning that recalls those of Carrel.

Clarke discusses other improvements of the same sort. We will probably be able, he asserts, to extend the range and sensitivity of our senses far beyond what they have at present. We may even, by means of telemetering

---

[25] *Ibid.,* p. 574. Huxley is discussing possibilities, but he does not seem very hopeful that they will actually occur.

[26] *Profiles of the Future,* p. 199.

[27] *Ibid.,* p. 200.

devices, be able to "know the way of an eagle in the sky, of a whale in the sea, or a tiger in the jungle"—and thereby "regain our kinship with the animal world, the loss of which is one of man's most grievous deprivations."[28] We will also be able, he predicts, to decrease sharply the amount of time we sleep, and thus, in effect, lengthen our lives. We may even, he suggests—at this point he appears to be talking about a real change for the better in man's nature—be able to produce human beings who are able to alternate periods of sleep and waking of such duration that in effect they live for hundreds or thousands of years.

Indeed, Clarke raises the possibility that man will be able to attain a kind of immortality. He questions whether death is "biologically inevitable, even if it is an evolutionary necessity,"[29] observes that our bodies are not like machines in that they never really wear out—the parts are continuously being replaced—and suggests that the way to bring about immortality is "to keep better records."

> Perhaps one day we will be able to help our bodies to do just that. The invention of the alphabet made mental forgetfulness no longer inevitable; the more sophisticated tools of future medicine may cure physical forgetfulness, by allowing us to preserve, in some suitable storage device, the ideal prototype of our bodies. Deviations from the norm could then be checked from time to time and corrected, before they became serious.[30]

And even if we cannot preserve our bodies from deterioration, says Clarke, we may be able to replace them, while there is still time, with machines.

> One can imagine a time when men who still inhabit organic bodies are regarded with pity by those who have passed on to an infinitely richer mode of existence, capable of throwing their consciousness or sphere of attention instantaneously to any point on land, sea, or sky where there is a suitable sensing organ. In adolescence we leave childhood behind; one day there may be a second and more portentous adolescence, when we bid farewell to the flesh.[31]

This would appear to be a change indeed in human nature.

[28] *Ibid.*, p. 203.
[29] *Ibid.*, p. 207. It should be mentioned, in the context of our study, that Clarke declares that "death (though not aging) is obviously essential for progress, both social and biological. Even if it did not perish from overpopulation, a world of immortals would soon stagnate" (*ibid.*).
[30] *Ibid.*, p. 208.
[31] *Ibid.*, p. 209. Clarke never loses sight of the possibility that some of these changes in human nature might be for the worse instead of for the better.

THE MARXIST POSITION REGARDING PROGRESS IN HUMAN NATURE

In a sense, the Marxists are not parties to the dispute being considered in this chapter, for they deny the validity of the notion of human nature, as it is conceived by the other writers here discussed. For example, Bukharin, in an essay in which he outlines and explains Marx's teaching, observes, from the Marxist point of view, that

> hidden, so-called "natural resources" do not function socially. They must cease to be "hidden." Only when they are transformed from matter into material, from "things in themselves" into "things for us," entering the stream of artificial material transformation, that is the stream of the material labour process, becoming objects of change, are they changed (both qualitatively and quantitatively), as "elements" of social development.[32]

This is to apply to "nature" the general "materialist" conception that everything that exists, or everything that exists as an object of knowledge and thought, must be viewed in its practical aspect, that is, as affecting, and as affected by, ourselves. This conception is insisted upon by Marx in all of his writings, notably the "Theses on Feuerbach." But if this be so of "nature" in the sense described by Bukharin in the above passage, it must equally be true of "nature" in the sense of "human nature." "It is just the same," Bukharin goes on to declare,

> with biological "human nature," that is with the other aspect of "the nature premises" for social development. "Corporeal organization," man of the "race" or "species," is the historical premise of social or historical man, and a relatively constant one. Once again, a change in "human nature" (either a corporeal one or its spiritual correlation) is derived from social development. The law of its development is determined by the law of the development of society as a whole at the basis of which lies the law of the development of productive forces, that is a specifically social law.[33]

[32] "Marx's Teaching and Its Historical Importance," in *Marxism and Modern Thought*, p. 40.

[33] *Ibid.*, p. 41. Marx declares in the "Theses on Feuerbach" that "the chief defect of all materialism up to now . . . is, that the object, reality, what we apprehend through our senses, is understood only in the form of the *object* or *contemplation*; but not as *sensuous human activity*, as *practice*. . . . The question whether objective truth is an attribute of human thought—is not a theoretical but a *practical* question. . . . The dispute over the reality or nonreality of thinking that is isolated from practice is a purely *scholastic* question. . . . The essence of man is no abstraction inherent in each separate individual. In its reality it is the *ensemble* (aggregate) of social relations. . . . The philosophers have only *interpreted* the world differently, the point is, to *change* it" (*The German Ideology*, pp. 197–9).

In other words, the Marxists maintain that, whatever may have been the case with primitive man, civilized man has no fixed or definable nature; the changes that seem to occur in the innate capacities of human beings are merely the result of changes in society, which shapes human beings in various ways.[34]

In spite of the refusal of the Marxists to accept the central notion involved in the discussion of progress in human nature, they nevertheless often write in a manner very similar to that of others who give the affirmative answer to the question, whether improvements in man's nature occur or at least will occur in the future. According to their view, modern bourgeois man—himself a product of social forces—is not much of an improvement, if any improvement at all, over feudal man; and he may represent a change for the worse when compared to primitive man, for whom "primitive communism" was the normal social condition. But the man of the future, socialist or communist man, will be a different story. When the Revolution is completed, when, in Engels' phrase, the realm of freedom is attained, improvements of many kinds will occur. The human species, "the coagulated *homo sapiens*," as Trotsky puts it,

> will enter once more into a state of radical transformation, and, in his own hands, will become an object of the most complicated methods of artificial selection and psycho-physical training. . . . Man will make it his purpose to master his own feelings, to raise his instincts to the heights of consciousness, to make them transparent, to extend the wires of his will into hidden recesses, and thereby to raise himself to a new plane, to create a higher social biologic type, or, if you please, a superman.[35]

This conception seems to be shared by some of the non-Marxist authors who have been discussed previously. Fourier, Godwin, and Condorcet also maintain that progress in human nature will be accelerated by the establishment of an "ideal" state. Fourier, in particular, seems to be in the main line of Marxist thought on this question. He confidently asserts that the organization of the world into *phalanstères* will result in an immense increase in human talents; there will be thirty-seven million poets the equal of Homer, a like number of Newtons and Molières, and a vast efflorescence of talent in every other sphere. Trotsky makes a prophecy that is strikingly similar. It is difficult to predict, he says,

---

[34] Perhaps the Marxists denied the validity of the notion of a "fixed" human nature in order to counter the argument, so often expressed by antisocialists, that socialism "is contrary to human nature." They conceded that socialism was contrary to the "nature" of "bourgeois man," but they insisted that even "bourgeois man" was the product of social forces.

[35] *Literature and Revolution*, pp. 254–5.

the extent of self-government which the man of the future may reach or
the heights to which he may carry his technique. Social construction and
psycho-physical self-education will become two aspects of one and the same
process. All the arts—literature, drama, painting, music and architecture will
lend this process beautiful form. More correctly, the shell in which the
cultural construction and self-education of Communist man will be enclosed, will develop all the vital elements of contemporary art to the highest
point. Man will become immeasurably stronger, wiser and subtler; his body
will become more harmonized, his movements more rhythmic, his voice
more musical. The forms of life will become dynamically dramatic. The
average human type will rise to the heights of an Aristotle, a Goethe, or a
Marx. And above this ridge new peaks will rise.[36]

PROGRESS IN HUMAN NATURE AS INDEPENDENT OF PROGRESS IN THE CONDITIONS OF LIFE

Among the authors who give the affirmative answer to the question,
whether progress occurs in human nature, a few seem to say that this
kind of progress occurs independently of progress in the conditions of human existence, though the former may have a reciprocal relation with
the latter.[37]

Teilhard de Chardin holds that there is a cosmic or universal progress
of life, the steps or phases in which are marked by "spheres" (other writers
use the term "kingdoms"). First comes the inorganic; the panpsychic
hypothesis requires that this be conceived as somehow alive. Next appears
the unicellular sphere, which remains more or less unchanged for billions
of years. A third phase is represented by the vegetable sphere, which "surrounds" the unicellular sphere much as the outer leaves surround an
onion. On this is superimposed the sphere or kingdom of the animals, and
last of all, surrounding all, is the sphere of reflexive consciousness—the
noosphere.

The change from the animal sphere (zoosphere) to the noosphere is
not, strictly, human progress. It is life not man that has progressed when
man appears, when the first "reflective being" is born. With his birth the
noosphere comes into being. But the development of the noosphere itself
is in the main line of progressive evolution. The general process is reflected
in the particular one.

The general process is an advance toward universal self-consciousness;
hence the particular one is the progress of humanity toward consciousness

---

[36] *Ibid.*, p. 256.

[37] As we have noted, no progress author asserts that progress occurs *only* in man's
nature.

of itself as itself. At first this is shadowy. The first men are only dimly aware of themselves as men. Their progress in self-understanding is slow. It is at least a million years before they begin to comprehend with any clarity the idea of "mankind."

> "Mankind" was at first a vague entity, felt rather than thought out, in which an obscure feeling of perpetual growth was allied to a need for universal fraternity. . . . Mankind was the object of a faith that was often naive. . . . Whether one takes part in the cult or makes fun of it . . . to-day no one can escape being haunted or even dominated by the idea of mankind.[38]

Man's first faint recognition of his own being and of the fact that he is *a member of a species* has now grown so that we speak of "the family of man" and understand, as Teilhard puts it, that "the whole earth . . . is required to nourish each one of us."

> Is this not like some great body which is being born—with its limbs, its nervous system, its perceptive organs, its memory—the body in fact of that great Thing which had to come to fulfil the ambitions aroused in the reflective being by the newly acquired consciousness that he was at one with and responsible to an evolutionary All?[39]

Man, in short, is a "collective reality, and therefore *sui generis."* Hence,

> mankind can only be understood to the extent that, leaving behind its body of tangible constructions, we try to determine the particular type of conscious synthesis emerging from its laborious and industrious concentration. It is in the last resort only definable as a mind.[40]

"Knowledge," says Teilhard, "is the twin sister of mankind."[41] It grows with man, and its fate is bound up with his own. But knowledge is not man; it is one of his possessions. Indeed, its growth, for Teilhard as for so many others, is the paradigm of progress in the conditions of human life. The growth of "that great Thing" that is "in the last resort only definable as a mind" is not progress of that sort. In some sense, this is progress in man's nature.

This sort of progress in human nature has an effect on progress in the conditions of life; and the latter sort has an effect on the former. Teilhard may be read as saying that technology leads the progressive advance of mankind—for sophisticated means of global communication are probably

---

[38] *Phenomenon of Man,* p. 245.
[39] *Ibid.,* pp. 245–6.
[40] *Ibid.,* pp. 247–8.
[41] *Ibid.,* p. 248.

required if humanity as a whole is to become aware of itself as an entity. Nevertheless, progress in human nature is to some extent an independent phenomenon. Technology directs man's progress, perhaps; but, in another sense, technology thereby serves the cause of progressive evolution itself.[42]

No progress author seems to affirm only progress in human nature, as we have observed. However, one or two writers emphasize this kind of progress almost to the exclusion of progress in the conditions of life. One of these is P. Lecomte du Nouÿs, who writes:

> Evolution continues in our time *no longer on the physiological or anatomical plane but on the spiritual and moral plane.* . . . The transition from the ancestral animal, still squirming within us, to Man is too recent for us to be able to understand . . . it, but we are actually living in the midst of a revolution, a revolution on the scale of evolution.[43]

The proof of this, says Nouÿs, is the existence among us of a minority of men who "master" their instincts, impulses, and pleasures, and regard the spiritual "values" of Christianity and the other "higher" religions. That the new type of man is in the minority does not tell against the theory, for "we are still at the dawn of human evolution." If only one man out of a million were endowed with a conscience we would still have to recognize, according to Nouÿs, that a change in nature is overtaking humanity before our very eyes.[44]

Nouÿs points out that evolution acts directly only on individuals, although its ultimate results affect entire species. Hence human progress— "there is no other," Nouÿs declares—occurs through "mutant" changes that occur from time to time in individuals (for example, Socrates, Buddha, Jesus), and that are perpetuated by means of the "evolutionary mecha-

---

[42] The question might be framed thus: Would mankind have advanced as far, or in the same fashion, toward consciousness of itself without modern technology? The answer appears to be that it would have, although not perhaps along the same route. Teilhard declares that "we are faced with a harmonized collectivity of consciousnesses equivalent to a sort of super-consciousness. The idea is that of the earth not only becoming covered by myriads of grains of thought, but becoming enclosed in a single thinking envelope so as to form, functionally, no more than a single vast grain of thought on the sidereal scale, the plurality of individual reflections grouping themselves together and reinforcing one another in the act of a single unanimous reflection" (*ibid.*, p. 251).

Indeed, several science fiction writers have imagined future societies in which men communicate in this way without the aid of technical devices, but by "seeing" directly into each others' minds. The point seems to be that this is the direction in which progressive evolution is tending, technology or no technology.

[43] *Human Destiny*, p. 78. This work is severely criticized by many scientific evolutionists; see, for example, Simpson's *The Meaning of Evolution*, p. 44, note. Whatever his supposed incompetence in science, Nouÿs' predictions are very much in line with those of some writers who base their theories on "scientific truths."

[44] *Ibid.*, p. 82.

nisms" of language and tradition. Thus the race is being subjected to a slow evolutionary process that has been going on for many centuries and by which more and more individual human beings are genetically so constituted that they freely choose the essentially human rather than the essentially animal mode of existence.[45]

Historically, the first indication of the new orientation of man was given by the ancient artifacts, the coarse flint implements and the traces of fire, says Nouÿs. But these discoveries were not the cause but rather the effect of a change in the very nature of man. The main constituent of evolutionary progress is a change for the better in the genetic makeup of mankind. The technical and other improvements that are so often discussed by progress authors seem to be of relatively little importance in Nouÿs' view.

The last remark applies equally to the millennialists, notably Lessing and the Joachimites. They do not speak of changes in the genetic makeup of human beings, nor do they consider the improvements in man's nature to be caused by desirable mutations. The cause of improvement, in their case, is Providence rather than nature or evolution, and the changes occur in the soul of man rather than in his genes. Nevertheless, the result is the same. With the advent of the Eternal Gospel, human beings will be by nature virtuous and will naturally desire the right. As a result, the world will be better; there will be progress in the conditions of human life. But progress in human nature will happen first.[46]

Spencer also foresees internal improvement in man, though the source of this once again differs. His argument in favor of the perfectibility of man is similar to his argument for progress in general. He defines imperfection as "unfitness to the conditions of existence," and declares that unfitness "must consist either in having a faculty or faculties in excess; or in having a faculty or faculties deficient; or in both."[47] A faculty in excess is one to which the conditions of life do not afford full exercise; a deficient

---

[45] Nouÿs sees a symbolic representation of this progress in Genesis. He points to "the two successive creations reported in the first and second chapters," and concedes that the "orthodox exegesis" views the two accounts as describing the same occurrence. According to Nouÿs, however, "on the eighth day, God creates *another* living being having the human form also, and for the first time the sacred text uses a different language. God first breathes in the soul through man's nostrils, and then commands him *not* to eat of the fruit of the tree of the knowledge of good and evil, knowing that he will eat it." This use of a prohibition instead of a command is the heart of the matter. "It signifies that the most important event of evolution has taken place. It signifies the appearance of a new discontinuity in nature, a discontinuity as deep as that which exists between inert matter and organized life. It signifies the birth of conscience, and of the last freedom" (*ibid.*, p. 85).

[46] The improvement discussed here is not that change in human nature that is the result of grace, as usually conceived by Christian writers.

[47] *Social Statics*, pp. 78–9.

faculty is one from which the conditions of life demand more than it can perform.

> But it is an essential principle of life that a faculty to which circumstances do not allow full exercise diminishes; and that a faculty on which circumstances make excessive demands increases.
>
> And so long as this excess and this deficiency continue, there must continue decrease on the one hand, and growth on the other.
>
> Finally, all excess and all deficiency must disappear; that is, all unfitness must disappear; that is, all imperfection must disappear.
>
> Thus the ultimate development of the ideal man is logically certain.[48]

Most of the examples Spencer gives to support his argument—that a tree becomes bulky when it stands alone, and slender if one of a group; that the blind attain a more delicate sense of touch; that the musician learns to detect an error of a semitone amidst what seems to others a very babel of sounds, and so forth—are examples not of changes in nature but of the adaptibility of organisms to their environment. As such, the examples do not prove that there is progress in human nature. But a few examples—that the same creature assumes the different forms of cart horse and race horse, according as its habits demand strength or speed, and so forth—are of the sort required. And it is clear enough that Spencer is speaking of an improvement in human nature and not merely of an adaptation of existing human nature to social circumstances. The human faculties *will* be molded into complete fitness for the social state, he declares; the things we call evil and immorality *will* disappear; man *will* become perfect. With equal certainty, these changes for the better must be in the very nature of man.

THE POSITION THAT PROGRESS DOES NOT OCCUR IN HUMAN NATURE

The progress authors who deny progress in human nature may be divided into three groups. The first includes the many authors, most of them writing either in the eighteenth or the twentieth century, who maintain that human nature is always and everywhere the same, that progress occurs only in the conditions of life, and that improvements in men's behavior are merely the result of improved conditions of life.

The second group includes the writers who foresee a progressive development, realization, or fulfillment of human nature, partly as the result of improved conditions of life, but who do not conceive such development

---

[48] *Ibid.*, p. 79.

or fulfillment as a change in human nature *per se.* According to them, the men of the future will be more fully human, and thus in some sense better men, but they will not be essentially or fundamentally different from the men of today. For these writers, too, human nature remains the same.

The third group includes the writers who concede that the nature of man can change, and who concede also that it may change in the future, but who maintain that the changes are reversible and thus do not constitute permanent improvements in human nature.

The progress authors who hold that there is no progress in human nature are listed below.[49]

Pascal	Henry George
Fontenelle	Bellamy
Mandeville	Tolstoy
Leibniz	Sumner
Voltaire	Henry Adams
Adam Smith	Dewey
Kant	Broad
Turgot	Inge
Helvétius	Ortega
Herder	Maritain
Chateaubriand	Simon
Malthus	De Rougemont
Hegel	Ginsberg
Buckle	Childe
J. S. Mill	C. G. Darwin
Charles Darwin	E. H. Carr

HUMAN NATURE IS ALWAYS AND EVERYWHERE THE SAME

A number of eighteenth-century writers assert that men are the same at all times and places. Turgot, for example, writes:

The resources of nature and the prolific seeds of science are found wherever there are men. The loftiest heights of knowledge are and can be nothing but developments or combinations of the first ideas given us by the senses, just as the edifice whose height most astonishes our eyes rests of necessity upon the same earth we press beneath our feet. And the same senses, the same organs, the spectacle of the same Universe have everywhere given men the same

[49] Progress authors not shown in this list or the one on p. 288 do not take an ascertainable position on the question being considered in this chapter.

ideas, just as the same needs and the same propensities have everywhere taught them the same arts.[50]

Turgot speaks of perfectibility, a term often used by authors who affirm progress in human nature. But he is careful to say that he means the perfectibility of institutions, not of men. "Humanity moves onward to perfection," he declares, but not individual human beings. As individuals, men are subject to "nature," which is cyclical.

> Everything is born and born again, everything perishes; and in . . . successive generations . . . time does but restore . . . the image of what it has already made to disappear.[51]

The situation is different with humanity, with the human race taken as a whole. For mankind has

> formed from individual stores of knowledge a common treasure, that one generation transmits to another, like unto a heritage continually augmented by the discoveries of each century.[52]

The idea being presented here is of successive generations of men who, because of increasing knowledge—continuously increasing because each generation adds to it—may *seem* to differ from their forebears. In fact, however, the difference is only superficial, and man remains essentially the same.

Helvétius concurs. "Everyone knows," he declares,

> that he is not of a different nature from the Romans; that the difference of his education produces the difference of his sentiments, and from thence he is shocked at the bare recital of a spectacle which custom would doubtless have rendered agreeable, had he been born on the banks of the Tiber.[53]

Making use of a figure used by Fontenelle, Helvétius goes on to ask:

> Who can assert that men are not like those trees of the same species, whose seed, being absolutely the same, but never sown exactly in the same earth, nor exposed entirely to the same winds, the same sun, or the same rain, must in unfolding themselves necessarily produce an infinity of different forms?[54]

Fontenelle also holds that just as the trees of the ancient world were no different from modern trees, so the men were no different, either. Apparent differences between epochs are the result of education and changed en-

---

[50] *Tableau philosophique des progrès successifs de l'esprit humain*, p. 5.
[51] *Ibid.*, p. 6.
[52] *Ibid.*
[53] *De l'esprit; or Essays on the Mind and the Several Faculties*, p. 180.
[54] *Ibid.*, p. 198.

vironment. This is to say that progress occurs only in the conditions of life, and not in human nature; the contrast is presented, in Fontenelle's essay, between the fixity of species and the changeability of society.

The same view is held by Voltaire. "Men in general have ever been what they now are," he declares:

> by this I would not mean to say that they always had fine cities, large cannon, comic operas, and religious convents; but man always had the same instinct, which prompted him to love himself, in the companion of his pleasures, in his children, in his grandchildren, in the works of his hands.[55]

The position that human nature does not change, and that progress is confined to the conditions of human life, finds expression in our own time as well as in the eighteenth century. E. H. Carr makes a distinction that, he says, Hegel also makes, between "history," which is progressive, and "nature," which is not.

> The Darwinian revolution appeared to remove all embarrassments by equating evolution and progress: nature, like history, turned out after all to be progressive. But this opened the way to a much graver misunderstanding by confusing biological inheritance, which is the source of evolution, with social acquisition, which is the source of progress in history. The distinction is familiar and obvious.[56]

Evolution by inheritance must be measured in the millions of years, Carr points out, and he declares that no measurable biological change is known to have occurred in man since the beginning of written history. However, progress by social acquisition can be measured in generations.

> Modern man is said to have no larger a brain, and no greater innate capacity of thought, than his ancestor 5,000 years ago. But the effectiveness of his thinking has been multiplied many times by learning and incorporating in his experience the experience of the intervening generations.[57]

Others also hold this view. Childe, for example, declares that

> since the time when the skeletons of *homo sapiens* first appear in the geological record, perhaps 25,000 years ago, man's bodily evolution has come virtually to a standstill, though his cultural progress was just beginning.[58]

Ginsberg has a similar thing to say, though he speaks specifically of moral progress, where Childe's "cultural progress" is mainly in the realm of science and technology.

[55] "The Philosophy of History," in *Essays and Criticisms*, p. 28.
[56] *What Is History?*, p. 150.
[57] *Ibid.*, pp. 150–1.
[58] *Man Makes Himself*, p. 34.

The moral progress I have so far discussed is essentially a progress in ethical conceptions acting through tradition. It consists in the clarification of ideals, in obtaining a firmer grasp of the conditions of their realization and in the widening of human sympathies through an extension of the power of imaginative identification. There is no reason to believe that any improvement has been affected in the human breed, or that the hereditary basis of character has undergone a change for the better or for the worse.[59]

And Dean Inge puts the case with considerable force. "There has been no physical progress in our species for many thousands of years," he asserts.

The Cro-Magnon Race, which lived perhaps twenty thousand years ago, was at least equal to any modern people in size and strength; the ancient Greeks were, I suppose, handsomer and better formed than we are; and some unprogressive races, such as the Zulus, Samoans, and Tahitians, are envied by Europeans either for strength or beauty. . . . Mentally . . . the men of the Old Stone Age, ugly as most of them must have been, had as large brains as ours; and he would be a bold man who should claim that we are intellectually equal to the Athenians or superior to the Romans. . . . If progress means the improvement of human nature itself, the question to be asked is whether the modern civilized man behaves better in the same circumstances than his ancestor would have done. Absence of temptation may produce an appearance of improvement, but this is hardly what we mean by progress. . . . It seems to me doubtful whether when we are exposed to the same temptations we are more humane or more sympathetic or juster or less brutal than the ancients. . . . It is difficult to feel with any confidence that either the lapse of time or civilization has made the *bête humaine* less ferocious.[60]

Several nineteenth-century authors also maintain that progress in human nature does not occur. An interesting case is Bellamy. The Marxist authors tend, on the whole, to assert that progress in human nature will occur after the millennium. Bellamy is usually found in the same camp with the Marxists. On this point, however, he seems to differ. He is explicit in stating that the change, observed in *Looking Backward*, from a society based on class antagonism and greed (our own), to one based on social harmony (that of the year 2000), involves no change in human nature. Viewing all the improvements that have occurred by the year 2000, Bellamy's protagonist, West, speaks to his host, Dr. Leete:

"Human nature itself must have changed very much," I said.
"Not at all," was Dr. Leete's reply, "but the conditions of life have changed, and with that the motives of human action."[61]

59 *Reason in Society*, p. 315.
60 *The Idea of Progress*, pp. 22–3.
61 *Looking Backward*, p. 61.

Another interesting case is that of Buckle, who suggests the possibility, at least, that improvements in man's nature may have occurred, but who points out that there is no way of knowing whether they have or not. "It may be," he writes,

> that, owing to some physical causes still unknown, the average capacity of the brain is, if we compare long periods of time, becoming gradually greater; and that therefore the mind, which acts through the brain, is, even independently of education, increasing its aptitude and the general competence of its views. Such, however, is still our ignorance of physical laws, and so completely are we in the dark as to the circumstances which regulate the hereditary transmission of character, temperament, and other personal peculiarities, that we must consider this alleged progress as a very doubtful point; and in the present state of our knowledge, we cannot safely assume that there has been any permanent improvement in the moral or intellectual faculties of man, nor have we any decisive ground for saying that those faculties are likely to be greater in an infant born in the most civilized part of Europe, than in one born in the wildest region of a barbarous country.[62]

The last sentence in this passage constitutes a direct denial of Comte's position on this matter.[63]

The laws to which Buckle refers are those of genetics; the scientific study of them was not effectively undertaken until after his death. Nevertheless, the possibility of bringing about improvement in human nature by means of controlled human breeding was being considered in his time, and before. Malthus, for example, declares that "in human life, though there are great variations from different causes, it may be doubted whether, since the world began, any organic improvement whatever in the human frame can be clearly ascertained."[64] That this kind of progress has not occurred in the past, however, does not, according to Malthus, absolutely rule it out for the future. Malthus continues:

> It does not . . . seem impossible, that by an attention to breed, a certain degree of improvement, similar to that among animals, might take place among men. Whether intellect could be communicated may be a matter of doubt: but size, strength, beauty, complexion, and perhaps even longevity are in a degree transmissable.

The breeding of animals can be controlled by human beings, Malthus observes; the question is, whether men have the capacity to control their own breeding. In fact, he is doubtful.

[62] *History of Civilization in England*, p. 177.
[63] See above, pp. 288–9.
[64] *Population*, p. 60.

As the human race . . . could not be improved in this way, without condemning all the bad specimens to celibacy, it is not probable, that an attention to breed should ever become general.

Furthermore, even if some improvement in man's nature could be brought about in this way, it would not be much. This indeed is Malthus' main point of contention with Godwin and, especially, with Condorcet. "The error does not seem to lie," he declares,

in supposing a small degree of improvement possible, but in not discriminating between a small improvement, the limit of which is undefined, and an improvement really unlimited.[65]

Malthus' dispute with Godwin is based not so much on the latter's belief that progress in human nature will be unlimited, as on his assertion that the mind has power over the body and can improve it almost at will. We recall Godwin's contention that cheerfulness and ardor can overcome illness and fatigue.[66] "The instances here mentioned," Malthus declares, in reply to Godwin's remarks on the subject,

are chiefly instances of the effects of mental stimulants on the bodily frame. No person has ever doubted for a moment the near, though mysterious connection, of mind and body. But it is arguing totally without knowledge of the nature of stimulants to suppose, either that they could be applied continually with equal strength, or if they could be so applied, for a time, that that they would not exhaust and wear out the subject. In some of the cases here noted, the strength of the stimulus depends upon its novelty and unexpectedness. Such a stimulus cannot, from its nature, be repeated often with the same effect, as it would by repetition lose that property which gave it its strength.

In the other cases, the argument is from a small and partial effect, to a great and general effect, which will in numberless instances be found to be a very fallacious mode of reasoning. The busy and active man may in some degree counteract, or what is perhaps nearer the truth, may disregard those slight disorders of frame, which fix the attention of a man who has nothing else to think of; but this does not tend to prove that activity of the mind will enable a man to disregard a high fever, the smallpox, or the plague.

The man who walks twenty miles with a motive that engrosses his soul, does not attend to his slight fatigue of body when he comes in; but double his motive, and set him to walk another twenty miles, quadruple it, and let him start a third time, and so on; and the length of his walk will ultimately depend upon muscle and mind. . . . A motive of uncommon power acting upon a frame of moderate strength, would, perhaps, make the man kill himself by his exertions, but it would not make him walk an hundred miles

[65] *Ibid.*
[66] See above, p. 289.

in twenty-four hours. This statement of the case, shews the fallacy of supposing, that the person was really not at all tired in his first walk of twenty miles, because he did not appear so, or, perhaps, scarcely felt any fatigue himself.[67]

As it were in reply to criticism of this kind, Malthus quotes Godwin saying that

> nothing would be more unphilosophical than to conclude, that, because a certain species of power is beyond the train of our present observation, it is beyond the limits of the human mind.[68]

But this statement calls forth from Malthus an even more indignant denial. "I own," he says, "my ideas of philosophy are in this respect widely different from Mr. Godwin's. The only distinction that I can see, between a philosophical conjecture, and the assertions of the Prophet Mr. Brothers, is, that one is founded upon indications arising from the train of our present observations, and the other has no foundation at all."[69] It is clear that Malthus considers Godwin's predictions to belong in the latter class, and not in the former.

In short, the position of Malthus in regard to the question being considered is similar to that of Buckle. Neither denies categorically that there has been improvement in human nature in the past, and both consider at least the possibility that improvement in this respect may occur in the future. At the same time, however, they concur in asserting that there is no real evidence for past improvement, and little probability for it in the future. Hence they may properly be assigned to the group of progress authors who deny the occurrence of progress in human nature.

THE PROGRESSIVE FULFILLMENT OF HUMAN NATURE

Kant maintains as primary and incontrovertible principles, first, that "all the capacities implanted in a creature by nature, are destined to unfold themselves, completely and conformably to their end, in the course of time"; and second, that "in man, as the only rational creature on earth, those natural capacities which are directed toward the use of his reason, could be completely developed only in the species and not in the individual."[70] These two statements, taken together, constitute a clear denial

[67] *Population*, pp. 77–8.
[68] Qu. in Malthus, *ibid.*, p. 81.
[69] *Ibid.*
[70] *Idea of a Universal History*, in W. Hastie (ed.), *Principles of Politics*, p. 4; see also Teggart (ed.), *The Idea of Progress*, p. 293.

that progress occurs in human nature, or, what is the same thing, an assertion that progress occurs only in the conditions of human life. All men
are born with the same human nature. However, later men will be able to
realize their innate capacities more fully than earlier men.

That realizing or fulfilling human nature is easily understood or effected
is questioned by Kant in another work. "The question next arises," he
declares, "as to the means by which this continuous progress to the better
may be maintained."

> When carefully considered, we soon see that as this process must go on to
> an incalculable distance of time, it cannot depend so much on what we do
> of ourselves, for instance, on the education we give to the younger genera-
> tion, or on the method by which we may proceed in order to realize it, as on
> what human *Nature* as such will do *in* and with us, to compel us to move in
> a track into which we would not readily have betaken ourselves.[71]

In other words, the progressive fulfillment of human nature being a
natural necessity, our (artificial) efforts to further it are as likely to impede as to hasten it.

Herder, who is found with Kant on other questions, is found with him
on this one, too. "Every beast attains what his organization can attain,"
he declares: "man only reaches it not, because his end is so high, so extensive, so infinite; and he begins on this earth so low, so late, and with
so many external and internal obstacles." Man, in short, "has everything
that pertains to reason and to humanity to learn." But in spite of the fact
that he is now "retarded by chains" in his "progress to truth and liberty,"
man *will* learn all; he *will* become a "nobler, freer creature"; and the
"simular of man will become man in reality."[72] The last statement clearly
supports the proposition that human nature itself does not change, but
that man progressively realizes or fulfills his nature in time.

Leibniz and Hegel concur in this view. The fact, for Leibniz, that our
happiness must consist in a perpetual progress to new pleasures and new
perfections, does not mean that man will improve in his nature; indeed,
exactly the contrary is the case, for as man advances in this kind of happiness he becomes more and more fully what he now is potentially. And
the progress in the consciousness of freedom that for Hegel is the essence
of human progress carries the same connotation. All men are and always
were born free, or at least with the capacity for freedom; the conditions

[71] "On the Saying: That a Thing May Be Right in Theory but Does Not Hold
in Practice," in Hastie, p. 71; see Teggart, p. 307. Here again we have direct opposition to Comte's position, and that of other writers, that education (in the broad
sense) will bring about improvements in man's nature.
[72] *Outlines of a Philosophy of the History of Man*, V, p. 124; see also Teggart,
p. 312.

of life must, however, improve (this means, primarily, that the modern state must be invented and developed) before that innate capacity for freedom can be realized.

The same position is held by modern writers like Maritain and Simon. According to them, a human being in the state of grace has an improved nature, but this is not a transmissible or inheritable improvement, and therefore does not constitute progress in human nature. At the same time, the conditions of life, especially those reflected in what may be called the moral climate, are susceptible of improvement. This means that later men have a greater opportunity to realize or fulfill their innate capacity for virtue than do earlier men. But it does not mean that the capacity of later men is any greater than that of earlier men. The human capacity for virtue and for all other attainments remains the same—until the end of history, when man will recover the better nature that he had, in the person of Adam, in Paradise. But that change, since it occurs outside of time, cannot be considered an instance of progress in human nature.[73]

REVERSIBLE IMPROVEMENTS IN HUMAN NATURE

In spite of the "dogma" that measures progress by increase in the sentiments of altruism, kindliness, peaceful feelings, and so forth, Dewey declares,

> there is no reason that I know of to suppose that the basic fund of these emotions has increased appreciably in thousands and thousands of years. Man is equipped with these feelings at birth as well as with emotions of fear, anger, emulation and resentment. What appears to be an increase in one set is, in reality, a change in their social occasions and social channels.[74]

Dewey explains his point by means of a physical analogue. One need not assume that civilized man has "a better endowment of ear or eye than savage man" to understand why civilized man hears and sees "better" than his primitive forebears. It is merely that social surroundings give civilized man "more important things to see and hear." Furthermore, civilized man "has the wit to devise instruments to reinforce his eye and ear—the telegraph and telephone, the microscope and telescope." In like manner, there is no reason to suppose that civilized man has less natural aggressiveness or more natural altruism than the savage. However, he may live in social conditions that create a

[73] For further discussion of the views of Maritain and Simon on the progress of morality, see Chapter 25.

[74] "Progress," in *International Journal of Ethics*, 1916, p. 516.

greater demand for the display of kindliness and which turn his aggressive
instincts into less destructive channels. There is at any time a sufficient
amount of kindly impulses possessed by man to enable him to live in
amicable peace with all his fellows; and there is at any time a sufficient
equipment of bellicose impulses to keep him in trouble with his fellows.[75]

Apparent changes in human nature, whether or not they are improvements, could as easily be reversed, Dewey is saying. They are the result
of society's demands upon its members; there is no fixed human nature,
and such changes as occur are relative to the society in the context of
which they are observed. The similarity between this view and that of
the Marxists is manifest. Dewey, like the Marxists, asserts that human nature is "plastic," and that man can only be fully understood as a social
being.

However, the Marxists are found on the affirmative side of the question, whether progress occurs in human nature; Dewey on the negative
side. What is the reason for this difference?

It appears to consist in their different conceptions of the progress
in the conditions of human life that is ultimately the cause of improvements in man's "nature." For the Marxists, progress of that kind is necessary; what is more, it will result in an ideal society, one in which "the
free development of each is the condition of the free development of all."
Dewey has no such conception. For him, progress is highly contingent
and, one feels, always at least potentially reversible (if it were necessarily
reversible he would of course not be a progress author at all). Even more
important, progress, in Dewey's view, will never result in an ideal or
"perfect" society. Society may, he believes, be improved; progress is a
possibility for the future. But even such progress as occurs will be fundamentally limited in extent, if not in duration. Men may act better in the
future, and they may construct a better world. But the possibility will
always remain that social conditions will call forth their worst instead of
their best instincts. Men will always be born with the same capacities for
good and for evil.

All mankind, declares C. G. Darwin,

display the same characteristics of pugnacity, ambition, envy, laziness,
selfishness, unselfishness, loyalty, kindliness, sociability, sense of humour and
so on. There are of course obvious differences in behaviour between individuals on account of differences of condition and of training or education
. . . but it is correct to say that man really is one species and that as such

[75] *Ibid.* See also Dewey's *Human Nature and Conduct* for more extensive consideration of the "plasticity" of man's nature, although not in the context of a
treatment of progress.

it will take a million years before anything notably different will arise in his nature. This is a fixed point.[76]

In spite of the incontrovertible character of this assertion, Darwin concedes that the future practice of eugenics may be able to bring about improvements in the average nature of human beings. The point is, however, that, in his view, these are necessarily impermanent. Hence the concession does not contradict his primary assertion.

The argument runs as follows. Eugenics is one of the perennial dreams of the human race, and is seen to be all the more desirable as progress is made in the development of animal species along lines that are held to constitute improvements in their nature. Therefore, Darwin predicts, human eugenics will be practiced in the future. However, the practice of eugenics requires that the species to be improved must be tamed. The question is, therefore, whether a species *can tame itself*, for, in order for human eugenics to be practiced with any consistent success, man must be treated as a domesticated and not a wild animal. But who is to do the taming? Darwin asks. He concedes that a despot could tame the majority or even the great majority of the human beings under his control, but he points out that even if the despot could control his own breeding he could not control that of his descendants, and the likelihood of their retaining their control over themselves, to say nothing of their subjects, is, in Darwin's opinion, nil. Hence whatever temporary improvements in human nature may be brought about by eugenics as practiced in the future, these will be obliterated by subsequent uncontrolled breeding, and the nature of man will therefore remain constant, or at least relatively constant, throughout the million years that Darwin expects the human species to endure on earth.[77]

Darwin's position thus is seen to be the same as Dewey's, though it is based on entirely different premises. Both foresee the possibility of future improvements in human nature, but both maintain that these are fundamentally transitory and impermanent. The result, in each case, is that human nature will remain the same and not progress, and such improvements as may occur will be the result only of progress in the conditions of human life.

[76] *The Next Million Years*, p. 58.
[77] *Ibid.*, pp. 84–98.

II

Subordinate Issues
Concerning the Respects in
Which Progress Occurs

18

Kinds of Progress in Human Products and Institutions

I n the remaining chapters in Book Two we will treat a number of questions, all of them of primary interest to progress authors, about the different areas or respects in which progress in the conditions of human life occurs. Is there progress, for instance, in morals, or is progress restricted to knowledge and technology? If there is progress in both areas, is one sort the condition or cause of the other, do the two occur independently, or is there a relation of reciprocal causality between them? Does progress in knowledge precede technological progress, or the other way around? Is technological progress the condition of political and social progress, or vice versa? Does political progress occur at all, and, if so, what constitutes political progress? If it occurs, does it necessarily or usually precede improvement in behavior (moral progress), or is moral progress the condition of other (social) types?

DIVISION OF THE SUBJECT MATTER

We have previously indicated that those who affirm progress in the conditions of human life assert that improvements occur in one or more of these areas:

1. Knowledge
2. Technology
3. Wealth
4. Social and political institutions
5. Morality.

This division is convenient, but of course no claim is made that it is the only feasible one. Authors treat progress in many different ways. A glance at the tables of contents of half a dozen works on the subject, taken almost at random, shows the extreme diversity of kinds of progress in institutions discussed in the literature. It would have been possible to distinguish fifty different kinds of progress instead of five.

Nor is it claimed that the five kinds listed above are exhaustive. There may be realms of human activity that are not included, although these are not likely to be realms in which progress is said to occur.[1] We must concede, as well, that the lines between the various kinds cannot always be drawn with precision. A given author's discussion of progress in religion, for instance, might have to be treated from two points of view: from the point of view of progress in social and political institutions, and from the point of view of moral progress. Another author's discussion of progress in health might well touch on matters considered in the chapters on technological progress and on progress in wealth; if he emphasized public-health institutions, we might treat him in the chapters on progress in social and political institutions; and he might even mention or even treat as of primary importance the subject of public morality, which we would consider in the chapters on moral progress. Depending on the author's general social and philosophical orientation, what he calls progress in knowledge may mean knowledge *of* the world (knowledge of nature and of human nature), knowledge of *how to control* or change the world (technological progress), or knowledge of *how to behave* in the world (moral progress).

In most cases, however, the lines between the various kinds of progress in the outward conditions of life are drawn clearly enough for our purposes. It usually is possible to discern what an author is mainly talking about, and to place him either as agreeing with, or as opposing, others who are talking about the same thing.[2]

The five kinds of progress in man's products and institutions fall into two rather distinct groups. The first group includes progress in knowledge, progress in technology, and progress in wealth (economic progress). The

[1] Fine art is an important case in point. See the Appendix.
[2] In spite of the diversity mentioned, it is also true that several important progress authors follow a scheme of division that is roughly the same as ours.

second group includes progress in social and political institutions, and moral progress.

It appears that no progress author denies that knowledge increases in time. It may be objected, of course, that during certain periods of history mankind forgets more than it learns, that its stock of knowledge decreases rather than increases. Such a period is the so-called Dark Ages, when Western man is said to have lost much of the culture inherited from the Greeks and Romans.[3] Progress authors tend to meet this objection in one of two ways. Either they say that progress was "working unawares" during such periods,[4] that the progress in knowledge that occurred was hidden, only to be revealed at a later date; or they point to the *overall* increase of knowledge throughout man's history on earth, and ask whether it can be seriously maintained that man knows no more now than he did, say, 50,000 years ago.

Similar considerations apply to technology. Man is now capable of doing certain things, and exercising certain controls over external nature, that were not possible in earlier times. Once more it may be asked whether man's technical facility grows steadily with the passage of time; there may be times during which technology suffers an eclipse. But taking all of history into view, it is hard to deny that mankind is absolutely more capable than it used to be. Nor is there much reason not to expect technological advance in the future.

Here, the question that seems to be important for progress authors is not whether technology advances, but whether its advance is for the better. A few progress authors question whether progress in knowledge is desirable, but the majority seem to feel that it is. A large number of authors seriously question whether technological advance is desirable, and thus whether it constitutes human progress.

Finally, it appears to be undeniable that the human race is increasing in numbers. The fact that there are constantly[5] more people alive on the

---

[3] The period 1200–800 B.C. is also called a Dark Age by historians. "The art of writing disappeared," declares M. I. Finley, "the centres of power crumbled, there was much petty warfare . . . and all in all the material and cultural levels were poverty-stricken by contrast with the Mycenean civilization" (*The Ancient Greeks,* p. 2).

[4] Interestingly enough, Finley notes that certain achievements occurred even during the early Greek Dark Age. "The story is not just one of decay and decline," he says, "for it was in this Dark Age, by a process we can only vaguely glimpse in archaeological finds and in the myths as told by later Greeks, that a major technological revolution occurred—the coming of iron—and that Greek society was born" (*ibid.*). The similarity to the happenings of the Dark Ages between A.D. 600–1000 is striking.

[5] The earth's population may not be increasing constantly. Various eighteenth-century writers speculated, with some evidence, that the population of Europe between A.D. 400 and 1400 had decreased. But the general tendency seems to be in the direction of increase.

earth must mean that there is an increase in the production of certain basic economic goods, and hence that there is an increase of wealth, at least in this primary sense. Increase or advance in the economic sphere is thus as indisputable as advances in knowledge and in technology. But there is not general agreement, even among progress authors, as to whether this advance is for the better. Indeed, perhaps the majority of them hold that progress would be hastened if there were fewer rather than more human beings on earth, and most of them concur in urging limitation on the future population. Hence, here, as before, the question that interests progress authors is not whether there is increase in wealth but whether increase in wealth is progress.

Advances in the political and the moral realms do not, on the contrary, have the same automatic character. They are far from being indisputable. The position that there is no advance at all in these areas can be ably defended. There is apparently no question that knowledge grows, that technology moves forward, and that wealth increases. But there is considerable question whether the changes—in themselves undeniable—in political and social institutions, and in moral behavior and practice, constitute any sort of orderly advance whatever.

If any sort of measurable or orderly advance is seen as occurring in these realms, it is almost always held to be progressive—*i.e.*, for the better —by progress authors. It is precisely the fact that advances may be talked about in knowledge, technology, and wealth without asserting that they are progressive, and that any advance in social or political institutions and in morals is almost always judged to be progressive, that most sharply distinguishes the two groups of kinds of progress in the conditions of human life.

The distinction that we have previously discussed between irreversible change for the better (*i.e.*, progress) and irreversible cumulative change that is not for the better (*i.e.*, ICC) is relevant here. One may speak meaningfully of *more* knowledge, of *more* technology, and of *more* wealth. But what does it mean to speak of more politics, and of more morals? If these phrases mean anything, they mean something more complex and subtle than the first three phrases. One is inclined, instead, to speak of *better* politics and of *better* morals. Conversely, it seems to make less sense to discuss better knowledge, better technology, and better wealth than to discuss the increase of these things.

Of course it does make some sense to speak of better knowledge, and there is some meaning in the notions of more politics and more morals. However, a discussion of more politics, for example, usually involves an affirmation of more *knowledge* of politics (or more understanding of the political art); more *technical capacity* to disseminate knowledge of political issues to the people, and to instruct them in order that they can make intelligent choices; or more *wealth* with which to support political activities, including political education. In other words, more politics may mean more knowledge, technology, or wealth. And a discussion of better knowledge may involve questions about moral and political behavior; this applies also to technology and even to wealth, which is often held to be good or bad according to whether it is used for good or bad social purposes. In other words, better knowledge, technology, or wealth may mean better morals.

It would be rash to claim that progress in knowledge, in technology, and in wealth always has an underlying basis of ICC, and that progress in social and political institutions, and in morals, is always intrinsically meliorative. Nevertheless, the distinction between progress and ICC helps to throw light on the distinction between the two main kinds of progress in the conditions of life.

The question, whether progress is necessary or contingent, is also relevant. Progress in knowledge, in technology, and in wealth tends to be seen as necessary; progress in politics and in morals tends to be seen as contingent. There are many exceptions to these rules, particularly to the second one, a fair number of writers holding that progress of all kinds is necessary. And a few progress authors maintain that technological and economic progress need not occur in the future, even if progress in knowledge necessarily and inevitably will occur.

The Shape of the Subordinate Controversy

In the following chapters, we do not consider it to be our task merely to distinguish the five kinds of progress in the conditions of life, and to identify the authors who maintain that this or that kind does or does not occur. These are not always the questions of greatest concern to progress authors. What they often emphasize is another sort of question, that of the hierarchy of the kinds of progress: whether, if one kind occurs, another kind will be brought about.

In other words, the questions treated in the following chapters tend to be more programmatical than those treated heretofore. The earlier questions were largely existential or conceptual. Here a majority of writers are interested in the relations among the various kinds of progress, and the effects that one kind may have on another. Above all, they are interested in the question—How may progress be brought about?

One author, for example, may say that political liberty must obtain before economic development can occur, and may therefore urge, for the sake of economic progress, the establishment of institutions conducive to political progress. Another writer, on the contrary, may hold that economic progress must precede political progress, and therefore urge investment, industrialization, and so forth—but always keeping liberty as the end in view. One writer may say that a good moral climate must precede good laws, on the grounds that morality cannot be legislated, and, as a consequence, urge that progress be first made in education for the sake of progress in political institutions; another may say that law is in some sense an educational institution, and that good laws will therefore improve morals.

There are many differences of this sort among progress authors. Each kind of progress in conditions has been put forward by some writers, at least, as the most important, and as the condition for other kinds. The discussion in the subordinate controversy about the respects in which progress in the conditions of life occurs is therefore divided into seven chapters,[6] in each of which two main questions are treated:

1. What do progress authors mean by this kind of progress, and do they hold that it occurs?

2. Do progress authors conceive this kind of progress as the condition of other kinds, and, if so, what kinds of progress are dependent on it, and in what way?[7]

The treatment in the following chapters differs from that in the earlier chapters in another way, as well. Previously, we have tried to consider the views of all of the progress authors studied, and have ranged them on one or the other side of the questions at issue. Henceforth, we will not undertake full-scale analyses of that sort. No lists of authors holding that this or that kind of progress does or does not occur will be found; and, in many cases, mention will be made of writers who have not been previ-

---

[6] There are two chapters each on political progress and on moral progress.

[7] Another way of describing the difference between the matters previously discussed and those discussed in the following chapters is to say that our treatment of progress has so far not touched upon intimate human concerns. Progress is a topic of everyday conversation. Progress is common in headlines. In a newspaper supplement, "Economic Review of an Emerging Africa" (*The New York Times,* Jan. 20, 1964), the word appeared no less than 374 times in 83 pages. Hardly a political speech could be made anywhere in the world that did not mention progress. And what public man does not claim, in addition, that he is helping to bring it about?

The "ordinary man" is not greatly concerned, perhaps, with the questions, whether progress is necessary or contingent, whether it will continue indefinitely or "plateau out," and whether or not it occurs in man's very nature. Instead, he wants to know what progress is, and how much of it, if any, he can expect. Most of all, he wants to know what he should do to make it happen.

It is mainly with matters of this sort that the following chapters deal.

ously discussed. Often, these are authors who do not have full-fledged theories of progress, but who nevertheless have something to say that is relevant to the subject at hand.

All progress authors concur in holding that some sort of progress in knowledge occurs, and most say that technological progress is also a fact. The chapters that deal with these kinds of progress are therefore relatively short, for not a great deal needs to be said on these matters that has not already been said. However, political and moral progress are considered by progress authors from many points of view. The extremely complex discussion of them in the literature requires more extensive treatment, and the chapters dealing with these important kinds of progress in the conditions of human life are relatively long.

19

Progress in Knowledge

I T is difficult to conceive a theory of human progress that would not involve some sort of progress in the knowledge of something.

The "something" varies, of course, from author to author. They question whether the increase of knowledge is always desirable. They question whether it is necessary. They question whether it will continue indefinitely or come to a stop. And they have different conceptions of knowledge itself. These run all the way from what has been called "tissue knowledge" to what might correspond to Aristotle's "wisdom."

Progress authors concur, however, in holding that knowledge in some sense grows with time, and that this growth is, on the whole, a progressive change. Indeed, for many of these writers, progress in knowledge *is* human progress; progress in knowledge is coextensive with the progress of mankind. At the very least it is the clue, the underlying basis, the "motor," of humanity's advance, of its forward motion, of its progress.

Perhaps there are two basic notions, among progress authors, regarding the reason why knowledge progresses. Either mankind is taught by some power outside it—God, or Providence, or "the Idea"; or mankind learns by itself.

For Lessing, as we have seen, the history of mankind is the story of God's effort to "educate" humanity. The Old and the New Testaments are but the first and second "primers" of the race; still to come is the "eternal gospel," which will contain the truth as mature men can finally know it.

Few writers are as explicit as Lessing, for whom Scripture is the sole source of man's progress in knowledge. For Chateaubriand, Christianity as a whole is the source of progress: "the modern world is indebted to it for every improvement, from agriculture to the abstract sciences." Christianity

> encourages genius, corrects the taste, develops the virtuous passions, imparts energy to the ideas, presents notable images to the writer, and perfect models to the artist. . . . There is no disgrace in being believers with Newton and Bossuet, with Pascal and Racine.[1]

A somewhat different view is held by Leibniz, who maintains that mankind progresses in the most important kind of knowledge when and as it learns more and more about God. God, being infinite, can never be completely known. But mankind enjoys a perpetual progress to new pleasures and new perfections that involve increasing understanding of the Divine Will.

Pascal, in contradistinction to the writers mentioned above, holds that it is in the realm of our knowledge of God that progress does *not* occur.

> It is in theology that authority has its chief weight because there it is inseparable from truth, which we know only through it.[2]

There cannot be cumulative knowledge of God, in the ordinary sense of progress,

> because the principles of theology are above nature and reason, and the mind of man, too feeble to reach them by its own efforts, can arrive at this highest knowledge only if carried there by an all-powerful and supernatural force.[3]

Perhaps God is in some sense the "teacher" of these sublime truths. Pascal insists, however, that authority is not required in the case of "subjects accessible to sense or reasoning."[4] Authority, here, is not only useless;

---

[1] *The Genius of Christianity*, pp. 48–9. The last sentence in this passage, which serves to show that science, history, philosophy, and literature have all been improved, is also a defense of Christianity against its attackers who, like Condorcet, suggest that progress and religion are opposed.

[2] *Preface to the Treatise on the Vacuum*, in GBWW, Vol. 33, p. 355; see also Teggart (ed.), *The Idea of Progress*, p. 165.

[3] *Ibid.*

[4] *Ibid.*, p. 356; see Teggart, p. 165.

it is an obstacle. In this realm, knowledge progresses; man learns by himself.

> Not only does each man advance from day to day in the sciences, but all men together make a continual progress as the universe grows old.[5]

KINDS OF PROGRESS IN KNOWLEDGE

The kinds of progress in knowledge can be distinguished according to the things the knowledge of which is said by progress authors to increase. Of particular interest to them are progress in knowledge of external nature, in knowledge of man and his relation to society, in moral knowledge, in philosophical knowledge, and in knowledge of the fine arts.

PROGRESS IN KNOWLEDGE OF EXTERNAL NATURE

The Pascalian analogy is probably the paradigm of all affirmations of progress in our knowledge of external nature. It is noteworthy, however, that the sphere in which knowledge progresses is restricted by Pascal to that of external nature. C. G. Darwin concurs in the restriction. His view of the "history" of the next million years foresees severe pressure from excess population, a "consequent callousness about the value of the individual's life," and cruelty "to a degree of which we do not willingly think." There will be vast amounts of humbug, deceit, and hypocrisy.

> This however is only one side of the history. On the other side there will be vast stores of learning, far beyond anything we can now imagine, and the intellectual stature of man will rise to ever higher levels.[6]

From time to time, "new discoveries" will result in "golden ages" during which men will be free to create "wonderful flowerings" in science, philosophy, and the arts. These, however, are not progressive. They are not irreversible; what is gained will be lost again. Nevertheless, knowledge itself will continue to grow.

The same point is made by Inge, who, like Darwin, casts doubt on the occurrence of any kind of progress except in the knowledge of the world of nature that surrounds us. We are driven to the conclusion, Inge declares,

[5] *Ibid.*, p. 357; see Teggart, p. 167.
[6] *The Next Million Years*, p. 149.

that neither science nor history gives us any warrant for believing that humanity has advanced, except by accumulating knowledge and experience and the instruments of living.[7]

The "instruments of living" mentioned in this passage may denote technological progress. However, the emphasis seems to be on knowledge simply, or in general.

Most of the writers who hold that there is progress in man's knowledge of external nature—of "subjects accessible to sense or reasoning"—agree that the present age is an era of particularly marked progress in this regard. It is almost a commonplace that the mid-twentieth century is the scene of a "knowledge explosion." This, the "prevailing view of the evolution of science," is the occasion for some remarks by M. King Hubbert on the relation of authority to progress in knowledge.

> Scientific knowledge has become so vast as compared with the limited capabilities of the individual human intellect that one man can only hope to know "authoritatively" a minute fraction of the whole. Hence we are constrained, if we are to avoid being scientific dilettantes, to select some limited domain—our "specialty"—of such small size that we are capable of reading all the pertinent literature and hence of mastering all that is known about it. By this premise, all other scientists must do the same with respect to other domains, so that the only way of knowing anything outside of one's own specialty is to accept the word of an authority or specialist in that field. Hence, according to this view, we are condemned to accept authoritarianism by the very immensity of human knowledge.[8]

Hubbert is distressed by this state of affairs. The infinite divisibility of knowledge, and our consequent dependence on authority for almost all that we "know," is not a sign, for him, of true progress in knowledge. He declares that Galileo, "the individual above all others to whom physical science owes its origin," fought throughout his life to establish the truth that the final appeal in science is to "a valid observation or experiment," and not to "a human authority, either ancient or modern."[9] The "present . . . state of confusion" in science and, indeed, in knowledge

> arises from a fundamental misconception regarding the nature of science and its evolution. The evolution of science is, in fact, not a progression from the simple to the complex, but quite the opposite. It is a progression from the complex to the simple. . . .[10]

[7] *The Idea of Progress*, p. 24.

[8] "Are We Retrogressing in Science?", in *Science*, Vol. 139, No. 3558, 8 March 1963, p. 888.

[9] *Ibid.*, p. 884.

[10] This, of course, is in fundamental opposition to the view of Spencer and his followers.

The common denominators of all phenomenological sciences are (i) an initial chaos of phenomena, infinite in amount, and (ii) the simplicity and finite capacity of the human intellect. Since it is impossible for human beings to understand chaotic phenomena, it is necessary that these be reduced to a state of simplicity if they are ever to be understood. The entire history of science has been the history of progressive reduction of one chaos of phenomena after another into a form that is within the powers of comprehension of an average human being. . . .

In the whole field of science these master generalizations number at most but a few tens.[11]

However, despite Hubbert's somewhat unorthodox view[12] that the present epoch is not necessarily one of real progress in knowledge, he concurs in holding that, *in general,* knowledge of external nature has progressed and will continue to progress.

Progress in Knowledge of Social Man

C. D. Broad, conceding that there has been a great deal of progress in our knowledge of external nature, denies that there has been much if any progress in our knowledge of man.

The beginnings of a genuine science of organisms exists, and progress in this science might at any moment become rapid. . . . But, so far as I can see, there are not even the beginnings of a scientific psychology of the individual or of communities.[13]

This assertion is opposed by a number of authors writing both before and after Broad. Comte, Condorcet, Godwin, and Mill, among others, hold that there is much progress in precisely these respects; and B. F. Skinner may be allowed to stand for the many modern psychologists and behaviorists who maintain that, whatever may be the failings of psychoanalysis,[14] there is recognizable progress in our knowledge of social systems. Thus far, Skinner declares,

men have designed their cultures largely by guesswork, including some very lucky hits; but we are not far from a state of knowledge in which this can be changed.[15]

[11] *Ibid.,* pp. 888–9.
[12] This view is, of course, held by a number of antiprogress authors. Cf. the remarks of Burckhardt, qu. above, p. 198.
[13] *The Mind and Its Place in Nature,* p. 664.
[14] Most behaviorists seem to agree that the progress of individual psychology—primarily, psychoanalysis—is at the best minute. Freud, on the contrary, holds that the invention of psychoanalysis is an important sign of man's progress in knowledge. See, for example, *Civilization and Its Discontents,* Chapter VIII.
[15] "The Design of Cultures," in *Daedalus,* Summer 1961, p. 545.

We have not yet attained the level at which we can "describe some distant state of mankind toward which we are moving or 'deciding' to move." But this is not required for progress to occur.

> Early physical technology could not have foreseen the modern world, though it led to it. Progress and improvement are local changes. We better ourselves and the world as we go.[16]

Skinner's point is that by careful "conditioning" mankind can be led forward and upward. The same point was made by Helvétius, some two hundred years earlier; but Helvétius calls the mechanism "education" rather than "conditioning." Even the man of genius, Helvétius declares, "is only produced by the circumstances in which he is placed."

> Thus all the art of education consists in placing a man in such a concurrence of circumstances as are proper to unfold the buds of genius and of virtue. A love of paradoxes has not led me to form this conclusion; but the desire of promoting the happiness of mankind.[17]

E. H. Carr sums up the problem neatly, and reveals his own beliefs.

> At the present time, few people would, I think, question the fact of progress in the accumulation both of material resources and of scientific knowledge. . . . What is questioned is whether there has been . . . any progress in the ordering of society. . . . It seems to me simply untrue to say that our understanding of the problems of social organization or our good will to organize society in the light of that understanding have regressed; indeed, I should venture to say that they have greatly increased.[18]

Progress in Moral Knowledge

Helvétius holds that education can "unfold the buds of genius and of virtue." The question, whether progress in the knowledge of virtue—of morality—occurs, or can in the future be made to occur, is considered by many authors. A number maintain that while there may be no progress in the moral orientation of man—this might be progress in human nature,

---

[16] *Ibid.*, pp. 545–6.

[17] *De l'esprit*, p. 363. Helvétius' own age is seen by him as having attained such a degree of intellectual enlightenment and discernment that it can clearly see the "barbarism" inherent in the early history of Christianity. "In the simplicity of the ages of ignorance," he declares, "objects presented themselves under a very different aspect from that in which they appear to enlightened eyes. The tragedies of our Saviour's passion, edifying as they were to our ancestors, appear to me as scandalous" (*ibid.*, p. 137).

[18] *What Is History?*, pp. 156–7.

in any event—there is undoubted progress in man's knowledge of how he ought to act, whether he acts that way or not.

Yves Simon, for instance, although he refuses to compare "the total amounts of good and evil which exist in humanity . . . at two epochs of history," is nevertheless willing to discuss "the evolution of a factor in general morality, to wit, the knowledge of good and evil, the moral conscience."

> An examination of the moral conscience of just men during the last few centuries of the history of our societies reveals great progress. It does not follow that the world is better, absolutely speaking; it does not follow that today's saints are greater saints than the saints of old. It follows only that morality has risen to a higher *state* in the persons of its most perfect representatives. And this is not a negligible result.[19]

Simon cites as examples the treatment of prisoners of war, the "problem of destitution," the question whether aggressive war can be justified, child labor, and so forth. The point is not that prisoners of war are not still treated very badly, that some people are not still destitute, that the attempt is not still made to justify aggressive wars, and that children do not still labor. Rather, it is that just men no longer accept these practices, which were once accepted by nearly everybody. The just are shocked by these practices, they abhor them, they attempt to make them illegal and to end them in fact.

Numerous other expressions of this view are to be found in the literature. The entire question of moral progress is discussed at greater length, and from several points of view, in Chapters 24 and 25.

PROGRESS IN KNOWLEDGE OF FINE ART

A number of writers, while denying that there is progress in the sense of better art, concede that man knows more *about* art as time passes. Thomas Munro, for instance, argues that the arts evolve; if the arts do not progress, at least they advance in an orderly and measurable fashion. This thesis is questioned by many authors; and Munro concedes that it can be ably opposed. What is unquestionable, according to him, is that man knows more *about* art than he once did.[20]

Gilson concurs. "The philosophy of art," he declares, "is a clear case of progress achieved in our knowledge of reality."

[19] *Community of the Free*, pp. 126–7. For Maritain's treatment of some of the same topics, see below, 432–4.

[20] For a discussion of progress in the fine arts, including an analysis of Munro's view of the matter, see the Appendix.

It does not invent art itself, for art has always been there, but philosophers have been extremely slow in recognizing it for what it is. In this respect, the modern discoveries made in the field of perhistoric art are of the greatest importance for philosophical reflection. Just as significant as prehistoric painting and sculpture is the wave of skepticism which attends the discovery of every prehistoric site. Historians cannot convince themselves at first that many millennia ago there were men who were perfect artists although they knew next to nothing.[21]

Indeed, for Gilson, art is not at all in "the order of knowing," but rather in "the order of making"; there is therefore no possibility that increased knowledge could result in better art. But our knowledge not only of how to use materials but also of how to appreciate art, in general our understanding of what art is, have increased. This is undeniable progress in our knowledge of reality.

A similar point is made by Butterfield about the art of history. The "history of historical study often turns out to be a story of local decline," he declares, but it nevertheless shows "over-all progress . . . at certain levels." We know absolutely more about history and the writing of history than we once did; and it can be expected that we will continue to grow in our knowledge and appreciation of history in the future.[22]

Butterfield's remarks are typical of a wide range of modern opinion. One finds in the literature affirmations of progress in the "art" of the novel, of biography, of the etching, of printing, of industrial design, and so forth. Many of these affirmations do not involve an affirmation of overall human progress. They have in common with the views mentioned above, however, the notion that individual works of art are not necessarily better, but that our knowledge of the art in question improves.

PROGRESS IN PHILOSOPHY

Gilson's conception of progress "in our knowledge of reality" is of a sort called by other writers philosophical progress or progress in philosophy. Thus, "what true progress is, and how it is usually qualified by all sorts of backsliding and by incompatible movements in contrary directions, is well illustrated," George Santayana declares, "by the history of philosophy."

There has been progress in it; if we start with the first birth of intelligence and assume that the end pursued is to understand the world, the progress

[21] *The Arts of the Beautiful*, p. 76.
[22] *Man on His Past*, pp. vii, 35–6, 100.

has been immense. We do not understand the world yet; but we have formed many hypotheses about it corroborated by experience, we are in possession of many arts which involve true knowledge, and we have collated and criticized—especially during the last century—a great number of speculations which, though unverified or unverifiable, reveal the problems and the possibilities in the case; so that I think a philosopher in our day has no excuse for being so utterly deceived in various important matters as the best philosophers were through no fault of theirs, because they were misled by a local tradition, and inevitably cut off from the traditions of other ages and races.[23]

Santayana observes, however, that this does not mean that "the latest philosophers are the best: it is quite the other way." In this respect, he says, philosophy is like poetry.

> There is progress in that new poets arise with new gifts, and the fund of transmitted poetry is enriched; but Homer, the first poet among the Greeks, was also the best, and so Dante in Italy, and Shakespeare in England.[24]

The first fruits of a civilization and a language are the richest and best, Santayana declares; what follows is more valuable "in this respect or that"; but it does not equal that "first exuberance." Thus the history of a given philosophical position or view tends to show relative degeneration from its first expression, at the same time that philosophy as a whole shows steady improvement.[25]

Maritain makes some of the same points, and adds others; he emphasizes less the uncertain quality of philosophical progress, more its steady growth on the "speculative side." Metaphysics is, he declares, "the noblest science," and it "has the most purely intelligible object"; as a result, "the part played by accident" is more restricted than anywhere else. The "law of continuous progress" therefore applies.

> In [metaphysics], better than in any other [discipline], is realized the absolutely essential condition of this progress, namely, fixity of principles and stability of tradition: it does not require, for the discovery of its principles, extraordinary instruments and extraordinary conditions of research, but only the simplest evidence of the senses—used, it is true, by the purest intelligence. To repeat, then, in it is realized the absolutely essential condition of continuous progress, and therefore more than all other sciences it resembles, by the constancy of direction of its movement, the motionlessness of angelic knowledge.[26]

[23] "The Progress of Philosophy," in *Soliloquies in England and Later Soliloquies*, p. 208.
[24] *Ibid.*
[25] *Ibid.*, 209.
[26] *Theonas*, p. 159.

In spite of "the enormous deficiencies of the human subject," metaphysics, Maritain declares, moves steadily forward. In certain ages it slows down, he concedes, in others it even experiences "long intervals of stagnation," but it always "resumes its flight in a direction that does not vary." Its overall progress seems not very rapid, Maritain admits; nevertheless, "by its imperceptible additions of new things to old, it has built up a treasury of wisdom not to be exhausted." He adds that metaphysics, being "most certainly the Queen of the Sciences," must therefore be magnanimous, "and you know that Aristotle said that the magnanimous man advances slowly."[27]

CHARACTERISTICS OF PROGRESS IN KNOWLEDGE

For most progress authors it is better to have more knowledge than to have less. This means, in effect, that increase of knowledge is usually an instance of human progress in the most general sense. However, sev-

---

[27] *Ibid.*, pp. 159–60. Maritain goes on to observe that "philosophy is something other than the immense mass of the notions of philosophers, and that if all mathematicians co-operate in the growth of mathematics, and all scientists in the growth of science, all philosophers do not co-operate—at any rate directly—in the growth of philosophy" (*ibid.*, p. 160). He thus implies, here and elsewhere, that the progress of philosophy might be accelerated if philosophers co-operated, and suggests that one thing they could do together would be to undertake clarifications of the divergent views of philosophers, past and present, on given ideas. This indeed is the purpose of the studies of various ideas by the Institute for Philosophical Research, of which the present work is an example.

This point is made by M. J. Adler, who declares, in *The Idea of Freedom*, that "progress in philosophy depends on something more than the proliferation of philosophies or the novelty of their doctrines." Such proliferation is indeed a part of philosophical progress, he concedes, but he insists that "the progressive envelopment of philosophical truth by a multiplicity of doctrines must be matched by a progressive development of dialectical truth about their diversity. The controversies that underlie this diversity must be explicitly set forth as the background of continuing efforts to resolve basic issues. Sustained dialectical work is, therefore, the other condition of philosophical progress, on the side of the contribution to the pursuit of truth which can be made by the rational debate of basic issues" (Vol. I, pp. 75–6).

From this point of view, our study of the idea of progress—if in fact it is a dialectical clarification of the subject—is not only a contribution to the discussion of the literature about progress, and in that special sense an addition to that literature, but also an example of progress in philosophy. If, then, progress in philosophy is an aspect of progress in knowledge, and if, furthermore, progress in knowledge is an aspect of human progress in the most general sense, then this work is an example of progress.

Such reflexivity does not apply in the case of the Institute's other studies, of the ideas of love, happiness, justice, freedom, and so forth. Each of those works is about the literature in question, and in that sense an addition to that literature; each is also, perhaps, an example of progress in philosophy. But none is an example of the subject with which it deals: e.g., *The Idea of Freedom* is not an example of freedom. A study of the idea of knowledge would, however, have a like reflexive character.

eral writers question whether the advance or increase of knowledge
is for the better in every sense. Is humanity as a whole always better off
because mankind knows more?

Broad, for instance, raises this question when he suggests that there is
a race between our scientific knowledge of inorganic nature and our
scientific knowledge of man. If the former wins, the human race may
destroy itself; if the latter wins, human progress can be expected to continue indefinitely. Thus, Broad seems to be saying that increase in our
knowledge of inorganic nature is progress with respect to science itself,
but only questionably progress with respect to mankind as a whole.

Simon seems to be making a similar, but not the same, point when
he refuses to assert that "the world is better, absolutely speaking." The
increase of our moral knowledge, the advance of the "moral conscience,"
is improvement of a limited sort; it is a good thing to know more about
how one *should* act. It would be a much better thing if men *did* act in the
way that they know they should; more meaningful progress would have
occurred if there were improvement in behavior parallel and equal to improvement in our moral conceptions.

The position of Pascal appears once again to be similar. It is all very
well, Pascal seems to be saying, to have more rather than less knowledge
of external nature; the advance that necessarily occurs in this regard is in a
desirable direction. However, there is no sign that Pascal holds that this
advance is an indubitable improvement in the total "human condition."
Progress in the knowledge of nature is a limited good; above all, it does
not help man find his salvation. For Pascal, this is a more important
matter than understanding the world of nature.

In contradistinction to men like Broad, Simon, and Pascal, men like
Helvétius, Lessing, and Skinner seem to hold that progress in knowledge
is intrinsically meliorative with regard to the human race as a whole.
According to these writers, who perhaps conceive knowledge in a somewhat different way, mankind is necessarily better off because of its increased knowledge.

Descartes, too, for whom the discovery of *la méthode* is an intellectual
advance of the first importance for man's moral betterment, holds that
progress in knowledge—at least in this sense—is meliorative with regard
to the interests of the race as a whole.[28] However, Descartes does not seem
to be saying that all increase of knowledge is meliorative in this general
sense. Only the knowledge of the new method—and the knowledge that

[28] It is on this point, perhaps, that Pascal and Descartes most strikingly part
company. "I cannot forgive Descartes," Pascal declares. "In all his philosophy he
would have been quite willing to dispense with God" (*Pensées*, II, 77, p. 29).

derives from it, of nature, of human nature, and of Providence—is so regarded.

That knowledge must *increase* is the opinion of most progress authors. According to Lessing, the Joachimites, and a few others, the necessity is imposed; God wills that man shall grow in knowledge. According to the majority of writers, however, it is in the very nature of knowledge that it should increase. This is especially true of the authors who make use of the Pascalian analogy.

It is quite another thing to say that *progress* in knowledge must occur, and in fact, relatively few authors explicitly assert this. Perhaps Leibniz holds not only that progress must occur in knowledge, but that mankind must also progress at the same time; Comte, Condorcet, Godwin, and a few others seem to concur. A more widely held opinion, however, is that the sort of knowledge that is most valuable to mankind—knowledge of social systems, of good and evil, and of like matters—is to a large extent contingent on man's desire to seek it, and on his efforts in that direction, as well as on his inherent capacity to find it. Broad, for instance, raises the question whether, even if thoroughgoing knowledge of social organization were obtained, it could be applied "without deliberately alter[ing] the emotional constitution of mankind." Such progress "could arise," he goes on to declare, "only on the basis of a profound theoretical knowledge of the factors which produce, modify, and remove non-rational beliefs." One cannot be certain, says Broad, that such knowledge is attainable; if it is not, significant human progress is improbable.[29] In any event, it is clearly contingent.

In the view of the Marxist writers, the really important advances in knowledge that man can expect in the future must wait until the attainment of the ideal socialist state. This will inevitably be attained, after which knowledge will inevitably grow; but this means that progress in knowledge is ultimately necessary. Other writers who conceive a certain state of society as a prerequisite of progress in knowledge of the highest sort—for example, Fourier, who does not consider that the *phalanstères* will inevitably be founded—seem to see this progress as ultimately contingent and not necessary. Still others holding the latter position are discussed below.

How much can man know? How much *more* can he know than he already knows? If very little more, then the question—Is progress necessary?—might at some time have to receive a negative answer.

[29] *Op. cit.*, p. 665.

The same consideration applies to the question—Will progress in knowledge continue indefinitely or "plateau out?"—or, indeed, has it already done so? Most progress authors either assert explicitly or imply that there is no limit to human knowledge, and that mankind will go on learning as long as it inhabits the earth. This is the view of authors like Kant, Herder, Guizot, Buckle, and Carr. Comte, however, holds that although man will continue always to learn, the rate of increase of knowledge will slow down, since mankind approaches (although it never actually reaches) an intellectual condition in which positive knowledge of everything is available, if not already present in everyone.

Jeans suggests, going even further than Comte, that knowledge is essentially limited, as we have seen, and Becker concurs in this view, although he is not, as we have also seen, strictly speaking a progress author. When all technological knowledge has been attained, and no new sources of power are discoverable, "the outward conditions of life will change less and less rapidly," Becker declares,

> will in time become sufficiently stable perhaps to be comprehended, sufficiently stable therefore for a relatively complete adjustment of ideas and habits to the relatively unchanging body of matter-of-fact knowledge of man and his outer world in which he lives.[30]

At this point, some sort of progress—moral or political—appears still to be going on, but it is not progress in knowledge. Thus progress in this very limited sense will ultimately "plateau out."

There is considerable question as to whether the millennialists hold that progress in knowledge will ever come to an end. Perhaps writers like Lessing and the Joachimites are saying this; for if man learns, or is taught, what it is most important for him to know, he need not, and in fact may not, struggle to learn anything else. If salvation is assured and men naturally live well, why should they study science? However, in spite of the Marxist contention that progress in history will come to an end when the ideal society is achieved, they do not foresee a subsequent end to the advance of knowledge. Indeed, just the opposite is the case, for only then will mankind be free at last to attain true knowledge of the world as it is.

It cannot be proved that all progress authors affirm progress in knowledge, for this is a "falsifiable" proposition that requires only one exception for disproof. All that we can say is that we have found no author not affirming progress in knowledge of some sort.

[30] *Progress and Power*, pp. 111–2.

The next question to be considered is whether progress authors hold that progress in knowledge is prior to other kinds of progress in the conditions of human life—progress, that is, of the sort that is opposed to progress in man's very nature. One answer to the question seems to be that in the same sense in which some sort of knowledge must precede any willing or acting whatsoever, progress in knowledge is basic to other kinds.

Some writers are clear in asserting that progress in knowledge—what they often call theoretical knowledge—has logical and temporal priority. Condorcet, for example, declares that

> nature has joined together indissolubly the progress of knowledge and that of liberty, virtue and respect for the natural rights of man; and . . . these, the only real goods that we possess, though so often separated that they have been held to be incompatible, must on the contrary become inseparable from the moment when enlightenment has attained a certain level.[31]

That Comte concurs may be inferred from the fact that he sees the progress of all institutions as modeled on the law of the three states of the human mind. Mill, Fontenelle, Carr, Ortega, and other proponents of the Pascalian analogy also concur, as does Godwin, who declares that "everything may be trusted to the tranquil and wholesome progress of knowledge,"[32] and that man's "moral improvements will keep pace with his intellectual."[33] Indeed, says Godwin,

> Sound reasoning and truth, when adequately communicated, must always be victorious over error: Sound reasoning and truth are capable of being so communicated; Truth is omnipotent: The vices and moral weakness of man are not invincible: [therefore] Man is perfectible, or in other words, capable of perpetual improvement.[34]

At the present day, a more common way of affirming the priority of progress in knowledge is to emphasize the importance of research. Stevan Dedijer, for instance, declares that the leaders of the two most "advanced" countries in the world—the United States and the Soviet Union—agree on at least one thing.

> They both say that we are living in a scientific technological revolution. They both act in the belief that scientific research is the sine qua non for the welfare and survival of their countries. In most of the developed nations to-

[31] *Sketch for an Historical Picture of the Progress of the Human Mind*, p. 10.
[32] *Enquiry Concerning Political Justice*, I, p. 362.
[33] *Ibid.*, p. 110.
[34] *Ibid.*, p. 86.

day every product and service is increasingly based on research; in some, the research potential is increasing exponentially.[35]

Two-thirds of the world's population are "passive bystanders" in the scientific revolution. And those countries that do not have active research programs are falling farther and farther behind those that do.

> The developed countries are using research more and more in a socially planned way as the motor power of their social progress, while the un-developed countries still lack this motor. . . . Progress does not just happen any more; it is manufactured, made to order, planned by using the knowledge of social behavior as systematized by social science. . . . In the political phase of the scientific revolution, new inventions increase the productivity of science and its social effects. The most important of these is planned development of science on a national scale by means of the set of decisions called research policy.[36]

Whether the research is being undertaken into the facts of external nature, the organization of social behavior, or political "decision-making," it is always, Dedijer maintains, the research and the consequent new knowledge that comes first, and that must come first, before social progress can occur. Progress in knowledge is unquestionably prior, in this view, to all other kinds.

Dedijer's notion of research is that of a highly formalized knowledge, the quest for which obeys certain rules, and the sign of the attainment of which is a new power over external phenomena. By this very token, knowledge has priority. Other writers have a conception that is less clear. L. H. Morgan, for example, explicitly asserts that human progress is measured by certain discoveries and achievements that would be termed technological: the discovery that fish are good to eat, the invention of iron weapons, and so forth.[37] These technological advances are prior, in Morgan's view, to economic, political, and moral progress, and even to progress in the arts. But he nevertheless implies that some sort of progress in knowledge is prior even to the technological advances. Men must "know" something about the environment before they discover that fish are good to eat; they must "know" what a weapon is before making one out of iron.

Indeed, the organism, in "feeling hungry," and in ceasing to "feel hungry" after a meal, is expressing some sort of knowledge. One may posit some mechanico-chemical device or the existence of a psychic "awareness" that is called by some psychologists "tissue knowledge" or "instinctual

[35] "Research: The Motor of Progress," in *Bulletin of the Atomic Scientists,* Vol. XVIII, No. 6, June 1962, p. 4.
[36] *Ibid.*
[37] Morgan's scheme of human progress is discussed in the next chapter.

knowledge." Whatever it is called, and in whatever circumstances, "knowledge" in this sense is prior to all the activities of even a rational animal.

However, to claim, on these grounds, that all progress authors maintain that progress in knowledge is more important than any other kind would be to distort the literature. Whatever the logical priority involved, many writers emphasize other kinds of progress more than they do progress in knowledge. Their notion of knowledge is like the more familiar one of Dedijer, involving a formal system with a hierarchy of propositions, relations between groups of propositions, and so forth. This "theoretical knowledge" is, in the view of many authors, not prior at all to other kinds of progress, but a consequence of one or more of them. For instance, it is often held that mankind could not attain any formal, organized, theoretical knowledge of the world before there was a class of men with the leisure to seek such knowledge. This is to make economic progress (progress in wealth) at least temporally prior to progress in knowledge. And still other notions regarding the conditions on which progress in knowledge depends will be discussed in the following chapters.[38]

[38] There are important differences between the authors who emphasize progress in knowledge and those who emphasize other kinds of progress. This is seen when the question is asked: What does a given author say ought to be done to bring about or hasten progress? Whatever his conception may be of the logical priority of progress in knowledge, he is saying different things when he maintains that progress is mainly dependent on education or research, and when he says that it is mainly dependent on new technological discoveries, on advances in political institutions, on the improvement of behavior, or on more just economic arrangements.

Indeed, the hallmark of the true priorist of progress in knowledge is usually one of three terms: enlightenment, research, or education. The first has become passé; the field is therefore left to the last two.

20

Technological Progress

M os t progress authors concur in affirming technological progress. No author denies that technological *advance* occurs; the question, here as in the previous chapter, is whether the advance is progressive (*i.e.,* for the better). Progress authors who deny technological progress in this sense usually reserve the term "progress" for advances in other realms (political and moral).

Affirmations of technological progress are especially common in the twentieth century; indeed, the word "progress" as it is used in ordinary speech usually means little more than technological progress. At the same time, the twentieth century also has seen a number of discussions, by progress authors, of whether technological advance is meliorative with regard to the human race as a whole.[1]

No very subtle distinction is made in this book between progress in knowledge and technological progress. The Aztecs are supposed to have known the wheel but to have used it only to make mobile toys for their children. From our point of view, their invention would count as prog-

[1] Such questions have been particularly prevalent since World War II and the invention of the atomic bomb.

ress in knowledge, not as technological progress; but in the Western world, the wheel is a prime example of technological advance, if not of progress. The difference, perhaps, is between knowledge *about* and knowledge *how to;* technology is in some sense applied knowledge. But it is not merely that. Men can discover, invent, and act without formal, theoretical knowledge. And it is precisely discoveries, inventions, and actions that (according to most progress authors) constitute technological progress.

SCHEMES OF TECHNOLOGICAL PROGRESS

A number of writers propose schemes of man's history in which his progress is based on, or marked by, significant inventions and discoveries. A variety of such schemes is found in the literature. However, a few inventions are mentioned by many writers, over and over again.

Perhaps printing, gunpowder, and the compass are most commonly called significant inventions by the older writers, while the discoveries of fire, of agriculture, of city life, and of science itself are most often discussed by the twentieth-century accounts, which often have a more abstract view of the subject.

Turgot, for example, among the older writers, declares that the discovery of the art of printing made possible almost unlimited progress, for "the merest accidents are put to use as a source of discovery" when they can be recorded for later generations.[2] Henry Adams remarks:

> Of the compass, as a step towards demonstration of the dynamic law, one may confidently say that it proved, better than any other force, the widening scope of the mind, since it widened immensely the range of conduct between nature and thought. The compass educated. This must prove itself as needing no proof.[3]

The invention of gunpowder is conceived not only as a prime example of human ingenuity but also as the cause of much other progress. Levi Woodbury, for instance, observes that

> it is contended . . . by some, and not without plausibility, that the introduction of firearms has assisted much to elevate the lower classes, making their military services equally efficient with those of the feudal nobility, and has thus helped to pave the way earlier to the abolition of serfism, and all that menial dependence of the many on the few which characterized previous ages.[4]

[2] *Tableau philosophique des progrès successifs de l'esprit humain,* p. 17.
[3] *Education,* p. 482.
[4] "On Progress," in G. E. Probst (ed.), *The Happy Republic,* p. 276.

Printing, gunpowder, and the compass date from the Dark and Middle Ages, during which, in the opinion of some progress authors, there is question as to whether progress continued to occur. The three inventions, therefore, are signs, in the view of those who would quiet these doubts, that progress was "working unawares" in those times. The phrase itself is Turgot's, and he lists other inventions, besides printing, that date from the same period:

> What a surge of inventions unknown by the ancients and due to these barbaric centuries! Our art of musical notation, letters of exchange, our paper, window glass, large mirrors, windmills, clocks, spectacles. . . . Facts were being amassed in the obscurity of the times of ignorance, and the sciences whose progress was not the less real for being hidden were destined one day to reappear increased by these new riches.[5]

L. H. Morgan also measures progress by certain inventions and discoveries, but they are not the same ones, and they date from a much earlier period of human history. Morgan divides that history into seven epochs, in each of which a new and higher "status" is acquired by mankind.

I. Lower Status of Savagery	From the Infancy of the Human Race, to the commencement of the next Period.
II. Middle Status of Savagery	From the acquisition of a fish subsistence and a knowledge of the use of fire, to etc.
III. Upper Status of Savagery	From the Invention of the Bow and Arrow, to etc.
IV. Lower Status of Barbarism	From the Invention of the Art of Pottery, to etc.
V. Middle Status of Barbarism	From the Domestication of animals in the Eastern hemisphere, and in the Western from the cultivation of maize and plants by Irrigation, with the use of adobe-brick and stone, to etc.
VI. Upper Status of Barbarism	From the Invention of the Process of Smelting Iron Ore, with the use of iron tools, to etc.

[5] *Loc. cit.*

VII. Status of Civilization   From the Invention of a Phonetic
                                    Alphabet, with the use of writing, to
                                    the present time.[6]

C. G. Darwin counts four "revolutions," based, respectively, on the discovery of fire, of agriculture, of city life, and of science. A similar scheme is proposed by Mumford, Butterfield, and several others. Childe also speaks of revolutions, but he views them as based on a much larger number of inventions. Nineteen inventions and discoveries led, he declares, to the development of "civilization" around 600 B.C. The first fifteen "contributions to man's progress" were the fruit of the two millennia before 3000 B.C. They are:

> Artificial irrigation using canals and ditches; the plow; the harnessing of animal motive-power; the sailboat; wheeled vehicles; animal-husbandry; fermentation; the production and use of copper; bricks; the arch; glazing; the seal; and . . . a solar calendar, writing, numeral notation, and bronze.[7]

The fifteen[8] culminated in what Childe calls the urban revolution. The two succeeding millennia—from about 2500 B.C. to about 600 B.C.—were less productive.

> Perhaps only four achievements deserve to be put in the same category as the fifteen. . . . They are: the "decimal notation" of Babylonia (about 2000 B.C.); an economical method for smelting iron on an industrial scale (1400 B.C.); a truly alphabetic script (1300 B.C.); aqueducts for supplying water to cities (700 B.C.).[9]

Childe offers a rationale for measuring progress—and for studying history—in terms of "significant achievements." History is not just political history, he says. Realist history, which views changes in forces of production, in economic structure and social organization as largely dependent on changes in tools and technologies, makes much more sense. It is better political history as well, Childe feels.

The tone of these remarks is characteristic of the authors who emphasize technological progress. Indeed, their view of progress is sometimes thought to be harsh. Bagehot, for instance, supports the notion of "verifiable progress" by pointing to the "undeniable" differences "by which a village of English colonists is superior to a tribe of Australian natives

[6] *Ancient Society,* p. 12.
[7] *Man Makes Himself,* p. 180.
[8] We count sixteen, although Childe says several times that there are fifteen items in this list.
[9] *Ibid.*

who roam about them." The most marked difference, and therefore sign of progress, Bagehot declares, is that the English

> can beat the Australians in war when they like; they can take from them anything they like, and kill any of them they choose.[10]

The schemes of technological progress considered above emphasize past achievements of the race. Many authors, while not denying those, consider as of greater importance technological advances that remain to be achieved. Harrison Brown discusses some of these, although his hopes for their attainment are tinged by the recognition that mankind stands at a crossroads of history.[11]

> Given adequate supplies of energy, man can, in principle, extract everything that he needs for his existence at a high standard of living from substances which exist abundantly in the earth's surface—air, seawater, and ordinary rock. . . . Within the rock itself there is sufficient energy to carry out the processing and also to provide power for the operation of industrial machinery. . . . When we look at the situation solely from the point of view of technological and energetic feasibility, we must conclude that the resources available to man permit him, in principle, to provide adequately for a very large population for a very long period of time.[12]

Many authors concur in projections of this sort, although they put emphasis on the contingent nature of these achievements. The Marxists,

[10] *Physics and Politics*, p. 151. In like manner, Becker, who refuses, as we have seen, to call technological advance meliorative, holds that the sign of human progress is that men put apes in zoos, and not the other way around.

Aside from this refusal to make moral judgments regarding the historical advance of man, Becker's position is much the same as those discussed above. "Since we wish to correlate progress with the expansion of human power and intelligence," he writes, "the best plan is to look for those discoveries or inventions that have been followed by a marked change in man's activities and ways of living. The discovery of fire is certainly one of these; the invention of writing is another. For a third we might take the invention of the steam engine; but since our last period must be long enough to turn around in at least, it will be better to take an earlier discovery—the discovery of magnetic force (China, A.D. 1160?). These three events give us four periods which may be bracketed along the Time-Scale within very roughly approximate dates" (*Progress and Power*, pp. 29–30).

Becker's four periods occupy, respectively, 9/10, 1/10, 1/100, and 1/500 of the total past of the human race. Hence his scheme, like Henry Adams', is accelerative.

[11] Brown uses this phrase in several of his writings. The pamphlet "Community of Fear" expresses his anxiety regarding the future; his projections of progress must be seen in this light. See above, pp. 145–6.

[12] *The Challenge of Man's Future*, p. 220. The size of the earth's population, Brown declares, might reach 50, or 100, or even 200 billion persons. However, many of our current notions of comfort would have to be given up. Brown also points out that technological progress is dependent on maintaining a certain level of technology —which might be lost in another world war.

however, do not share the doubts. Lenin's "great formula" for progress —"Communism is Soviet power plus the electrification of the whole country"—is quoted with approbation by the authors of the *1961 Draft Program*. They go on to declare that

> the main economic task of the Party and the Soviet people is to create a material and technical basis of communism within two decades. This means the complete electrification of the country and the perfection on this basis of the techniques, technologies, and organizations of social production in industry and agriculture, the comprehensive mechanization of productive operations and a growing degree of their automation, the widespread use of chemistry in the national economy, the vigorous development of new, economically effective branches of production, new types of power and new materials, the all-round and rational utilization of natural resources, the organic fusion of science and production, and rapid scientific and technical progress, a high cultural and technical level for the working people, substantial superiority over the more developed capitalist countries in productivity of labor, which constitutes a most important prerequisite for the victory of the Communist system.[13]

There is no question, the *Draft Program* seems to say, that these technological advances will actually be achieved.

Many of the writers who feel that future technological progress is contingent point to the fact that it will depend, above all, on the availability of energy. Those who hold that the sources of energy are limited and will become even more limited in the future predict little future progress; those who do not are more hopeful. C. G. Darwin exemplifies the former, A. C. Clarke the latter, view. Darwin feels that when the fossil fuels that we already know about—including uranium—are exhausted, which they inevitably will be within a few hundred years, man will have to return to a style of life similar in most respects to that of European man of the sixteenth and seventeenth centuries. Clarke, on the other hand, declares that "in this inconceivably enormous universe, we can never run out of energy or matter." (We can, he concedes, "all too easily run out of brains.")[14]

---

[13] *Program of the Communist Party of the Soviet Union (Draft), 1961*, pp. 161–3. This work reflects the great interest of Khrushchev in chemical technologies. It will be noted that the document projects technological exploitation of human as well as natural resources.

[14] *Profiles of the Future*, p. 155. In a book called *Engineers' Dreams* (subtitled "Great Projects That *Could* Come True"), Willy Ley reviews some of the methods that are commonly suggested for the future replacement of fossil energy sources. However, he doubts that any of these—particularly the control of fusion power—will ever be an adequate substitute. Thus he throws considerable doubt on future technological progress, and hence on human progress.

Clarke schedules future inventions in a way similar to that of writers who propose complex schemes of past technological progress. His "time table for the future" includes these items:

1970—Manned lunar landing; translating machines.

1990—Fusion power;[15] personal radiophones; landing on Mars.

2010—Weather control; robot mining vehicles exploring deep under the earth's crust.

2030—Mining the moon and planets; contact with extra-terrestrial intelligences.

2050—Gravity control;[16] artificial breeding of intelligent animals.

2100—Actual meeting with extra-terrestrials; human immortality.[17]

The last item, which is, as we have observed, an example of progress in human nature, will have far-reaching effects. Immortal human beings

> will have time enough, in those endless aeons, to attempt all things, and to gather all knowledge. They will not be like gods, because no gods imagined by our minds have ever possessed the powers they will command. But for all that, they may envy us . . . for we knew the universe when it was young.[18]

One limiting factor emerges in the course of Clarke's discussion of future technological progress. Man, he declares, may eventually become obsolete. "The old idea that man invented tools," he says, "is . . . a misleading half-truth; it would be more accurate to say that tools invented man."[19] The point, as Clarke develops it, is that tools were first used by "prehuman anthropoids"; their use resulted in the emergence of the species *Homo sapiens;* and the invention, by *Homo sapiens* in turn, of more and more efficient tools may produce a species of machines, able to "live" independently of *Homo sapiens* and able also to reproduce their kind,[20] and possessing a "civilization" to which *Homo sapiens* will be

[15] In contrast to Ley and Darwin, Clarke views the future control of fusion power (the thermonuclear reaction) as inevitable. It will solve the energy problem once and for all.

[16] According to Clarke, this is the "final solution" of the problem of terrestrial locomotion.

[17] *Ibid.,* p. i. See also the chart on pp. 234–5. Clarke observes that his "chart of the future" is not to be taken "too seriously, but it is both amusing and instructive to extrapolate the time scale of past scientific achievement into the future. If it does no more, the quick summary of what has happened in the *last* hundred-and-fifty years should convince anyone that no present-day imagination can hope to look beyond the year 2100. I have not even tried to do so" (*ibid.,* p. 233).

[18] *Ibid.,* p. 232.

[19] *Ibid.,* p. 213.

[20] The mathematician John von Neumann is said by Clarke to have shown theoretically that it is possible to construct machines that exactly reproduce themselves if

only an adjunct. The earth will become an enclave of the universe, and human beings, bound as they will always be to terrestrial life, will inhabit a backwater of the future "world culture."

> Creatures of flesh and blood such as ourselves can explore space and win control over infinitesimal fractions of it. But only creatures of metal and plastic can ever really conquer it, as indeed they have already started to do. The tiny brains of our Prospectors and Rangers barely hint at the mechanical intelligence that will one day be launched at the stars.[21]

Man in space, Clarke points out, is worse than a fish out of water. As a result, "most of our energies will be devoted to protecting our frail and sensitive bodies against the extremes of temperature, pressure, or gravity found in space and on other worlds." Within wide limits, machines are indifferent to these extremes. More important, they can "wait patiently through the years and the centuries that will be needed for travel to the far reaches of the universe."

> It may well be that only in space, confronted with environments fiercer and more complex than any to be found upon this planet, will intelligence be able to reach its fullest stature. Like other qualities, intelligence is developed by struggle and conflict; in the ages to come, the dullards may remain on placid Earth, and real genius will flourish only in space—the realm of the machine, not of flesh and blood.[22]

Mankind need fear nothing in all of this, Clarke assures us. The popular idea that intelligent machines would be hostile to man is

> so absurd that it is hardly worth wasting energy to refute it. I am almost tempted to argue that only *un*intelligent machines can be malevolent. . . . The higher the intelligence, the greater the degree of cooperativeness. If there is ever a war between men and machines, it is easy to guess who will start it.[23]

---

the necessary "nutriment" is present in their environment in an assimilable state—e.g., minerals dissolved in seawater. The machines would cruise under their own power for a year or more, reproduce their kind several times over, and then return to base to be "harvested" for the minerals, such as gold and molybdenum, that they contain.

[21] *Ibid.*, p. 222.

[22] *Ibid.*, pp. 222–3.

[23] *Ibid.*, pp. 226–7. It is easy to guess, too, who would win such a war. All of this, however, may be somewhat irrelevant to the concern of this study. The machines, the existence of which is predicted by Clarke and a host of other science-fiction writers, will not be human. The progress of intelligence, which Clarke affirms in these remarks, is not human progress *per se*. Such speculations are discussed only to show the lengths to which technology's advocates will go.

Projections of the sort represented by these remarks of Clarke are to be found not only in contemporary writing on the subject of future technological progress. In 1843, Thoreau reviewed a work by J. A. Etzler, *The Paradise Within the Reach of All Men, without Labor, by Powers of Nature and Machinery.* Thoreau shows characteristic doubt about Etzler's predictions, the optimistic tone of which is revealed by the following passage, quoted by Thoreau:

> Fellow Men! I promise to show the means of creating a paradise within ten years, where everything desirable for human life may be had by every man in superabundance, without labor, and without pay; where the whole face of nature shall be changed into the most beautiful forms, and man may live in the most magnificent palaces, in all imaginable refinements of luxury, and in the most delightful gardens; where he may accomplish, without labor, in one year, more than hitherto could be done in thousands of years; may level mountains, sink valleys, create lakes, drain lakes and swamps, and intersect the land everywhere with beautiful canals, and roads for transporting heavy loads of many thousand tons, and for travelling one thousand miles in twenty-four hours; may cover the ocean with floating islands movable in any desired direction with immense power and celerity, in perfect security, and with all comforts and luxuries, bearing gardens and palaces, with thousands of families, and provided with rivulets of sweet water; may explore the interior of the globe, and travel from pole to pole in a fortnight; provide himself with means, unheard of yet, for increasing his knowledge of the world, and so his intelligence; lead a life of continual happiness, of enjoyments yet unknown; free himself from almost all the evils that afflict mankind, except death, and even put death far beyond the common period of human life, and finally render it less afflicting. Mankind may thus live in and enjoy a world, far superior to the present, and raise themselves far higher in the scale of being.[24]

CHARACTERISTICS OF TECHNOLOGICAL PROGRESS

Many progress authors point to a danger in the rapid advance of technology—the danger that man will use his powerful new tools to harm himself. They ask whether advancing technology is for the good of the human race as a whole. Does technology improve the conditions of human life or, negatively, bring after it a kind of political or moral regress?

The position that technological advance is intrinsically regressive was

[24] Thoreau's review, in the course of which he quoted this passage, was published in *The Democratic Review,* and is republished in Curti, Thorp, and Baker, *American Issues: The Social Record,* pp. 421–6. René Dubos discusses predictions of this kind in *The Dreams of Reason.*

treated in Chapter 8. We are concerned here with affirmative answers to the question. Among these, perhaps the most common is inherent in the position that technological advance is neither good nor bad in itself, but that it can be used by men for good or for ill. It is this fact about technology that is the basis, according to De Rougemont, of what he calls "the ambivalent character of all progress."[25] Thus he discusses a number of common "mistakes," as he terms them, all resulting from the false opinion that technology is intrinsically harmful. First, there is "the mistake about the bomb."

> The Bomb is not at all dangerous. It is a thing. What is horribly dangerous is man. He it was who made the Bomb and gets ready to use it. To control the Bomb is absurd. . . . If the Bomb is left alone, it will do nothing, plainly. It will stay quiet in its crate. So please let us hear no more tales. What we need to control is man.[26]

There are also the mistakes about the telephone, about the fine car, about the standardization of work, and about inventions in general. No one is a "slave to the telephone."

> If you run to answer, irritated by the noise, it is you who expected something which you wanted not to miss. So you are only your own slave.[27]

In the case of the fine car, the tyranny is exerted by our passions, not by technics on their own. With regard to the standardization of work,

> it is not the machine that turns a man into a slave. It is a certain behavior which other men impose on a workman, not so much to facilitate his handling of his machine as to ensure that he will keep up with it for the sake of a standard output.[28]

Finally, the "mistake about inventions" is the belief that any invention could be employed *only* for good.

> I say that such an invention would be the work of the Devil: it would deprive man of his freedom, which God has willed for him.[29]

That technological advance is intrinsically meliorative and therefore necessarily contributory to human progress is perhaps not held so commonly in these days of rapid growth of science and control over the en-

[25] *Man's Western Quest*, p. 156.
[26] *Ibid.*, p. 145.
[27] *Ibid.*
[28] *Ibid.*, p. 146.
[29] *Ibid.* Others who hold, with De Rougemont, that progress is essentially ambivalent, include Maritain, Simon, and such writers as Marcuse and N. O. Brown, who are treated in this work as anti-progress authors.

vironment as it was when such growth was not so rapid. Thomas Mann's passionate humanist, Herr Settembrini, can speak for those who hold what is probably an older view.[30] Settembrini maintains, in his conversations with Hans Castorp, that technological advance inevitably and necessarily brings after it progress in justice, happiness, and peace.

> In paying due honour . . . to commerce and technology . . . Settembrini apparently did so not for the sake of these forces themselves, but purely with reference to their significance for the ethical development of mankind. For such a significance, he declared, he joyfully ascribed to them. Technical progress, he said, gradually subjugated nature, by developing roads and telegraphs, minimizing climatic differences; and by the means of communication which it created proved itself the most reliable agent in the task of drawing together the peoples of the earth, of making them acquainted with each other, of building bridges to compromise, of destroying prejudice; of, finally, bringing about the universal brotherhood of man.[31]

According to Settembrini, humanity has sprung upward out of the depths of darkness and fear, moving ever onward toward a goal of fellow-feeling and enlightenment, of goodness and joyousness; and upon this path the industrial arts were the vehicles conducive to the greatest progress.

That technological progress is necessary is maintained by many progress authors—though once again, it should be pointed out that they sometimes mean that technological *advance* is necessary or inevitable, and that progress in this regard, or as a result of this, depends on man's decision to use technology for good. Thus, Charles Frankel, referring to the fact (reported by Toynbee) that during the "social cataclysm" of the fall of the Minoan and Hellenic civilizations the technique of ironworking was not lost, observes:

> The discovery of fire, the use of metals, the invention of the wheel, the development of writing, the introduction of money as a means of exchange—

[30] This older view is that of writers like Condorcet, Comte, and Buckle, to name only three.

[31] *The Magic Mountain*, pp. 198–9. "All of this made a confused impression on Hans Castorp," Mann goes on to say. "Herr Settembrini seemed to bring together in a single breath categories which in the young man's mind had heretofore been as poles asunder—for example, technology and morals! Positively, he made the statement that Christ had been the first to proclaim the principle of equality and union, that the printing-press had propagated the doctrine, and that finally the French Revolution had elevated it into law!"

These statements reduce, of course, to the position that technological advance constitutes meliorative progress for mankind.

it is difficult to say whether all or any of these are the products of transfigur-
ing visions. But they have an ability to ride through the fashions, to move
across cultural boundaries, and to live through social disasters. And they have
a cumulative tendency to improve, and to engender other techniques which
also become part of the permanent legacy of the race.[32]

Carr, in his neo-Pascalian formulation of the principle of progress—
"progress in history . . . rests on the transmission of acquired assets"—
concurs.

> These assets include both material possessions and the capacity to master,
> transform, and utilize one's environment. Indeed, the two factors are closely
> interconnected, and react on one another.[33]

Barrett Moore, although he gives no specific reason why technological
progress is inevitable, speaks of it as if it were.

> There is at least one area, technology, in which there is overwhelming factual
> evidence of continual advance from the earliest record of *homo sapiens* down
> to the present day. Even the most confirmed opponent of cultural evolution
> must concede this point in the face of the evidence accumulated by now.
> To be sure, there are occasional setbacks. But there can be no doubt about
> the general trend.[34]

And C. G. Darwin makes a point on which several authors concur. A
culture based on science—which ours has been for at least three hundred
years—cannot be lost, and must advance toward more and more efficient
control of nature. The reason is that the methods of science are universal;
technology has only to survive in the minutest fragment of the race
(supposing a near-general cataclysm) in order to continue its progress.[35]

Many writers hold, on the contrary, that technological progress, like
other kinds of progress, is contingent on human freedom. And they particularly emphasize the fact that technological progress will cease if man
destroys the world by means of his own technology.

The destruction need not be the result of an overt act, for example, the
nuclear holocaust that is feared by the authors of the *Einstein-Russell
Manifesto*, or by Brown and Real.[36] Ritchie Calder, for one, points to
another danger. "With the resources of modern science and technology,
tempered by wisdom," he declares, "we can escape from the limitations

[32] *The Case for Modern Man*, pp. 186–7, Note.
[33] *What Is History?*, pp. 155–6.
[34] "On the Notions of Progress, Revolution, and Freedom," in *Ethics*, January,
1962, pp. 106–7.
[35] *The Next Million Years*, p. 146.
[36] See Note 11, above.

of past civilizations and succeed where they failed."[37] However, such an escape depends on our finding a solution for the problem of excess population, a problem that results from our very successes in technology. Too many people can swamp any technological advance, and drown it in the agonizing frustrations consequent on unfulfilled needs. Calder, like Broad, conceives the situation in terms of a race between two forces, both potent, the one working for good and the other for harm. "Remembering the 4,000,000,000 people who will share this planet in twenty years' time," he warns, "science and statesmanship will have to work fast."[38] Calder's position may be described thus: Technology, if given time enough, can solve all our problems. But it may not have the time.

Brown views the situation differently. He imagines what would happen to the world if technological progress ceased; one result would be a severe limitation on population.

> Without the existence of an industrialized society somewhere in the world, disease could not be effectively controlled and transportation would not be in existence which would permit shipment of food from areas of surplus to areas of deficiency. In the absence of the availability of the products of industrialization, the population of the Indian sub-continent would probably not exceed about 100 million persons. Similarly, if industrialization should for some reason cease to exist in the world, and human life were to be supported entirely by intensive agriculture, the population of human beings would probably never exceed about 5 billion persons.[39]

And even "intensive agriculture" is to some extent dependent on technology. The general point is clear: Technology may cease to advance; its progress is not a necessary fact in the future.[40]

Writers like Morgan, Childe, Darwin, and the others who measure human progress by various past achievements, such as the attainment of a fish subsistence or the discovery of fire, seem to be saying that technological progress is prior to other kinds. These remarks by Moore also seem to support that position:

> As soon as one concedes the fact of technical advance, one must make other concessions as well. There is no need to be a technological determinist to

[37] *After the Seventh Day,* p. 440.
[38] *Ibid.* These words were written in 1961.
[39] *The Challenge of Man's Future,* p. 221.
[40] Whatever the reason given for the cessation of this kind of progress, the fact that it is conceived as possibly ceasing is sign enough that it is contingent and not necessary. Indeed, it is suggested by some writers—for example, Aldous Huxley, in *Brave New World Revisited*—that a universal revolt against the "technical menace" might bring about the end of technological progress.

realize that changes in technology are accompanied by changes in social structure. . . . In a civilization, for example, that uses electricity and internal combustion engines as its main sources of energy, we are unlikely to find the gathering of shellfish as the chief way of obtaining food, or the tribe as the main form of social organization.[41]

However, not all of the authors who affirm technological progress hold that it is prior. De Rougemont, Simon, Maritain, and the others who maintain that progress in general, and especially this kind of progress, is essentially ambivalent, are saying that something else besides technology is the basis of "real" or "true" progress.

These writers tend to use the term "progress" when they speak of advances in technology. Such progress is, in their view, somewhat dangerous, and not entirely to be trusted; they seem to have doubts as to whether they should approve of it, at least give it unqualified approval. Other authors, who do not differ with them very much, perhaps, decline to use the term at all in reference to this kind of advance. Dewey, for example, insists that the "rapid change of conditions" to be observed in recent times affords only the opportunity for progress, and is not progress in itself. The contingent progress that man can attain if he wants it, is, according to Dewey, mainly in the political and moral realms. He is emphatic in dismissing technological advances—changes that others call progressive—as in no sense intrinsically changes for the better.

Dewey at least concedes the possibility of future progress, based at least in part on advances in technology. It is but one more step—however, it is a step that takes us out of the progress camp altogether—to the position of the authors like Juenger and Ellul. Juenger holds that technological advance is essentially a pejorative change. Progress in other respects cannot, therefore, occur as a result of technological "progress" (Juenger's use of the term is always highly ironic); indeed, progress is almost ruled out by the powerful effect of technological advance. The technologists are taking over the world, Juenger is saying, and the possibility of progress grows every day more unlikely.

If it is true, however, that men "vote with their feet and with their pocketbooks" (as it is sometimes claimed), then the support for the position that technological advance is not only intrinsically progressive but is the cause of other kinds of progress may be stronger than the progress literature indicates. A large number of progress authors question the value of this kind of progress, point to its ambivalent character, or declare that it is not really progress at all. Nevertheless, the governments of the world spend vast sums to encourage technology, and the movement of peoples

[41] *Op. cit.*, p. 107.

and power in the world of today is in the direction of the technologically advanced countries, and away from those that are backward in this respect.[42]

[42] The progress literature as a whole suggests that six different positions regarding the relations of progress and technological advance can be distinguished. They are:

1. Technological progress occurs and it is the only kind of progress that occurs.
2. Technological progress occurs and it is prior to all other kinds that occur.
3. Technological progress occurs and it is always in some way associated with other kinds that occur, though it is not clearly the cause or condition of their occurrence.
4. Technological advance occurs but it is not intrinsically meliorative, and the most important kind of progress—meliorative, or "real," progress—occurs to some extent independently.
5. Technological advance is not progress at all but it is in some sense a condition of "real" progress.
6. Technological advance occurs but it is human regress rather than human progress in any sense.

2I

Economic Progress

WHAT do progress authors mean by economic progress? What is advancing? What is growing or increasing? What is there more of? And how is the advance or increase measured?

It is hard to find answers to these questions in the progress literature. Nevertheless, progress authors speak often of economic progress. Indeed, this is a leading notion of our time. Governments may stand or fall on issues about economic progress, and wars are fought about it.

If there is any specific economic progress—a kind of progress that differs from technological progress, or progress of power, or increase of population—it must, in some sense, be in wealth. What increases, when economic progress occurs, is wealth. However, questions remain. What is wealth —how is it to be defined? And assuming that it has been defined, how is increase in it to be measured?

Is the progress of wealth the increase of national wealth? Is it increase in the sum of economic power wielded by the aggregate of individuals in a society? Or of all human beings in the world? That sum might be very great at the same time that there was a severe inequality of distribution, with a few individuals very rich and most very poor. Would a situation in which an absolute increase of wealth was concentrated in fewer and fewer hands be termed progressive by progress authors? Or would they insist that the wealth be distributed equitably?

Probably most writers take the position that wealth must be distributed among a large number of persons. A. J. Todd, for instance, declares that

> if we take material wealth as a criterion of social progress it must be from the standpoint of general participation in real wealth. . . . Social progress involves the harmonious development of every constituent member and group in society, this harmony to be determined by the fitness of the society to meet the exigencies of nature and self-conscious life, to grapple with its problems of to-day, and to provide for going on to-morrow.[1]

"Put in still another way," says Todd, "the economic test for social progress is the satisfaction of the needs of the individual more and more efficiently by means of community life." From this point of view, progress

> means for every member of society a wider share in life, the life more abundant, and not merely in the means of increased production. . . . Progress may be measured by the decreasing ratio of those who live . . . from hand to mouth.[2]

However, even though this position seems to be widely held, it is not explicitly expressed by many writers. And, sometimes, especially in the case of the earlier writers, one receives the impression that it matters little whether wealth is well distributed or not, as long as it increases. Thus Asa Briggs, for example, points out that "the underdeveloped countries of today" seemed, in the sixteenth century, "to be the great centers of wealth: the 'gorgeous East' and the South American El Dorado." But he also points out that countries like India, though relatively wealthy, did not have anything like an equitable distribution of wealth; there were teeming millions in India in 1700, just as there are today. However, the notion that progress in wealth involves the more equitable distribution of increasing wealth does not seem to have been discussed by anyone at that time.[3]

The present chapter is divided into four sections. In the first are treated some typical affirmations of economic progress by progress authors. On the whole, these are not complex; usually, they are little more than assertions

---

1 *Theories of Social Progress,* pp. 123–4.
2 *Ibid.,* pp. 124–5.
3 "Technology and Economic Development," in *Scientific American,* September 1963, p. 55. The entire September 1963 issue of this magazine was devoted to questions discussed in this chapter.

that wealth, however defined and distributed among men, tends "naturally" to increase, and that this increase is meliorative and hence inherently progressive. One or two denials of economic progress in this relatively simple and straightforward sense are also considered. In fact, though many progress authors fail to discuss economic progress, few explicitly deny it.

The second section treats the Marxist theory of economic progress. This is probably the only carefully argued affirmation of this kind of progress in the literature.

The third section deals with the question of the relation of economic progress to population increase. The "natural" increase of human population is considered by some writers to be the cause or at least the best sign of general progress; by others to be associated with general progress but not the cause of it; and by still others—particularly contemporary authors —to be the leading obstacle to progress in the future.

The last section contains a discussion of two points raised by the previous sections. The distinction between technological progress and economic progress is, in the view of many progress authors, not a very clear one. Hence we will address ourselves to the question of how economic progress differs from technological progress. Is the latter the cause of the former? Is it a necessary condition of it? Or are the two kinds of progress separate and distinguishable phenomena?

The attempt to answer such questions leads to the discussion of the priority of economic progress over other kinds of progress. Is economic progress always the result of other kinds of advance, or is it, in some sense, a condition of improvement in other realms? And if so, in what sense is this true?[4]

The Natural Progress of Opulence

Several progress authors maintain that it is in the very nature of wealth to increase. The leading spokesman of this position is Adam Smith, who, in speaking of "the natural progress of opulence," writes:

The uniform, constant, and uninterrupted effort of every man to better his condition, the principle from which public and national, as well as private opulence is orginally derived, is frequently powerful enough to maintain the

---

[4] There is still another reason why the discussion in the literature of economic progress is hard to analyze. Economists tend to use more technical terms than do writers about progress in knowledge, moral progress, and so forth. The present work does not pretend to expert knowledge of economics; it cannot be involved, for instance, in a discussion as to whether economics itself progresses.

natural progress of things towards improvement, in spite both of the ex-
travagance of government and of the greatest errors of administration. Like
the unknown principle of animal life, it frequently restores health and
vigour to the constitution, in spite, not only of the disease, but of the absurd
prescriptions of the doctor.[5]

This is also the position of Mandeville, for whom the economic progress
of the hive is founded on a natural and healthy selfishness. The notion
that free competition is the source of this kind of progress is put forward
as well by Buckle, who pays tribute to Smith.

When these great truths were recognized [*i.e.*, those expounded in *The
Wealth of Nations*], all the old notions concerning the balance of trade, and
the supreme importance of the precious metals, at once fell to the ground.
These enormous errors being dispersed, the true theory of barter was easily
worked out. It was perceived, that if commerce is allowed to be free, its
advantages will be shared by every country which engages in it; [and] that,
in the absence of monopoly, the benefits of trade are of necessity reciprocal.[6]

And Dugald Stewart provides a gloss of Smith's work that makes his idea
even more clear:

The most effectual plan for advancing a people to greatness, is to maintain
that order of things which nature has pointed out; by allowing every man, as
long as he observes the rules of justice, to pursue his interest in his own way,
and to bring both his industry and his capital into the freest competition
with those of his fellow-citizens.[7]

Bellamy, writing only a few years after Buckle, vigorously denies the
proposition that free competition promotes economic progress. The spokesman for Bellamy's Utopia, Dr. Leete, criticizes the world of 1887 on just
these grounds.

I suppose [he says] that no reflection would have cut the men of your wealth-
worshipping century more keenly than the suggestion that they did not know
how to make money. Nevertheless, that is just the verdict history has passed
on them. Their system of unorganized and antagonistic industries was as
absurd economically as it was morally abominable. Selfishness was their only
science, and in industrial production selfishness is suicide. Competition,
which is the instinct of selfishness, is another word for dissipation of energy,
while combination is the secret of efficient production; and not till the idea
of increasing the individual hoard gives place to the idea of increasing the

[5] *The Wealth of Nations*, p. 326.
[6] *History of Civilization in England*, pp. 217–8.
[7] *Adam Smith, Works, with an Account of His Life and Writings*, Vol. V, p. 492.

common stock can industrial combination be realized, and the acquisition of wealth really begin.[8]

Marx, Engels, Bukharin, and other Marxists also emphasize the importance of cooperation over competition for economic progress, although they concede that at certain epochs competition is inevitable and serves the cause of progress. Despite these differences, however, all of these writers concur with Smith, Stewart, Mandeville, and Buckle in holding that wealth increases in fact.

Other writers who also concur in this judgment are Gibbon, Guizot, Priestley, Carr, Mumford, and Bryce, who, for different reasons, maintain that the natural tendency of wealth is to increase. We may "acquiesce in the pleasing conclusion," says Gibbon,

> that every age of the world has increased and still increases the real wealth, the happiness, the knowledge, and perhaps the virtue, of the human race.[9]

Priestley predicts that "nature, including both its materials and its laws, will be more at our command; men will make their situation in this world abundantly more easy and comfortable; they will probably prolong their existence in it and will grow daily more happy."[10] Guizot converts this confidence about the future into a definition of progress itself. What is progress? he asks, and replies:

> On the one hand there is a manifold increase in the power and well-being of society at large; and on the other a more equitable distribution of this power and this well-being among the individuals of which society is composed.[11]

Carr asserts that "at the present time, few people would . . . question the fact of progress in the accumulation both of material resources and of scientific knowledge."[12] Mumford foresees a time when life will no longer be dominated by work, when work will be integrated into a "more abundant and significant life."[13] And, finally, Bryce sees signs all around him that mankind's total wealth grows with the passage of time.

> There is much more food available for the support of life, much more production of all sorts of commodities. . . . [There is also] the greater abun-

---

[8] *Looking Backward*, p. 244.
[9] *Decline and Fall of the Roman Empire*, Ch. 38, Vol. II, p. 98.
[10] Qu. by Stringfellow Barr, *The Pilgrimage of Western Man*, p. 295. This work, incidentally, markedly lacks an affirmation of the overall progress even of Western man. Evidently a "pilgrimage" is different from a "progress."
[11] *History of Civilization in Europe*, p. 11.
[12] *What Is History?*, p. 156.
[13] *The Transformations of Man*, p. 177.

dance of . . . clothing, the better condition of housing, the diffusion of property through all classes of the community. Along these lines the improvement has been extraordinary.[14]

Not all progress authors hold that economic progress occurs in the sense of increasing wealth. Malthus is a striking figure in this regard. He argues in *Population* that food is necessary to existence, and sexual passion will not cease to be dominant in human affairs; but the amount of food is limited, while the amount of passion is unlimited. Hence the power of population is indefinitely greater than the power in the earth to produce sustenance for man. The only checks on population are misery—*i.e.*, starvation—and vice—*i.e.*, all kinds of corruption, degradation, and disease, and ultimately war. The argument is conclusive, says Malthus, against any general increase of wealth in the future.[15]

These assertions are echoed by C. G. Darwin, a confessed Malthusian. We must look forward, he declares, over the next million years, to very long stretches of time during which mankind will enjoy no economic advantage over Renaissance man, say, or European man of the Dark Ages. There will usually, if not always, be a "starving margin," many of whom will "have to live in a state which, whatever it may be called, will be indistinguishable from slavery." From time to time there will be new "golden ages," but these will always be temporary, and the overall picture is dark.[16]

Many other writers deny economic progress, but most of them are not progress authors. Indeed, it is fairly rare to find a progress author saying that wealth does not increase. Several suggest that if the "technical venture" fails, economic progress will cease—but that is merely to make economic progress contingent, not to deny it. And, of course, many progress authors fail to discuss economic progress or progress in wealth at all.

The Marxist Theory of Economic Progress

Marx and Engels have a more complex theory of how economic progress occurs than is to be found in the writings of the authors discussed in the previous section. This is partly because they maintain that the

---

[14] "What Is Progress?", in the *Atlantic Monthly*, August 1907, pp. 148–9.

[15] Malthus affirms progress in knowledge, and he may see some future moral progress as well (resulting from the spread of Christianity over the world). But he denies permanent economic advance, and thus denies progress in this sense. By implication, he also denies social and political progress in the future.

[16] Cf. *The Next Million Years*, pp. 42–56.

social, political, and even the cultural characteristics of societies are determined by their stage of economic development. An expression of this basic Marxist view is found in Engels:

> *All* past history, with the exception of its primitive stages, was the history of class struggles . . . these warring classes of society are always the products of the modes of production and of exchange—in a word, of the *economic* conditions of their time . . . the economic structure of society always furnishes the real basis, starting from which we can alone work out the ultimate explanation of the whole superstructure of juridical and political institutions as well as of the religious, philosophical, and other ideas of a given historical period.[17]

Feudal societies—the first step away from the primitive societies in which there is no division of labor and hence no class struggle[18]—grow up and flourish but are destroyed by the middle class that they allow to develop in their midst, and whose interests depend on the expansion of trade and manufactures. This middle class creates a superstructure of politics, law, culture, and so forth, that is conducive to the profit of its creators.

The destruction of feudal societies is a progressive advance, both in the most general sense, as pointing the way to ultimate Communism, and insofar as the middle class increases the absolute wealth of mankind by developing new means of production. Thus the advent of bourgeois capitalism serves the cause of progress. But bourgeois capitalism is destroyed in its turn, for it allows a class—a lowest class this time, not a middle one—to grow up in its midst: the proletariat. Once again new means and methods of production increase manufacturing capacity, but this involves an internal contradiction. Wages remain low, so that the proletariat cannot satisfy the demand for new markets, which must therefore be sought outside the society. This situation leads to the creation of monopolies, as capacity expands, which make more efficient use of existing markets. These expand also, but are essentially limited. On the one hand, centralization of control over production is achieved, but, on the other, the proletariat is goaded beyond endurance. A succession of crises and imperialist wars for markets finally produces a situation in which the proletariat steps in and takes over the already centralized

---

[17] *Socialism: Utopian and Scientific*, p. 124. These remarks apply to all past history, but not to the future, for in the final stage of Communism, mankind, having attained release from the struggle for existence, will be able to make its own history. History will no longer be materially determined.

[18] There is some question whether the step from primitive communism to feudal society is progressive, according to Marx. Perhaps mankind would be better off if it had remained simple—Marx is a Rousseauian to this extent.

authority and converts it to the first stage of socialism—the dictatorship of the proletariat.

So capitalism falls, but we have not yet arrived at true Communism. It is first necessary to drive production ever and ever forward, for as long as men must struggle for the needs of life they are not free of the torment of class antagonism. The secret is to make labor the essence of life. As Marx writes:

> In a higher phase of Communist society, after the enslaving subordination of individuals under division of labor, and therewith also the antithesis between mental and physical labor, has vanished; after labor, from a mere means of life, has itself become the prime necessity of life; after the productive forces have also increased with the all-round development of the individual, and all the springs of co-operative wealth flow more abundantly—only then can the narrow horizon of bourgeois right be fully left behind and society inscribe on its banners: from each according to his ability, to each according to his needs![19]

The final stage of the Marxist historical process is thus marked by abundance of wealth and comfort as well as by social justice, moral integrity, artistic excellence, and other desirable characteristics.

The Marxist position is stated in slightly different terms by the authors of the *1961 Draft Program,* but it remains recognizable.

> As the country advances toward Communism, personal needs will be increasingly met out of public consumption funds, whose rate of growth will exceed the rate of growth of payments for labor. The transition to Communist distribution will be completed after the principle of distribution according to one's work will exhaust itself, that is, when there will be an abundance of material and cultural wealth and labor will become life's prime necessity for all members of society.[20]

A number of non-Marxist writers accept some of the elements in the Marxist theory while rejecting others. W. W. Rostow, for instance, whose *The Stages of Economic Growth* is "a *non*-Communist Manifesto," denies that economics necessarily dominates social development, though he admits its importance. He denies that class struggle is the whole story, though he admits there are economic conflicts between classes. He disagrees with the proposition that "economic interests and motives [are] an ultimate cause of war-making," though he admits that they helped "determine the setting out of which certain wars arose." Finally, though Rostow agrees with Marx's prediction that a new kind of abundance and

[19] *Critique of the Gotha Program,* p. 52. This short document is replete with affirmations of economic progress.
[20] *Program of the Communist Party of the Soviet Union (Draft), 1961,* p. 184.

affluence will be attained by mankind, he is not nearly so certain as Marx about what man will do with it. "And then the question beyond," he remarks,

> where history offers us only fragments: what to do when the increase in real income loses its charm? Babies, boredom, three-day weekends, the moon, or the creation of new inner, human frontiers in substitution for the imperatives of scarcity?[21]

ECONOMIC PROGRESS AND INCREASE OF POPULATION

It has been agreed for a century that the number of humans on earth has been pretty steadily growing since man first became man.[22] Population increase has become particularly rapid in the twentieth century. And the rate of increase seems to be growing as well.

This fact is of import for the discussion of progress in wealth (economic progress). Authors react to it in various ways. A few hold that the increase in population is in itself progress. Others suggest that it is irreversible cumulative change (ICC) but not progress. A fair number say that it is the sign or symbol of progress, but not progress itself.

A large group of writers holds that population growth is an obstacle to progress if it proceeds beyond a certain point. They ask whether progress is possible at all if the human race continues to grow in numbers. They wonder whether anything can be done to inhibit this growth. And they suggest that if it could be stopped or slowed to a reasonable rate of increase, man might enjoy unparalleled progress.[23]

The notion that population increase is intrinsically progressive is probably contained in the Biblical injunction to "Be fruitful, and multiply." It also appears to be expressed by Comte.

> The natural increase of population, which contributes more than any other influence to accelerate the speed [of progress] . . . has always been regarded as the clearest sympton of the gradual amelioration of the human

---

[21] *The Stages of Economic Growth*, p. 16.

[22] This was not, however, the consensus two centuries ago. In his essay, "On the Populousness of Ancient Nations," Hume concludes, on the basis of the available evidence, that the nations of antiquity were blessed with larger populations than those of his time, and that the world seems, on the whole, to be decreasing in population. Hume is unable to suggest a reason why this should be so.

[23] There is a very large literature that is concerned with the problem of population growth and its effect on the future of mankind. We have not attempted to analyze it here; but our discussion of the views of a few progress authors reveals most of the commonly held opinions on the subject.

condition; and nothing can be more unquestionable when we take the whole race into account.[24]

Here Comte is saying that the "natural" increase of population is intrinsically cumulative in the sense of ICC, and the "clearest symptom" of progress itself.

Comte's argument runs like this: Increase in population implies condensation of population; condensation of population produces pressure both on the means of subsistence and on the ingenuity of mankind; the pressure is met by "a division of employments" that would not be favored by smaller numbers; and this in turn hastens progress.

> By creating new wants and new difficulties, this gradual concentration develops new means, not only of progress but of order, by neutralizing physical inequalities, and affording a growing ascendency to those intellectual and moral forces which are suppressed among a scanty population.[25]

Bryce also sees population growth as a sign of progress, if it is not, for him, intrinsically progressive. The fact that the population of Europe was "probably three or four times, that of North America probably twenty times," as large in 1900 as in 1700 proves, says Bryce,

> that there is much more food available for the support of life, much more production of all sorts of commodities, and in particular an immense increase in the area of land used for producing food, with an improvement in the methods of extracting food from the land.[26]

But for Bryce such progress and "improvement" is far from being "amelioration in the human condition" in the sense in which it is that for Comte. Bryce questions whether improvements of this sort facilitate intellectual and moral progress, and whether they bring about an increase in intelligence, in virtue, and in happiness.

"Upward kinks in the population curve" are, for Childe, signs of the occurrence of the historical "revolutions" that have brought about man's progress. As we have seen, these revolutions are mainly technical advances and discoveries; the historian is able to date them by noting the sharp increases in world population that succeed them. The thinking is

---

24 *Positive Philosophy*, pp. 519–20. "Natural" does not mean quite the same thing here as "necessary"—though Comte seems to feel that population increase is also inevitable. Elsewhere, Comte declares that "one fact is enough to silence sophistical declamation on this subject [*i.e.*, the question whether progress occurs]: the continuous increase of population all over the globe, as a consequence of civilization, while the wants of individuals are, as a whole, better satisfied at the same time" (p. 467).

25 *Ibid.*, p. 520.

26 *Op. cit.*, p. 148.

familiar, for similar views are held by writers such as C. G. Darwin, Mumford, and Butterfield, to name only three who speak of "kinks," "nodal points," and "revolutions" both in progress and in the curve of population growth.

Like Bryce, these authors tend to withhold from population growth alone the judgment that it itself is progressive. It is for them a sign of progress, a result of progress in other respects. Yet it is closely associated with progress.

However, although population growth tends to be viewed by the writers just mentioned, and by others who emphasize either the contingency or the limited quality of progress, as symbolic of past progress, they often suggest that it is a possible cause of future regress. Thus, C. G. Darwin, for example, declares that

> there can never be more people than there is food for. There will not be less, because man, like every other animal, tends to increase in numbers.[27]

The net result is that population will increase as the supply of food increases. Past "revolutions" produced sharp increases in human numbers. The present epoch, marked as it is by the discovery of many new techniques as well as rich supplies of energy, is one in which population can expand at its "natural" rate without undue pressure on food production. But we are now nearing the end of this golden age, if we have not already reached it. Soon there will be again a starving margin, some ten percent of humans who live "on the margin of existence." Indeed, this is the perennial human situation, for

> the central feature of human history must always be the pressure of population. Man, the wild animal, will obey the laws of life and will tend to multiply until he is limited by the means of subsistence.[28]

In the past, this perennial situation did not grow markedly worse. Technical advances allowed increased populations to exist; population leveled off at the new, higher level, and the starving margin remained more or less constant. But it is characteristic of our time that we are living far beyond our energy "income." When our "capital" runs out, we will have to retrench at a lower level of population. This adjustment will be cataclysmic. And future golden ages will also produce violent historical wrenches.

> If at any time some discovery, usually an agricultural one, should make a greater supply of food available, then, reckoning on the long-term time-

[27] *Op. cit.*, p. 27.
[28] *Ibid.*, p. 124.

scale, instantaneously the population will rise to a new level, and after that things will go on as before, but now with a larger starving margin in the larger population. It is by no means evident that the world will be any the better for it, but the point is not whether it is a good thing, but whether it will happen, and the answer is that undoubtedly it will.[29]

Viewing man over "the next million years," Darwin is relatively sanguine; while he points to severe troubles in the next two or three centuries, he holds that the average future of man will not be really worse than the average past—it is just that it will not be really better. Other contemporary writers emphasize more strongly the immediate danger of the "population explosion." Predictions that the world will "shortly" be burdened by a population of 5 billion, or 10 billion, or even 100 billion persons are commonplaces of our time. Within the next two centuries, according to one set of figures, there will be a human being for every square yard of the earth's surface. It is obvious, of course, that these "predictions" are not meant seriously. Since the earth could not possibly "support" so many people, they will not be "on" it. Nevertheless, the threat to mankind's progress is real.

Darwin's pessimism is based, as we have indicated, on his doubts about the possibility of future technological progress. According to him, technology was able to support a growing population in the past, but this is no longer true; technology has itself produced a situation which it can no longer control. Some progress authors dispute just this point. Harrison Brown, for example, denies that the pressure of population "indefinitely exceeds" the capacity of the earth to produce food. He concedes that Darwin's and Malthus' reasoning is sound, but shows how they came to an incorrect conclusion. Malthus' extrapolation into the future suffered, he declares,

> not from lack of proper reasoning, but from lack of sufficient knowledge of the potentialities of technological development. . . . In short, the scientific knowledge of his time was too meagre to permit his drawing valid conclusions, no matter how sound his reasoning was.[30]

Even a population of 200 billion persons is conceivable, Brown suggests.

Brown makes the point that the capacity of the earth to produce food need not be indefinitely extended, for technology, at the same time that it is extending this capacity, can also discover an effective method of limiting population growth. The implication is that if the *rate* of population increase can be contained, we have nothing to fear from our growing

---

[29] *Ibid.*, p. 126.
[30] *The Challenge of Man's Future*, p. 6. These remarks apply as well to C. G. Darwin, for whose reply see below, p. 367.

numbers. The same point is made by Ritchie Calder. At the lowest estimate, he declares, the earth could, by various means,

> support a population of at least 10,000,000,000. So, however much we may deplore them, we need not be terrified by figures like 4,000,000,000—except that they are only twenty years away. It is the time factor, not the numbers, that is the real cause for concern.[31]

With the resources of modern science and technology, "tempered by wisdom," it should be possible "to escape from the limitations of past civilizations and succeed where they failed." There need not be a starving margin; all men can have enough to eat, and can enjoy a "human" existence. But, Calder warns,

> remembering the 4,000,000,000 people who will share this planet in twenty years' time, science and statesmanship will have to work fast.[32]

The danger is in the rate of the increase, not in the increase itself.

One does not know how Malthus would reply to these arguments, but C. G. Darwin may perhaps be allowed to speak for him. He holds that whatever improvement there may be in the technical methods of producing food, there will always be pressure from population because man is a "wild animal" and will not, indeed cannot, control his birthrate, except for short periods. Various methods may work for a time, even for a rather long time over much of the earth—perhaps as much as a hundred years. But sooner or later something will go wrong. One nation will allow its population to increase unchecked, perhaps intentionally, perhaps simply by accident; it will, therefore, begin to weigh disproportionately in the world's power structure; other nations will feel they have to follow suit; and the "Malthusian trap" will once more be sprung.

The essence of Darwin's argument is his notion that man is a wild animal who has no "superior" animal to "domesticate" him and force him to limit his numbers. This deficiency is supplied, in imagination at least, by Leo Szilard, who, in *The Voice of the Dolphins*, tells how these intelligent mammals, recognizing the danger to them and to the whole world in human population increase, invent a cheap and effective method of birth control. They retain the patent on this chemical device and with the immense income derived from the sale of it manage to insure continuing world peace. They bribe prime ministers when that is necessary, develop ingenious schemes for mutual protection, and support the costs of a world police force, which, since it is very well paid, remains loyal only to them.

[31] *After the Seventh Day*, p. 438.
[32] *Ibid.*, p. 440.

Another kind of answer to Darwin and Malthus is given by John R. Platt. He too recognizes the danger in uncontrolled population increase. He concedes that our very numbers may overwhelm us within a very few generations, with the inevitable result a nuclear war that will destroy all life on earth, or at least all human life. But, says Platt, this may not happen. The situation is simple: *either* mankind will destroy itself, *or* it will control its numbers; and, if it persists, it will inevitably control its numbers. Platt suggests no one method by which this might be done; perhaps he has no particular method in mind. He merely points out the absolute necessity that such a method be found and applied. Hence, as we might have observed in Chapter 15, a special kind of necessity is involved here; a solution to the population problem will inevitably be found—*if* man in fact remains on earth for another hundred years.

It should be pointed out here that the points made by Brown, Calder, Darwin, Szilard, and Platt—from their different points of view—actually are not new. Comte, more than a century ago, clearly recognized the problem that disturbs modern demographers. He wrote:

> It must be observed . . . that if the condensation [of population] and rapidity [of population growth] were to pass beyond a certain degree, they would not favour, but impede this acceleration [of progress]. The condensation, if carried too far, would render the support of human life too difficult; and the rapidity, if extreme, would so affect the stability of social enterprises as to be equivalent to a considerable shortening of our life. As yet, however, the increase of population has never nearly reached the natural limits at which such inconveniences will begin; and we have really no experience of them, unless in a few exceptional cases of disturbance caused by migrations, ill-managed as to their extent of numbers and of time. In an extremely distant future, our posterity will have to consider the question, and with much anxiety; because, from the smallness of the globe, and the necessary limitation of human resources, the tendency to increase will become extremely important, when the human race will be ten times as numerous as at present, and as much condensed everywhere as it now is in the west of Europe. Whenever that time comes, the more complete development of human nature, and the more exact knowledge of the laws of human evolution, will no doubt supply new means of resistance to the danger.[33]

Of course, the situation has changed since Comte's time; the increase of population *has* reached "the natural limits at which . . . inconveniences . . . begin." One has the impression, nevertheless, that Comte

[33] *Op. cit.,* p. 520. Comte's view as here expressed differs from that of many modern writers in only one important respect: he feels that "the more complete development of human nature" will aid in finding a cure for the problem of population, whereas most moderns seem intent on finding a mechanical solution.

A change in human nature would of course be of extreme importance in this regard. The Malthusian argument is based on the assumption that man will remain fundamentally the same.

would remain sanguine, for he, in several places, expresses his belief that as men progress their basic needs decrease, however their numbers may increase. "We cannot but observe," he declares, "that men take less food as they advance in civilization." He adds that "nobody supposes that men will ultimately cease to eat," but it is obvious that if human needs decrease sufficiently a very much larger population could subsist comfortably on the earth.[34]

A similar solution—though a more radical one—is suggested by Godwin. Not only will human hunger for food decrease in the "rational society" of the future, but human sexual passion will also abate. "The men whom we are supposing to exist," says Godwin, "when the earth shall refuse itself to a more extended population, will probably cease to propagate." This of course is the final answer to the Malthusian argument.[35]

Still other progress authors approach the population problem, and its relation to progress in general, from another point of view. A. J. Todd, for example, reviews contemporary opinions[36] on the question of whether "progress mean[s] necessarily a large and growing population," and declares that "the most serious-minded Eugenists now agree that not large populations, but good populations, are the ideal of civilized man."[37] The same position is taken by L. P. Jacks, who writes:

> Consider the growth of population—the immense increase in the total bulk and volume of the human race. Whether this constitutes a clear gain to humanity obviously cannot be answered without reference to moral considerations. To increase the arithmetical quantity of life in the world can be counted a gain only if the general tendencies of life are in the right direction. If they are in the wrong direction, then the more lives there are to yield to these tendencies the less reason has the moralist to be satisfied with what is happening.[38]

We have first to be convinced that the human race is not on the wrong road, he goes on to say, before we can look with complacency on the increase of its numbers.

CHARACTERISTICS OF ECONOMIC PROGRESS

The majority of progress authors seems to feel that economic progress is dependent on technological progress; indeed, most fail to make a care-

[34] *Ibid.*, p. 484.
[35] *An Enquiry Concerning Political Justice,* II, p. 528. This is one of the points in Godwin's work regarding which Malthus is most scornful.
[36] As of c. 1910.
[37] *Op. cit.*, p. 119.
[38] "Moral Progress," in F. S. Marvin (ed.), *Progress and History,* p. 142.

ful distinction between the two kinds of progress. We have observed this tendency in writers like Brown, Calder, and Szilard; and the fact that C. G. Darwin denies future technological advances, and therefore also denies future economic progress, lends support to this judgment.

It is true that the Marxists often make use of the term "economic progress," but they do not thereby seem to be making the distinction. Bukharin, for example, holds that economic progress occurs, and that it is allied with the ever increasing division of labor; but the latter phenomenon is a kind of technological advance. The essential difference, in his view, between a primitive society of men who "are hardly more than monkeys, tribal animals," and a highly developed capitalist society, a "sublime 'mental culture,' a great Babylonian confusion," is to be observed in the difference of technical economic arrangements.

> How was it possible for this mind to develop? What were the conditions for its growth? The growth of *material production,* the increase in the power of man over nature, the increase in the *productivity of human labor.*[39]

Bukharin speaks in another place of the relatively undeveloped economies of ancient times, and again measures the difference between them and our own highly developed economies in technological terms.

> It is evident that the relations between people in the labor process are determined by the stage of advance in the evolution of technology. . . . Just as the ancient technology determined the ancient form of economy, so capitalist technology determines the present-day capitalist economy.[40]

From one point of view, then, the Marxists hold that technological progress is prior to economic progress. In fact, however, their notion of "means of production," the evolution of which is the key to understanding human progress, draws from both conceptions. It is both economic and technological; progress occurs, perhaps inseparably, in both respects. This view of the matter is characteristic of many modern authors, Marxists and non-Marxists alike.

Certain other authors emphasize the priority of economic progress over other kinds of progress, whether or not economic progress itself is ultimately dependent on technological progress. Thus, Mumford and Childe, for example, assert that the creation of an agricultural surplus was the condition of the specialization of function which led, in the past, to many kinds of progress—to progress in knowledge, and to technological, social, or political, and even moral progress. An initial increase in wealth

[39] *Historical Materialism,* pp. 60–1.
[40] *Ibid.,* pp. 138–40.

—itself the result, perhaps, of a prior technological discovery—is seen by these authors and by many others as the absolutely necessary condition of further human progress. If all men still practiced subsistence agriculture, there would be no cities, no science, and no possibility of ameliorating the general conditions of human life.

Maritain occupies a special position in this part of the controversy. His *True Humanism* is written mainly against the Marxist contention that economic forces are the spring of history; nevertheless, he places heavy emphasis on the importance of economic progress for progress of other kinds. Economic progress is not in itself sufficient; it must be accompanied by advances of other kinds. But it is necessary for social progress.

Maritain's differences with the Marxists do not keep him from sharply criticizing the capitalist system. We must choose, he declares, between the idea of an essentially industrial civilization and an essentially human one, for which industrialism would be only a means. And he asks:

> Under the capitalist system is not an industrial enterprise a hive composed of, on the one side, salaried workers and, on the other, of capital united in a company—a grouping not of men but of paper and of money, of symbols of wealth, whose soul is the desire to create new rights of possession? . . . If we imagine in the place of the capitalist system a future system whose spirit and economic structure would be in conformity with the communal and personalist conception of society, this collectivization would not be suppressed by its economic regulation, it would be organized on entirely other lines and for the benefit of the human person.[41]

Maritain's aim is what he calls "pluralist economics," *i.e.*, a system in which there are goods for the many rather than for the few. "It is an axiom for the 'bourgeois' economic order and mercantile civilization that *one gets nothing for nothing*: an axiom bound up with the individualistic conception of ownership." In the "new Christendom," however,

> the law of *usus communis* would lead to there being, at least and first of all in what is concerned with the primary spiritual and material needs of human beings, *as many things as possible for nothing*. . . . That the primordial necessities of the human person should *be served* is, after all, nothing but the first condition of any economic order not meriting the name of barbarous.[42]

The main point of Maritain's remarks is that progress has, as he says, "two poles: one economic, on the side of the most urgent necessities of the ethico-biological order; the other religious, on the side of the most

---

[41] *True Humanism*, p. 158.
[42] *Ibid.*, pp. 185–6.

urgent necessities of the life of the soul."[43] In fact, he declares, the Christian "must strive for some proportionate realization . . . of the claims of the Gospel . . . in the socio-temporal order."[44] This would involve, he makes clear, the satisfaction of basic human needs for food, shelter, health, and other goods usually deemed economic.[45]

Other positions with regard to the relative priority of economic progress are found, or at least hinted at, in the literature. Thus for Adam Smith, Stewart, and Mandeville, the progress of wealth, though it is a natural phenomenon, is to some extent dependent on the lack of—or rather on the application of the proper—social and political controls. This is to make political progress prior to economic progress. Buckle, who supports this view, also emphasizes that knowledge of social and economic laws precedes economic progress—without knowledge, wealth will not increase. And an author such as L. P. Jacks is probably saying that moral progress is the condition of economic progress, for progress in wealth is not "really" progress unless it occurs in a moral context. However, the predominant modern view of this matter is that of the Marxists—namely, that economic progress is a necessary, though perhaps not the sufficient condition of further progress, and that economic progress is based on technological progress. Without the latter, almost all contemporary writers agree, the possibility of future progress of any kind is extremely slim.

[43] *Ibid.*, p. 89.
[44] *Ibid.*, p. 120.
[45] Yves Simon concurs with Maritain in most of these judgments.

22

Political Progress: I

MANY writers discuss the historical changes that, following their usage, may be termed social or political progress. (The earlier writers tend to call this kind of progress political, the later writers social, but they appear to be talking about the same thing.) Political progress is clearly distinguished from progress in knowledge and from technological progress; however, these kinds of progress are sometimes said to underlie political progress. It is also distinguished from economic progress, although increase in wealth may be associated with it.

Political progress and moral progress are not always carefully distinguished by progress authors. In this work, we take the former term as applying to changes that clearly concern large groups of human beings—i.e., changes that occur to man considered as a social animal. We take moral progress as applying to changes that usually manifest themselves in the behavior of individual human beings, although they may also be manifested in social behavior.

Discussions of political progress in the progress literature can be grouped under five heads. One group of authors sees, and emphasizes as a constituent of human progress, an historical trend toward control over man's selfish or "unsocial" nature. The idea is that men participate in a "social contract," and that it is progress to do so. This group of writers is opposed by those who view security—at least, too much security—as an obstacle to progress. The dispute centers not on the question of whether man should have government but on the question of whether he should have a minimum of government or, supposing different kinds of government, the right kind.

Another group of writers sees an historical trend toward larger and larger political units, a trend that culminates, for many of them, in a future union or "planetization" of the entire human race in one community. Most of the authors who perceive this change judge it to be progressive, but a few question whether it is desirable in every sense. And several others question whether man will actually reach the world government that, they agree, is his proper end.

Still another group speaks of the increasing efficiency of political or governmental organization. Their notion is that reason either must or may be increasingly applied to the problems of men living together, and that progress is a result. Denials of this position sometimes take the form of assertions that rationalization of social organization is a sign of an excessive "technologization" of mankind—in itself a regressive change.

Several writers, notably Condorcet and Tocqueville, discern a steady advance of mankind toward greater equality, and see in this the main constituent of political progress. Others deny that such an advance is a feature of history, and, if it is, that it is a progressive change.

Finally, a large and disparate group of progress authors holds that the advance of, in, or toward freedom is basic to the idea of human progress. These writers differ among themselves about what constitutes freedom, although they all use the term. In some cases the freedom they discuss is political, in others it is not. However, they all seem to be discussing a social phenomenon. Here, too, there are writers who deny that advance in or toward freedom, in at least some sense of the term, is progress.

The first three controversies, as outlined above, are treated in the present chapter. The controversies regarding equality and freedom are treated in Chapter 23.[1]

We have found it to be impossible to discuss these matters without at the same time considering authors' views as to the priority, or relative importance, of one kind of political progress as against others, and as against other kinds of progress in general. Hence there is no particular section of Chapters 22 and 23 in which these questions are treated. However, some general remarks can be made here.

[1] Fewer authors than one might expect discuss progress in justice; those who do are discussed from another point of view in Chapter 25.

Progress in circumstantial freedom, in the view of those who affirm it, is dependent on technological progress. For most progress authors, however, other types of political progress seem to be basic constituents of progress itself. Many of the authors who affirm them also affirm that other kinds of progress follow from them. A good society, in their view, is a leading cause, or perhaps merely a condition, of progress in the most general sense.

Hobbes and Rousseau, for example, view the progressive step that is represented by the social contract as the condition of every other sort of progress. Bagehot and Mill have a similar regard for the political liberty that is, for them, the *sine qua non* of a progressive society. Kant and Dante conceive world government as the condition of the fullest realization of man's rational nature. Wells, inverting the relation just mentioned, sees world government as resulting in a vast increase of power; and Teilhard views it as the necessary step toward man's future progress—but what this will be he cannot tell. For Condorcet, progress in equality is probably more fundamental than any other type except progress in knowledge. For Tocqueville, if there is to be any other progress it will follow from the increase of equality—but of that he is not sure.

Perhaps progress in or toward freedom has the highest priority of all, at least in the view of the authors who emphasize it. We have noted that this is the case for Bagehot and Mill. In some sense, progress in acquired freedom is the be all and end all for Hegel. And collective freedom, according to Comte, Marx, Engels, Bakunin, and the others who say that man will ultimately attain it, is the condition of all further progress. What this progress will be like—whether, for example, it will be primarily in human nature, as several writers seem to suggest—is hard to tell. In a sense, mankind can hope for no more than to possess collective freedom. Indeed, the prospect is glittering enough. But if there is to be any change in this earthly paradise, if perfection can be improved upon, it will necessarily be on the basis, and as a result, of this state of man in which the free development of each is indissolubly connected with the free development of all.

PROGRESS AND SECURITY

In a classic description of the "state of nature," Hobbes describes its disadvantages and, by implication, shows how much mankind has progressed.

> Whatsoever . . . is consequent to a time of war, where every man is enemy to every man; the same is consequent to the time, wherein men live

without other security, than what their own strength, and their own invention shall furnish them withal. In such condition, there is no place for industry; because the fruit thereof is uncertain; and consequently no culture of the earth; no navigation, nor use of the commodities that may be imported by sea; no commodious building; no instruments of moving, and removing, such things as require much force; no knowledge of the face of the earth; no account of time; no arts; no letters; no society; and which is worst of all, continual fear, and danger of violent death; and the life of man, solitary, poor, nasty, brutish, and short.[2]

Hobbes' view is that political organization is basic to every aspect of civilization and progress. Without it there is no knowledge, no technology, no wealth, no art, no morality, and, of course, no progress in these things. Above all, there is no security and safety. Men live in continual fear. There can be no human progress in these circumstances. Hence, political progress is prior to every other type.

In a passage that is equally celebrated, Rousseau describes the first action of men to overcome the disadvantages of this unhappy primal state. He imagines a situation in which there is no right but that of the strongest, and supposes

men to have reached the point at which the obstacles in the way of their preservation in the state of nature show their power of resistance to be greater than the resources of the disposal of each individual for his maintenance in that state. That primitive condition can then subsist no longer; and the human race would perish unless it changed its manner of existence.[3]

The resolution of the situation is a "social compact." The problem is, Rousseau says, to find a form of association that will defend and protect with the whole common force the person and goods of each associate, and in which each, while uniting himself with all, may still obey himself alone, and remain as free as before. This requirement is met by

the total alienation of each associate, together with all his rights, to the whole community; for, in the first place, as each gives himself absolutely, the conditions are the same for all; and, this being so, no one has any interest in making them burdensome to others.[4]

The alienation being without reserve, Rousseau says, the union is as perfect as it can be; moreover, each man, in giving himself to all, gives himself to nobody. The result is the essential social compact, to wit:

[2] *Leviathan*, pp. 96–7.
[3] *The Social Contract*, in *The Social Contract and Discourses*, p. 14.
[4] *Ibid.*, p. 15.

Each of us puts his person and all his power in common under the supreme direction of the general will, and, in our corporate capacity, we receive each member as an indivisible part of the whole.[5]

The passage from the state of nature to the civil state substitutes justice for instinct, Rousseau goes on to say, and gives men's actions the morality they had formerly lacked. This is of course a progressive change; its character in terms of the change from one type of freedom to another will be mentioned in the next chapter. It is sufficient here to note that human progress has occurred when the social compact is made, and that this advance is as relatively important for Rousseau as it is for Hobbes.[6]

The idea that movement toward more social security and safety is primary to other types of progress is affirmed by many progress authors. J. S. Mill, for instance, notes that "in savage life there is little or no law, or administration of justice," and declares that

> we accordingly call a people civilized, where the arrangements of society, for protecting the persons and property of its members, are sufficiently perfect to maintain peace among them; i.e. to induce the bulk of the community to rely for their security mainly upon social arrangements, and renounce, for the most part, and in ordinary circumstances, the vindication of their interests (whether in the way of aggression or of defense) by their individual strength or courage.[7]

Progress in this respect "is a good," Mill says, it is "the cause of much good," and it is "not incompatible with any." But he warns that

> there is other good, much even of the highest good, which [the progress of] civilization in this sense does not provide for, and some of which it has a tendency (though that tendency may be counter-acted) to impede.[8]

These other goods are cultural and moral, as well as political; the point is that too much "security"—that, for instance, of a despotism, no matter how benevolent—tends to stifle progress in these other respects. Nevertheless, a certain amount of social and political security is essential to the occurrence of other kinds of progress. Hence Mill is in general agreement with the position of Hobbes and Rousseau.[9]

[5] *Ibid.*

[6] The unquestioned differences between Hobbes and Rousseau with regard to their conception of the state of nature, its conversion into civil society, and the character of the social contract, are not relevant here.

[7] "Civilization," in *Dissertations and Discussions*, Vol. 1, p. 162.

[8] *Ibid.*, p. 160.

[9] Once again the differences among Mill, Hobbes, and Rousseau on many questions are not relevant. We will return to Mill's notion of progress in political liberty in Chapter 23.

T. H. Huxley, in making much the same point, employs a colorful image. The state of nature may be compared, he says, to a wild field full of weeds. In such a field, there is constant struggle, and the losers do not survive. Society, on the other hand, may be compared to a garden. Here man interferes with nature; he inhibits "the antagonistic influences of the general cosmic process." The struggle for existence is limited, although not so much as to obliterate the desirable effects of natural competition.

> Laws, sanctioned by the combined force of the colony . . . restrain the self-assertion of each man within the limits required for the maintenance of peace.[10]

Technological and economic innovations progressively convert the wild natural state to an ordered state of art. In a sense, then, political progress is dependent on such prior changes. However, the first achievement of mankind is the garden, in the rich soil of which other kinds of progress flourish.

Huxley points out that even in a highly evolved society the struggle for existence has not entirely ceased. Unlike bees in a hive, he says, social man remains an individual, and continues to possess aggressive instincts. These instincts are held in check by his desire to be liked by his fellows. Hence, human society is a balance between self-assertion and self-restraint, brought on by social pressure. Society must contain elements of self-assertion because it was forged as a weapon in the struggle for existence. The elements of self-restraint permit it to adhere. Its members must restrain themselves if they are to continue to live together. The battle is unending.

> That which lies before the human race is a constant struggle to maintain and improve, in opposition to the State of Nature, the State of Art of an organized polity; in which, man may develop a worthy civilization, capable of maintaining and constantly improving itself.[11]

Other writers who maintain that political progress is measured by the degree to which men create social controls over their selfish aggressiveness are Comte, Condorcet, and a host of French eighteenth-century authors. In the form of pleas for support of an organization such as the United Nations, the position is also commonly held in the twentieth century.[12]

[10] "Evolution and Ethics," in *Evolution and Ethics and Other Essays,* p. 18.
[11] *Ibid.,* pp. 44–5.
[12] Hobbes' comparison of the state of nature to that of war is interesting. This conception of political progress involves the notion that it is a movement away from a situation in which war is either actual or likely to one in which peace obtains or is progressively more possible.

Huxley's assurance that men in highly developed societies are not like bees in a hive is notable in the light of several modern attacks on the idea that increase in rational social controls constitutes political progress. Lewis Mumford may be mentioned particularly in this connection.[13] Maritain and De Rougemont, with their notion of the desirability of political "pluralism," perhaps join in this attack, though not with so much vehemence.[14] Mandeville and C. G. Darwin also oppose the position, though for different reasons. Mandeville holds that social controls impede progress—they are regressive. Darwin says that they are impossible (*i.e.*, necessarily ineffectual in the long run).

Mandeville, of course, makes specific mention of bees. In his hive the bees make progress when they are vicious—as long as their social demands are not too exacting, as long as they are not "honest." When the state of nature becomes too much like a garden, in which, in Huxley's words, "the rows of plants are straight and there is no longer a struggle for existence," the hive ceases to progress.[15]

C. G. Darwin's point is that man remains a wild animal no matter how much domesticity he may temporarily assume. In Huxley's terms, once more, society always tends to the wild state, and cannot be maintained in a state of art—the garden will inevitably grow to weeds. There will be periods when social controls make possible significant progress. But these will not and cannot endure.[16]

PROGRESS TOWARD A WORLD COMMUNITY

Many writers conceive political progress in terms of a tendency for human social units to increase in population and in territorial extent. The goal of this process is often said to be the unification of all mankind in one world government or community.

According to Guizot, "political centralization" is an important aspect of progress. In the history of Europe "the actual accomplishment of this change [political centralization] belongs," he says, "to the sixteenth and seventeenth centuries."

[13] Mumford is discussed in another context below, pp. 385–6.

[14] De Rougemont is discussed in Chapter 23, p. 413.

[15] Mandeville's position is similar to that of Adam Smith and other "liberal" economists. They frown on too many social controls. But they recognize the necessity of having some controls on selfishness. Mandeville, perhaps exercising the right to exaggerate in a fable, suggests that any controls—any imposed "virtue"—are detrimental.

[16] Underlying Darwin's view is the notion that man will remain essentially the same. If men were to improve in their nature, the garden might have a better chance to endure.

It is this preparation, this silent and hidden process of centralization, both in the social relations and in the opinions of men—a process accomplished, without premeditation or design, by the natural course of events—that we . . . make the subject of our enquiry.[17]

The centralization that Guizot describes is confined mainly to Europe, but its significance is universal. For "it is thus that man advances in the execution of a plan which he has not conceived, and of which he is not even aware." The plan is human progress in the widest sense, providentially ordered and insured.

Others see the tendency toward political unity as anthropogenic. Harrison Brown suggests, for example, that it is in the very nature of civilization not only to make possible but to produce larger unions of human beings. From this increase in the size of communities flows other sorts and types of progress.[18]

Guizot and Brown describe a general tendency. Its goal, in the opinion of a number of progress authors, is the eventual unification of mankind. Bellamy's Dr. Leete, for example, declares that

we all look forward to an eventual unification of the world as one nation. That, no doubt, will be the ultimate form of society, and will realize certain economic advantages over the present [*i.e.*, as of A.D. 2000] federal system of autonomous nations.[19]

The Marxists concur in holding that such an eventuality is to be expected; the world, they say, will be one under Communism.[20] The millennialists —the Joachimites, Lessing, the Jehovah's Witnesses—are no less certain of the ultimate unity of mankind.

H. G. Wells also foresees the existence of a world state, but he emphasizes the difficulties that will be met on the way to it.

There can be little question that the attainment of a federation of all humanity, together with a sufficient measure of social justice, to ensure health, education, and a rough equality of opportunity to most of the children born in the world, would mean such a release and increase of human energy as to open a new phase in human history. . . . Without supposing any change in human quality, but merely its release from the present system of inordinate waste, history justifies this expectation.[21]

[17] *History of Cvilization in Europe*, p. 291.
[18] Brown's theory is not very different from Aristotle's, as we have it in the *Politics*. See *The Challenge of Man's Future*, pp. 14–22.
[19] *Looking Backward*, p. 143.
[20] Khrushchev's threat that the Soviet Union will "bury" the capitalist world is a prediction that Communism will finally rule the entire earth.
[21] *The Outline of History*, pp. 1094–5.

Will such a federation be attained in fact? Wells concedes that there will be many catastrophes before the final world order arrives. "One cannot foretell the surprises or disappointments the future has in store," he says. "Yet, clumsily or smoothly, the world, it seems, progresses and will progress."[22] And such progress toward unification is the basic constituent of human advance.

Wells wrote, of course, before the discovery of the atom bomb, which makes some writers fear that one of the intervening "catastrophes" may end the quest for world unity. In a typical statement of this view, Barrington Moore writes:

> Conceivably humanity may have to pass through another major war, even a series of them. If a world state emerges from the slaughter and destruction, one could still call it progress. Naturally there is nothing inevitable about such an outcome, and there is a very strong possibility that all civilization, indeed all life, may be destroyed first.[23]

Progress is here highly contingent. Nevertheless, it still consists mainly in the advance toward world unity.

Dante also discusses the idea that a world government is the goal of man's (secular) history. Whatever is the universal goal of human civilization, he says, if there be such a goal, will serve as a first principle. In fact, there is such a goal, for man's basic power is

> to be sensitive to intellectual growth, for this trait is not found in beings either above or below man. For though there are angelic beings that share intellect with man, they do not have intellectual growth, since their very being is to be intellect and nothing else and hence they are intellectual continuously, otherwise they would not be changeless.[24]

Therefore, it is clear, Dante writes, that man's basic capacity is to have a potentiality or power for being intellectual. And since this power cannot be completely actualized in a single man or in any of the particular communities of men, there must be a multitude in mankind through whom this whole power can be actualized.

> I have now made clear enough [says Dante] that the proper work of mankind taken as a whole is to exercise continually its entire capacity for intellectual growth, first, in theoretical matters, and, secondarily, as an extension of theory in practice.[25]

[22] *Ibid.*, p. 1100.
[23] "On the Notions of Progress, Revolution, and Freedom," in *Ethics*, January 1962, p. 115.
[24] *On World Government or De Monarchia*, p. 4.
[25] *Ibid.*, p. 5.

The best means toward this end is universal peace. "Let this, then, be our principle . . . and let it serve as a standard set before us by which to test the truth of whatever we shall try to prove."[26]

We must next consider, Dante goes on to say, what condition of things is most conducive to universal peace. The answer is world government. "To achieve this state of universal well-being," he declares, "a single world government is necessary."[27] Any particular institution needs unity of direction; therefore mankind as a whole also needs it. Human government is but a part of that single world administration which has its unity in God; man is by nature in God's likeness and therefore should, like God, be one. These are the basic theoretical arguments; in addition, Dante shows that "the world-government is apt to be least greedy and most just,"[28] as well as most reasonable. Furthermore, as human freedom consists in being ruled by reason and in living for the goal of mankind, such freedom is possible only under world government. All of these arguments show that the goal of man's history is a single community, advances toward which constitute progress for mankind.

Will mankind actually reach this state? Here Dante is even less certain than are the writers mentioned before. A condition of "world" peace prevailed during the Augustan Empire, he reminds us, but will it be again attained before the end of time? In fact, disunity is the mark of Dante's own era. "O race of men," he cries,

> how many storms and misfortunes must thou endure, and how many shipwrecks, because thou, beast of many heads, strugglest in many directions! Thou art sick at heart and sick in mind, both theoretical and practical! No irrefutable arguments appeal to thy theoretical reason, and no amount of experience to thy practical intelligence, and even thine emotions are not moved by the sweet, divine persuasiveness which sounds to thee from the trumpet of the Holy Spirit: "Behold how good and how pleasant it is for brethren to live together in unity."[29]

Dante's theoretical arguments, including his notion that the basic power of man is to grow in intellect and that the final result will be a universal community, are echoed in Kant's *Idea of a Universal History*. In *Perpetual Peace*, Kant sketches the steps necessary to the attainment of such a world state, as well as its basic requirements. He declares that the "guarantee" of perpetual peace "is nothing less than the great and ingenious artist, nature."

[26] *Ibid.*, pp. 5–6.
[27] *Ibid.*, p. 6.
[28] *Ibid.*, p. 11.
[29] *Ibid.*, pp. 20–1.

Her mechanical march evidently announces the grand aim of producing among men, against their intention, harmony from the very bosom of their discords. Hence it is that we call it *destiny*, viewing it as a cause absolute in its effects but unknown as to the laws of its operations. But the regular order which we observe in the course of the events of this world, makes us call it *Providence*.[30]

There is more here than a mere exigency of our nature. "When I say that nature wills that this or that arrive," Kant explains, "this does not mean that she makes it a duty to us; it is practical reason alone that can prescribe laws to free beings without constraining them; but it means, that nature does it herself, whether we will or no. *Fata volentem ducunt, nolentem trahunt*."[31] And Kant concludes:

If it is a duty, if the hope can even be conceived, of realizing, though by an endless progress, the reign of public right—perpetual peace, which will succeed to the suspensions of hostilities, hitherto named treaties of peace, is not then a chimera, but a problem, of which time, probably abridged by the uniformity of the progress of the human mind, promises us the solution.[32]

Among modern authors, only Teilhard de Chardin, perhaps, affirms the future attainment of a world community with as much confidence as Kant. Indeed, the "idea of mankind" is almost, for Teilhard, the heart of the idea of human progress. We have "forged all sorts of economic and cultural links . . . around us," he writes, "and they are multiplying in geometrical progression."

It is no longer a simple field, however big, but the whole earth which is required to nourish each one of us. If words have meaning, is this not like some great body which is being born—with its limbs, its nervous system, its perceptive organs, its memory . . . ?[33]

"There are two ways, through two stages, in which we can picture the form mankind will assume tomorrow," Teilhard declares, "—either (and this is simpler) as a common power and act of knowing or doing, or (and this goes much deeper) as an organic super-aggregation of souls. In short, knowledge or unanimity."[34] Knowledge we understand; through it and by it man progresses; he learns as he grows older. Unanimity, on the other hand, implies a "megasynthesis."

[30] *Perpetual Peace*, p. 27.
[31] *Ibid.*, p. 32. Interestingly enough, the same quotation is used by Spengler to reinforce his assertion of a theory of cycles in history—and particularly his prediction of the downfall of the West. See above, p. 163.
[32] *Ibid.*, p. 67.
[33] *The Phenomenon of Man*, pp. 245–6.
[34] *Ibid.*, p. 248.

This, which on the biochemical level is equivalent to a "process of super-molecularisation on the planet," is the inevitable end result of a process that is the most remarkable fact of current history. Teilhard writes in another work:

> Underlying all the surface-changes of present-day history, the reality and paramount importance of a single basic event is becoming daily more manifest: namely, the rise of the masses, with its natural corollary, the socialisation of Mankind. The supreme interest and significance of this process lies in the fact that, scientifically analysed, it may be seen to be irresistible in two ways: in the *planetary* sense, because it is associated with the closed shape of the earth, the mechanics of generation and the psychic properties of human matter; and in the *cosmic* sense because it is the expression and prolongation of the primordial process whereby, at the uttermost extreme from the disintegrating atom, psychic force is born into the Universe and continuously grows, fostered by the ever more complicated grouping of matter.[35]

Projected forward, this process "makes it possible for us to envisage a future state of the Earth in which human consciousness . . . will have attained a maximum . . . of concentration by total 'reflexion' (or *planetisation*) of itself upon itself."[36]

Our instincts may rebel against this, says Teilhard, but they do so vainly and also wrongly.

> In vain, because no power in the world can enable us to escape from what is in itself the power of the world. And wrongly because the real nature of this impulse that is sweeping us towards a state of super-organisation is such as to make us more completely personalised and human.[37]

Human collectivization will pass, Teilhard says, beyond the *enforced* phase, where it now is, into the *free* phase:

> that in which (men having at last understood that they are inseparably joined elements of a converging Whole, and having learnt in consequence to *love* the preordained forces that unite them) a natural union of affinity and sympathy will supersede the forces of compulsion.[38]

The surest sign that mankind is moving in the direction Teilhard describes is, he says, the existence, more and more commonly on earth, and furthermore in every nation and clime, of "a new element, not yet catalogued but of supreme importance: We might call it *Homo progressivus*,

[35] *The Future of Man*, p. 124.
[36] *Ibid.*
[37] *Ibid.*, pp. 124–5.
[38] *Ibid.*, p. 125.

that is to say, the man to whom the terrestrial future matters more than the present."

A new type of man indeed, when we consider that, less than two hundred years ago, the notion of an organic evolution of the World in Time had acquired neither form nor substance in the human mind. When we come to look for them, men of this sort are easily recognisable. They are scientists, thinkers, airmen and so on—all those possessed by the demon (or the angel) of Research.[39]

Indeed, the existence of this new type of man, who believes in, demands, and hence will ultimately attain the collectivization or unification of mankind, is beginning already to result in a new division of the race. The old Marxist conflict between producers and exploiters is becoming outdated, is, at the best, a misplaced approximation. What divides the men of today into two camps is not class but an attitude of mind—"the spirit of movement."

On the one hand there are those who simply wish to make the world a comfortable dwelling-place; on the other hand, those who can only conceive of it as a machine for progress—or better, an *organism that is progressing*. On the one hand the "bourgeois spirit" in its essence, and on the other the true "toilers of the Earth," those of whom we may safely predict that, without violence or hatred, simply by biological predominance, they will tomorrow constitute the human race. On one hand the cast-offs; on the other, the agents and elements of planetisation.[40]

Many other writers foresee a future unification of all of mankind in one social state, but all of them do not hold that such a tendency is desirable. Seidenberg, for instance, predicts that mankind will indeed achieve this unity, but that it will spell the end of progress. "Post-historic man" will no longer change. He will live like the ants[41] and the bees that serve as exemplars for so many progress—and antiprogress—authors. Seidenberg is not a progress author; but Mumford is. Mumford warns that the dead end that Seidenberg sees as inevitable is *one* possibility that confronts man, but not the only one. Posthistoric man will be a reality if we allow ourselves to become totally subservient to our machines. That hopeless and final stage of man's career on earth will be reached if our civilization continues to give increasing emphasis to the practices that mark our epoch, and that were "originally brought in by capitalism, machine

[39] *Ibid.*, p. 137.
[40] *Ibid.*, p. 139. Teilhard discusses this topic throughout *The Future of Man*. See esp. pp. 155–84, 227–37, 270–80, 281–8, and 289–98.
[41] For Teilhard's specific denial that human society will ever be antlike, see *ibid.*, pp. 38, 40.

technics, the physical sciences, bureaucratic administration, and totalitarian government."[42] However, mankind *can* choose (and attain) a "world culture" that will control, instead of being controlled by, the machine. Mankind may become one, may go beyond the "axial" religions, all forms of sectarianism, regionalism, nationalism, and so forth. Mumford is perhaps not much more optimistic than Dante, though he has much the same vision.

Maritain, too, sees dangers in the future unification of the human race in one social state. Such an eventuality can only be termed progressive if the state is pluralistic, he declares; that is, if it is based on both "economic . . . and juridical pluralism."

> The idea of an organized political fraternity of a political order holds indubitable promise of important historic destinies. But in a pluralist and personalist city it would be realized in a novel way. . . . These formations will be founded on freedom; and they will be multiple, that is the capital point.[43]

In other words, only if a future world order insures freedom will it be progressive.

C. G. Darwin does not question the desirability of the political unification of mankind; he holds, however, that it is impossible (for more than relatively short periods of time). It is to be expected, he writes, that a single government of the earth will not arise very frequently. Most of the time the natural, geographic divisions of the earth's surface will be nearly independent states, which will form alliances with one another so as to compete against rival alliances. Here again, he notes, much depends on the "fuel problem."

> If transportation is easy, world conquest would be easier both for military reasons and because the more uniform culture should make the world government more acceptable.[44]

Darwin looks forward over a very great stretch of time. In this he differs from some of the writers considered above, who seem to imagine a kind of "United States of the World" fairly soon.[45] He does, however, share his long view with many writers of science fiction. It is interesting that

[42] *The Transformations of Man*, p. 155.
[43] *True Humanism*, pp. 164–5.
[44] *The Next Million Years*, p. 141. A. C. Clarke, conceiving the "fuel problem" to be soluble, predicts a future world community based on advanced communications and transportation. See *Profiles of the Future*, pp. 186–96. Teilhard agrees with Clarke on this point.
[45] However, Kant looks forward to a vast future, while Orwell predicts a situation much like the one Darwin describes, as already in existence in 1984.

while they see tremendous changes in a "million years," Darwin sees almost none, at least not very significant ones. It is of the essence of his predictions about the future that it will be very much like the past—with the exception of knowledge, which will continue to grow.

PROGRESS TOWARD A SOCIETY BASED ON REASON

A number of authors, while they may also take some of the other positions discussed in this chapter, put particular emphasis on the relation between political progress and reason. The idea is, simply, that political progress mainly occurs when, or if, man introduces reasonableness into his social arrangements.

Comte holds that progress toward the rational (*i.e.*, the positive) society is inevitable; he also urges his contemporaries to act in such a way that the great goal may be more quickly attained. Indeed, this is the point of his whole philosophy. Positive science has brought about much increase of man's control over nature. Now, with the invention of the sciences of social statics and social dynamics, society will also be improved according to positive principles.

The Positive Philosophy contains relatively few predictions regarding the future. These are reserved for a later work of Comte's, *A System of Positive Polity*. This work is the vehicle for the expression of Comte's hopes, expectations, and programs for the future of Europe and the world. The future social state will, Comte says, secure the victory of social feelings over self-love.[46]

It is noteworthy that Comte does not approve the tendency toward unreserved liberty of expression that he sees as characteristic of his epoch. It is the result of the convulsions attendant on the revolutionary change of values that is ushering in the positive state, and is not itself progressive. Physicists and mathematicians, he points out, must abide by rules of discourse, evidence, proof, and so forth. In a rational society the same will be true of politicians and moralists. In the positive state

the principles of free enquiry will abide within . . . natural and permanent limits: that is, men will discuss, under appropriate intellectual con-

[46] Altruism is a feeling, Comte says, and it must be treated as such. It will therefore be necessary to found a new religion. This will be based on Man and not on God. Its power will be in social Man, in the positive stage of Humanity, conceived, in Comte's phrase, as "The Great Being." For an extensive analysis of Comte's proposed religion, see, for example, F. E. Manuel, *The Prophets of Paris*, pp. 268–96.

The Positive Polity has received, on the whole, much more stringent criticism than *The Positive Philosophy*. See Manuel, and also Mill's *Auguste Comte and Positivism*, pp. 125–200.

ditions, the real connection of various consequences with fundamental rules uniformly respected.[47]

Godwin is another who affirms that political progress will be the result of the application of reason to social matters. In a state enjoying political justice we may look forward to near-perfect health and an almost indefinite life-span.

> Other improvements may be expected to keep pace with those of health and longevity. There will be no war, no crimes, no administration of justice, as it is called, and no government. Besides this, there will be neither disease, anguish, melancholy, nor resentment.[48]

This sort of prediction comes in for sharp criticism by Yves Simon. He speaks with disapproval of "the extremely seductive idea of substituting for the control of the passions by virtue, prudence, and authority, a judicious arrangement of social relations which makes the rigors of ascetism and obedience superfluous."[49] No social system can ever be so reasonable, Simon is saying, as to work automatically and without effort and dedication on the part of its members.

However, that such a system can exist and indeed will inevitably exist is the opinion of Comte and Godwin. It is also the opinion of certain Marxist writers. Godwin notes that government will not be required in a society based on reasonableness. Engels concurs.

> State interference in social relations becomes [he declares], in one domain after another, superfluous, and then dies out of itself; the government of persons is replaced by the administration of things, and by the conduct of processes of production. The State is not "abolished." *It dies out.*[50]

Or, as he puts it elsewhere, "the State will not be 'abolished'; it will wither away."

That the State will wither away in the last stage of history is a prime notion in the Marxist idea of human progress. Why will the State disappear? What will replace it? Godwin predicts that every man will seek, with ineffable ardor, the good of all. The Marxists have a similar conception—men will be comrades, brothers. As Bukharin says, in the society of the future there are not even contradictions between personal and social interests. "We are now dealing with a friendly brotherhood of workers *with a common plan of production.*"[51] The emphasis is on the rational

---

[47] *Positive Philosophy,* p. 835.
[48] *An Enquiry Concerning Political Justice,* I, p. 528.
[49] *Community of the Free,* p. 94.
[50] *Socialism: Utopian and Scientific,* p. 141.
[51] *Historical Materialism,* p. 41.

planning of production and therefore of social relations. Marx, Lenin, Trotsky, and Bellamy speak in similar fashion. And the *1961 Draft Program* declares that

> for all their diversity, the requirements of people will express the sound, reasonable requirements of perfectly developed persons. . . . The social economy reaches the highest stage of planned organization, and the most effective and rational use is made of the material wealth and labor reserves to meet the growing requirements of the members of society.[52]

Most writers taking the view that mankind will attain a reasonable society agree that such a society must have a rational economic basis. One expression of this is the formula, from each according to his ability, to each according to his needs.[53] Maritain, who objects to many features of the Communist program, accepts this one, but points out that it is basically a Christian idea. The "new Christendom" must extend really, and not only figuratively, he says, to human social structures, and so bring about "a veritable socio-temporal realization of the Gospels." The bourgeois axiom, *one gets nothing for nothing*, must be converted to a new social formula, *as many things as possible for nothing*. For no other condition is reasonable.[54]

For other writers, the rule of law is the rule of reason, and (social) progress is marked by the increasing rule of the former. Henry Maine, for instance, holds that the various influences operating on society have produced a general tendency in law itself, which can be defined as a transition from customary or status law to rational or contract law. Less and less are things done and actions proposed because they have always been done that way, more and more because it is reasonable to act in that way.[55] This position, however, is often opposed in the progress literature. Law is usually conceived as the repository and representative of traditional values, which are not conducive to progress. Laws must be broken for progress to occur. Maine himself concedes this. Social necessities and social opinion are always in advance of law, he says.

> We may come indefinitely near to the closing of the gap between them, but it has a perpetual tendency to reopen. Law is stable; the societies we are speaking of are progressive. The greater or less happiness of a people depends on the degree of promptitude with which the gulf is narrowed.[56]

[52] *The Program of the Communist Party of the Soviet Union (Draft), 1961,* p. 160.
[53] This is a moral principle and as such is discussed in Chapter 25.
[54] *Op. cit.,* p. 128.
[55] *Ancient Law,* Ch. 1, *passim;* see also pp. 26–9.
[56] *Ibid.,* p. 29.

C. D. Broad also conceives political progress in terms of an advance toward a society based on reasonableness. He points to "the complete absence" of a scientific psychology and sociology with which to "deliberately alter the emotional constitution of mankind, and deliberately construct more sensible forms of social organization." Such alterations doubtless constitute significant political and social progress, but the point is that effective methods of persuasion are lacking that "could arise only on the basis of a profound theoretical knowledge of the factors which produce, modify, and remove non-rational beliefs." And if these are not found in time, human society, rational or not, may be destroyed by the pure science that deals with nature and not with man.[57]

Broad agrees that a rational society is desirable, although he thinks it is not likely that it will be attained. Others point out dangers inherent in such a society. This is of course preeminently the view of such anti-progress authors as Seidenberg and Juenger, who assert that advance toward rational social control—rationality or intelligence is opposed in their conception to instinct, of which they approve—will stifle initiative and make the individual a slave to a system. But some writers who affirm progress are in full concurrence on this criticism. Henry Adams does not like the progressive rationalization of society that proceeds, he suggests, on the analogy of progressive science. And De Rougemont holds that such progress is at best ambiguous; like technology, it can be used for good or for evil; it could serve tyranny as well as freedom.

Spencer, however, among progress authors, presents what is perhaps the most thorough indictment of advance toward a rational society. He concedes that political organization may serve progress in two ways. It secures the means for cooperation and strengthens the social structure, which gives progress a more solid base; and by enlarging the social group it permits an extensive division of labor. Both developments are examples of the progressive complexification of phenomena, which is, according to him, the essence of progress. These gains are not wholly the work of government, of course, but Spencer declares that political organization based on reason contributes largely to their accomplishment.

But there are liabilities, too. Unchangeableness of structures is a concomitant of arrested growth, he asserts, calling on a biological principle to support his contention that too much organization can stifle continuing progress and development. Political organization may tend toward a

[57] *The Mind and Its Place in Nature*, pp. 662–6. Opposed to Broad are, on the one hand, those who maintain that we do in fact have more than the beginnings of scientific sociology—such as Skinner—and, on the other hand, those who suggest the possibility that some kind of mass psychoanalysis might bring about real progress—such as N. O. Brown and Marcuse. However, most neo-Freudians are not enthusiastic about societies supposed to be built on "reason."

static persistence of forms that resist change, that cling to the past, and that hinder even new forms of cooperation and new departures in specialization of function. Moreover, a rational society, Spencer declares, is too expensive. Political regulation and planning cost more than they are really worth. Finally, political organization hinders progress by inhibiting individual initiative. Reason acts coercively on invention and tends to produce a society where status is fixed. In effect, it stops the movement toward greater complexification at a certain level and allows it to go no farther. But that, of course, is to stop progress itself.[58]

Spencer's "liberal" position is taken by many of his contemporaries. We have noted that Maine decries the tendency of law to solidify and hence to impede progress. Bagehot insists on the same point. Even a society based on reason is likely, he says, to become customary and traditional, at which point free discussion must be allowed to "break it open" again. And Buckle is almost contemptuous of the idea that any society can ever be reasonable enough not to require change. Furthermore, the changes must be imposed, as it were, from without. "No great political improvement," he says, "no great reform, either legislative or executive, has ever been originated in any country by its rulers." The perfect positive state is a pure fiction, and the worst possible thing would be to obey Comte's restrictions against free discussion and criticism. In fact,

> the first suggesters of improvements have invariably been bold and able thinkers, who discern the abuse, denounce it, and point out how it is to be remedied. At length, if circumstances are favourable, the pressure from without becomes so strong, that the government is obliged to give way; and, the reform being accomplished, the people are expected to admire the wisdom of their rulers, by whom all this has been done.[59]

Comte might reply that Buckle's criticism applies only to imperfect societies; they must, indeed, make provision for improvement, and Buckle's methods are probably effectual. In the positive state, Comte would insist, there is no room for improvement. Any change would be for the worse. Buckle's reply, in turn, would be to the effect that no society is ever perfect. Their ideas of political freedom differ, as will be seen, and this is perhaps enough to account for their difference in views.

The above is no more than a sketch of some of the opinions of progress authors regarding political progress toward a more reasonable society. Many other names might be mentioned in this connection—Hegel, Augustine, St. Pierre, the authors of the U.S. Constitution and of the U.N.

---

[58] *Principles of Sociology*, Sections 340 ff.
[59] *History of Civilization in England*, pp. 272–3.

Charter, Saint-Simon, Locke—the list is long. For what is being considered here is, in fact, an age-old dream of man. And on the other hand, the idea that a reasonable society might turn into a tyranny all the more effective for its rational basis has been a philosophical nightmare for an equally long time.

23

Political Progress: II

PROGRESS TOWARD EQUALITY

O ur hopes for the future condition of the human race can be sub-
sumed under three important heads," says Condorcet:

the abolition of inequality between nations, the progress of equality within
each nation, and the true perfection of mankind.[1]

With regard to the abolition of inequality between nations, Condorcet
feels that increased facility of communication among them, partly as the
result of the advance of science and partly as the result of ever widening
commercial activities, will insure that the more backward nations will soon
catch up to those that have already attained a measure of progress. Indeed, "the progress of these [less progressive] peoples is likely to be
more rapid and certain than our own because they can receive from us
everything that we have had to find out for ourselves."[2]

The time will therefore come when the sun will shine only on free men
who know no other master but their reason; when tyrants and slaves, priests
and their stupid or hypocritical instruments will exist only in works of his-

[1] *Sketch of an Historical Picture of the Progress of the Human Mind*, p. 173.
[2] *Ibid.*, p. 178.

tory and on the stage; and when we shall think of them only to pity their victims and their dupes; to maintain ourselves in a state of vigilance by thinking on their excesses; and to learn how to recognize and so to destroy, by force of reason, the first seeds of tyranny and superstition, should they ever dare to reappear among us.[3]

With regard to the progress of equality within each nation, Condorcet asserts that the differences that exist between individuals have three main causes:

inequality in wealth; inequality in status between the man whose means of subsistence are hereditary and the man whose means are dependent on the length of his life, or, rather, on that part of his life in which he is capable of work; and, finally, inequality in education.[4]

"It is easy to prove," says Condorcet, "that wealth has a natural tendency to equality."[5] Since this is true, all that is needed to attack the first cause of inequality between individuals is to insure that no artificial barriers are allowed to impede its natural movement. This is a fairly simple matter; it is a question of improving the body of civil laws having to do with the economic and financial activities of citizens.

The second cause of inequality—inequality in status—is overcome with more difficulty. The laborer must provide his family "what is rather like a life annuity, save that it is more dependent on chance; and in consequence there is a very real difference between people living like this and those whose resources are not at all subject to the same risks, who live either on revenue from land, or on the interest on capital which is almost independent of their own labour."

Here then is a necessary cause of inequality, of dependence and even of misery, which ceaselessly threatens the most numerous and most active class in our society.[6]

The real problem is the insecurity of life of this class of people. Condorcet suggests several solutions. One is a system of social insurance that will guarantee old people a means of livelihood, will provide funds for widows and orphans, and will give young people sufficient capital to make a good start in life. The system will be based on actuarial and social statistics.

It is to the application of the calculus to the probabilities of life and the investment of money that we owe the idea of these methods which have al-

[3] *Ibid.*, p. 179.
[4] *Ibid.*
[5] *Ibid.*, p. 180.
[6] *Ibid.*, p. 181.

ready been successful, although they have not been applied in a sufficiently comprehensive and exhaustive fashion to render them really useful, not merely to a few individuals, but to society as a whole, by making it possible to prevent those periodic disasters which strike at so many families and which are such a recurrent source of misery and suffering.[7]

This arrangement for social security will be initiated by the state, but Condorcet feels certain that if it is operated on sound mathematical and financial principles it will produce more wealth than it uses. It will pay for itself at the same time that it relieves much misery.

Also helping to solve the problem, according to Condorcet, will be the establishment of private rather than public insurance companies. These, "the work of private associations . . . will be formed without any real risk, once the principles for the proper working of these schemes have been widely diffused." He foresees a time, too, when credit will cease to be the exclusive privilege of wealth, and when industrial and commercial activities will be made more independent of "the existence of the great capitalists."[8] All of these suggestions not only should be, but will be, put into effect—as many of them have been, in fact, in the nearly two centuries since the publication of Condorcet's book.

The third cause of social inequality is inequality of education. Condorcet does not expect all men to be educated equally, but he does not consider this necessary. The degree of equality in education that "we can reasonably hope to attain, but that should be adequate, is that which excludes all dependence, either forced or voluntary."[9] This condition can be "easily" attained even by those who can study for only a few years in their childhood, and in their few hours of leisure thereafter.

By a suitable choice of syllabus and of methods of education, we can teach the citizen everything that he needs to know in order to be able to manage his household, administer his affairs and employ his labour and his faculties in freedom; to know his rights and to be able to exercise them; to be acquainted with his duties and fulfil them satisfactorily; to judge his own and other men's actions according to his own lights and to be stranger to none of the high and delicate feelings which honour human nature; not to be in a state of blind dependence upon those to whom he must entrust his affairs or the exercise of his rights; to be in a proper condition to choose and supervise them; to be no longer the dupe of those popular errors which torment man with superstitious fears and chimerical hopes; to defend himself against prejudice by the strength of his reason alone; and, finally, to escape the deceits of charlatans who would lay snares for his fortune, his

[7] *Ibid.*
[8] *Ibid.*, pp. 181–2.
[9] *Ibid.*, p. 182.

health, his freedom of thought and his conscience under the pretext of granting him health, wealth and salvation.[10]

With such an educational system in effect, the inhabitants of a country will no longer be distinguished by their use of language and by other social and cultural signs. Above all, they will be able to govern themselves, they will have more than merely a "mechanical knowledge" of the procedures of art, science, industry, and business, and they will no longer have to depend for every trivial affair on "clever men who rule over them in virtue of their necessary superiority." And so, Condorcet says, "they will attain a real equality."[11]

The various causes of inequality do not act in isolation, nor do those of equality;

> they unite, combine and support each other and so their cumulative effects are stronger, surer and more constant. With greater equality of education there will be greater equality in industry and so in wealth; equality in wealth necessarily leads to equality in education; and equality between the nations and equality within a single nation are mutually dependent.[12]

"Then the social art will have fulfilled its aim," says Condorcet, "that of assuring and extending to all men enjoyment of the common right to which they are called by nature." And that is not all.

> The real advantages that should result from this progress [toward equality], of which we can entertain a hope that is almost a certainty, can have no other term than that of the absolute perfection of the human race.[13]

Condorcet sees a general historical tendency toward greater equality, but his main concern, perhaps, is with the future; progress is not contingent, but the greatest achievements of the race are nevertheless still to come, and depend to some extent at least on actions taken now. Tocqueville, although he concurs in these points, subtly shifts the emphasis on each of them. He writes:

> It is evident to all alike that a great democratic revolution is going on among us, but all do not look at it in the same light. To some it appears to be novel but accidental, and, as such, they hope it may still be checked; to others it seems irresistible, because it is the most uniform, the most ancient and the most permanent tendency that is to be found in history.[14]

10 *Ibid.*
11 *Ibid.*, p. 183. These remarks of Condorcet constitute one of the most enthusiastic recommendations of education to be found in the progress literature. As such, they might have also been considered in Chapter 19.
12 *Ibid.*, pp. 183–4.
13 *Ibid.*, p. 184.
14 *Democracy in America*, Vol. I, "Author's Introduction," p. 3.

Tocqueville belongs in the latter class. The history of his own country shows "scarcely a single great event of the last seven hundred years that has not promoted equality of condition," he says.[15] Nor is this, he finds, peculiar to France. Wherever we look, we perceive the same revolution going on.

> The various occurrences of national existence have everywhere turned to the advantage of democracy: all men have aided it by their exertions, both those who have intentionally labored in its cause and those who have served it unwittingly; those who have fought for it and even those who have declared themselves its opponents have all been driven along in the same direction, have all labored to one end; some unknowingly and some despite themselves, all have been blind instruments in the hands of God.[16]

"The gradual development of the principle of equality is, therefore," Tocqueville says, "a providential fact. It has all the chief characteristics of such a fact: it is universal, it is lasting, it constantly eludes all human interference, and all events as well as men contribute to its progress."[17]

This great "primary fact" of history was brought to Tocqueville's attention by his studies of America. Nothing struck him more forcibly during his stay in the United States, he says, "than the general equality of condition among the people." The influence of this characteristic of the Americans extends far beyond the politics and laws of the country. It has no less effect on civil society than on the government. "It creates opinions, gives birth to new sentiments, founds novel customs, and modifies whatever it does not produce." Indeed,

> the more I advanced in the study of American society the more I perceived that this equality of condition is the fundamental fact from which all others seem to be derived and the central point at which all my observations constantly terminated.[18]

This being so, what is the relevance to the future of mankind? Tocqueville is struck by "a kind of religious awe produced . . . by the view of that irresistible revolution which has advanced for centuries in spite of every obstacle and which is still advancing in the midst of the ruins it has caused."[19] Nevertheless, he cannot answer the question, whither are we tending? For "the magnitude of what already has been done pre-

[15] *Ibid.*, p. 5.
[16] *Ibid.*, p. 6.
[17] *Ibid.*
[18] *Ibid.*, p. 3.
[19] *Ibid.*, p. 7.

vents us from foreseeing what is yet to be accomplished."[20] In this regard Tocqueville differs sharply from Condorcet.

He is certain of two things: first, that the advance is irresistible; second, that

> if the men of our time should be convinced, by attentive observation and sincere reflection, that the gradual and progressive development of social equality is at once the past and the future of their history, this discovery alone would confer upon the change the sacred character of a divine decree.[21]

But he has an almost equal uncertainty—and here he departs farthest from the view of Condorcet—as to whether he approves the change. There is no question that Condorcet believes that future progress toward equality will be a change for the better. But Tocqueville's conviction that, "sooner or later, we shall arrive, like the Americans, at an almost complete equality of condition,"[22] fills him with misgivings. He writes at the end of his work:

> When I survey this countless multitude of beings shaped in each other's likeness, amid whom nothing rises and nothing falls, the sight of such universal uniformity saddens and chills me and I am tempted to regret that state of society which has ceased to be.[23]

The world that Tocqueville had known, the death knell of which had already sounded, was "full of men of great importance and extreme insignificance, of great wealth and extreme poverty, of great learning and extreme ignorance." He does not approve that vanishing world; nevertheless, he regrets its passing. He is not certain that the new equality will be better—or even as good. But he concedes that he cannot see with the eye of the Almighty, "whose gaze necessarily includes the whole of created things and who surveys distinctly, though all at once, mankind and man."

> We may naturally believe that it is not the singular prosperity of the few, but the greater well-being of all that is most pleasing in the sight of the Creator and Preserver of men. What appears to me to be man's decline is, to His eye, advancement; what afflicts me is acceptable to Him. A state of equality is perhaps less elevated, but it is more just: and its justice constitutes its greatness and its beauty. I would strive, then, to raise myself to this point of the divine contemplation and thence to view and to judge the concerns of men.[24]

20 *Ibid.*
21 *Ibid.*
22 *Ibid.*, p. 14.
23 *Ibid.*, Vol. II, p. 350.
24 *Ibid.*, p. 351.

Tocqueville is saying that the advance toward equality, which is the primary fact of history, is not necessarily progress. He declares that it is impossible to say that the change is for the better in the most general sense. "No man on the earth can as yet affirm," he asserts, "absolutely and generally, that the new state of the world is better than its former one; but it is already easy to perceive that this state is different."[25] The advance of man toward greater equality is necessary: "the nations of our time cannot prevent the conditions of men from becoming equal."[26] But there is much that men can do, in the way of knowing and of acting, to insure that this development is real progress, and not regress, for the human race. "It depends upon themselves whether the principle of equality is to lead them to servitude or freedom, to knowledge or barbarism, to prosperity or wretchedness."[27]

Condorcet and Tocqueville hold that advance toward equality is a characteristic of man's history, and that this advance is allied with progress. Others concur on the second point, but not on the first. According to J. B. Bury, Proudhon held that progress depends on the energy of individuals, that liberty is a condition of its advance, "and that the end to be kept in view is the establishment of justice, which means equality."[28] This is to say that progress depends upon, and to some extent consists in, the increase of equality among men, but it is not to say that equality will necessarily increase.

A similar point is made by Henry George, who compares society to a boat.

[25] *Ibid.*

[26] *Ibid.*, p. 352.

[27] *Ibid.* Like Condorcet, Tocqueville holds that education can be an aid in averting the possible ill effects of increasing equality. "The first of the duties that are at this time imposed upon those who direct our affairs," he writes, "is to educate democracy, to reawaken, if possible, its religious beliefs; to purify its morals; to mold its actions; to substitute a knowledge of statecraft for its inexperience, and an awareness of its true interest for its blind instincts, to adapt its government to time and place, and to modify it according to men and to conditions. A new science of politics is needed for a new world" (*ibid.*, I, p. 7). Condorcet would agree with most of this, probably, but he would not concur in holding that religious beliefs ought to be reawakened.

[28] J. B. Bury, *The Idea of Progress*, p. 317. Bury quotes Proudhon as saying: "What dominates in all my studies, what forms their beginning and end, their summit and their base, their reason, what makes my originality as a thinker (if I have any), is that I affirm Progress resolutely, irrevocably, and everywhere, and deny the Absolute. All that I have ever written, all I have denied or affirmed, I have written, denied or affirmed in the name of one unique idea, Progress. My adversaries, on the other hand, are all partisans of the Absolute, *in omni genere, casu, et numero,* to use the phrase of Sganarelle" (*ibid.*, pp. 317–8).

Bury also analyzes the views of Leroux, a French Socialist who seems to affirm progress toward equality. See p. 319.

Her progress through the water will not depend upon the exertion of her crew, but upon the exertion devoted to propelling her. This will be lessened by any expenditure of force required for bailing, or any expenditure of force in fighting among themselves, or in pulling in different directions.[29]

What, then, are the conditions under which men may pull together and advance the social boat, which is to say, progress? They are, says George, two: association and equality.

Improvement becomes possible as men come together in peaceful association, and the wider and closer the association, the greater the possibilities of improvement. And as the wasteful expenditure of mental power in conflict becomes greater or less as the moral law which accords to each an equality of rights is ignored or is recognized, equality (or justice) is the second essential of progress.[30]

"Thus association in equality is the law of progress," George goes on to declare. "Association frees mental power for expenditure in improvement, and equality, or justice, or freedom—for the terms here signify the same thing, the recognition of the moral law—prevents the dissipation of this power in fruitless struggles." And he adds that inequality of conditions or of power tends to lessen the tendency toward progress, and can even reverse it.[31]

Not all progress authors hold that mankind is progressing in equality, nor, even if equality is increasing among men, that this is a desirable development. Saint-Simon, for instance, along with his followers, the so-called Children of Saint-Simon, maintains that the doctrine of equality of the eighteenth-century *philosophes* is a notoriously ignorant misreading not only of the facts of history but also of the facts of physiology. Actually, these writers insist, there are three distinct and quite different types of men: the brain type, sometimes called the Aristotelian type; the motor type; and the feeling type, sometimes called the Platonic type. The capacity of the first type is intellectual; they will be the scientists of the new world. The capacity of the second is manual only; they will be the laborers. And the capacity of the third is emotional or "sentimental"; they will be the artists, the poets, the religious leaders, and the ethical teachers.

Progress, according to the Saint-Simonians, is a natural phenomenon; it consists in advance toward a society that is based on, and congruent to,

29 *Progress and Poverty*, p. 508.
30 *Ibid.*
31 *Ibid.*

what is natural in man. Equality is not natural, because of the fundamental differences between men; therefore the ideal society of the future,
toward which progress inevitably tends, will be marked by social inequality. It will be a harmonious association of men fundamentally dissimilar, organized in three natural classes. It will be above all harmonious,
for men naturally desire not equality but the expression of their intrinsic
and immutable—and different—physiological aptitudes. Inequality in the
social hierarchy is thus beneficent and desirable. In fact, it is inconceivable that men could be happy unless society reflected, and was organized
according to, their natural inequality.[32]

> Our religion does not stifle liberty, it does not absorb sacred personality. It
> holds each individual to be saintly and sacred. Since it promises classification
> according to capacity, does this not guarantee each man the preservation and
> development of his own native physiognomy, his own particular aptitude,
> under a name which belongs only to him?[33]

An example of the application of this rule is the Saint-Simonian attitude toward communistic schemes of property.

> We must foresee that some people will confound this system with what is
> known under the name of *community of goods*. There is nevertheless no
> relationship between them. In the social organization of the future each
> one . . . will find himself *classified* in accordance with his capacity, re-
> warded in accordance with his work; this should sufficiently indicate the
> inequality of the division.[34]

Comte does not accept many elements of the Saint-Simonian idea of
progress, but he agrees that equality is not desirable, and that social progress is in the direction of inequality. In discussing the "metaphysical
polity," he describes some of the dogmas that mark it, and that must be
overcome when the "positive polity" is finally established.

> The dogma which ranks next in importance to that of free inquiry is that
> of Equality; and in the same way, it is taken to be absolute when it is only
> relative, and permanent, while it expresses merely the position of minds
> employed in breaking up the old system.[35]

The dogma of equality helped to overthrow the old polities, says Comte,
but it is an obstacle to progress toward the positive state. The latter is

---

[32] These remarks are to a large extent drawn from Manuel's discussion of Saint-
Simon in *The Prophets of Paris*, pp. 124–9. Manuel observes that the Saint-Simonians
opposed their idea of social "organicism" to that of social equality.
[33] Père Barrault, a Child of Saint-Simon, qu. in Manuel, p. 176.
[34] *Doctrine de Saint-Simon*, qu. in Manuel, *ibid.*
[35] *Positive Philosophy*, p. 411.

based on the natural intellectual and moral differences between men, and it would be threatened by the dogma of equality if this were allowed to continue to hold sway. In fact, the progress of civilization tends to increase these differences (at the same time that it tends to decrease physical differences—here Comte is in opposition to the Saint-Simonians), so the dogma of equality will become more and more inimical to progress. Finally, it becomes "anarchical, and directly hostile to its original destination."[36]

Fortunately, there will be no place for equality in the positive state—or rather, there will be no place for artificial inequality. Men endowed with superior moral and intellectual capacities will undertake the tasks to which they are uniquely fitted, and the inferior will find their social and political niche as well. Comte is impatient with proponents of the idea of political liberty. True freedom consists in obedience to the exigencies of nature, and that will be the mark of the positive society.[37]

John C. Calhoun is another who holds that the tendency toward greater equality is inimical to progress. "To . . . make equality of condition essential to liberty would be to destroy both liberty and progress," he declares.

> The reason is that inequality of condition, while it is a necessary consequence of liberty, is, at the same time, indispensable to progress. In order to understand why this is so, it is necessary to bear in mind that the main-spring to progress is the desire of individuals to better their condition. . . . It is, indeed, this inequality of condition between the front and rear ranks, in the march of progress, which gives so strong an impulse to the former to maintain their position and to the latter to press forward into their files. This gives to progress its greatest impulse.[38]

C. G. Darwin does not seem to prefer inequality, but he nevertheless holds that the future will be marked by inequality rather than equality. The reason is the basic facts and exigencies of life. For instance, Darwin writes, "it is quite safe to say" that there will always be rich and poor.

> Wealth will be the mark of success, so the abler people will tend to be found among the wealthy, but there will always be many among them of a far less estimable character. These are the people who are interested not in the work, but only in the reward, and they will all too often succeed in gaining it in a variety of discreditable ways, such as by currying favour with an autocrat.[39]

---

36 *Ibid.*, p. 412.
37 For Comte's idea of collective freedom, see below, pp. 414–5.
38 "A Disquisition on Government," in *The People Shall Judge*, Vol. I, p. 686. W. G. Sumner holds similar views; see his "The Challenge of Facts," in *ibid.*, Vol. II, pp. 83–91.
39 *The Next Million Years*, p. 138.

Furthermore, future communities will have to live on their "real earnings," which means that their standard of living will be comparatively low. The threat of frequent starvation will operate with special force against the least efficient members of society. As a result, "in the long run it is inevitable that the lower types of labour will have an exceedingly precarious life." Indeed, it will be worse than precarious.

> One of the triumphs of our own golden age has been that slavery has been abolished over a great part of the earth. It is difficult to see how this condition can be maintained in the hard world of the future with its starving margins, and it is to be feared that all too often a fraction of humanity will have to live in a state which, whatever it may be called, will be indistinguishable from slavery.[40]

The idea that the future will see the return of slavery is in direct opposition to the view of almost all authors who affirm political progress. Even Comte and the Saint-Simonians would blanch at it; despite their belief that the future will be marked by inequality, they hold that no one will be forced to be what he does not want to be.

PROGRESS IN OR TOWARD FREEDOM

Many progress authors discuss progress in, or toward, freedom; this is a favorite topic in the literature. However, anyone conversant with the literature of freedom will not be surprised to learn that they hold different notions of what freedom is, and therefore of what it means to make progress in or toward it.

In order to understand the relation between progress and freedom, it is necessary to distinguish the kinds of freedom that progress authors are talking about. This can be done by following M. J. Adler's scheme, as it is developed in *The Idea of Freedom*. We can then analyze our authors' views according to a similar scheme.

Adler finds that five different kinds or types of freedom are discussed in the literature of freedom. All are relevant to progress. They are, following Adler's terminology:

1. *Circumstantial freedom*, which is possessed by any individual who, under favorable circumstances, is able to act as he wishes for his own good as he sees it.

2. *Acquired freedom*, which is possessed only by those men who, through acquired wisdom or virtue, are able to will or live as they ought in conformity to the moral law or an ideal befitting human nature.

[40] *Ibid.*, p. 139.

3. *Natural freedom,* which is possessed by all men, in virtue of a power inherent in human nature, whereby a man is able to change his own character creatively by deciding for himself what he shall do or shall become.

4. *Political liberty,* which is a freedom possessed only by citizens who, through the right of suffrage and the right of juridical appeal against the abuses of government, are able to participate in making the positive law under which they live and to alter the political institutions of their society.[41]

5. *Collective freedom,* which is a freedom that will be possessed by humanity or the human race in the future when, through the social use of the knowledge of both natural and social necessities, men achieve the ideal mode of association that is the goal of mankind's development and are able to direct their communal life in accordance with such necessities.[42]

Very roughly, progress authors affirm progress *in* circumstantial freedom, *in* acquired freedom, and *in* political liberty. They affirm progress *toward* collective freedom. And they conceive natural freedom to be a condition of progress in other respects.

PROGRESS AND NATURAL FREEDOM

Natural freedom is more or less the equivalent of "free will." There is, of course, a dispute in the freedom literature as to whether the will is actually free. But authors disagree on the point whether *man* has free will or not, not whether *some men* have it or not. Hence, there can be no progress in natural freedom simply.[43]

However, natural freedom—man's free will—is considered to be an important prerequisite of progress by several writers. Dobzhansky, for instance, argues that evolution is of two kinds. One kind is organic or biological evolution; this, man shares with all living species. The other is cultural evolution and is unique to man. Organic evolution occurs in the genes. Culture, the exclusive property of man, is transmitted by

[41] This freedom is a variant of circumstantial freedom. Circumstances—especially the political circumstances in which an individual finds himself—are essential to it. However, individuals who are not citizens of states enjoying political liberty may still possess circumstantial freedom. They cannot govern themselves in the sense of political liberty, but they may still be able to do as they please.

[42] This freedom is a variant of acquired freedom. It is acquired; but it differs in that it is not acquired by an individual but by the human race as a whole.

[43] It might be said that at some epoch man did not have natural freedom—"free will"—but that at a later epoch he gained it. This might constitute an affirmation of progress. If so, it would probably involve a change in human nature.

"instruction, precept, imitation, and learning." The two kinds of evolution are of course interrelated. But they are also distinct. Organic evolution goes on to a large extent—perhaps totally—outside of man's awareness. It is, in a sense, the domain of necessity. Cultural evolution, on the contrary, is the domain of freedom.

> Biological evolution has produced the genetic basis which made the new, specifically human, phase of the evolutionary process possible. But this new evolution, which involves culture, occurs according to its own laws, which are not deducible, from, although also not contrary to, biological laws. *The ability of man to choose freely between ideas and acts is one of the most fundamental characteristics of human evolution.* Perhaps freedom is even the most important of all the specifically human attributes.[44]

Maritain also sees a relation between natural freedom and progress. Progress is "an essential impulse of human nature," he says, "but is in itself a work of our spirit and our freedom acting in co-operation with nature."[45] History and progress are not

> fixed in advance by evolution; rather [they depend] on an enormous mass of accumulated necessities and fatalities, but one in which the interventions of . . . freedom can take effect; [they are] only fixed in advance in the degree . . . to which man renounces his own freedom.[46]

Indeed, all those authors who hold that progress is contingent are saying implicitly, if they do not say explicitly, that natural freedom underlies progress. For the main contingency on which progress depends is human freedom, the freedom to choose to progress or not to progress. However, even if progress is held to be necessary, this does not mean that natural freedom is not involved in it. Kant, Guizot, Herder, and others attempt to maintain freedom in this sense in the context of affirmations of the necessity of progress.

PROGRESS IN CIRCUMSTANTIAL FREEDOM

Bagehot, in discussing the concept he calls "verifiable progress"—progress that every sensible person would agree has occurred—asks us to con-

---

[44] *The Biological Basis of Human Freedom*, p. 134. Emphasis added. Dobzhansky quotes G. G. Simpson as saying that "the old evolution was and is essentially amoral. The new evolution involves knowledge, including the knowledge of good and evil" (*ibid.*, p. 135).

[45] *True Humanism*, p. 88.

[46] *Ibid.*, p. 124.

sider the difference between a village of English colonists and the tribe of natives who roam about them.

> Indisputably in one, and that a main, sense they are superior. They can beat the Australians in war when they like; they can take from them anything they like, and kill any of them they choose.[47]

This difference, which signifies other things as well (e.g., progress in knowledge, technological progress, etc.), also represents progress in circumstantial freedom. The colonists have more freedom than the natives, for they can do what they like, while the tribesmen cannot. The means at their disposal are greater, and these enabling means increase their freedom.

The occurrence of this type of progress in freedom is recognized by many writers. Probably nearly every progress author who affirms the occurrence of technological progress (and that is nearly all of them) also affirms, perhaps implicitly, progress in circumstantial freedom for at least some human beings.

However, the assertion that technology *advances* does not necessarily imply an affirmation of progress in freedom in this sense. Juenger and Seidenberg, for example, concede technological advance, and they even term it, ironically, "progress"; but they view it as inhibiting, rather than enlarging, circumstantial freedom. We have treated their position as a denial of progress. Some who affirm progress raise the same point.

De Rougemont, for instance, holds that the ambiguity of progress is its prime characteristic. He speaks of the "ambivalent character of all progress," of the "ideal of personal progress, the *ambiguous* enlargement of man's powers over himself and over the cosmos in which he exists," and of the idea of progress as combining with the idea of an "enlargement of the human hazard."[48] What De Rougemont seems to mean is that the increase of circumstantial freedom that accompanies technological progress is itself ambiguous and ambivalent. Simply, it can be used for good or for ill. But there is also implied a notion of increasing responsibility that goes along with increasing freedom. The idea of freedom, for De Rougemont, includes more than just circumstantial freedom. It also includes a notion of responsibility to natural, civil, and moral law.[49] The more circumstantial freedom one has, he is saying, the more complicated one's freedom becomes. Juenger and Seidenberg, denying progress, hold that technological advance really decreases our freedom of action, our circumstantial freedom. De Rougemont does not say that. But he declares that in a sense

---

[47] *Physics and Politics*, pp. 150–1.
[48] *Man's Western Quest*, pp. 156, 169, 171.
[49] That is, a notion of acquired freedom.

it is true that the more freedom of action we have, the more we are hedged in by considerations of what ought to be done—and what ought not to be done. To return to Bagehot's example, the English colonists cannot really kill any of the natives they choose, De Rougemont is saying. The situation is not as simple as that.

Mumford points to another limitation on the progress in circumstantial freedom that attends technological progress. Arguing against any "official system of inspecting armaments," he asserts that

> only in an open world, where every nook and corner is exposed to the curiosity of the chance visitor, where every citizen may be freely heard if he raises his voice, can mankind sleep safely, even supposing that it has achieved a firm basis for coexistence between governments now hostile to each other.[50]

In a sense, Mumford implies, no one really has circumstantial freedom unless all have it.[51] Rather, there are two types of circumstantial freedom, one of which increases as technological progress occurs, the other of which increases as the world advances in the direction of "openness." The one does not follow necessarily from the other. Hence the progress in circumstantial freedom that is dependent on technological progress is ambivalent.

The type of circumstantial freedom that is signified, for Mumford, by an open world is discussed by many authors. They conceive increase in freedom of speech, of investigation, of inquiry, of research to be the major component of progress in circumstantial freedom, which they consider to be the condition of other sorts of progress.

Lord Acton, for instance, holds that the "constancy of progress, of progress in the direction of organized and assured freedom, is the characteristic fact of modern history, and its tribute to the theory of Providence," and that "achieved liberty is the one ethical result that rests on the converging and combined conditions of advancing civilization."[52] The new world is distinguished from the old, Acton says, by

> the universal spirit of investigation and discovery which did not cease to operate, and withstood the recurring efforts of reaction, until, by the advent of the reign of general ideas which we call the Revolution, it at length prevailed. This successive deliverance and gradual passage, for good and evil, from subordination to independence is a phenomenon of primary importance.[53]

[50] *The Transformations of Man,* p. 156.
[51] This is not, however, collective freedom.
[52] *Essays on Freedom and Power,* pp. 35–6.
[53] *Ibid.,* pp. 27–8.

For Acton, too, progress in this type of freedom is ambivalent; it is a phenomenon that is for good and for ill; he shares with De Rougemont a notion of the responsibilities that attend increasing liberty. Nevertheless, progress in this sense is not to be doubted, Acton is saying.

Guizot has a similar notion. Discussing a particular historical period, the Reformation, he speaks in terms that are applicable, as he elsewhere indicates, to all periods, though in lesser degree.

> It is evident . . . simply from the consideration of the state of the human intelligence at this period, and of the power which then governed it, that the Reformation must have been . . . a sudden effort made by the human mind to achieve its liberty, a great insurrection of human intelligence. This, doubtless, was the leading cause of the Reformation, the cause which soared above all the rest; a cause superior to every interest either of sovereigns or of nations, superior to the need of reform properly so called, or of the redress of the grievances which were complained of at this period.[54]

The human mind, in attempting to free itself from the shackles of error, ignorance, and superstition, brings about great social and political advances that are properly called progress. It is in the very nature of the mind to attempt this, and to grow in this type of freedom.[55]

We have seen how much Comte disapproves of this sort of advance— he does not call it progress at all—in the direction of freedom of inquiry. The Marxists concur in this judgment, as our discussion of collective freedom will show. But one does not have to be a Marxist or a Comtian to maintain that the increase of circumstantial freedom, either in the sense of the increase of enabling means of action or in the sense of free inquiry and expression, is not progress in itself. Moore, for example, using the word "progress" in two ways, meaning first technological advance, second "advance in the prerequisites of freedom," questions whether "technological advance with all its consequences implies movement toward freedom." And he declares that

> it is doubtful that there has been any trend toward greater freedom in the course of human history. The most that the facts allow us to assert with

---

[54] *History of Civilization in Europe*, p. 328.

[55] This is a commonplace of the eighteenth and early nineteenth centuries. Buckle is a spokesman for the view. Some modern authors also hold it. For instance, Herbert J. Muller says that "a person is free to the extent that he has the capacity, the opportunity, and the incentive to give expression to what is in him and to develop his potentialities." Knowledge, science, and the humanities did not progress during the Middle Ages, Muller declares, because men were not free in this sense. "Faith remained primary; reason could never openly question the fundamentals of faith, its main business was always to support faith." However, the Renaissance was "plainly a movement toward intellectual and imaginative freedom, and effected a lasting emancipation of mind and spirit" (*Freedom in the Western World*, pp. 37–9).

any confidence is an advance in important prerequisites of freedom, through the elimination of the necessity for hunger, disease, and toil.[56]

What another writer might call (circumstantial) freedom is thus, for Moore, not freedom at all, but merely a condition of it. Hence there is no progress in freedom in this sense. There is, nonetheless, progress in the prerequisites of freedom.[57]

PROGRESS IN POLITICAL LIBERTY

Political liberty is given a limited meaning in *The Idea of Freedom.* The term refers only to the kind of liberty possessed by a citizen insofar as he participates in his government, and especially in making or approving the laws under which he lives. This kind of freedom is carefully distinguished from both circumstantial and acquired freedom. On the one hand, political liberty, although circumstantial, differs from circumstantial freedom in that it is possessed *only* by those who participate in their government. On the other hand, it differs from acquired freedom (even though it may in fact be acquired—otherwise there could be no progress in it) in that participation in government constitutes an additional freedom beyond that of obeying just laws. One may possess acquired freedom—"spiritual liberty," or "moral freedom," as it is sometimes called—without participating in making the laws under which one lives. For example, a man may possess acquired freedom in a benevolent despotism, but he could never possess political liberty there.

In *The Science of Right*, Kant shows why (in his day) the suffrage must be limited to those who are qualified for "active citizenship." This "presupposes," Kant says, "the independence or self-sufficiency of the individual citizen among the people," a qualification which all cannot meet. In contrast, the majority of citizens have mere "passive citizenship."

> The apprentice or a merchant or tradesman, a servant who is not in the employ of the state, a minor . . . all women, and generally everyone who is compelled to maintain himself not according to his own industry, but as it is arranged by others (the state excepted), are without civil personality, and their existence is only, as it were, incidentally included in the state.[58]

Passive citizens do not possess political liberty; but, says Kant, they will have it in the future. They have a right to claim

[56] "On the Notions of Progress, Revolution, and Freedom," in *Ethics,* January 1962, p. 107.
[57] Moore's idea of freedom may be closer to that of acquired freedom.
[58] *The Science of Right,* in GBWW, Vol. 42, p. 437.

that whatever be the mode in which the positive laws are enacted, these
laws must not be contrary to the natural laws that demand the freedom of
all the people and the equality that is conformable thereto; and it must
therefore be made possible for them to raise themselves from this passive
condition in the state to the condition of active citizenship.[59]

Kant envisages a progressive amelioration of society and with it the
progressive extension of the suffrage to all its members. As we know from
his *Universal History*, he looks forward to a time when all men necessarily
will enjoy—because it is in the nature of history that they will do so—
the political liberty of active citizenship which (in his day) is confined
to a few.

Maritain's idea of political liberty differs subtly from Kant's, as is indicated in *The Idea of Freedom*.[60] From the point of view of the idea of
progress, the differences are less important than the similarities. The
major difference between the two authors is this: Kant sees progress in
political liberty as necessary and inevitable; Maritain sees it as contingent on man's willingness to bring it about. For Maritain, this sort of
progress is far from inevitable.

For Tocqueville, the prime constituent of political progress is advance toward equality. This includes the notion of an increasing participation of all citizens in their government. "Gradually the distinctions of
rank are done away with," he says; "the barriers that once severed mankind are falling; property is divided, power is shared by many, the light
of intelligence spreads, and the capacities of all classes tend towards
equality. Society becomes democratic, and the empire of democracy is
slowly and peaceably introduced into institutions and customs."

> I can conceive of a society in which all men would feel an equal love and
> respect for the laws of which they consider themselves the authors; in which
> the authority of government would be respected as necessary, and not divine;
> and in which the loyalty of the subject to the chief magistrate would not be
> a passion, but a quiet and rational persuasion. With every individual in
> possession of the rights which he is sure to retain, a kind of manly confi-
> dence and reciprocal courtesy would arise between all classes, removed alike
> from pride and servility. The people, well acquainted with their own true
> interests, would understand that, in order to profit from the advantages of
> the state, it is necessary to satisfy its requirements. The voluntary association
> of the citizens might then take the place of the individual authority of the
> nobles, and the community would be protected from tyranny and license.[61]

If such a society of all men is achieved, it will of course represent progress in political liberty. The only question, therefore, is whether it will be

[59] *Ibid.*
[60] See Vol. I, pp. 343–4.
[61] *Democracy in America*, Vol. I, pp. 9–10.

achieved. Tocqueville is not as certain of this as he is certain of the advance toward equality. The latter is the tendency of history, but it may not result in the society described in the passage just quoted. Hence, for Tocqueville, as for Maritain, progress in political liberty is contingent. It mainly depends, it seems, on education; all citizens cannot intelligently participate in their own government unless they are instructed in their rights, duties, and civic and social responsibilities.

Bagehot and J. S. Mill seem more inclined to view political liberty as a condition of progress than as a constituent of it. Of the two, Bagehot is perhaps the more explicit. Only those nations can progress, he says, that defend and make use of the right to differ. The right to differ is institutionalized in a certain kind of government—"government by discussion."

> It was "government by discussion" which broke the bond of ages and set free the originality of mankind. Then, and then only . . . "the tendency in every man to ameliorate his condition" begins to be important, because then man can alter his condition, while before he is pegged down by ancient usage.[62]

Government by discussion—in itself a progressive step—is the source of most other kinds of progress. As soon as governments by discussion have become strong enough to be stable, Bagehot says,

> and as soon as they have broken the fixed rule of old custom, and have awakened the dormant inventiveness of men, then, for the first time, almost every part of human nature begins to spring forward, and begins to contribute its quota even to the narrowest, even to "verifiable," progress.[63]

Mill, in general, concurs. But he emphasizes, where Bagehot does not, the importance of the extraordinary individual in the occurrence of progress. "The despotism of custom is everywhere the standing hindrance to human advancement," he says, "being in unceasing antagonism to that disposition to aim at something better than customary, which is called, according to circumstances, the spirit of liberty, or that of progress or improvement."[64] This is Bagehot's point. But Mill declares further that the spirit of improvement is not the same as the spirit of liberty, for improvements may be forced on unwilling people, and the spirit of liberty may temporarily ally itself with the opponents of improvement. Nevertheless,

[62] *Physics and Politics*, p. 159.
[63] *Ibid.*, p. 101.
[64] *On Liberty*, in *On Liberty, Representative Government, the Subjection of Women*, p. 87.

the only unfailing and permanent source of improvement is liberty, since by it there are as many possible independent centres of improvement as there are individuals.[65]

PROGRESS IN ACQUIRED FREEDOM

It has been suggested that several progress authors combine a notion of circumstantial freedom with one of acquired freedom. Usually the former is seen as having to be tempered by the latter, the idea being that increasing freedom (in the sense of increasing means) must be controlled, lest it be dangerous or licentious, by some sort of acquired wisdom, virtue, or knowledge.

Among progress authors, the one who most clearly affirms progress in acquired freedom is Hegel. For Hegel, human progress is defined as advance in or toward freedom. But what kind of freedom is this, in which, and toward which, the Spirit moves?

Hegel asserts that the conception of freedom as the ability of each man to do as he pleases "reveals an utter immaturity of thought."[66] Circumstantial freedom is therefore no freedom at all, and certainly not the freedom by which man's progress is measured. Instead, true freedom for Hegel is the perfection of the will in the fulfillment of duty. Only the will "which purifies its object, content, and aim, and raises them to this universality . . . is genuinely a free will," he says.[67] Furthermore, only the will that obeys law is free; for it obeys itself when the subjective will of man submits to laws, and the contradiction between liberty and necessity vanishes.

The very process of history is, furthermore, movement in the direction of the free will. The attainment of freedom, says Hegel, is the highest good of history and the sole aim of Spirit. This is the result at which the process of the world's history has been continually aiming,

> and to which the sacrifices that have ever and anon been laid on the vast altar of the earth, through the long lapse of ages, have been offered.[68]

For Hegel, the ideal form of government is monarchy; this is the form of the State toward which all history tends and progresses. He thus differs sharply in his notion of progress in freedom with those authors who hold that, whatever the degree of "moral" or "spiritual" freedom an individual

---

[65] *Ibid.* See also *Representative Government, ibid.,* pp. 160–4, where Mill discusses the relation between progress and order.

[66] *Philosophy of Right,* p. 27.

[67] *Ibid.,* p. 30.

[68] *Philosophy of History,* p. 19.

may possess, he is not in possession of political liberty unless he is able to participate in his government. In fact, participation in government is irrelevant to Hegel's idea of progress in freedom.

Several other progress authors appear to speak of progress in acquired freedom. De Rougemont, for example, sees "responsibility" as the leading quality of a member of a good society; and he also sees an increase in responsibility with the passage of time. This is perhaps only to say that for him circumstantial freedom—particularly insofar as it is advanced by technological progress—must be tempered and controlled by a sense of obligation. This would be no more than prudence in the presence of such weapons, for example, as the atomic bomb. But De Rougemont appears to be saying more than this. Let us assume, he writes,

> that the Goal of the whole of human history, as viewed in the Christian perspective, is this: *the community of persons,* set free and set in relation by virtue of faith.[69]

He seems here to be discussing a concept, called by some authors "Christian liberty," that is more than mere prudence in the presence of power.

Maritain expresses similar views. He too emphasizes responsibility; all freedom must be regulated, he says, but

> all exterior regulation is vain if its aim is not to develop the sense of the person's own creative responsibility, and his sense of communion. To feel responsible for one's brothers does not diminish our freedom but weights it with deeper responsibility.[70]

The good society toward which mankind *may be* progressing (for Maritain, progress is always contingent) will enjoy circumstantial freedom in the sense of liberty of conscience. "The commonweal could and should tolerate (to tolerate is not to approve) ways of worship more or less distant from the truth." Nevertheless, "the positive pole of its direction would be integral Christianity."[71] In such a society, more and more men would find the truth and thereby acquire the highest and truest freedom.

PROGRESS TOWARD COLLECTIVE FREEDOM

We turn now to a type of freedom to be acquired in the future by mankind as a whole. Since man does not yet possess it, and since it is a good, the movement toward it is human progress.

[69] *Man's Western Quest,* p. 40.
[70] *True Humanism,* p. 176.
[71] *Ibid.,* pp. 160–1.

Collective freedom, though applicable to individuals as well as to humanity as a whole, is not circumstantial freedom; it is not the freedom to do as one pleases in propitious circumstances. If it were, some individuals would possess it now, but none do. On the other hand, it is not simply acquired freedom; it will not be possessed by good men alone, or by any portion of mankind, but by all men. Either all men will have it, or no man will have it. It is a freedom that will be possessed by the whole human race collectively in that future toward which mankind, historically, is inevitably moving.[72]

Nevertheless, collective freedom is similar to acquired freedom. It, too, is acquired. Furthermore, acquired freedom involves willing compliance with certain laws—either moral laws or ideals of what humanity is or ought to be.[73] Collective freedom also involves compliance with laws, but these are not primarily moral or political. They are the laws of nature and of human nature.

Compliance with natural and societal laws is not voluntary in the same sense for collective-freedom authors as for acquired-freedom authors. Moral laws are violable; some men obey them and some do not, and this type of freedom is possessed by only a portion of human beings. Compliance with natural and societal laws, on the contrary, is necessary. Man cannot disobey the law of gravity, for example; nor can he disobey the law of history. But his compliance can be with or without understanding. Without understanding of them, men are slaves to natural forces. Authors who affirm progress toward collective freedom foresee a time when all men—humanity as a whole, collective man—will not only obey but also understand the laws that determine human life. Then, and only then, will man be free.

He is not free now because, first, he does not sufficiently understand the laws that he must obey, and second, because he is, as a consequence, subject to the arbitrary rule of other men. In the absence of willing compliance with the laws of nature and society, man is, as Comte puts it, the slave of man. What Comte calls true liberty begins only when all arbitrariness has been eliminated from human life and society.

When man submits only to the objective laws that positive science teaches him, he will, Comte says,

> no longer be the slave of man; he [will yield] only to external law; and to this, those who demonstrate it to him [will be] as submissive as himself. . . . The more perfectly they are known, the more free will our conduct become from arbitrary command or servile obedience.[74]

[72] All of the authors who affirm progress toward collective freedom hold that progress in general, and particularly such progress, is necessary.
[73] Hence it is often called "moral" or "spiritual" freedom.
[74] *Positive Polity*, Vol. I, p. 296.

There will be substituted "the empire of genuine convictions for that of arbitrary will"; for

> true liberty is nothing else than a rational submission to the preponderance of the laws of nature, in release from all arbitrary personal dictation.[75]

Comte does not believe that this future freedom will involve the "withering away" of the state. On the contrary, "society can no more exist without a government, than government can exist without a society."[76] Other writers disagree on this point. The state, for Bakunin, is the prime enemy of freedom, for it embodies everything arbitrary. "Authority," he says, "is the negation of liberty."

> The state is the sum of all the negations of the individual liberty of all its members. . . . The liberty of each is the limit or rather the natural negation of the liberty of all the others. Well! this absolute limitation, this negation of the liberty of each in the name of the liberty of all or of the common right—that is the State. Thus, where the State begins, individual liberty ceases, and vice versa.[77]

But the time is coming, Bakunin predicts, when man will obey, not other men but the laws of nature. Then man will no longer be a slave, "since he is obeying only laws which are inherent in his own nature, under the conditions of which he exists, which make up his entire being. When he obeys them, he obeys himself."[78]

"There is no good outside liberty, and liberty is the source and absolute condition of all good which really deserves that name," says Bakunin, "the good being nothing else than liberty."[79] Man will attain this good; to it, history tends. There is movement toward, if not in, freedom; the change is meliorative; and it is necessary.

Both Comte and Bakunin recognize that the slavery under which man now lies is imposed not only by the arbitrary rule of other men but also by what may be termed social and economic necessities. "The chains of slavery which nature places on all her children," says Bakunin, include

> hunger, privations of all kinds, pain, the influence of climate, the seasons, and, in general, the thousand conditions of animal life which maintain the human being in a quasi-absolute dependence on the environment which surrounds him.[80]

[75] *Positive Philosophy*, p. 435.
[76] *Positive Polity*, Vol. II, p. 162.
[77] *Oeuvres*, I, pp. 283–4.
[78] *Ibid.*, III, p. 235.
[79] *Ibid.*, I, p. 204.
[80] *Ibid.*, pp. 110–1.

The remedy is to transform the earth into a place more and more favorable to humanity. This point is, of course, made by Marx, Engels, and their followers in great detail. Marx says:

> The realm of freedom does not commence until the point is passed where labor under the compulsion of necessity and of external utility is required.[81]

There is a kind of freedom in primitive society, but it is soon lost; it will only be attained again when men are no longer forced to labor but instead labor because they wish to, because they recognize and positively affirm the social necessity of labor. But this cannot occur without much technological and economic progress of another sort. Until the productive forces at man's disposal reach the point where all men enjoy substantial leisure as well as ample subsistence, society will remain divided into classes—those who control production and those whose labor is exploited for the sake of the others.

This explains the Marxist emphasis on technological progress. It must occur in order to "free" man from economic slavery. But man will achieve another kind of freedom as well. The state, since it involves the government of a politically and economically class-divided society, is nothing but an instrument of the dominant class. Hence, for true liberty to be achieved, the state must wither away. Full or true or "collective" freedom will not be attained, for Marx, Engels, and their followers, until all class distinctions have disappeared and all production has been concentrated in the hands of a vast association of the whole nation. Then the public power will lose its political character and the state will simply disappear.

These remarks may seem to imply that collective freedom is the same as circumstantial freedom. Indeed, the freedom that the Marxists foresee will be possessed by individuals. But this is because, and not in spite, of the fact that mankind will possess freedom *collectively*. Humanity will acquire collective freedom, and *thereby* individual men will be free. However, they will not be free simply to please themselves. They will not be free, for example, not to work, not to love, not to adhere to the society. On the contrary, they will freely desire to do all of these things. In that will their freedom consist.

In one sense, the attainment of collective freedom involves, for all the authors who affirm it, the attainment of knowledge—scientific knowledge, knowledge of the natural necessities that determine all phenomena, social as well as physical. It is conceded by them that man already possesses some knowledge of these matters. Why then is freedom reserved to the future? Why is man not free now—at least to some extent?

---

[81] *Capital*, Vol. III, Part VII, Ch. XLVII, Sect. III, p. 954; qu. in *The Idea of Freedom*, Vol. I, p. 375.

The answer is that what is involved is not merely knowledge but the social use of knowledge. What will be achieved is not simply a recognition of the necessities under which men live but also the ability to conduct one's life in accordance with them. Such knowledge, being practical, involves more than theory. Mankind must grow into freedom, which it will slowly but surely attain by practice.[82]

Such, at least, is the view of the authors who hold this position.

[82] "The present generation of Soviet people shall live under Communism," declares the *Program of the Communist Party of the Soviet Union* (*Draft*), *1961* (p. 230). Marx, Engels, and other early Marxists may have felt that Communism was farther off in time; Lenin thought that it would take centuries, rather than decades, to attain it. It may also be a new idea to the Soviet people—only a portion of the earth's Marxists seem to have believed that all men, everywhere, must have collective freedom before anyone could.

24

Moral Progress: I

DURING the three or four centuries in which progress has been
a leading (if not the leading) idea in the West, probably no single
topic has been of such great concern to those who thought and wrote
about it—and none has brought forth such passionate affirmations and denials—as moral progress. There are several reasons why this is so.

First, the judgment that progress occurs at all is based on the judgment
that there are changes for the better in human life, and that judgment,
in turn, has a moral basis. "Better" is the comparative of "good," and
good is a moral idea.

Second, even those modern writers who attempt to treat the idea of
progress as though it were not a moral idea recognize that, for the great
majority of other writers on the subject, it is a moral idea, inescapably.

Third, as so many commentators point out,[1] the idea of progress is in
some sense the heir of the faith and the passion that another age devoted to Christianity. Most particularly, progress is the concrete secularization of the Christian idea—and virtue—of Hope. And it goes with-

[1] For example, John Baillie, in *The Belief in Progress*, and Carl Becker, in the
article "Progress," in the *Encyclopedia of the Social Sciences*.

out saying that the ideas that give Christianity its power to move men's minds are moral, too.

Finally, the idea of progress incorporates, and makes explicit, the highest hopes—whether religious or not—of the human race. To question the moral basis of these hopes is to question the idea of humanity itself.

We should not be surprised, therefore, to discover that moral progress is, for many writers, the *sine qua non* of human progress, of progress in general. In the opinion of most progress authors, improvements of the kind signified by moral progress are the goal of all progress. And if moral progress itself does not occur, the progress (in other senses) that remains is somehow cast in doubt.

What is moral progress? In what does it consist (whether or not it actually occurs)? Progress authors answer this question in different ways. For some, merely acting better is not true moral progress. That is —or would be, if it occurred—an improvement in human nature. It would involve the existence on earth of more moral human beings—either a *fixed number* of men who are consistently more moral, or an *increasing number* of persons who are moral, or both. The main idea here is that better actions on the part of men in general do not necessarily mean that moral progress has occurred. The improvement in action may be the result of social pressures, themselves impermanent, so that progress is reversible. Different circumstances may force people to act better, superficially, but if they are not changed in their nature they will act worse again when circumstances change back to what they were. In that case, the supposedly "better" people would revert to a "primitive" or "savage" or "natural" condition of morality.

Other writers subtly change the emphasis on the notion of morality in relation to progress. That is, they hold that the only progress, or perhaps the only real, true, or meaningful progress, is moral progress. Let us concede that there are advances in knowledge and techniques, these writers say. Let us concede that the human being is a healthier animal, and that he now enjoys a longer average life-span. But these changes— these advances—are not examples of human progress. That involves an improvement in actions or in nature, or in both. That must occur before it can be said that human progress occurs. All of these other developments are either irrelevant to progress, or they are, in some sense, conditions of progress. Human progress *is* moral progress. No other change deserves the name.[2]

[2] The assertion that progress is equivalent to moral progress, when it is accompanied by the further assertion that such progress does not occur at all, is of course a denial of progress and is therefore not considered here. However, the authors who

A third conception of moral progress involves a less stringent conception of progress in general. No betterment of human nature is demanded; and it is accepted that not much real improvement in character has yet occurred. At the same time, the writers who hold this position say it is wrong to deny that men act better toward each other on the whole. They promulgate better laws and expect more from one another, which in turn improves behavior. Thus, although men still do not live truly well, they live better than they did in the past—at least the distant past. There is a clear advance from "savage" or "primitive" morality, even if, from time to time, modern men continue to act "savagely" or "primitively." The surest sign of this, it is held, is that when modern man acts badly he blames himself. Standards of action are higher than they used to be.

A variant of this position is often proposed. It is that, although there may not be much moral improvement observable in history, at least men *know* more about how they should act than they once did. Their understanding of what they ought to do progresses even if they do not progress in their behavior.

Three different positions, then, regarding moral progress are taken by progress authors. Progress is

1. affirmed in knowledge, technology, etc., but denied in morals;
2. equated with moral progress;
3. affirmed in morality as well as in other respects.

The first position is associated with the contention that moral progress would mean a change in human nature, which does not occur. The third involves a notion of limited moral improvement.

Authors taking the first two positions are discussed in the present chapter. Affirmations of moral progress in the sense of the third position are analyzed in Chapter 25.

Moral Progress and Change in Human Nature: Denials of Moral Progress

A number of writers maintain that "real" or "true" moral progress involves, or would involve if it occurred, a change in human nature.[3] This

say that progress *is* moral progress do not usually deny progress absolutely in that sense. They seem more concerned to de-emphasize technological progress and progress in knowledge; to say, in effect, that man should not pride himself on such achievements, since moral progress is (or would be) more significant. They often end by conceding that some progress occurs, after vigorously denying that much of it occurs. And they usually suggest that moral progress may occur in the future.

[3] This section, thus, mainly treats denials of moral progress, for the authors who maintain that (moral) progress actually occurs in human nature were discussed in Chapter 17.

view of the topic is almost always accompanied by a denial that moral progress actually has occurred. Thus, Dewey, for instance, says:

Man is equipped with these feelings [*i.e.*, altruism, kindliness, peaceful feelings, etc.] at birth as well as with emotions of fear, anger, emulation and resentment. What appears to be an increase in one set is, in reality, a change in their social occasions and social channels.[4]

"There is at any time," he continues, "a sufficient amount of kindly impulses possessed by man to enable him to live in amicable peace with all his fellows; and there is at any time a sufficient equipment of bellicose impulses to keep him in trouble with his fellows." Most if not all of the supposed moral progress of the past is therefore an illusion. Men are not any different; varying circumstances call forth varying responses.

However, Dewey emphasizes that the possibility of future moral progress must be taken seriously. "For the first time in history mankind is in command of the possibility of progress," he declares. "The rest is for us to say."[5] Even if human beings do not change fundamentally, the social occasions of behavior can be improved. Advances in science, in technology, and an increase in wealth allow the creation of a better social milieu. Thus, although human nature remains constant, human behavior can improve.

Dewey also emphasizes the role of education in this process. Walter Lippmann, taking a similar position with regard to moral progress, emphasizes the part played by the statesman in producing an improved environment for moral action.

It is probably true that the impulses of men have changed very little within recorded history. What has changed enormously from epoch to epoch is the character in which these impulses appear. The impulses that at one period work themselves out into cruelty and lust may at another produce the richest values of civilized life. The statesman can affect that choice.[6]

It should be recognized, however, that both Dewey and Lippmann are denying the occurrence of moral progress in the past, and questioning the possibility of permanent moral progress in the future. If progress in this respect is nothing more than an effect of other developments, and if these are not intrinsically progressive—as, for these two authors, they do not seem to be—then hopes for lasting moral progress are illusory.

C. G. Darwin holds the same position, except that he more strongly asserts that the apparent moral progress of recent times will be reversed. This phenomenon is the result of the special situation in which man has

[4] "Progress," in *International Journal of Ethics*, April 1916, p. 316.
[5] *Ibid.*, p. 314.
[6] *A Preface to Politics*, p. 300.

found himself in the last two or three centuries, a situation that cannot endure. The truth is, Darwin says,

> that all our present codes about the sanctity of human life are based on the security of life as it is at present, and once that is gone they will inevitably be revised, and the revision will probably shock most of our present opinions.[7]

Darwin foresees a future "callousness about the value of the individual's life, and . . . cruelty to a degree of which we do not willingly think."[8] He expects that wars will continue to be fought, increasingly for land, which will grow more scarce and valuable as population more and more exceeds food supplies. The fact that land is so valuable may mean that certain kinds of destruction will not be practiced as in the past; he expects, for example, that atomic bombs will not be used in future wars, since they would invalidate precisely the gains sought. But "in view of the cheapened value of human life there is little likelihood," he says, "that the hostile population will be treated in a more humane manner than has been the custom in the past."[9]

Darwin sees another reason, perhaps a more basic one, why moral progress should not be expected in the future. Speaking of various character types, or "roles," that have less or more success in life, and are thus less or more likely to be dominant in future populations, he describes one type that can be expected to produce more trouble as time goes on. This is the "hero,"

> using the term not in the modern sense of a man embodying all the virtues, but in the original sense used by Homer. The Homeric hero, who has his counterparts in many other semi-barbaric conditions of life, is brave and reckless, but selfish, undisciplined and something of a bully.[10]

His very selfishness confers an advantage on his type, Darwin points out, and, since he revolts against discipline, he is likely to have his way. In addition, it is characteristic of him that

> he is usually by no means monogamous, but very much the reverse, so that his qualities are likely to be reproduced and multiplied many times in the next generation.[11]

---

[7] *The Next Million Years,* p. 136.

[8] *Ibid.,* p. 149.

[9] *Ibid.,* p. 144. It should be pointed out that Darwin holds that the moral regress in question is relative only to the high standards now in effect. Man will probably not sink, in the future, below what he has *usually* been in the past.

[10] *Ibid.,* p. 69.

[11] *Ibid.,* p. 70.

Is it possible, Darwin asks, that in the long run the earth will be wholly peopled by heroes? The fact that this would make it a very disagreeable world is irrelevant, "for there is nothing in nature to dictate that the world has got to be agreeable." However, it is not, it seems, very likely. Heroes (bullies) need room, as it were, to move.[12] The world of the future is going to have little waste space. Nevertheless, Darwin feels that there will be more bullies rather than fewer. And since it is characteristic of bullies that they "positively enjoy making their fellows miserable," an increase in their numbers seems to indicate not only a lack of moral progress but positive moral regress. This is the more true since the class of men he calls bullies is one of the prime causes of the relapse from civilization into barbarism that Darwin sees as a frequent occurrence in the past, and regards as an equally frequent one in the future.

> Such men are apt to be brave and self-confident, but selfish and concerned only with their personal interests, and above all indifferent to the sufferings of those around them. Such men, always ready to assume leadership, only interested in their own advantage, and indifferent to the fate of their fellows, are perfectly adapted instruments for destroying the delicate balance of civilization.[13]

Darwin himself probably does not regard such destruction as true moral regress. The average condition of human life, in his view of it, is not much above barbarism. Civilization is the exception rather than the rule. It occurs infrequently and cannot be expected to endure. Hence there is no more reason to expect that life will grow radically worse—except from the viewpoint of a "golden age" morality—than there is to expect that it will grow radically better. Over the next million years the picture is neither black nor white, but a rather consistent gray.[14]

There are hints that the above writers are suffering from disillusion because of the events of the twentieth century—two world wars and other catastrophes—that seem to provide evidence that there has been no thorough moral improvement in mankind. Other writers specifically mention these events and admit that they are disillusioned. Heilbroner, for

[12] Are we to think of F. J. Turner's frontiersman? Turner admires the character Darwin is here criticizing—or at least recognizes its beneficial effect on American history. Actually, Turner never says flatly that the frontier type is the source of human progress in general. But these implications of his famous essay seem sometimes to be expressed by later writers. See, for example, *Europe's Steppe Frontier: 1500–1800*, by W. H. McNeill.

[13] *Op. cit.*, p. 119.

[14] All in all, Darwin paints a gloomy picture. His position, simply—one he shares with Mandeville—is that immorality confers an advantage in the struggle for existence. It is interesting to note that Sir Charles' grandfather, Charles Darwin, is one of the leading exponents of the position that morality confers just such an advantage.

instance, lists some occurrences that are not conducive to moral optimism. We often imagine, he says, that life is much better today than, say, in the Dark Ages, but this depends very much on whose lives we conjure up in these two periods.

> After all, we live at a time when German brutality reached what may be, statistically, a record for the systematic extermination of life, and when Russian despotism at its worst took us back to the level of morality of the crueler Biblical kings.[15]

Freud also discourses at length on the disillusion felt by believers in progress as a result of the cruelties and barbarism of the First World War. The essay "Thoughts for the Times on War and Death," published in 1915, expresses a kind of despair. We are constrained to believe, he says,

> that never has any event been destructive of so much that is valuable in the commonwealth of humanity, nor so misleading to many of the clearest intelligences, nor so debasing to the highest that we know.[16]

Freud is particularly overcome by the immorality of "science herself," which supplies weapons of more and more horror, and which, in the person of the anthropologist, "is driven to declare the opponent inferior and degenerate," and, in that of the psychiatrist, to publish a diagnosis of "the enemy's disease of mind or spirit."

Freud sees immorality and betrayal of civilization everywhere. He is shocked by the reflection that it is precisely "the great ruling powers among the white nations upon whom the leadership of the human species has fallen" that have so eagerly run into conflict with one another. If *they* have not progressed morally, then the human race has not done so through any of its representatives. Indeed, it is just this conclusion that leads Freud to the position taken by the other authors discussed above. We may derive this consolation, Freud says

> —that our mortification and our grievous disillusionment regarding the un-civilized behavior of our world-compatriots in this war are shown to be unjustified. They were based on an illusion to which we had abandoned ourselves. In reality our fellow-citizens have not sunk so low as we feared, *because* they had never risen so high as we believed.[17]

In the heart of every one of us, he declares, is a murderous intent that is not eradicated by civilization, and is only feebly held in check by it.

[15] *The Future as History*, pp. 191–2.
[16] In *Collected Papers*, Vol. IV, p. 288.
[17] *Ibid.*, p. 300.

To sum up: Our unconscious is just as inaccessible to the idea of our own death, as murderously minded towards the stranger, as divided or ambivalent towards the loved, as was man in his earliest antiquity.[18]

Moral progress is only an illusion. Man remains the same.

In another work, Freud is no less firm in denying the supposed improvement in moral character that would be, for him, the basis of true moral progress. Men are not gentle, friendly creatures wishing for love, he says, who simply defend themselves if they are attacked. On the contrary,

> a powerful measure of aggression has to be reckoned as part of their instinctual endowment. The result is that their neighbour is to them not only a possible helper or sexual object, but also a temptation to them to gratify their aggressiveness on him, to exploit his capacity for work without recompense, to use him sexually without his consent, to seize his possessions, to humiliate him, to cause him pain, to torture and kill him.[19]

"Homo homini lupus," he adds; "who has the courage to dispute it in the face of all the evidence in his own life and in history?"

At the same time, the story of what man "by his science and practical inventions has achieved on this earth, where he first appeared as a weakly member of the animal kingdom, and on which each individual of his species must ever again appear as a helpless infant—O inch of nature!—is a direct fulfillment of all, or of most, of the dearest wishes in his fairytales."[20] Progress in knowledge, in techniques, in wealth, is an indisputable fact. But it does not result in moral progress. Man has always been, and probably will remain, a wolf to man.[21]

MORAL PROGRESS AS COEXTENSIVE WITH HUMAN PROGRESS

The position, just discussed, that moral progress would constitute, if it occurred, a change in human nature, that such a change is not observable, and that moral progress therefore, strictly speaking, does not occur in history—this position usually, as is evident from the mere statement of it, comes down to a denial of moral progress. The position, with which we

[18] *Ibid.,* p. 316.
[19] *Civilization and Its Discontents,* p. 85.
[20] *Ibid.,* p. 52.
[21] Perhaps a universal psychoanalysis might soften man's wolflike character, but even it would not change his nature. Thus Freud might have been considered in Chapter 17 as one of the authors who oppose the notion that progress occurs in human nature.

now deal, that moral progress is coextensive with human progress—that man progresses morally or not at all—does not, on the other hand, always constitute a denial that moral progress occurs, for it is said by some writers who hold this conception that progress does occur in this sense. No other changes except moral improvements deserve the name of progress; but such improvements are to be observed.

This view is explicitly stated, for example, by L. P. Jacks. Any writer on progress, he says, at least any writer who affirms the occurrence of progress, must be dealing with the question of moral progress. This is inevitable, he declares, because every progress author deserving of that appellation

> must show that the particular sort of progress he is dealing with is real or genuine progress, and this it cannot be unless it is moral.[22]

Progress is not progress in the abstract, he declares, "whatever that may mean, but progress *for us* constituted as we are; and since our constitution is essentially moral all progress that we can recognize as such must be moral also."

> Science, Industry, Government, might all claim progress on their own ground and in their own nature, but this would not prove progress as we understand the word, unless it could be shown further that these things contribute to human betterment in the highest sense of the word. *Their* progress might conceivably involve *our* regress.[23]

Having stated his understanding of the meaning of the terms "progress" and "moral progress," Jacks goes on to state his belief concerning them. "To believe in moral progress as an historical fact, as a process that has begun, and is going on, and will be continued—that is one thing, and it is my own position. To believe that this progress is far advanced is another thing, and is not my position." Moral progress is a fact, Jacks holds, but it is also a fact that we are much nearer to the beginning of it than to the end of it. And he remarks that

> we should do well to accustom ourselves to this thought. Many of our despairs, lamentations, and pessimisms are disappointments which arise from our extravagant notions of the degree of progress already attained.[24]

He lists some of the signs educed for significant moral progress—that we read books, ride in airplanes, eat dinner with a knife and fork, pay taxes cheerfully, study human science, "talk freely about humanity, and

22 "Moral Progress," in F. S. Marv:.. (ed.), *Progress and History*, p. 134.
23 *Ibid.*
24 *Ibid.*, pp. 134–5.

spend much . . . time in making speeches on social questions." It is true that these things are signs that we have progressed morally, he says, but we should not flatter ourselves; they are not cause for complacency. A good rule for optimists would be: "Believe in moral progress, but do not believe in too much of it." Morally considered, we are still in "a Neolithic age, not brutes indeed any longer, and yet not so far outgrown the brutish stage as to justify these trumpetings." Indeed, there would, he thinks, be more optimists in the world, more cheerfulness, more belief in moral progress if this fact were admitted and understood.

And he makes particular reference to the first world war that, in the view of the authors discussed in the previous section, was a cause of absolute dejection. The war has revealed us to ourselves as nothing else in history has ever done, Jacks declares. Thus he counters Freud's point about the lesson of the war. The war

> has not discredited science, nor philosophy, nor government, nor anything else that we value, but it has shown that these things have not brought us as far as we thought. That very knowledge, when you come to think of it, is itself a very distinct step in moral progress. Before the war we were growing morally conceited; we thought ourselves much better, more advanced in morality, than we really were, and this conceit was acting as a real barrier to our further advance. A sharp lesson was needed. . . . This sudden awakening to the truth is full of promise for the future.[25]

J. A. Froude concurs in holding that progress reduces to moral progress. What is often called progress, he says, is only change, and change that is sometimes for the worse. "Mere" heaping up of wealth, "mere" extension of the suffrage, is not necessarily progress at all. "Purity, justice, right, unselfishness" are the criteria of real social advance. The progress of civilization depends on the extent of the domain that is reclaimed, as he puts it, under the moral law.[26] Stephen Alexander holds that not only does progress mean moral progress but morality also means progress. All morality is a process of change, of development, and this change is always for the better.

> Progress, the most important of the dynamic conceptions, will be found to be involved in all morality. . . . It will be found that moral ideals move by a process which, allowing for differences, repeats the law by which natural species develop, and of this process the dynamical conceptions represent different elements. . . . Progress is essential to morality. Every moral ideal is an arrested moment in the passage from one ideal to a higher.[27]

[25] *Ibid.*, pp. 135–6.
[26] See the essay, "Progress," in *Short Studies*, Second Series, esp. pp. 274–5.
[27] *Moral Order and Progress*, pp. 18–9; see also pp. 369, 399–400. Alexander was a nineteenth-century American astronomer.

And for W. W. Campbell, progress is essentially the development of new and higher moral imperatives—new moral values, new ideals. It is idealism alone that civilizes man.

> That which is purely practical, containing no elements of idealism, may sustain existence and to that extent be valuable, but it does not civilize. I believe it is the idealism of pure knowledge, the idealism in applied knowledge, the idealism in industry and commerce, the idealism in literature and art, the idealism in personal religion, which leavens the life of the world and pushes forward the boundaries of civilization.[28]

[28] "Presidential Address to the American Association for the Advancement of Science, 1915," in *Science,* 42:238.

25

Moral Progress: II

T H E statement that progress *is* moral progress, that no historical de-velopments except moral developments can be called progressive, is not the same as the statement that progress means change for the better. There are changes for the better—for example, the increase of knowledge—that are not in themselves moral improvements. More important, equating moral progress with progress in general rules out of consideration a num-ber of questions that deeply concern many progress authors. Is the growth of scientific and perhaps of theoretical and philosophical knowledge pro-gressive—*i.e.*, is it good for man? Is the realm of technology (the control of nature) the primary one, or indeed the only one, in which man has a really progressive capacity? Is increase in specialization of function an es-sentially progressive characteristic of the human species? Of all living species? Does history show a progressive tendency toward the planetization of social structures? Is the fact that human numbers tend to increase a mark of progress, a condition of progress, or the greatest obstacle to prog-ress? These and other questions become, by implication, irrelevant if it is claimed that human progress is coextensive with moral progress, in the limited sense of the latter term.[1]

In fact, most authors do not insist on the equivalence. They are willing to consider, and they discuss, aspects of progress that are not primarily moral, as we have seen. And they also affirm moral progress in limited senses. This chapter is devoted to the analysis of their affirmations—and of a few denials—of moral progress in the respects which are most often considered by them.

The analysis is divided into three parts. It is convenient to follow A. J. Todd, who says that

> we all recognize three more or less distinct lines of possible moral development, namely, (1) in ethical concepts; (2) in the established principles of social organization and societal relations; (3) in the character of human beings.[2]

This breakdown is useful to us, although several remarks must be made. Progress in ethical concepts, from one point of view, is an aspect of progress in knowledge, and was so considered in Chapter 19. Hence, a less than exhaustive treatment of this topic is needed here. Progress in the established principles of social organization and relations is an aspect of what we have called political progress and was so considered in Chapters 22 and 23. Once more we need not, therefore, go into it here as thoroughly as we otherwise would have to do. And progress in the character of human beings might be, and by some authors is, considered as progress in human nature. This topic, too, has already been treated.

There remain, nevertheless, a number of positions regarding moral progress to be discussed.

Progress in Ethical Concepts

Buckle is a leading exponent of the view that moral progress mainly consists in, and is largely the result of, what he calls intellectual progress— *i.e.*, progress in knowledge. Advances in human conduct, says Buckle, are stationary as compared with intellectual advances. The progressive aspect of intellectual truths, *including moral truth*, is sometimes startling. The intellectual element is not only more progressive and powerful but more permanent. Intellectual gains are more easily gathered, preserved, and transmitted than behavioral ones.

---

[1] The authors who affirm this equivalence may be saying no more than that a judgment that a change is for the better (*i.e.*, progressive) must be made on moral grounds.

[2] *Theories of Social Progress*, p. 127.

Nevertheless, the latter do occur. Buckle takes war as a typical example. War, he says, is the expression of unintelligence, backwardness, and ignorance. Militarism is not so much immoral as stupid. It is not moral advances—general improvement in character or behavior—that have brought about the decline of war but intellectual ones. The invention of gunpowder resulted in a special war class, a standing army; the rest of the population was left to peaceful pursuits and forgot war. Discoveries in the science of political economy undercut many of the old causes of jealousy and suspicion among nations, hence made war less likely. And technological advances in transportation and communication broke down the barriers of ignorance between nations. "That this barbarous pursuit [*i.e.*, war] is, in the progress of society, steadily declining, must be evident, even to the most hasty reader of European history," Buckle declares.[3] And that decline, itself an example of moral progress, is the direct result of intellectual progress on other fronts.

Progress in knowledge produces yet other moral improvements.

> It is to the diffusion of knowledge, and to that alone, that we owe the comparative cessation of what is unquestionably the greatest evil men have ever inflicted on their own species. For that religious persecution is a greater evil[4] than any other, is apparent, not so much from the enormous and almost incredible number of its known victims, as from the fact that the unknown must be far more numerous and that history gives no account of those who have been spared in the body, in order that they might suffer in the mind.[5]

The conclusion from this and other examples is that progressive changes in ethical conceptions are dependent mainly, if not solely, on the amount of knowledge possessed by the ablest among living men, the direction that knowledge takes, and, above all, the extent to which knowledge is diffused throughout society.

Mill agrees in general with this view of the relative importance of intellectual and moral progress, although he makes a significant proviso. "Some . . . (among whom is Mr. Buckle himself) have inferred," Mill says,

> or allowed it to be supposed that they inferred, from the regularity in the recurrence of events which depend on moral qualities, that the moral qualities are little capable of being improved, or are of little importance in the general progress of society, compared with intellectual or economic causes.[6]

[3] *History of Civilization in England,* p. 190.
[4] War is the *second* greatest evil.
[5] *Ibid.,* p. 189.
[6] *A System of Logic,* p. 610.

But we are not to conclude that moral progress in the sense of improved conduct and behavior does not occur, Mill declares. Buckle—so Mill has been assured, he says, by a mutual friend—

> never intended to affirm or imply that mankind are not progressive in their moral as well as in their intellectual qualities. . . . He desired to make abstraction of the intellect as the determining and dynamical element of the progression, eliminating the more dependent set of conditions, and treating the more active one as if it were an entirely independent variable.[7]

Intellectual progress (progress in the knowledge of ethical concepts, among other things) is the independent, progress in conduct the dependent, variable. The latter occurs, but the former is the more important phenomenon.

Maritain goes further than Buckle and Mill. As for "the field of human *action,* or morality, which has its source principally in the will"—this, he says, shows little or no progress, certainly no necessary progress.

> In the field of the moral life . . . there is no unvarying progress for humanity, but endless vicissitudes: because matter—our own animated matter —is hard to control.[8]

It is not correct to point to the advent of Christianity as an "immense moral progress," for Christianity is a divine fact, and gratuitous; it is not a *natural* progress of humanity. Besides, the advent of Christianity provides the possibility of disastrous regress.

> Humanity continues to be directed in its movement towards a divine goal unknown to itself; yet if it breaks with the life of the Church it makes its own wounds worse than if Christ had not come. *Si non venissem, et locutus fuissem eis, peccatum non haberent.* Never forget that the same light that lightens some blinds others.[9]

Nevertheless, in "the speculative order, the order of knowledge," there is remarkable as well as measurable progress in moral conceptions.

In another work, Maritain posits the existence of a "law of the progress of moral conscience."[10] This is the law according to which man knows more and more about the natural law as time goes on. It is not a law of conduct; "allow me to stress that I am not pointing to any progress in human moral behavior," Maritain declares. "I am pointing to a progress of

---

[7] *Ibid.,* pp. 610–11, Note. Mill remarks that Buckle's method is like that of the political economists who isolate one factor in economic development for special study.

[8] *Theonas,* p. 154.

[9] *Ibid.,* pp. 155–6. Teilhard makes a similar point in *The Phenomenon of Man,* p. 311.

[10] *On the Philosophy of History,* p. 104.

moral conscience as to the *knowledge* of the particular precepts of natural law."[11] For example, Abraham was a saint, Maritain explains, and what is more, a saint of "incomparable stature." But he did not know that certain actions are contrary to the natural law.

> Hence we must conclude that mankind's state of nature was not a state in which natural moral laws were perfectly known and practised. As a matter of fact, the precise knowledge of these natural moral laws—with the exception of the self-evident primary principle, *good is to be done and evil to be avoided*—is acquired slowly and with more or less difficulty. . . . In other words, our knowledge of moral laws is progressive in nature. The sense of duty and obligation was always present, but the explicit knowledge of the various norms of natural law grows with time.[12]

Maritain cites several examples of progress in moral conscience. "We are now aware," he says, "that slavery is contrary to the dignity of the human person." The fact that there are nations that enslave persons does not invalidate this point. They are ashamed of the fact—"that's why propaganda is so necessary." Another example is the treatment of prisoners of war. It used to be considered proper to kill an enemy whether or not he was still fighting. Now we have "a completely different view of our obligations towards prisoners of war," although we still kill prisoners from time to time, and othewise harm them. Child labor is no longer considered legitimate—this is still another example. And there are numerous other areas into which the natural law has been extended in recent centuries.[13]

According to Maritain, moral knowledge must be based on experience. "Metaphysics is not a reflective knowledge," he says; it is not a reflection of common sense. But moral knowledge is reflective in this sense of the term. Hence the work of theoretical reflection cannot replace in moral matters the slow advance of consciousness, conscience, and experience in mankind.

> This means not only an advance in rational knowledge, but primarily an advance in our lived awareness of our basic inclinations—an advance which may be conditioned by social changes. Thus for many centuries moral philosophers and common consciousness stressed the obligations of man prescribed by natural law. But there are also rights of man, which were, of course, implicitly recognized, especially by Christian thinkers.[14]

[11] *Ibid.*, pp. 105–6.

[12] *Ibid.*, pp. 103–4.

[13] *Ibid.*, pp. 106–7. Some of the same examples are cited by Yves Simon, and were discussed above, p. 330.

[14] *Ibid.*, p. 110. Westermarck is another who maintains that there is progress in the field of moral judgments. "Society is the birthplace of the moral consciousness," he declares, and whatever broadens the area of wholesome social contact and sym-

Yet it seems that it was necessary, Maritain declares, to wait until the eighteenth century, and the related social changes in human history, "to have the basic inclination on which an explicit awareness of these rights depends liberated in us."

Yves Simon, agreeing in general with this position, lays particular stress on the part that positive law can play in the progress of the moral conscience. "The discovery of moral truth," he says, "is generally an obscure, anonymous, secret thing." He traces the evolution of a progressive innovation in morals through the first vague recognitions and "individual adherences"—perhaps on the part of saints—to the moment when it is

> embodied in a deathless work—the writings of a great thinker, or the career of a hero. Thereafter its sociological existence is definitely consolidated. Happen what may, the idea will never disappear from history.[15]

However, this stage is still "far below what the service of man demands." As yet, only a sprinkling of individuals, the "moral elite," has cognizance of the new idea. It must now reach down to the "morally normal man" and be numbered among the principles that he "will never openly call into question." The distribution of moral truth is as important as its discovery.[16]

The diffusion of moral innovations does not occur in the same way that scientific and technical innovations are disseminated, Simon maintains—"that is to say, through spontaneous social relations." New scientific truths easily impose themselves on the majority of minds. Not so new moral truths. To keep the struggle from being too unequal, the conscious centers of society must pronounce in favor of the new idea and ensure its distribution, as well as its preservation, "by putting at its service the unequaled pedagogical force constituted by the machinery of positive law."

> By being incorporated into legal practice, moral truth penetrates the very citadel of ignorance and error, into that obscure realm of familiar, tenacious, and dominating images, the purification of which is the absolute condition of lucidity of conscience.[17]

---

pathy enriches moral consciousness. The change of cognitions or ideas thus produces a change of emotions. "Now the evolution of the moral consciousness partly consists in its development from the unreflecting to the reflecting stage, from the unenlightened to the enlightened. This appears from the decreasing influence of external events upon moral judgments and from the growing discrimination with reference to motives, negligence and other factors in conduct which are carefully considered by a scrupulous judge" (*Origin and Development of the Moral Ideas,* Vol. II, p. 740).

[15] *Community of the Free,* p. 132.

[16] This notion is also implied by Buckle. See above, p. 430.

[17] *Ibid.,* p. 134.

According to L. T. Hobhouse, the notion of obligation is the basis of "the ethical idea," and the historical steps in the conception of obligation constitute moral progress.

> Obligation is the general expression for the relations in which men . . . stand, and it is (a) in the way in which obligation is conceived, and (b) in the conduct which it covers, that ethical evolution is principally seen.[18]

The advance from primitivism to the present day requires many pages to describe, but, Hobhouse says, it can be epitomized thus:

> At the beginning is custom, with its blend of the ethical and unethical, accepted without criticism and guiding life without system or general plan. At the end is the rational order of conduct founded on the conditions of human development, and directed to the furtherance of that development as its supreme end.

"The evolution of mind in man, from being a blind, unconscious, fitful process has become a purposive, self-directed movement. This is the fundamental change effected in the course of human history."[19]

Morris Ginsberg has a similar conception of the steps or phases of moral progress. In his view the basic tendency is "the extension of the range of persons to whom moral judgments are held to apply." For instance, Ginsberg says, "the unity of mankind" once meant "the unity of Christian mankind"; now, even among Christians, it means the unity of all men.[20]

Other signs of moral progress, according to Ginsberg, are "the internalization and individualization of the conscience," and the growing rationalization of moral judgments. Primitive people require external sanctions; civilized people have sanctions within themselves. With regard to the increasing rationalization of morals, Ginsberg distinguishes three phases:

> In the first, morality is dominantly customary and there is little or no reflection on the grounds of action, though if challenged traditional explanations will be forthcoming. . . . In the second, there is growing reflection by story tellers, poets and moralists and later by philosophers who seek to disentangle the rules of action and the ideals of conduct by the method of critical analysis. . . . In the third phase dialectical analysis begins to be combined with empirical study of the conditions and consequences of actions and the study of the conditions under which they can be brought to fruition.[21]

[18] *Morals in Evolution*, pp. 622–3.
[19] *Ibid.*, p. 631.
[20] *Reason and Unreason in Society*, p. 308. The unity of mankind meant the unity of all men for Augustine. This does not invalidate Ginsberg's point; it merely combines it with Maritain's. Augustine possessed a knowledge of the natural law that was in advance of his time.
[21] *Ibid.*, p. 311.

The clearest evidence of moral progress, Ginsberg declares, is to be found in the "gradual moralization of religion." The conception of God and of an afterlife are "gradually transformed," and there is a tendency to identify the spiritual with the ethical. "The demand is then made that religious beliefs must satisfy ethical tests."[22]

Ginsberg meets the charge that our time is one of moral regress by declaring that the moral problems we face are more difficult than those our fathers had to deal with. The attempt is made, he says,

> to apply moral principles to the solution of economic and political problems by a larger number of people and on a scale hitherto unparalleled. There is an increasing demand that economic and political institutions shall conform to justice.[23]

The old, relatively simple moral principles tend to break down and to be found inadequate when called upon to solve problems of vast scope and implication. Another source of trouble is the "growing realization" of the gulf between public and private morals. Men are beginning to feel that they can no longer commit immoral acts in the name of a state or nation. A third difficulty is the fact that European morals have never effectually incorporated the dissident elements of barbaric and Christian tradition. Nonviolence as taught by Christ, which is opposed to the older ethic, has never been well learned.

> The result is a real lack of clarity in dealing with problems connected with the right use of force, and the reconciliation of freedom with order; and the erection of a fundamentally false, but superficially plausible, antithesis between the good of the individual and the good of the community.[24]

Despite these difficulties, which might be enough, one feels, to explain even more distress than we have suffered, Ginsberg sees the "moral content" of ideas—for instance, the idea of freedom—as constantly growing with the passage of time. This growth is likely to continue. It is not, however, inevitable that it should.

> Further progress depends upon whether we can formulate a coherent and comprehensive good common to mankind, whether we can acquire sufficient knowledge of the conditions which are necessary for its realization, and whether we can, in the light of such knowledge, generate a common or cooperative will with sufficient energy to bring these conditions into being.[25]

Ginsberg's is, therefore, an affirmation of contingent moral progress.

[22] *Ibid.*, p. 313. Do these remarks, when compared with those of Maritain, reflect the difference between modern Catholic and Jewish conceptions of religious and moral progress?

[23] *Ibid.*, p. 318.

[24] *Ibid.*, p. 319.

[25] *Ibid.*, p. 323.

For W. T. Stace, moral progress consists in the diffusion of a set of ideas —a "cluster," because they cling together and imply one another.

> The chief members of this cluster are the ideas of (1) the infinite value of the individual; (2) the equality of all men . . .; (3) individualism; (4) liberty. Of these ideas the first, that of the infinite value of the individual, is the *key* idea.

In fact, the other three "are really only aspects or facets of this one idea."[26]

Stace shows by a number of examples that this cluster of ideas underlies almost all moral notions. The doctrine of equality, for example, is manifested, not only in formal laws and institutions but in many of the instinctive reactions of human beings to one another.

> It is a commonplace that mothers often love and value their troublesome or even wicked children as much as—sometimes more than—their good ones. But how is it possible to value equally two persons of entirely unequal merit? The reason is that the mother does not value her child as a means to some benefit to herself. She loves him for himself, that is as an end.[27]

Stace holds that the idea of the infinite value of the individual is a peculiarly Western, a Christian, idea, and that moral progress is thus, so far, mainly (though not entirely) confined to the West. However, the idea is beginning to spread over the rest of the world. Hence moral progress will continue in the future—not necessarily, but probably.

Progress in Social Relations

The authors just discussed emphasize the intellectual or ideational content of moral progress, but some of them—particularly Stace and Mill— do not deny a consequent improvement in social morality. Other writers, while not denying progress in ethical conceptions—in the moral conscience, as Maritain puts it—place greater emphasis on improvements in individual and social behavior.

Bagehot educes many instances of moral progress in this sense. For example, he sees an historical increase of "prescriptive governability." We take without thought and as a *datum,* he declares, what the ancient political philosophers took as a *quaesitum.* He asserts, too, that the military vices

> of civilization seem to decline just as its military strength augments. Somehow or other civilization does not make men effeminate or unwarlike now

---

[26] *The Destiny of Western Man,* p. 124.

[27] *Ibid.,* p. 155. Stace might have added that the mother can value each of her unequal children equally because she values each of them infinitely.

as it once did. There is an improvement in our fibre—moral if not physical.
. . . The breed of ancient times was impaired for war by trade and luxury,
but the modern breed is not so impaired.[28]

And he affirms progress in toleration, in sympathy, in kindness, and particularly in prudence—the capacity to postpone the present to the future.
We may be sure, he declares, that the morality of prehistoric man was as
imperfect and as rudimentary as his reason.

> The same sort of arguments apply to a self-restraining morality of a high
> type as apply to a settled postponement of the present to the future upon
> grounds recommended by argument. . . . Exactly also like a shrewd far-
> sightedness, a sound morality in elementary transactions is far too useful a
> gift to the human race ever to have been thoroughly lost when they had
> once attained it. . . . If any reasoning is safe as to pre-historic man, the
> reasoning which imputes to him a deficient sense of morals is safe, for all
> the arguments suggested by all our late researches converge upon it, and
> concur in teaching it.[29]

Bagehot views what he calls "animated moderation" as an important
constituent of morally progressive races; indeed, he states that this is a
leading mark of progress. Most of the ills of the world, he suggests, are
the result of too much haste—in belief, in judgment, in action. The essential temperateness of the English is a sign of their progressive national
character.

> In action it is . . . this quality in which the English . . . excel all other
> nations. There is an infinite deal to be laid against us; and . . . no want
> of people to say it. But, after all, in a certain sense, England is a success in
> the world; her career has had many faults, but still it has been a fine and
> winning career upon the whole. And this on account of the exact possession
> of this particular quality. What is the making of a successful merchant?
> That he has plenty of energy, and yet that he does not go too far. And if
> you ask for a description of a great practical Englishman, you will be sure
> to have this, or something like it: "Oh, he has plenty of go in him; but he
> knows when to pull up."[30]

Indeed, it is just the lack of this quality in the Russians, Bagehot declares,
that is the reason for their notable lack of worldly success. And he seriously doubts, too, whether the Americans will ever be able to overcome
what seems to him their natural hastiness. In general, he holds that an
imposing manner is a dignified usage that tends to preserve itself and

[28] *Physics and Politics*, p. 35.
[29] *Ibid.*, pp. 84–5.
[30] *Ibid.*, p. 146.

also other usages along with it. It tends to induce obedience, and as such helps to bring about progress.[31]

We have seen that the basic source or principle of progress, for Bagehot, is struggle and conflict, and this applies in morals as well as in other realms. Morality confers an advantage in the battle of life. This notion is also put forward by Charles Darwin, whose *Origin of Species* was the inspiration for Bagehot's theory. Darwin's *The Descent of Man,* in turn, shows the effect of Bagehot's ideas about progress.[32] In order that primeval man, or apelike progenitors of man, should become social, they must, Darwin says, have acquired the same instinctive feelings that impel other animals to live in a body; and they no doubt exhibited the same general disposition.

> They would have felt uneasy when separated from their comrades, for whom they would have felt some degree of love; they would have warned each other of danger, and have given mutual aid in attack or defense. All this implies some degree of sympathy, fidelity, and courage.[33]

When two tribes of primeval man came into competition, if one tribe—other things being equal—included a "great number of courageous, sympathetic, and faithful members, who were always ready to warn each other of danger, to aid and defend each other, this tribe would succeed better and conquer the other. . . . Thus the social and moral qualities would tend slowly to advance and be diffused throughout the world."

Darwin mentions several types of moral qualities that are advantageous in the same way. However, he is not as enthusiastic about this kind of progress as Bagehot; and he is much more doubtful regarding the increase of virtue in modern times. In one respect, however, Darwin seems to agree wholly with Bagehot. "Obedience," Darwin says, "as Mr. Bagehot has well shown, is of the highest value, for any form of government is better than none."[34] If obedience is of value, then it will tend to increase—and we arrive at Bagehot's progress in "governability."[35]

[31] One of the great difficulties for the United States, says Bagehot, is that there has not been any cultivation of an impressive manner among the Americans. This leads to their overhastiness.

[32] *The Origin of Species* was published in 1859, *Physics and Politics* in 1869, and *The Descent of Man* in 1871.

[33] *The Descent of Man,* in *The Origin of Species and the Descent of Man,* p. 498.

[34] *Ibid.*

[35] The twentieth century has seen a lively dispute regarding the character and temperament of "primitive" man. The observations of such writers as Turnbull, Van der Post, and others may lead us to believe that the Pygmies, the Bushmen, and other "primitive" African races are gentle, loving people, alas! only waiting to be "spoiled" by civilization; and we are, therefore, to conclude that man has tended toward savagery rather than sweetness in his career on earth. On the other hand,

Sympathy, feelings of general humanity, and brotherhood are considered by a large number of progress authors to be signs of moral progress. Signs of it—but in the opinion of many there is not much progress of this sort to be observed. However, at least one group of writers emphasizes moral progress of this type apparently above all others. Bellamy, for instance, discovers that "the solidarity of the race and the brotherhood of man," which were not more than faint hopes in the nineteenth century, are "ties as real and as vital as physical fraternity" in the year 2000.[36] Bukharin, too, looks forward to improvements along this line:

> Let us now consider the state of affairs in organized society. In such a society there is no anarchy in production; there are no classes, no oppositions of class interests, etc. There are not even contradictions between personal and social interests. We are now dealing with a friendly brotherhood of workers.[37]

Marx and Engels foresee a social milieu in which men will be comrades and brothers. And the *1961 Draft Program* predicts moral progress of this and many other types.

> Harmonious relations will be established between the individual and society. . . . Family relations will be freed from material considerations and will be based solely on mutual love and friendship.[38]

In the course of the transition to Communism, the *1961 Draft Program* goes on to declare, the moral principles of society become increasingly important, the sphere of action of the moral factor expands, and the importance of the administrative control of human relations diminishes accordingly.

> The Party holds that the moral code of the builder of communism should comprise the following principles:
>
> Devotion to the Communist cause, love of the Socialist motherland and of the other Socialist countries;
>
> Conscientious labor for the good of society—he who does not work, neither shall he eat;
>
> Concern on the part of everyone for the preservation and growth of public wealth;

Robert Ardrey, in *African Genesis* and in *The Territorial Imperative*, argues the case for "primitive" man's being naturally aggressive. Actually, the dispute is a perennial one. It can be traced back to the Greeks.

[36] *Looking Backward*, p. 134.

[37] *Historical Materialism*, p. 41.

[38] *Program of the Communist Party of the Soviet Union (Draft)*, 1961, p. 160.

A high sense of public duty, intolerance of actions harmful to the public interest;

Collectivism and comradely mutual assistance: one for all and all for one;

Humane relations and mutual respect between individuals—man is to man a friend, comrade, and brother;

. . . Friendship and brotherhood among all peoples of the U.S.S.R., intolerance of national and racial hatred;

. . . Fraternal solidarity with the working people of all countries, and with all peoples.[39]

Comte, who shares with the Marxists the notion that mankind is advancing in the direction of collective freedom, also shares with them some of their ideas about the future moral condition of mankind. It is unquestionable, he declares,

that civilization leads us on to a further and further development of our noblest dispositions and our most generous feelings, which are the only possible basis of human association, and which receive, by means of that association, a more and more special culture.[40]

Moral progress, for the Marxist authors, is mainly the result of prior technological and economic progress. For Comte, the prior development appears to be primarily in knowledge. There is at present, he says, a certain "antagonism" between the intellectual and moral spheres, but this is merely provisional, and another effect of the breakdown of the old "metaphysical" societies; it will be "dissolved at once when the sociological point of view is established as the only true one." The positive philosophy, when it is applied to moral questions, will produce moral progress of three sorts: in personal morality, domestic morality, and social morality. The action of a universal education, says Comte—echoing Condorcet—and then the steady intervention of a wise discipline, both public and private—this side of the matter is *not* emphasized by Condorcet—carried on by the same moral power that had superintended the earlier training, will have marked effects in all three areas. In the first, one will observe

a noble boldness in developing the greatness of Man in all directions, free from the oppression of any fear, and limited only by the conditions of life itself.[41]

[39] *Ibid.,* pp. 208–9.
[40] *Positive Philosophy,* p. 516.
[41] *Ibid.,* p. 832.

As for domestic morality, "we have seen what is the subordination prescribed by nature in the cases of sex and of age."[42] The ordered relation of the sexes and generations, according to Comte, will be a vast improvement over the present anarchy in this respect. Finally, the positive philosophy is the first to have ascertained the true point of view of social morality.

> The metaphysical philosophy sanctioned egotism; and the theological subordinated real life to an imaginary one; while the new philosophy takes social morality as the basis of its whole system. . . . We have yet to witness the moral superiority of a philosophy which connects [as the positive philosophy does] each of us with the whole of human existence, in all times and places. . . . For instance, the scrupulous respect for human life, which has always increased with our social progression, must strengthen more and more as the chimerical hope dies out which disparages the present life as merely accessory to the one in prospect.[43]

There is the strongest conceivable evidence, Comte concludes, of the possibility of developing, on human grounds alone, "a sense of general morality complete enough to inspire an invincible repugnance to moral offense, and an irresistible impulse to steady practical devotedness."

"The characteristic of Education is this, above all," says Comte: "a Being naturally inclined to live for self and in self is to be made disposed to live for others so as to live again in others by others."[44] Perhaps the character of such selfless altruism is best described in the phrase of Godwin, who foresees a time when everyone shall seek, with ineffable ardor, the good of all.

According to many progress authors, there are other signs of progress in social morality besides the increase of brotherhood and altruism. One is the decline of war, in which several nineteenth-century progress authors believe. Buckle's views on the subject have been noted; Comte agrees that war tends to grow less important in social life; and so does Levi Woodberry. Woodberry declares that

> cruelty of all kinds has been gradually lessening. This has aided to strip war throughout of many of its horrors. It makes prisoners where it once extirpated; and prisoners to be exchanged, rather than enslaved. It exonerates

[42] *Ibid.* This remark reflects Comte's fiercely held early belief in the natural inferiority of women (see also pp. 498–508). See below for some discussion of his later change of heart.

[43] *Ibid.*, pp. 832–4.

[44] Qu. by Todd, *op. cit.*, p. v. Todd also quotes Leslie Stephen as saying that "the progress of civilization depends, I should say, on the extension of the sense of duty which each man owes to society at large."

even from imprisonment all not in arms, and thus relieves helpless infancy and the feebleness of woman from the bitter sufferings of captivity. It has, in truth, rendered war itself less frequent, substituting reason and negotiation and arbitration more often for the battle-field; and the frivolous grounds for hostilities which often have deluged nations in blood would not in this age rouse public feeling, nor arm any free government, either with the sinews of war, or the lion hearts which are indispensable to its success.[45]

On no other subject than this is there a greater difference of opinion, perhaps, among authors writing in the half century before the First World War and those writing in the half century after it.

A large number of progress authors discuss the question whether war and its attendant cruelties abate or increase. An equally large number put emphasis on the social position of women as a prime element in moral progress. Maritain, for instance, remarks that Christianity's endowment of women, "otherwise and particularly in the East regarded as an object of property, with a sense of dignity and personal liberty," is a gain "of immense historical importance."[46] Improvement in the treatment accorded women by men is a mark of moral progress. Maritain also holds, with many others, that woman is herself a civilizing, a progressive influence. He quotes Raïssa Maritain on this point:

> In this story of human progress which we are endeavoring to read word by word in Genesis, be it noted, whatever be the possibility of other interpretations, that woman has jumped a stage. She was not made from the earth, from "the dust of the earth" like man. . . . She was made of human stuff, created in the heart of paradise, while man only entered therein after his creation.
>
> Thus, according to the Bible, the physical origin of woman is nobler than that of man. The price of this privilege is that the claims of God and of man are by so much the higher with regard to her, and even, dare one say, in the eyes of God. . . . God has permitted the laws which man has made, either by himself or under His inspiration, always to demand a greater humanity, abnegation and purity from woman. The traces, the memory of his animal and earthly stage press more heavily on man. But Eve is full of resemblances to the better Adam.[47]

Mill declares that "the principle which regulates the existing social relations between the two sexes—the legal subordination of one sex to the other—is wrong in itself, and now one of the chief hindrances to human

---

[45] "On Progress," in Probst (ed.), *The Happy Republic*, pp. 276-7.
[46] *True Humanism*, p. 190.
[47] Qu. by Maritain, *ibid.*, pp. 192-3, Note.

improvement."[48] And even Comte, whose strictures on the natural inferiority of woman are a notable element in his *Positive Philosophy*, expresses in a later work, written after his meeting with the woman he called his "angel,"[49] his feeling that respect, not to say adoration, of woman is one of the great goals of human progress. He declares, in fact, that masculine sexuality will eventually cease altogether, and woman will be the sole progenitor of the race.

> Such a perfection is presaged by the growing development of chastity, which, proper to the human race, at least among males, shows the physical, intellectual, and moral efficacy of a sound employment of the vivifying fluid. . . . Thus one conceives that civilization not only disposes man to appreciate woman more but continually increases the participation of the female sex in human reproduction, ultimately reaching a point where birth would emanate from woman alone.[50]

Of all the influences tending to promote progress in social morality perhaps none is cited more often than religion. We have noted Maritain's opinion that the advent of Christianity is not an example of human *natural* progress, but many progress authors consider this objection to be irrelevant to the real question, which is whether moral progress occurs, whatever its source. Thus Chateaubriand, for instance, declares that religion, as it became more widely known and discarded fanaticism, imparted a greater mildness to Christian manners.

> This change was not the effect of letters; for the spirit of humanity has not been the more respected in those countries which could boast of their superior knowledge.[51]

This view, which is in direct opposition to that of Buckle, is shared by Madame de Staël. Commiseration for sufferings must, in every age, have naturally existed in the human heart, she says; nevertheless, "how different are the morals of antiquity from those of Christianity! The one is founded upon violence, and the other upon sympathy."[52] And even Malthus admits some improvement in manners as a result of the introduction of Christianity. It is slight enough, perhaps, and it is furthermore

[48] *The Subjection of Women,* in *On Liberty, Representative Government, the Subjection of Women,* p. 427.
[49] Manuel tells the story of this meeting and Comte's subsequent change of heart toward all women in *The Prophets of Paris,* pp. 260–3.
[50] *Positive Polity,* Vol. IV, pp. 276–7, qu. by Manuel, p. 292. The change in question would surely be in man's very nature.
[51] *The Genius of Christianity,* p. 684.
[52] *The Influence of Literature Upon Society,* p. 196.

confined to a few; the mass of men show as yet little or no moral progress. But it is there.[53]

Progress authors less often deny the occurrence of some sort of progress in social morality than might be supposed. Yet there is at least one uncompromising denial to be found in the literature. It is a curious and ironic view, and one hardly knows how seriously to take it. It must nevertheless be noted that Mandeville holds a position clearly opposed to all of those discussed above. His bees once lived like men and acted like men "in small." The hive was naturally filled with vice, yet the whole mass was a paradise. The source of social action—and of progress—was the endeavor of millions to supply each other's lust and vanity. The worst cheats and knaves were, of course, the ones who cried the loudest against dishonesty and fraud:

> And all the rogues cry'd brazenly,
> Good Gods, had we but honesty!

Whereupon Jove, appropriately indignant, rid the hive of fraud. The reign of honesty in this complex society turned out to be catastrophic. Pride, envy, and emulation waned. Luxuries were no longer needed. Industry and trade declined. A once flourishing civilization became vulnerable to its enemies. Defeated in a final battle, the remaining bees retreated into a hollow tree to lead temperate, frugal lives, blessed with content and honesty. They had given up their vices, but at a fearful cost. They had given up progress as well.[54]

Progress in the Character of Human Beings

Little remains to be said on the subject of moral progress. For the most part, authors who affirm that there are progressive changes in the character of human beings hold that such changes are in human nature, and their views have already been treated. Several of the writers discussed in the preceding paragraphs, too, seem to speak of improvements in character, and might have been considered here. Nevertheless, a few progress authors seem to place emphasis on what may be termed private moral progress, as opposed to public or social melioration. This would doubtless have a social effect. But the more important effect would be on individuals.

[53] *Population*, pp. 138–9.
[54] We have previously pointed out that Mandeville's fable exaggerates in a way that expository works seldom do.

We have examined Kant's theory of progress in other contexts, and have seen that progress, for him, is based on strife (itself providentially ordained) and is necessary because, nature being so constituted as to do nothing in vain, the very possibility of general progress insures its actuality. But general progress is not the same thing as moral progress. The distinctive characteristic of moral progress, considered in itself, is that it is *not* inevitable. The argument runs like this.

Morality, says Kant, is an obligation founded in the nature of reason. This obligation presupposes a goal, and the goal is a reign of reason under which men treat one another not as means but as ends. This ideal condition is a necessary postulate of reason and is therefore factually possible. The question is whether it will ever actually be attained. The answer is that it *probably* will. For what is the alternative to moral progress?

> It is a spectacle most unworthy—I will not say of a Divinity, but even of the commonest well-disposed man—to see the human race making a few steps upward in virtue from one period to another, and soon thereafter falling down again as deep into vice and misery as before. To gaze for a while upon this tragedy, may be moving and instructive; but the curtain must at last be let fall upon it. For when prolonged in this manner, it becomes a farce; and although the actors may not become weary, being fools, yet the spectator will become tired of it, having enough in one or two acts, where he has got grounds to infer that this play that never comes to an end is but an eternal repetition of the same thing. . . . [This] is—at least according to our ideas—altogether opposed to the morality of a wise Creator and Governor of the world.[55]

It is the innate sense of duty of every man toward posterity that pretty well assures moral progress, for, as Kant says, every man is, in fact, prompted so to act that the successive generations may always become better, and the possibility of this must be assured. Kant also points to contemporary advances in civil and religious liberty, which are, he declares, the conditions of real moral progress. Hence, it is not only highly likely, from a theoretical viewpoint, that this type of progress will occur, but it is also observable that it does occur.

This is not to say, however, that any one man, or even a sequence of generations of men, has a good idea of what moral progress consists in, or what direction it should take. Progress occurs, in Kant's conception of it, over a vast number of generations, during which there are doubtless many pitfalls to be avoided and strait ways to be negotiated. It is for this reason

[55] "On the Saying: That a Thing May Be Right in Theory, But May Not Hold in Practice," in W. Hastie (ed.), *Principles of Politics*, pp. 68–9. See also Teggart (ed.), *The Idea of Progress*, p. 305.

that he recommends against taking progress, as it were, into one's own hands. Men, with their limited vision, are likely to do as much harm as good.

It is for the same reason that moral progress, in the last analysis, must be seen as essentially contingent. Progress toward the universal rule of reason is inevitable; it is insured by Nature herself. But morality is a private matter. The individual's innate sense of duty cannot be determined in the same way as the general progress of the human race. To say that it could would be to deny man natural freedom. In Christian terms, to assure man salvation is to deny him free will, and without that he cannot deserve salvation. The individual's capacity—perhaps never to be exercised—for immorality can never be taken from him, even in a world that is entirely and thoroughly reasonable. Therefore, moral progress, even though it is in the highest degree probable, cannot be said to be inevitable.

Most of the progress authors who look forward to anything like Kant's future moral progress conceive it as the result of a deep and abiding change in human nature. The Marxists hold this view of the matter, as we have seen, although they say the improvement in human nature will be the result of social progress. Lessing, the Joachimites, and other evangelists of the "eternal gospel" predict that in the next and last dispensation of the world, mankind will naturally seek the good for its own sake, and not for the sake of anything else. This too is progress within human nature, not in man's exterior arrangements and conditions of life. And Hermann J. Muller foresees a similar eventuality. Not only will it be possible, he says, to breed men with better minds—with more searching, more analytic intellects—we can also make them pleasanter to live with. To be worked for, "by both cultural and genetic means," are

> a genuine warmth and fellow feeling and a cooperative disposition, a depth and breadth of intellectual capacity, moral courage and integrity . . . a strengthening and extension of the tendencies toward kindliness, affection, and fellow feeling in general. . . . As regards other affective traits, there is much room for broadening and deepening our capacity to appreciate both natural and man-made constructions, to interpret with fuller empathy the expressions of others, to create ever richer combinations of our own impressions, and to communicate them more adequately to others.[56]

Insofar as these changes are the result of manipulation of the genes, they occur in the makeup of the human being. But if, as Muller seems to sug-

[56] "Should We Weaken or Strengthen Our Genetic Heritage?", in *Daedalus*, Summer 1961, pp. 445–6.

gest, they could also be brought about by cultural means, then they might involve no important change in human nature.

In this sense, perhaps, it is possible to speak of moral progress in the character of human beings as a change in the general conditions of human life. Moral progress of this sort might occur by the historical selection of certain character traits over others, all of which are present in the human being from the beginning. This is probably the view of Bagehot, and we are not surprised, therefore, to find him suggesting that human character improves along with human knowledge and power. And Charles Darwin can be interpreted as concurring on this point.

Ptirim Sorokin sees the situation somewhat differently. He looks not to the past but to the present and future, and observes at least thirteen different ways in which love confers social and other advantages. Progress, for Sorokin, is highly contingent, for hatred is also a great force in the world. Nevertheless, if progress does in fact continue to occur, it will be because of, as well as consist in, the increase of the rule of love in human affairs. Progressive men love better and will do so increasingly if the human race survives. The energy of unselfish love

> ennobles all familistic persons, communities or nations, inspires them with great and constructive tasks, and blesses them with the strength and creativity necessary for realization of these high objectives.[57]

Lewis Mumford also conceives progress as contingent; and he too holds that love progresses, grows stronger and richer. Since man started on his career, Mumford declares,

> there has not been merely an increase in the quantity of mind, but also in its qualitative attributes: in man's sensitiveness, his feeling, his capacity for love. . . . Despite many setbacks and diversions, mind has matured, and love, which first sprang out of the needs of reproduction and nurture, has widened its domain. No theory of human development is adequate that does not include this widening of the province of love: it is this, rather than intelligence and the division of labor (which man shares with rats and termites), that marks man's full emergence into the human estate. In the act of maturation man has made existence more lovable by multiplying the objects and the ways of love.[58]

It is the growth of the idea of the person that underlies this remarkable increase of love, Mumford says. Love, like mind itself, has been slowly gathering momentum through the organic world; by reason of its late in-

[57] *Power and Morality*, p. 153.
[58] *The Transformations of Man*, p. 173.

troduction into the drama conceived and enacted by man, it has absorbed only a small share of man's working and learning activities.

> But in the development of the person love is actually the central element of integration: love as erotic desire and procreativeness, love as passion and aesthetic delight, lingering over images of beauty and shaping them anew, love as fellow feeling and neighborly helpfulness, bestowing its gifts on those who need them, love as parental solicitude and sacrifice, finally, love with its miraculous capacity for overvaluing its own object, thereby glorifying and transfiguring it, releasing for life something that only the lover at first can see.[59]

There is no essential change in human nature to be observed here; man always had the capacity for love, and history is the record of its growing actualization. Past and present history, at least—there is question about the future. The possibility exists that man may go the way of posthistoric sterility and spiritual death. If he does not, if he takes the better road, love will continue to grow and to reach out into the universe. What is more, no limit can be set to its effects. "Who can set bounds," Mumford asks, "to man's emergence or to his power of surpassing his provisional achievements?" And he adds:

> Every goal man reaches provides a new starting point, and the sum of all man's days is just a beginning.[60]

CHARACTERISTICS OF MORAL PROGRESS

At several places in the foregoing discussion we have considered the question whether moral progress, in whatever sense, is necessary. In general it seems that progress authors hold that this kind of progress, more than any other, is contingent, since morality, being essentially the domain of freedom, escapes the domination of historical tendencies in a way that knowledge, for example, may not do. Nevertheless, it is noteworthy that writers like Comte and the Marxists hold that moral progress, since it is the inevitable result of an historical process that they see as necessary, is necessary, too. And perhaps Lessing and the Joachimites would agree, since future progress is assured by Providence's plan for the world.

It is possible that Lessing and the Joachimites feel that moral progress will cease when men are as good as they can be, but it appears that no

[59] *Ibid.*, p. 176.
[60] *Ibid.*, p. 184.

other progress authors hold this position. There is manifestly no limit to what love may do, nor is there, even for Comte and the Marxists—those authors, in other words, who maintain that humanity progresses toward collective freedom—any limit to the amelioration of social and personal relations to be expected when the good society is finally attained.

Progress in knowledge is, in the view of Buckle and Mill, a phenomenon prior to moral progress; the latter is dependent and, at least for Mill, contingent (where progress in knowledge is in some way necessary and inevitable). Thomas Mann's character, Herr Settembrini, sees moral progress as one effect—perhaps the leading one—of technological progress; and Dewey views technological advance as the condition of moral progress, though it is not progress in itself. Writers like Mumford and Childe suggest that the increase of wealth is in some sense a prior condition of some sorts of moral progress, at least. Mankind, when released from the pressures of the struggle for existence, is more likely to make changes for the better in its social and moral relations. There is no question that the Marxists hold this view: only when the problems of subsistence are finally solved by the application of technological ingenuity, and when the economic progress represented by the cessation of the struggle between classes for control of the means of production has occurred, will mankind enter upon a course of real progress in morality.

Comte agrees, perhaps, although his emphasis is rather on the growth of knowledge than on economic developments. Moral progress will be a result of the progress of equality, which in turn is dependent on the progress of knowledge, in Condorcet's conception of the priorities. If, in Teilhard's view, there is to be moral progress at all—one is not entirely certain of this—it will probably be one of the effects of the inevitable future planetization of mankind. For Kant, moral progress will be aided, if not insured, by the necessary advance of rationality in the system of the world. Finally, the attainment of more freedom, of whatever kind, is held by many writers to be a condition, in one way or another, of moral progress, in the sense of the progress of ethical conceptions, the progress of social relations, and progress in the character of human beings.

Although no progress author clearly asserts that moral progress is a prior condition of other types of exterior progress, it is probable that few fail to recognize the reverse effect (as it may be called) of moral progress on others kinds. As Herman J. Muller might put it, there is a positive feedback between moral progress and progress in knowledge, technology, wealth, politics, and so forth. If moral progress occurs, this cannot be conceived as harming man in any way. What is being implied here, of course, is a priority of another sort. Moral progress may be an effect of other types of progress; it may be, temporally, the posterior or subsequent phenomenon. Logically, however, moral progress is not posterior, but absolutely prior. In the opinion of most progress authors, moral progress—in the old Aristotelian phrase—is *that for which* all human progress occurs.

The Problem of Progress
in the Fine Arts

The Problem of Progress
in the Fine Arts

T H A T progress occurs in knowledge and in technology is almost universally affirmed by progress authors—that is, by writers who say that progress occurs at all. The majority of progress authors seem to agree that there is at least some progress in wealth. A fair number—perhaps a minority, but nevertheless an important one—assert that political and moral progress are future possibilities, if they are not (as for many they are not) clearly discernible facts of past history. But few progress authors maintain that progress in the fine arts occurs, or even that it can occur. And even the small number of assertions to this effect that can be found in the literature are, when analyzed, in one way or another defective.

This is not to say, of course, that there are not many assertions to be found, in the literature of art criticism and in general historical writing, to the effect that the art of one time is better than that of another time, or that the artists of one time are more skilled, more aware, or more effective as artists than those of another. What is hard to find are assertions to the effect that there is a more or less steady change for the better in the history of art, such that it is true in general that the art of a later time is clearly superior to that of an earlier time. And predictions that the art of the future will be clearly superior to that of the past and of the present are exceedingly rare.

They are not nonexistent, however, and so it behooves us to treat this difficult aspect of our subject. What is more, the progress literature is by no means deficient in *denials* of progress in art.[1] Indeed, it is the denials, rather than the affirmations, of this kind of progress that are of greatest interest. At the same time, the denials must be in opposition to something, and one has the impression—not a very clear one—that there are implicit affirmations of progress in art in the literature. It is this quality of the affirmations that makes the subject difficult to treat.

Before attempting to do so, it should be said that progress authors are probably inclined to agree that progress occurs in our *knowledge* of art; histories of art are a relatively modern invention, and they tend to be fuller, and more detailed, with the passage of time. This, however, is progress in knowledge, not progress in art. Writers are also inclined to agree that there is some sort of increase in the number of artistic techniques that can be (but, of course, need not be) studied, and perhaps mastered, by modern artists, as opposed to ancient ones. Photography is an obvious example; another is the development of oil pigments; still another is the modern use of the blowtorch in sculpture. These inventions allow later artists to do things with their materials, and to create kinds of artistic works, that were impossible for their forebears. But this is not progress in art, either; it is technological progress. In discussing progress in art it is essential to keep in mind, and to search for in the writings of authors, some artistic or aesthetic criterion for determining whether progress occurs in this respect. Above all, the error of mistaking moral progress as expressed in art for artistic progress itself should be avoided.

In what follows, we will first treat denials of progress in art, for these afford no difficulty. We will then turn to the few apparent affirmations of this kind of progress to be found in the literature.[2]

Denials of Progress in the Fine Arts

The position that progress cannot occur in art because of the nature of progress, or of art, or of both, is taken by many progress authors. Other

[1] In general, denials of progress in art by authors who do not concern themselves with the subject of progress in general—either to affirm or to deny it—are not considered in this Appendix.

The question of evolution, including or not including progress, in the arts is treated extensively by Thomas Munro, in *Evolution in the Arts*. Frequent reference to this work is made in what follows.

[2] Denials are treated first, rather than affirmations, as elsewhere in the book. The reason is that the denials of progress in art by progress authors usually raise a question about the existence of a cumulative principle in art that several of the authors who affirm progress in art attempt to answer.

denials are made by writers who feel that art may once have progressed, but can no longer do so. We will treat the former position first.

For De Rougemont, the notion of "development" is essential to progress. Progress cannot occur where there is no development. It is a mistake, he declares, to apply the idea of progress "to spheres in which it is not development but the moment and the action that count."

> If it is true that Einstein's relativity represents a progression over Newtonian physics, and if the electronic brain is an advance on Vaucanson's automata, it does not follow that the latest in time of our atonal or sound-effects modes marks any progress on Mozart. For there is no going "beyond" Mozart: he is sufficient unto himself. He is not a transitory stage in some collective pursuit or inquiry, never ended; he is a completed work, a creative act. . . . The arts do not progress, for they are not made up of "currents" but of significant works. . . . The measure of great art is love, not the manner of expression; sublimity, not difference; an achievement valid for all, not some small variation momentarily odd.[3]

This view, a familiar one, is also expressed by A. C. Brock. "At one time the arts flourish," he says, "at another they decay." The reason is to some extent mysterious.

> One nation cannot take up an art where another has left it. That is where art seems to differ from science. . . . Art . . . is always a growth of its own time which cannot be transplanted, and no one can tell why it grows in one time and among one people and not in another.

Besides, there is no accounting for tastes—"and in saying that we despair of progress in the arts."

> For it is ultimately this unaccountable thing called taste, and not the absence or presence of genius, which determines whether the arts shall thrive or decay in any particular age or country.[4]

[3] *Man's Western Quest*, pp. 168–9.
[4] "Progress in Art," in F. S. Marvin (ed.), *Progress and History*, pp. 224–7. In a sense, Brock answers his own points later on in this article. Progress has never yet occurred in art, he declares, but this does not mean that it will never occur. "What do we mean by progress except the successful exercise of the human will in a right direction?" he asks. If this is what progress is, then it can occur in art as well as in other areas, for there is no reason why we cannot turn our will to bringing about artistic progress, as we have turned it to bringing about progress in knowledge, in science and technology, and in morals. The directed and improved will is not all that is required, of course. We must also learn all that we can about the art of the past; we must establish a tradition in art, and build on it. This, too, is possible, although it has never been done; "though genius is born, it is also made."
Hence, Brock's position is that progress in art is possible; it can occur in the future. The remarks quoted in the text are representative, however, of many denials of progress in art.

Brock is saying the same thing as De Rougemont. There is no "development" in art; that is, no criterion or rule according to which one work of art (or school of art) may be said to follow necessarily after another, and not precede it; in short, no cumulative principle.

The question of progress in the arts is a "very difficult problem," says Lord Bryce. A modern high-school student knows more than Euclid; does this mean we have produced mathematicians greater than Euclid? The English of the nineteenth century knew more about the drama than the Greeks, but did any of them write greater plays than Aeschylus or Sophocles? Once more there is no—rather, Bryce finds no—cumulative principle. Knowledge accumulates. It progresses. But art does not.[5]

The difference between art and science is also emphasized by Théophile Gautier. "Art differs from science in this," he writes: "it begins again with each artist. . . . There is no progress in art."[6] Aldous Huxley agrees. "Every artist begins at the beginning," he declares. "The man of science, on the other hand, begins where his predecessor left off."[7] And John Caird holds that

> the achievements of the painters, sculptors, poets of the past are not handed on to their successors like those of the men of science. . . . Here what a man does depends comparatively little on what others have done before him, but mainly on the quality and temper of his own mind. . . . The perfection of a work of art lies in that which is deeper than expression—the creative faculty, the ineffable gift of genius. . . . Now, this is an element which cannot be transmitted or handed down. It is independent of tradition and education, it comes as an inspiration on elected souls fresh from the eternal fount of light, and the men of later times have no nearer or freer access to it than those of ages the most remote.[8]

Wanda Landowska also emphasizes the singularity of works of art that prohibits art from being truly progressive. We are told that "everything advances, everything progresses in life," she writes; "the earth itself is not immobile. Yes, but fortunately it does not try with gigantic strides to reach the sun; it seems that while rotating around it the earth gets closer at times, farther at others, only to return to about the same place." Some sort of cyclicity applies to art as well.

> Similarly art does not run in the direction of just one preconceived ideal; each generation has its own, and each generation reaches it more or less. From that spring the numerous aspects of beauty in works of art which are perfect in themselves, although different from each other.

[5] See "What Is Progress?", in *The Atlantic Monthly*, August 1907, p. 150.
[6] Qu. by Munro, *op. cit.*, p. 26.
[7] Qu. by Munro, *ibid.*
[8] Qu. by Munro, *ibid.*, pp. 26–7.

That is why, Mme Landowska goes on, we equally enjoy Homer and Shakespeare, Sophocles and Molière, Phidias and Michelangelo, Watteau and Rodin. She objects that only in music "are we supposed to accept the idea" of progress.

If this religion of progress went on, coupled with ignorance, we would read in two hundred years, "Ravel may be considered the father of music because the composers who preceded him, such as Beethoven and Wagner, were still in an embryonic stage and have fallen into a just oblivion."[9]

Her historical studies have shown that "each generation [is] proud of having reached the apogee of perfection after one or two centuries of progress," Mme Landowska remarks. Thus progress in knowledge, instead of supporting, undermines the notion of progress in art.

The denial in her case is somewhat limited—it applies mainly to music. But she quotes Victor Hugo as making the more general point:

Beauty in art is its immunity to improvement. Art as such does not by itself advance or regress. Transformations in poetry are merely undulations of beauty useful to human motion. Art is not capable of intrinsic progress. Retrogress as far as you please, from the palace of Versailles to the castle of Heidelberg; from the castle of Heidelberg to Notre-Dame de Paris; from there to the Alhambra; from the Alhambra to St. Sophia; from it to the Coliseum; from the Coliseum to the Acropolis, and from there to the Pyramids; you may go backward in centuries, but you will never regress in art. Art does not depend on any betterment of the future, or any transformation of language, or on any death or birth of an idiom. It is as pure, as complete, as divine amid total barbarism as it is in the midst of civilization. Such is the little known law of art![10]

Despite the fact that Hugo takes his examples from architecture, this is a general denial of the occurrence of progress in art. Hugo believes, like the other writers mentioned, that no principle of cumulation or development is to be found in the history of art. Each work of art is unique and is complete in itself. Historical comparisons between works of art are not valid; hence, progress in this respect is not possible.

In the view of Turgot, art can no longer progress—though, in a sense, it once did. The reason is that art is essentially limited, and the limits have already been reached. "Knowledge of nature and of truth is as infi-

[9] "Is Music a Progressive Art?", in *Landowska on Music,* p. 41.
[10] Qu. by Mme Landowska, *ibid.,* pp. 39–40. She also quotes Picasso as saying that the cave paintings of the Dordogne Valley have never been bettered.

nite as they," he says. Progress in knowledge and technique will continue indefinitely. However,

> the arts, whose object is to give us pleasure, are as limited as ourselves. Time unfolds continually new discoveries in the sciences; but poetry, painting, music, have a fixed limit, which is determined by the nature of languages, imitation of nature, and the limited sensibility of our organs; which they approach gradually and which they cannot pass.[11]

"The great men of the Augustan era reached it," Turgot observes, "and are still our models." This might be interpreted as an assertion that art is progressive but that it "plateaued out" a long time ago. However, that does not seem to be the intent of Turgot's remarks. He distinguishes between art and science—knowledge—on the grounds of their relation to us. The one is limited, the other not. Presumably, the absolute limits of art could have been met at the very beginning—as, indeed, some say they were, in the work of Homer—which would imply that art does not progress at all. In fact, Turgot's position is not unlike that of the writers previously mentioned. The sciences advance because they have a cumulative principle of progress. Art does not.

Fontenelle agrees with Turgot, although he sets the limits of artistic improvement in the future, at least for some of the arts. "Eloquence and poetry are rather limited in scope," he says. There must, therefore,

> come a time when they are developed to their highest perfection; and I hold that for eloquence and for history that time was the century of Augustus. I can imagine nothing superior to Cicero and Livy; it is not that they are without their faults, but I do not believe that it is possible to have fewer imperfections combined with so many noble qualities; it is universally allowed that it is only to this extent that men can be said to be perfect in anything.[12]

However, Fontenelle doubts whether all kinds of poetic perfection have yet been reached. He holds that Virgil is superior to Theocritus and Homer, and declares that "the most beautiful verse in the world is that of Virgil." Nevertheless, he admits that

> I shall never be greatly surprised to see Virgil excelled; and our modern romances, which are poems in prose, have already made us aware of this possibility.[13]

---

[11] *Tableau philosophique*, in F. J. Teggart (ed.), *The Idea of Progress*, p. 252. Turgot's contention, incidentally, is hotly disputed by many advocates of the moderns in the controversy between Ancients and Moderns. See, for instance, Dryden's *Essay on Dramatic Poesy*.

[12] *Digression sur les Anciens et les Modernes*, in Teggart, p. 182. This essay is rich in affirmations of possible improvement in certain genres. In general, however, Fontenelle seems to doubt future artistic progress.

[13] *Ibid.*

As to the drama, though the Greeks far excelled the Romans in this respect, says Fontenelle, "the best works of Sophocles, of Euripides, and of Aristophanes will hardly rank beside *Cinna, Horace, Ariane, Le Misanthrope*."[14] Improvement is, therefore, still possible in this branch of literature. In addition,

> we have even some new varieties, such as the courtly epistles, the tales, the operas, each of which has given us an excellent author, to whom antiquity has no one to oppose, and whom posterity will probably never surpass. . . . We see by a great many poetical works that verse can have to-day as much nobility as it ever had, and at the same time much greater exactness and precision.[15]

Nevertheless, although he allows the possibility of new invention in art, Fontenelle's position is not really different from that of previous authors. He affirms the essentially limited character of art, and the necessity, therefore, that whatever progress occurs in it must sometime cease, if it has not done so already. Knowledge is not like this, he asserts. Progress in knowledge goes on and on.

It may be argued that progress once occurred in art, but can no longer do so, on other grounds than the essentially limited character of artistic work. Art is expression, says Mumford, and a reward of craftsmanship in many branches of art and technics used to be that

> the worker could pass, with further technical skill, from the operational to the expressive parts of his job. Through acquiring skill in technics, he became licensed, as it were, to practice art. At that stage, the machine itself makes a contribution to creative release. . . . Up to a point, then, in all the industrial arts, technical development and symbolic expression go hand in hand.[16]

In the nineteenth century, however, a new stage of human development was reached. Machines became almost divine and were almost worshiped; they were treated as autonomous, while human beings were considered servile. Men were "thing-conditioned, externalized, de-humanized—disconnected from their historic values and purposes."[17] As a result, man is now no longer able to express his inmost needs, his most exalted ideals, his most daring dreams. He is stifled by the machine instead of inspired by it.

> The maimed fantasies, the organized frustrations, that we see in every comprehensive exhibition of modern painting today are so many symptoms of

[14] *Ibid.,* p. 186.
[15] *Ibid.*
[16] *Art and Technics,* p. 63.
[17] *Ibid.,* p. 14.

this deep personal abdication. Pattern and purpose have progressively disappeared, along with the person who once, in his own right, embodied them. Man has become an exile in this mechanical world; or rather, even worse, he has become a displaced person.[18]

A similar point is made by Valéry, who defines progress in such a way as to show how it is inimical to art.

Eliminating all considerations of a moral, political, or aesthetic character, I found that progress came down to the rapid and obvious growth of the (mechanical) *power* at man's disposal, and of the *accuracy* he can attain in his predictions. Horsepower and the number of varifiable decimals: these are indexes that, beyond any doubt, have greatly risen in the last hundred years.[19]

However, "our progress must be paid for," Valéry warns. The price is our inability to indulge in

refined leisure, in profound enjoyment, in the true, intimate, and contemplative understanding of works of art.[20]

A number of authors hold the view expressed by Mumford and Valéry. On the whole, however, they do not affirm the occurrence of progress in other respects, and thus are not considered here. Among these might be mentioned Juenger, Ellul, and Seidenberg, who indict modern art on the same grounds as Valéry and Mumford. Advances in technology, they maintain, spell the death of art.

Mumford and Valéry are contingent progress authors; they are not certain of future progress, but they do concede its possibility. And this is inherent in their view of art. At present, art is regressing because of the conditions of life in which it exists. If those conditions changed, art might advance. Nevertheless, even though their denial of the occurrence of artistic progress is therefore not absolute, they may be placed in the same category with writers like Turgot and Fontenelle, who, for different reasons, see future progress in art as either impossible or very unlikely, and, if possible at all, limited in scope.

We have, then, two kinds of denial of the occurrence of this type of progress. The one is based on a conception of society and of man—it is perhaps a contingent denial, which, by inversion, may be viewed as a contingent affirmation. The other is an absolute denial. It derives from

18 *Ibid.*, p. 9.
19 *History and Politics*, p. 164.
20 *Ibid.*, p. 339. In short, progress—and also what Valéry calls its opposite, tradition—are both opposed to "humanity." "Clearly," he writes, "tradition and progress are the two great enemies of the human race" (*ibid.*, p. 394).

the assertion that there is no cumulative or developmental principle in art, hence, no progress. It is the latter position that is opposed by progress authors who affirm progress in art.

Affirmations of Progress in the Fine Arts

Thomas Munro examines at length "the argument of anti-evolutionists that art can not evolve because it is not cumulative. Art, they say, is fundamentally different from science in that (a) it is constantly 'beginning at the beginning,' (b) does not retain and incorporate its innovations, and (c) does not become obsolete." He attempts to counter each of these arguments.

> There is a real difference between art and science in these respects, but it is one of degree and is gradually diminishing. It is an example of cultural lag which is due to temporary causes. Science was not systematically cumulative in its early stages. Art is becoming more so as modern methods of preserving and transmitting its products, aims, and techniques develop. . . . A closer look at the history of art shows that it is often highly cumulative. Innovations in its form, style, and mental content as well as those in technique have been transmitted from one generation to another on a vast scale. Few artists or schools of art really "begin at the beginning." They build on the work of previous artists. . . . Types and examples of art in each age . . . differ as to the extent to which they become obsolete.[21]

Munro defines artistic evolutionism as "the belief that a large-scale process of descent with adaptive, cumulative, complicative change has occurred and is still occurring in the arts." This is a belief that he shares. He is careful to point out, however, that artistic evolution "does *not* mean . . . that the arts are progressing or getting better."

> Whether the arts progress is essentially an evaluative question, involving standards for judging improvement or deterioration. . . . Increasing complexity . . . does not necessarily make for improvement in its quality. Adaptation to environment, as judged in terms of fitness for survival, does not always coincide with improvement in the moral, intellectual, or aesthetic quality of life.[22]

In fact, Munro probably does not believe that the arts actually progress. Nevertheless, his contention that the arts evolve, that they are subject to a process of cumulative development, seems to be a prerequisite of an affirmation of progress in art. The belief in artistic evolution is opposed to

[21] *Op. cit.*, p. 367.
[22] *Ibid.*, pp. 220–2.

the position of De Rougemont and others who hold that art is not subject to development. Munro insists that art is *somewhat* cumulative, that no artist ever starts *entirely* from the beginning, that some works of art *do* become obsolete, and that a *certain amount* of tradition is handed on from generation to generation. This would be sufficient, in the view of a few progress authors, to support an affirmation of progress in art. However, Munro does not apply the term "progress" to this developmental process, mainly, it appears, because he wishes to restrict the term to changes in the human social condition that are manifestly for the better in the most general sense. Hence, although he opposes the basic argument of those who deny progress in art, he does not make a clear affirmation of this kind of progress.

Hobhouse, while conceding that a given work of art is unique and cannot, in a sense, be improved upon or "developed," goes further than Munro, and attempts to save progress in art. He compares progress in art with progress in knowledge and in morals. "Knowledge . . . takes the lead in progress," he says, "because each generation can acquire the whole possessions of the past unimpaired and add to them its own." In morals, the situation is more complex, for the problem is that "we have not only to learn, but to come to be. . . . Nevertheless, the road once trodden is always easier to traverse anew." Art is even more complex, and its improvement is far from being continuous. Nevertheless, some sort of progressive advance occurs even here.

> In art there seem to be epochs of progress in which some new vein is struck out by pioneers. This is worked by one artist after another, each learning from the last, till the best that can be done along that line is reached. The vein is then exhausted, and subsequent work along that line produces less and less ore and more and more dross. . . . Meanwhile other pioneers are striking out in a fresh direction, and art revives in a new place. The cause of this brokenness of its history seems to be that the function of art is to give perfect expression—that is, expression in which the feeling-tone of the sense-symbols used precisely fits the thought expressed—to whatever facet of experience the artist seeks to approach. When this is once done adequately it cannot be done again.[23]

Hobhouse's theory combines elements found in the theories of Mumford and Turgot. The function of art is not only to express but to express perfectly; it therefore contains an essential "plateauing out" principle, as it may be called. By its very nature it cannot go on and on in one direction. But, in another sense, it can and does go on and on. The source of this progress is tradition, as it is the source of other kinds of progress. Tradition

[23] *Morals in Evolution*, p. 635, Note.

is used by the artist in a special way. At the last stage, when the ore is worked out, tradition becomes a real barrier to progress. The artist must know how and when to discard the old lode and to search for a new. But he nevertheless will work the new according to rules and skills derived from his knowledge of the art of the past.[24]

If the function of art is to express something, and if this something changes as the world progresses, then it may be that the cumulative principle—the principle of progress—that underlies progress in art is really social rather than aesthetic. This, indeed, seems to be the case with Hobhouse; it is perhaps the case with most progress authors who see progress in this respect. Comte, for instance, writes at the end of *The Positive Philosophy*:

> One of the least anticipated results of this working out of opinions, morals, and institutions under the guidance of positive philosophy is the development which must take place in the modes of expressing art.[25]

Art "must gain much" by being incorporated into "the social economy, from which it has hitherto been essentially excluded." The positive world —the world of industry, of science, of order, and of progress—has so far maintained an uneasy peace with art, and has scorned its methods and powers as it has been scorned in return. Art once enjoyed a close relation with "the public and military existence of antiquity," but this is now ended.

> The laborious and pacific activity proper to modern civilization is scarcely yet instituted, and has never yet been aesthetically regarded; so that modern art, like modern science and industry, is so far from being worn out, that it is as yet only half formed.

By and large, modern art has treated of private life, "for want of material in public life."

[24] A. L. Kroeber points out in *Style and Civilization* that the development of science is in some respects similar to that of art, at least when the aim of science is understanding rather than utility or profit. Advances in understanding come in bursts, says Kroeber, each dedicated to a particular problem or set of problems, and, when these have been solved by the available methods, science slacks off until a new set of problems arises. Fundamental or pure science thus progresses "in not too different a way from development in the arts." Applied science develops along a more even course. However, advance in pure science, as in Greece, is often not accompanied by technological progress at all. In modern times, pure science has tended to progress "more uniformly or steadily, perhaps because of its massive organization and great practical success" (pp. 61 ff.).

Munro, who discusses Kroeber in this connection, also cites other writers who see a cumulative, developmental, or evolutionary principle in the arts. See *op. cit.*, pp. 35–209, *passim*.

[25] *Positive Philosophy*, p. 836. For another treatment of Comte's theory of progress in art, see Munro, pp. 46–54.

But public life will be such as will admit of idealization: for the sense of the good and the true can not be actively conspicuous without eliciting a sense of the beautiful; and the action of the positive philosophy is in the highest degree favorable to all the three.[26]

The main difference, according to Comte, between the art of antiquity and that of the coming positive society is in its view of man in relation to nature. There will be a systematic regeneration of human conceptions, he says. The positive conception of Man views him as "the supreme head of the economy of Nature, which he modifies at will, in a spirit of boldness and freedom, within no other limits than those of natural law."[27] The so-called divine law will have no place in this art, nor will there be any room at all for the supernatural. It will be the epic of Man—and it will not be a tragedy.

This great work can be broken down, Comte declares, into two parts. There is first "the marvelous wisdom of Nature"; this has already been "sung, in imitation of the ancients, and with great occasional exaggeration." There remain "the conquests of Man over nature, with science for his instrument, and sociality for his atmosphere," which promise

> much more interest and beauty than the representation of an economy in which he has no share, and in which magnitude was the original object of admiration, and material grandeur continues to be most dwelt upon.[28]

It is required only to add that all of this applies to the graphic and plastic arts as well as to literature, and we have a prediction of advances in art to be expected in the future. The cumulative social progress of man will help determine the form of this new art; the art will be about something new and itself progressive. But the art will be better, too.

Comte goes on to meet an objection that is raised by more than one author.

> While the positive spirit remained in its first phase, it was reproached for its anti-aesthetic tendency; but we now see how, when it is systematized from a sociological centre, it becomes the basis of an aesthetic organization no less indispensable than the intellectual and social renovation from which it is inseparable.[29]

In other words, the conflict between art and science will not continue; indeed, art will draw from science and enrich itself thereby. Comte's hope that the dawning age of science will see a renaissance of art based

[26] *Op. cit.*, p. 837.
[27] *Ibid.*
[28] *Ibid.*
[29] *Ibid.*, p. 838.

on the discoveries of science and also, it may be said, on the triumph of the scientific world view, is shared by a few other writers. For instance, Ernest Renan feels that scientific knowledge will provide a new and richer source of poetical inspiration.

> Although the tales of fiction have been assumed so far to be essential to poetry, the true wonders of nature will provide a far more sublime subject once they have been unveiled in all their splendor; they will be the source of a poetry that will be reality itself, that will be at the same time science and poetry.[30]

That is what Comte might call the intellectual side of the matter. Bellamy emphasizes the moral and social side. Dr. Leete looks backward to the changes that have overtaken the world since its conversion to rational socialism. "It has been," he says, "an era of unexampled intellectual splendor."

> When men came to realize the greatness of the felicity which had befallen them, and that the change was not merely an improvement in details of their condition, but the rise of the race to a new plane of existence with an illimitable vista of progress, their minds were affected in all their faculties with a stimulus, of which the outburst of the medieval renaissance offers a suggestion but faint indeed.

As a result, "there ensued an era of mechanical invention, scientific discovery, art, musical and literary productiveness to which no previous age of the world offers anything comparable."[31]

The Marxists, too, seem to hold that art is progressive. Like Comte, they maintain that it changes as the economic basis of society changes, and this, of course, is a progressive change. New forms of art develop as a result of new forms of society, there is a cumulative artistic tradition, and artists, even in "unjust" societies, produce works that affirm enduring human values.[32]

---

[30] *L'Avenir de la science*, qu. by René Dubos, *The Dreams of Reason*, p. 8. Other writers have a similar conception, as Munro points out. Madame de Staël, he writes, "did not assert that modern art was better than ancient in form or expression, for the ancients had achieved perfection in organizing the limited range of thoughts and feelings known to them. But now, she said, a much wider range of these psychological materials has become available. Society has changed; the sum of ideas has increased, and emotions have been more subtly discriminated. . . . Guizot . . . developed this point by saying that in modern literature the total fund of sentiments and ideas is stronger and richer; one sees that the human soul has been moved at more numerous points and to a greater depth. Hence the formal imperfections in modern writing" (*op. cit.*, pp. 46–7).

[31] *Looking Backward*, p. 161.

[32] Munro offers an analysis of the Marxist theory of evolution in art, *op. cit.*, pp. 92–104.

However, the great age of art will occur in the future, when men are finally free. Trotsky describes some of the achievements to which humanity may look forward:

> Social construction and psycho-physical self-education will become two aspects of one and the same process. All the arts—literature, drama, painting, music and architecture will lend this process beautiful form. More correctly, the shell in which the cultural construction and self-education of Communist man will be enclosed, will develop all the vital elements of contemporary art to the highest point. Man will become immeasurably stronger, wiser and subtler; his body will become more harmonized, his movements more rhythmic, his voice more musical. The forms of life will become dynamically dramatic.[33]

It appears that all men will be artists; life itself will have become a work of art. This, however, cannot occur in the context of a philosophy of "art for art's sake." That is a decadent capitalistic notion, says Trotsky. Instead, art and artists will exist for the sake of mankind—for the sake of social justice, equality, and right.

The main idea here is that, when a rational and just social order is established, art will progress along with other cultural factors. The same idea underlies Fourier's prediction that the establishment of his phalansteries will result in the simultaneous existence of 37,000,000 poets the equal of Homer. Godwin, too, seems to expect improvements in art as a result of the establishment of political justice. And the notion is almost a commonplace in science-fiction utopias. Since it is difficult to describe better works of art than yet exist, the authors of such books usually content themselves with describing the amazement of visitors to these future societies. The visitors are overwhelmed by the beauty and richness of the art that they see, although they cannot say exactly why.[34]

The authors discussed above have their eye on the future. One or two other writers point to past artistic progress as the result of the injection of some new element into the world of art. This new element may be technological or political—for example, the discovery of a new technique, such as perspective, or a new freedom of expression for artists. The ad-

---

[33] *Literature and Revolution*, p. 256.

[34] In a grisly story, Ray Bradbury tells of how, in a future civilization, subjects allow their hands, feet, and scalps to be removed so that they may be attached to wires that "broadcast" programs—direct artistic experiences—into their minds. The subject has the feeling that he participates in the action. He is cared for by attendants who see to it that his body receives nutrient fluids. The most popular "programs" are ones in which the subject is the hero of successive Western melodramas and of successive seductions. The treatment is expensive, since it involves a lifetime of care; however, since the subjects will never have another waking thought, to say nothing of any moment of anxiety, as long as they exist, they are willing to pay the high price.

vent of Christianity is also cited as a new (moral) element that allows the production of better art.

Chateaubriand is the leading exponent of this view. He asserts that Christianity has brought about the improvement of all the fine arts, as well as the arts of production, industry, agriculture, etc. He sees progress in the forms of worship, in the construction of churches and the organization of parishes, in religious and other ornaments, in singing, in prayers, in the building of tombs, in the "General View of the Clergy," in missions, in the military orders (Chivalry), in hospitals, education, monasteries, and so on. The list is practically endless.

As to poetry, Chateaubriand begins with the epic. He admires Homer and Virgil, and it may be suspected that he thinks them greater poets, *per se,* than any modern (Christian) poet. But he emphasizes the potentialities that the modern poet possesses and the ancient poet lacked. Having admitted that, in a sense, the old epics were greater *wholes,* he points to

> the incalculable advantage which poets ought to have observed in the Christian religion, instead of obstinately trying to decry it. For it is equal to polytheism in the *marvelous,* or in the relations of *supernatural things,* as we shall . . . attempt to prove; it has moreover the drama and moral part which polytheism did not embrace.[35]

For instance, Chateaubriand compares the meeting of Ulysses and Penelope, after their twenty-year separation, to the first love of Adam and Eve in *Paradise Lost.* The former is great and true, he says.

> But neither the love of Penelope and Ulysses, nor that of Dido for Aeneas, nor of Alceste for Admetus, can be compared with the tenderness displayed by the august pair in Eden. The true religion alone could have furnished the character of a love so sacred, so sublime.[36]

He cites the famous scene in the *Iliad* wherein Priam comes to Achilles to reclaim the body of his son; but "we shall find in the tragedy of *Zara* a father to contrast with Priam," says Chateaubriand.[37]

> Racine's *Andromache* has greater sensibility, is more interesting in every respect, than the ancient *Andromache.* That verse which is so simple, yet so full of love—

[35] *The Genius of Christianity,* p. 233. Chateaubriand must show, he says, that "the divinities of paganism, in a poetical point of view," have no "superiority over the Christian divinities." He thus tries to prove that angels and devils are more interesting than the pagan gods and goddesses. He suggests, for instance, that the character of Satan in *Paradise Lost* is unequaled in ancient literature (*ibid.,* p. 309).

[36] *Ibid.,* p. 241.

[37] Voltaire is not one of Chateaubriand's favorite authors, but he is at least more Christian than Homer.

> Je ne l'ai pas encore embrassé d'aujourd'hui
> (I've not yet kissed him [my child] today)—

is the language of a Christian mother, and is not in accordance with the Grecian taste, still less that of the Romans.[38]

"*Zara*, as a tragedy, is, in our opinion, more interesting than *Iphigenia*," Chateaubriand declares. He writes also that,

> setting aside the particular genius of the two poets, and comparing only man with man, the characters of the *Jerusalem* appear to us superior to those of the *Iliad*.[39]

The point here, as in many other remarks, is that, although Tasso was not so great a poet as Homer, he could do more, despite his inferior talents, because he had the power, the beauty, and the profundity of Christianity to draw on. He could hence surpass Homer in at least one respect; a poet *equally* talented would surpass him in every respect.

Chateaubriand prefers Racine's *Phèdre* to the plays on the same theme of Euripides and Seneca. Racine's work

> exhibits a gradation of feeling, a knowledge of the sorrows, the anguish, and the transports of the soul, which the ancients never approached. Among them we meet with fragments, as it were, of sentiments, but rarely with a complete sentiment; here, on the contrary, the whole heart is poured forth.[40]

And St. Pierre's *Paul et Virginie* surpasses all the pastorals of the ancients.

> This pastoral is not like the idyls of Theocritus, or the eclogues of Virgil; neither does it exactly resemble the grand rural scenes of Hesiod, Homer, and the Bible; but, like the parable of the *Good Shepherd*, it produces an ineffable effect, and you are convinced that none but a Christian could have related the evangelical loves of Paul and Virginia.[41]

Christianity brings about progress not only in poetry. It also improves music and painting.

> Christianity has created a dramatic department in painting far superior to that of mythology. It is religion also that has given us a Claude Loraine, as it has furnished us with a Délille and a St. Lambert. But what need is there of so many arguments? Step into the gallery of the Louvre, and then assert, if you can, that the spirit of Christianity is not favorable to the fine arts.[42]

[38] *Ibid.*, p. 248.
[39] *Ibid.*, p. 263.
[40] *Ibid.*, p. 276.
[41] *Ibid.*, p. 290.
[42] *Ibid.*, pp. 279–80.

Even Christian ruins are preferable to ancient ones. "Sacred relics of Christian monuments," cries Chateaubriand, "ye remind us not, like so many other ruins, of blood, of injustice and of violence! Ye relate only a peaceful history, or at most the mysterious sufferings of the Son of man!"[43]

The view that *Paradise Lost* is greater than the epics of antiquity because its "fable" is morally superior was held by others in the century before Chateaubriand's.[44] Some of his other judgments are shared by his contemporaries. But there is probably no other writer who so unequivocally approves the influence of the spirit of Christianity upon art, and sees so much artistic improvement as a result of it.

Comte, Godwin, Fourier, and the Marxists see progress in art as occurring because of underlying social progress; a better world will call forth better art, both because of its inherent exigencies and because, art being in some sense imitation, the improvement in the model will result in improvement in the finished work. Chateaubriand sees improvement in art as the result of the injection of a new element into the human scene, which otherwise, perhaps, does not markedly change. Still another way to view the progress of art is to conceive it as advancing according to the rule of progress in general. This notion, which is sometimes called cultural evolutionism, is associated with Spencer.[45]

The rule that the simple becomes complex applies in literature, says Spencer, as it does in other realms:

> in the manifold effects of the primitive mystery-play as originating the modern drama, which has variously branched; or in the still multiplying forms of periodical literature which have descended from the first newspaper, and which have severally acted and reacted on other forms of literature and on each other. The influence which a new school of painting—as that of the pre-Rafaelites—exercises upon other schools; the hints which all kinds of pictorial art are deriving from photography; the complex results of new critical doctrines, as those of Mr. Ruskin, might severally be dwelt upon as displaying the like multiplication of effects.[46]

Although Spencer conceives his rule of progress as being fundamentally meliorative, it is not, when applied to art, an exclusively aesthetic principle. That more complex art is "better" than less complex art is a judgment of the historian, not, it seems, a fact intrinsic to art itself. The principle of artistic advance is unidirectional—a later work is necessarily more com-

[43] *Ibid.*, p. 472.
[44] Addison, in his *Spectator* papers, was a leading apologist for this judgment.
[45] Other cultural evolutionists are discussed by Munro, *op. cit.*, pp. 55–91.
[46] *Progress: Its Law and Cause*, in Teggart, p. 447.

plex—but it is hard to know why this means that it should necessarily be more beautiful. A similar unidirectional theory, without, however, the cosmic overtones found in Spencer, is proposed by Morgan and Tyler. Once more, however, the progress or evolution of art is considered by them to be only tangentially an aesthetic matter. The arts evolve along a set path and according to determined steps or stages, and this progress or evolution is good. But its goodness, its meliorative component, is not aesthetic.[47]

CHARACTERISTICS OF PROGRESS IN THE FINE ARTS

For Spencer and other cultural evolutionists progress in art is as inevitable as any other kind of progress, for it is the result of the same (or a similar) principle. For Comte, the Marxists, and other social evolutionists, progress in art is as inevitable as the social, economic, political, and moral progress that underlies it. Art will improve because the world will grow better. For Chateaubriand, progress in art follows from the advent of Christianity; the latter is a fact of history, and so the former probably is, too.

Necessary progress authors seem, on the whole, to be more inclined to discuss future progress in art than are contingent progress authors. However, a few of the latter make known their views. Mumford and Valéry, to name but two, hold that progress in art may occur in the future if the world is fashioned or refashioned according to their view of how it ought to be. Perhaps Maritain holds the same opinion. It is certainly the opinion of Fourier, who contends that the world will not see 37,000,000 Homers, Molières, etc., unless it forms good societies.

Turgot, Fontenelle, and others hold that art is essentially limited, and that its progress, if it occurs at all, is limited, too. It will "plateau out" when perfection is attained; it may already have "plateaued out." Hegel appears to concur. He writes:

> The theory was finally to emerge that art and literature, like laws and institutions, are an expression of society and therefore inextricably linked with other elements of social development—a theory which . . . has discredited the habit of considering works of art in a vacuum, dateless and detached.[48]

[47] Munro quotes J. M. Fischer as saying that "as the evolution of humanity from a state of nature progresses by stages up to civilization, so do art and science, the outstanding manifestations of progress. . . . The main evolutionary periods of music coincide with the main epochs in the history of man" (*op. cit.,* p. 48).

[48] *The Philosophy of History,* qu. by Munro, p. 49. Hegel also discusses these questions in *Aesthetik.*

He also conceives progress in general as "plateauing out" in the German state, the ultimate embodiment of the Idea. For this reason, it seems appropriate to assume that he believes that artistic progress will also come to an end.

Others, however, place no limits on future progress in art. It is particularly notable that the Marxists do not claim that this type of progress will "plateau out," although they hold that economic and social progress will cease when the last stage of history—true Communism—is attained.

Progress authors usually conceive progress in art (if they affirm it at all) as dependent on other kinds of progress. For writers like Mme de Staël, Guizot, and Godwin, it is probably most dependent on the progress of knowledge; as we know more, our art also improves. For the Marxists, it is mainly dependent on economic and political advances that are, perhaps, in turn dependent on technological ones. Progress in the means of production will result, eventually, in better art. For Comte, Fourier, and other "radical socialists," artistic progress will come when the new and more perfect world comes into being. (For Comte this is a necessary development; for Fourier it is no more than a possibility.) And for writers like Chateaubriand, the prior change would seem to be moral, or spiritual. Perhaps, however, Chateaubriand is also emphasizing progress in knowledge.

In the case of Spencer and other cultural evolutionists, there may be no priorities among the various types of progress. They all occur for the same reason—in the case of Spencer, because of the universal law that the simple always becomes complex.

Are there, then, any progress authors who hold that progress in art is prior to other kinds of progress? Does any writer hold that artistic progress is more important than any other kind?

When Shelley declares, in his *Defence of Poetry,* that poets are unacknowledged legislators of the world, he states a proposition that might be developed into an assertion of the priority of artistic progress. However, Shelley does not seem to be saying that progress actually occurs in art, and hence cannot be considered an exponent of this position. The same is true of Whitman, who writes:

> Though it may not be realized, it is strictly true, that a few first-class poets, philosophers, and authors, have substantially settled and given status to the entire religion, education, law, sociology, etc., of the hitherto civilized world, by tinging and often creating the atmospheres out of which they have arisen.[49]

[49] *Democratic Vistas,* in *Complete Poetry and Selected Prose,* p. 662.

But Whitman does not offer a clear affirmation of progress in art, either. If there is no progress in this respect, then it cannot be said that he holds that it is prior to other kinds of progress.

The case of Tolstoy is more complex. In *What Is Art?*, he first defines progress as movement toward the universal union of men with one another. The art of the future will then, he says,

> consist not in transmitting feelings accessible only to members of the rich classes, as is the case to-day, but in transmitting feelings embodying the highest religious perception of our times. Only those productions will be esteemed art which transmit feelings drawing men together in brotherly union, or such universal feelings as can unite all men. . . . Nor will the artists producing the art be as now merely a few people selected from a small section of the nation. . . . Artistic activity will then be accessible to all men. . . . The artist of the future will live the common life of man, earning his subsistence by some kind of labour. . . . The artist of the future will understand that to compose a fairy-tale, a touching little song, a lullaby, an entertaining riddle, an amusing jest, or to draw a sketch which will delight dozens of generations or millions of children and adults, is incomparably more important than to compose a novel or a symphony, or paint a picture, which will divert some members of the wealthy class for a short time and then for ever be forgotten.[50]

This is probably an assertion that progress will occur in art. Some art is better than other art, says Tolstoy; the future will see more of the better, less of the worse. So far, others agree with him; but these remarks do not constitute an affirmation of the priority of progress in art. However, Tolstoy takes a further step. He ends his essay with a discussion of the relation of science and art. He uses a homely simile:

> Science and art are like a certain kind of barge with kedge-anchors, which used to ply on our rivers. Science, like the boats which took the anchors upstream and made them secure, gives direction to the forward movement; while art, like the windlass worked on the barge to draw it towards the anchor, *causes the actual progression.*[51]

It is true, according to Tolstoy, that "a false activity of science inevitably causes a correspondingly false activity of art." But the opposite seems to be true as well. "The task of art," Tolstoy says, "is enormous."

> Through the influence of real art, aided by science, guided by religion, that peaceful co-operation of man which is now maintained by external means,— by our law-courts, police, charitable institutions, and so forth,—should be

[50] *What Is Art?*, pp. 268, 269, 271, 273.
[51] *Ibid.*, p. 270. Emphasis added.

obtained by man's free and joyous activity. Art could cause violence to be set aside.[52]

Furthermore—and in saying this Tolstoy appears to be alone among progress authors—"it is only art that can accomplish this."
He concludes thus:

> The task for art to accomplish is to make that feeling of brotherhood and love of one's neighbour, now attained only by the best members of society, the customary feeling and the instinct of all men. . . . The destiny of art in our time is to transmit the truth that well-being for men consists in their being united together, and to set up, in place of the existing reign of force, that kingdom of God—that is, of love—which we all recognize to be the highest aim of human life.[53]

In other words, progress in art is prior to moral and social progress. It is doubtful whether Tolstoy would say that it was prior to progress in wealth—but he might not call that progress at all. There is some question whether progress in art is prior to progress in knowledge. The two seem to be more or less coordinate and on the same plane. However, Tolstoy appears to hold that art is the prior activity of mankind at the present time.

The progress literature, then, seems to contain a number of affirmations of progress in art. For the most part, however, the progress that is affirmed is not essentially, certainly not exclusively, aesthetic. Progress in art is often primarily a matter of progress in knowledge or technological progress, at other times the result—more or less inevitable—of progress in still other respects. Authors who attempt to retain a purely aesthetic definition of art—that its essence is beauty, for example, or that its essence is the expression of feeling—usually, though not always, hold that art does not progress. Perfection in these terms is attained in any *great* work of art, or at least in many great works; and it can be attained at any time—not necessarily after a long process of (cumulative) development. The first worker in an artistic field is by this view as likely to be the best as the last. And that, of course, is an outright denial of progress.

[52] *Ibid.*, pp. 286–7.
[53] *Ibid.*, p. 288.

Bibliography

Acton, John Emerich Edward Dalberg. *Essays on Freedom and Power*. Ed. by Gertrude Himmelfarb. New York: Meridian Books, 1957.

Adams, Brooks. *The Law of Civilization and Decay*. New York: Vintage Books, 1959.

Adams, George P. "The Idea of Civilization," in Dennes, ed., *Civilization* (*q.v.*), pp. 45–68.

Adams, Henry. *The Degradation of the Democratic Dogma*. New York: Capricorn Books, 1958.

——. "A Letter to Teachers of American History," in *ibid*.

——. "The Rule of Phase Applied to History," in *ibid*.

——. *The Education of Henry Adams*. Modern Library, New York: Random House, 1931.

Adler, Mortimer J. *The Conditions of Philosophy*. New York: Atheneum, 1965.

——. *The Idea of Freedom*. 2 vols. New York: Doubleday and Co., 1958, 1961.

Alexander, Stephen. *Moral Order and Progress*. New York, 1899.

Aratus. [*Phaenomena*]. Tr. by G. R. Mair. London: Loeb Classical Library, 1921. See also Teggart, ed., *The Idea of Progress* (*q.v.*), p. 77.

Ardrey, Robert. *African Genesis*. New York: Delta Books, 1961.

——. *The Territorial Imperative*. New York: Atheneum, 1966.

Aristotle. *Metaphysics* (*Metaphysica*). Tr. by W. D. Ross, in vol. VIII, *The Works of Aristotle*, ed. by W. D. Ross. Oxford: Oxford University Press, 1940.

——. *Meteorology* (*Meteorologica*). Tr. by E. W. Welsten, in vol. III, *ibid.*, 1923.

——. *On the Heavenly Bodies* (*De Caelo*). Tr. by J. L. Stocks, in *ibid*.

——. *On Generation and Corruption* (*De Generatione Et Coruptione*). Tr. by H. H. Joachim, in vol. II, *ibid.*, 1930.

——. *Politics* (*Politica*). Tr. by B. Jowett, in vol. X, *ibid.*, 1921.

Aron, Raymond. *Introduction to the Philosophy of History*. Tr. by G. J. Irwin. Boston: Beacon Press, 1962.

Augustine, St. *The City of God*. Ed. by W. C. Greene. Cambridge: Harvard University Press, 1960.

Ayres, C. E. *Toward a Reasonable Society*. Austin: University of Texas Press, 1961.

Bacon, Francis. *Advancement of Learning and Novum Organon*. New York: Willey Book Co., 1944.

———. "The Sphinx," in *Gateway to the Great Books* (*q.v.*), vol. 8.

Bagehot, Walter. *Physics and Politics*. Boston: Beacon Press, 1956.

Baillie, John. *The Belief in Progress*. New York: Charles Scribner's Sons, 1950.

Bakunin, Mikhail A. *The Political Philosophy of Bakunin*. Ed. by G. P. Maximoff. Glencoe: The Free Press, 1953.

Barr, Stringfellow. *The Pilgrimage of Western Man*. Philadelphia: J. B. Lippincott Co., 1962.

Becker, Carl. *Progress and Power*. New York: Vintage Books, 1965.

———. "Progress," in *The Encyclopedia of the Social Sciences*. New York: Macmillan Co., vols. 11–12, pp. 495–499.

Bellamy, Edward. *Looking Backward, 2000–1887*. The Riverside Library, Boston: Houghton Mifflin Co., 1931.

Berdyaev, Nicolas. *The Fate of Man in the Modern World*. Ann Arbor Paperbacks, Ann Arbor: University of Michigan Press, 1961.

———. *The Meaning of History*. New York: Charles Scribner's Sons, 1936.

Berenson, Bernard. *Aesthetics and History*. Anchor Books, New York: Doubleday & Co., 1954.

Bergson, Henri. *Creative Evolution*. Tr. by Arthur Mitchell. Modern Library, New York: Random House, 1944.

Bierstedt, Robert (ed.). *The Making of Society*. Modern Library, New York: Random House, 1959.

Bird, Otto A. *The Idea of Justice*. New York: Frederick A. Praeger, 1967.

Blum, Harold F. *Time's Arrow and Evolution*. New York: Harper & Bros., 1962.

Boas, Franz. *The Mind of Primitive Man*. New York: The Free Press, 1965.

Borkenau, Franz. "The Concept of Death," in *The Twentieth-Century*, vol. CLVII, no. 938, April 1955, pp. 313–329.

Bossuet, J. B. *An Universal History*. London, 1778.

Boulding, Kenneth E. "Decision-Making in the Modern World," in Bryson, ed., *An Outline of Man's Knowledge of the Modern World* (*q.v.*), pp. 418–442.

Briggs, Asa. "Technology and Economic Development," in *Technology and Economic Development*. New York: Alfred A. Knopf, 1963, pp. 3–18.

Broad, C. D. *The Mind and Its Place in Nature*. International Library of Psychology, Philosophy and Scientific Method. Patterson, New Jersey: Littlefield Adams & Co., 1960.

Brock, A. C. "Progress in Art," in Marvin, ed., *Progress and History* (*q.v.*), pp. 224–247.

Brown, Harrison. *The Challenge of Man's Future*. New York: Viking Press, 1956.

Brown, Harrison; Bonner, James; and Weir, John. *The Next Hundred Years*. New York: The Viking Press, 1957.

Brown, Harrison, and Real, James. *Community of Fear*. Santa Barbara, California: Center for the Study of Democratic Institutions, 1960.

Brown, Norman O. *Life Against Death: The Psychoanalytic Meaning of History*. New York: Vintage Books, 1961.

Bryce, James. "What is Progress?," in *Atlantic Monthly*, August, 1907, pp. 143–156.

Bryson, Gladys. *Man and Society: The Scottish Enquiry of the Eighteenth Century*. Princeton: Princeton University Press, 1945.

Bryson, Lyman (ed.). *An Outline of Man's Knowledge of the Modern World*. New York: McGraw-Hill Book Co., Inc., 1960.

Buchanan, Scott. *Essay in Politics*. New York: Philosophical Library, 1953.

Buckle, Thomas Henry. *History of Civilization in England*. 3 vols. New ed. London: Longmans, Green and Co., 1872.

Bukharin, N. I. "The Theory of Historical Materialism," in *Marxism and Modern Thought*, by N. I. Bukharin *et al.*, tr. by Ralph Fox. London: George Routledge & Sons, Ltd., 1936.

Burckhardt, Jacob. *Force and Freedom: Reflections on History*. Ed. by J. H. Nichols. Boston: Beacon Press, 1964.

Burke, Edmund. *Reflections on the Revolution in France*. London: Everyman's Library, 1940.

Butterfield, Herbert. *Man On His Past*. Boston: Beacon Press, 1960.

Bury, J. B. *The Idea of Progress*. New York: Dover Publications, 1955.

———. *Selected Essays*. Ed. by H. Temperley. Cambridge: Cambridge University Press, 1930.

Cairns, Grace E. *Philosophies of History*. New York: The Citadel Press, 1962.

Calder, Nigel (ed.). *The World in 1984*. 2 vols. Baltimore: Penguin Books, 1965.

Calder, Ritchie. *After the Seventh Day*. New York: Simon & Schuster, 1961.

Calhoun, John C. *A Disquisition on Government*, in *Calhoun: Basic Documents*, ed. by J. M. Anderson. State College, Pa.: Bald Eagle Press, 1952, pp. 27–97. See also *The People Shall Judge* (*q.v.*), vol. I, pp. 676–686.

Calverton, V. F. (ed.). *The Making of Man*. Modern Library, New York: Random House, 1931.

Campbell, W. W. "Presidential Address to the A. A. A. S., 1915," in *Science*, 42:238.

Camus, Albert. *The Myth of Sisyphus and Other Essays*. New York: Vintage Books, 1960.

Carlyle, Thomas. "On History," in *Critical and Miscellaneous Essays*. New York, 1900.

Carr, Edward Hallett. *What is History?* New York: Alfred A. Knopf, 1962.

Carrel, Alexis. *Man, the Unknown*. New York: MacFadden Books, 1961.

Carver, T. N. *Sociology and Social Progress*. New York, 1905.

Casson, Stanley. *Progress and Catastrophe: An Anatomy of Human Adventure*. London: Hamish Hamilton, 1937.

Chateaubriand, Viscount de. *The Genius of Christianity, or the Spirit and Beauty of the Christian Religion*. Tr. with notes by Charles White. 2nd ed. rev. Baltimore: John Murphy & Co., 1856.

Childe, V. Gordon. *Man Makes Himself*. Mentor Books, New York: New American Library, 1951.

———. *What Is History?* New York: Abelard, 1953.

Cicero. *De Officiis*. With an English translation by Walter Miller. London: The Loeb Classical Library, 1913. See also Teggart, ed., *The Idea of Progress* (*q.v.*), pp. 89–91.

————. *De Natura Deorum*. Tr. by Francis Brooks. London: Methuen, 1896. See also Teggart, ed., *The Idea of Progress* (*q.v.*), pp. 87–88.

Clark, Colin. *The Conditions of Economic Progress*. 2nd. ed. London: Macmillan & Co., Ltd., 1951.

Clarke, Arthur C. *Childhood's End*, in *Across the Sea of Stars*. New York: Harcourt, Brace and Co., 1959.

————. *Profiles of the Future*. New York: Bantam Books, 1964.

Clough, Shepard B. *The Rise and Fall of Civilization*. New York: Columbia University Press, 1961.

Coblentz, Stanton A. *The Decline of Man*. New York: Minton Balch & Co., 1925.

Cohen, Morris R. *The Meaning of Human History*. The Paul Carus Lectures. Lasalle, Illinois: Open Court Publishing Co., 1961.

Cohn, Norman. *The Pursuit of the Millennium*. 2nd ed. Harper Torchbooks, New York: Harper & Bros., 1961.

Collingwood, R. G. *The Idea of History*. A Galaxy Book, New York: Oxford University Press, 1956.

Coleridge, S. T. *The Friend*, vol. III, Essay 10, London, 1818.

The Communist Blueprint for the Future: The Complete Text of All Four Communist Manifestos 1848–1961. New York: E. P. Dutton & Co., 1962.

Comte, Auguste. *The Positive Philosophy of Auguste Comte*. Tr. by Harriet Marineau. New York: Calvin Blanchard, 1855.

————. *System of Positive Polity*. 4 vols. Tr. by J. H. Bridges *et al*. London: Longmans, Green & Co., 1875–1877.

Condorcet, Antoine-Nicolas de. *Sketch for a Historical Picture of the Progress of the Human Mind*. Tr. by June Barraclough. New York: The Noonday Press, 1955.

Cram, Ralph Adams. "Why We Do Not Behave Like Human Beings," in *Convictions and Controversies*. Boston: Marshall Jones Co., 1935.

Croce, Benedetto. *History as the Story of Liberty*. Tr. by Sylvia Sprigge. New York: W. W. Norton & Co., 1941.

Crow, James F. "Mechanisms and Trends in Human Evolution," in *Daedelus*, Summer, 1961, pp. 416–431.

Danto, Arthur C. *Analytical Philosophy of History*. Cambridge: Cambridge University Press, 1965.

D'Arcy, M. C. *The Meaning and Matter of History*. New York: Meridian Books, 1961.

Darwin, Charles. *The Origin of Species and The Descent of Man*. Modern Library, New York: Random House, n.d.

Darwin, Charles Galton. *The Next Million Years*. Dolphin Books, New York: Doubleday & Co., 1952.

Dawson, Christopher. *Progress and Religion*. New York: Doubleday & Co., 1931.

Dedijer, Stevan. "Research: The Motor of Progress," in *Bulletin of the Atomic Scientists*, vol. XVIII, No. 6, June 1962, pp. 4–7.

Dennes, William R. (ed.). *Civilization*. Berkeley: University of California Press, 1959.

Descartes, Rene. "Rules for the Direction of the Mind," in vol. I, *The Philosophical Works of Descartes*, ed. and tr. by Haldane and Ross. Cambridge: Cambridge University Press, 1931.

Dewey, John. *Intelligence in the Modern World.* Ed. by Joseph Ratner. Modern Library, New York: Random House, 1939.

————. "Progress," in *The International Journal of Ethics,* April, 1916, pp. 311–322.

Dobzhansky, Theodosius. *The Biological Basis of Human Freedom.* New York: Columbia University Press, 1960.

————. *Mankind Evolving.* New Haven: Yale University Press, 1962.

————. "Changing Man," in *Science,* vol. 155, no. 3761, January 27, 1967.

Dryden, John. *An Essay of Dramatic Poesy,* in *The Best of Dryden,* ed. by L. I. Bredvold. New York: The Ronald Press Co., 1933.

Dubos, Rene. *The Dreams of Reason.* New York: Columbia University Press, 1933.

Dunning, John R. "The Consequences of Power," in Bryson, ed., *An Outline of Man's Knowledge of the Modern World* (*q.v.*), pp. 256–278.

Dray, William H. *Philosophy of History.* Foundations of Philosophy Series. Englewood Cliffs, N.J.: Prentice-Hall, 1964.

Eddington, Arthur. *The Nature of the Physical World.* Ann Arbor: University of Michigan Press, 1958.

Edwards, Jonathan. *Selections.* Ed. by C. Faust and T. H. Johnson. Rev. ed. New York: Hill and Wang, 1962.

Eiseley, Loren. *Darwin's Century.* Anchor Books, New York: Doubleday & Co., 1961.

————. *The Immense Journey.* Vintage Books, New York: Random House, 1958.

Eliade, Mircea. *Cosmos and History.* Tr. by Willard R. Trask. Harper Torchbooks, New York: Harper & Bros., 1959.

Ellul, Jacques. *The Technological Society.* Tr. by John Wilkinson. New York: Alfred A. Knopf, 1964.

Emerson, Ralph Waldo. *The Complete Essays and Other Writings.* Modern Library, New York: Random House, 1950.

Engels, Frederick. *Dialectics of Nature.* Tr. and ed. by Clemens Dutt. New York: International Publishers, 1940.

————. *Socialism: Utopian and Scientific,* in *The Essential Left* (*q.v.*).

Epicurus. "Letter to Heredotus," tr. by C. Bailey, in *The Stoic and Epicurean Philosophers,* ed. by W. J. Oates. New York: Random House, 1940.

Eranos Yearbooks. Tr. by Ralph Manheim and R. F. C. Hull, ed. by Joseph Campbell. The Bollingen Foundation Series XXX. New York: Pantheon Books. Vol. I, *Spirit and Nature,* 1954. Vol. III, *Man and Time,* 1957. Vol. IV, *Spiritual Disciplines,* 1960.

The Essential Left. London: George Allen & Unwin, Ltd., 1961.

Faraday, Michael. *Observations on Mental Education,* in *Gateway to the Great Books* (*q.v.*), vol. 7.

Feuerbach, Ludwig. *The Essence of Christianity.* Tr. by M. Evans (George Eliot). London, 1854.

Finley, M. I. *The Ancient Greeks.* New York: Viking Press, 1963.

Fiske, John. *The Destiny of Man.* Boston: Houghton Mifflin & Co., 1884.

Flint, Robert. *History of the Philosophy of History.* Edinburgh, 1893.

Florus, Lucius Annaeus. *Epitome of Roman History.* With an English translation by E. S. Forster. London: Loeb Classical Library, 1929.

Fontenelle, Bernard Le Bovier de. "On the Ancients and Moderns," in Teggart, ed., *The Idea of Progress (q.v.)*, pp. 176–187.

Frankel, Charles. *The Case for Modern Man*. Boston: Beacon Press, 1959.

———. *The Faith of Reason: The Idea of Progress in the French Enlightenment*. New York: Columbia University Press, 1948.

Freud, Sigmund. *Civilization and Its Discontents*. Tr. by Joan Riviere. Chicago: University of Chicago Press, n.d.

———. *The Future of an Illusion*. Tr. by W. D. Robson-Scott. Garden City: Doubleday Anchor Books, n.d.

———. *Outline of Psychoanalysis*. Tr. by James Strachey. New York: W. W. Norton & Co., 1949.

———. *Totem and Taboo*, in *Basic Writings of Sigmund Freud*. Modern Library, New York: Random House, 1952.

———. "Thoughts for the Times on War and Death," tr. by Joan Riviere, in *Collected Papers*, vol. IV. London: Hogarth Press and The Institute of Psycho-Analysis, 1950.

Friedmann, Georges. *La Crise du progrès: esquisse d'histoire des idées, 1895–1935*. Paris, 1936.

Froude, J. H. "Progress," in *Short Studies on Great Subjects*. Everyman's Library, New York: E. P. Dutton & Co., 1964.

Gamow, George. *The Creation of the Universe*. New York: Viking Press, 1952.

———. "Modern Cosmology," in *The New Astronomy*, ed. by the editors of *Scientific American*. New York: Simon & Schuster, 1955.

Gardiner, Patrick (ed.). *Theories of History*. Glencoe: The Free Press, 1959.

Gateway to the Great Books. Ed. by R. M. Hutchins and M. J. Adler. 10 vols. Chicago: Encyclopaedia Britannica, 1964.

George, Henry. *Progress and Poverty*. Modern Library, New York: Random House, n.d.

Geyl, Pieter. "Can We Know the Pattern of the Past?—A Debate," in Gardiner, ed., *Theories of History (q.v.)*, pp. 307–319.

Gibbon, Edward. *The Decline and Fall of the Roman Empire*. Modern Library, New York: Random House, 1932.

Gilson, Etienne. *The Arts of the Beautiful*. New York: Charles Scribner's Sons, 1965.

Ginsberg, Morris. *Evolution and Progress*, being vol. III of *Essays in Sociology and Social Philosophy*. London: William Heinemann Ltd., 1961.

———. *The Idea of Progress: A Revaluation*. London: Methuen & Co., Ltd., 1953.

———. *Reason and Unreason in Society*. Cambridge: Harvard University Press, 1948.

Godwin, William. *An Enquiry Concerning Political Justice and its Influence on General Virtue and Happiness*. Photographic Facsimile of the 3rd ed. 3 vols. Toronto: University of Toronto Press, 1946.

Great Books of the Western World (GBWW). Ed. by R. M. Hutchins et al. 52 vols. Chicago: Encyclopaedia Britannica, 1952.

Guardini, Romano. *The End of the Modern World*. Chicago: Regnery, 1967.

Guizot, François Pierre Guillaume. *General History of Civilization in Europe*. Ed. by G. W. Knight. New York: D. Appleton & Co., 1896.

Halacy, D. S., Jr. *Cyborg: Progressive Change in the Nature of Man,* New York: Harper & Row, 1965.

Hardin, Garrett. *Nature and Man's Fate.* New York: Mentor Books, 1961.

Hartmann, Eduard von. *The Philosophy of the Unconscious.* London, 1884.

Havelock, Eric A. *The Liberal Temper in Greek Politics.* New Haven: Yale University Press, 1957.

Heard, Gerald. *The Ascent of Humanity.* New York: Harcourt, Brace & Co., 1929.

Hegel, George Wilhelm Friedrich. *The Philosophy of History.* Tr. by J. Sibree. New York: Willey Book Co., 1944.

———. *Philosophy of Right.* Tr. by T. M. Knox. Oxford: Clarendon Press, 1945.

———. *Selections.* Ed. by J. Loewenberg. New York: Charles Scribner's Sons, 1929.

Heilbroner, Robert L. *The Future as History.* New York: Grove Press, 1961.

Helvétius, Claude Adrien. *De L'Esprit; or, Essays On the Mind and its Several Faculties.* Tr. by William Mudford. London: Albion Press, 1810.

Herder, Johann Gottfried. *Outlines of a Philosophy of the History of Man.* Tr. by T. Churchill. 2 vols. London, 1803. See also Teggart, ed., *The Idea of Progress* (*q.v.*), pp. 308–320.

Herrick, C. Judson. *The Evolution of Human Nature.* Harper Torchbooks, New York: Harper & Row, 1961.

Hertzler, Joyce O. *Social Progress.* New York, 1928.

Hesiod. *The Homeric Hymns and Homerica.* With an English translation by Hugh G. Evelyn-White. The Loeb Classical Library, Cambridge: Harvard University Press, 1936.

Heuer, Kenneth. *How the Earth Will Come to an End.* New York: Collier Books, 1963.

Hobhouse, L. T. *Development and Purpose.* London: Macmillan and Co., Ltd., 1913.

———. *Morals in Evolution.* London: Chapman & Hall, 1951.

———. *Social Development.* London: Macmillan and Co., Ltd., 1924.

Hobbes, Thomas. *Leviathan.* Oxford: Clarendon Press, 1929.

Hocking, William Ernest. *The Coming World Civilization.* New York: Harper & Bros., 1956.

———. *Human Nature and Its Remaking.* New Haven: Yale University Press, 1918.

Hoyle, Fred. *Encounter with the Future.* New York: Trident Press, 1965.

Hubbert, M. K. "Are We Retrogressing in Science?" in *Science,* vol. 139, no. 3558, March 8, 1963.

Huntington, Ellsworth. *The Pulse of Progress.* New York: Charles Scribner's Sons, 1926.

Huxley, Julian. *Evolution in Action.* New York: Mentor Books, 1961.

———. *Evolution, the Modern Synthesis.* London: George Allen & Unwin, Ltd., 1942.

Huxley, Thomas H. "Evolution and Ethics. Prolegomena," in *Evolution and Ethics and Other Essays.* New York: D. Appleton & Co., 1914.

Ibn Khaldun. *The Muqaddimah.* Tr. by Franz Rosenthal. 3 vols. Bollingen Series XLII. New York: Pantheon Books, 1958.

Inge, W. R. *The Idea of Progress.* Oxford: Clarendon Press, 1920.

Jackson, J. Hampden. *Marx, Proudhon and European Socialism*. New York: Collier Books, 1962.

Jacobs, Dan N. (ed.). *The New Communist Manifesto and Related Documents*. Harper Torchbooks, New York: Harper & Bros., 1962.

Jacks, L. P. "Moral Progress," in Marvin, ed., *Progress and History* (*q.v.*), pp. 134–150.

Jaspers, Karl. *The Future of Mankind*. Tr. by E. B. Ashton. Chicago: The University of Chicago Press, 1961.

Jeans, James. *The Universe Around Us*. 4th ed. rev. New York: The Macmillan Co., 1944.

John XXIII. *Pacem in Terris*, Encyclical Letter of His Holiness Pope John XXIII. Ed. by William J. Gibbons, S.J. New York: Paulist Press, 1963.

Jones, R. F. *Ancients and Moderns*. 2nd ed. Magnolia, Massachusetts: Peter Smith, 1961.

Juenger, Friedrich Georg. *The Failure of Technology*. Los Angeles: Gateway Editions, 1956.

Jung, C. G. *Civilization in Transit*. Bollingen Series XX. New York: Pantheon Books, 1964.

Kahler, Erich. *The Meaning of History*. New York: George Braziller, 1964.

Kallen, Horace M. *Patterns of Progress*. New York, 1950.

Kant, Immanuel. *Perpetual Peace*. New York: Columbia University Press, 1939.

————. *The Science of Right*, in *Great Books of the Western World* (*q.v.*), vol. 42.

————. *The Philosophy of Kant*. Ed. by C. J. Friedrichs. Modern Library, New York: Random House, 1949.

————. *Principles of Politics*. Ed. and tr. by W. Hastie. Edinburgh: Clark, 1891.

————. "Idea of a Universal History from a Cosmopolitical Point of View," in *Principles of Politics*, ed. and tr. by W. Hastie, and in *The Philosophy of Kant*, ed. by C. J. Friedrichs (*qq.v.*).

————. "On the Saying: That a Thing May Be Right in Theory, But May Not Hold in Practice," in *Principles of Politics*, ed. and tr. by W. Hastie, and in *The Philosophy of Kant*, ed., C. J. Friedrichs (*qq.v.*).

Kirk, G. S. and Raven, J. E. *The Presocratic Philosophers*. Cambridge University Press, 1960.

Kroeber, A. L. *An Anthropologist Looks At History*. Ed. by Theodora Kroeber. Berkeley, California: University of California Press, 1963.

————. *Style and Civilizations*. Berkeley: University of California Press, 1957.

Kubler, George. *The Shape of Time*. New Haven: Yale University Press, 1962.

Kuhn, Thomas S. *The Structure of Scientific Revolutions*. International Encyclopedia of Unified Science. Vol. II, No. 2. Chicago: University of Chicago Press, 1962.

Landowska, Wanda. *Landowska on Music*. Ed. and tr. by D. Restout and R. Hawkins. New York: Stein & Day, 1964.

Laurence, William L. *New Frontiers of Science*. New York: Bantam Books, 1964.

Lavoisier, Antoine. *Elements of Chemistry* (*Traité élémentaire de chimie*). Tr. by R. Kerr. Ann Arbor, Michigan: Edwards Bros., Inc., 1940.

Leibniz, Gottfried Wilhelm. *Discourse on Metaphysics, Correspondence with Arnauld, Monadology.* Tr. by G. R. Montgomery. La Salle, Illinois: Open Court Publishing Co., 1937.

––––––. *The Monadology and Other Philosophical Writings.* Tr. by Robert Latta. London: Oxford University Press, 1898.

Lenin, V. I. *The State and Revolution,* in *The Essential Left (q.v.).*

Lessing, Gotthold Ephraim. *Lessing's Education of the Human Race.* Ed. by John Dearling. New York: Teacher's College, Columbia University, 1908.

Lewis, C. S. *The Abolition of Man.* New York: The Macmillan Co., 1947.

Ley, Willy. *Engineer's Dreams.* Explorer Books, New York: Viking Press, 1960.

Lippmann, Walter. *A Preface to Politics.* Ann Arbor: University of Michigan Press, 1962.

"Look! I am Making All Things New." New York: Watchtower Bible and Tract Society of New York, Inc., International Bible Students Association, 1959.

Lovejoy, Arthur O. *Essays in the History of Ideas.* Capricorn Books, New York: G. P. Putnam's Sons, 1960.

––––––. *The Great Chain of Being.* Cambridge: Harvard University Press, 1948.

Lovejoy, Arthur O. and Boas, George. *Primitivism and Related Ideas in Antiquity.* Baltimore: Johns Hopkins University Press, 1937.

Löwith, Karl. *Meaning in History.* Phoenix Books, Chicago: University of Chicago Press, 1957.

Lucretius. *On the Nature of Things (De Rerum Natura).* Tr. by H. A. J. Munro, in the *Stoic and Epicurean Philosophers,* ed. by W. J. Oates. New York: Random House, 1940.

Machiavelli, Niccolò. *Florentine History.* Tr. by W. K. Marriott. New York, 1909. See also Teggart, ed., *The Idea of Progress (q.v.),* p. 133.

Maine, Henry Sumner. *Ancient Law.* London: John Murray, 1920.

Malthus, Thomas Robert. *Population: The First Essay.* Ann Arbor Paperbacks, Ann Arbor: University of Michigan Press, 1959.

Mandeville, Bernard. *The Fable of the Bees, or Private Vices, Publick Benefits.* Ed. by Irwin Primer. New York: Capricorn Books, 1962.

Mann, Thomas. *The Magic Mountain.* New York: Alfred A. Knopf, 1930.

Mannheim, Karl. *Ideology and Utopia.* New York: Harcourt, Brace & Co., 1936. See also Gardiner, ed., *Theories of History (q.v.),* pp. 241–249.

Manuel, Frank E. *The Prophets of Paris.* Cambridge: Harvard University Press, 1962.

––––––. *Utopias and Utopian Thought.* Boston: Houghton Mifflin, 1966.

Marcuse, Herbert. *Eros and Civilization.* New York: Vintage Books, 1962.

Maritain, Jacques. *Man and the State.* Phoenix Books, Chicago: University of Chicago Press, 1951.

––––––. *Moral Philosophy.* Tr. by Marshall Suther, *et al.* New York: Charles Scribner's Sons, 1964.

––––––. *On the Philosophy of History.* Ed. by J. W. Evans. New York: Charles Scribner's Sons, 1957.

––––––. *Scholasticism and Politics.* Ed. by M. J. Adler. Image Books, New York: Doubleday & Co., 1960.

––––––. *Theonas.* Tr. by F. J. Sheed. New York: Sheed & Ward, 1933.

————. *True Humanism.* Tr. by M. R. Adamson. New York: Charles Scrib-
ner's Sons, 1950.
Marvin, F. S. (ed.). *Progress and History.* London: Oxford University Press,
1916.
Marx, Karl. *Capital.* Modern Library, New York: Random House, n.d.
————. *Critique of the Gotha Program.* New York: International Publishers,
1933.
Marx, Karl, and Engels, Friedrich. *The Communist Manifesto,* in *Capital, The
Communist Manifesto and Other Writings of Karl Marx.* Ed. by Max East-
man. Modern Library, New York: Random House, 1932.
————. *The German Ideology,* Parts I & III. Ed. by R. Pascal. New York:
International Publishers, 1947.
Marx and Engels on Malthus. Ed. by Ronald L. Meek. Tr. by Dorothea L.
Meek and Ronald L. Meek. London: Lawrence and Wishart, 1953.
McNeill, W. H. *Europe's Steppe Frontier: 1500–1800.* Chicago: University
of Chicago Press, 1964.
————. *Past and Future.* Phoenix Books, Chicago: University of Chicago
Press, 1954.
Medawar, P. B. *The Future of Man.* New York: Basic Books, 1960.
Melden, A. I. "Judgments in the Social Sciences," in Dennes, ed., *Civilization*
(*q.v.*), pp. 121–146.
Meyerhoff, Hans (ed.). *The Philosophy of History in Our Time.* New York:
Doubleday Anchor Books, 1959.
Mill, John Stuart. *Auguste Comte and Positivism.* Ann Arbor Paperbacks,
Ann Arbor: University of Michigan Press, 1961.
————. *On Liberty, Representative Government, The Subjection of Women.*
London: Oxford University Press, 1946.
————. *A System of Logic.* London: Longmans, Green & Co., 1936.
————. "Civilization," in *Dissertations and Discussions, Political, Philosophi-
cal, and Historical.* 2 vols. London: John W. Parker & Sons, 1859, Vol. I.
Milton, John. *Areopagitica and Other Prose Writings.* New York: The Mac-
millan Co., 1927.
Montagu, M. F. Ashley. *Man: His First Million Years.* New York: Mentor
Books, 1958.
————. (ed.). *Culture and the Evolution of Man.* New York: Oxford Uni-
versity Press, 1962.
Montesquieu, Baron de. *The Spirit of Laws, Including D'Alembert's Analysis
of the Work.* Tr. by Thomas Nugent. 2 vols. Rev. ed. New York: The
Colonial Press, 1900.
Moore, Barrington, Jr. "On the Notions of Progress, Revolution, and Freedom,"
in *Ethics,* January, 1962, pp. 106–119.
Morgan, Lewis Henry. *Ancient Society.* Ed. by Eleanor Burke Leacock.
Meridian Books, Cleveland: World Publishing Co., 1963.
Muller, Herbert J. *Freedom in the Modern World.* New York: Harper &
Row, 1966.
————. *The Uses of the Past.* New York: Oxford University Press, 1957.
Muller, Hermann J. *Out of the Night: A Biologist's View of the Future.*
London: Victor Gollancz, 1935.
————. "Should We Strengthen or Weaken our Genetic Heritage?," in
Daedelus, Summer, 1961, pp. 432–476.

Mumford, Lewis. *Art and Technics.* New York: Columbia University Press, 1960.

――――. *The City in History.* New York: Harcourt, Brace & World, Inc., 1961.

――――. *The Human Prospect.* Ed. by H. T. Moore and K. W. Deutsch. Boston: Beacon Press, 1955.

――――. *The Transformations of Man.* New York: Collier Books, 1962.

Munro, Thomas. *Evolution in the Arts.* The Cleveland Museum of Art, n.d.

Nef, John U. *War and Human Progress.* Cambridge: Harvard University Press, 1950.

Niebuhr, Reinhold. *Faith and History, A Comparison of Christian and Modern Views of History.* New York: Charles Scribner's Sons, 1949.

――――. *The Nature and Destiny of Man.* Vol. II. *Human Destiny,* New York: Charles Scribner's Sons, 1964.

Nietzsche, Friedrich. *Thus Spake Zarathustra.* Tr. by Thomas Common. New York: Boni and Liveright, Inc., 1917.

Nock, Albert Jay. *Memoirs of a Superfluous Man.* New York: Harper & Bros., 1943.

Nordau, Max. "Degeneration," in the *Hibbert Journal,* vol. X. (Oct. 1911– July 1912), pp. 745–765.

Nouÿs, Lecomte du. *Human Destiny.* New York: Mentor Books, 1949.

Ortega y Gasset, José. *History as a System and Other Essays.* Tr. by Lelene Weyl. The Norton Library, New York: W. W. Norton & Co., 1961.

――――. *Man and Crisis.* Tr. by Mildred Adams. The Norton Library, New York: W. W. Norton & Co., 1962.

Ouspensky, P. D. *The Psychology of Man's Possible Evolution.* New York: Alfred A. Knopf, 1959.

Ovid. *Metamorphoses.* With an English tr. by Frank Justus Miller. The Loeb Classical Library. 2 vols. London, 1916.

Pascal, Blaise. *Pensées. Provincial Letters.* Tr. by W. F. Trotter. Modern Library, New York: Random House, 1941.

――――. "Preface to the Treatise on the Vacuum," tr. by Richard Scofield, in *Great Books of the Western World* (*q.v.*), vol. 33. See also Teggart, ed., *The Idea of Progress* (*q.v.*), pp. 164–169.

The People Shall Judge, ed. by the Staff, Social Sciences I, The College of the University of Chicago. 2 vols. Chicago: University of Chicago Press, 1949.

Perrault, Charles. "A Comparison of the Ancients and Moderns," in Teggart, ed., *The Idea of Progress* (*q.v.*), pp. 188–194.

Piaget, Jean. *The Child's Conception of Physical Causality* and *The Child's Conception of the World.* International Library of Psychology, Philosophy and Scientific Method. Paterson, New Jersey: Littlefield, Adams Co., 1960.

Piel, Gerard. *Science in the Cause of Man.* New York: Alfred A. Knopf, 1961.

Plato. *The Dialogues of Plato.* Tr. by Benjamin Jowett. 2 vols. New York: Random House, 1937.

Polybius. *Histories,* see Teggart, ed., *The Idea of Progress* (*q.v.*), pp. 78–79.

Popper, Karl R. *The Open Society and Its Enemies.* 2 vols. Harper Torchbooks, New York: Harper & Row, 1964.

――――. *The Poverty of Historicism.* Harper Torchbooks, New York: Harper & Row, 1964.

————. "Prediction and Prophecy in the Social Sciences," in Gardiner, ed., *Theories of History* (*q.v.*), pp. 275–285.

Price, Derek J. De Solla. *Little Science, Big Science.* New York: Columbia University Press, 1963.

Program of the Communist Party of the Soviet Union (*Draft*), 1961, in *The Communist Blueprint for the Future* (*q.v.*).

Proudhon, P. J. *Philosophie du progrès.* Paris, 1946.

Richter, C. P. "Rats, Man and the Welfare State," in *American Psychologist,* 14: 18–28.

Robertson, William. *The History of America.* 14th ed. 3 vols. London, 1821.

Robinson, J. H. *The Mind in the Making.* New York: Harper & Bros., 1921.

Ross, Alf. *On Law and Justice.* Berkeley: University of California Press, 1959.

Robinet, J. B. *De la Nature,* see Lovejoy, *The Great Chain of Being* (*q.v.*), pp. 269–283.

————. *Une Philosophie de la gradation naturelle des formes de l'être,* see *ibid.*

Rostand, Jean. *Can Man Be Modified?* Tr. by Jonathan Griffin. New York: Basic Books, 1959.

Rostow, W. W. *The Stages of Economic Growth.* Cambridge: Cambridge University Press, 1961.

Rougemont, Denis de. *Man's Western Quest.* Tr. by Montgomery Belgion. World Perspectives Vol. 13. New York: Harper & Bros., 1956.

Rousseau, Jean Jacques. *A Discourse on the Origin of Inequality,* in *The Social Contract and Discourses,* tr. by G. D. H. Cole. Everyman's Library, London: J. M. Dent and Sons, Ltd., 1932.

Russell, Bertrand. *The Future of Science.* Wisdom Library, New York: Philosophical Library, 1959.

————. *Mysticism and Logic.* Anchor Books, New York: Doubleday & Co., Inc., n.d.

Saint-Simon, Claude Henri de Rouvroy. *The Doctrine of Saint-Simon: An Exposition.* Tr. by G. G. Iggers. Boston: Beacon Press, 1958.

Salomon, Albert. *The Tyranny of Progress.* New York: Noonday Press, 1955.

Sampson, R. V. *Progress in the Age of Reason.* Cambridge: Harvard University Press, 1957.

Santayana, George. *Soliloquies in England.* New York: Charles Scribner's Sons, 1923.

Schlegel, Frederick von. *The Philosophy of History.* Tr. by J. B. Robertson. London: H. G. Bohn, 1852.

Schopenhauer, Arthur. *The Will to Live: Selected Writings of Arthur Schopenhauer.* Ed. by R. Taylor. New York: Doubleday Anchor Books, 1962.

Seidenberg, Roderick. *Anatomy of the Future.* Chapel Hill: University of North Carolina Press, 1961.

————. *Posthistoric Man, An Inquiry.* Boston: Beacon Press, 1957.

Selsam, Howard. *Ethics and Progress.* New York: International Publishers, 1965.

Seneca. *Epistulae Morales,* see Teggart, ed., *The Idea of Progress* (*q.v.*), pp. 94–104.

————. *Physical Science in the Time of Nero,* being a translation of the *Quaestiones Naturales,* by John Clarke. London, 1910.

————. *The Stoic Philosophy of Seneca.* Tr. by Moses Hadas. Garden City: Doubleday Anchor Books, 1958.

Shafer, R. *Progress and Science.* New Haven: Yale University Press, 1923.

Shapley, Harlow. *The View from a Distant Star.* New York: Basic Books, 1963.

Shaw, G. B. *Three Plays for Puritans.* London, 1900.

Shelley, Percy Bysshe. *A Defence of Poetry.* London: The Porcupine Press, 1948.

Simon, Yves. *Community of the Free.* Tr. by Willard R. Trask. New York: Henry Holt & Co., 1947.

————. *Philosophy of Democratic Government.* Phoenix Books, Chicago: University of Chicago Press, 1961.

Simpson, G. G. *The Meaning of Evolution.* New Haven: Yale University Press, 1964.

Skinner, B. F. *Walden Two.* New York: Macmillan Co., 1948.

————. "The Design of Cultures," in *Daedelus,* Summer, 1961, pp. 534–546.

Small, Albion W. "The Category of 'Progress' as a Tool of Research in Social Science," in *The American Journal of Sociology,* 28 (1923), pp. 554–576.

Smith, Adam. *An Inquiry into the Nature and Causes of the Wealth of Nations.* Ed. by Edwin Canna. Modern Library, New York: Random House, 1937.

Smith, Goldwin. *The Heritage of Man.* New York: Charles Scribner's Sons, 1960.

Smith, J. Maynard. *The Theory of Evolution.* Baltimore: Penguin Books, 1958.

Sorel, Georges. *Les Illusions du progrès.* Paris, 1908.

Sorokin, Ptirim and Lunden, W. A. *Power and Morality.* Boston: Porter Sargent Publishers, 1959.

Southey, Robert. *Sir Thomas More, or Colloquies on the Progress of Society.* London, 1829.

Spencer, Herbert. *First Principles.* New York, 1898.

————. *Social Statics, or The Conditions Essential to Human Happiness Specified and the First of Them Developed.* New York, 1865.

————. "Progress: Its Law and Cause," in *Essays, Scientific, Political and Speculative,* New York, 1891. See also Teggart, ed., *The Idea of Progress* (*q.v.*), pp. 435–447.

Spengler, Oswald. *The Decline of the West.* Tr. by C. F. Atkinson. New York: Alfred A. Knopf, 1932.

Stace, Walter T. *The Destiny of Western Man.* New York: Reynal & Hitchcock, 1942.

Staël-Holstein, Madame de. *The Influence of Literature Upon Society.* 2nd ed. 2 vols. London, 1812.

Stern, Fritz (ed.). *The Varieties of History.* Cleveland: Meridian Books, 1956.

Stevenson, C. L. *Ethics and Language.* New Haven: Yale University Press, 1945.

Steward, Julian H. and Shimkin, Dimitri B. "Some Mechanisms of Socio-cultural Evolution," in *Daedelus,* Summer, 1961, pp. 477–497.

Strong, Edward. "Civilization in Historical Perspective," in Dennes, ed., *Civilization* (*q.v.*), pp. 93–120.

Sumner, William Graham. *War and Other Essays*. Ed. by Albert Galloway Keller. New Haven: Yale University Press, 1919.

————. "The Challenge of Facts," in *The People Shall Judge* (*q.v.*), vol. II, pp. 82–90.

Swift, Jonathan. *The Battle of the Books*, in *Selected Prose and Poetry*, ed. by Edward W. Rosenheim, Jr. New York: Holt, Rinehart & Winston, 1959.

Szilard, Leo. *The Voice of the Dolphins and Other Stories*. New York: Simon and Schuster, 1961.

Tax, Sol (ed.). *The Evolution of Man*. Vol. II, *Evolution After Darwin*. Chicago: University of Chicago Press, 1960.

Teggart, Frederick J. *Theory and Processes of History*. Berkeley: University of California Press, 1960.

————. (ed.). *The Idea of Progress*. Rev. ed. with an introduction by George D. Hildebrand. Berkeley: University of California Press, 1949.

Teilhard de Chardin, Pierre. *The Future of Man*. Tr. by Norman Denny. New York: Harper & Row, 1964.

————. *The Phenomenon of Man*. Tr. by Bernard Wall. New York: Harper & Bros., 1959.

Thompson, D'Arcy Wentworth. *On Growth and Form*. Abridged edition, ed. by J. T. Bonner. Cambridge University Press, 1961.

Thoreau, Henry David. "Paradise (to Be) Regained," in *American Issues: The Social Record*, ed. by Curti, Thorp, and Baker. Chicago: J. B. Lippincott Co., 1960, pp. 421–426.

Tocqueville, Alexis de. *Democracy in America*. Ed. by Phillips Bradley. 2 vols. New York: Alfred A. Knopf, 1951.

Todd, Arthur James. *Theories of Social Progress*. New York: The Macmillan Co., 1918.

Tolstoy, Leo. *What is Art? and Essays on Art*. Tr. by Aylmer Maude. London: Oxford University Press, 1959.

————. "The Difficulty of Defining the Forces that Move Nations," and "The Problem of Free Will and Necessity," in Gardiner, ed., *Theories of History* (*q.v.*), pp. 166–177.

Toulmin, Stephen and Goodfield, June. *The Discovery of Time*. New York: Harper & Row, 1965.

Toynbee, Arnold. *Civilization on Trial and The World and the West*. New York: Meridian Books, Inc., 1958.

————. *A Study of History*. Abridged edition by D. C. Somervell. 2 vols. New York: Oxford University Press, 1947, 1954.

Trench, R. C. *Notes on The Miracles of Our Lord*. London, 1846.

Trotsky, Leon. *Literature and Revolution*. Ann Arbor Paperbacks, Ann Arbor, Michigan: University of Michigan Press, 1960.

Trueblood, E. J. *The Dawn of the Post-Modern Era*. New York: Philosophical Library, 1954.

Turgot, Anne-Robert-Jacques. *The Progress of the Human Mind* (*Tableau philosophique des progrès successifs de l'esprit humain*). Tr. by McQuilkin De Grange. Hanover, New Hampshire: The Sociological Press, 1929. See also Teggart, ed., *The Idea of Progress* (*q.v.*), pp. 242–259.

Tuveson, Ernest Lee. *Millennium and Utopia*. Harper Torchbooks, New York: Harper & Row, 1964.

Valery, Paul. *History and Politics*. Tr. by Denise Folliot and Jackson Mathews. Bollingen Series XLV : 10. New York: Pantheon Books, 1962.

Varros, V. L. "Human Progress, the Idea and the Reality," in *The American Journal of Sociology*, 21 (1915), pp. 15–29.

Vico, Giambattista. *The New Science*. Tr. by Thomas Goddard Bergin and Max Harold Fisch. Ithaca: Cornell University Press, 1948.

Volney, Constantin Francois. *A View of the Soil and Climate of the United States of America*. Tr. by C. B. Brown, Philadelphia, 1804.

———. *Volney's Ruins or Meditations on the Revolutions of Empires*. New York: G. Vale, 1853.

Voltaire (François Marie Arouet). "The Philosophy of History, or an Historical Dissertation on the Origin of Manners, Customs and Religions of the Different Nations of Antiquity; with a Concise Exposition of their Religious Superstitions," in *Essays and Criticisms, containing Letters on the Christian Religion; the Philosophy of History; the Ignorant Philosopher, and the Chinese Catechism*. New York: Peter Eckler Publishing Co., 1920.

Wallis, Wilson D. *Culture and Progress*. New York: McGraw-Hill Book Co., 1930.

Walsh, James J. "Christianity and Civilization," in *Modern Progress and History, Addresses on Various Academic Occasions*. New York: Fordham University Press, 1912.

Walsh, W. H. " 'Meaning' in History," in Gardiner, ed., *Theories of History* (*q.v.*), pp. 295–307.

Ward, Lester F. *Dynamic Sociology*. 2 vols. New York, 1883.

Warnock, Mary. *Ethics Since 1900*. Oxford University Press, 1960.

Wells, H. G. *The Outline of History*. 3rd ed. rev. New York: The Macmillan Co., 1921.

Wheeler, R. H. "The Effect of Climate on Human Behavior in History," in *Cycles*. Pittsburgh: The Foundation for the Study of Cycles, 1963.

Whitman, Walt. *Complete Poetry and Selected Prose and Letters*. Ed. by Emory Holloway. London: Nonesuch Press, n.d.

Whitney, Lois. *Primitivism and The Idea of Progress*. Baltimore: Johns Hopkins University Press, 1934.

Whyte, Lancelot Law. *The Next Development in Man*. New York: Mentor Books, 1950.

Wiener, Norbert. *The Human Use of Human Beings*. 2nd ed. rev. New York: Doubleday Anchor Books, 1954.

Williamson, C. C. H. "Progress," *International Journal of Ethics*, 31(1921), pp. 394–407.

Woodbury, Levi. "On Progress," in *The Happy Republic*, ed. by George Probst. Harper Torchbooks, New York: Harper & Bros., 1962, pp. 270–276.

Index